Christmas
Advertising, Marketing & Display

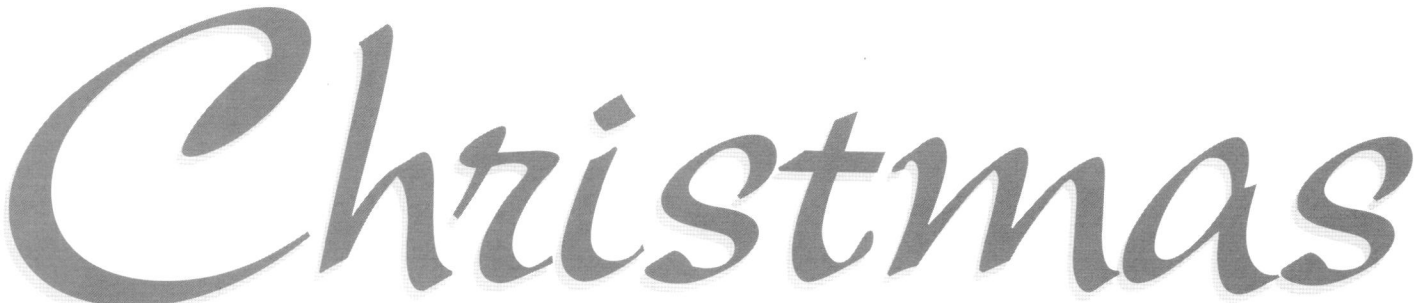

Advertising, Marketing & Display

Martin M. Pegler and the Editors of *Retail Ad World*

Visual Reference Publications, New York, NY

Copyright © 2001 by Visual Reference Publications, Inc.

All rights reserved. No part of this book may be reproduced
in any form or by any electronic or mechanical means,
including information storage and retrieval systems,
without permission in writing from the publisher.

Visual Reference Publications, Inc.
302 Fifth Avenue
New York, NY 10001

Distributors to the trade in the United States and Canada
Watson-Guptill
770 Broadway
New York, NY 10003

Distributors outside the United States and Canada
HarperCollins International
10 East 53rd Street
New York, NY 10022-5299

Library of Congress Cataloging in Publication Data:
Christmas Advertising Marketing & Display

Printed in China
ISBN 1-58471-062-4

CONTENTS

Display

Introduction	9
Accessories	10
Angels	12
Black	14
Calendar	16
Candy	18
Circus	20
Clocks	22
Deer	24
Disney	26
Evergreens	28
Fairy Tales	30
Foliage	32
Formalwear	34
Gingerbread	36
Glisten	38
Glitter	40
Gold	42
Home	44
Hearth	47
Ice & Snow	48
Icing	50
Interiors	52
Knights	56
Knight-ware	57
Lights	58
Miracle	60
Music	62
Musical Interludes	64
Nutcracker	66
Opulence	68
Ornaments	70
Over the Top	72
Peter Pan	74
Harry Potter	76
Red	78
Red & Green	80
Rich & Rococo	82
Santa	84
Time Travel	86
Vignettes	88
Visit to Santa	90
White Christmas	93

Advertising & Marketing

RETAILERS

Introduction	96
Dayton's Marshall Field's Hudson's	97
Disney Store	102
American Eagle Outfitters	106
Bergdorf Goodman	110
REI	114
Jacobson's	118
Alloy	120
Toys "R" Us	123
Laura Ashley	124
Neiman Marcus	126
FAO Schwarz	128
Ralph Lauren	130
Organized Living	132
Gucci	134
Kenneth Cole	135
Chiasso	136
Anthropologie	137
J. Crew	138
Pottery Barn	140
Carson Pirie Scott	142
L.L. Bean	143
Henri Bendel	144
Barneys New York	145
Banana Republic	146

SHOPPING CENTERS

Introduction	148
The Gardens	149
Lehigh Valley Mall/Montgomery Mall/ Quaker Bridge Mall	154
Plaza Las Américas	158
Bramalea City Centre	162
South Coast Plaza	167
King of Prussia	168
Hillsdale	170
South Shore Plaza	172
Bellevue Square/The Plaza	173
Newspaper Ads	174
Index	176

Foreword

CHRISTMAS is a magical time of year for everyone. Aside from all of the pomp, circumstance and festivities of the season, Christmas means much more. Christmas is the pivotal selling time that represents both your peak profit and volume time. It's crucial to prepare early for the Christmas selling season to make the most of seasonal window displays, marketing promotions and the right merchandise mix to capture a larger share of the dollars consumers are spending during the all-important Christmas season. Case in point: At the end of the Christmas 2000 period, a reported $195 billion was spent by shoppers at retail, plus an estimated $12 billion for on-line shopping in the United States alone. Will you be ready to capture your share of the big holiday dollars that the Christmas season is sure to bring?

We all know that successful retailers, whether they are a store, shopping center, catalog company, e-tailer or a combination, depend on smart strategizing, planning and execution to get the job done. That's why *Christmas Advertising, Marketing & Display* is your most important idea guide. This lavish, full-color reference shows and tells you what many other retailers in the U.S. and abroad—many just like yours—have done to attract customers and increase sales for this vitally important selling season. What's more, this book shows and tells you exactly how they did it!

For more than 60 years, Visual Reference Publications has published two highly specialized retail trade publications: *Views & Reviews*, a bimonthly photographic service showing the best in window display, and *Retail Ad World*, a monthly publication presenting the best in retail marketing, advertising and promotion. Each year, because of the importance of Christmas to our subscribers, both publications publish a specialized Christmas planning issue. We have reviewed our past material published in these specialized Christmas issues to present you with a book of the *best* in *Christmas Advertising, Marketing & Display*.

The lush edition is divided into two sections: Section 1, Display; and Section 2, Advertising & Marketing. The Display section is edited by the renowned authority in the field of visual merchandising and display, Martin M. Pegler. You'll see more than 200 photographs of some of the most interesting window and interior Christmas displays. Each photograph is accompanied by text, which explains to you what was done, how it was done, and how each window/interior can be adapted or expanded upon.

Advertising and Marketing is subdivided into two sections: the first, Retailers, covers stores, catalog companies and e-tailers; the second features Shopping Centers. In the Advertising and Marketing section you will read in-depth case studies that tell you about the marketing strategies and creative endeavors of a variety of leading companies. In addition, you'll view some of the best magazine/newspaper ads, direct-mail pieces and catalogs, including covers and intro pages.

As the publisher of both *Views & Reviews* and *Retail Ad World*, I have spoken to hundreds of advertising, marketing and display professionals. And, in my career, I have also been involved in creating Christmas advertising. I know how difficult it is to come up with new approaches and good ideas for Christmas, especially months and months before anybody but a retailer would even be thinking of Christmas.

But now, whenever *you're* ready to start planning for Christmas, this book will be at hand. If you're looking for fresh ideas that will produce maximum results, this book will get you in the mood, inspire you and get your creative juices flowing—whatever the time of year—whether it's March or December.

—John Burr

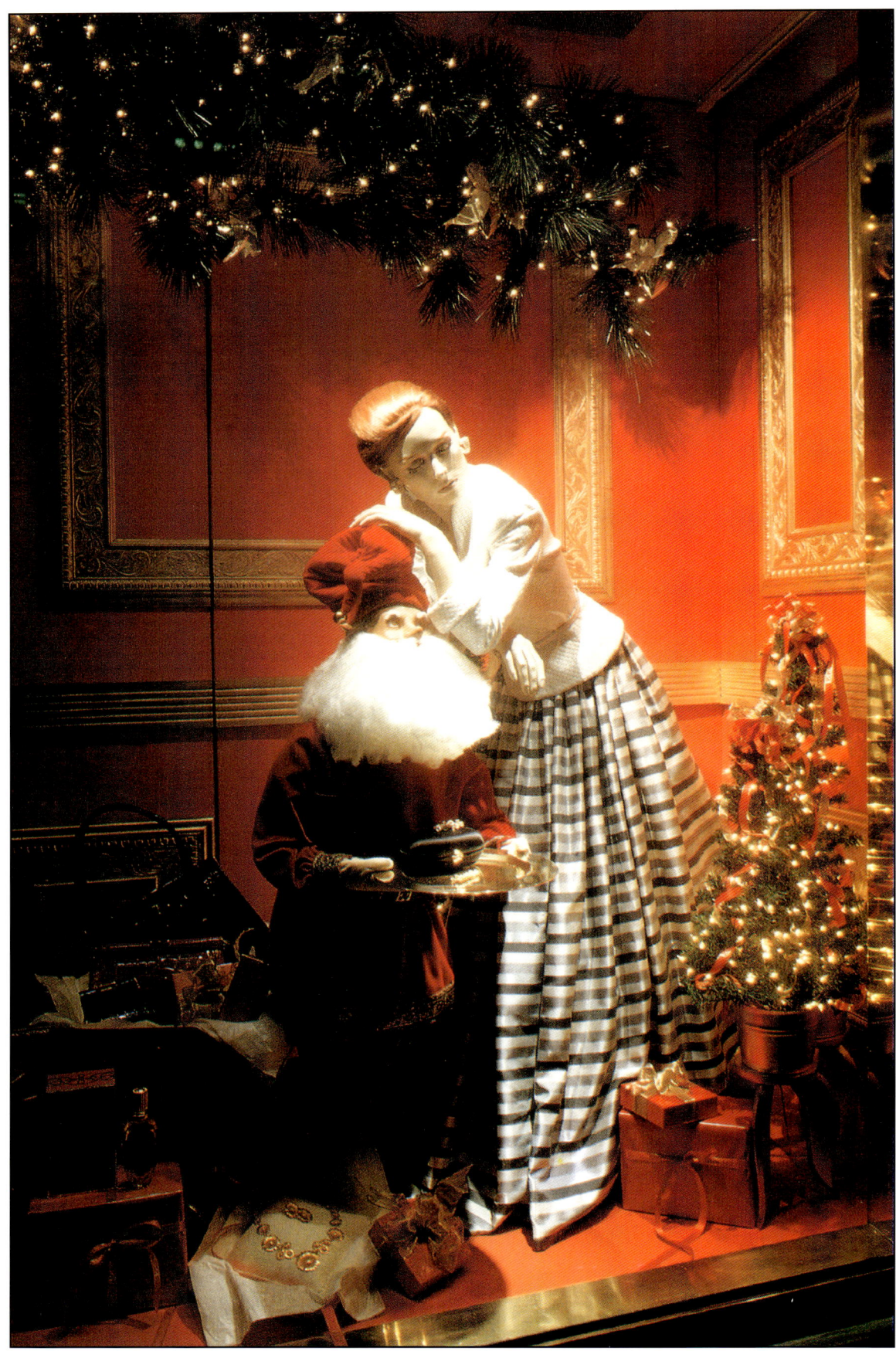

ESCADA, E. 57th St., New York, NY
Display Director: Christina DiCroce

Display

CHRISTMAS AND DISPLAYS are almost synonymous! If there was ever a time to display—to show off—your best in the best of all possible ways, then the Christmas season is the time because that is when your competition—all around you—is doing their best to show off their best in the best of all possible ways. With the street and the mall aisle, in front of your store, already enriched with lights, festive foliage and flaunting seasonal banners, how do you make your window displays attention-getting, alluring and more sales appealing?

Christmas displays generally fall into specific categories. There are the "Institutional" windows—windows filled with fantasy, fabulous animated figures, historic scenes and other "good will" messages from the store to the public at large and their customers specifically. Merchandise is rarely shown!!! This is a celebration of the season, the meaning of the holiday and a gracious gesture from the retailer to the consumer.

Then there are the "Promotional" displays. These are basically "gift-giving" idea windows. The retailer may fill the up-front area with mannequins in "Christmas morning" loungewear or "Going to a party" formalwear. It may be a "Clutter" display in which hundreds of gifts for the home are stacked, set out or just "tossed in" for a feeling of abundance. Or it can be a "one-of-a-kind" display where a single item gets the "star" treatment.

Whatever the promotional approach the retailer takes, more often than not the retailer will want to show more and more of the merchandise he has invested in and has in stock. Rather than overwhelming shoppers with one over-the-top or bursting-at-the-seams presentation with dozens of items that neither compliment or complement each other—and that stay in the windows for endless weeks. The ideal way, at Christmas time and for most of the year, is to show fewer items at a single showing but change the merchandise more frequently. Select a background, flooring, props and furniture that will go with a variety of product presentations so that these "investments" can stay the same through the frequent changes. However, rearrange and reorganize the placement of figures, forms, fixtures, furniture and props—and the dominant COLOR of the merchandise—so that the windows looks new and different from how they looked the week before. Sure, at this very busy time of the year who wants to go in and change windows weekly or biweekly? But at this time of the year and with all that stock-who can afford not to? If the shopper's eye records an image that says "this is last week's display" it tells the mind "nothing new here—keep walking!"

Christmas time is a time of tradition, of hearth and home, of fantasy and fun, of children's dreams come true and all the stuff those dreams are made of. It is more than Santa, his elves and his reindeer; more than evergreen trees all glittery and sparkling with lights; wreaths and garlands bedecked with ornaments and satin ribbons; angels and cherubs; candy, candles, clocks and calendars to mark off the date; Disney characters and fairy tales to be brought to "life"; gold, glitter and glistening accents; homes and hearths, jesters and jousters; knights in armor and all the other spellbinding things we came to hold dear as children. No matter how old we get or how smart and sophisticated we get, we still ache for and love to see (even if only once a year) these "memories" brought back and given new meanings. Even if they are used as settings for sweaters, sportswear and silver and glass.

To help you tread lightly through these "memories" that are now sources of inspiration for Christmas display settings, we have collected them in alphabetical order so that you may adapt them for use in your store and to further your store's image. An idea shown with formalwear may be changed to become an ideal setting for home giftware. What we have shown as an institutional display may be converted to a setting for a promotional display. These are ideas that have "worked;" that successfully were used in well known stores and shops and were created by today's top talents in visual merchandising and presentation.

May your Christmas be white—or red or green or gold—but what ever it is, may it be light, bright, attractive and successful.

—Martin M. Pegler

ACCESSORIES

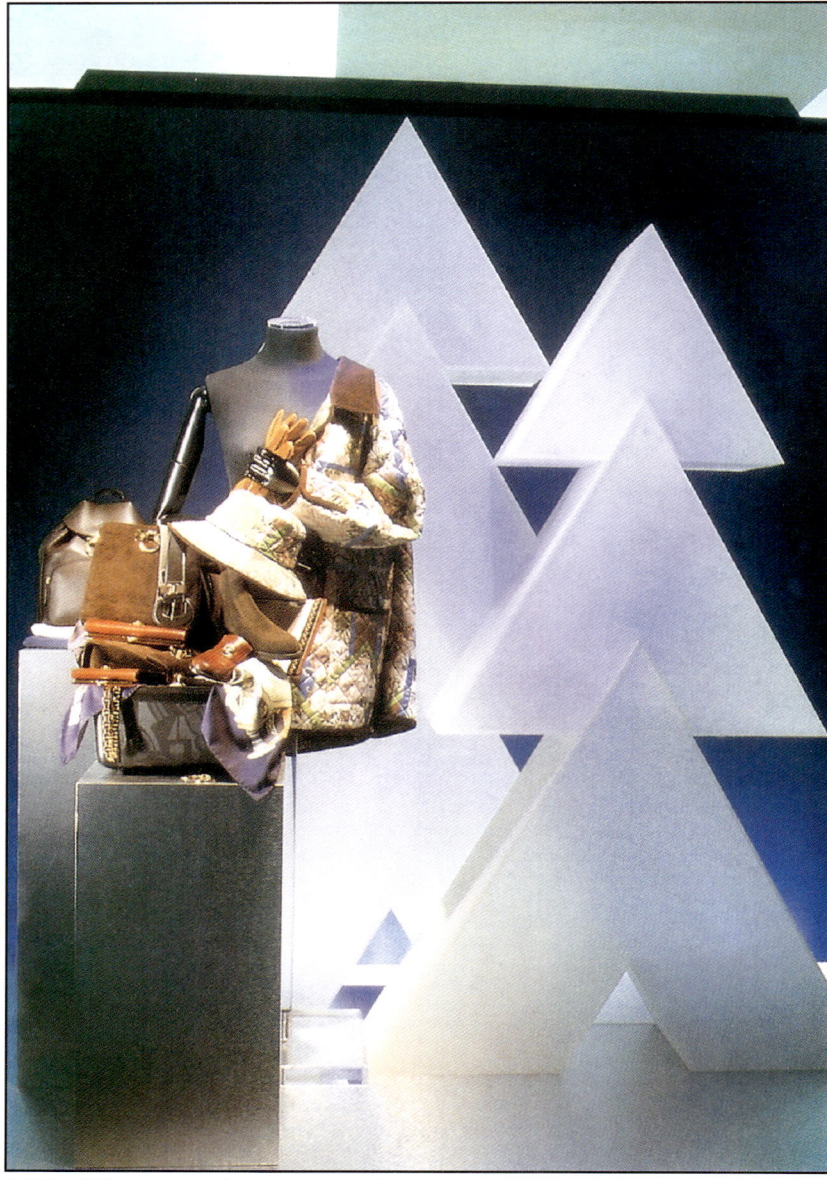

FERRAGAMO, E. 56th St., New York, NY
Visual Director: John Krenek
Asst. Director: Jesse Barber

Small and precious—much to be desired in little packages; the fashion accessories that appear in Christmas windows.

At Christmas time we find lots of small gift ideas presented that include fashion accessories such as bags, belts, shoes, jewelry, toiletries and cosmetics. The problem is—as it is all year round—how to make little "things" mean a lot when they are often presented in windows that are scaled for larger products.

It takes focus—it takes scale—it takes a good composition that elevates while it separates and makes sure that each object can be viewed on its own as well as part of an accessory ensemble. On these pages are some very effective accessory display solutions.

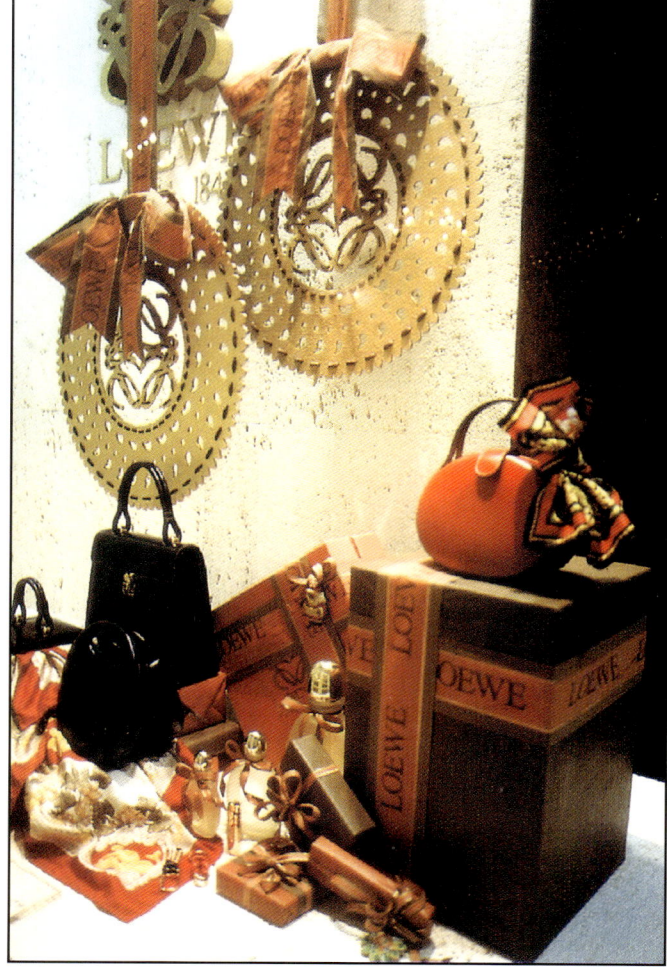

LOEWE, Raffles Hotel, Singapore

ACCESSORIES

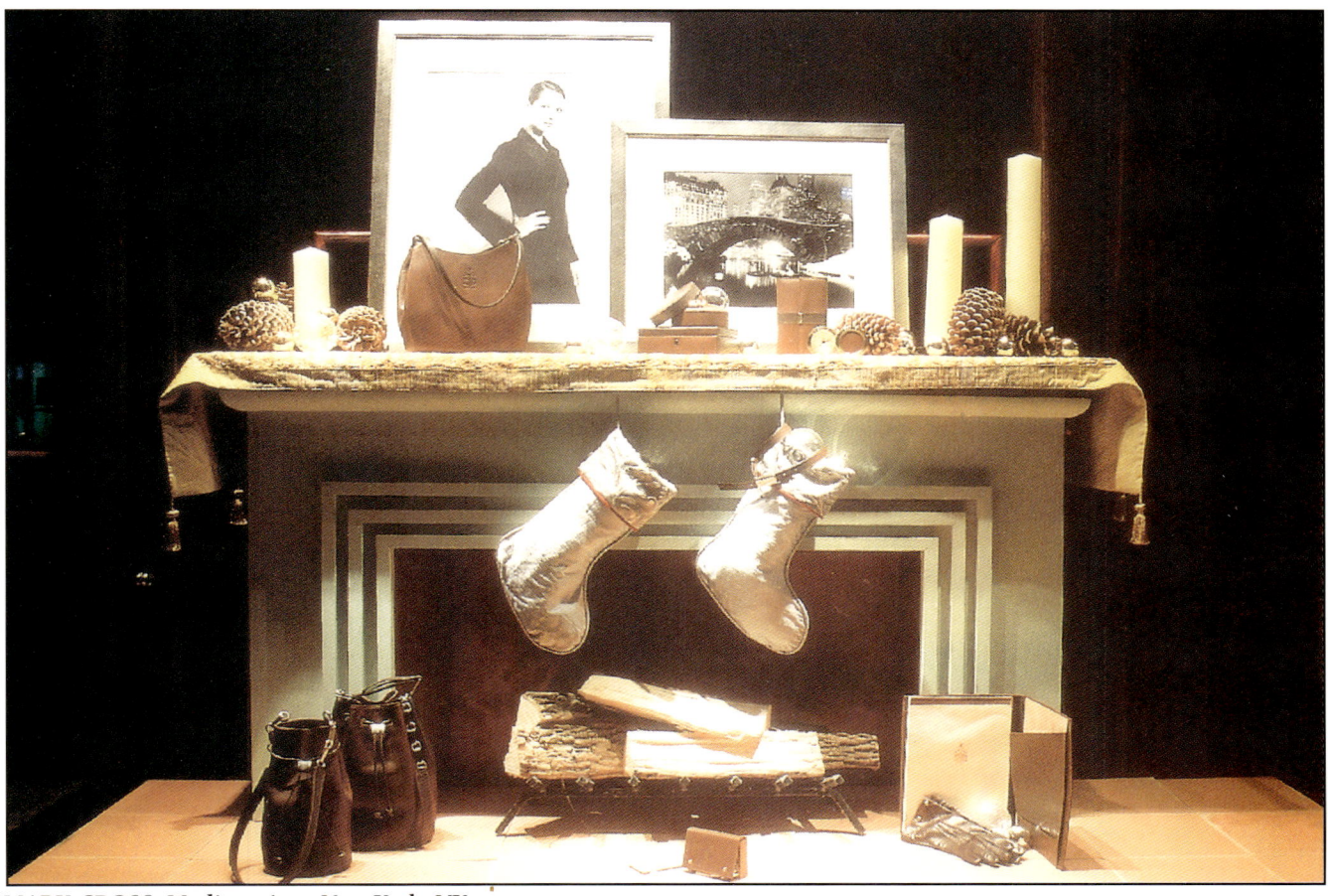

MARK CROSS, Madison Ave., New York, NY

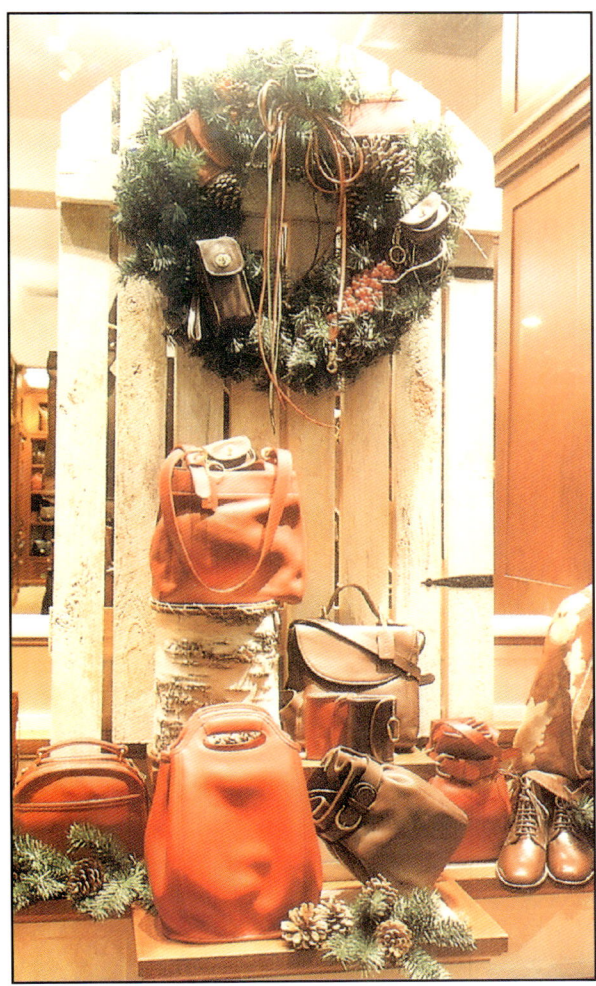

COACH STORE, Madison Ave., New York, NY

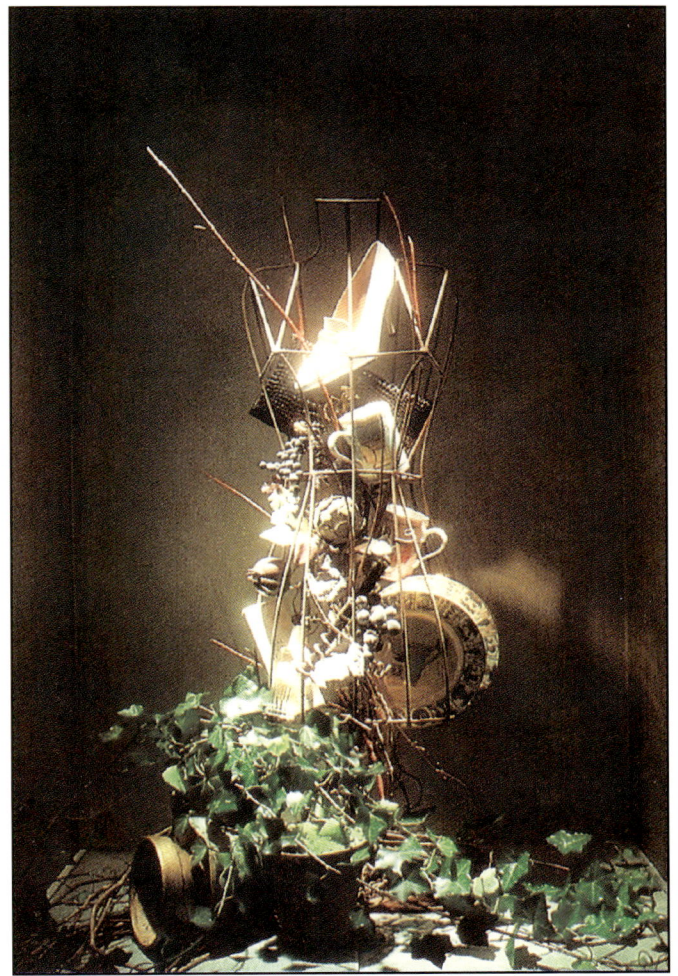

GUCCI, Fifth Ave., New York, NY
Cord. Dir. of Visual Presentation: James Knight

ANGELS

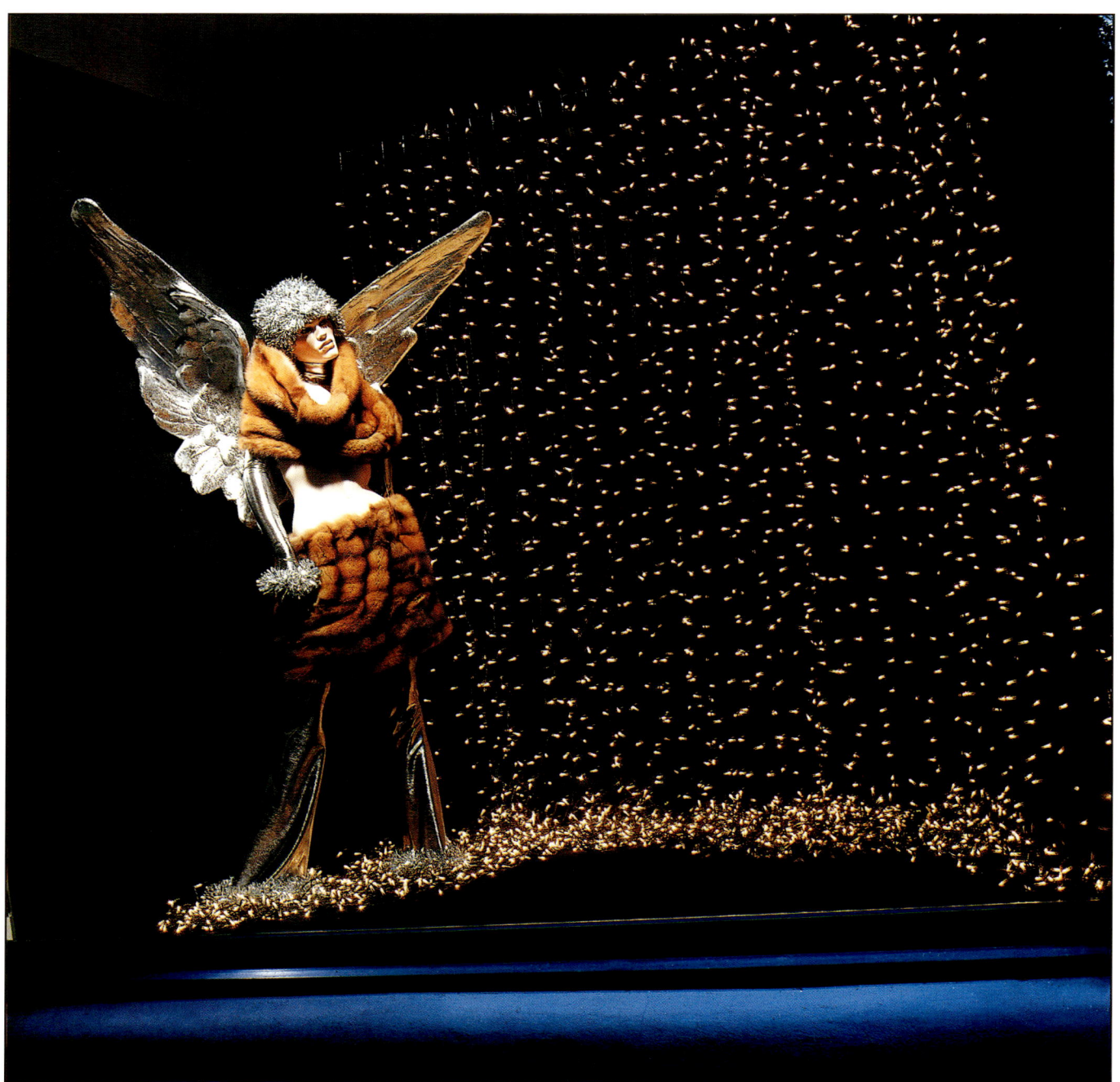

FROEHLICH FURS, Munich, Germany
Designed & Installed by: Peter Rank of Deko Rank, Munich, Germany

What would Christmas be without angels and angel's wings. Peter Rank of Deko Rank in Munich made effective use of the small sculptured figures-with wings added—to create a white and gold Christmas story for Sevigne, a Munich jewelry store.

White satin covered panels, tufted in gold, satin ribbons and satin covered boxes are combined in assorted ways with the figurines to affect a variety of compositions in the small, shadow box windows.

For Froehlich Furs, also in Munich, the designer created a background of dozens of strips of tiny, white lights and made a purely angelic gesture by adding the giant, silver-leafed wings to the mannequin dressed in fur, To carry through the new Millinneum look, Rank designed the silver and tinsel outfit to get into the festive mood.

ANGELS

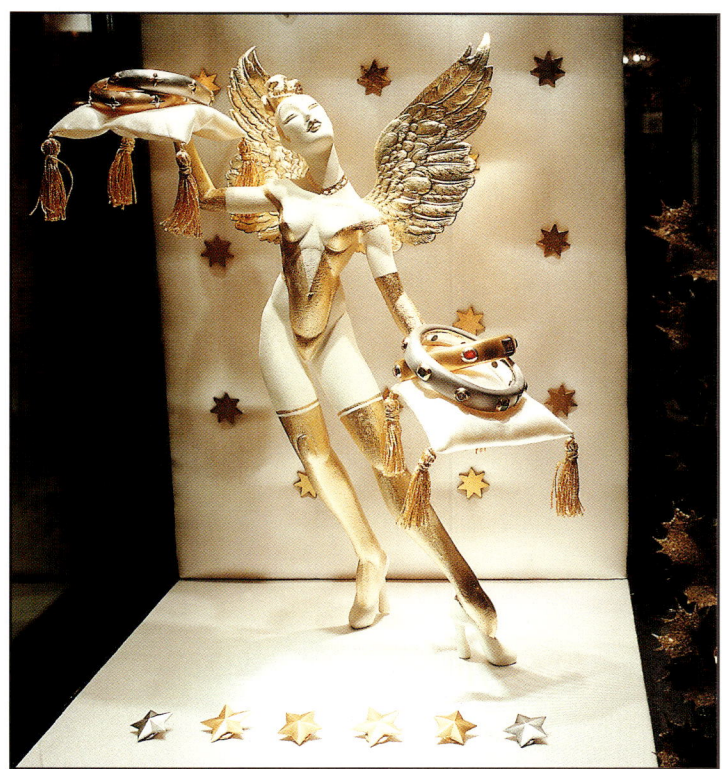
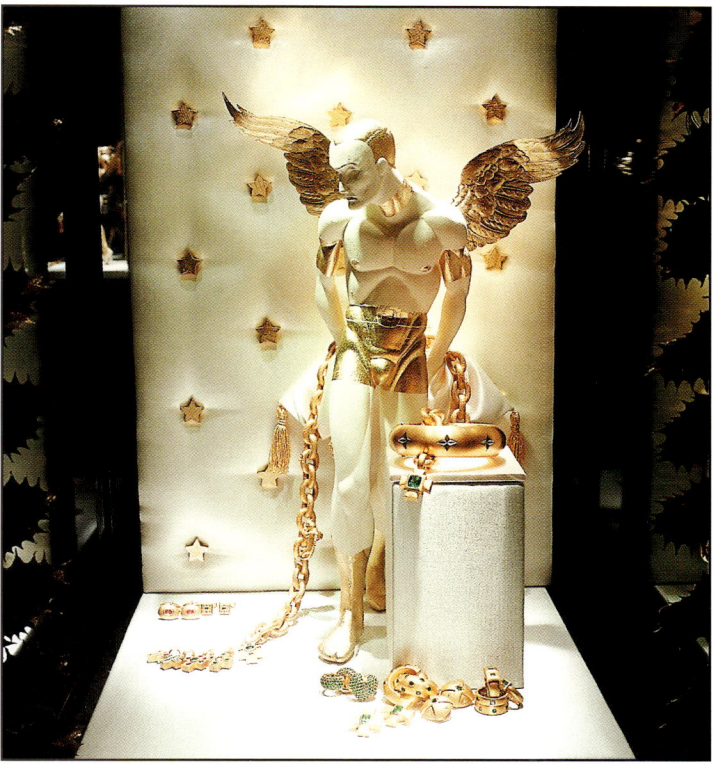
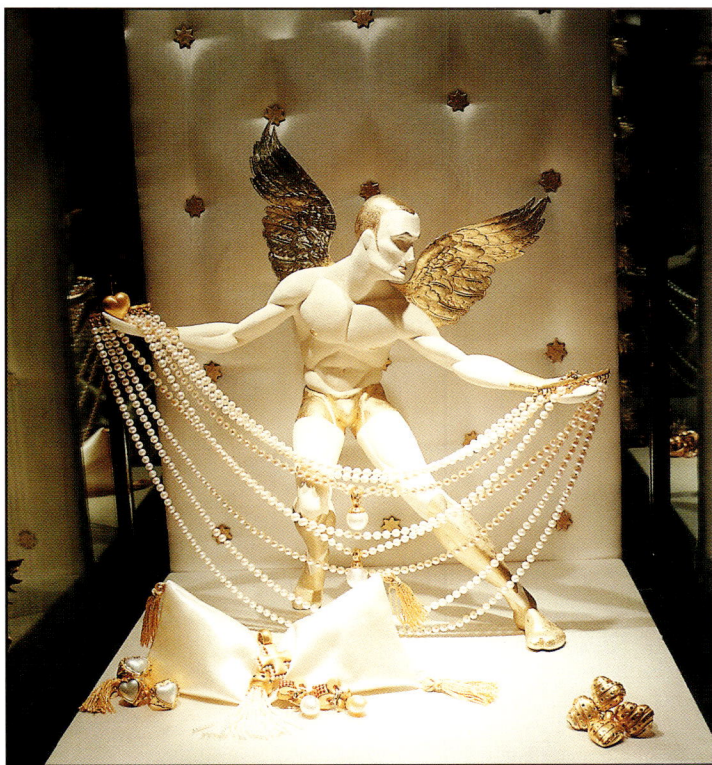
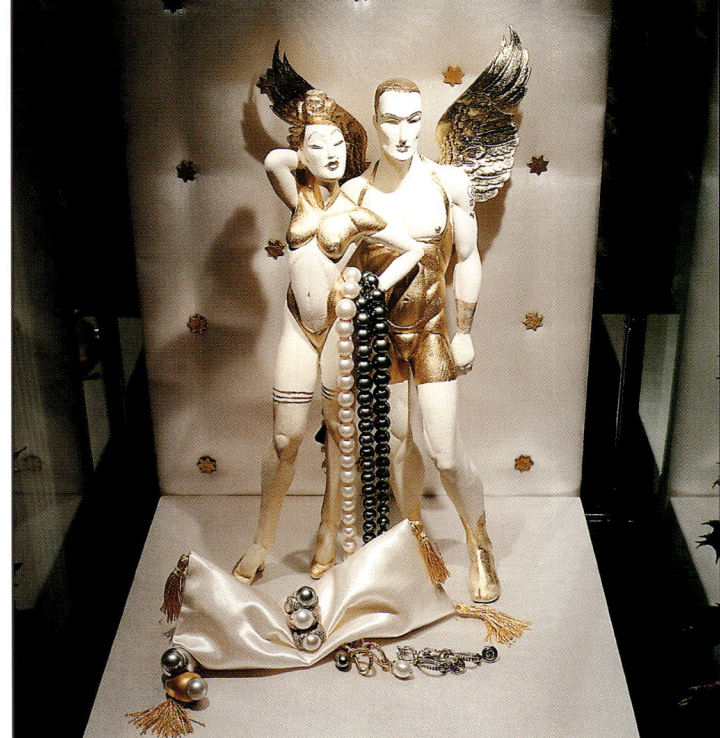

SEVIGNE, (ALL) Munich, Germany
Designed & Installed by: Peter Rank of Deko Rank, Munich, Germany

BLACK

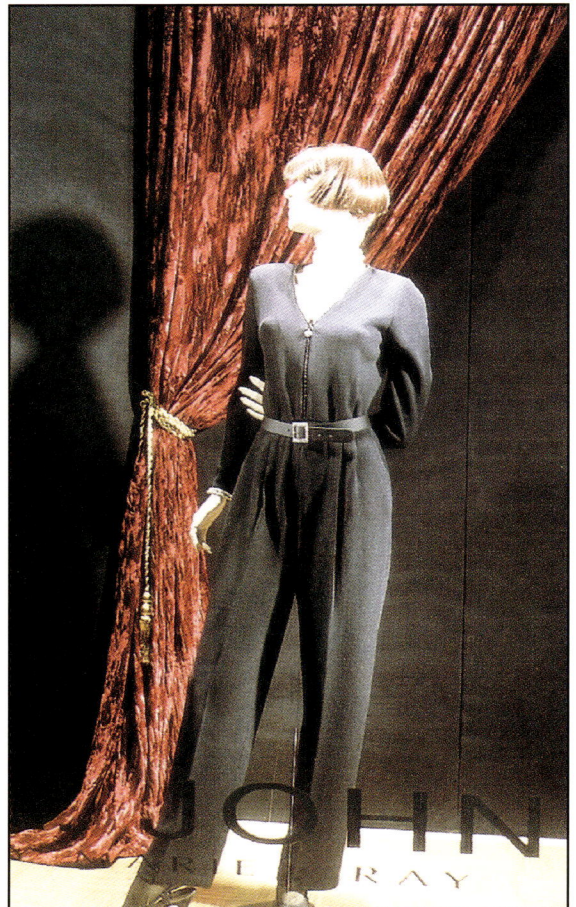

ST. JOHN, Fifth Ave., New York, NY
V.P. Creative Services: Kelly Gray

Black is always "back"—yet it never seems to leave! At Christmas time, when serious thought is given to dressing up, black is "new" and ready to be presented as a new arrival. Teamed up with red—or white—or accented with gold—black is fresh all over again.

Utterly simple—yet quite dramatic—is the pull back drape of crushed red velvet that sets off the black outfit on St. John's realistic mannequin.

In a stark Escada window stands the mannequin in the black ball gown relieved with gold on the encrusted bodice and on the diaphanous skirt. Behind here is a most unusual "wreath" made of voluptuous red velvet roses and dubonnet roses all accented with fiery red tree lights. The white on white frame provides emphasis without detracting from the gown.

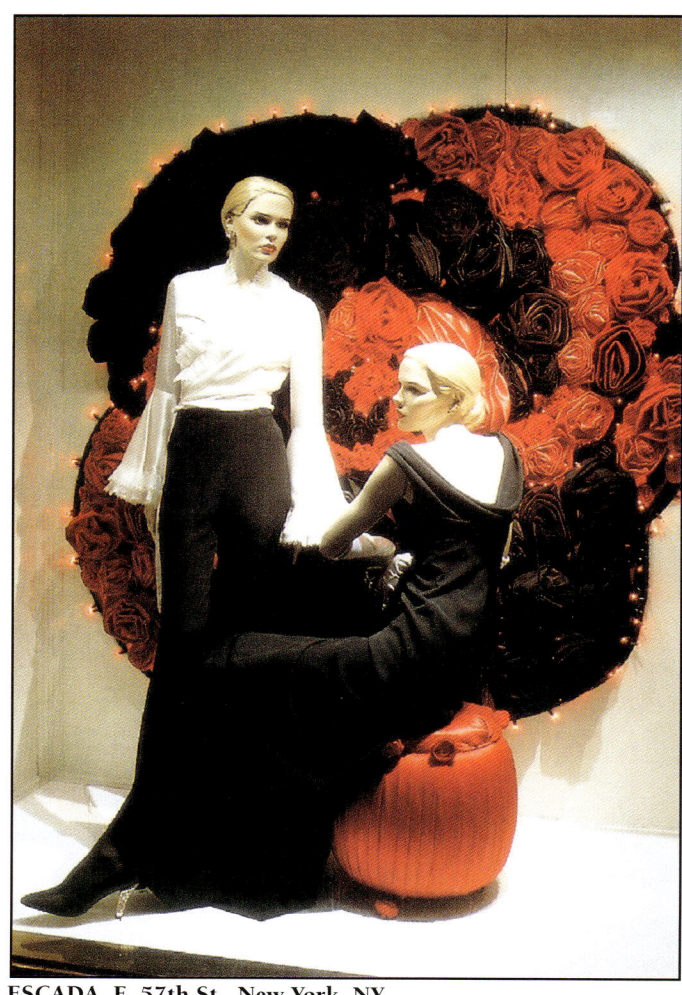

ESCADA, E. 57th St., New York, NY

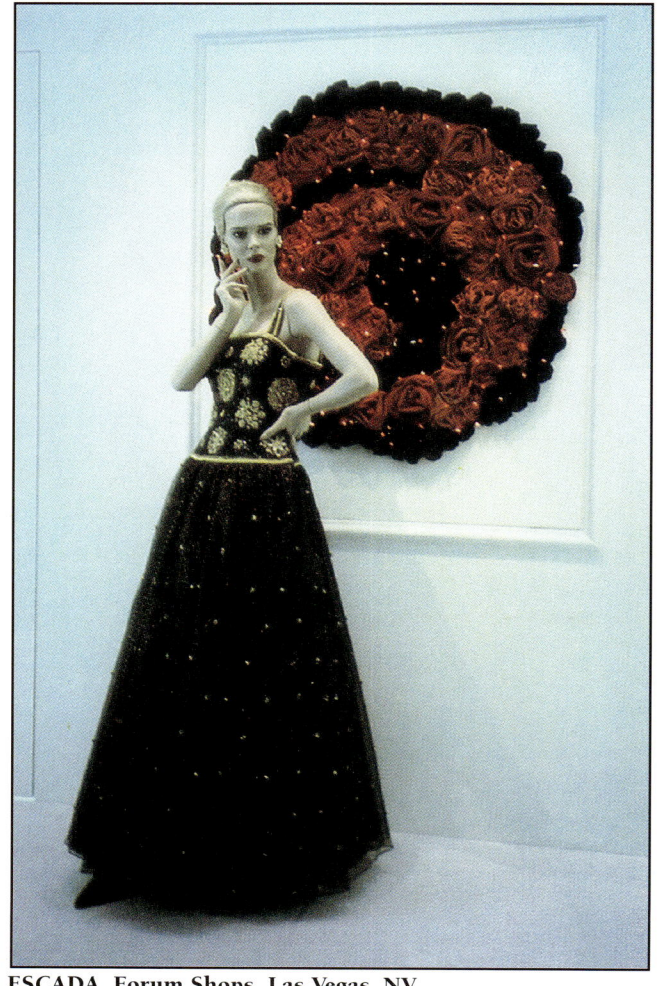

ESCADA, Forum Shops, Las Vegas, NV

BLACK

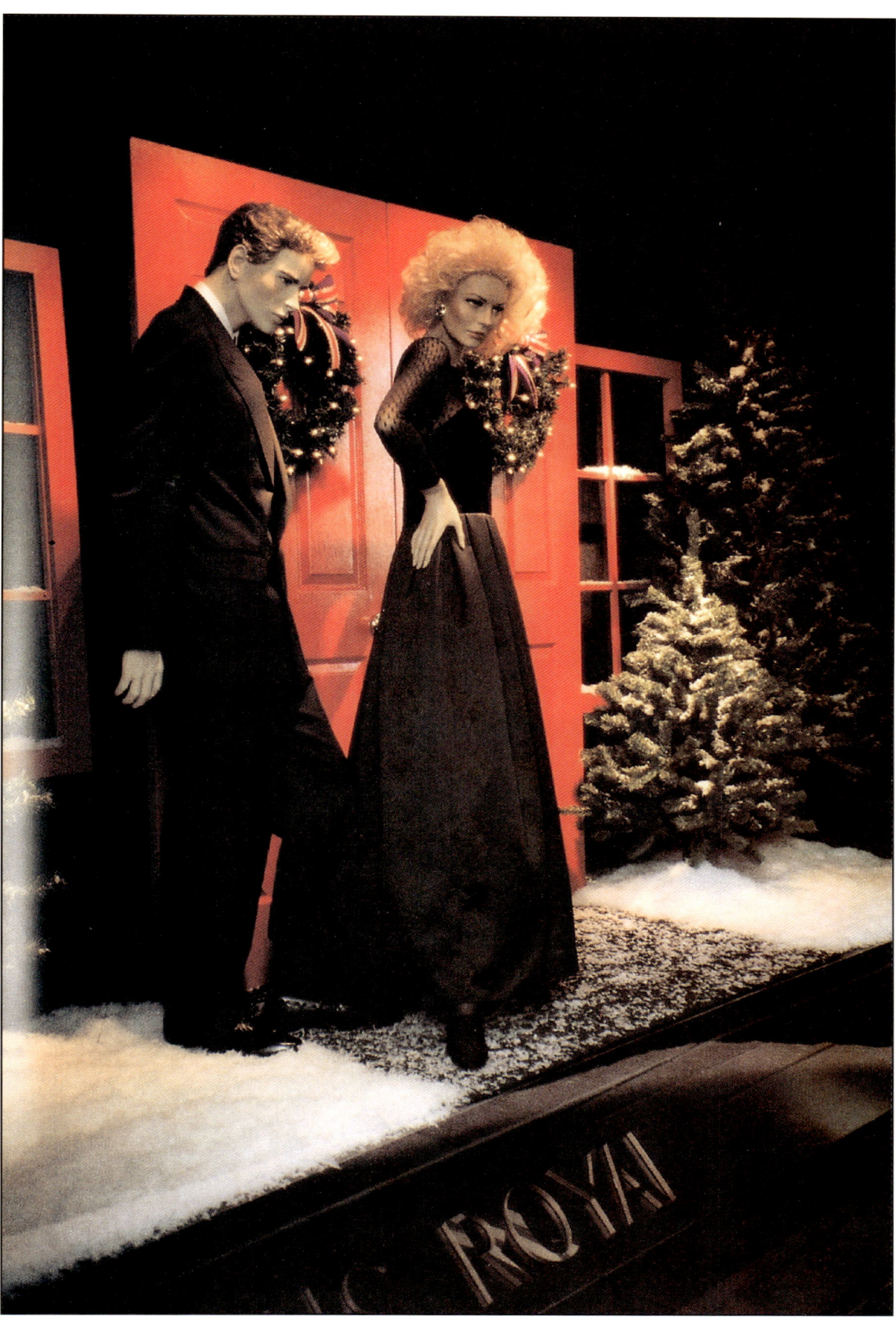

PALAIS ROYAL, Houston, TX
V.M. Director: Nancy Robison

The handsome couple at Palais Royal in Houston are stepping out and are about to step in to a holiday house party. The wreath laden red doors welcome them as well as provide a striking background for the black outfits. Red window frames floating in the black window space, the evergreen trees and the snow covered floor create a "real" setting for the holidays.

CALENDAR

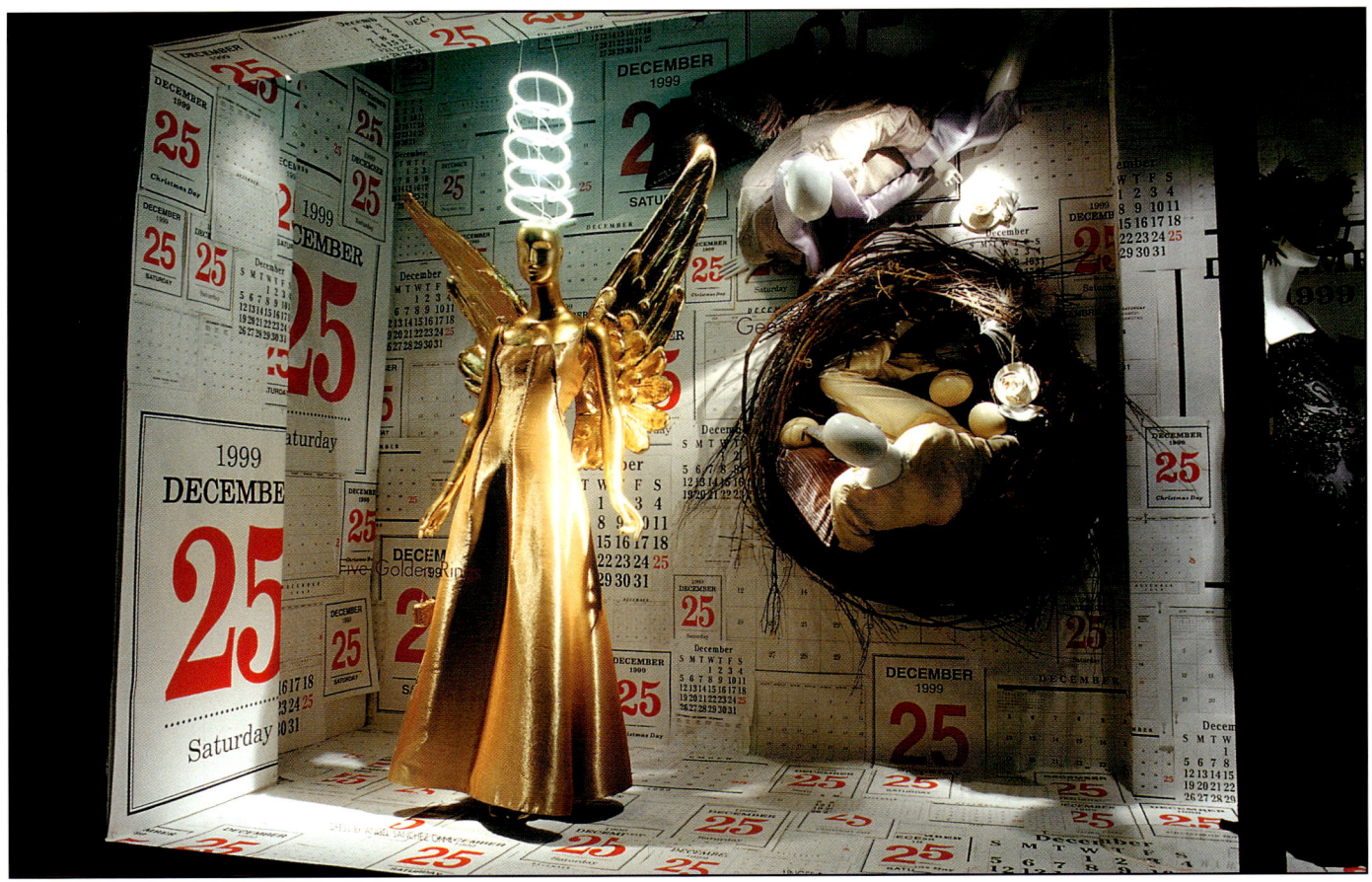

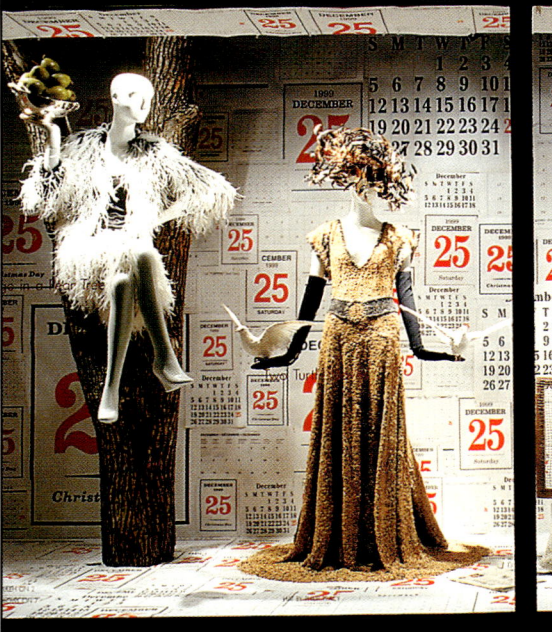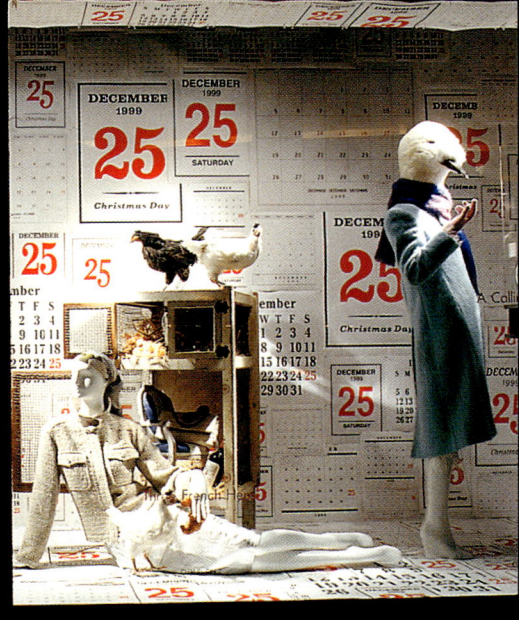

BERGDORF GOODMAN, (TOP AND ABOVE)
Fifth Ave., New York, NY
VP Visual Merchandising: **Linda Fargo**
Associate Creative Director: **David Hoey**
Production Manager: **Michael Metroka**

The count down continues in these Bergdorf Goodman windows where the background and floor are a collage of time-telling calendars: either of the month of December or just that red-letter date—the 25th. The viewer can't help but get the message even if it is delivered by "the birds": the assorted size, but always red, 25s demand the viewer's attention. If there is another message here it might have something to do with birds: stuffed birds, bird heads, bird seed, bird cages and a feathery outfit. Whatever—the birds do get the surprised and unsuspecting shopper on the street to stop and try to figure out what's going on. In the gold angel window (with the neon halo) it is the giant bird nest—on the wall—with the mannequins surrounded by the epic proportioned eggs and the juxta-positioning of planes that captures the viewer's eye and that turns the calendar page setting into a real stopper.

The "Men of the Millennium" windows in Bergdorf's Store for Men" are also royal treats for the eye. Each is crammed with rich details and unexpected surprises. All it takes is the shopper's willingness to stand before the glorious montage of paintings, props and merchandise and work through the exposition to get to the heart of the matter.

CALENDAR

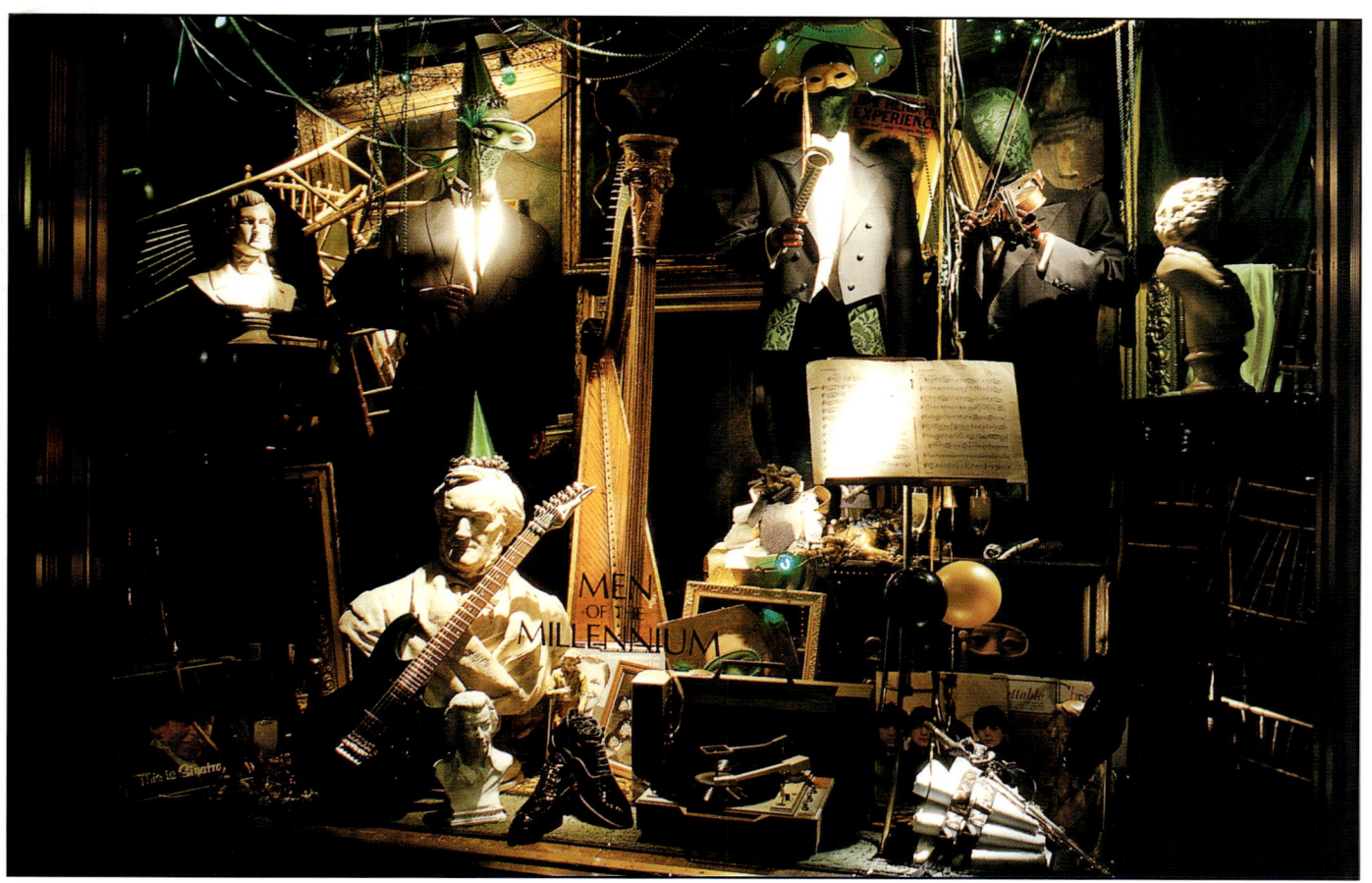

BERGDORF'S STORE FOR MEN, (ABOVE AND RIGHT)
Fifth Ave., New York, NY
VP Visuaal Merchandising: Linda Fargo
Associate Creative Director: David Hoey
Production Manager: Michael Metroka

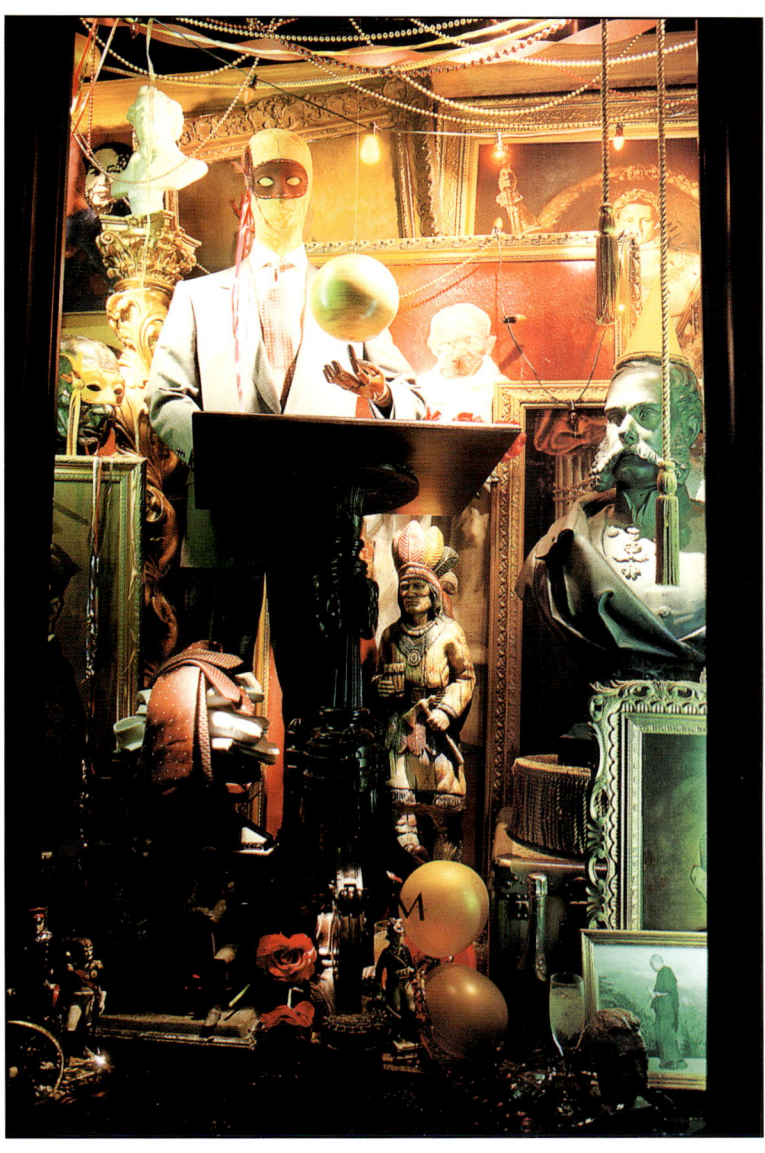

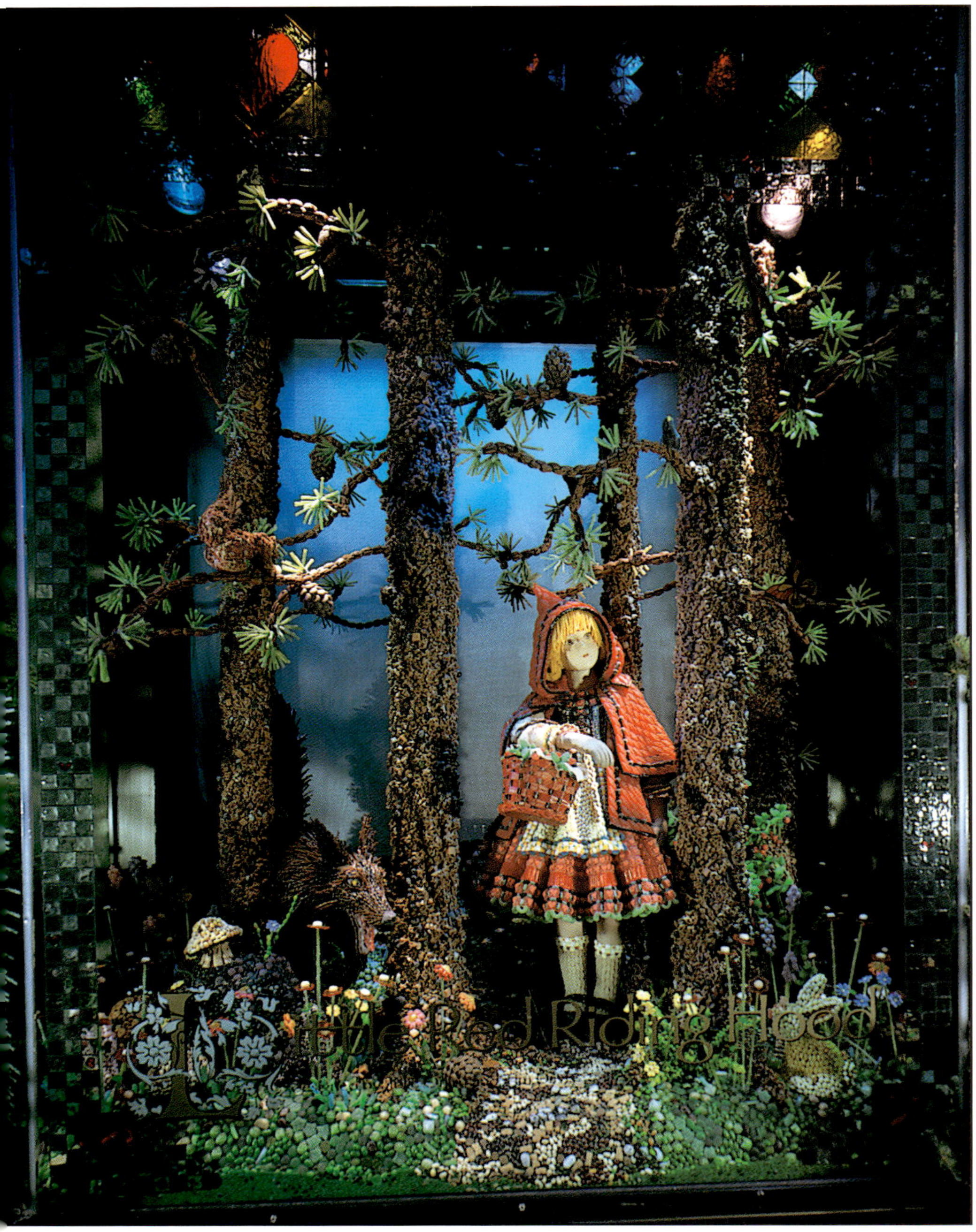

CANDY

ZCMI, (LEFT AND BELOW) **Salt Lake City, UT**
Visual Director: Mike Stephens

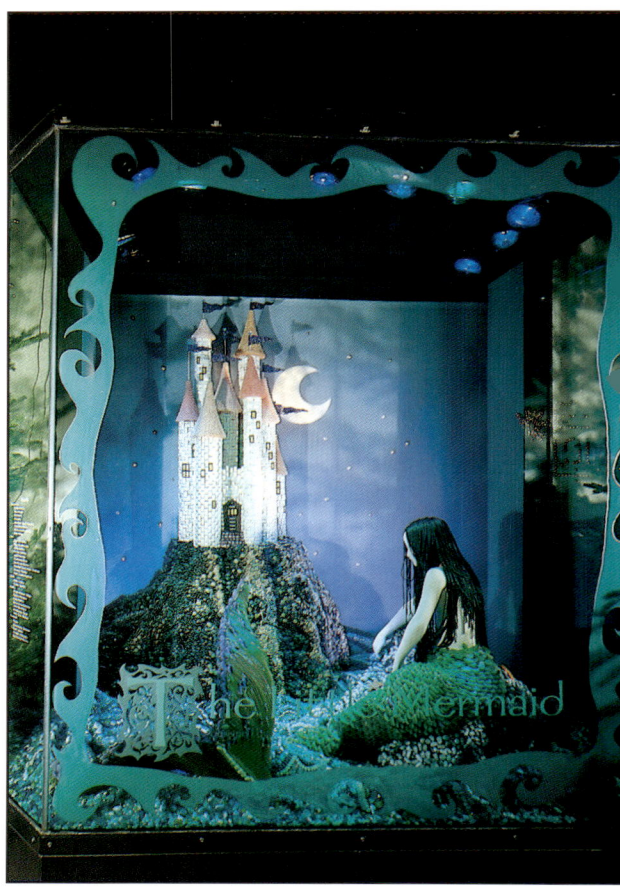

Fairy tales do come true—especially in display windows at Christmas time. For their institutional windows, ZCMI, with Mike Stephens, the visual director, leading his talented group of designers and decorators, presented the sweetest, most delectable and delicious versions of familiar fairy tales.

Tim Davison and Julie Orlob created their version of Little Red Riding Hood. She walks through a friendly forest filled with flowers, gravel, grass and animals all fashioned of and covered with candies and sweets. Alysa Revell's view of Anderson's Little Mermaid has her resting on jelly bean waves and rocks and admiring a Chiclet coated castle. Cinderella by Diane Call captures that magic moment when the pumpkin turns into the coach—again executed and covered in candies of all kinds and colors. Jack's Beanstalk just grows and grows even though the leaves are laden with candies as designed by Celeste Cecchini, and Anne Cook's Hansel & Gretal was just made to be smothered in candies. Along with Sherri Orton's Snow Queen (not shown) one can appreciate the creative talents and the imaginative use of candy applique that has made these Sweets windows so popular in Salt Lake City and why year after year the crowds come to "oh! and ah!" at the new "old" stories that the store candy coats for their customers' pleasure and delight.

CANDY

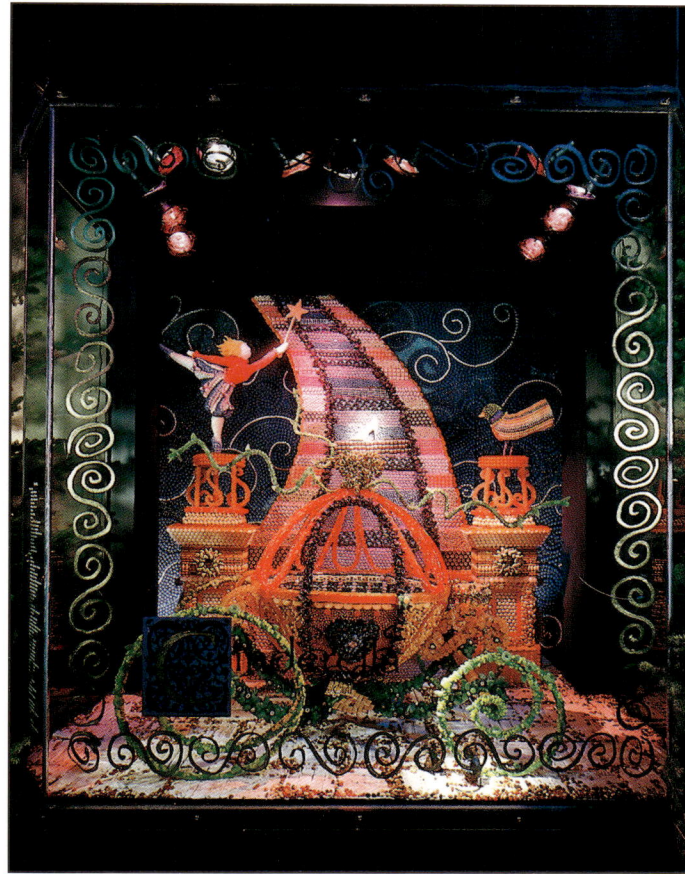

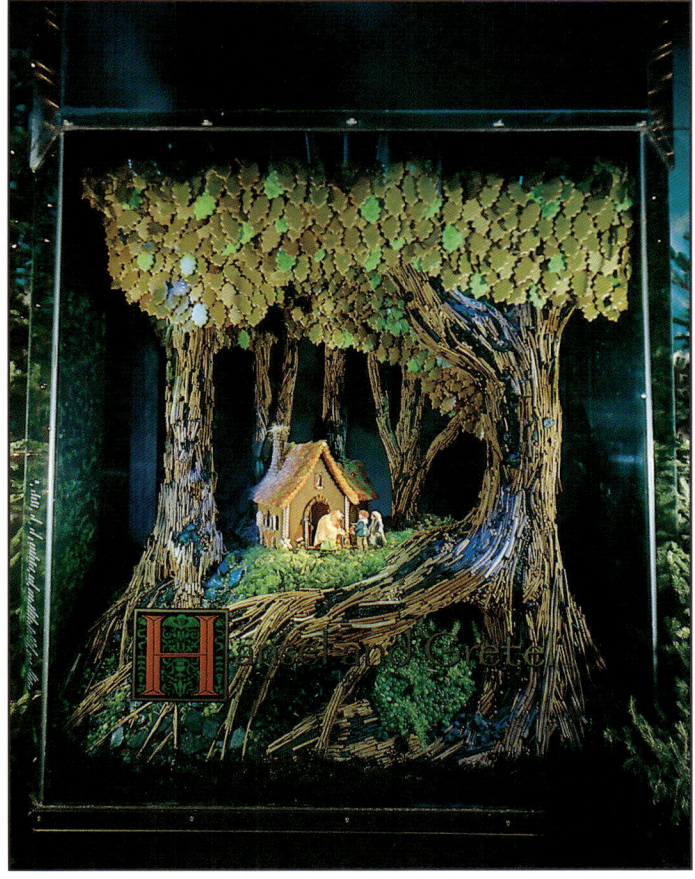

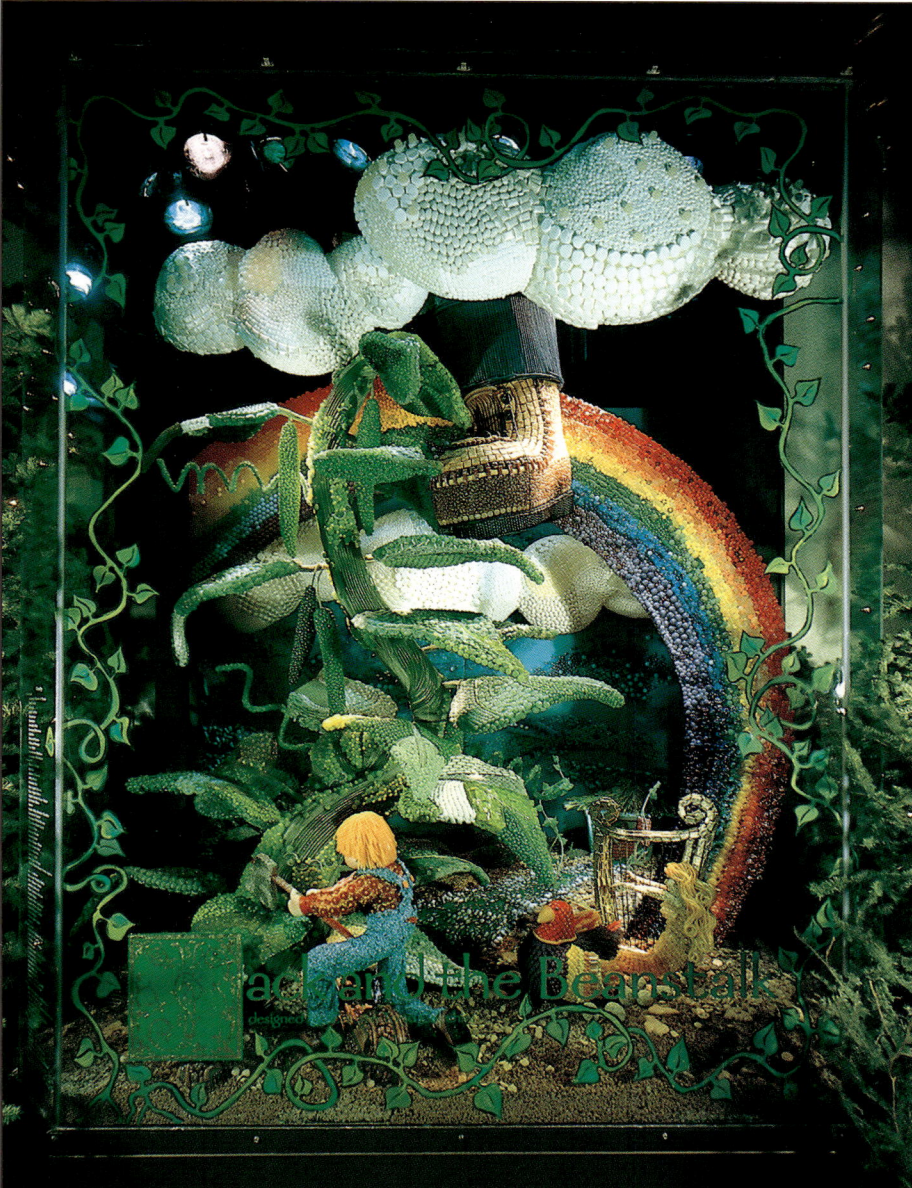

ZCMI, (ALL) Salt Lake City, UT
Visual Director: Mike Stephens

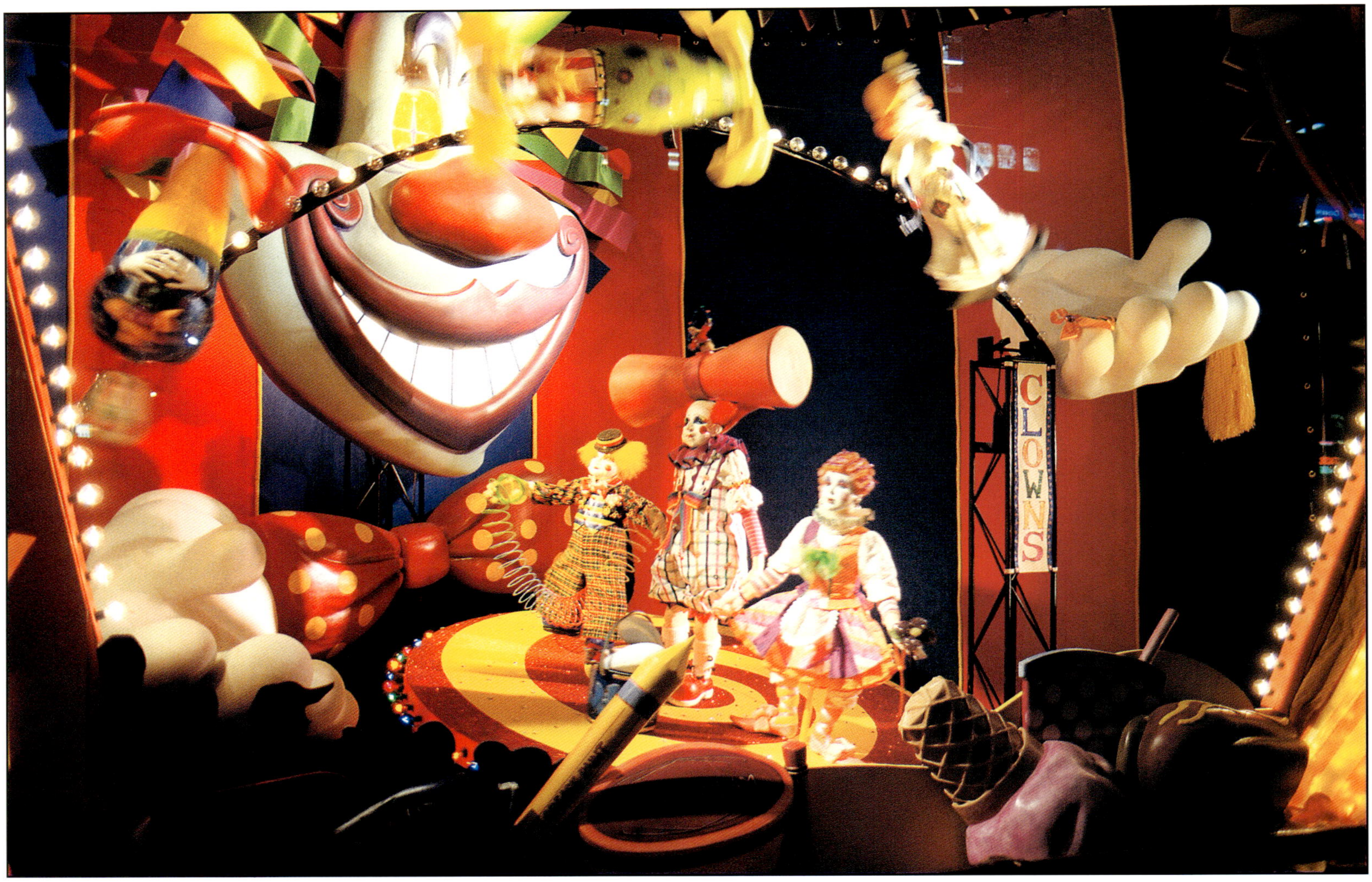

CIRCUS

LORD & TAYLOR, (ABOVE AND RIGHT),
Fifth Ave., New York, NY
Visual Creative Director: Manoel Renha

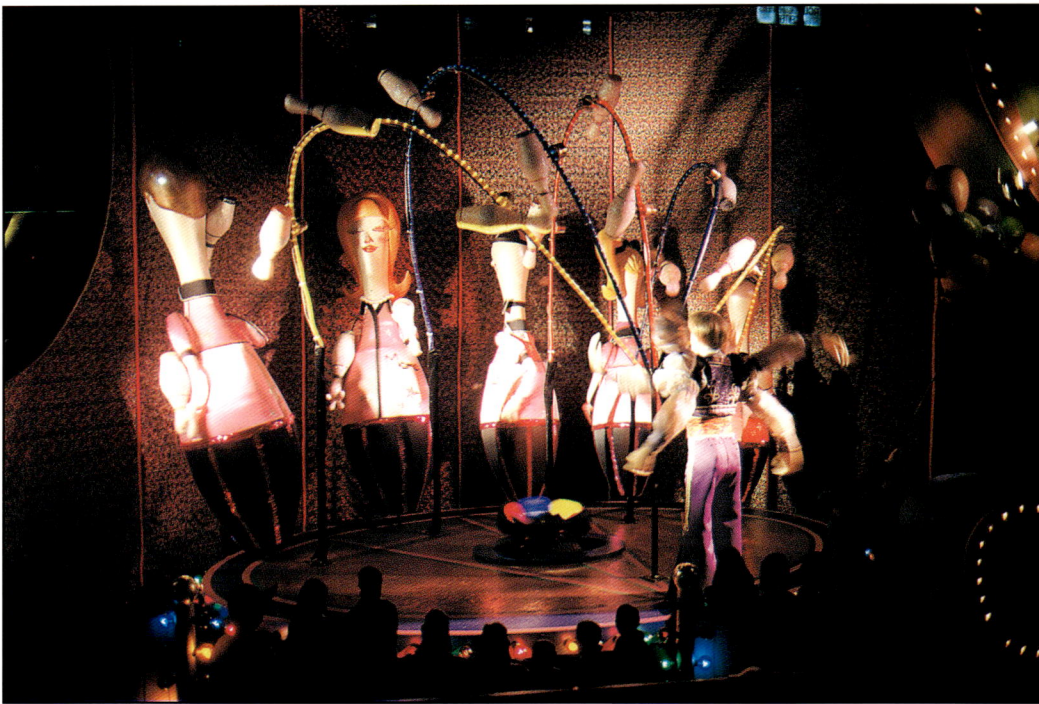

Even though we usually expect the circus to come to town along with the daffodils and the springtime flowers, Lord & Taylor suited all that glamour, glitz, color and music to the Christmas holidays with a spectacular array of circus entertainers that filled their Fifth Avenue windows—to please "children of all ages."

The universal appeal was evident from the crowds that lined up to watch "the acts"; the clowns in their dazzling, sequined, technicolor outfits, the jugglers and tight-rope walkers, the lion tamer. Manoel Renha, the store's creative director, created these fabulous scenes that are not only filled with color and light but with animation that enhances the displays and adds to the humor—such as the monkeys brushing the lion's teeth.

Adding to the spectacle and the surprise is the unexpected changes of scale with overly large figures mixed in with miniatures. Another clever device was adding the rows of small silhouetted heads up front against the glass. They became "the audience" in the bleachers and the viewer on the street was peeking a look over their heads. The children especially loved the elephant band and the mischievous monkeys while the adults took in all the razzle-dazzle as a memory of times gone by.

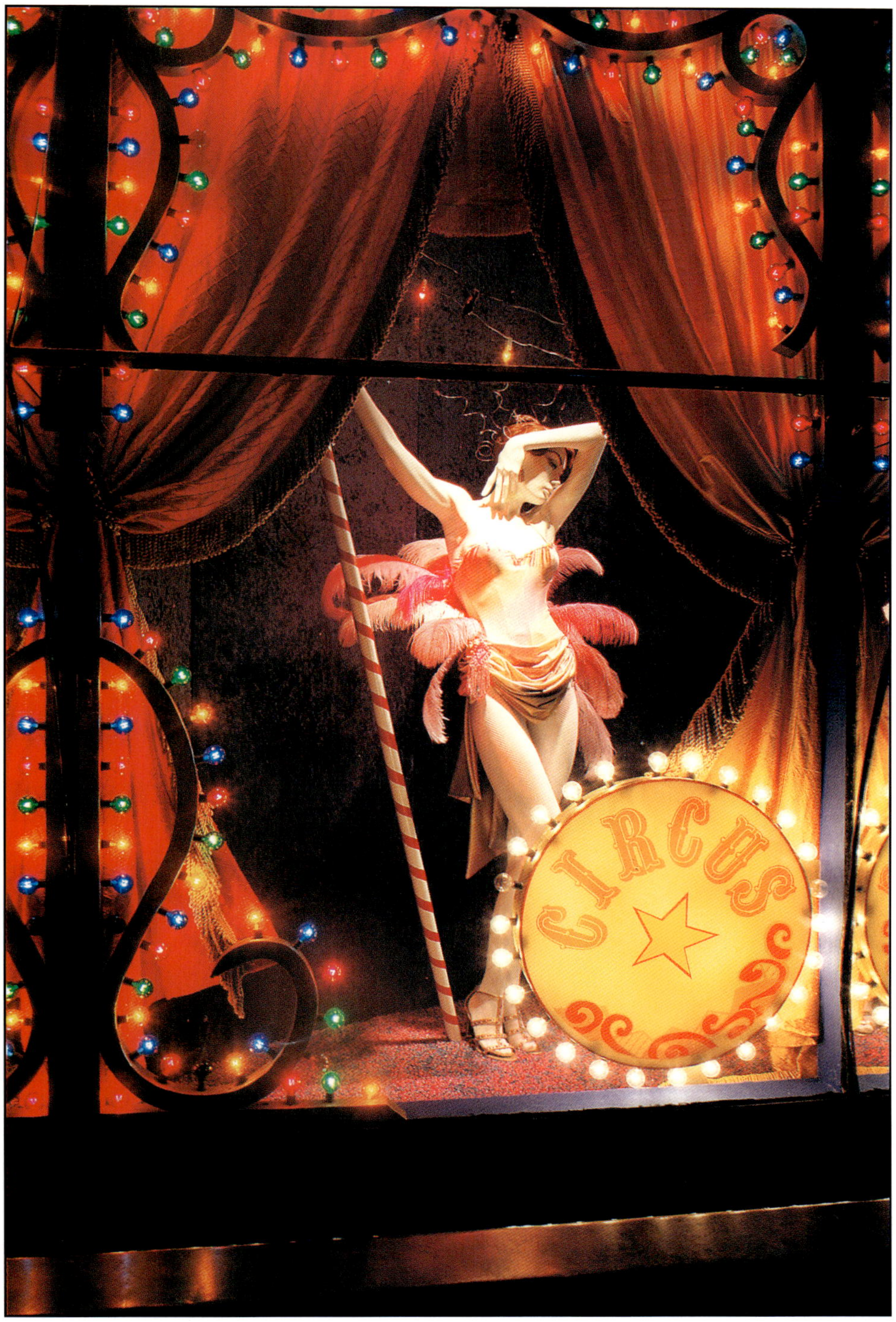

CIRCUS

LORD & TAYLOR, (ABOVE AND RIGHT)
Fifth Ave., New York, NY
Visual Creative Director: Manoel Renha

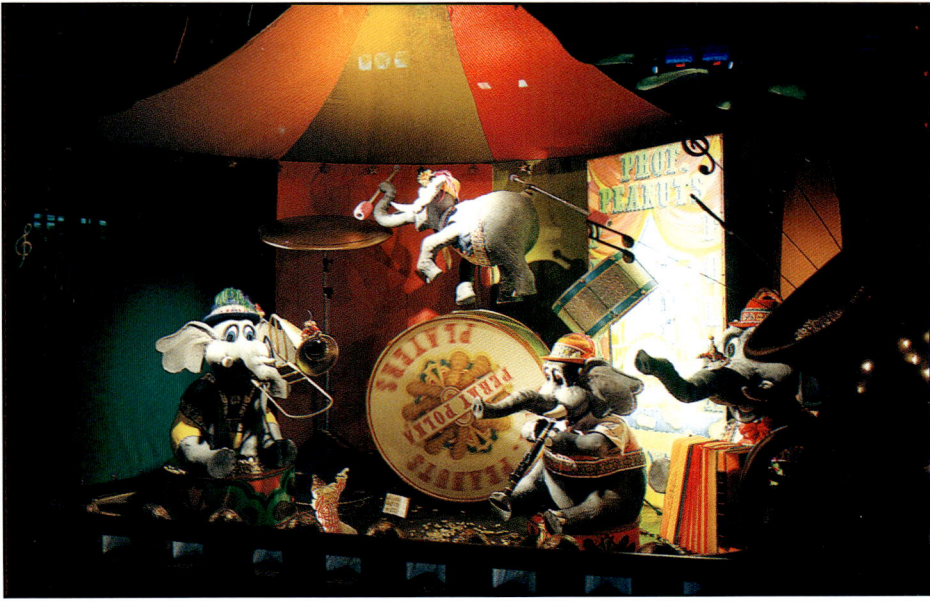

CLOCKS

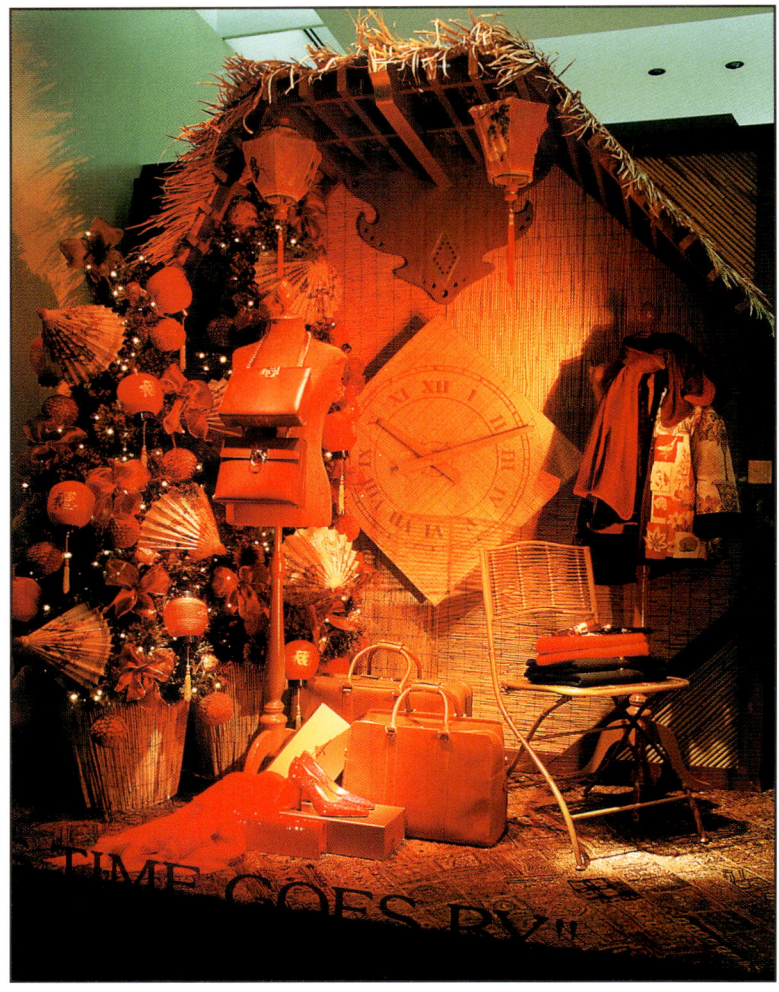

Ferregamo made a sophisticated bow to the Millennium talk by acknowledging the passage of time. In a series of vignettes in the store's open back windows, we are not only treated to a viewing of the designer garments and accessories but also to a play of time and places.

Red is the dominant color in the Asian inspired setting that combines tatami mats, woven bamboo and raffia with a Christmas tree almost smothered in painted silk lanterns, gold foil parasols, ornaments—and fashion accessories. In sharp contrast is the cool and chilly, ice and icicle trimmed setting for the frozen, snow bound whiter garments. The tree is this scene is trimmed with snowflakes, ribbons and twisted icicles. In a more rustic and provincial mood, the background is an overscaled, "carved" cuckoo clock and the more casual apparel is shown against a tree trimmed with red berries, ribbons, pine cones and other dried foliage. A golden glow permeates the rich and opulent Renaissance setting. Ornate gilt frames, fresco paintings, gauzy gold bows, cherubs and amorinos fill the space with a sense of luxury.

In each vignette there is a clock, cleverly contrived and integrated into the design in a central and focal spot that actually carries the message forward.

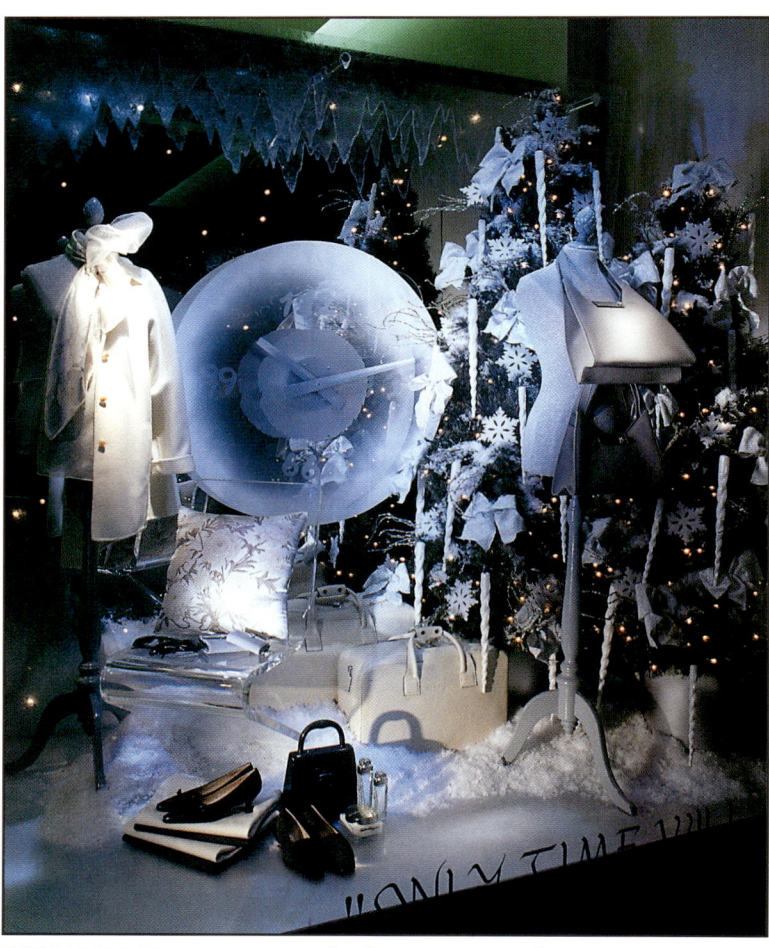

FERREGAMNO, (TOP AND ABOVE) 5th Ave., New York, NY
Dir. Of Visuals: John Krenek
Asst. Dir.: Jesse Barber

CLOCKS

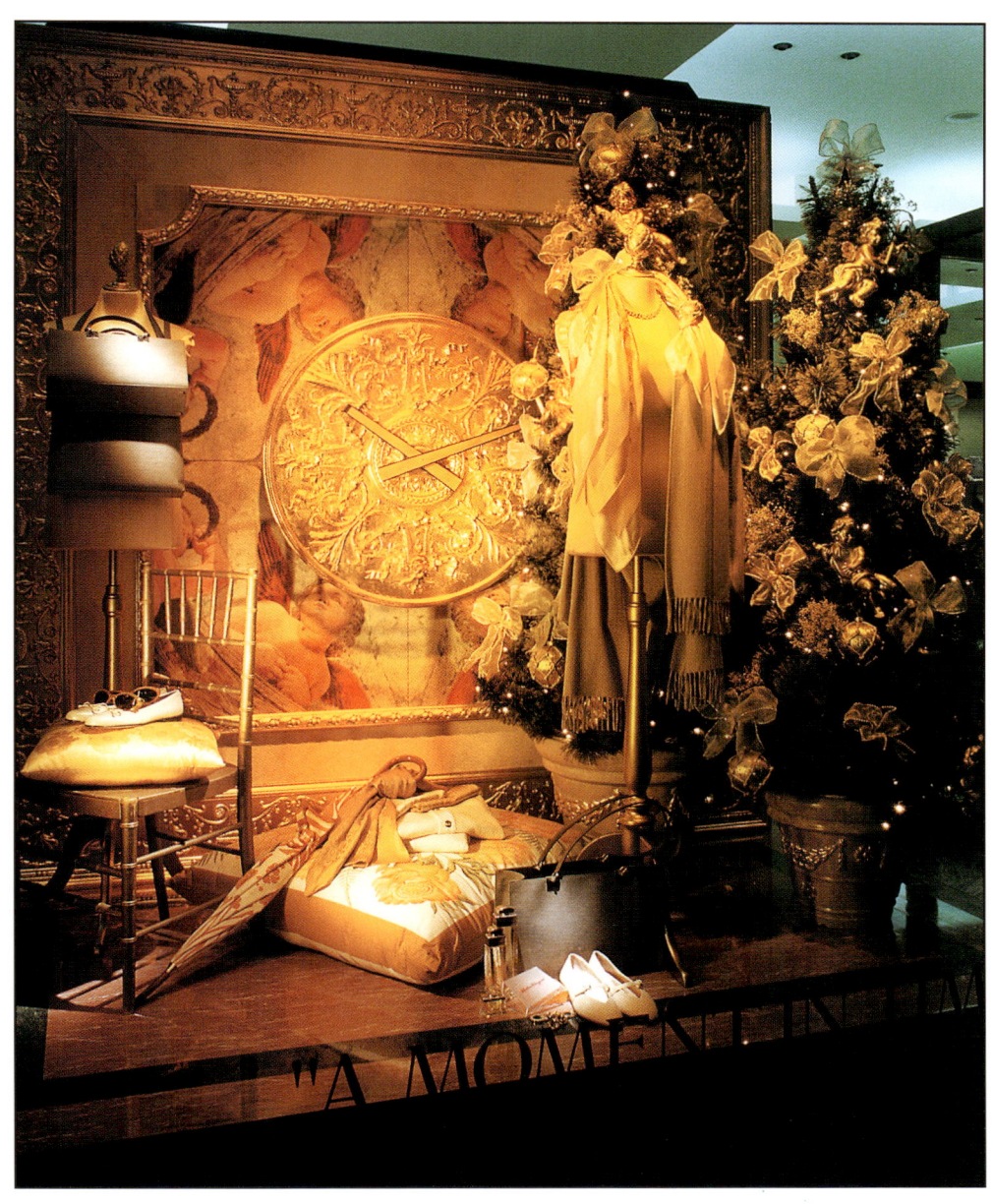

FERREGAMNO, (ABOVE AND RIGHT)
Fifth Ave., New York, NY
Dir. Of Visuals: John Krenek
Asst. Dir.: Jesse Barber

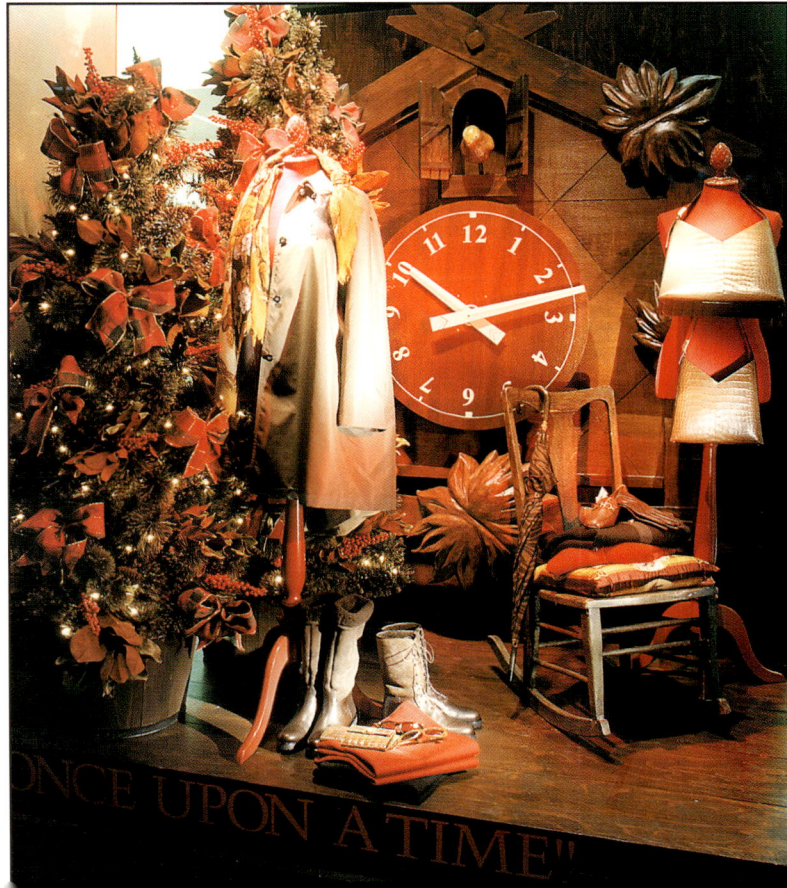

DEER

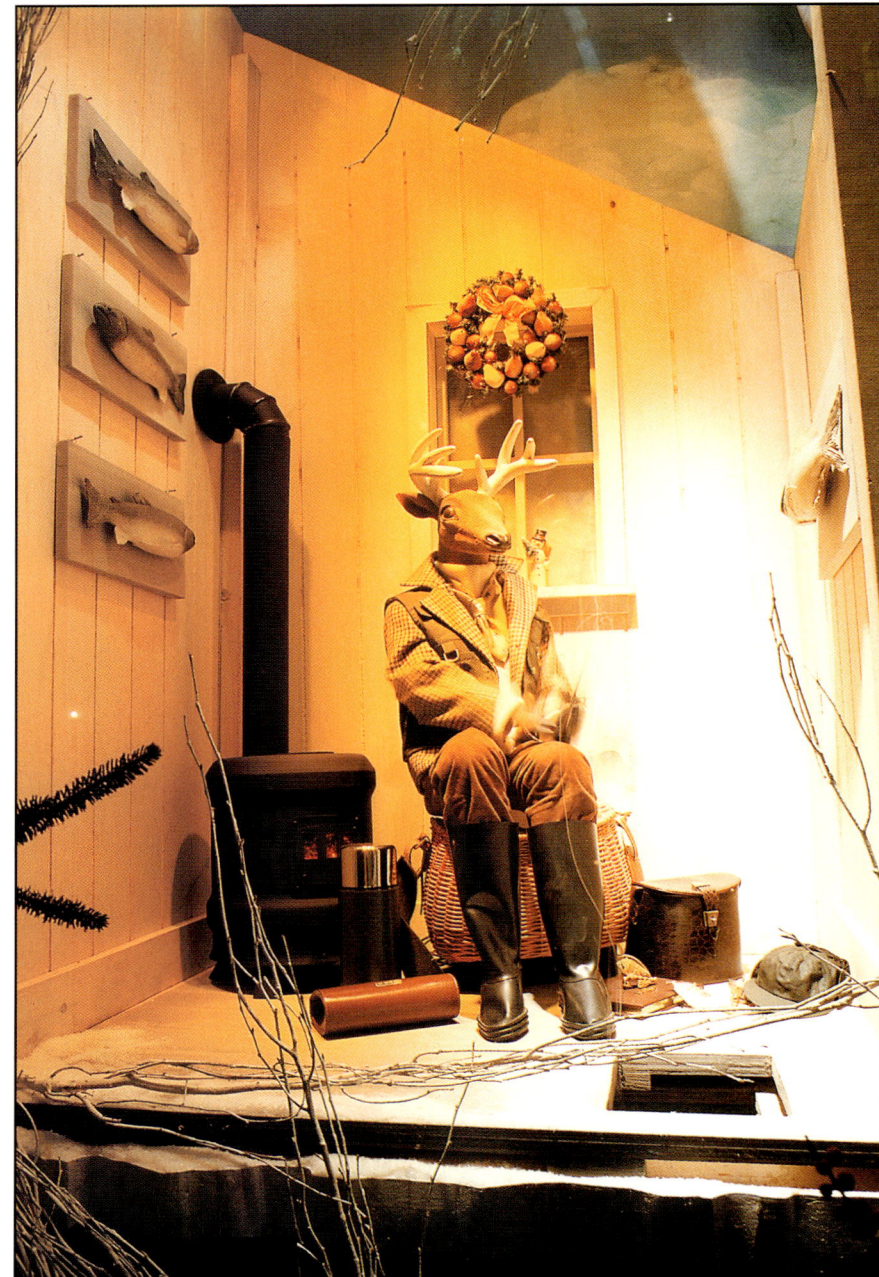

WATHNE LTD., W.57th St., New York, NY
Display Director: Jim Amen

Dear Oh Deer! What could be more Christmasy than one of Santa's ever-loving, ever bearing and ever pulling reindeer? However, as one century wanes and another starts, so does the image of the deer. Here we are showing four deer—half of Santa's usual team—in a variety of interpretations.

Most traditional and even then far from "old fashioned" is the dressed up deer in Wathne's window who is seen warming up by an old, wood burning stove before setting out on his rounds. His "rounds," this time, include some fishing and fly casting and that explains those rubber boots.

Beretta's deer—in silver and gold—is high styled and elegant. The gold pine cones on the floor and the gold gift box are the only other seasonal touches.

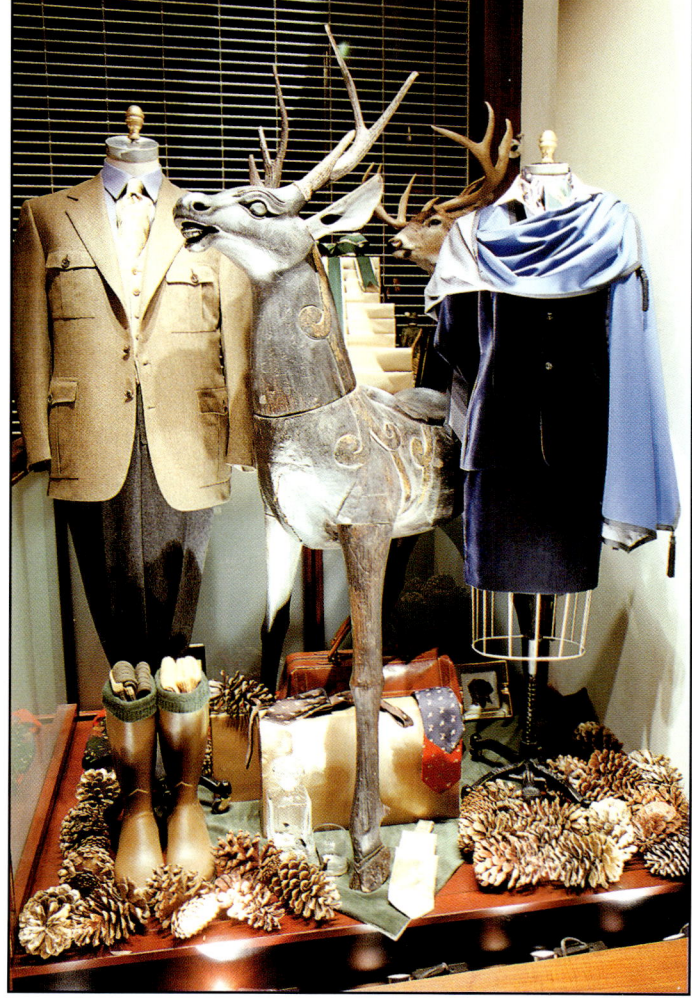

BERETTA, Madison Ave., New York, NY

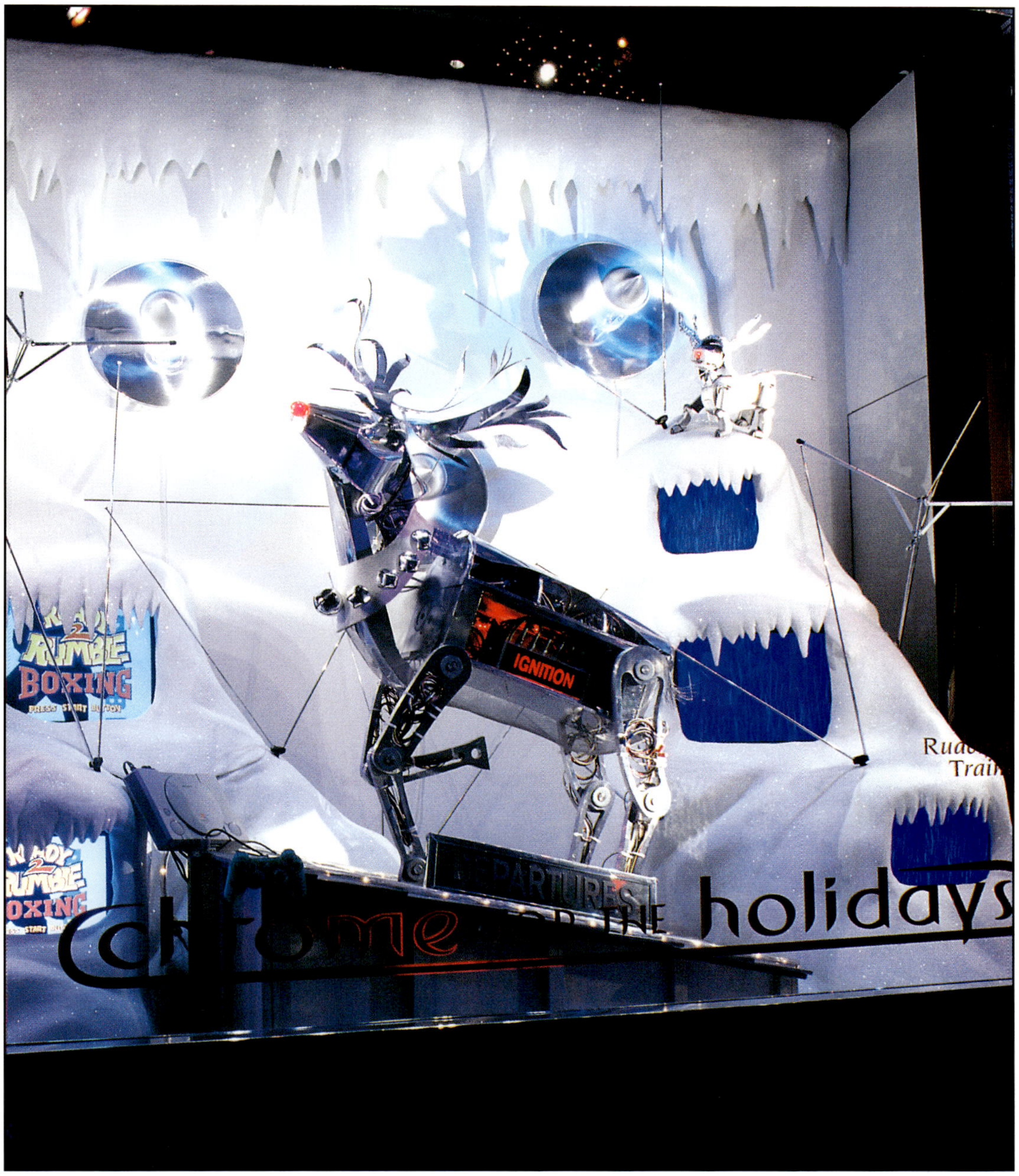

DEER

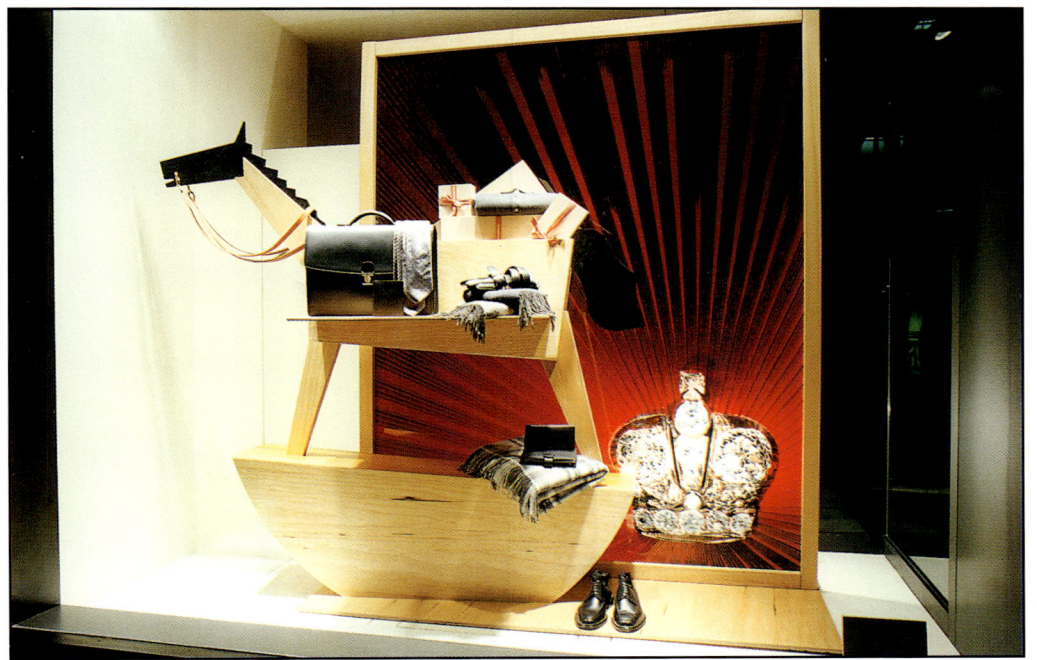

SONY, Madison Ave., New York, NY
Visual Events Director: Christine Belich

Zegna's rocking horse (but it could have been a deer) is simple and smart and provides a series of elevations for the men's fashion accessories. The pine wood frame around the red velour pleated background continues the simple, smart treatment while the red offers a bow to the season.

The robot-deer, a 21st Century deep sculpture, in Sony's window is definitely a thing of the future. Though recognizable as our dear, lovable deer, it has more in common with the computer age and cyber space. It is definitely "Chrome for the Holidays," Sony's, tongue-in-cheek look at traditional holiday icons.

ZEGNA, 5th Ave., New York, NY
VM Director: Mark Hoch

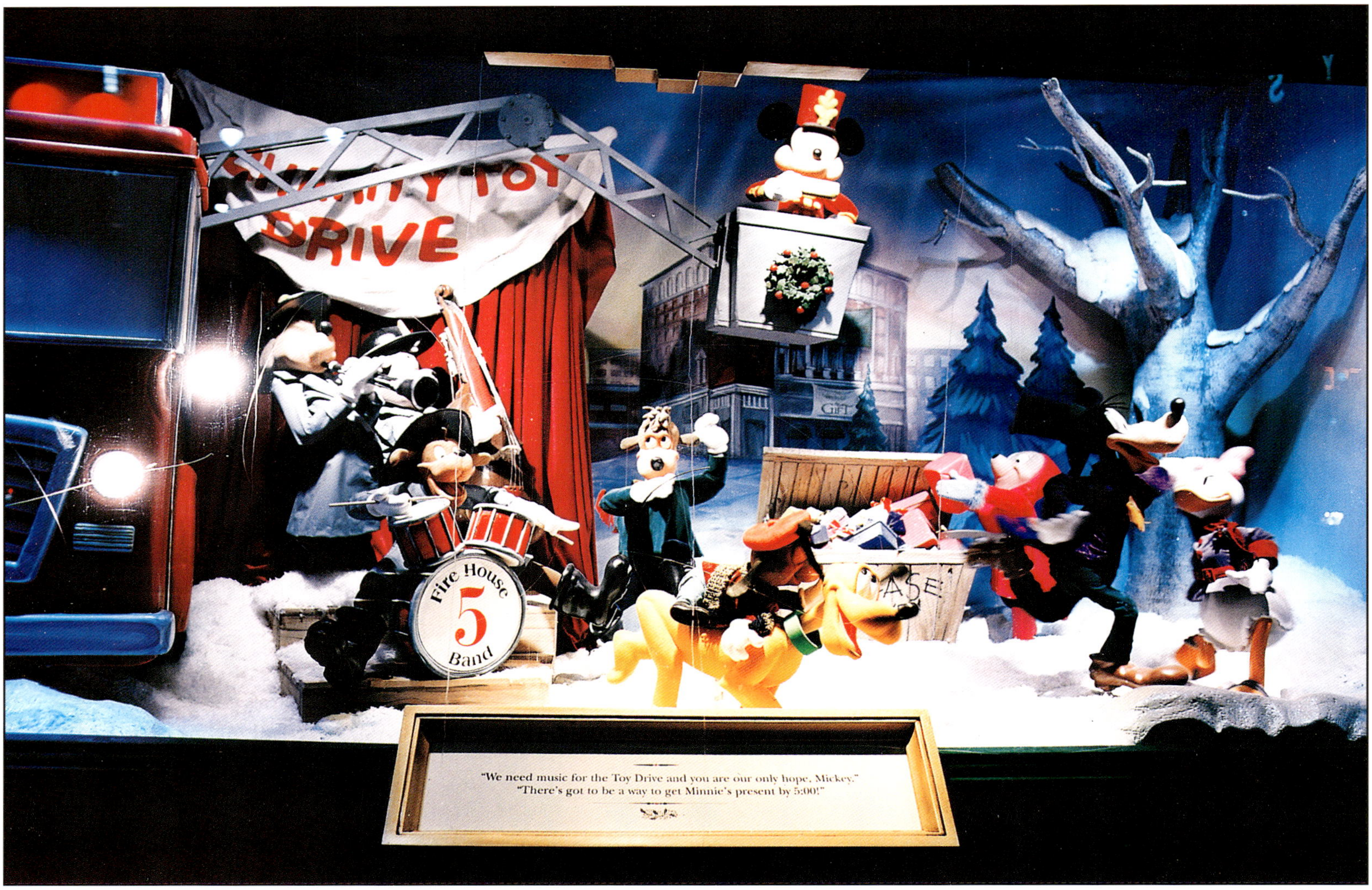

DISNEY

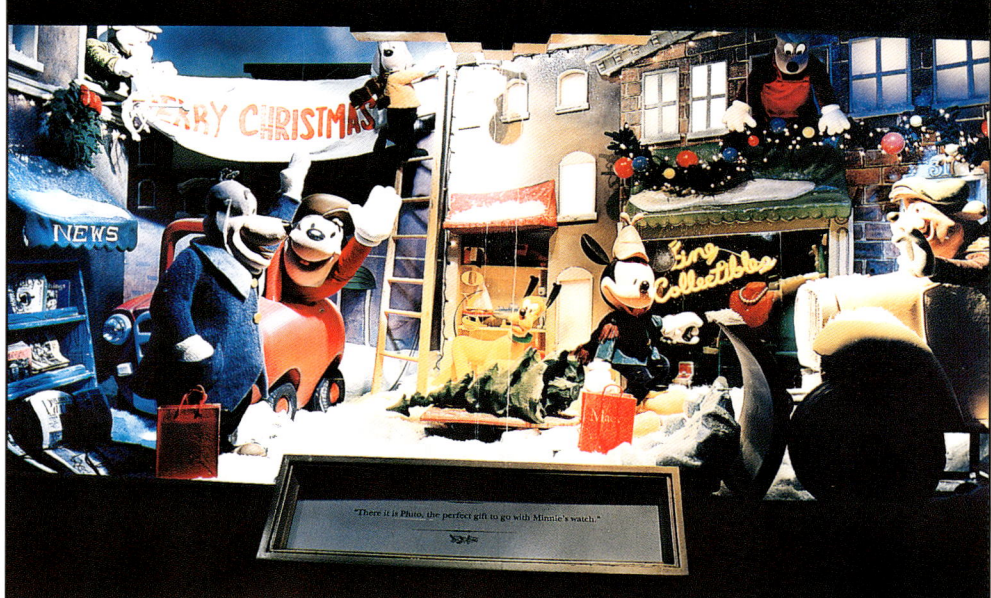

MACY'S, (ABOVE AND LEFT) Herald Square, New York, NY
Windows Director: Sam Joseph
Photographer: James Mulea, New York, NY

It was another "good old fashioned Christmas at Macy's with the perennial favorite of old and young making a star appearance. Mickey, Minnie, Pluto, Goofy and even Donald Duck put on new "hats" and took on new roles to give that all time favorite short story—"A Gift of the Magi" by O. Henry—a whole new flavor. The story now has Mickey selling his harmonica to buy Minnie a chain for the watch that she has just sold to buy Mickey a harmonica case.

Sam Joseph and his talented staff created three dimensional settings and incidents to fill out the six different scenes with loads of retro accents to please those who are old enough to remember when the "retro" was actually current and also please those young enough to find the "retro" fun-funky and cool. The old fashioned Christmas spirit is seen everywhere with trees aglitter with lights, decorated shop fronts, snowflakes and stars, and even "hearth and home" with the fireplace draped with Christmas stockings. There is music and song and the continuity is provided on plaques set up near the glass.

Of course, all's well that ends well and the holiday message comes through as "a gift from the heart is cherished and true. A present is best when love is given too." Just to remind you that you can get a love-ly present at Macy's—there are little red Macy bags scattered throughout the vignettes.

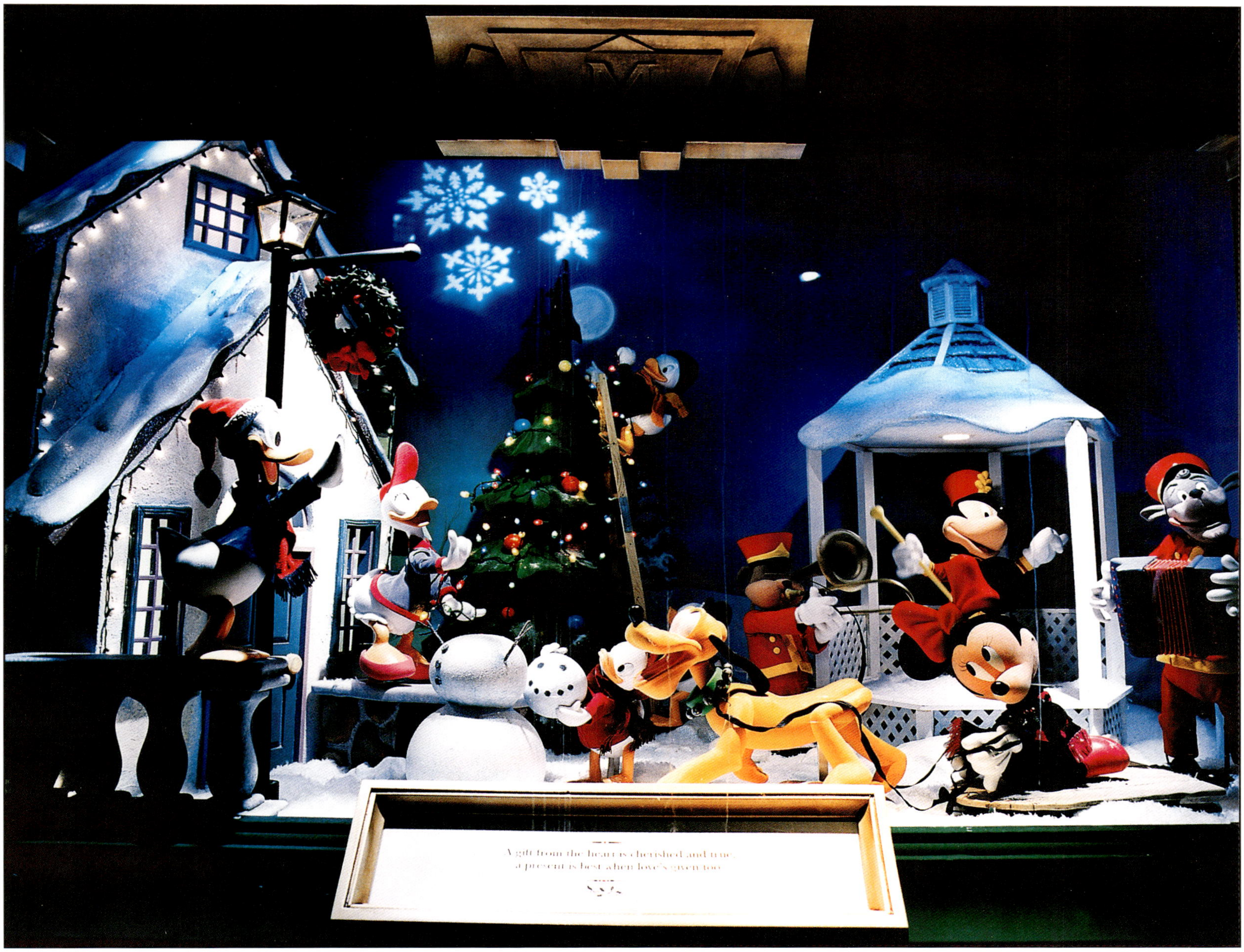

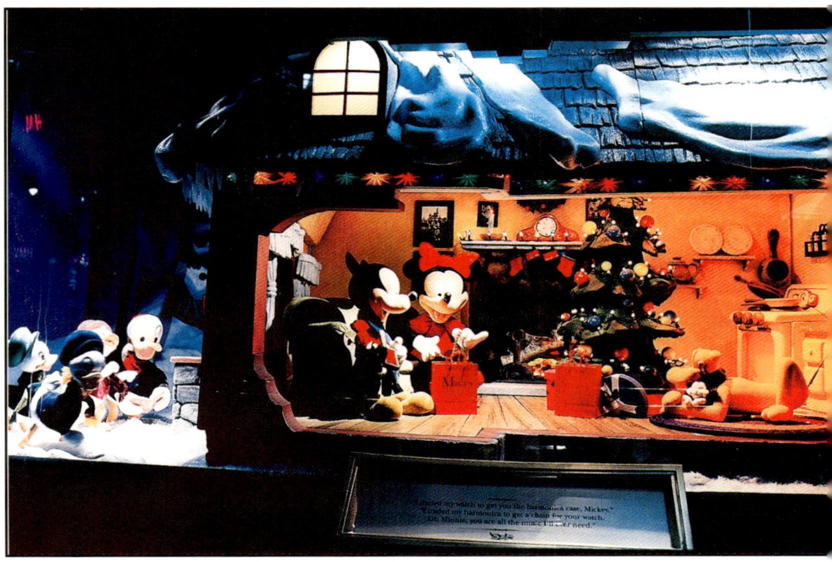

DISNEY

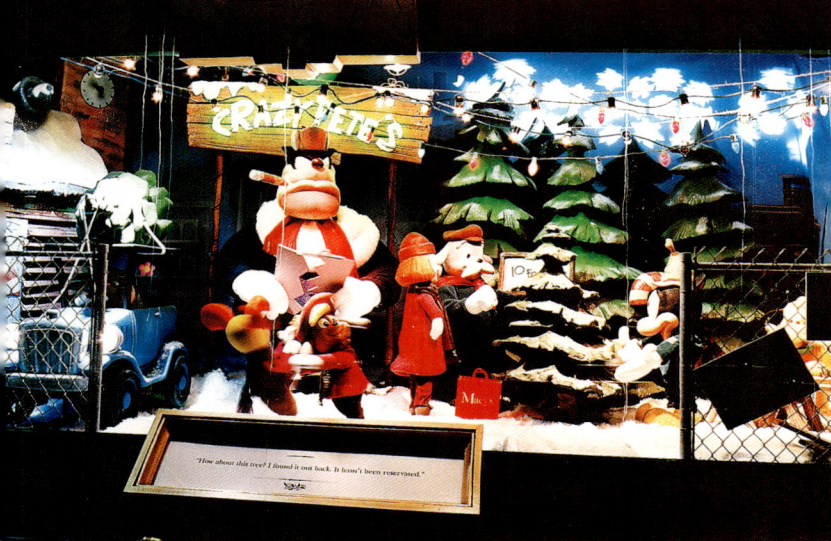

MACY'S, (ALL) Herald Square, New York, NY
Windows Director: Sam Joseph
Photographer: James Mulea, New York, NY

EVERGREENS

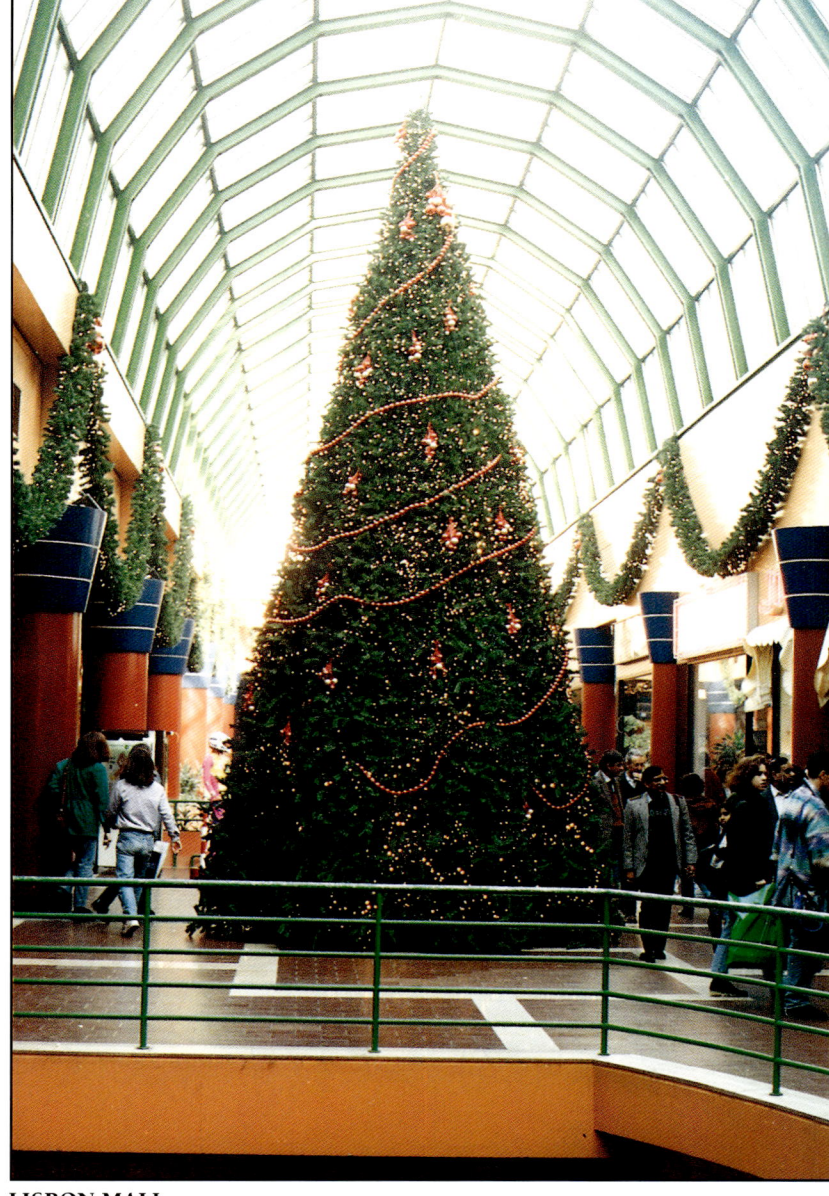

LISBON MALL
Designed & Executed by Barthelmess of Germany

What would Christmas be—or would it even be Christmas—without a Christmas tree??? In windows, in stores, in shopping malls and centers, in office buildings in public squares and most any place at this time of the year one is sure to find an evergreen tree—real or pretend—loaded and overwhelmed with ornaments, ribbons, berries, bows, toys, trinkets and thousands of flashing, flickering and twinkling lights. The Christmas tree is an international symbol and shown here are some that have graced malls in England, Portugal, France, Germany and the US. Throughout this issue the reader has seen smaller trees adapted to window or in-store use, but here we go for the spectacular.

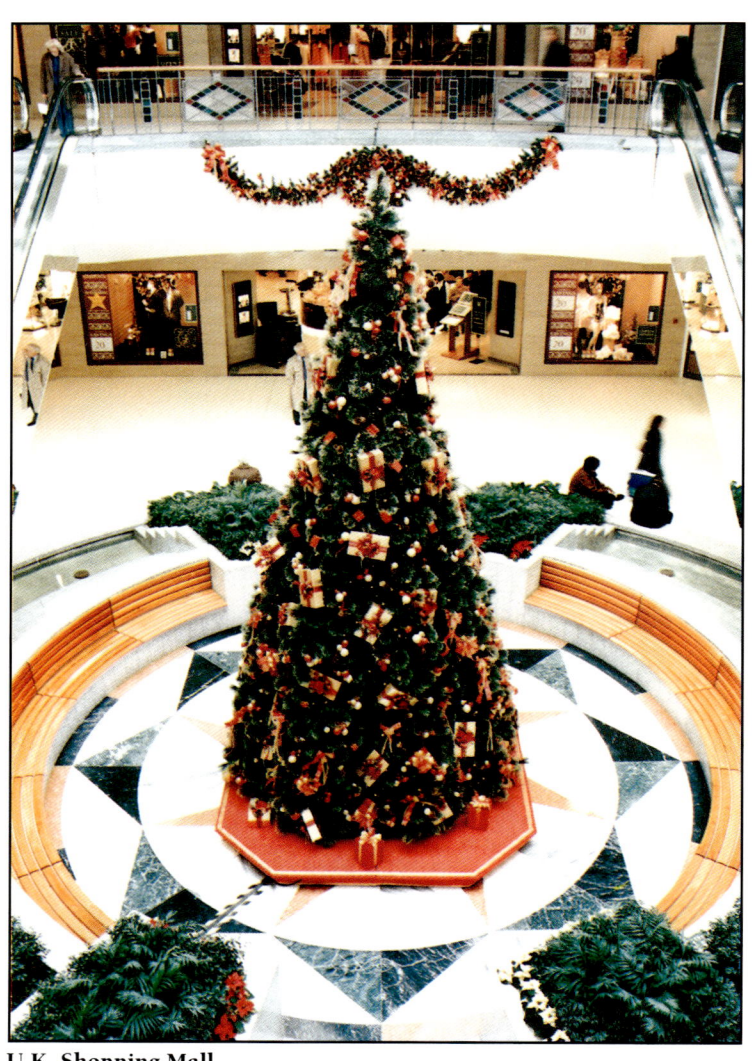

U.K. Shopping Mall
Designed & Executed by Barthelmess of Germany

EVERGREENS

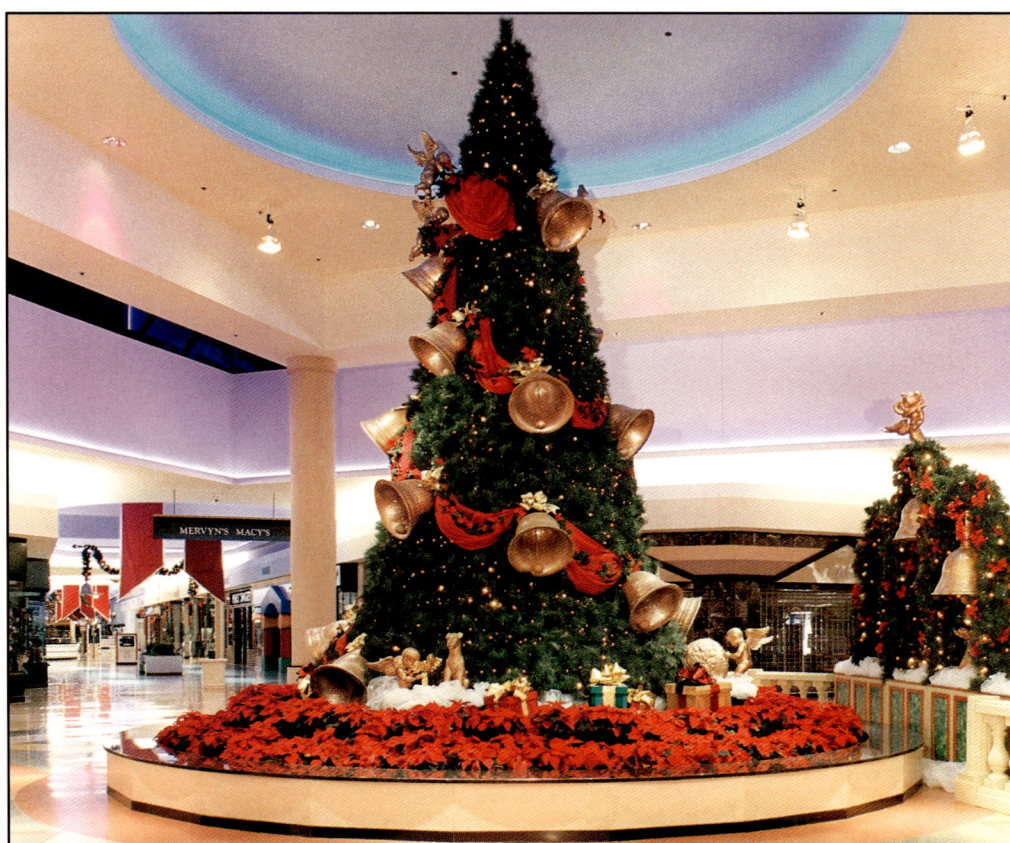

BAYBROOK MALL, Fleetwood, TX
**Designed & Executed by
The Design Centre, Wichita, KS**

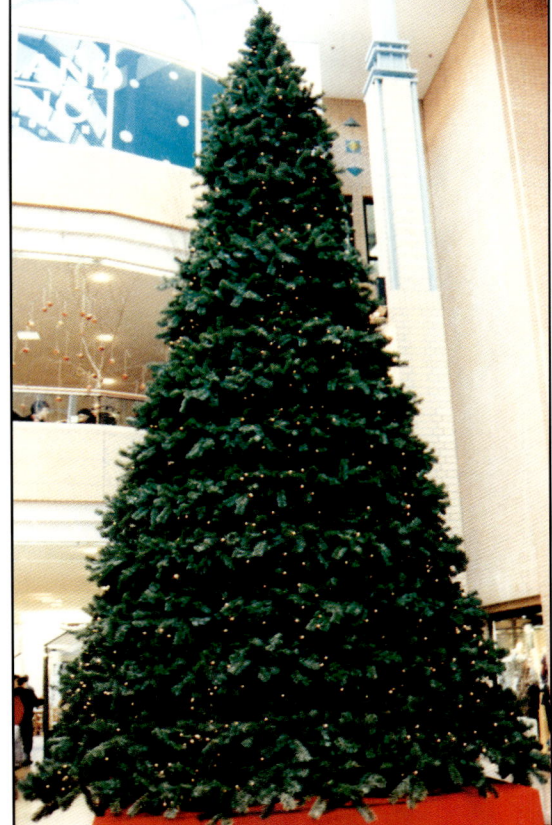

EIDHOVEN MALL
Designed & Executed by Barthelmess of Germany

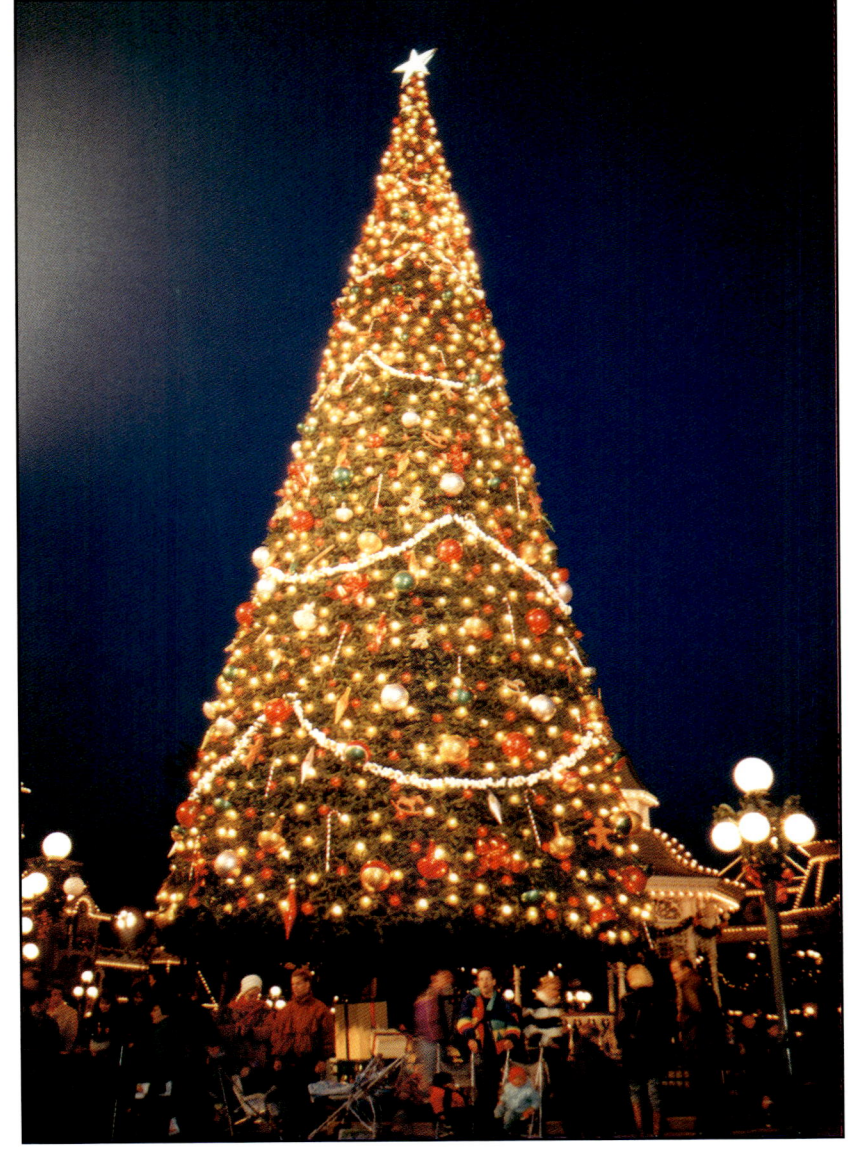

EURO DISNEY, Paris
**Designed & Executed by
Barthelmess of Germany**

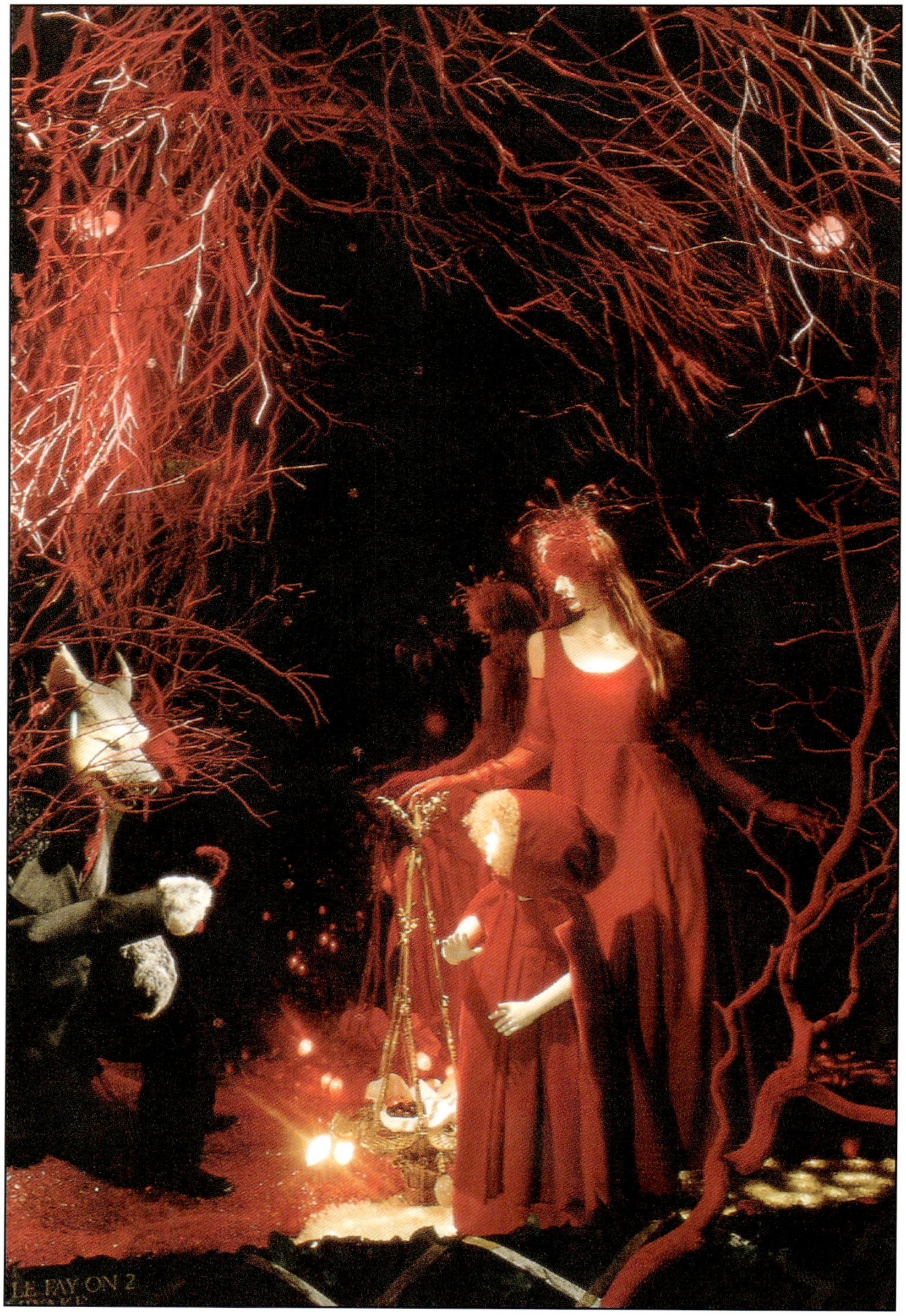

FAIRY TALES

"Fairy tales can come true—it can happen to you—" if you visited the Bergdorf windows which were devoted to updated versions of famous and familiarily fairy tales. You can be Red Riding Hood in a handsome red velvet gown while your daughter takes on the ingenue lead opposite the nasty old wolf lurking amid the silvery trees. You can be reassured that you are the "fairest in the land" in the elegant white gown while the "wicked queen"—in red—gives you a run for the title as she stands behind the richly embellished gold frame.

BERGDORF GOODMAN, (ABOVE AND RIGHT)
Fifth Ave., New York, NY
V.P. of Visual Presentation: Linda Fargo

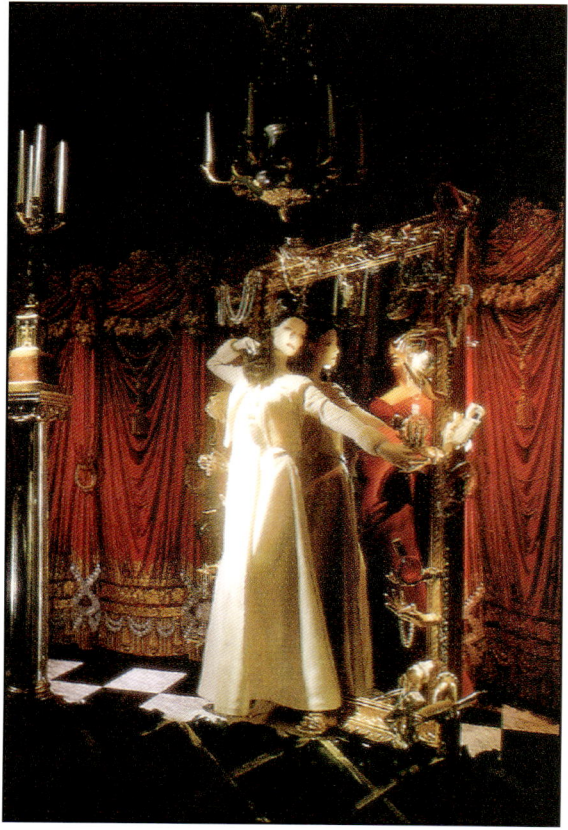

FAIRY TALES

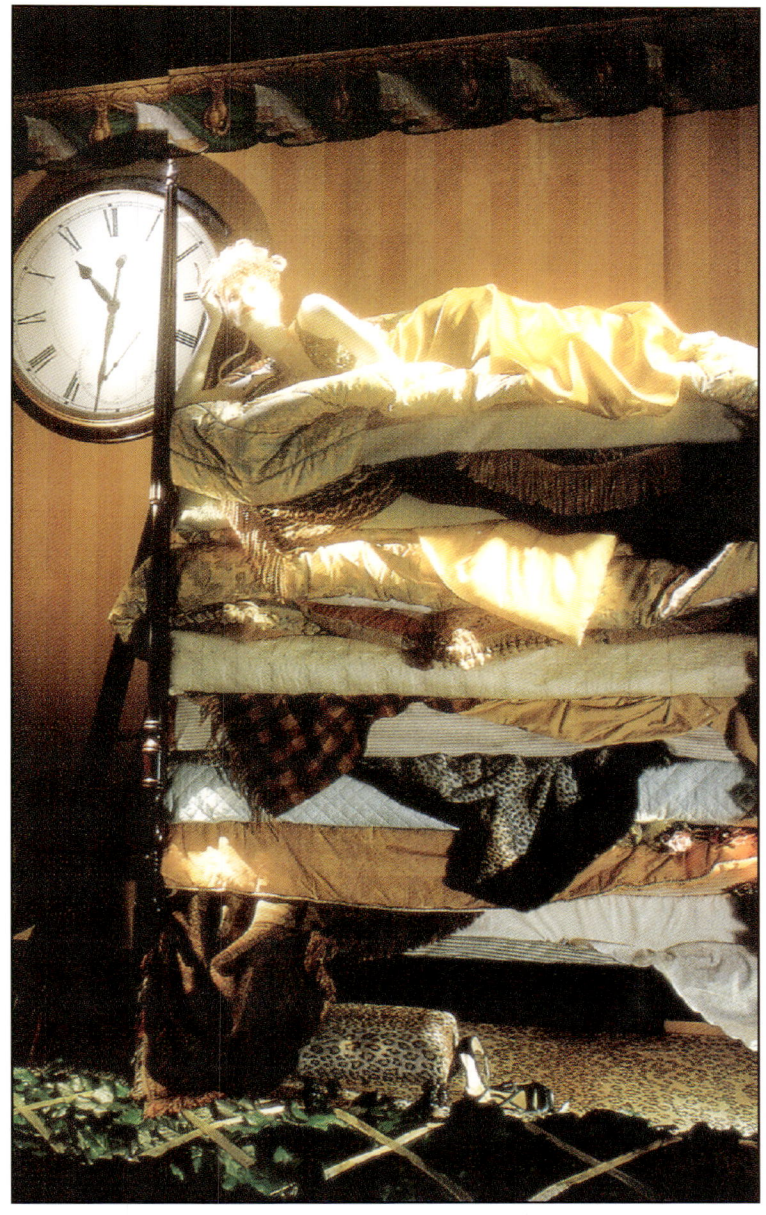

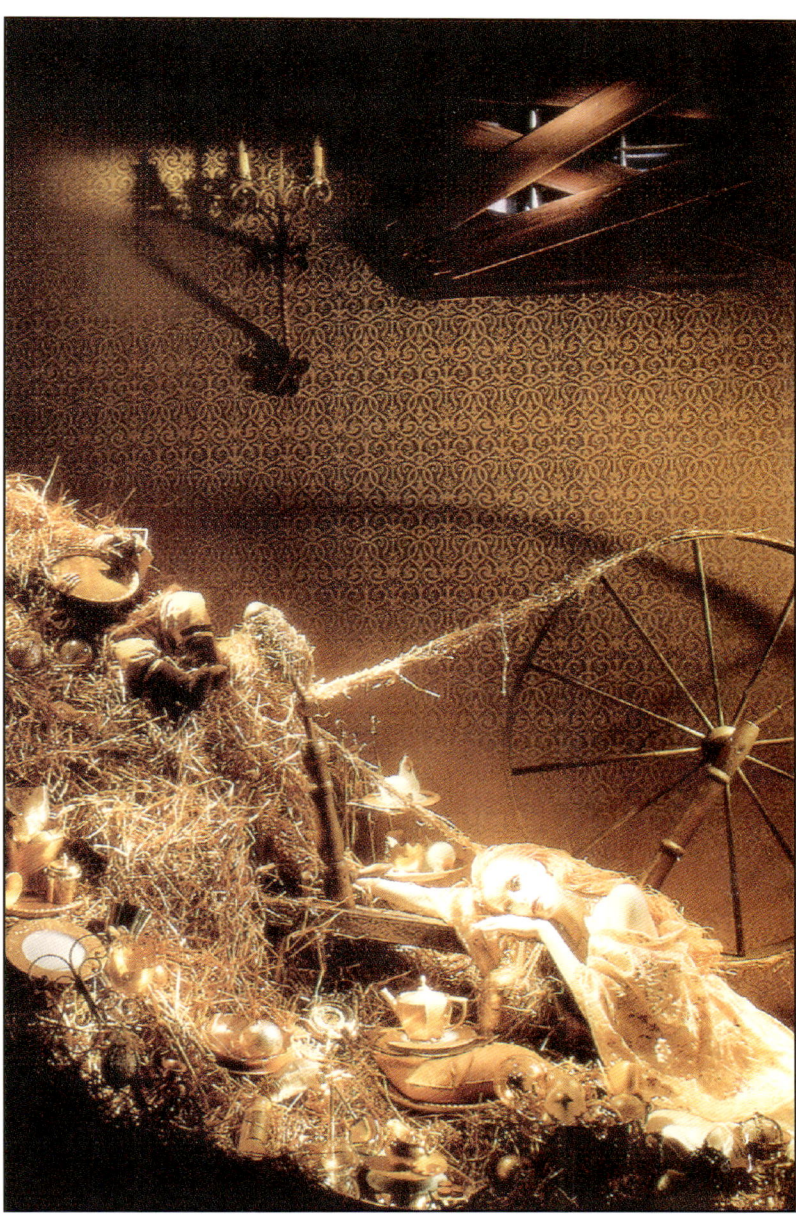

BERGDORF GOODMAN, (ABOVE AND ABOVE RIGHT)
Fifth Ave., New York, NY
V.P. of Visual Presentation: Linda Fargo

Nightgowns reach new levels of sophistication for the "princess" who doesn't know that the "pea" mattresses below, is keeping her from a restful night's sleep. The miller's daughter may not be able to spin straw into gold but she certainly has accumulated a wealth of stunning gifts for the home for her efforts. Ruplestilskin may not be pleased but most hostesses would love to share that collection. All in all, a delightful and decidedly UN-Grimm look at fairy tales.

FOLIAGE

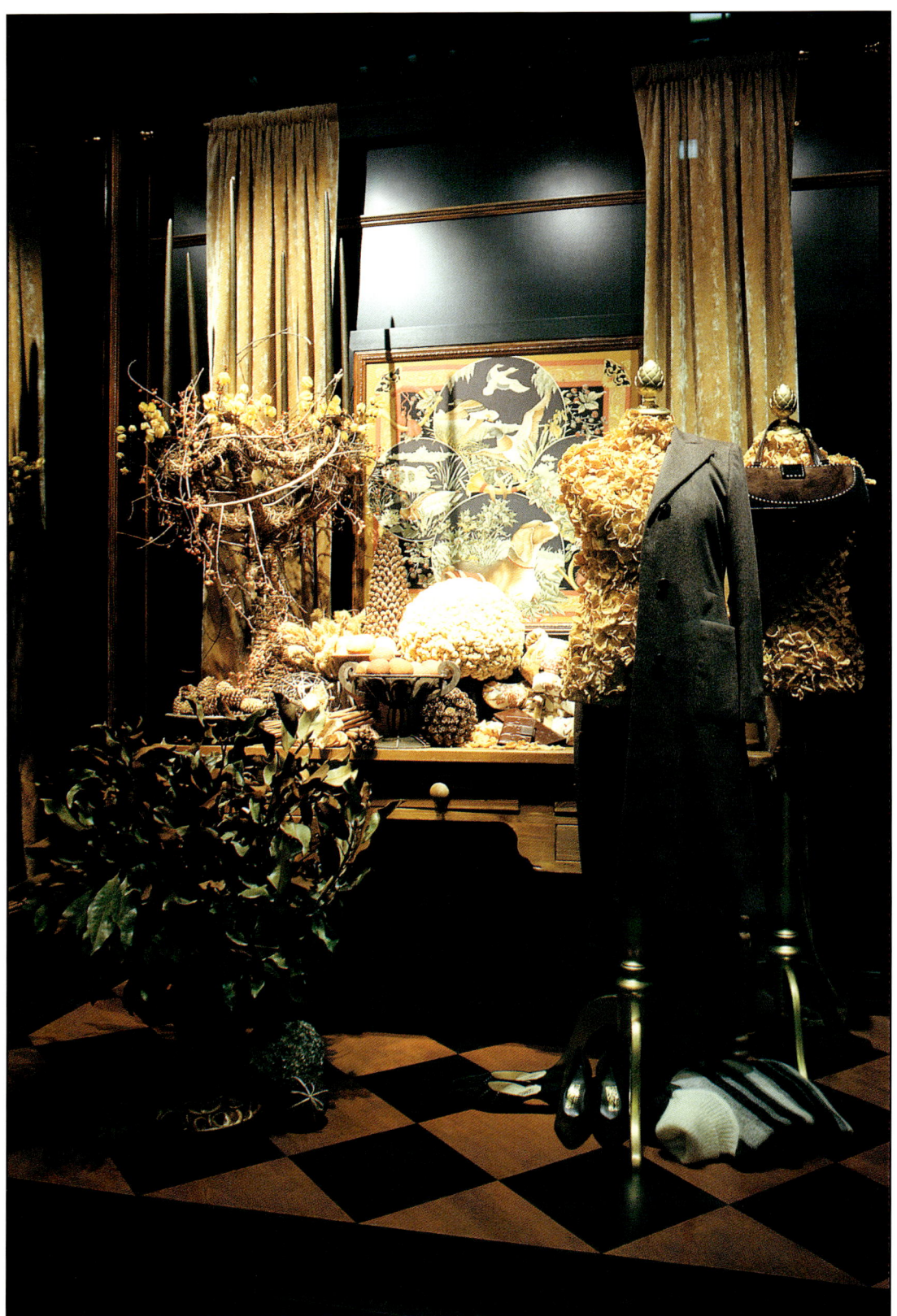

SALVATORE FERRAGAMO
Fifth Ave., New York, NY
Dir. Of Visuals: John Krenek
Assistant: Jesse Barber

Ferragamo's Christmas vignettes—all carefully color coordinated for impact—relied on foliage trim for their seasonal success. Whether it was an architectural setting for the black lined staircase on which the elegant collection of red shoes, bags and accessories were shown amid the lavish twig wreaths all bedecked with red ribbons, bows and berries, or the snowy white garden setting complete with chair, fence and Christmas trees encrusted with glittery ornaments, gold ribbons, pastel eucalyptus sprays and exotic berries—the windows showed off the Ferragamo products while smartly sending out "Best of the Season" greetings. Especially effective was the dress form finished with a flower head textured "blouse" for the smart black suit draped over it. This setting—all rich and opulent in black and gold—suggested a garden work table with the many different cones, berries, dried flowers, foliage and ornaments ready to be assembled for a lavish trim. The gold velvet curtains serve to frame the vignette while contrasting with the flat black woodwork which is accented with gilt.

FOLIAGE

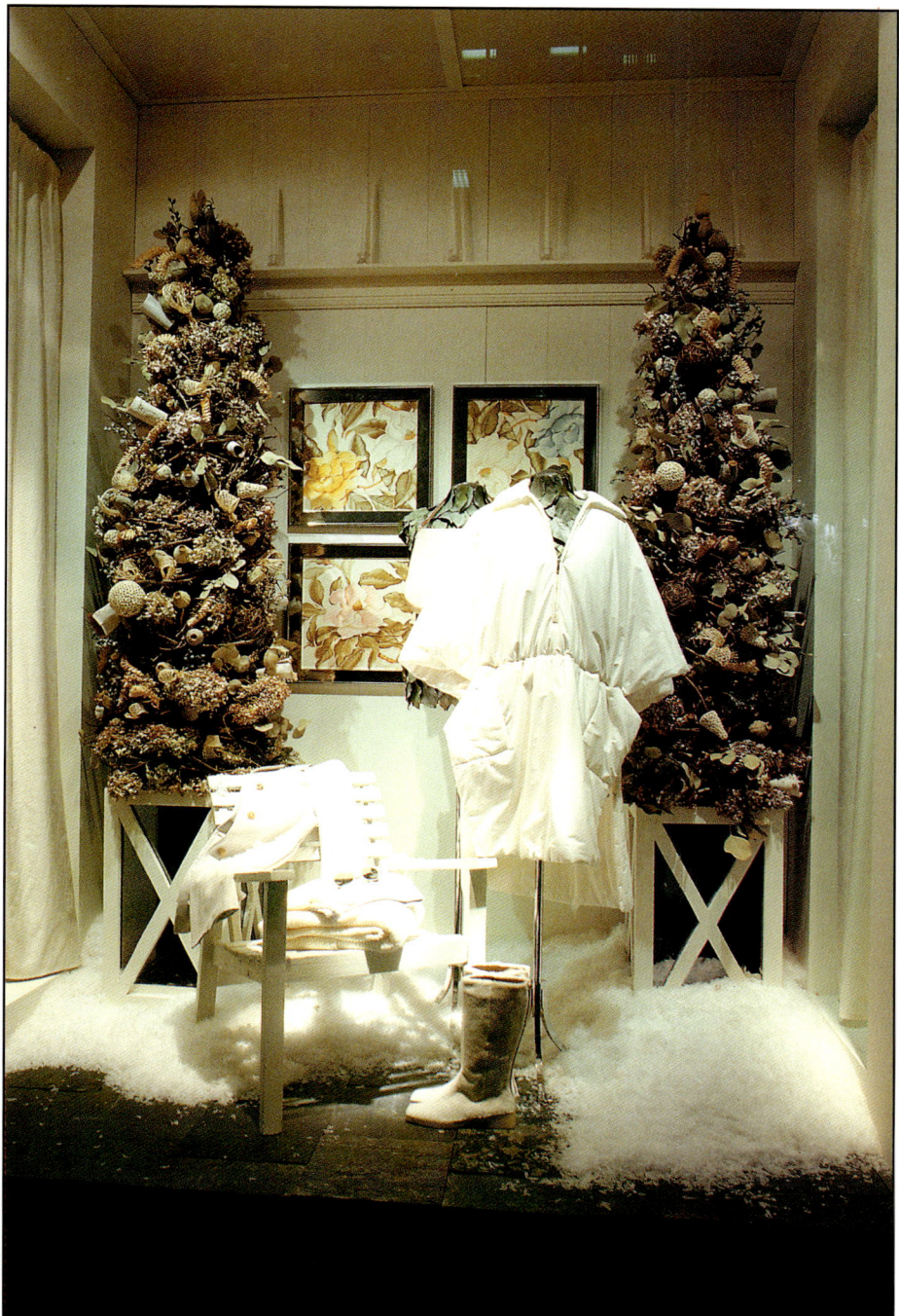

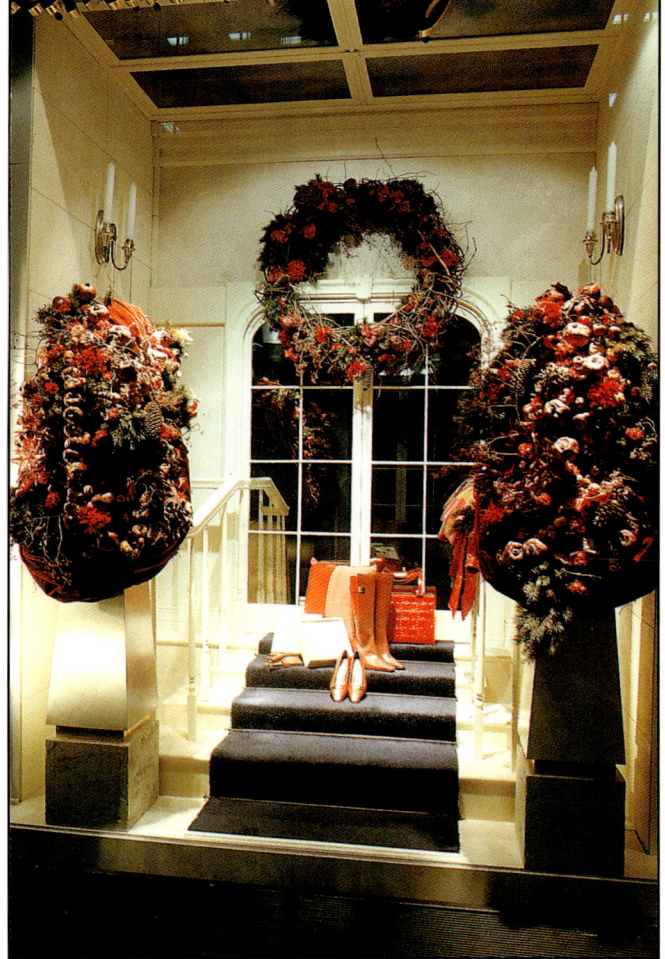

SALVATORE FERRAGAMO, (ABOVE AND LEFT)
Fifth Ave., New York, NY
Dir. Of Visuals: John Krenek
Assistant: Jesse Barber

FORMALWEAR

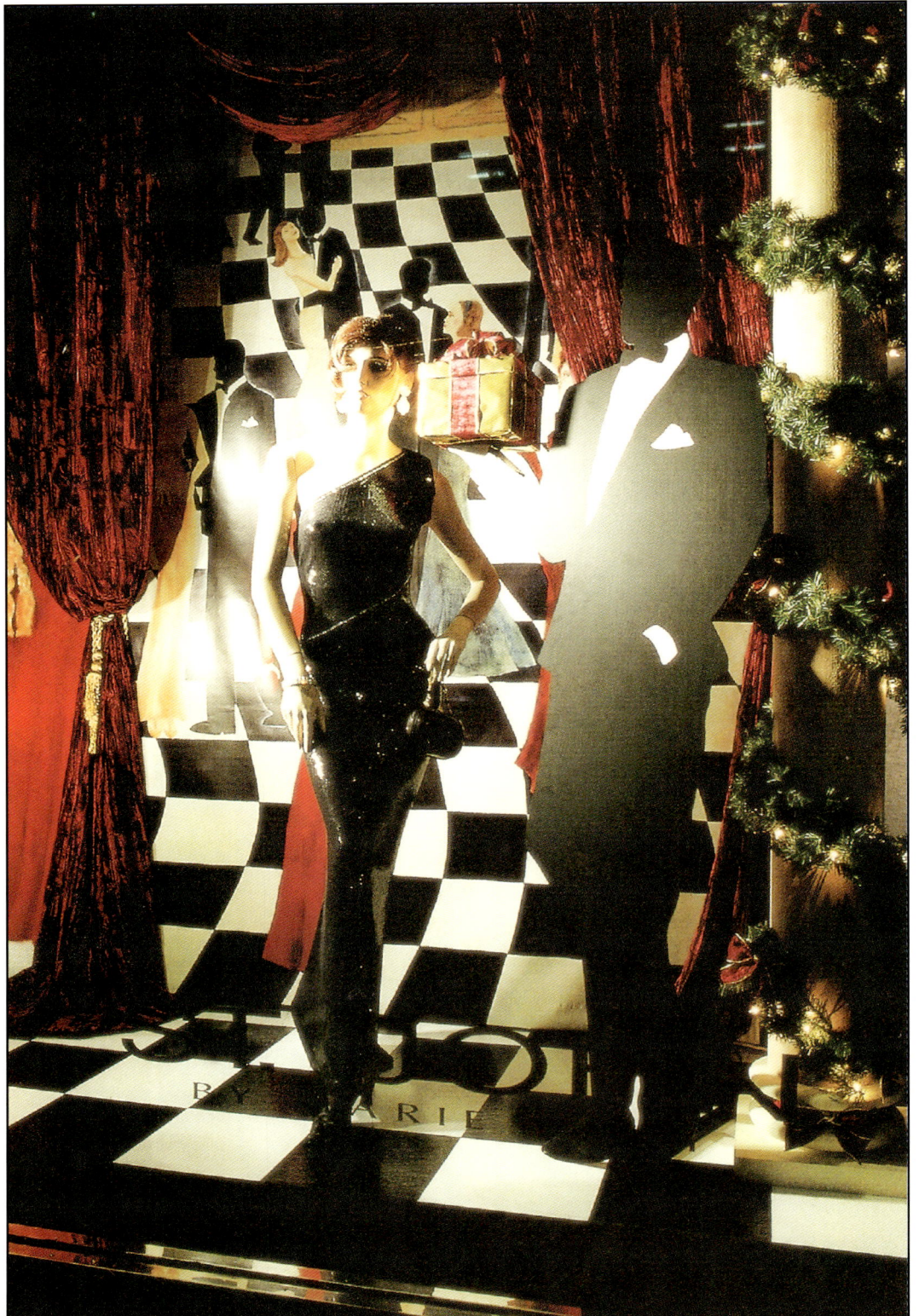

ST. JOHN BOUTIQUE,
Fifth Ave., New York, NY
V.P. Creative Design: Kelly Gray

Dressing up to celebrate the holiday season! On the following pages are some recent Christmas formal wear windows. Frequently menswear is featured along with the women's gowns: the tuxedo is the ideal fashion accessory for the formally dressed gown. At St. John's, on this page, a cut-out tuxedo-ed male figure escorts the lady dressed in black. The black and white checkered design cleverly adds depth and pattern to the display and the red draperies complete the holiday setting.

Bergdorf's Store for Men took off on flights to exotic places like the Imperial Palace, shown here, and in another window "ghost" musicians are backing up the headless songstress in a '40-ish musical night club setting.

Aquascutum also resorts to headless figures and combines formalwear for men and women are combined in a "homey" setting. She is perched on the fireplace mantel because the chair and floor are completely covered with gift suggestions and fashion accessories.

Pilar Rossi's realistic mannequin is dressed in red accented with black and it is surrounded by cut-out, silver leafed giant Christmas ornament forms. They serve to separate the mannequin up front from the store that is visible beyond the open backed window.

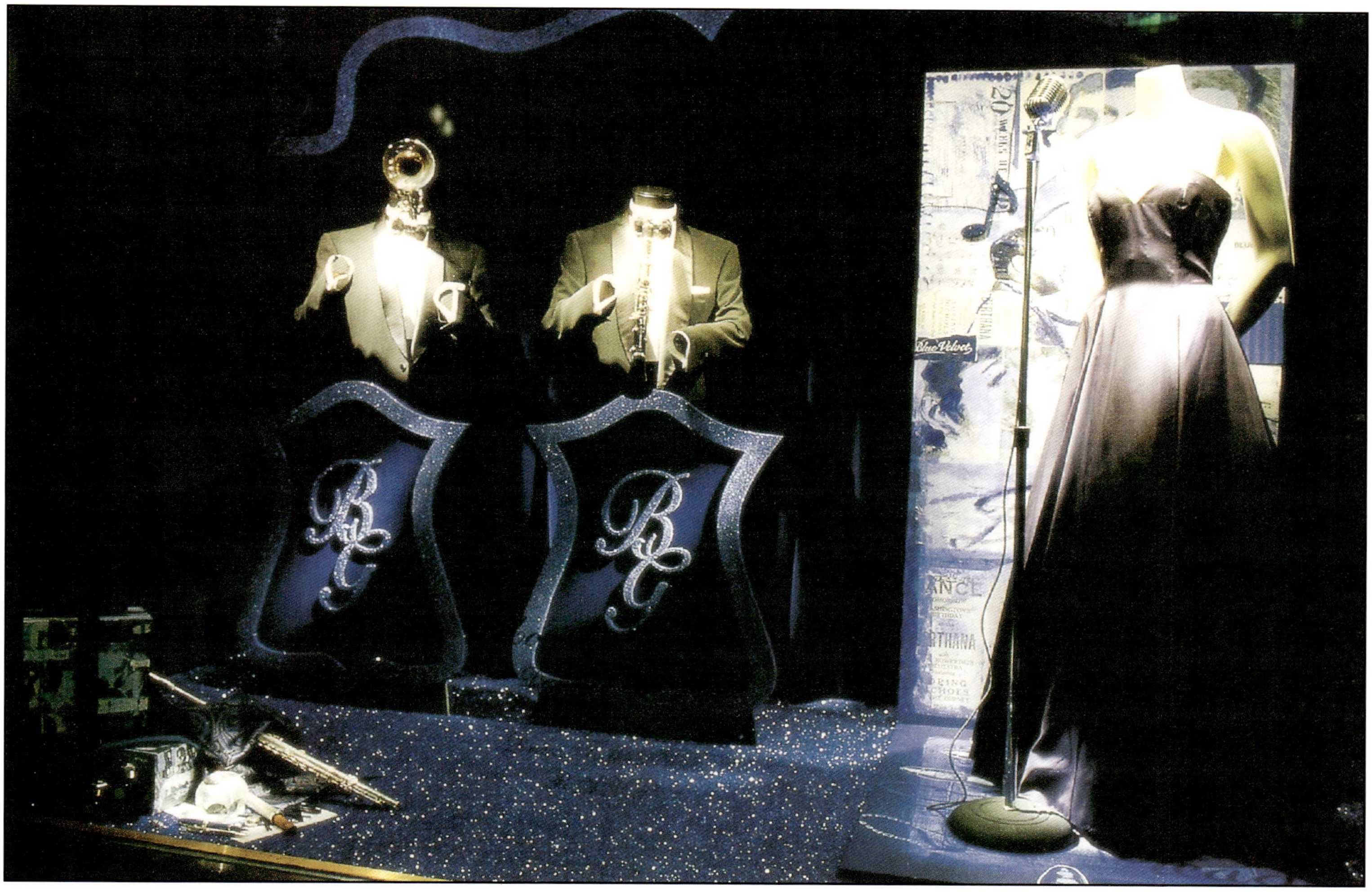

FORMALWEAR

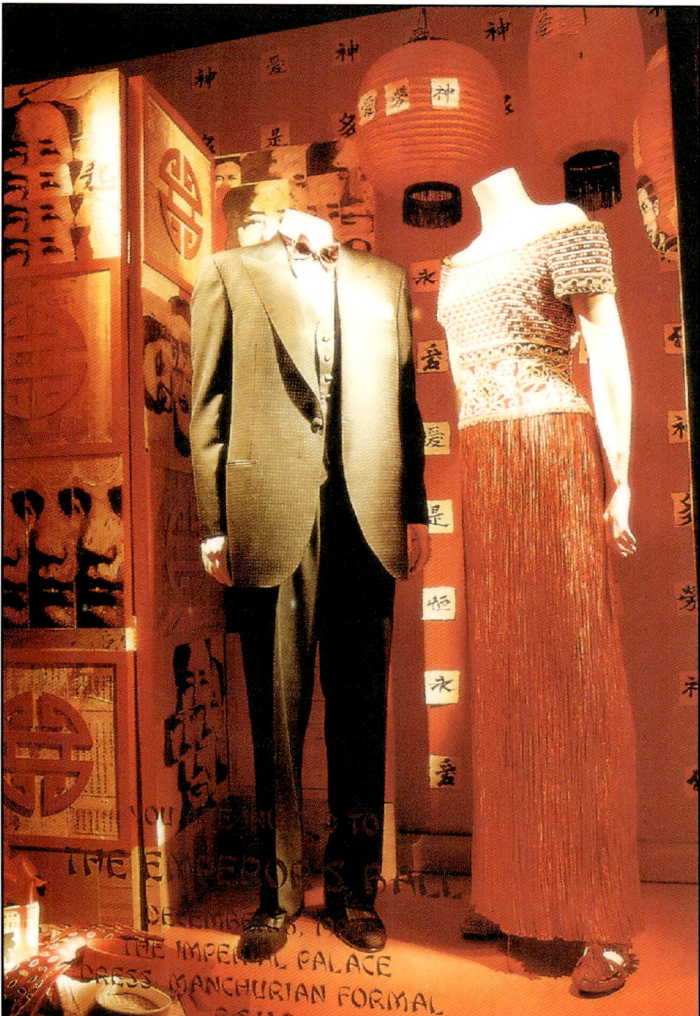

BERGDORF GOODMAN, (ABOVE AND LEFT)
Fifth Ave., New York, NY
V.P. Visual Presentation: Linda Fargo

GINGERBREAD

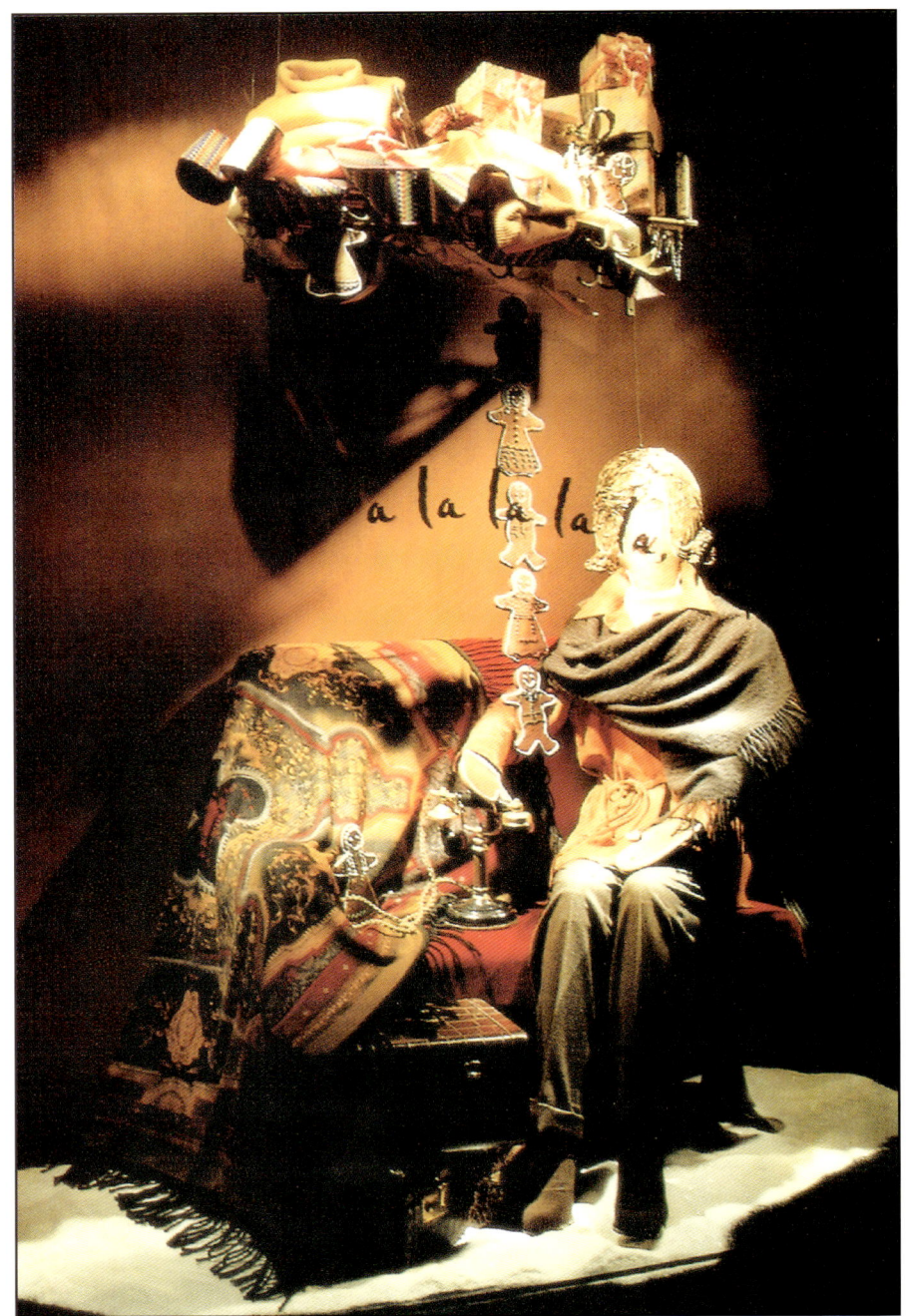

Paul Stuart's design team was off and running like the gingerbread man in the well remembered children's story. Iced "gingerbread" heads and hands over the beautifully draped and dressed suit forms serve as the continuity in this collection of windows that shows men's formal and casual wear as well as women's gift ideas. Blacked out window spaces, cleverly illuminated so the viewer sees only what the designers meant to be seen, are the focal attraction in these dramatic and amusing presentations. Almost a half ton of salt was used to provide the snowy setting for the merchandise arranged on the floor.

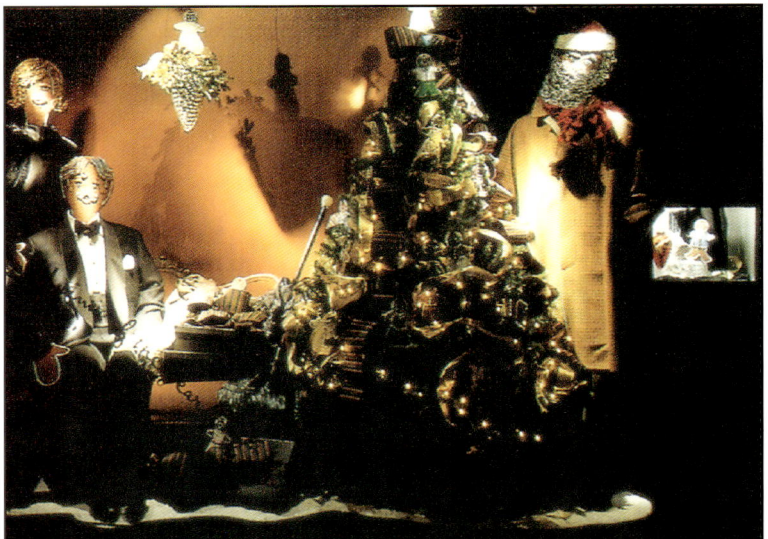

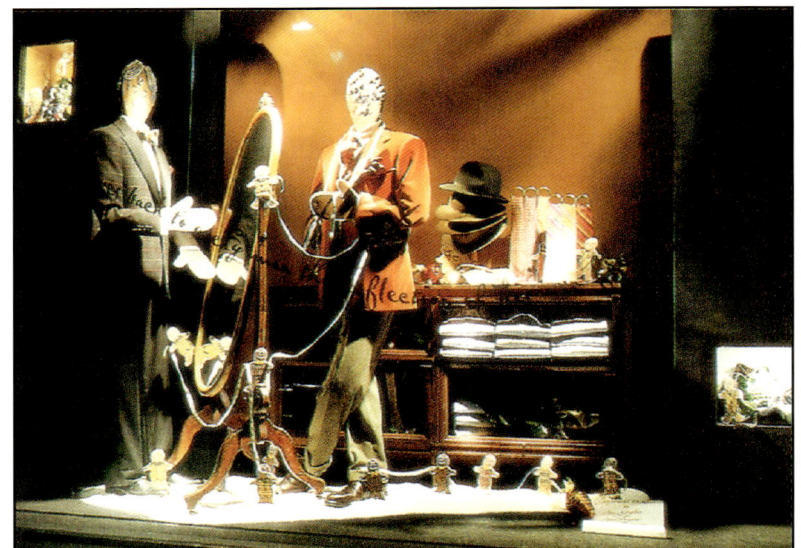

PAUL STUART, (ALL) Madison Ave., New York, NY
Creative Director: Tom Beebe
Display Managers: Gennaro Fredella/Michael Verbert
Gingerbread Fabrication: Amy's Bread, Chelsea Market, New York NY

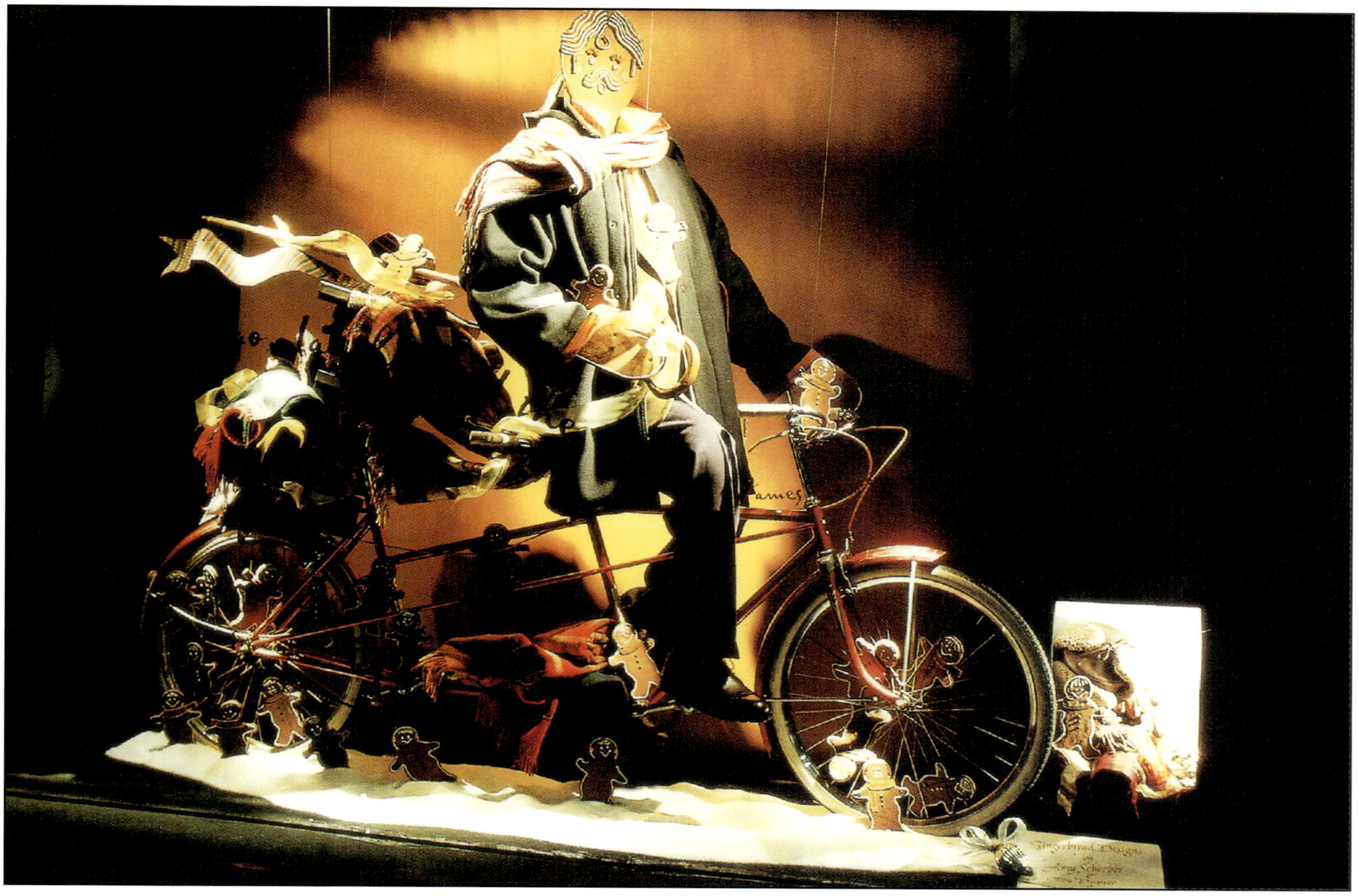

GINGERBREAD

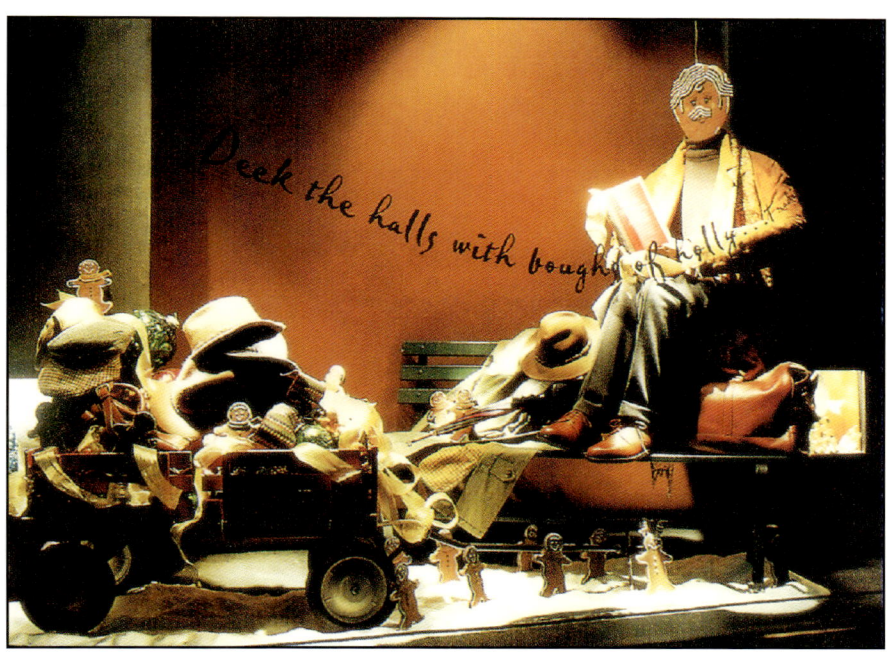

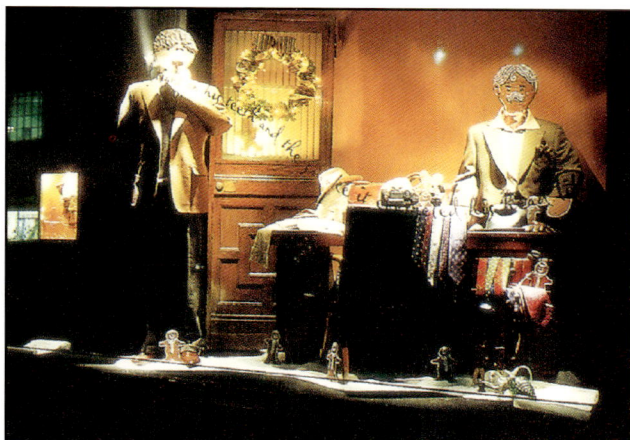

PAUL STUART, (ALL) Madison Ave., New York, NY
Creative Director: Tom Beebe
Display Managers: Gennaro Fredella/Michael Verbert
Gingerbread Fabrication: Amy's Bread, Chelsea Market, New York NY

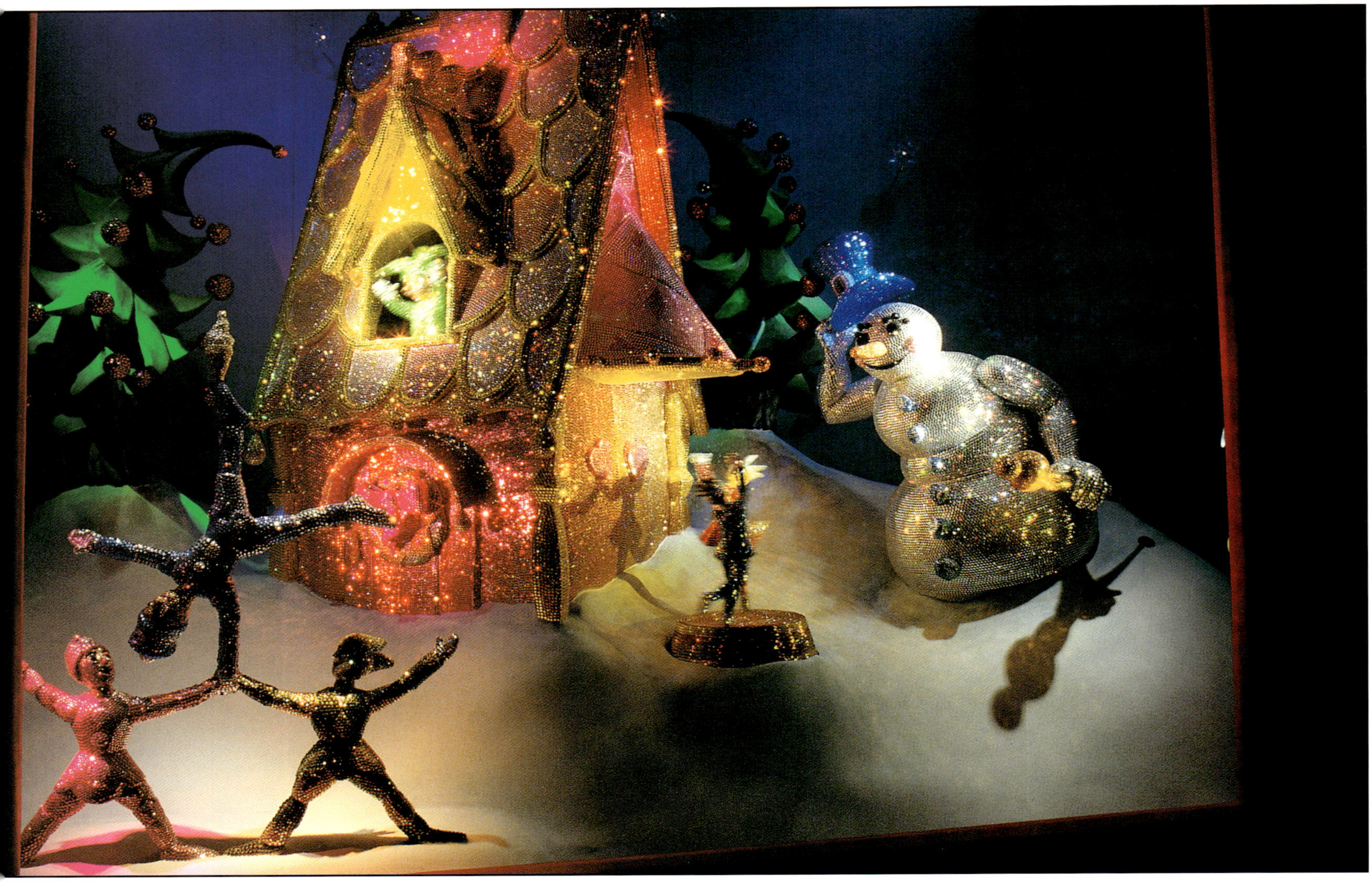

GLISTEN

BLOOMINGDALES, (ABOVE AND RIGHT), Lexington Ave., New York, NY
Creative Director: Mike Fisher

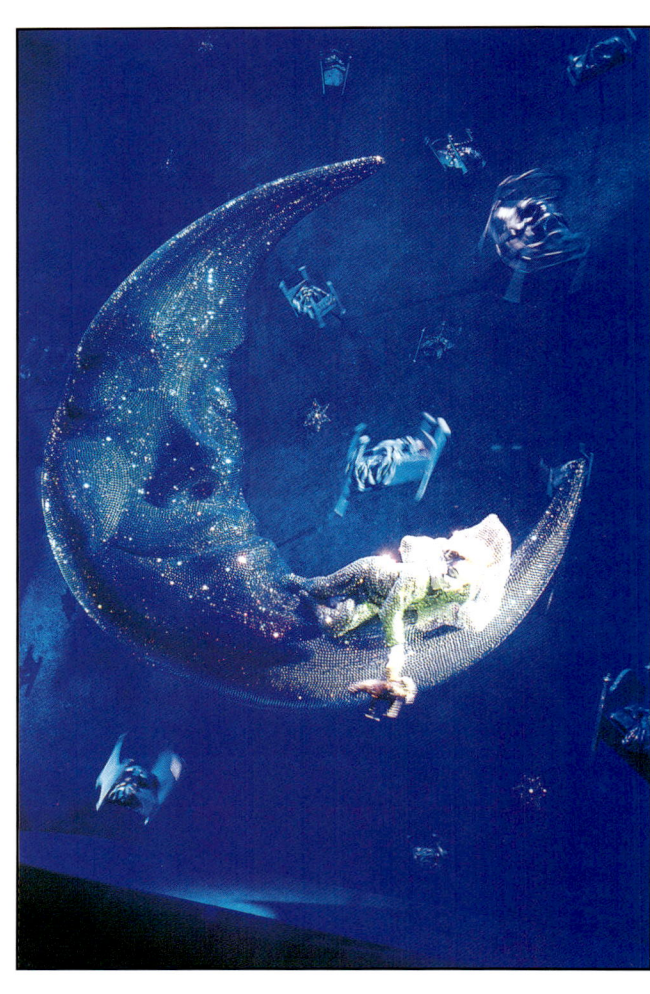

It took over 16,000 man and woman hours of labor and over one million crystals provided by the famous Swarovski company to affect the six Bloomingdale windows that filled Lexington Ave. with sparkle, shimmer and shine.

Under the supervision of Mike Fisher, Bloomingdale's creative director, each window was filled with traditional Christmas motifs and characters such as Rudolf of the noted red nose, Santa in his scarlet outfit, snow-people, stars and even a child sleeping blissfully on a crystal encrusted crescent moon and dreaming of all this wonder.

Also shown here is a gingerbread house afire with pinks, reds, and gold tinted crystals, acrobats in vivid colors and a silvery snowman with a brilliant blue hat. All this glitter and glow was set off by the dark background and the soft, snow covered floor.

GLISTEN

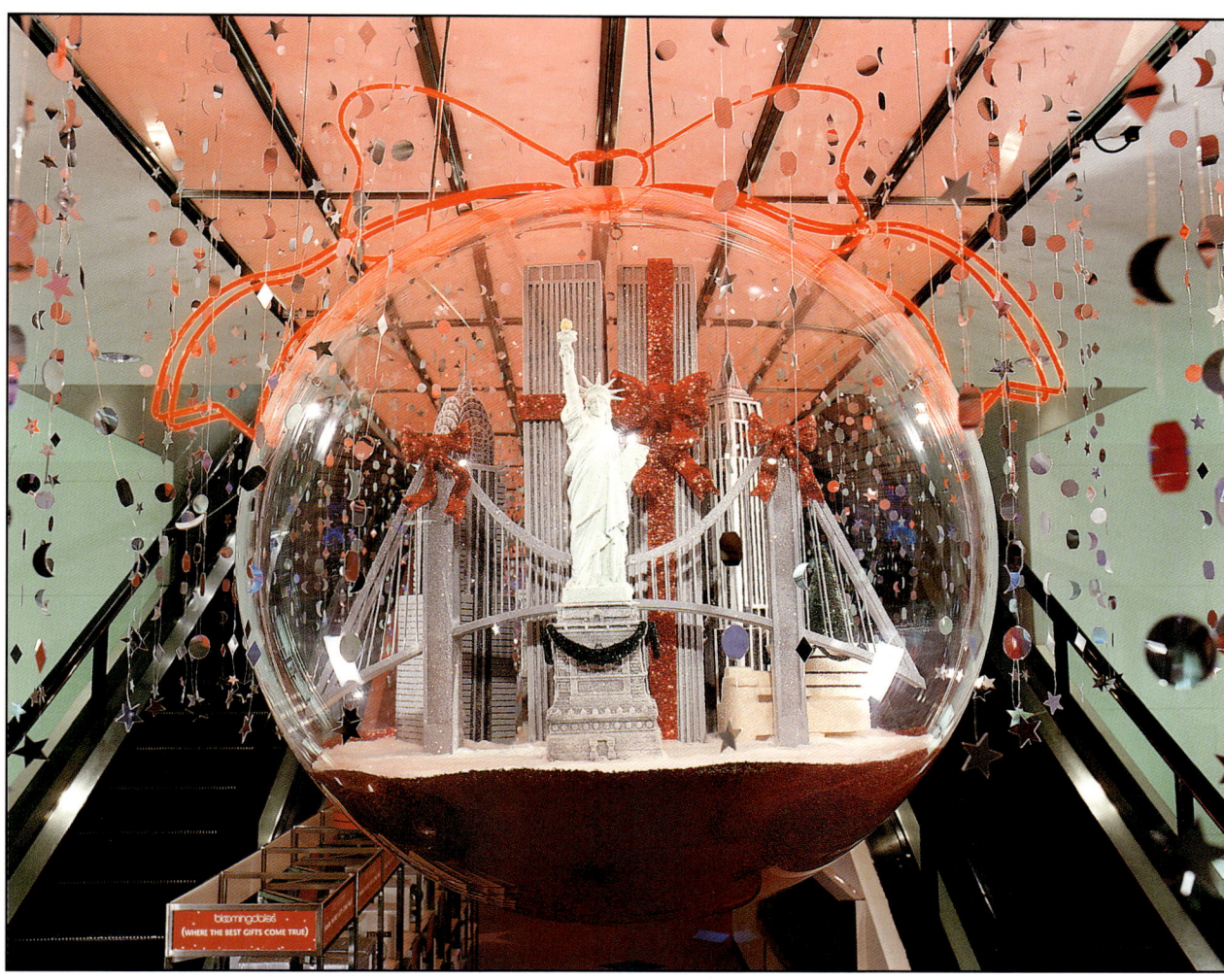

BLOOMINGDALES, (ALL)
Lexington Ave.,
New York, NY
VP of Visual Merchandising:
Jack Hruska

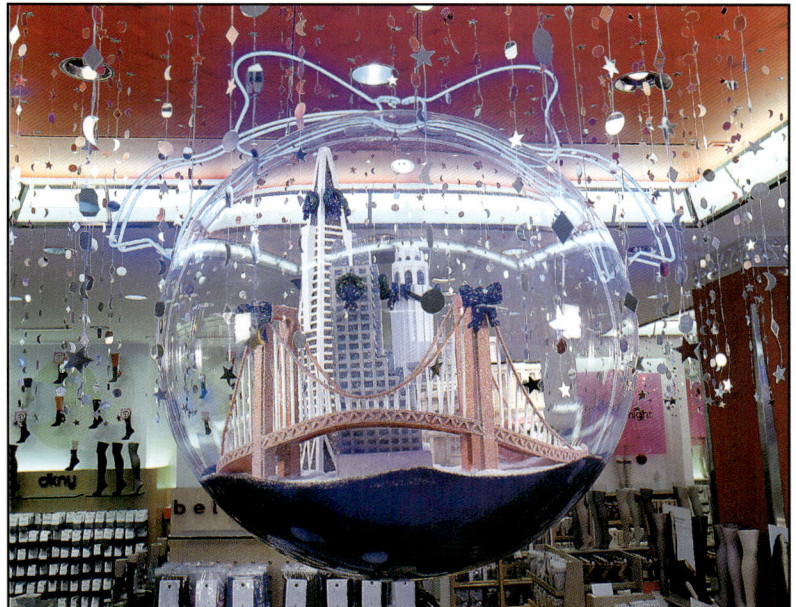

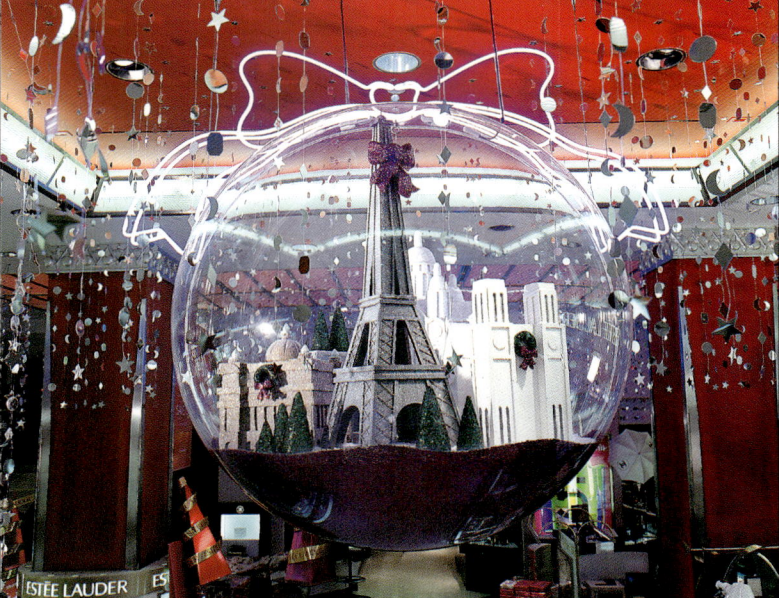

The glitter from the Swarovski crystal from the windows followed through into the interior. Floating overhead, in the main floor Cosmetics and Accessories areas, were these five ft. diameter acrylic globes resembling the snowball shakers so dear to children. Captured within the globes were hand carved famous landmarks of special cities: New York, Boston, Chicago, San Francisco, London, Paris and Venice. The scenes were painted and frosted with glitter as though snow and ice covered the structures. Each snowball was topped with a neon bow that also enhanced the glittery feeling while casting a pastel glow over the globes. Actual snowballs with the same city landmarks were on sale at Bloomingdales during the holiday season.

GLITTER

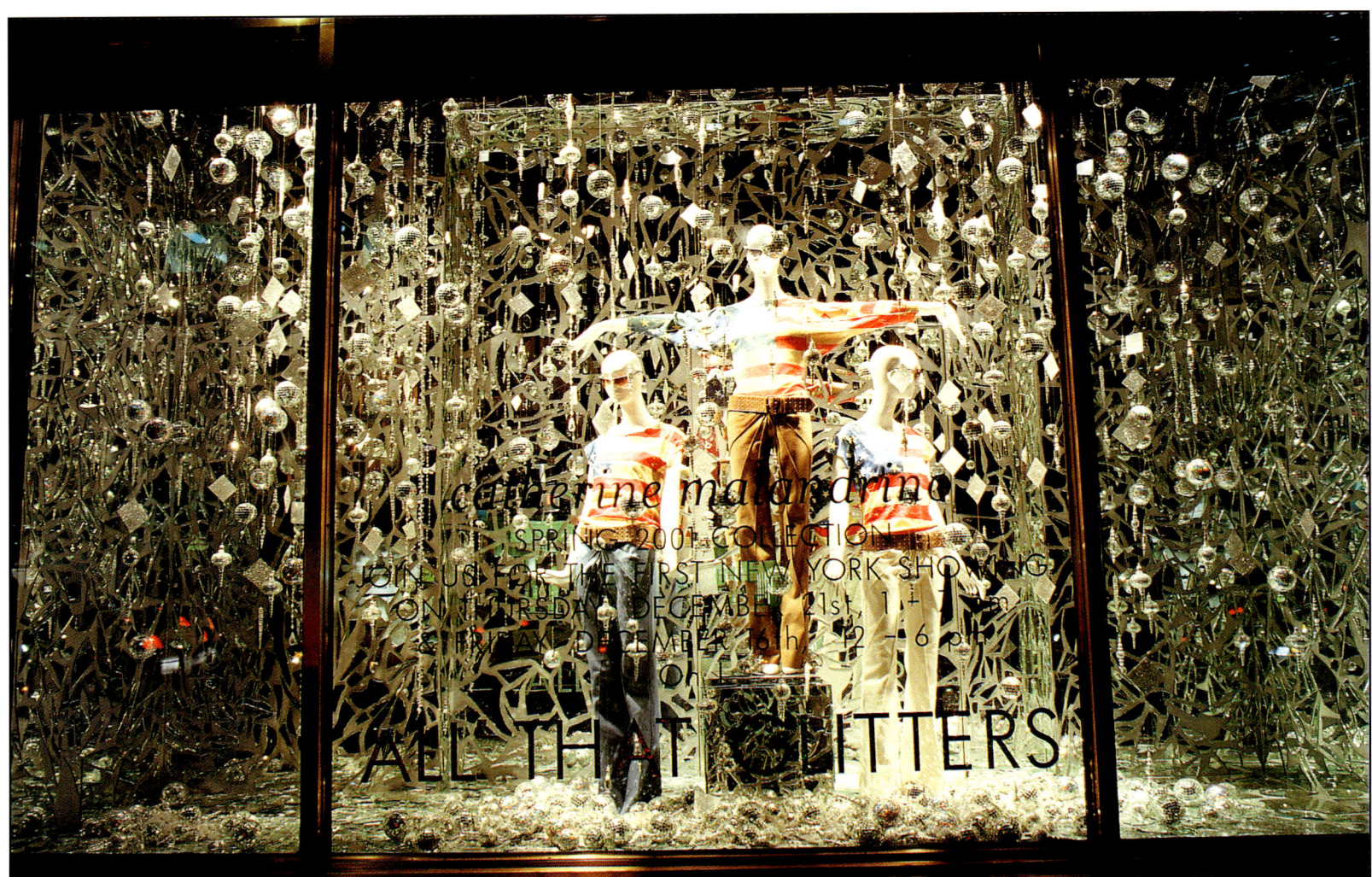

HENRI BENDEL, Fifth Ave., New York, NY
Display Director: Danuta Ryder

All that glitters and sparkles—and glitters and glitters seems to have ended up in Henri Bendel's fabulous open back window. Hundreds—maybe even thousands—of mirrored shapes and clear crystal ornaments were suspended throughout the high and wide space for a handsome and brilliant effect. The subtly striped tees on the white abstract mannequins barely record through the forest of crystal. What does come through in this season of strong colors and sharp contrasts is the crystal clear quality of the prisms and ornaments that fill the space and the floor and the "curtain" of crystal plastic shapes that add to the glittery clutter. It literally takes your breath away.

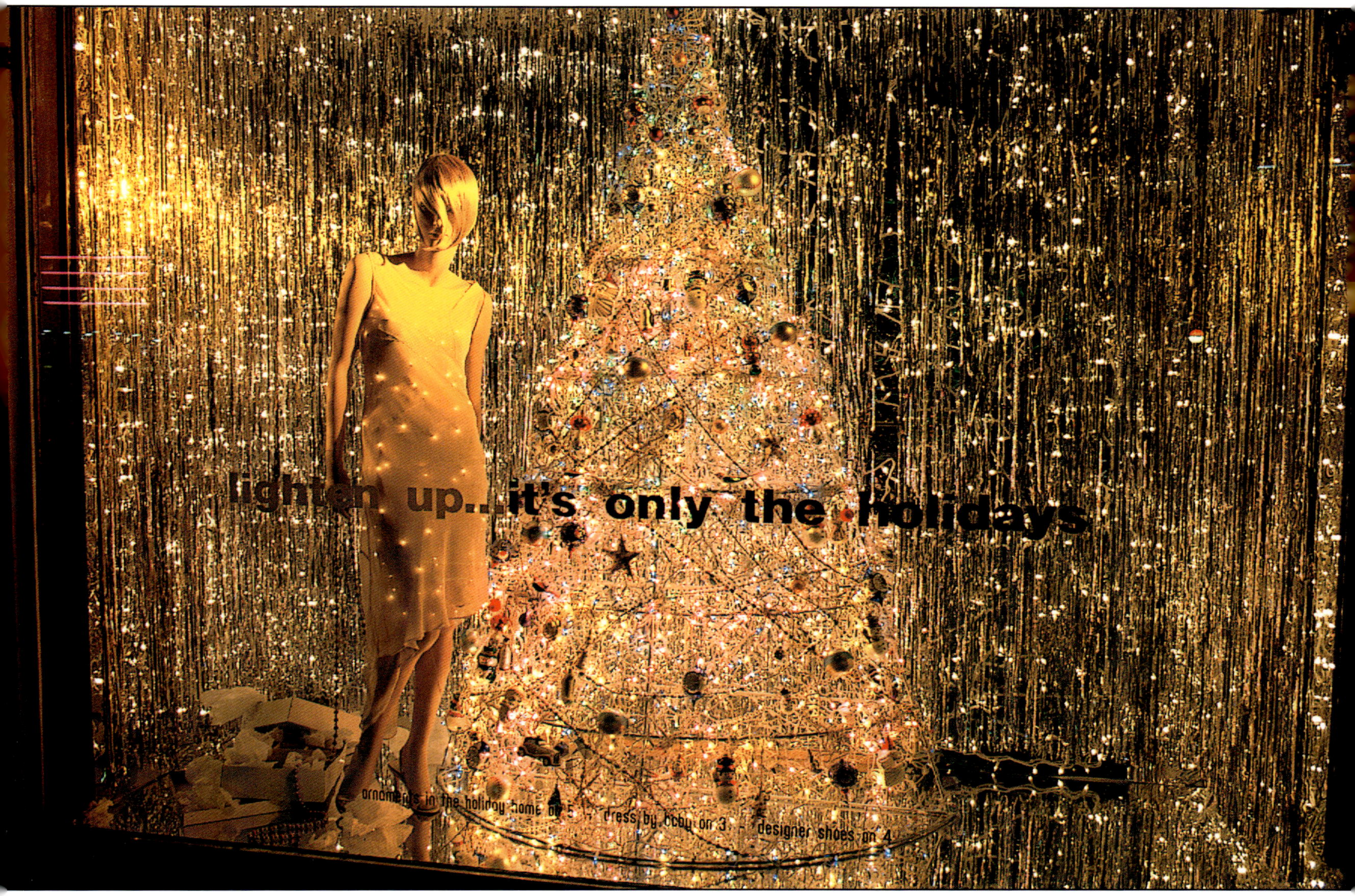

GLITTER

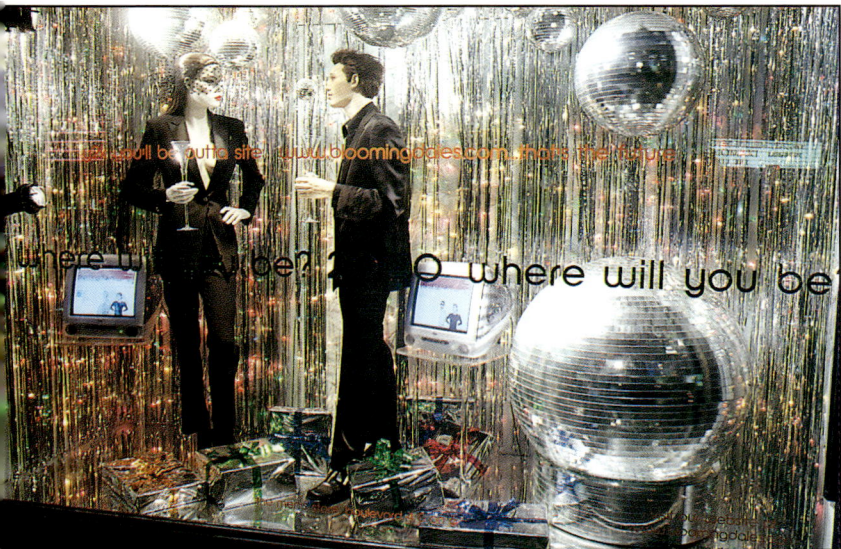

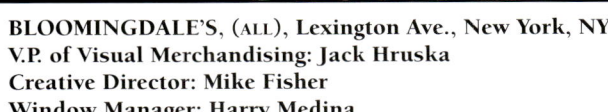

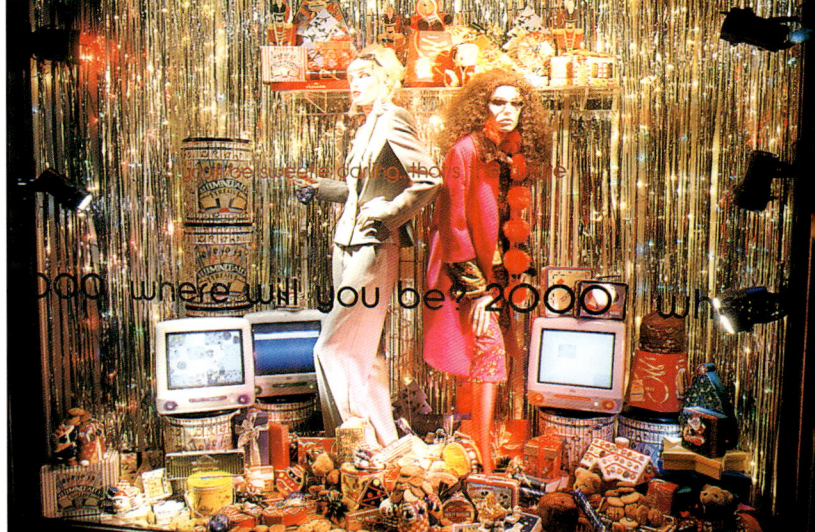

BLOOMINGDALE'S, (ALL), Lexington Ave., New York, NY
V.P. of Visual Merchandising: Jack Hruska
Creative Director: Mike Fisher
Window Manager: Harry Medina

GOLD

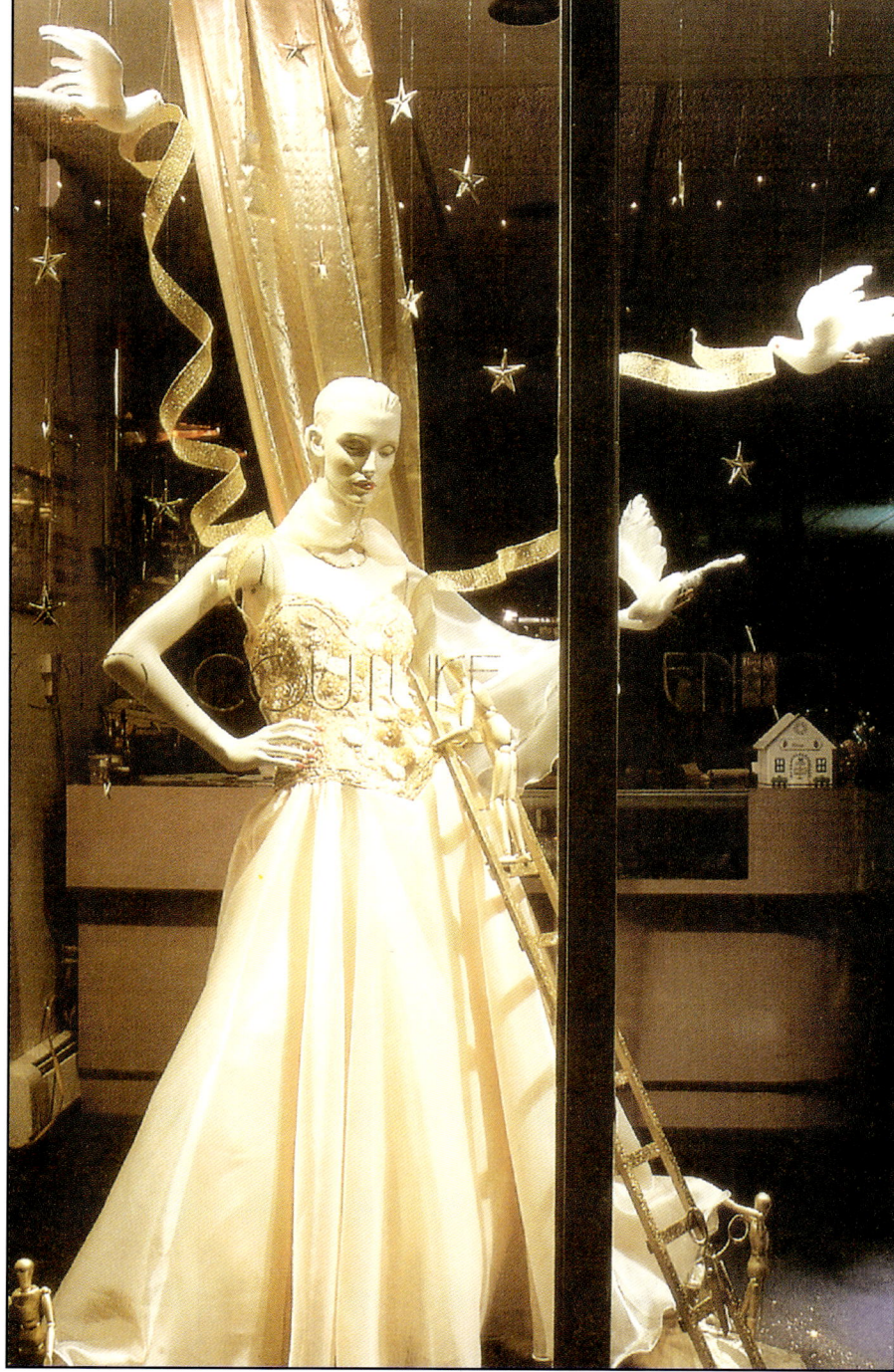

EN TOTO, Madison Ave., New York, NY

Gilt and gold, glistening and glittering, the richness, the elegance, the "treasure" of Christmas past—present—and future.

Gold bows and golden ribbons tied onto gift boxes, wreaths, trees and ornaments; gold leafed or antique gold rubbed rococo frames, ornate frames, musical instruments, furniture, cherubs and angels. Golden lights that suffuse the setting with the warmth of firelight or the setting sun. Or—gold satins, silks, brocades or velvets fashioned into festive gowns that would make Cinderella return to the fireside and start wishing all over again.

Bergdorf's golden gown steps out of a storybook, cut-out, softly tinted classic scenery to stand in the snow—in the light. The foamcore cut-out panels are lightly powdered with diamond dust to further enhance the ethereal, out-of-this-world setting.

The white, semi-realistic mannequin in gold in En Toto stands in an open back window with only a swath of gold lame fabric, some glame wired ribbons, gold sprinkled birds and shiny gold stars to separate the figure from the store beyond. To help keep the viewer's eyes up front some gilded wood artist's mannequins climb a gilded ladder to do some "adjustments" to the gown.

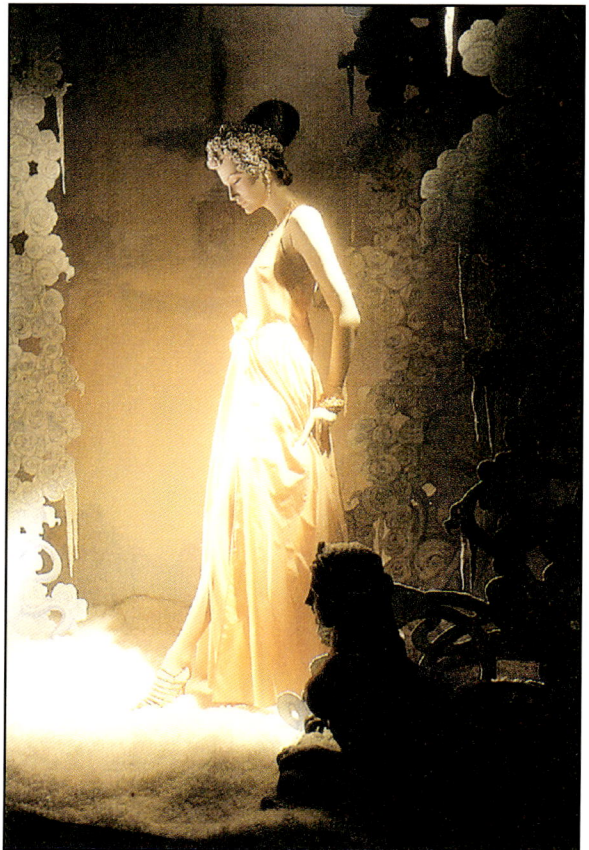

BERGDORF GOODMAN, Fifth Ave., New York, NY
Visuals Director: Linda Fargo

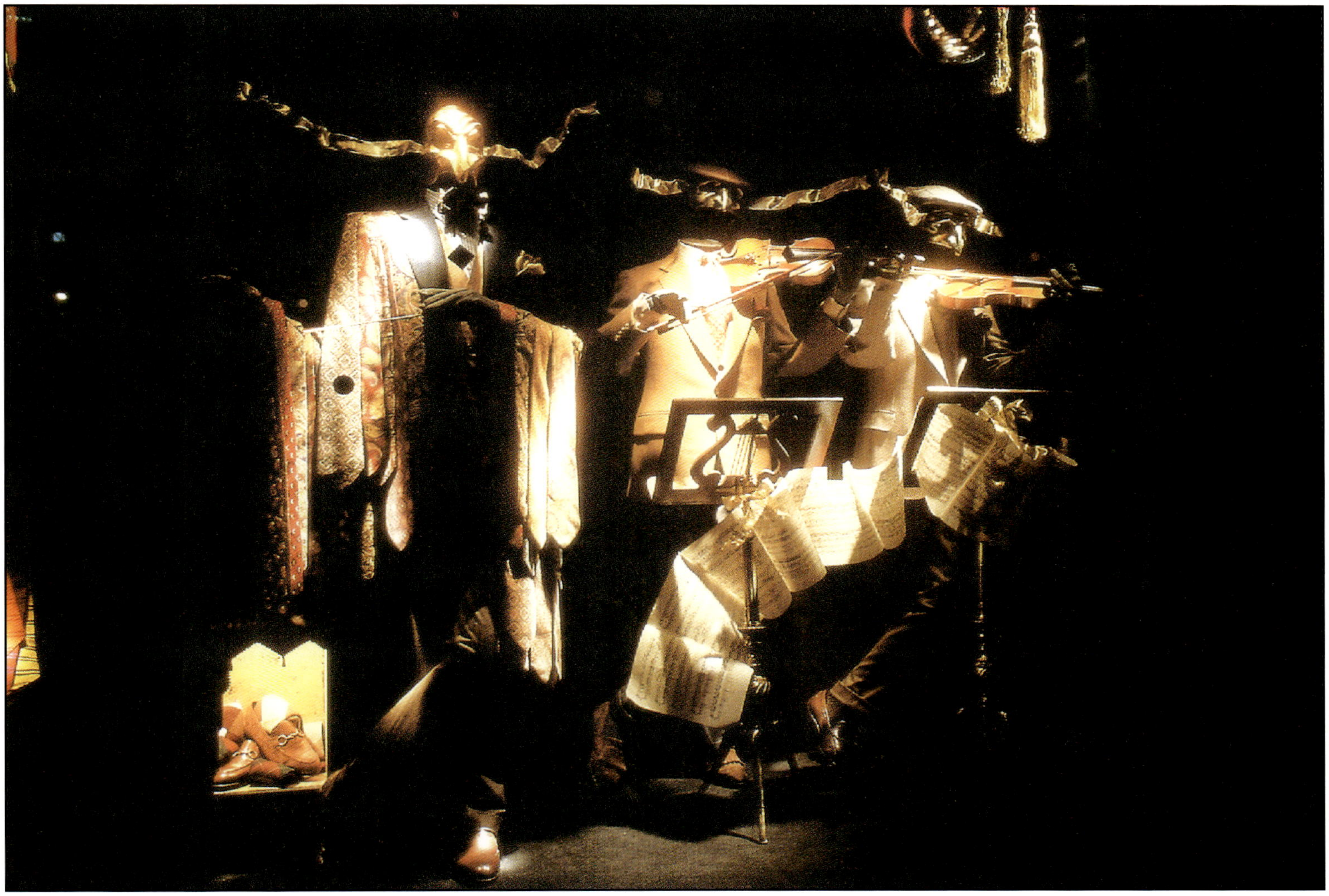

GOLD

PAUL STUART, Madison Ave., New York, NY
Creative Director: Thomas Beebe
Co-Visual Managers: Jerry Fredella/Michael Verbert
Display Team: Thomas Dang Vu

Ralph Lauren's realistic mannequin wears her gold gown to Paris where she will be the Belle of the Beaux Noelle ball. Gold wrapped gift boxes and a red velvet couch provide touchstones for the holiday season.

Gold ribbons, metallic gold music stands, golden masks and the rich, marvelous full golden light help to promote the products as well as the magic and illusion that is the Paul Stuart window.

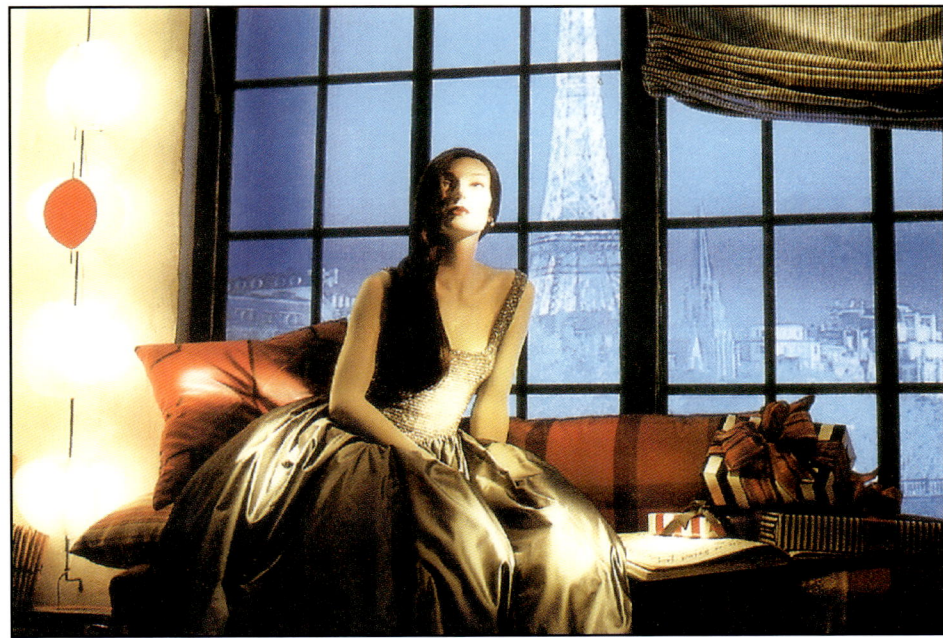

RALPH LAUREN, Madison Ave., New York, NY

HOME

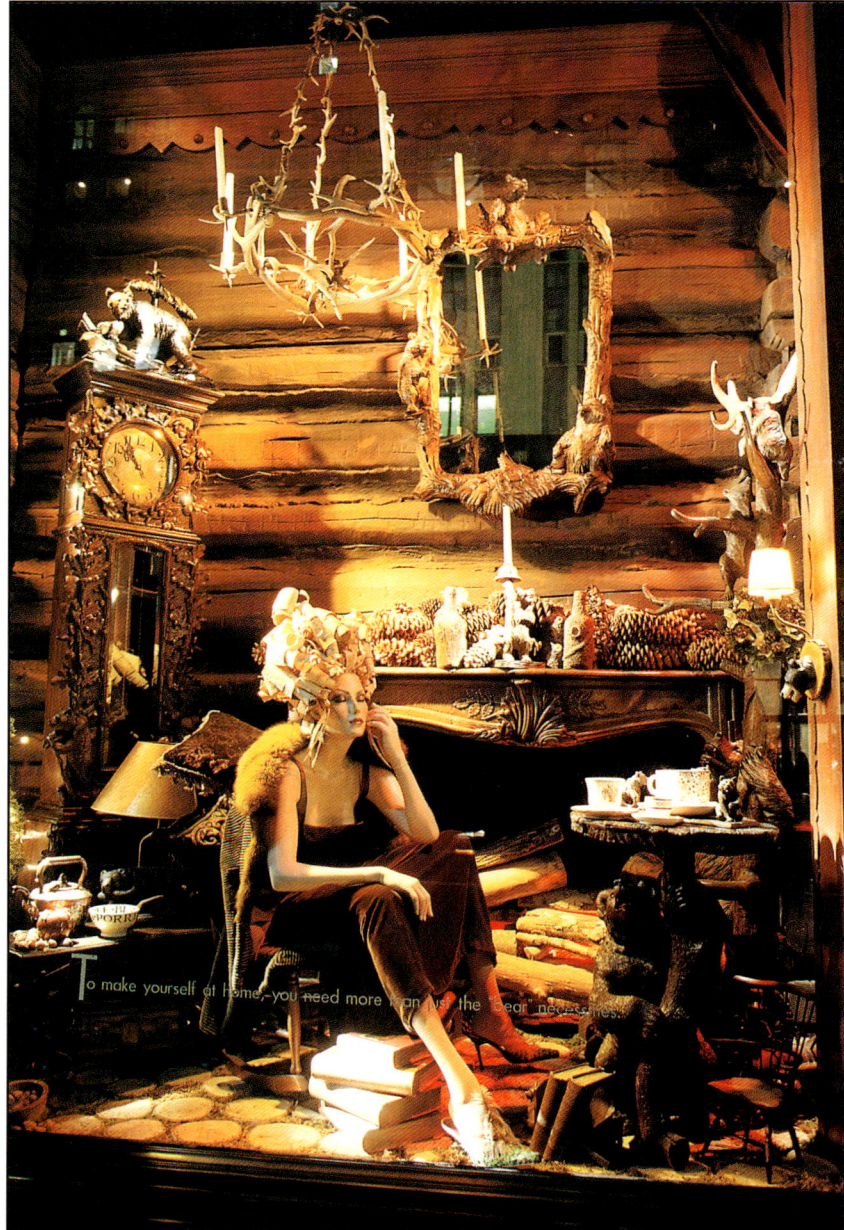

BERGDORF GOODMAN, (ABOVE AND RIGHT), **Fifth Ave.**, New York, NY
VP of Visual Presentation: Linda Fargo
Window Manager: David Hoey

At Bergdorf Goodman, the Fifth Ave. windows feature Home for the Holidays but it is doubtful if "home" was ever like those shown across the Fifth Ave. bank of windows. Each of the color coordinated windows was filled with dozens of delightful details and amusing contradictions that not only drew the shoppers over to see the display but kept them there "oh-ing and ah-ing" at how cleverly it was all done by David Hoey the window director and Linda Fargo, the VP of visual presentation. In the "log cabin" the accessories varied from gilt ormolu clocks and rococo fireplaces to antlered chandeliers and sconces. The mannequin's wig was fittingly made up of wood shavings and carrying through the "Goldilocks" theme—there are bears everywhere: atop the clock, holding up the table, etc.

The House of Cards was a winning hand in red and black and fun all over. The mannequins, in red gowns, where placed like royalty on the playing cards—one upright and one downright with red satin hearts to match.

The Tree House has a giant tree trunk falling into a gold brocaded sitting room. Mannequins are perched amid the foliage and the branches while parts of mannequins climb up from the floor to reach the leafy abode above which is hung with elegant Christmas stockings. Even the accessory windows got with the theme like the one with the furry deer in a wood planked barn standing watch over the assorted upscaled leather accessories.

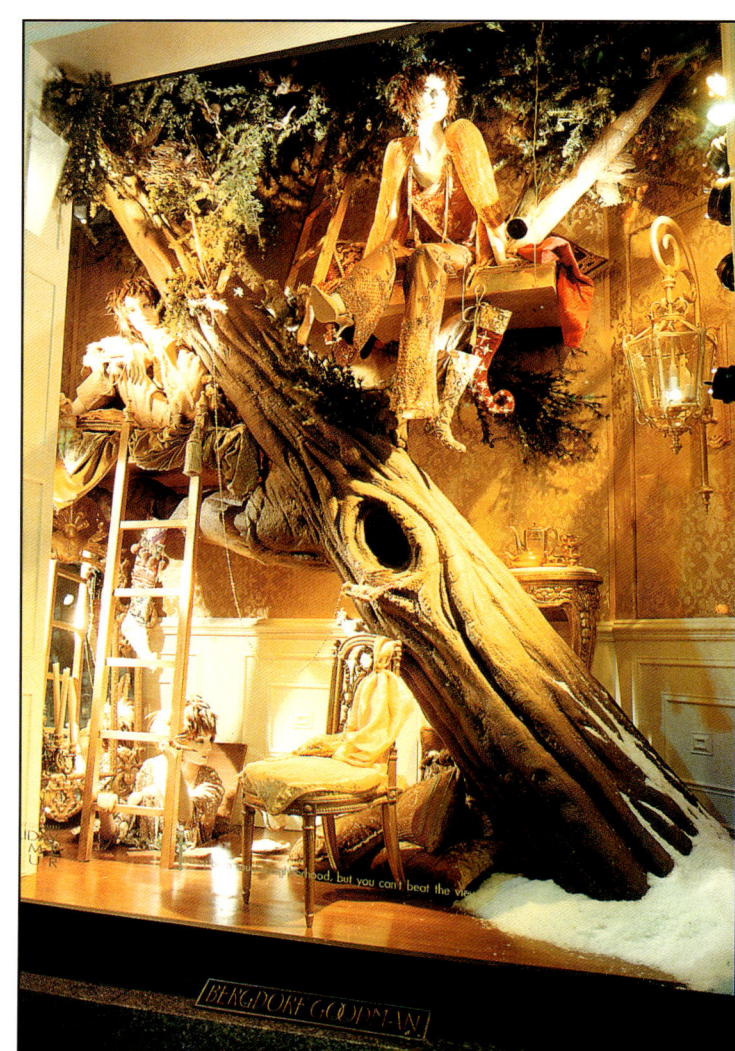

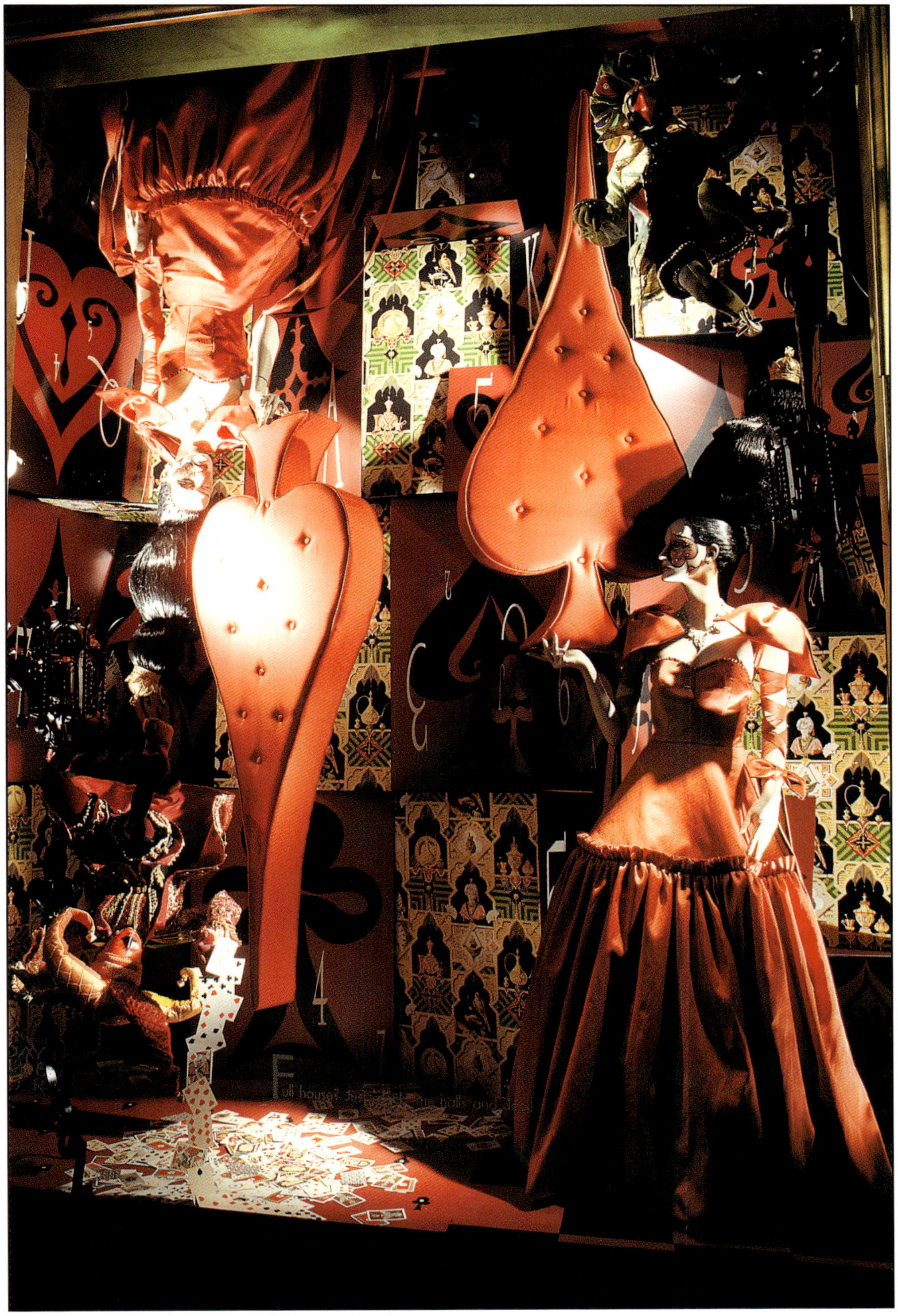

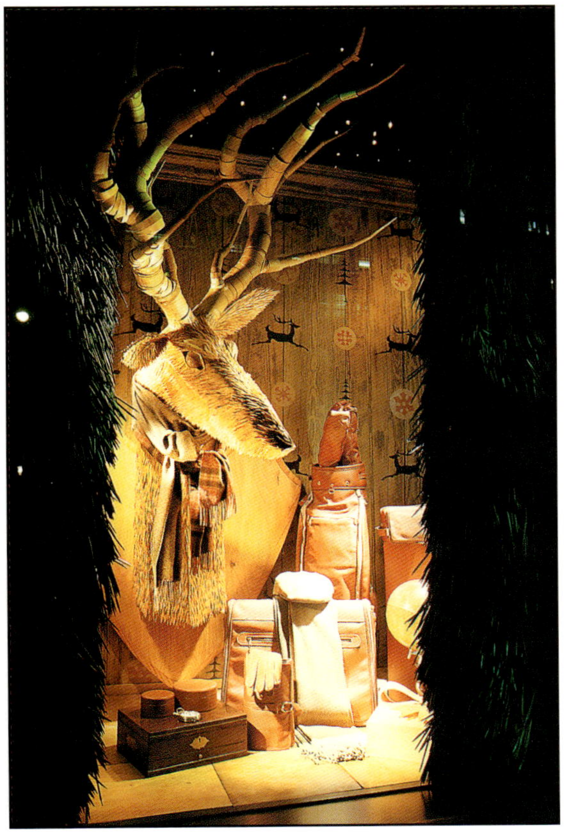

HOME

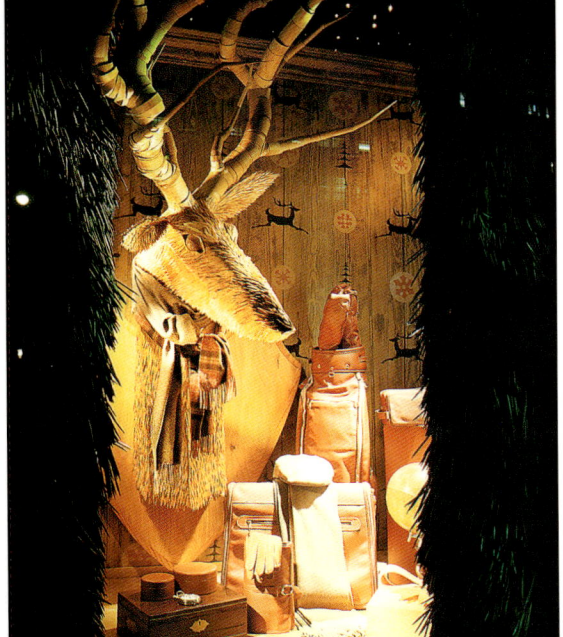

BERGDORF GOODMAN, (ABOVE AND LEFT), Fifth Ave., New York, NY
VP of Visual Presentation: Linda Fargo
Window Manager: David Hoey

HOME

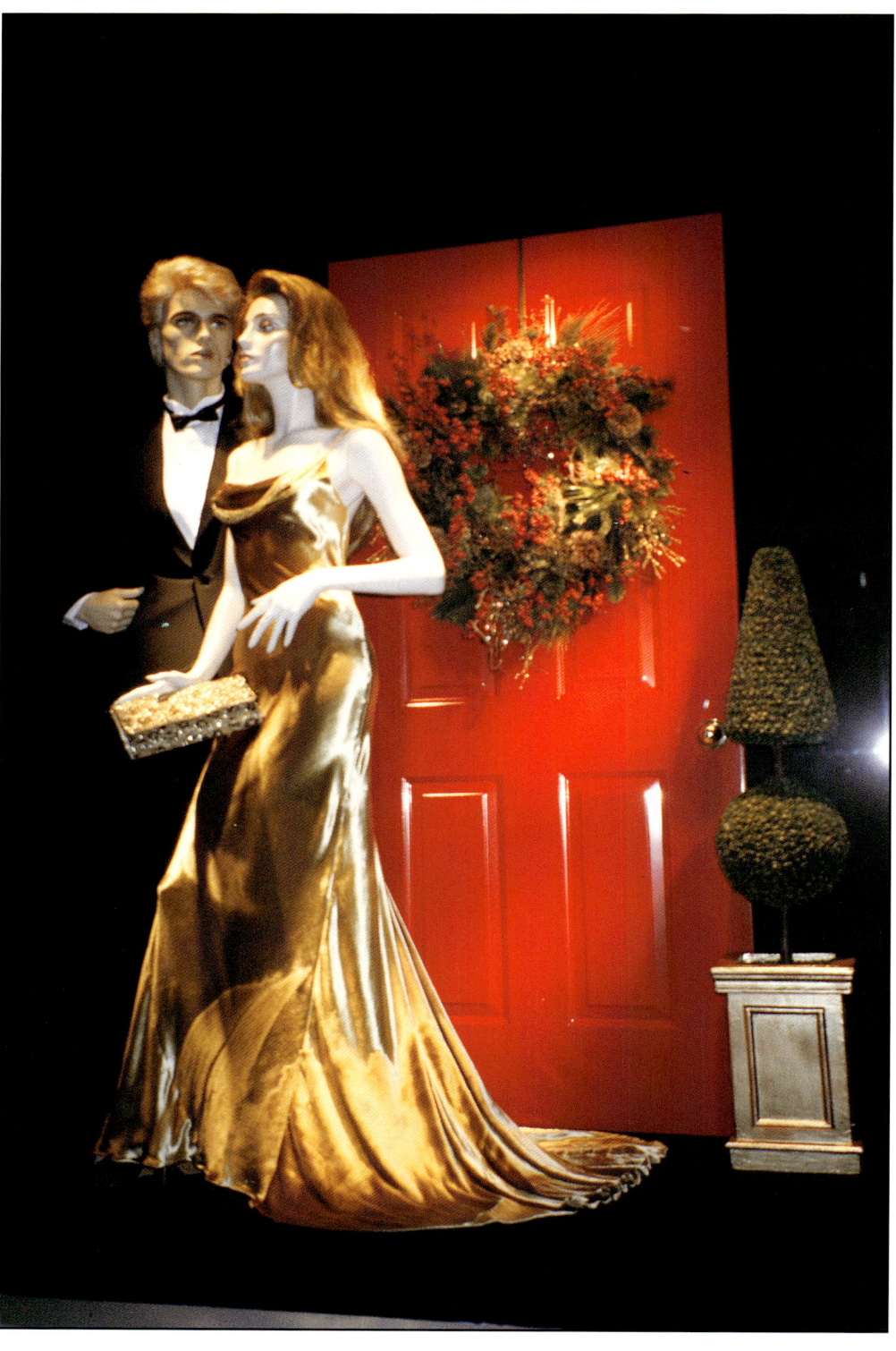

MISS JACKSON, Tulsa, OK
Art Director: Betty Batey

Miss Jackson in Tulsa, OK, is as upscale as a boutique can get—and at Christmastime Miss Jackson spreads a bountiful feast for the eye in their windows. Resplendent in red and gold—and the dominant theme of rich, rich red is played against lush and shimmering gold—whether the product is formal wear or gifts for the table and the home—the fabulous duo plays on and on.

It is definitely a night out as the formally clad mannequins step out from the brilliant red door for a night on the town. The red, green and gold trimmed wreath on the door and the green topiary in the gold planter beside the door are indicators of the holiday season. Once we step "inside"—in the windows—there are a series of lavish, lush and stunning displays of silver, china and crystal for holiday gift giving. Red candles, red gift boxes used as risers and green wreaths and foliage come together to create the eye-catching displays that are accentuated by the flickering bee lights.

HEARTH

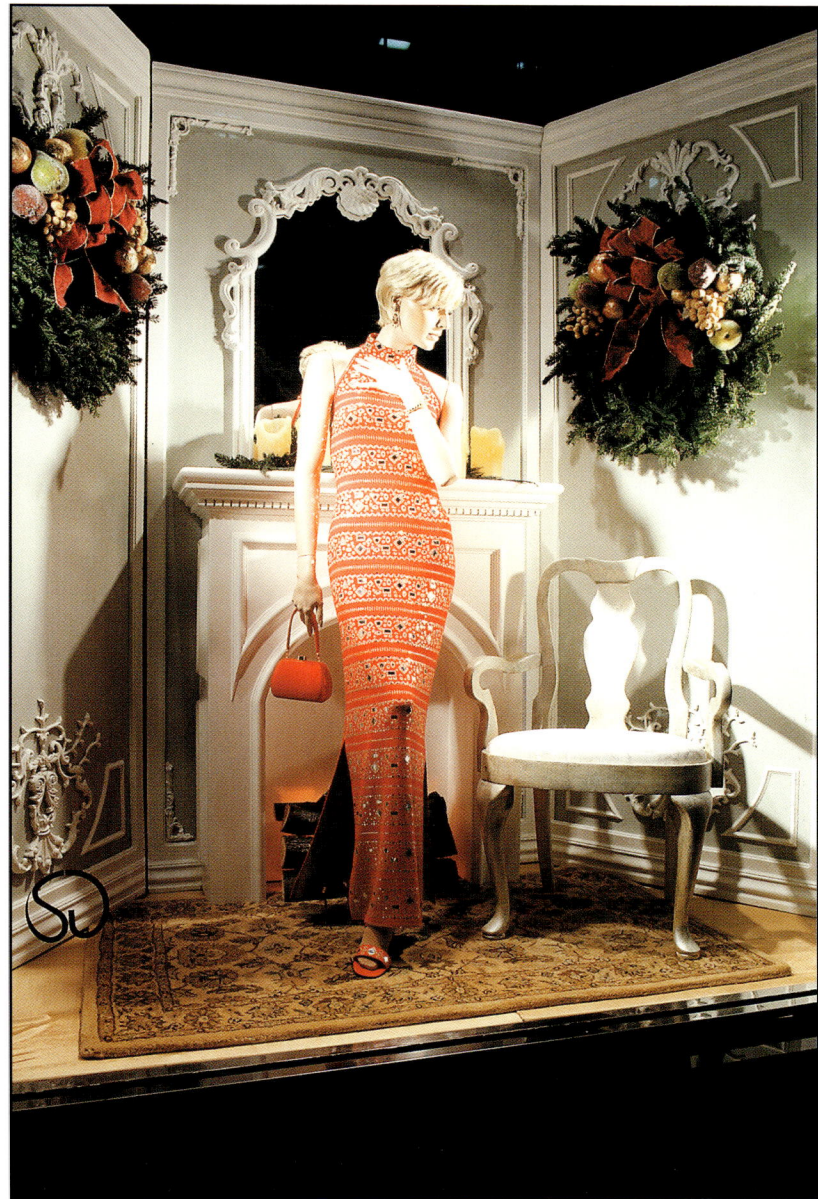

ST. JOHN BOUTIQUE, Fifth Ave., New York, NY
VP Creative Design: Kelly Gray

St. John takes a realistic approach to its setting for the realistic mannequin in the red, sequined gown. The small window space is enclosed by three "walls" painted gray and highlighted with white boiserie. The fireplace, mantle and mirror along with the white upholstered, silver-leafed chair create the "room." The lush green wreaths and the assorted candles on the mantle dress the room for the holiday.

Sony takes a more metallic approach to its setting for "Chrome for the Holidays." Here everything is slick, sleek, silvery and shiny from the metallic silver upholstered wing chair to the see-through plastic stockings on the metal faced fireplace, the lucite and clear glass candles and candlesticks to the deer head and wreath all crystal and crinkly. It is fun to compare the two settings since they are basically alike though they appear so different.

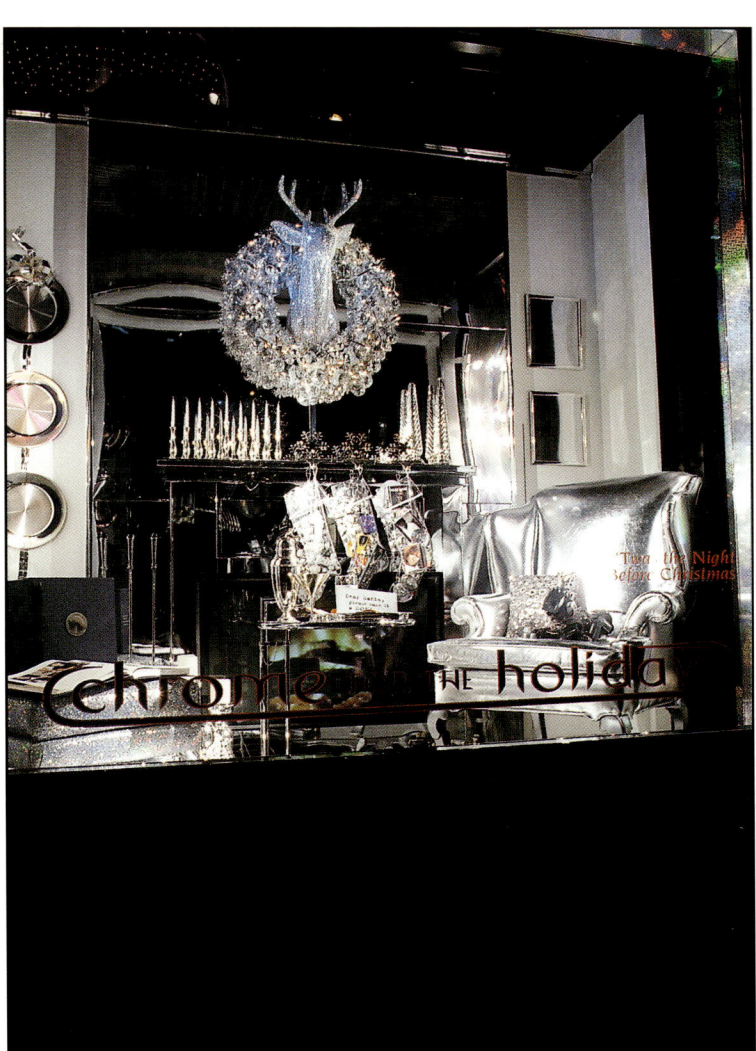

SONY, Madison Ave., New York, NY
Creative Director: Christine Belich
VP Retail Dept.: Helen Bratcher

ICE & SNOW

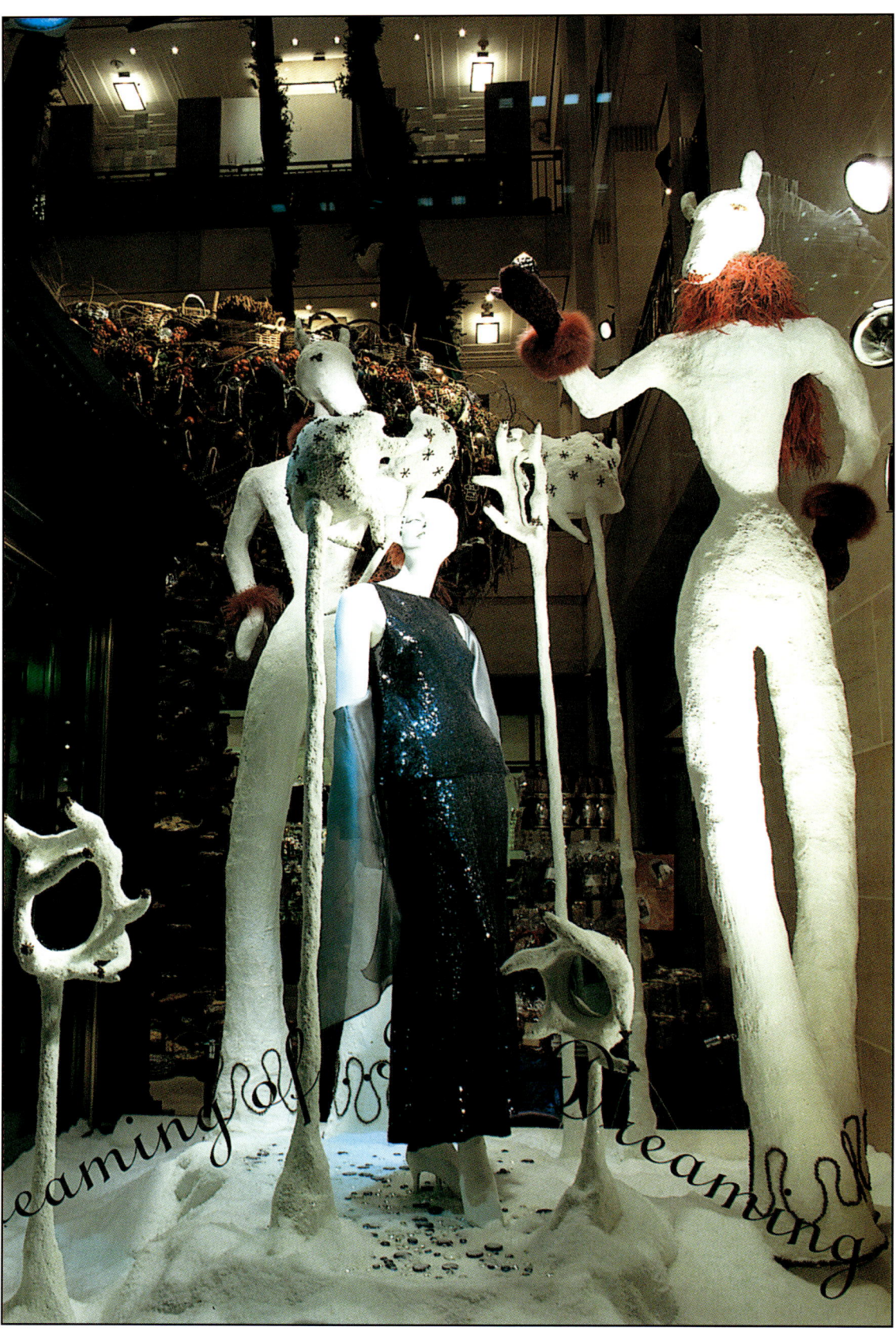

HENRI BENDEL, Fifth Ave.,
New York, NY
Dir. of Visual Presentation:
Barbara Putnam

Bendel's open back windows are really tall—and they were certainly tall enough for the giant snow figures in this white on white "I'm Dreaming Of…" surreal window presentation. The ten foot or more figures loomed over the stylized white mannequins in the display and some of the truly odd "people" wore some of the proposed gift items. White birds (?) fly through the open air space and strange and really unreal "trees" pop up out of the snow covered floor. Some of the highly stylized snow people are decorated with pearl icing and they add to the strangeness of the setting. Even the snow block architectural elements that serve as back dividers and the floating igloos overhead all contribute to these non-traditional but attention getting holiday windows.

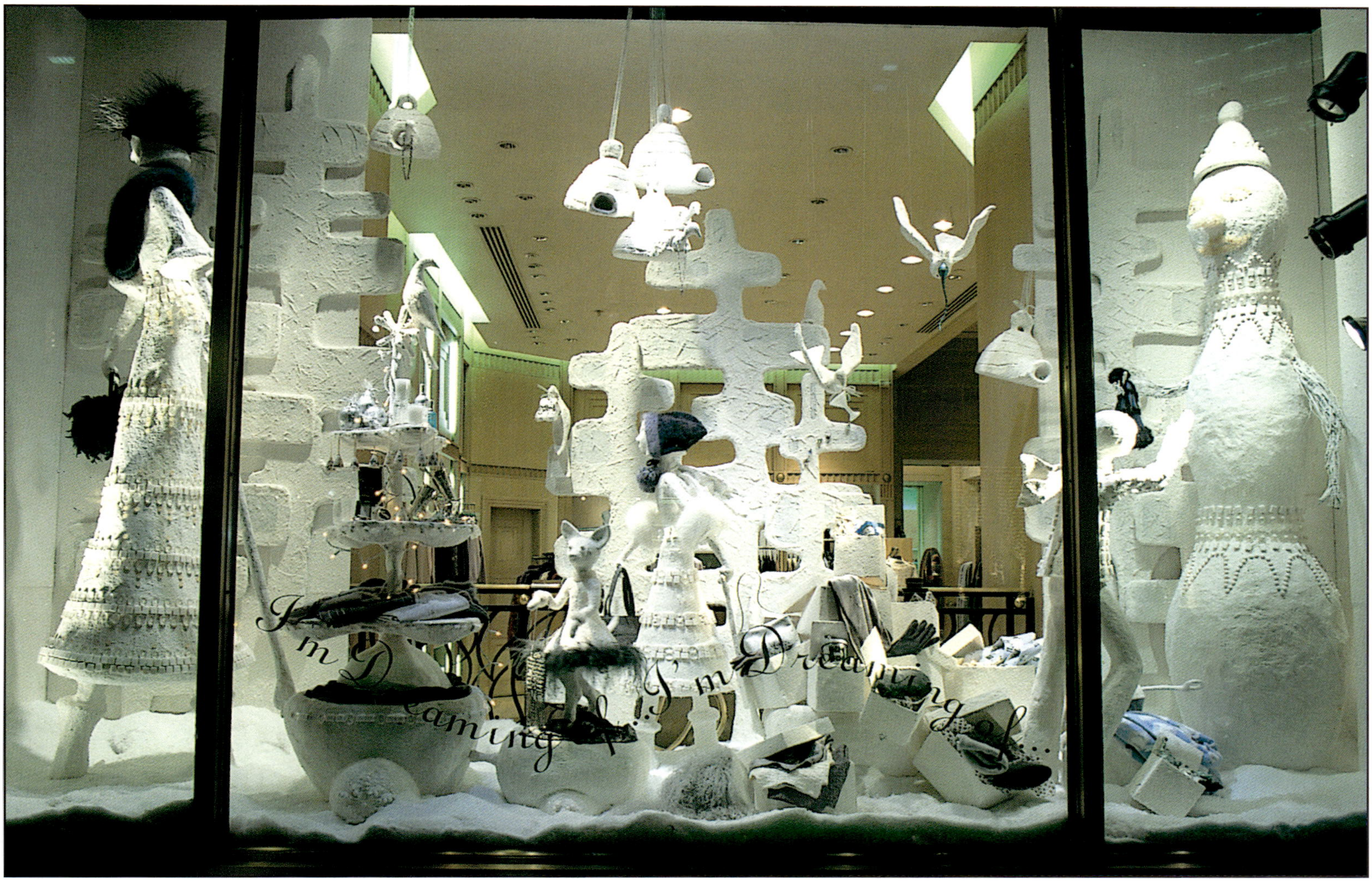

ICE & SNOW

HENRI BENDEL, (ABOVE AND LEFT)
Fifth Ave., New York, NY
Dir. of Visual Presentation: Barbara Putnam

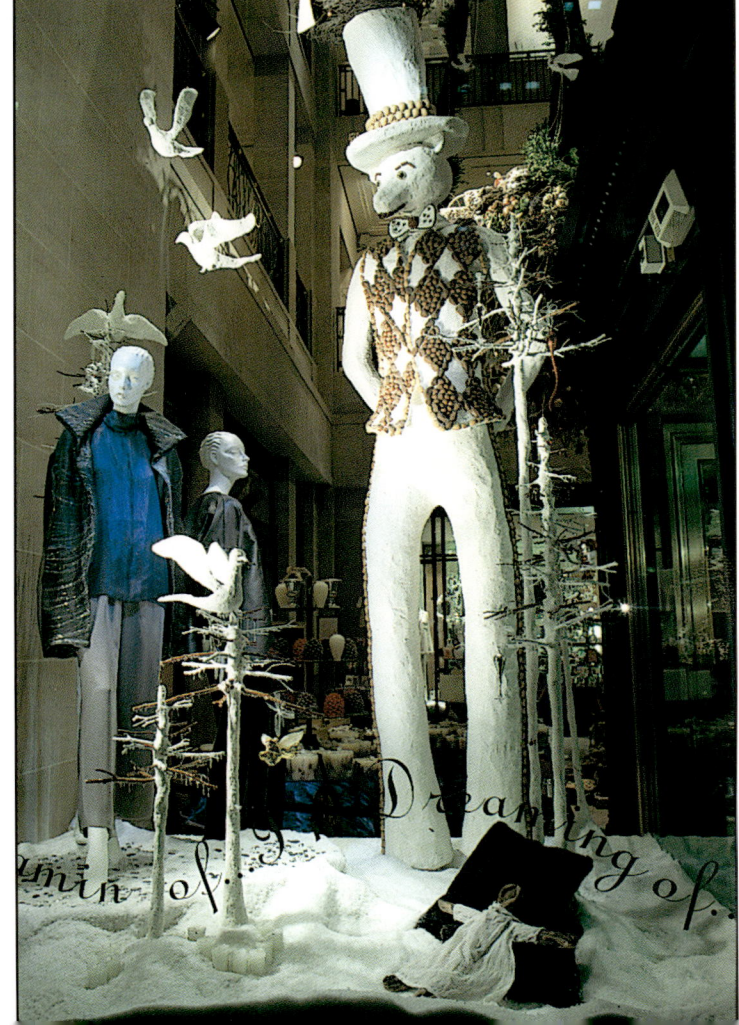

ICING

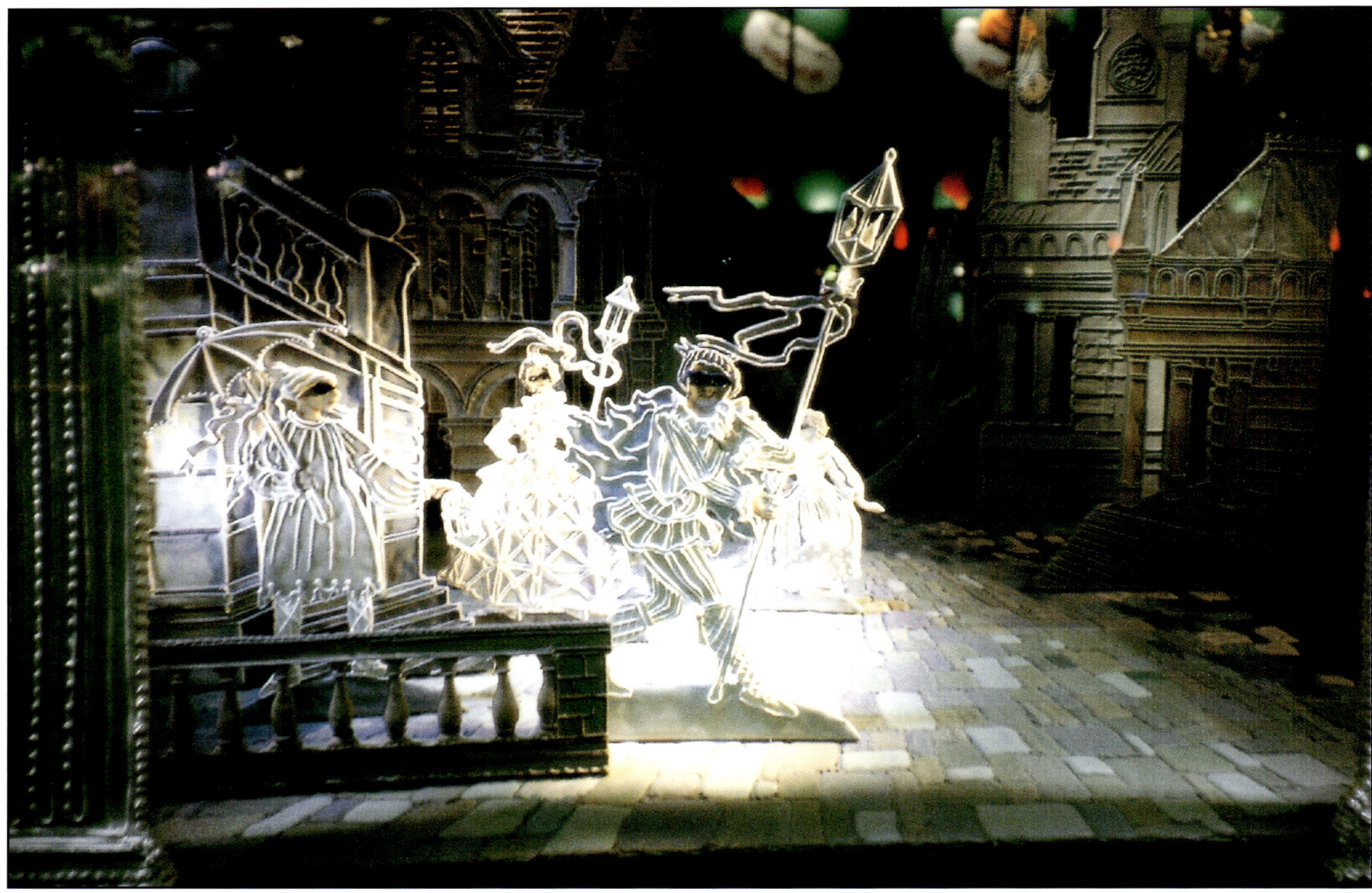

TIFFANY, Fifth Ave., New York, NY
V.P. Visual Merchandising: Robert Rufino

Inspired by the 18th century miniature theater sets, Tiffany's holiday windows recreated scenes of the holidays as they might have been celebrated long ago and far away. Cut out figures and "flats" are dimensionally "iced" to create exquisitely draw and detailed "gingerbread-type" figures but these are ballet-ish and ice-like in feeling. A decorative proscenium—up at the glass—sets the scene and helps add dimension as the flats are placed behind one another to further the feeling of depth. There is a setting for a festive ball with hanging chandeliers and dancing couples and in another window revelers are on their way to a party and must cross a village square filled with architectural cut-outs. The details and the "icing" are unbelievable—considering how small the figures and the props are.

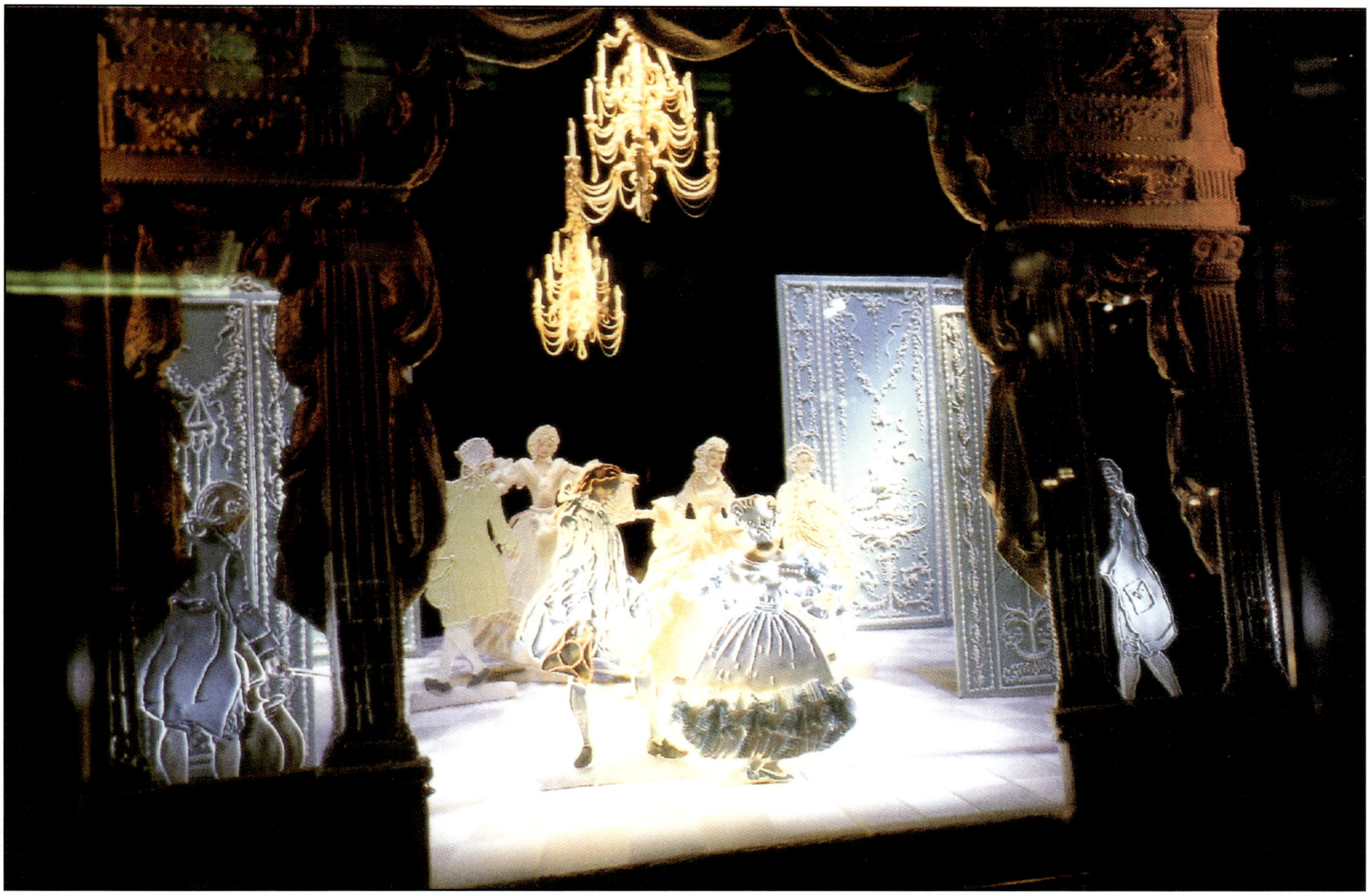

ICING

TIFFANY, (ABOVE AND RIGHT)
Fifth Ave., New York, NY
V.P. Visual Merchandising:
Robert Rufino

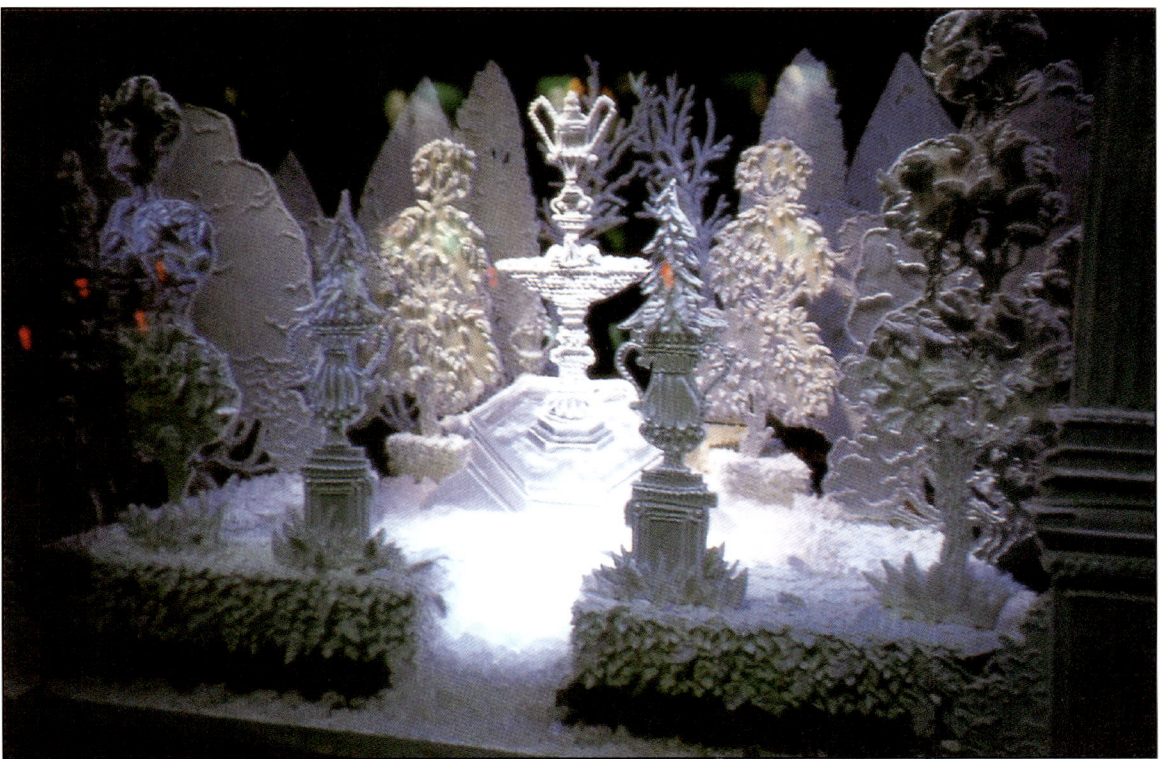

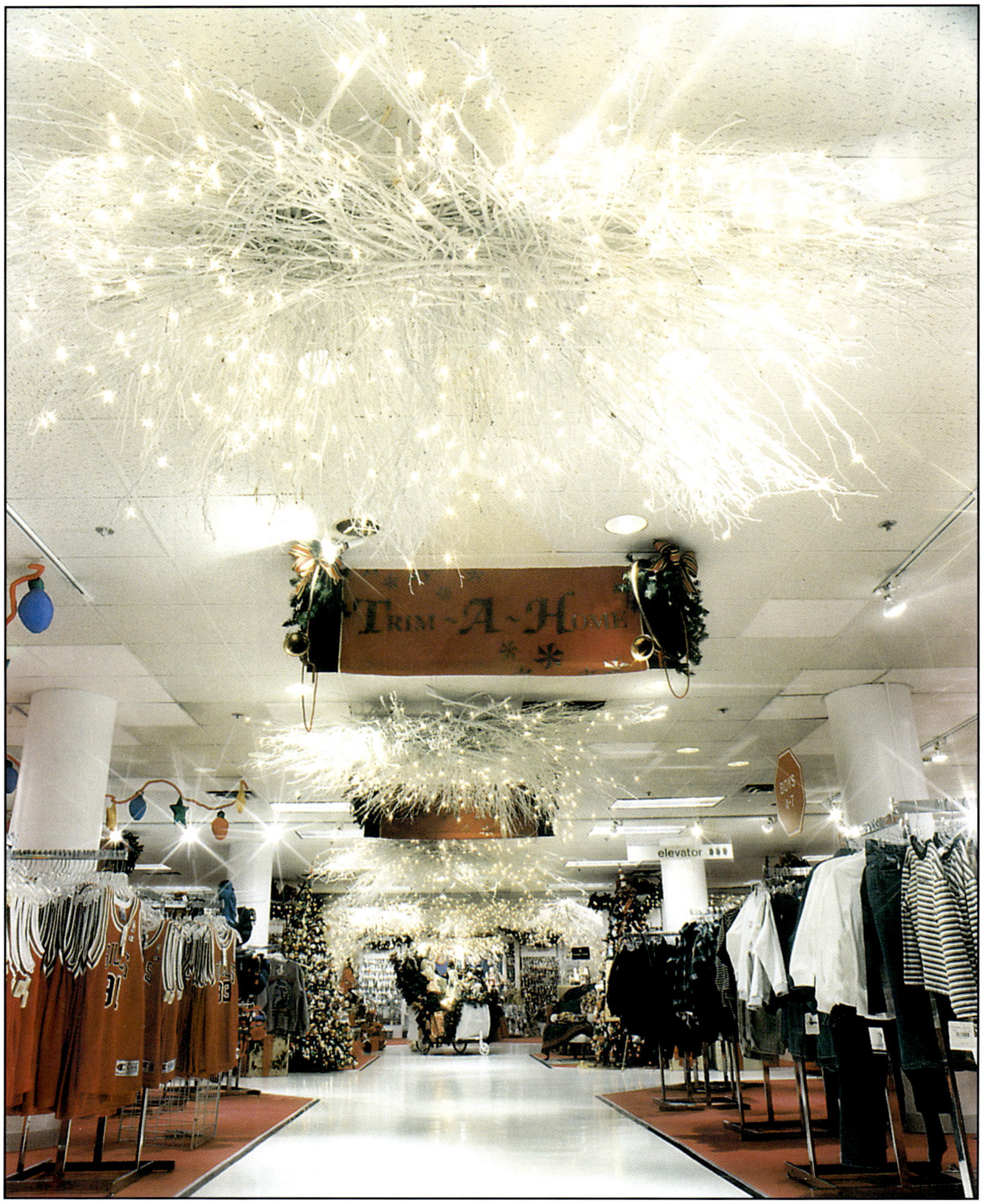

INTERIORS

CARSON PIRIE SCOTT, (LEFT AND BELOW), Chicago, IL
V.P. of Visual Merchandising:
Rick Schlenther
Reg'l. V.M. Director: Ted Georgiou
Photographer: Susan Kezon, Chicago, IL

Carson Pirie Scott on State St. in Chicago, went all out for Christmas with the selling floors sparkling with frosted white branches, twinkling lights and traditional red banners edged with green foliage trimmed with ornaments, ribbons and gold musical instruments. In the Trim-A-Tree Shop, red carpet was laid down in feature areas to stress the holiday theme. The space was redolent with fancifully trimmed Christmas trees, vignette settings, and a multitude of skirted selling tables layered in red, maroon and green and accented with gold. Fascias were decorated with green foliage wreaths wrapped with bee lights and red ribbons dangled off the ceiling—over special table top offerings—and they moved with the air circulating on the floor.

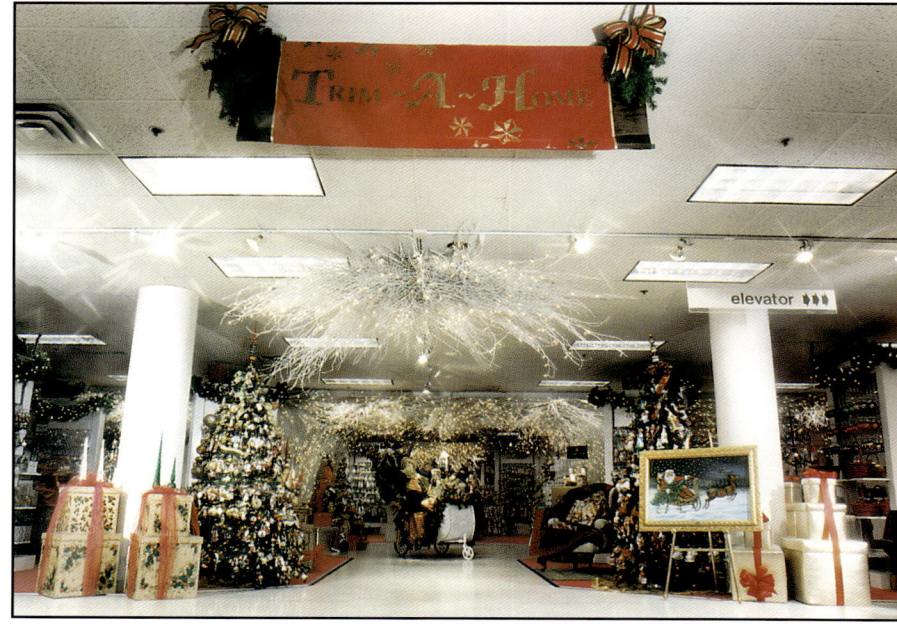

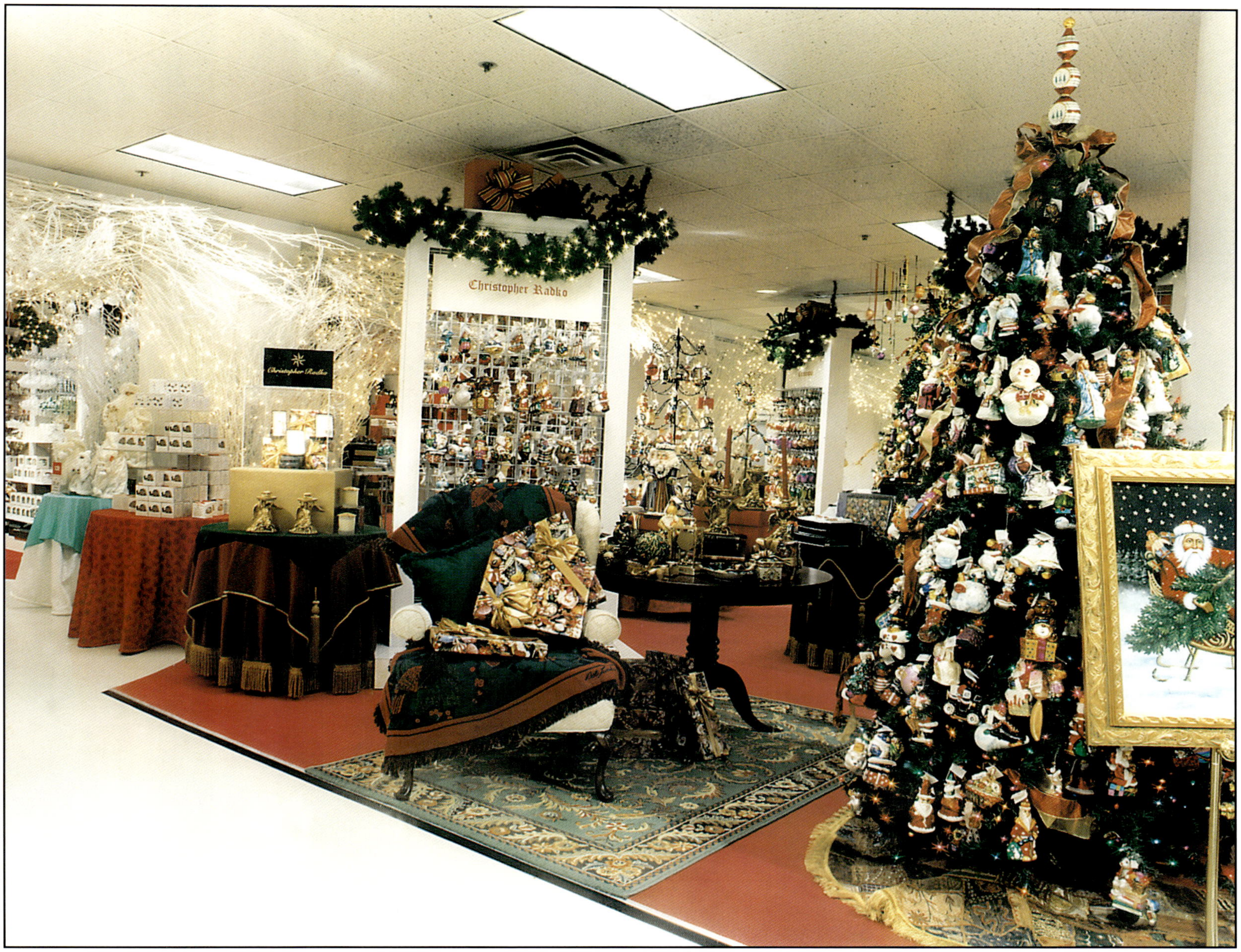

INTERIORS

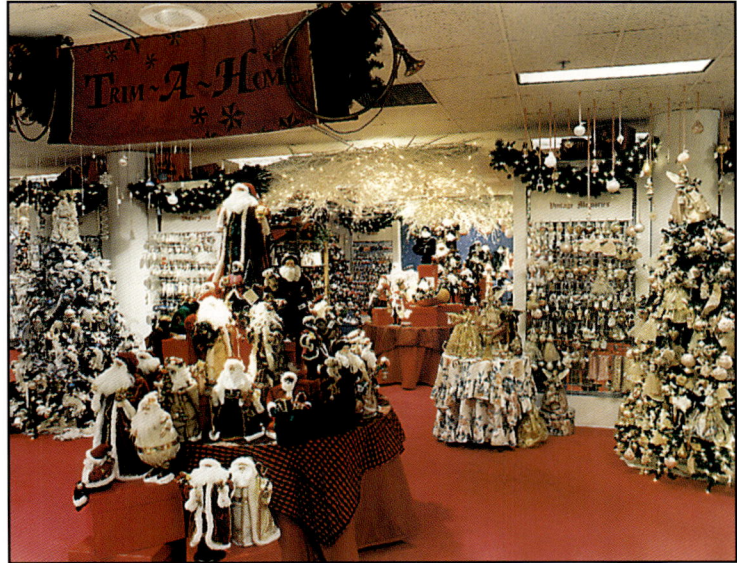
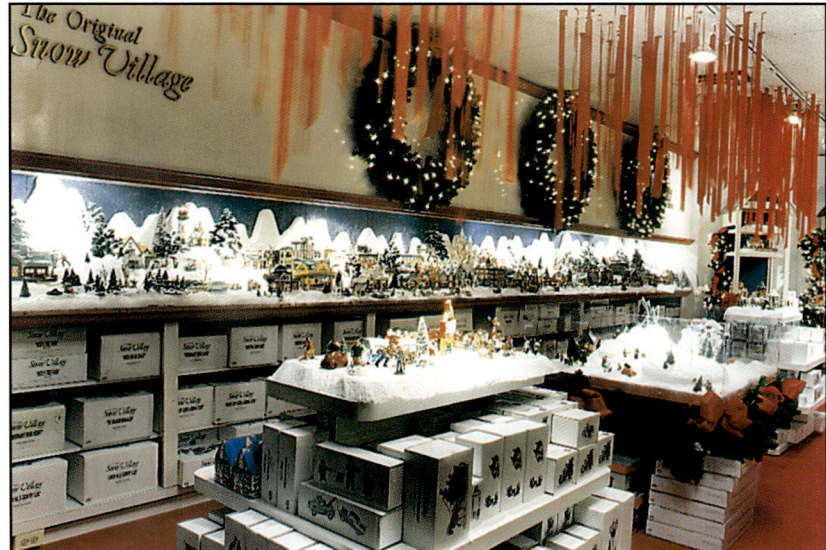

CARSON PIRIE SCOTT, (ALL), Chicago, IL
V.P. of Visual Merchandising: Rick Schlenther
Reg'l. V.M. Director: Ted Georgiou
Photographer: Susan Kezon, Chicago, IL

INTERIORS

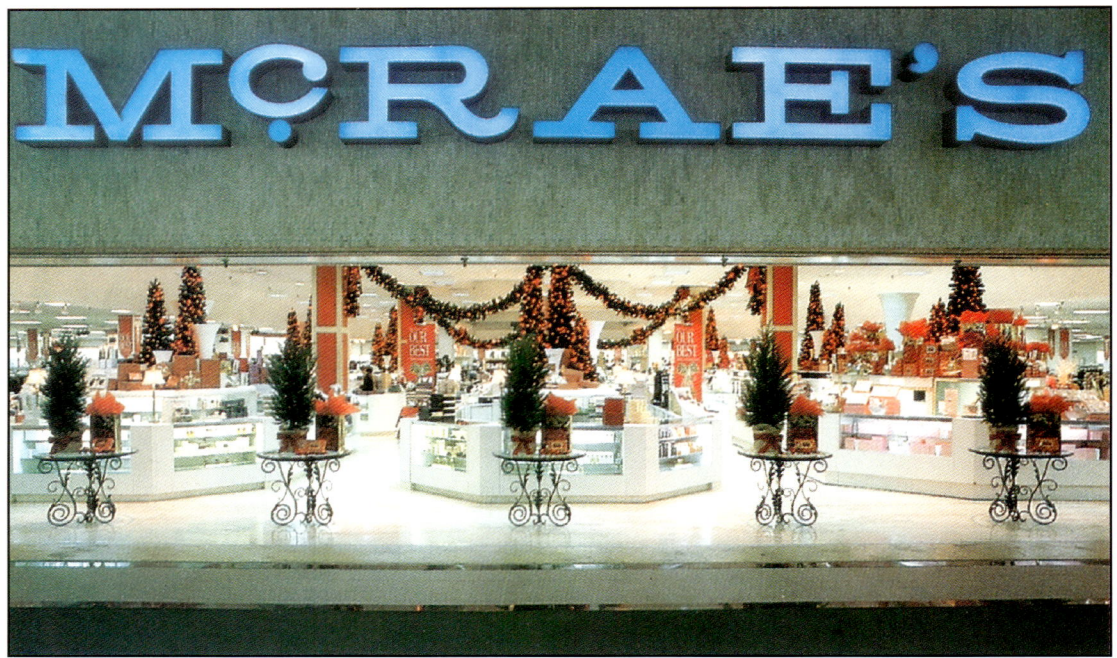

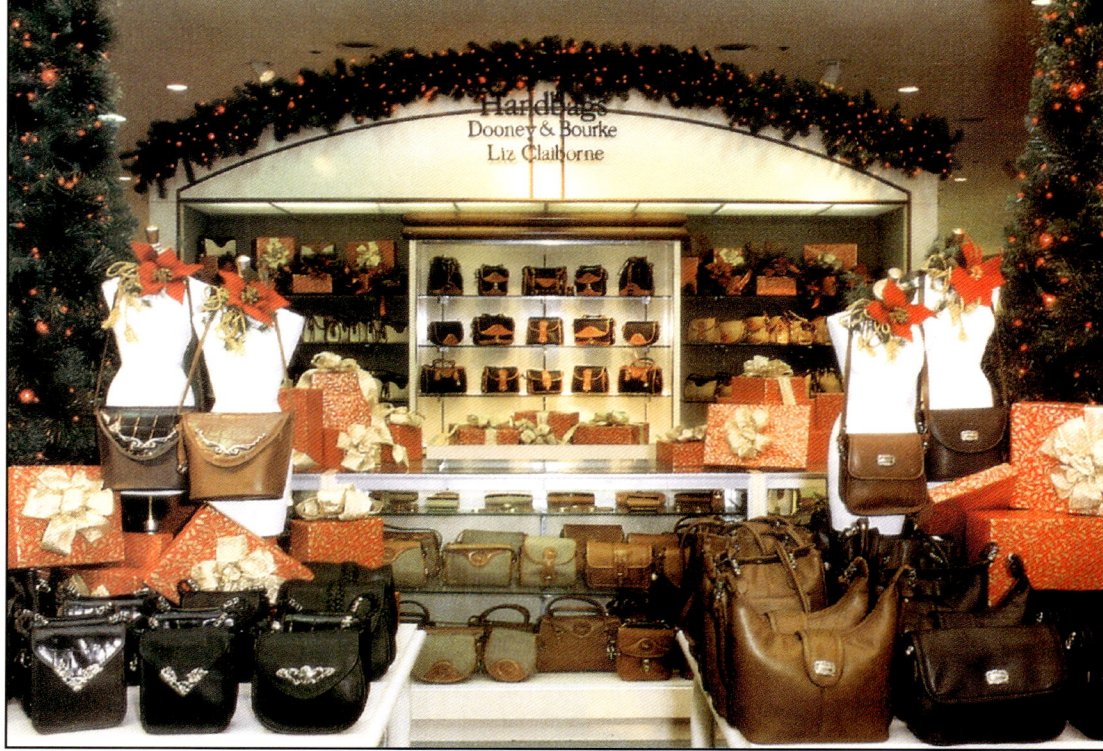

McRAE'S, Alabama
Director of V.M.: Rick Brown, SVM
DESIGN AND INSTALLATION TEAMS
Century Plaza: Steven Hadaway, Carmel Burgess, Sarah Eubanks, Eric Cannon, Michael McBride, Martin Cate
Brookwood Village: Steven Hadaway, Dorothy Allen, Eric Cannon, Carmel Burgess, Michael McBride, Martin Cate

Bringing Christmas inside the store! Where store windows have become obsolete, disappeared or just boarded over—more and more the store interior must carry out the Christmas greetings.

With the store-wide theme of "We Give You Our Best For Christmas" presented on red banners, streamers and signs in gold, the visual merchandising department, working under Rick Brown, SVM, featured a traditional Christmas palette of green foliage trimmed with red lights, red and gold gift boxes tied up with gold lame ribbon and the aforementioned signage to tell everybody that the season was here—and so were the gifts customers would be looking for.

The main floor (shown here is the Brookwood Village store) is swagged with green foliage brilliantly highlighted with the red lights, matching green trees on the ledges, red panels on the faces of the columns, and the store-wide banners that carry the message. Red and gold patterned boxes, red tissue poufs, gold ribbons and bows fill out the ledge trims and also add color to the cases below. The other store interior views (the Century Plaza Mall) show the handbag area on the main level, the men's casual department, the Ralph Lauren/Polo home boutique and a china/glass floor display.

INTERIORS

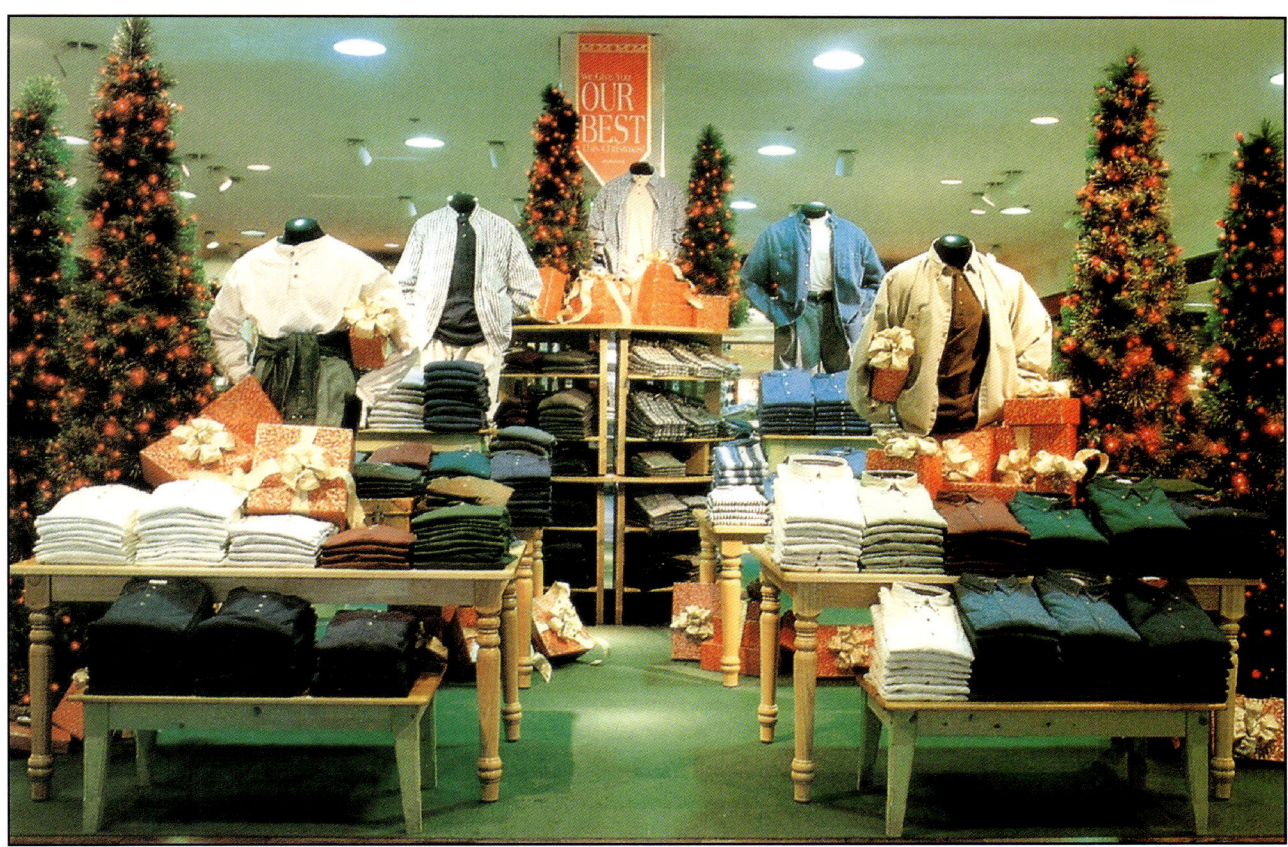

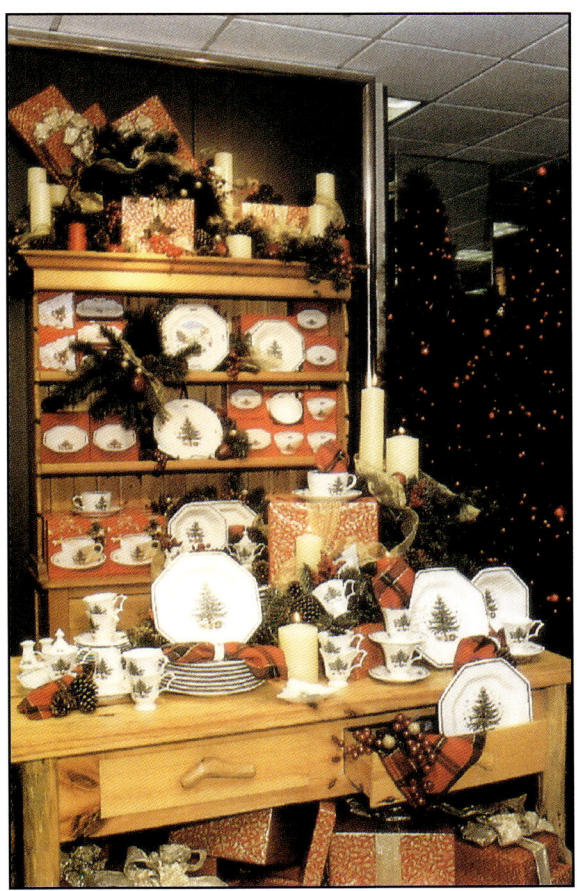

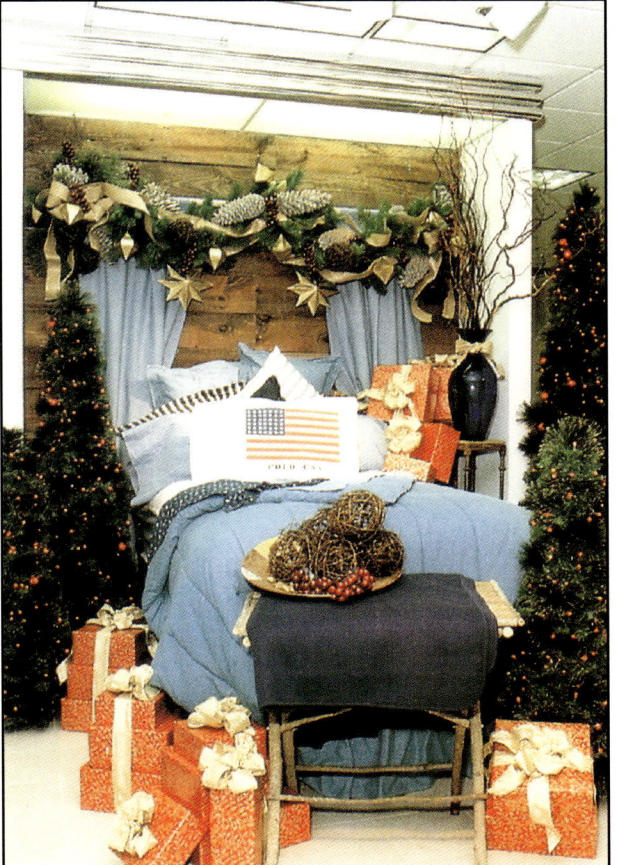

McRAE'S, (ALL) Alabama
Director of V.M.: Rick Brown, SVM
DESIGN AND INSTALLATION TEAMS
Century Plaza: Steven Hadaway, Carmel Burgess, Sarah Eubanks, Eric Cannon, Michael McBride, Martin Cate
Brookwood Village: Steven Hadaway, Dorothy Allen, Eric Cannon, Carmel Burgess, Michael McBride, Martin Cate

KNIGHTS

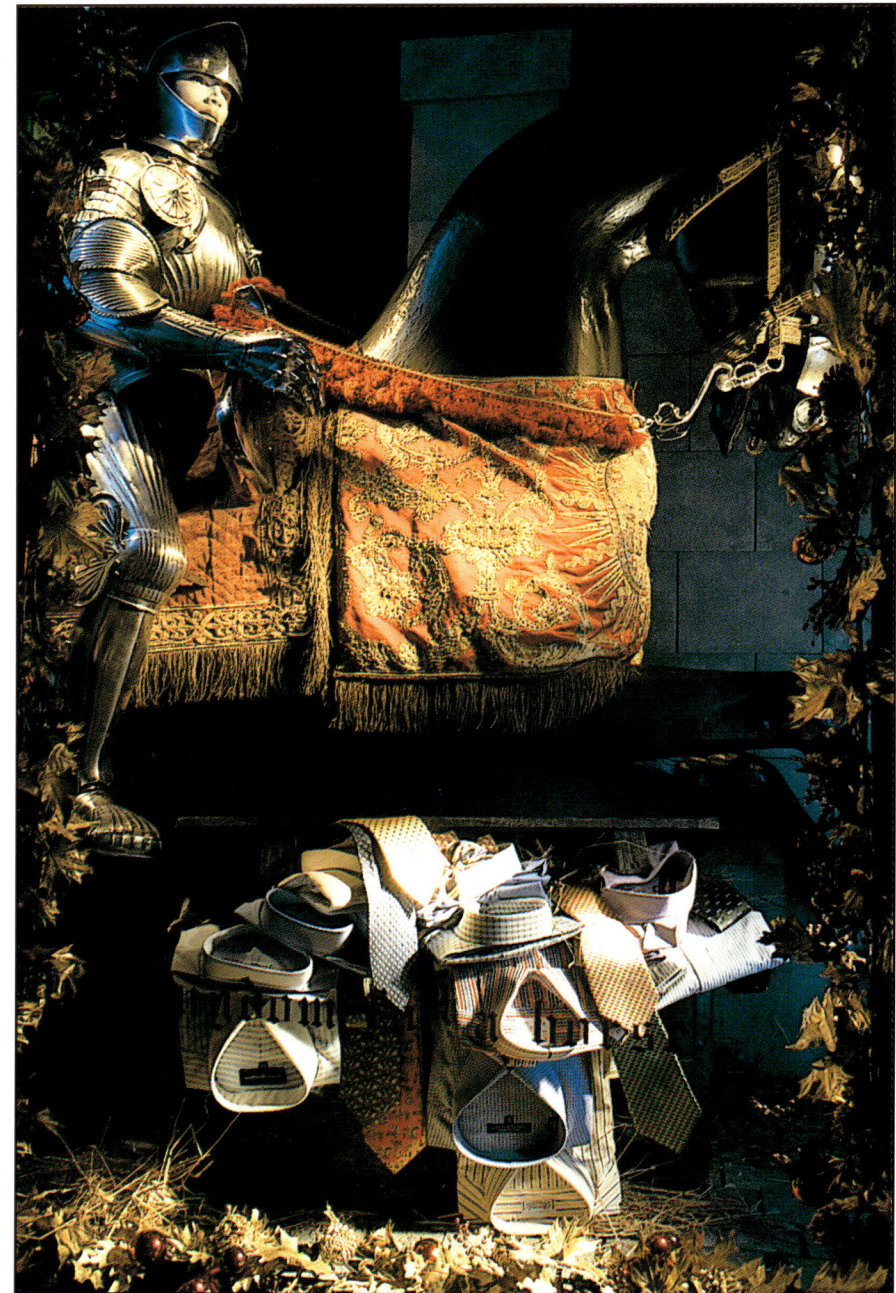

A knight in armor on a caparisoned steed charges through a maze of shirts and ties in one of Bergdorf's windows for men. In these renaissance inspired windows, gold leaves create a "frame" around the window and golden straw is scattered over the floor.

In the formal dress window, the "stone" arches in the background suggest a castle—maybe in Spain—and what could be more appropriate than knits in armor as attendants to the realistic mannequins. Red velvet drapery, seen through the arches, add to the richness of the setting and also reinforces the holiday message.

BERGDORF GOODMAN MEN'S STORE
(ABOVE AND RIGHT) **Fifth Ave., New York, NY**
V.P. of Visual Merchandising: **Linda Fargo**

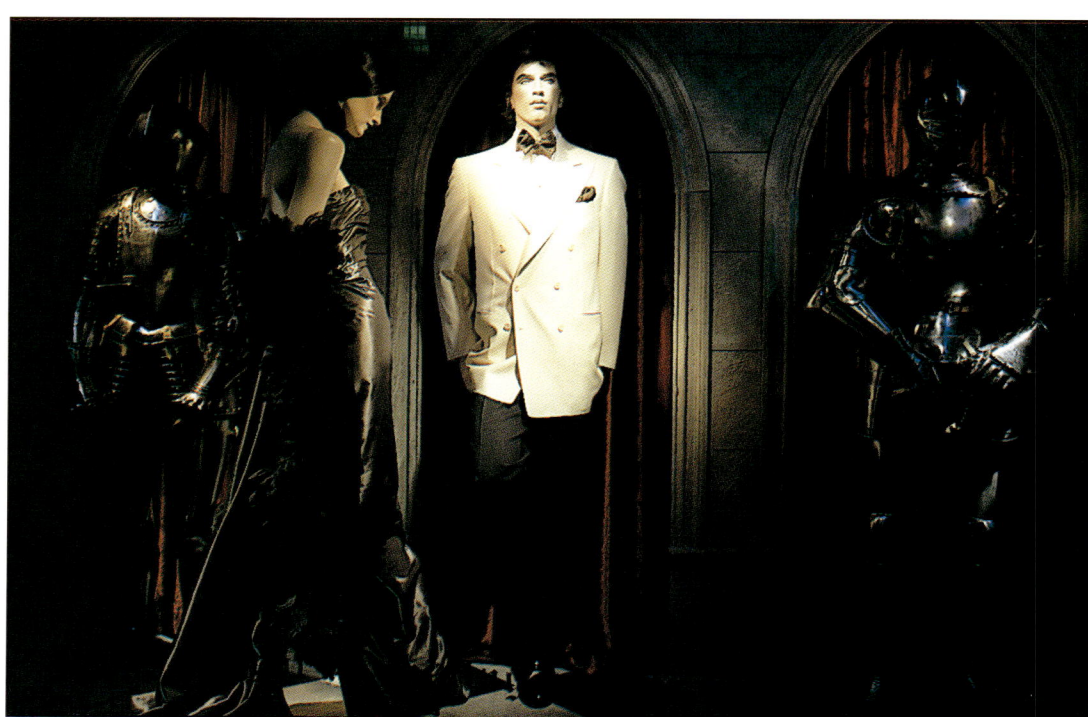

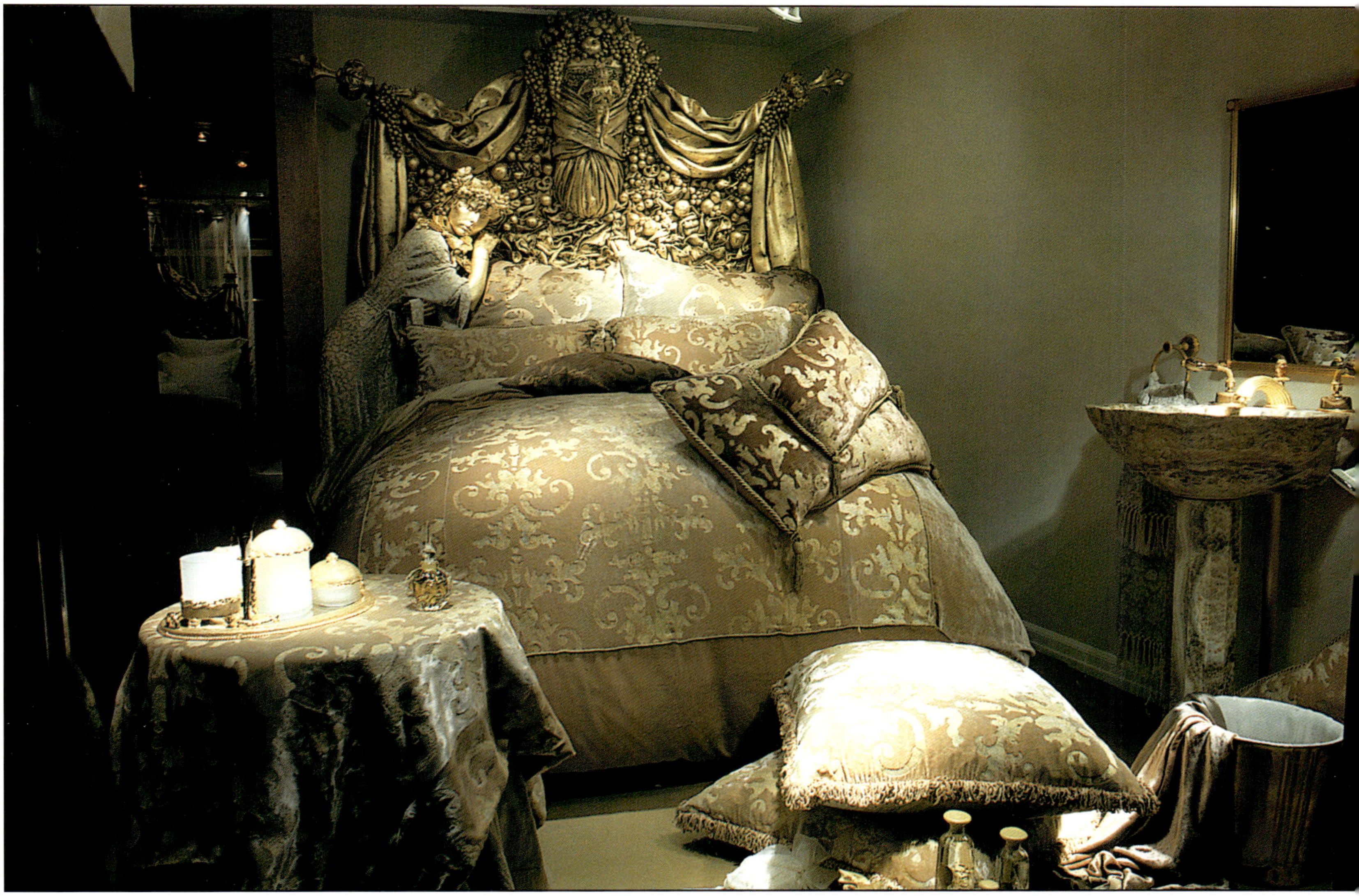

KNIGHT-WARE

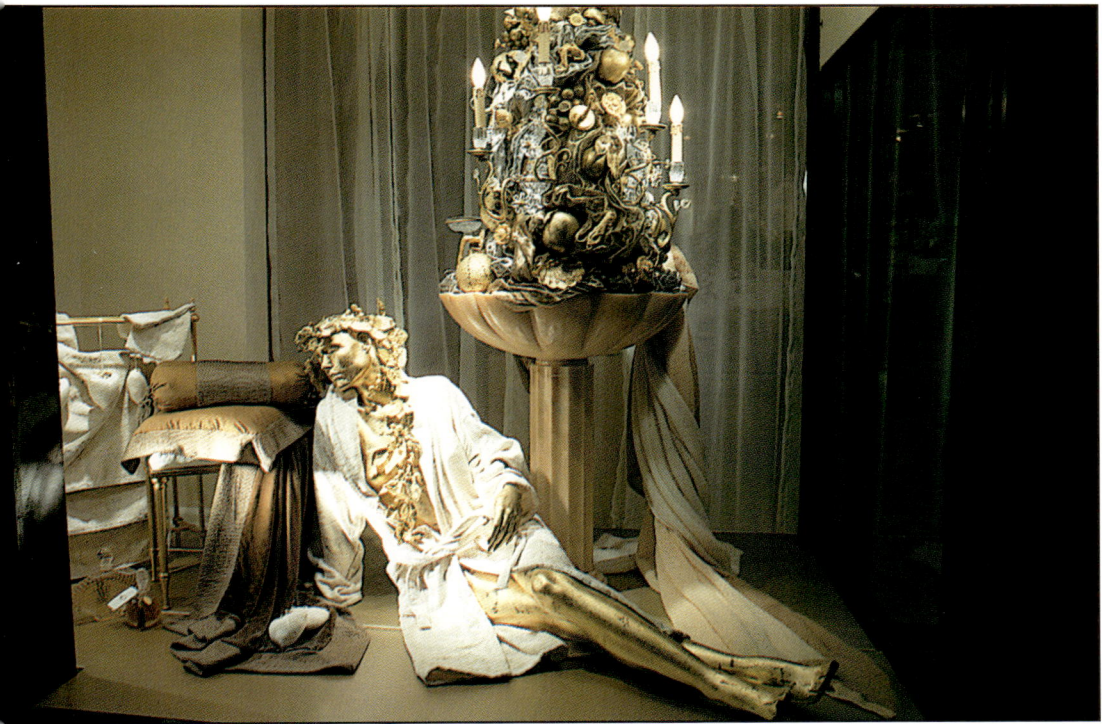

For utter luxury and loveliness, nothing can compare with the settings in Sherle Wagner's windows. Not only did they herald the holidays, they also served to introduce the company's new Bed Shop.

Rich damask fabrics and gilt Sherle Wagner hardware were combined with the ornate headboard created and executed by mary Costantini, and gold leafed mannequins to affect vignette settings that are lush, luxurious and still elegantly tasteful. The fanciful epergnes and mannequin styling were done by Ann Kong, the designer of the windows.

SHERLE WAGNER, (TOP AND ABOVE)
E. 57th St., New York, NY
Designer: Ann Kong
Headboard: Mary Costantini

LIGHTS

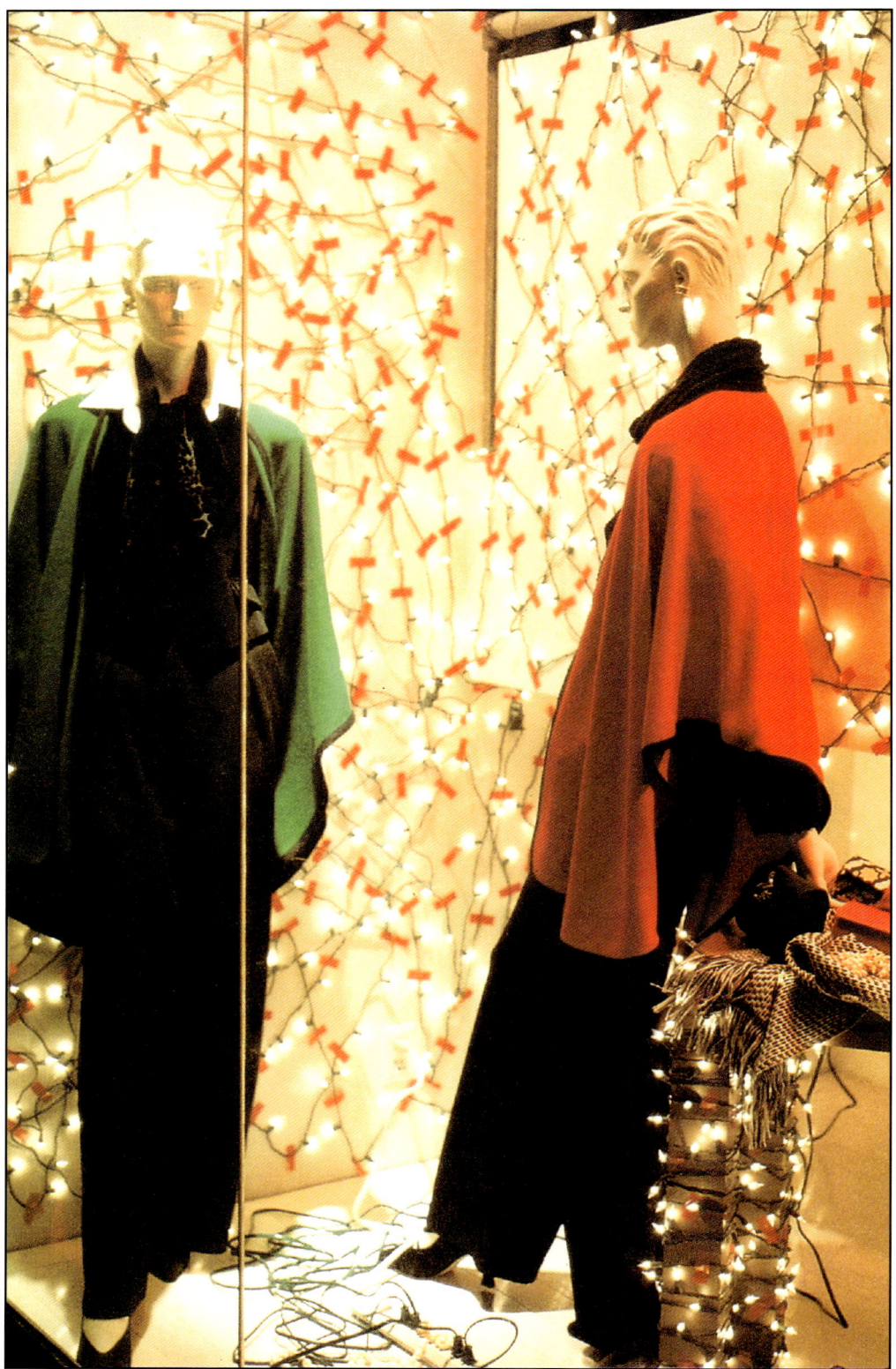

MOGA, Madison Ave., New York, NY
Display Designer: Stefano Corradi

What would Christmas be without bee lights? Without sparkling, twinkling and shimmering lights? They light up the season—put the "stars" in the skies—the sparkle in the snow—the twinkle in the trees, and the richness in the wreaths.

Showing festive red and green wraps for women in the Moga window is made even more festive and exciting by the myriad lights that fill the back wall panels and scatter down to the floor. The little red "band-aids" with which the strings are attached to the panels add to the fun and uniqueness of the display.

White is even whiter when the setting is frosty—and Frosty is there to escort the St. John woman in her classic white knit suit through the snow. The pinpoints of the white bee lights through the snow textured back panels add an extra dollop of sparkle to the frosting.

While the painted snowman hides behind the headless form in Bergdorf's men's window, it is the swag of lights all ready to swoop or drape that catch the viewer's eye. Rough birch logs "frame" the snowy scene and the assorted lengths of birch logs serve as elevations in the foreground for the toiletries.

LIGHTS

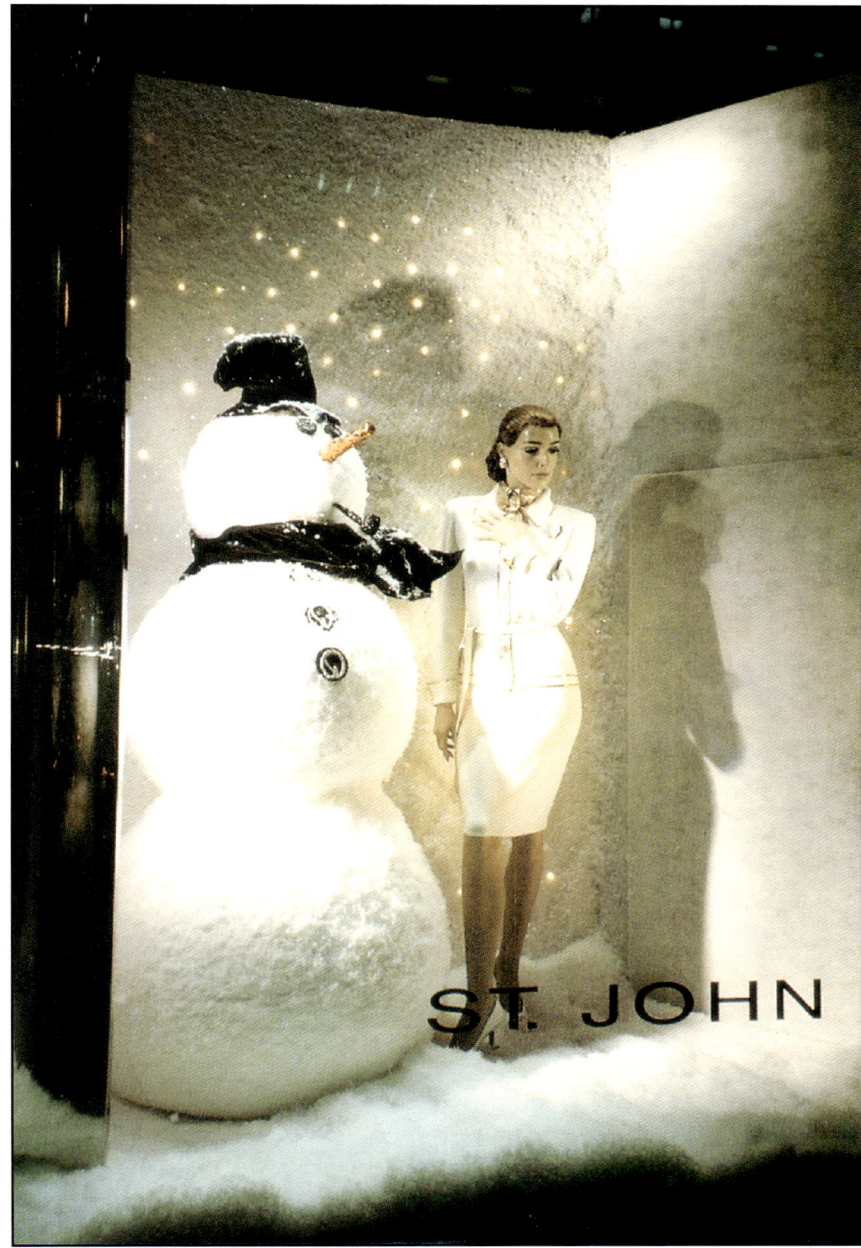

ST. JOHN, Fifth Ave., New York, NY
V.P. Creative Director: Kelly Gray

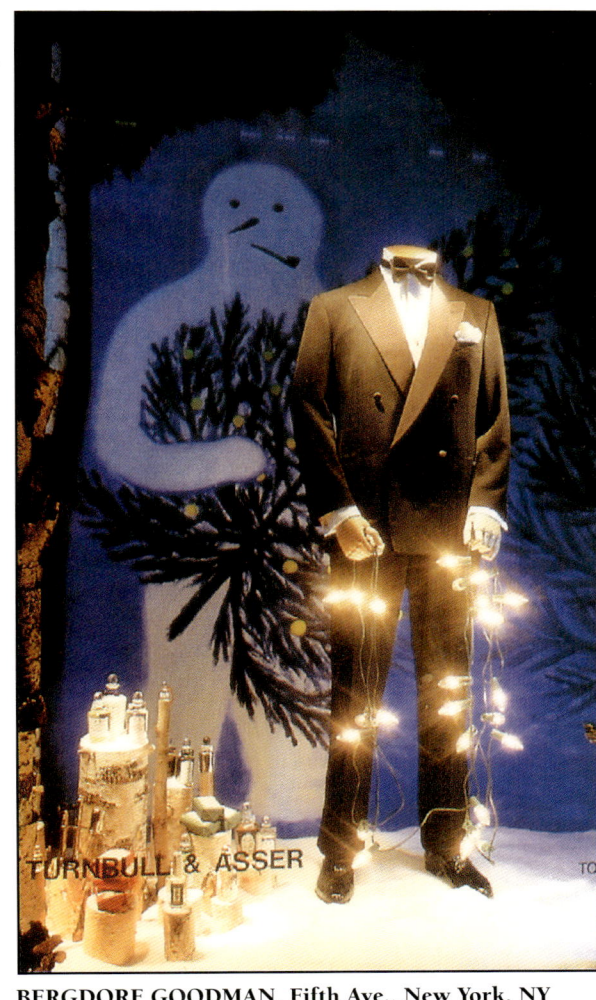

BERGDORF GOODMAN, Fifth Ave., New York, NY
Visuals Director: Linda Fargo

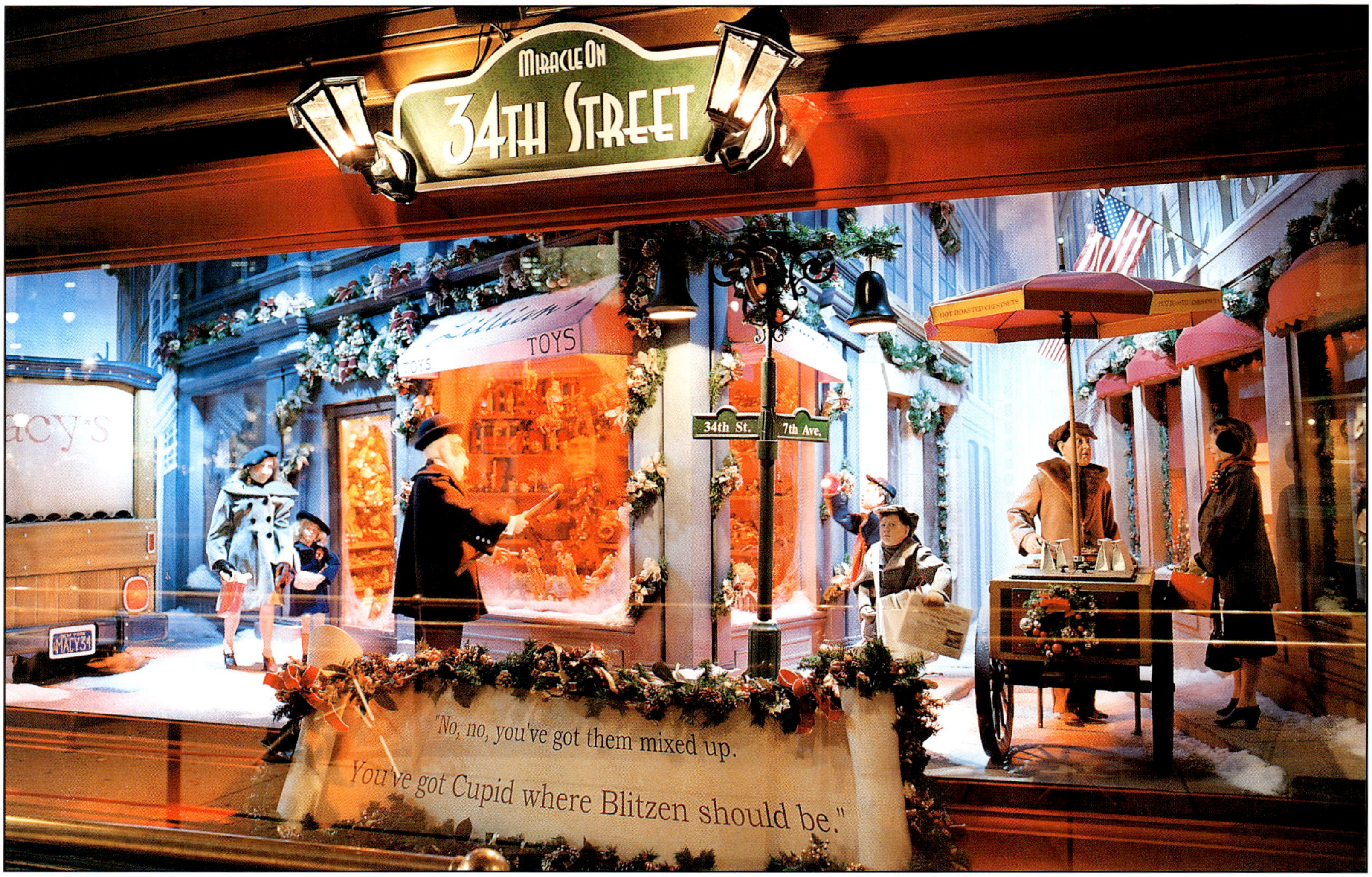

MIRACLE

MACY'S, (ABOVE AND RIGHT) 34th St., New York, NY
Sam C. Josephs: Window Director

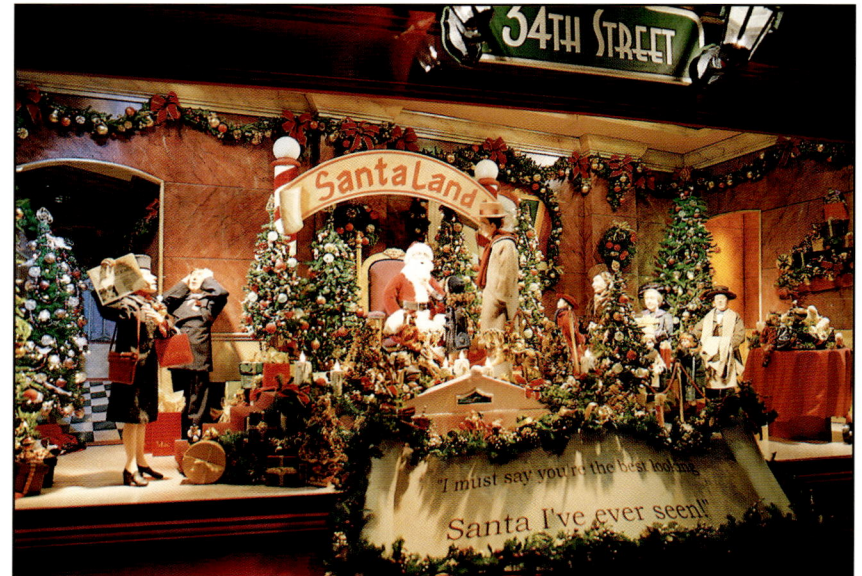

Christmas and Macy's. Almost synonymous. Just like holly goes with berries and pine trees and ornaments go together, so does the Christmas season seem to belong to Macy's Department Store. Other stores are just as festive and full of the holiday spirit but since 20th Century Fox produced the film classic "Miracle on 34th Street" a half century ago, Macy's—starting with its annual Thanksgiving parade—has become the criteria by which Christmas stores and stories are judged. And so, all these years later, many children whose parents weren't even born when the film was originally released, will at Christmas time, sit with their parents and watch reruns of the film about the little girl who comes to believe there really is a Santa Claus. The setting for "The Miracle" is Macy's.

Sam Josephs and his staff of "elves" recreated—at last—that story in miniature in the store's six major windows that stretch across the Broadway facade. Down to the smallest details like the individually wrapped mini-mini gift boxes-in a series of vignettes-the familiar story is retold. There were long, endless lines of parents and children lined up to once again relive the "classic" and to once again get to believe that there is a Santa Claus. Thank You, Mr. Macy and the entire display staff and their "friends" for finally bringing "The Miracle" back to 34th Street.

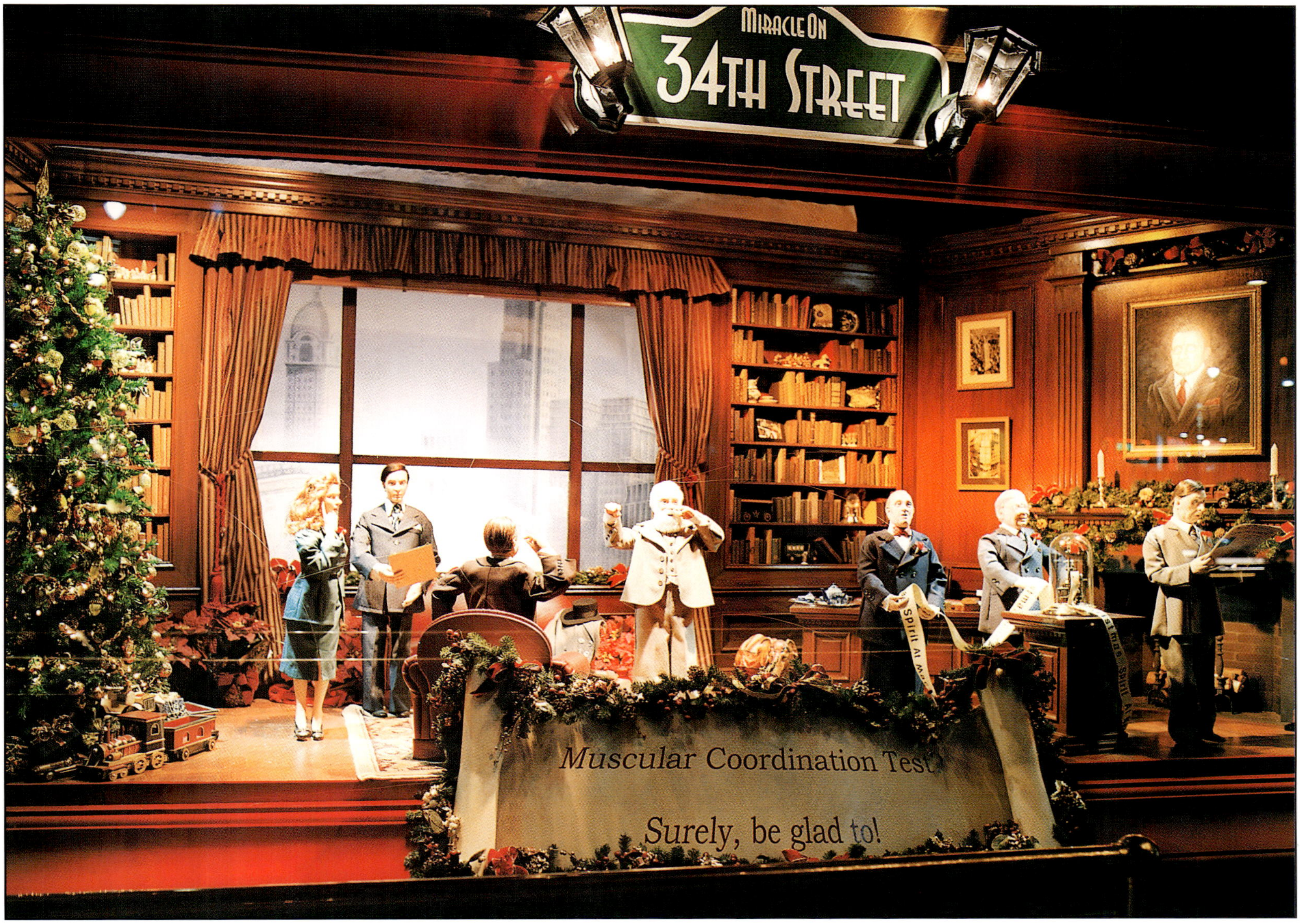

MIRACLE

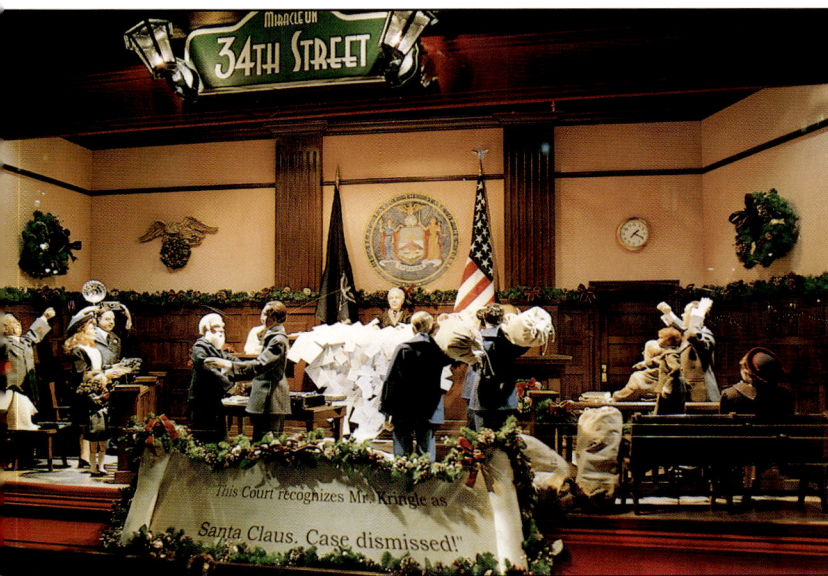
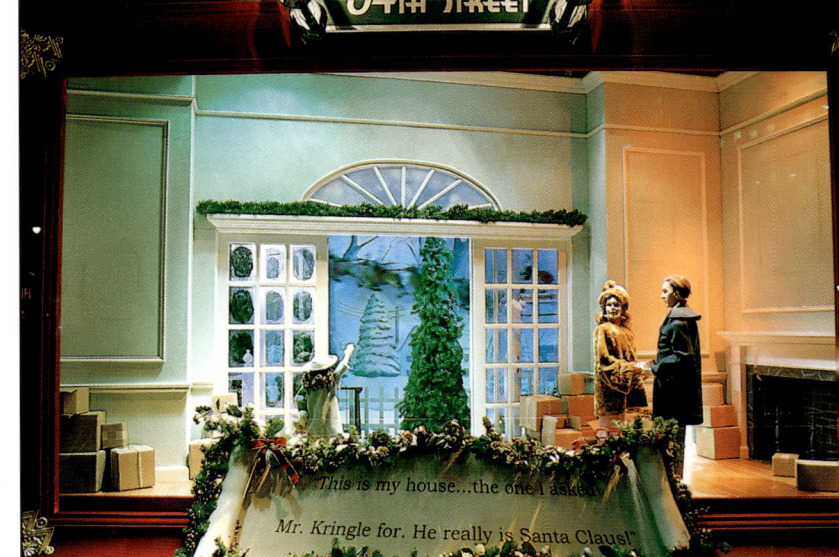

MACY'S, (ALL) 34th St., New York, NY
Sam C. Josephs: Window Director

MUSIC

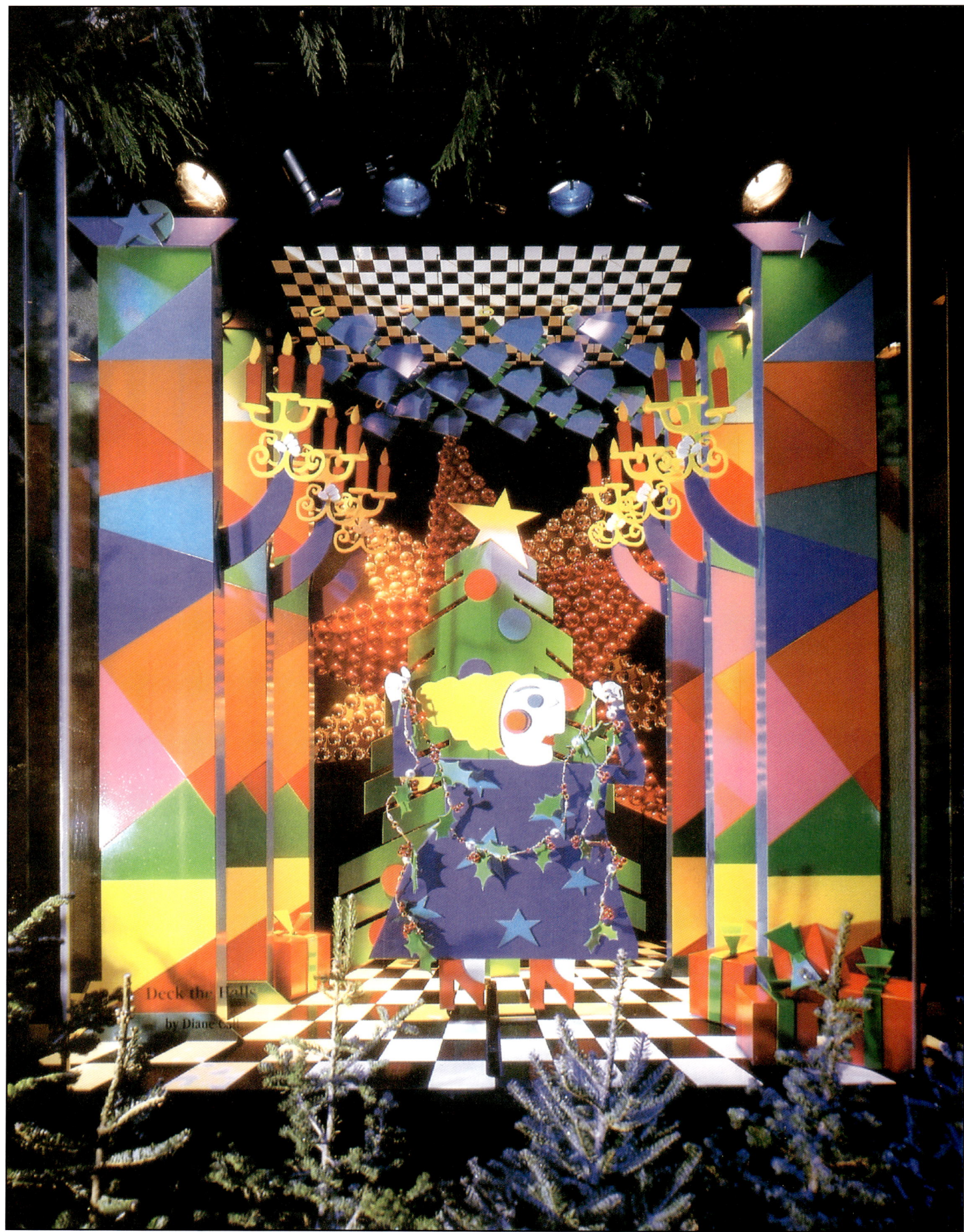

ZCMI, Salt Lake City, UT
Visuals Director: Mike Stephen
Designers: Celeste Cecchini, Diane Call, Annie Cook, Tim David and Alysa Revell

MUSIC

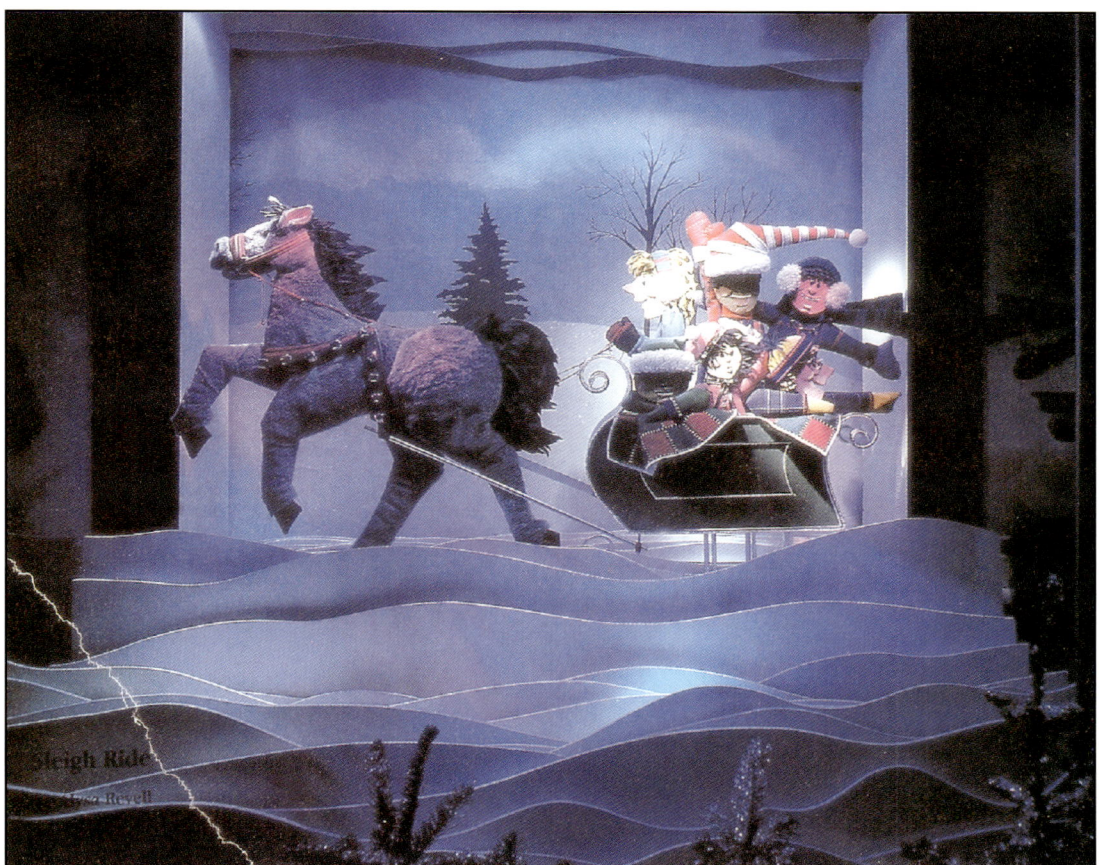

Christmas is the time for songs and singing. Music is Christmas and Christmas is music. ZCMI took its inspiration for a series of institutional windows from the music that is played over and over during the holiday season. Merchandise was kept inside the store while these windows sparkled with lights, with color, and with the glitter of shiny ornaments. Shown here are the familiar classics "Deck the Halls" and "Sleigh Ride," and, for the aging Baby Boomers, there is nostalgia in "Rock'n Round the Christmas Tree."

The visual director, Mike Stephen, and his able staff of designers took this opportunity to "interpret" three dimensionally the recognizable tunes as new and entertaining tableaux for the delight of the friends and shoppers of ZCMI.

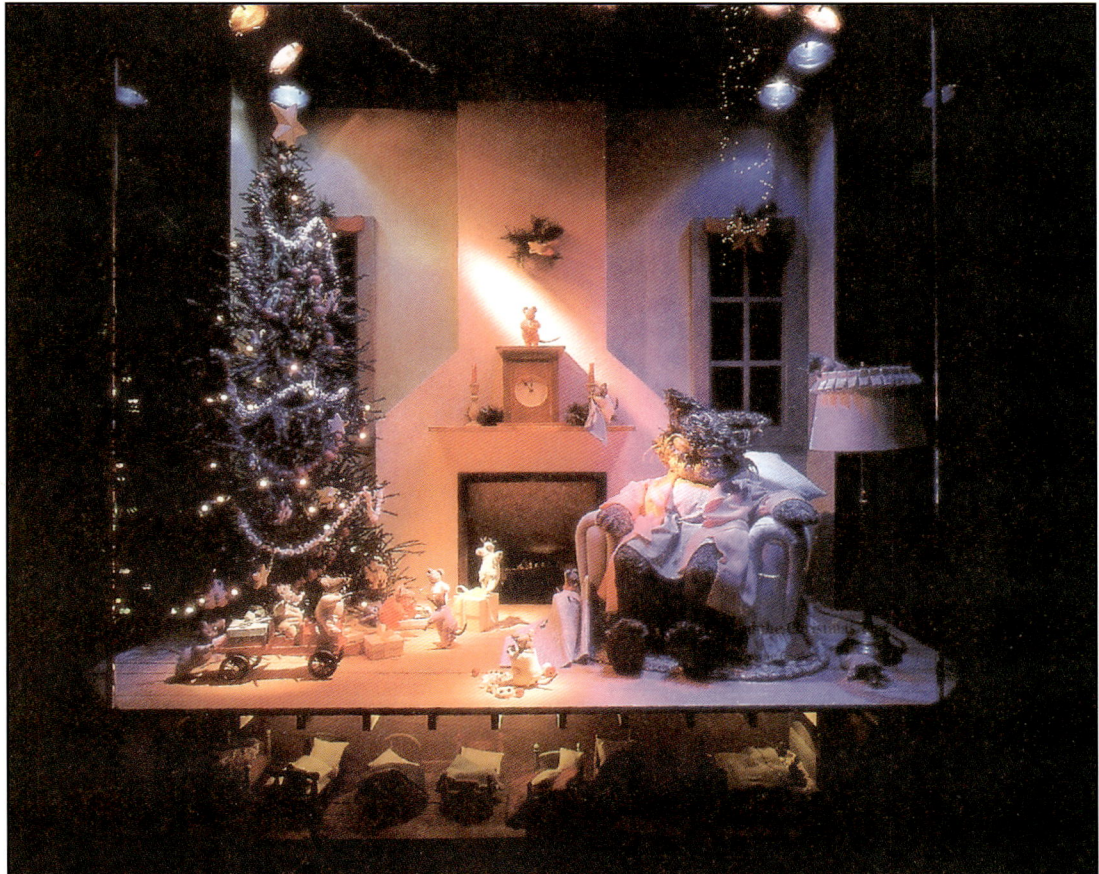

ZCMI, (TOP AND ABOVE) **Salt Lake City, UT**
Visuals Director: Mike Stephen
Designers: Celeste Cecchini, Diane Call, Annie Cook, Tim David and Alysa Revell

MUSICAL INTERLUDES

Simply stated with dramatic pull-back velvet drapes, some gold painted opera chairs, a musical instrument to set the music playing and the elegant holiday merchandise set out under warm and romantic lighting: that is how it was done this year at Paul Stuart's on Madison Ave.

The recurring element was the green foliage garland enriched with ornaments and ribbons. The glass ornaments were color coordinated with the window drapery: gold balls with gold drapery, pink ornaments with the deep pink curtain. Other unifying elements were the glittery mounds of snow that covered the floors of the windows and the elegant gilt chairs that served as elevations for the fashion accessories.

In the accessory window the chairs were lined up in a row against the subtly striped wall with the lush ribbon and ornament foliage swagged over the seats. As before—simply stated and neatly done but full of the season's sentiments.

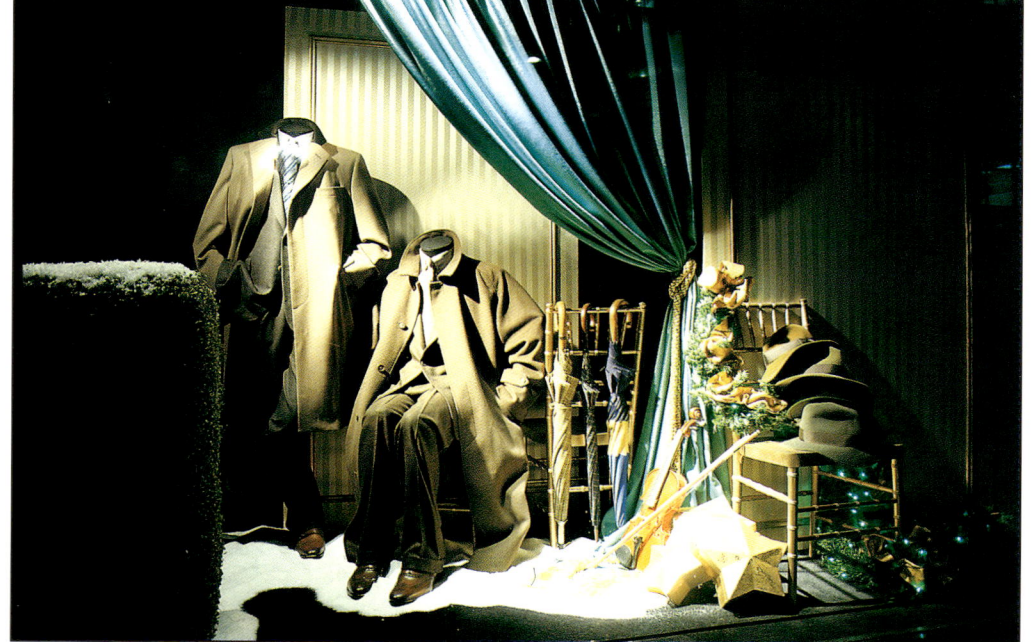

PAUL STUART, (ABOVE AND LEFT)
Madison Ave., New York, NY
Visual Managers: Jerry Fredella & Michael Verbert

MUSICAL INTERLUDES

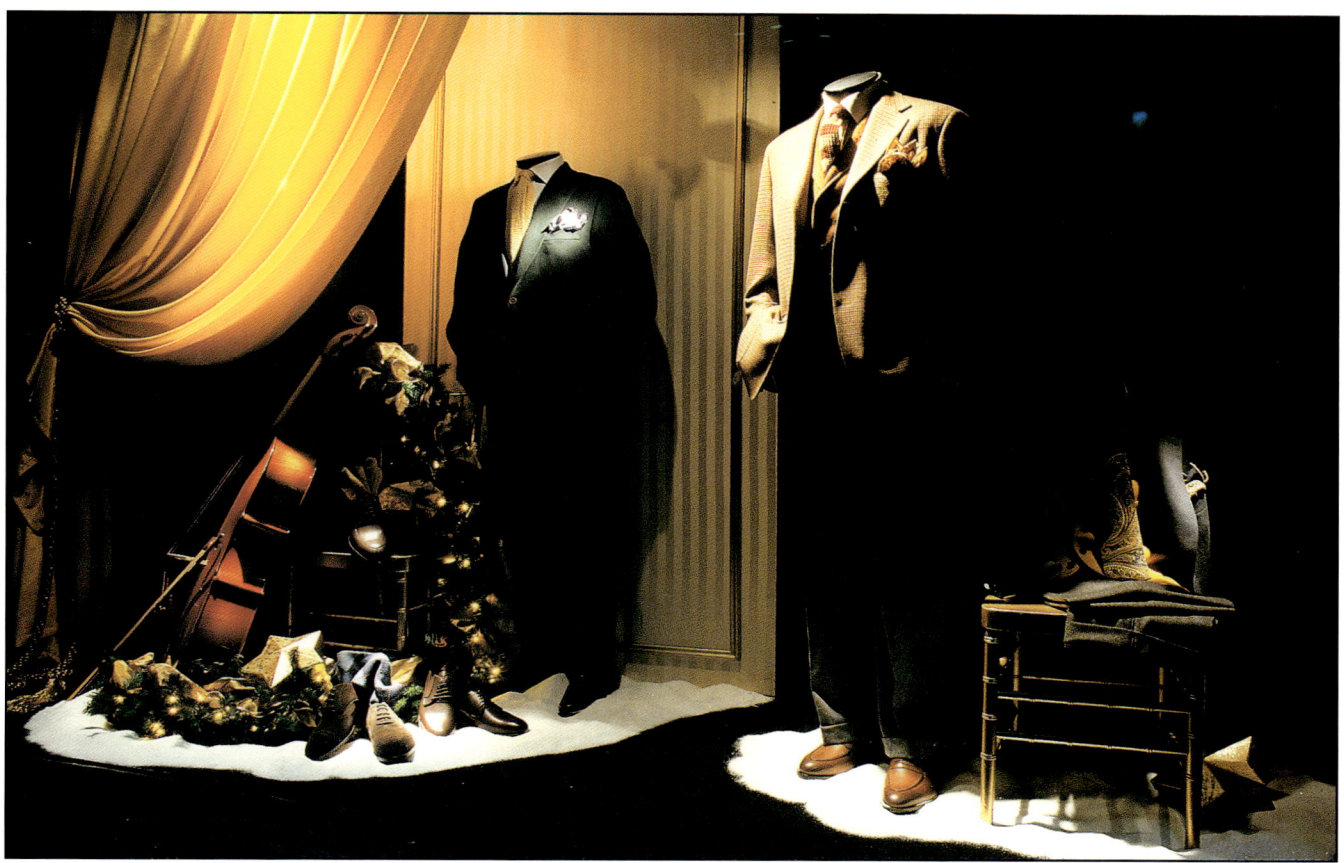

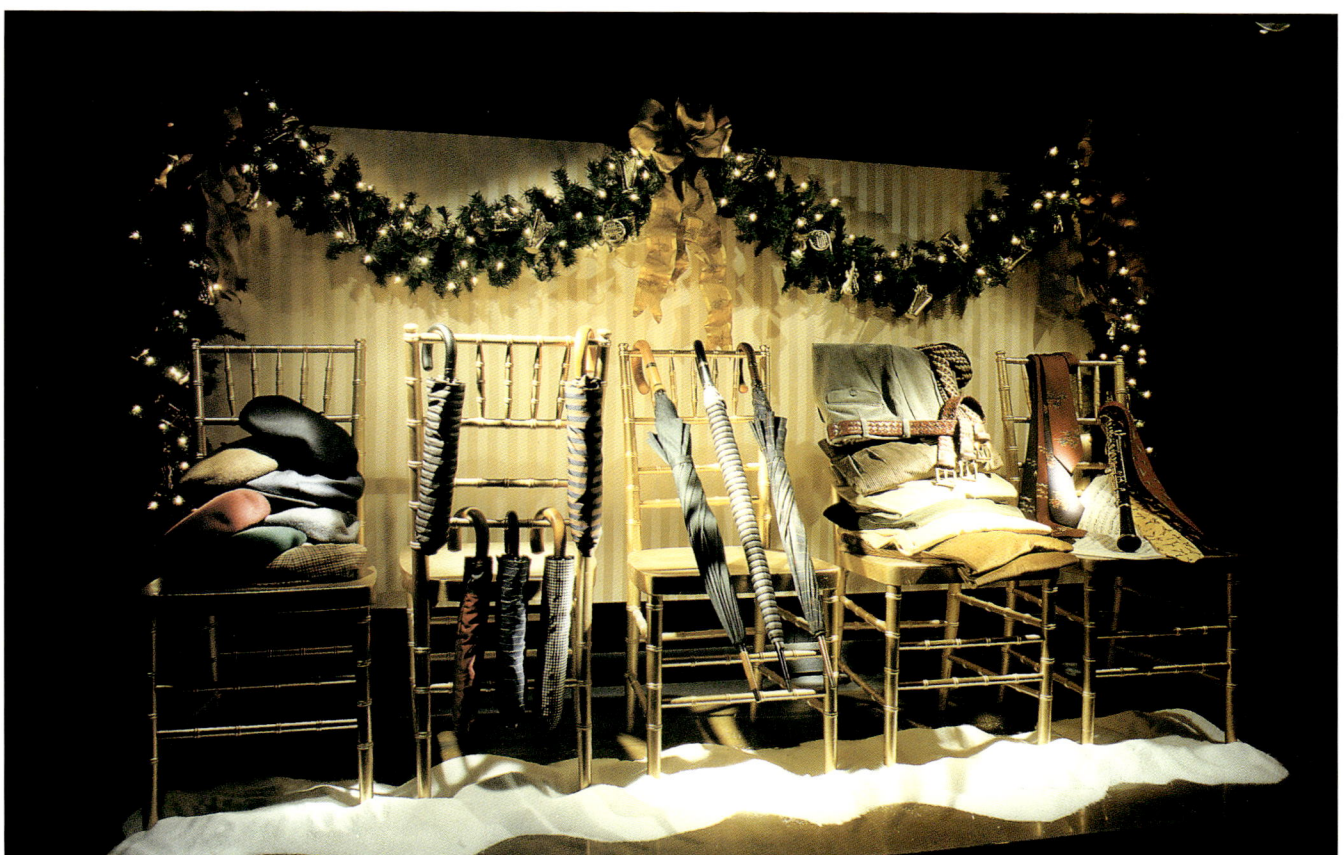

PAUL STUART, (TOP AND ABOVE), Madison Ave., New York, NY
Visual Managers: Jerry Fredella & Michael Verbert

NUTCRACKER

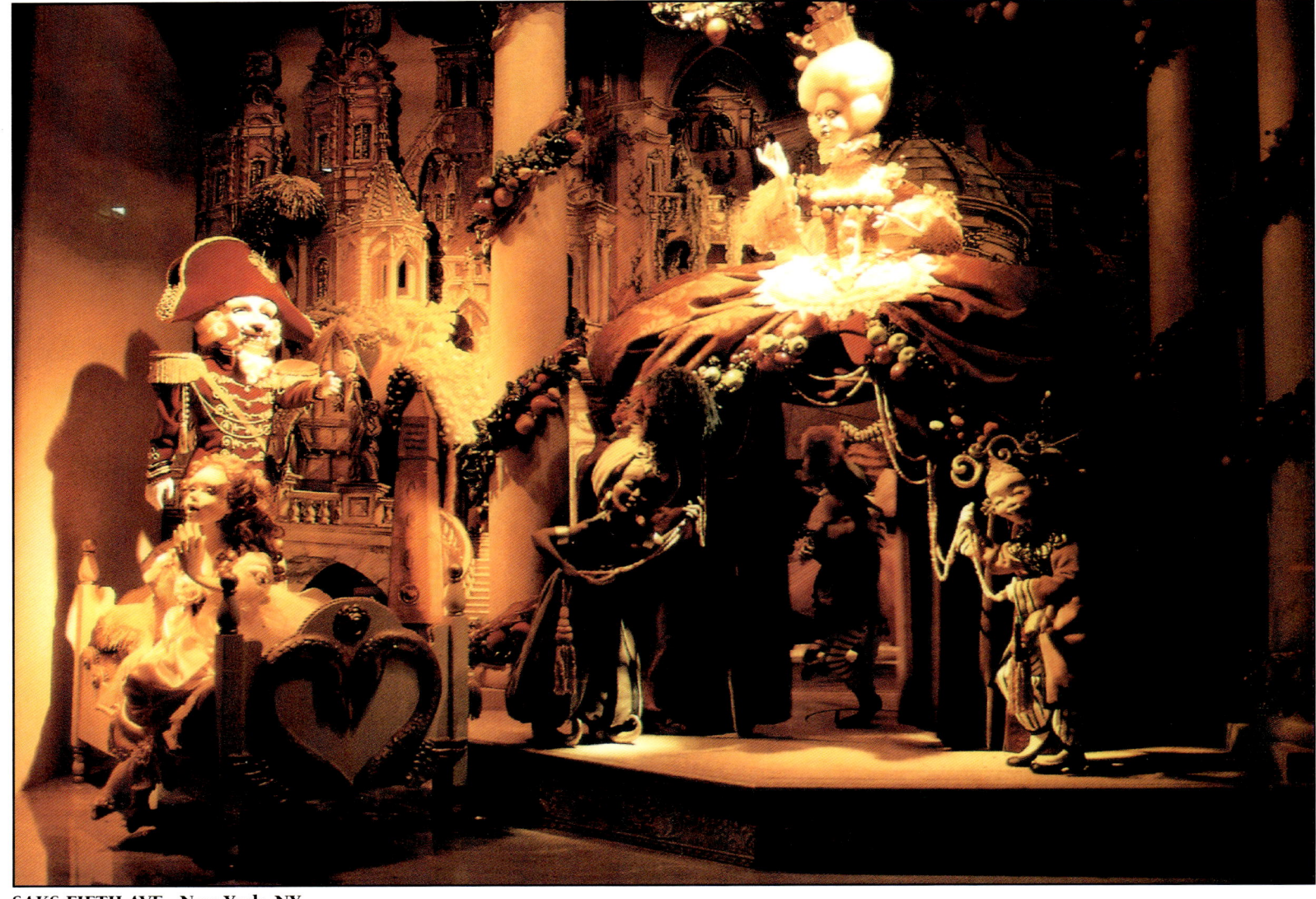

SAKS FIFTH AVE., New York, NY
V.P. of Visual Merchandising: Ken Smart
Visual Director of Windows: Randy Yaw

Saks Fifth Avenue took the familiar Nutcracker ballet as the source of inspiration for the animated windows on Fifth Avenue. While graphic reproductions of the Nutcracker Soldier King stood guard over the fashion presentation on the side streets, Fifth Ave. was lined up with visitors to see and hear this version of the Christmas story. The great moments of the ballet are beautifully reproduced in rich fabrics and in gilded settings while the music that fills the street is from the Tchaikovsky score. The "story" and the "continuity" is provided in each window so that the viewers can quickly pick up what is happening as they glide, spin and move down the waiting line in time to the happy music.

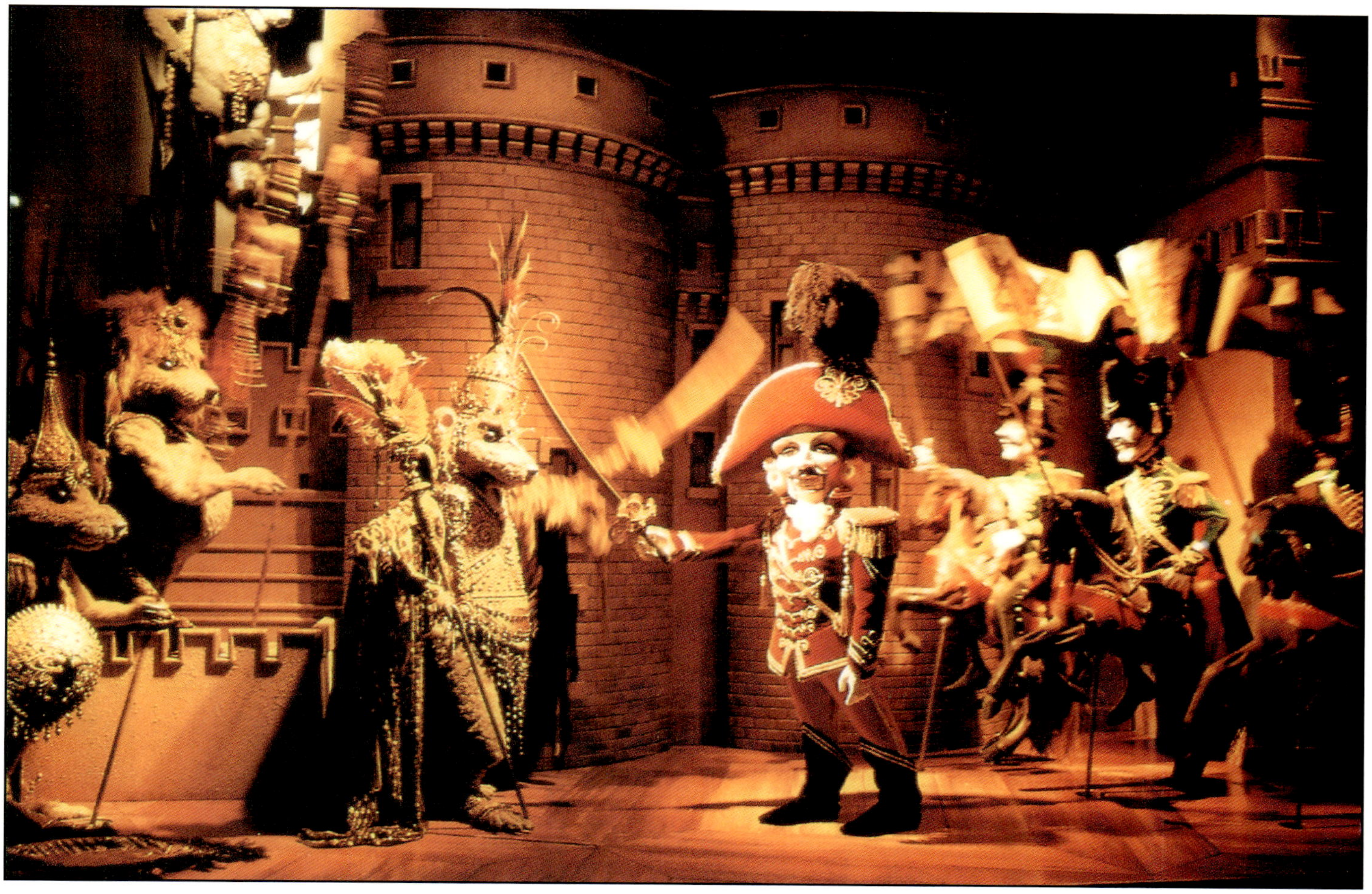

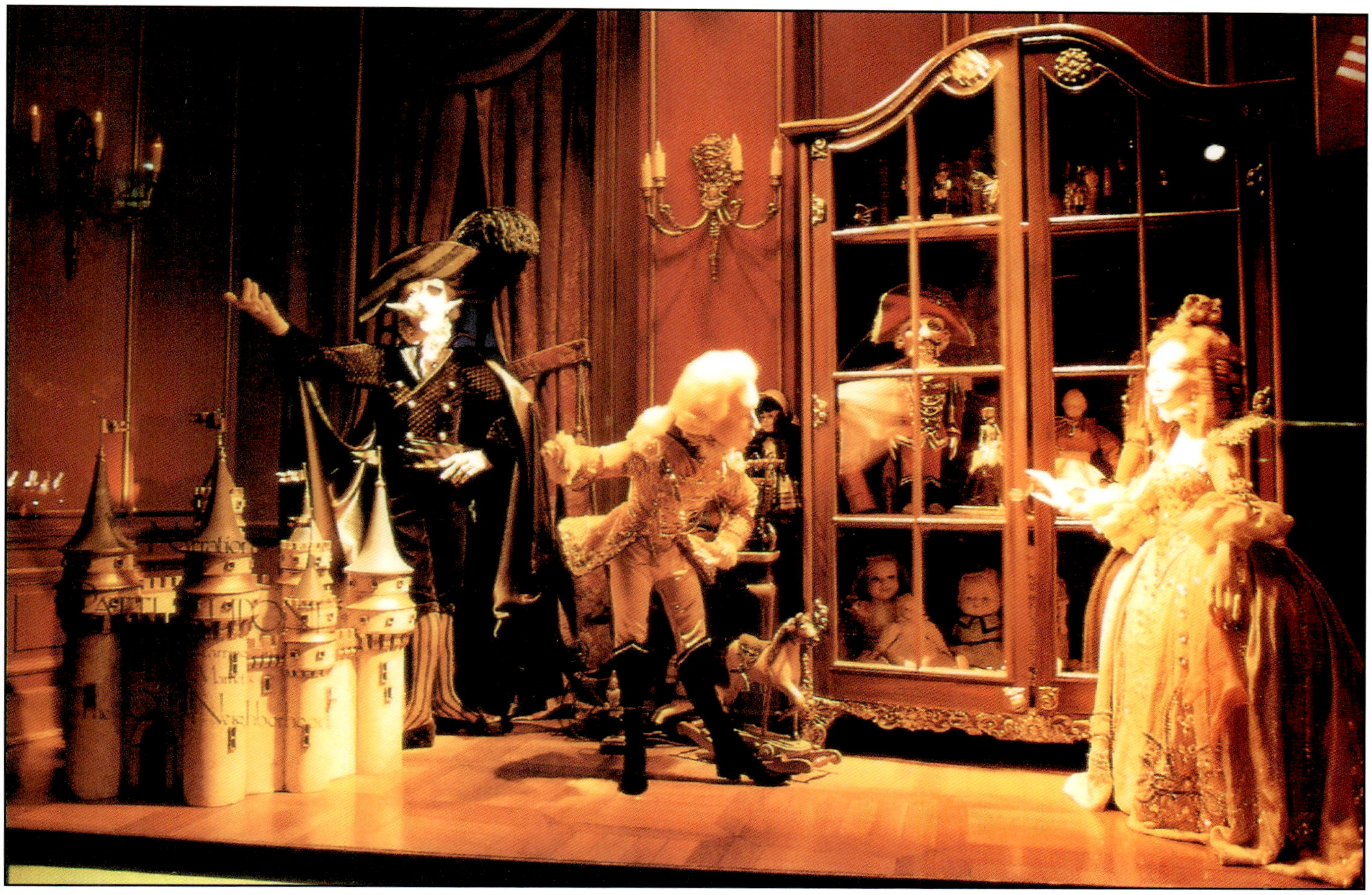

NUTCRACKER

SAKS FIFTH AVE., (TOP AND ABOVE) New York, NY
V.P. of Visual Merchandising: Ken Smart
Visual Director of Windows: Randy Yaw

OPULENCE

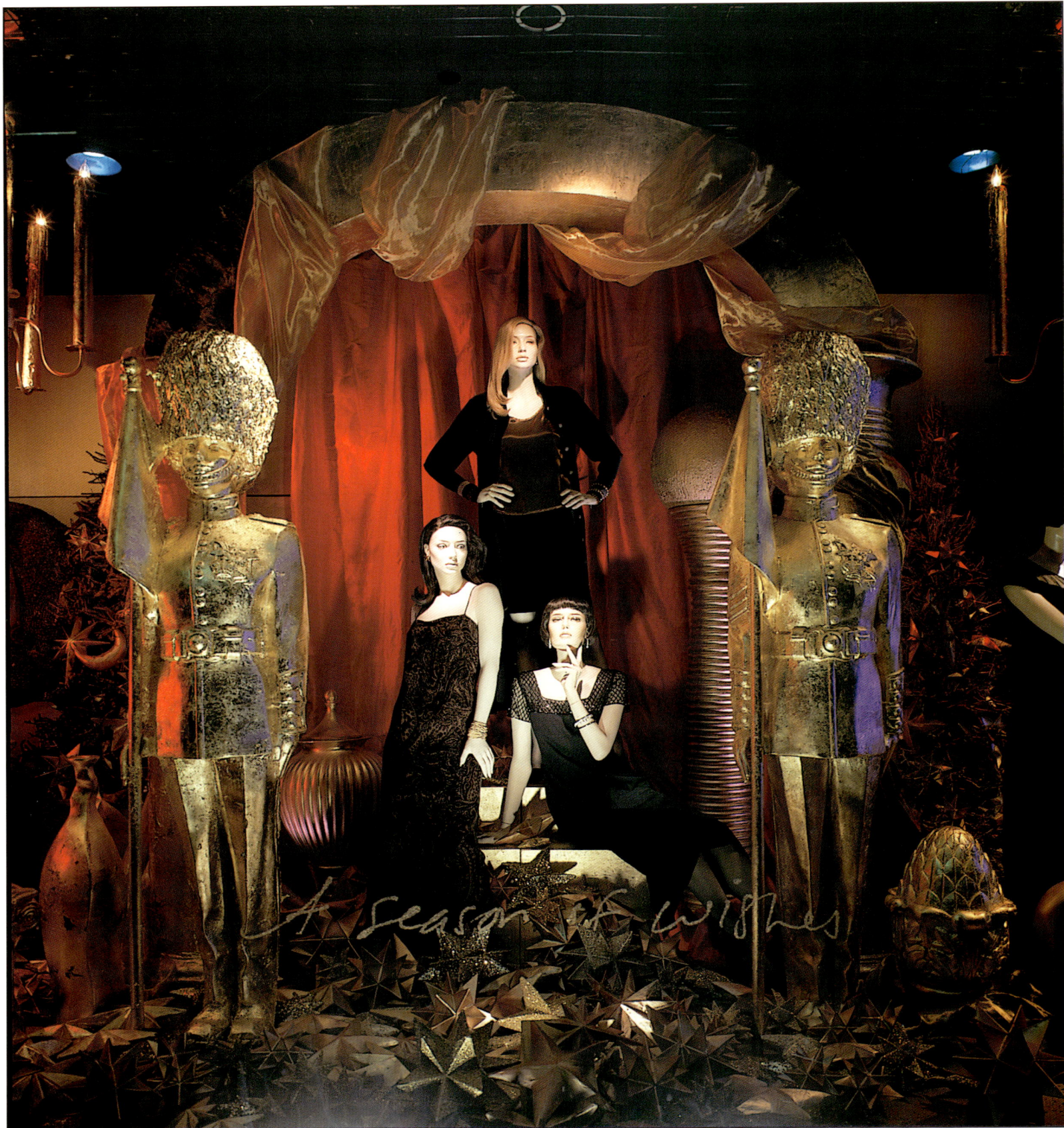

ZCMI, Salt Lake City, UT
Visual Director: Mike Stephens
Designer: Celeste Cecchini

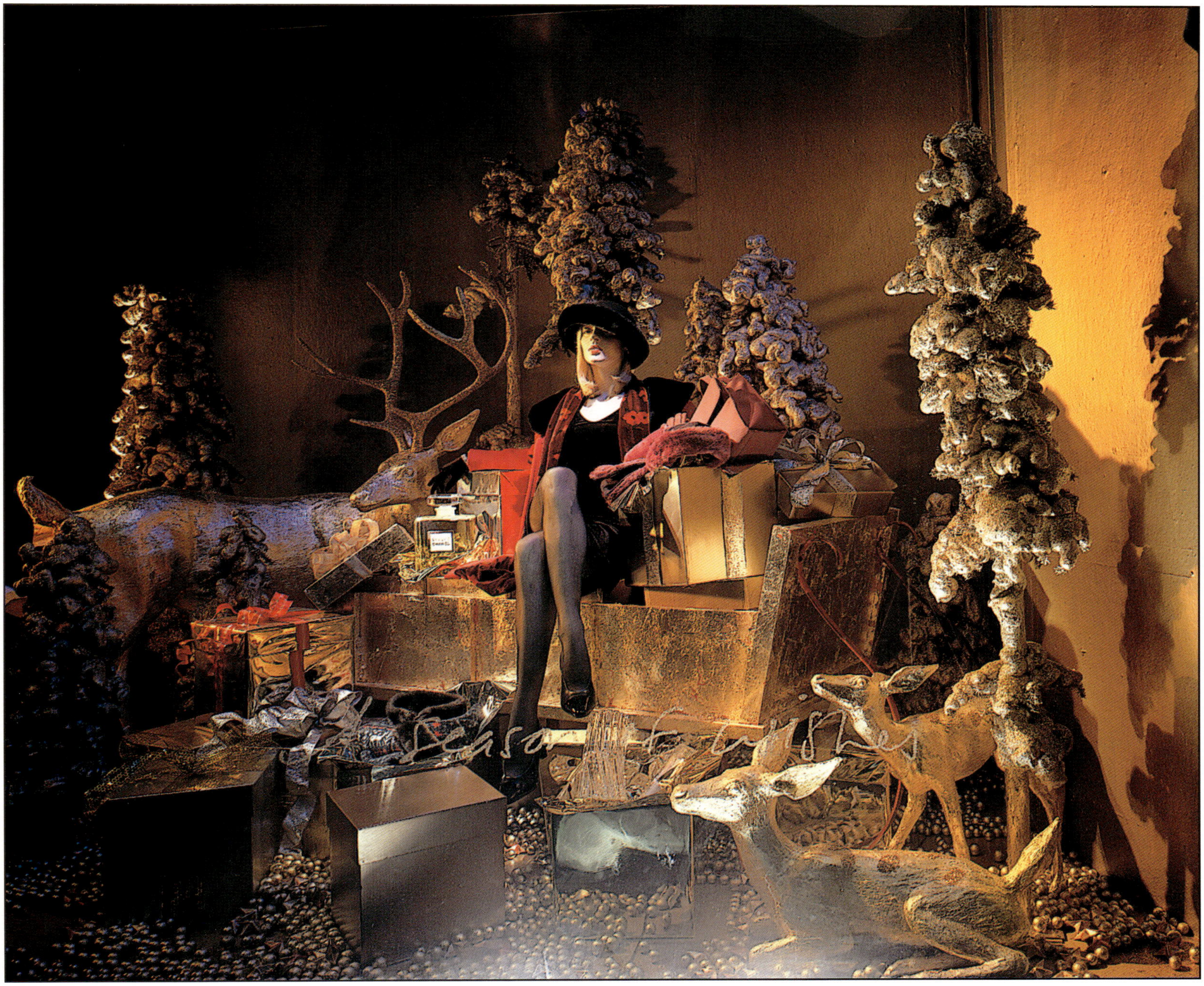

OPULENCE

At ZCMI in Salt Lake City, it was "Season of Wishes." It was wishing for special gifts and the gift fulfillment of the merchandise displays in the lavish window settings. In one setting, two stylized guards, finished in gold leaf, stand sentry duty in front of a gilded arch rich embellished with gossamer gold fabrics and lustrous red velvet drapes. The subtle but glittery setting presents black formalwear for the magical season. In another window, the bench and the assembled reindeer are also golf leafed as are the ornate epergnes filled with clusters of sculpted fruits. Shiny gold boxes tied with red ribbon complement the mannequin in black with the dashing red scarf.

Golf leafed stars and panels highlight a small perfume window. What makes this set of windows so ravishing is also what makes them such a great concept. It means using old and familiar props—revitalized with gold leaf finishes.

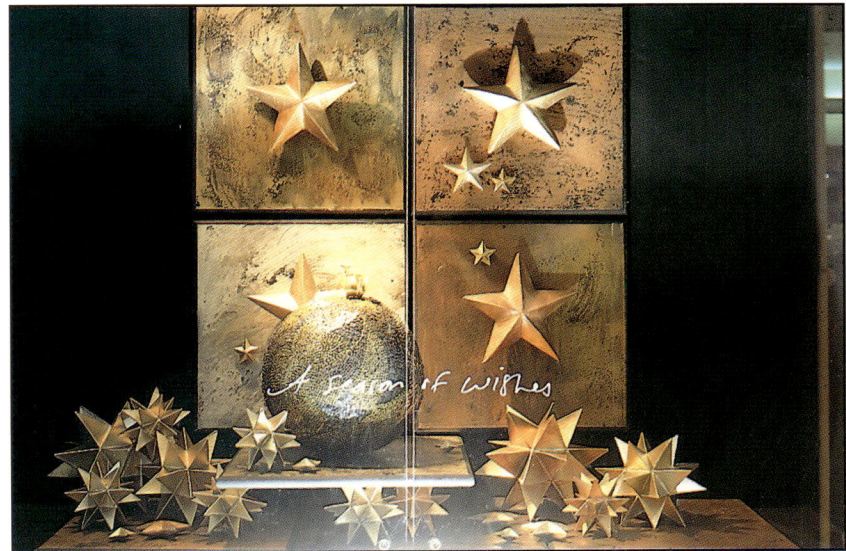

ZCMI, (TOP AND ABOVE) Salt Lake City, UT
Visual Director: Mike Stephens
Designer: Celeste Cecchini

ORNAMENTS

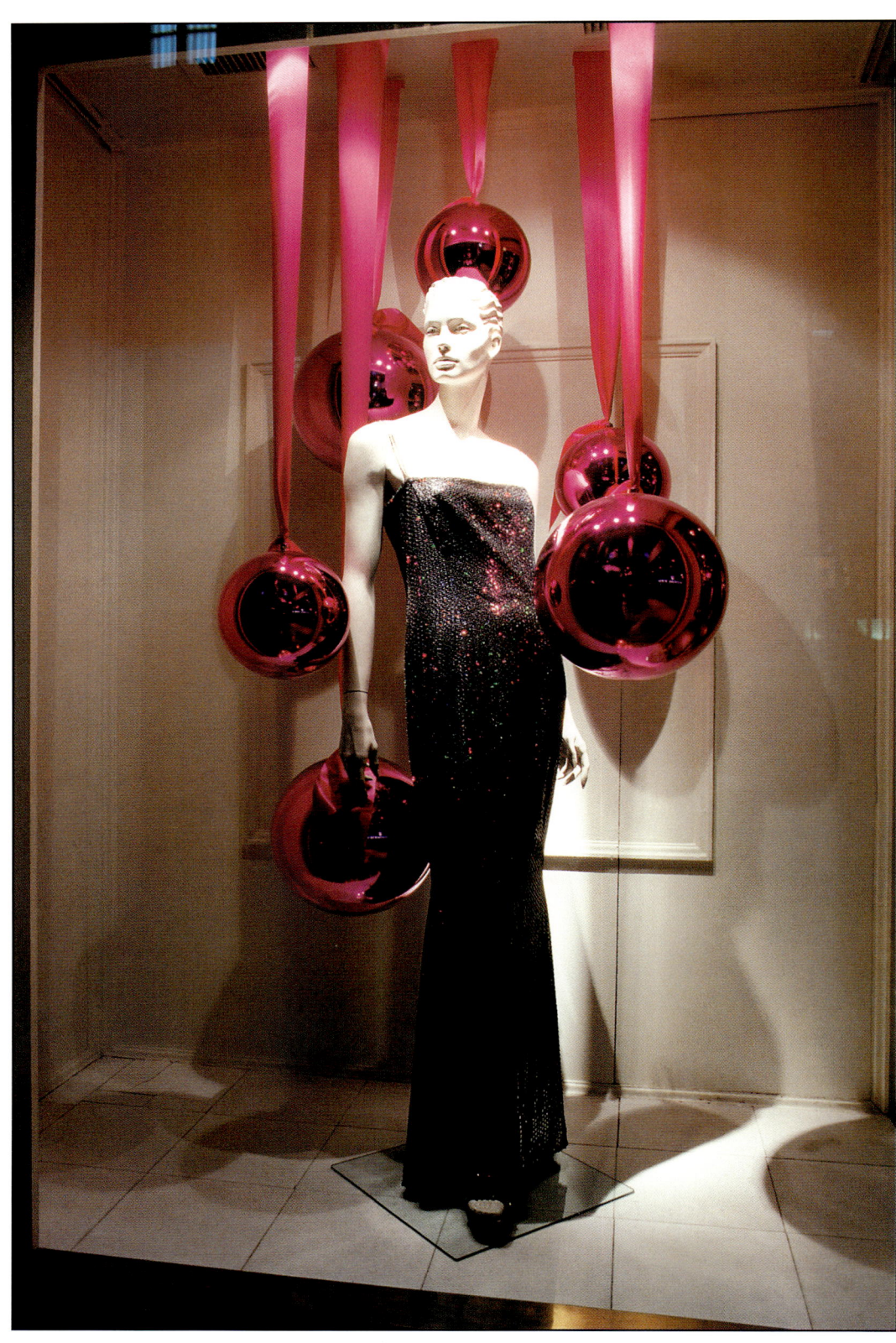

ESCADA, E. 57th St., New York, NY
Dir. Retail VM: Anthony Battaglia

Making it big and making it better is the way Burberry approached their holiday windows. The giant, cut-out and dimensionalized "ornaments" are wallcovered in the famous and familiar Burberry plaid. Making an ideal backdrop for the plaid is the bright red that is used for covering the walls and floors. Displayed on the shelves is a variety of giftable Burberry accessories. The abstract mannequin, dressed in a Burberry plaid skirt is examining the wares on display while the dog on the Burberry leash is making eye contact with the shoppers on the street. The theme—"Plaid Tidings"—what else?

Escada's simple setting complements the elegant, multi-flittered black gown. Hanging from cerise satin ribbons are the oversized cerise ornaments that pick up the red/violet glitter on the dress. The all-white setting and the sophisticated white stylized mannequin sit back and let the message be told.

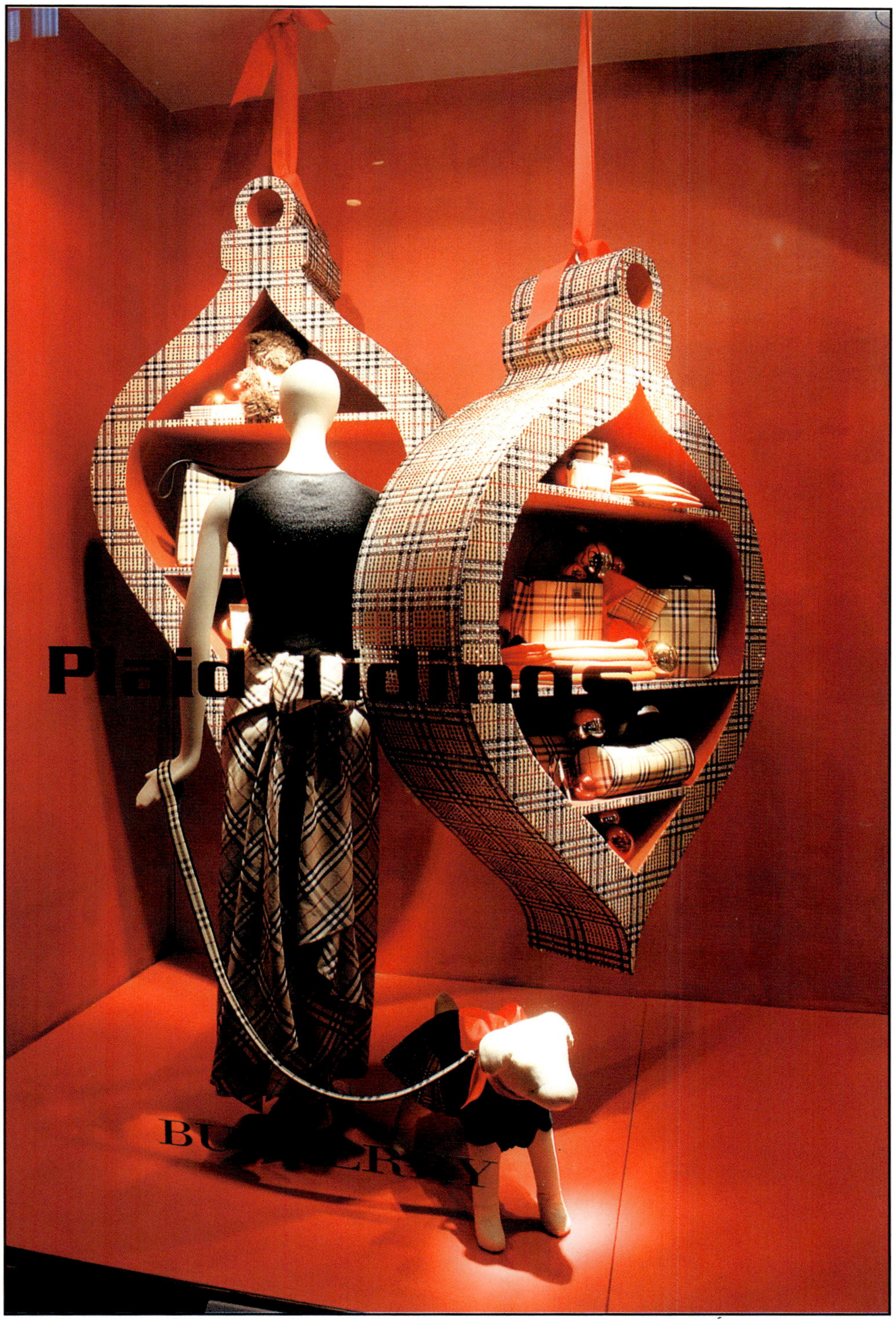

ORNAMENTS

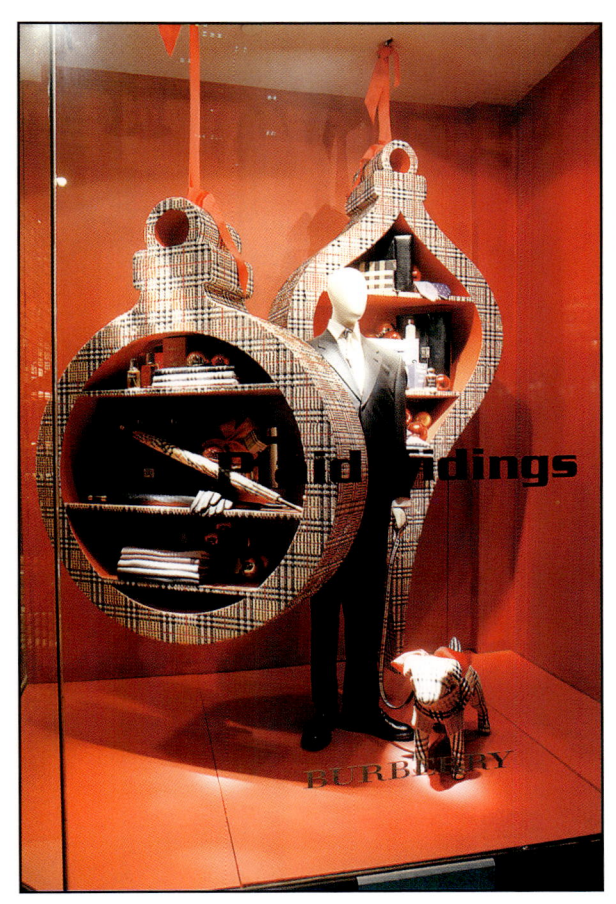

BURBERRYS, (ABOVE AND LEFT) E. 57th St., New York, NY
VP Store Design & VM: Diane Gatterdam

OVER THE TOP

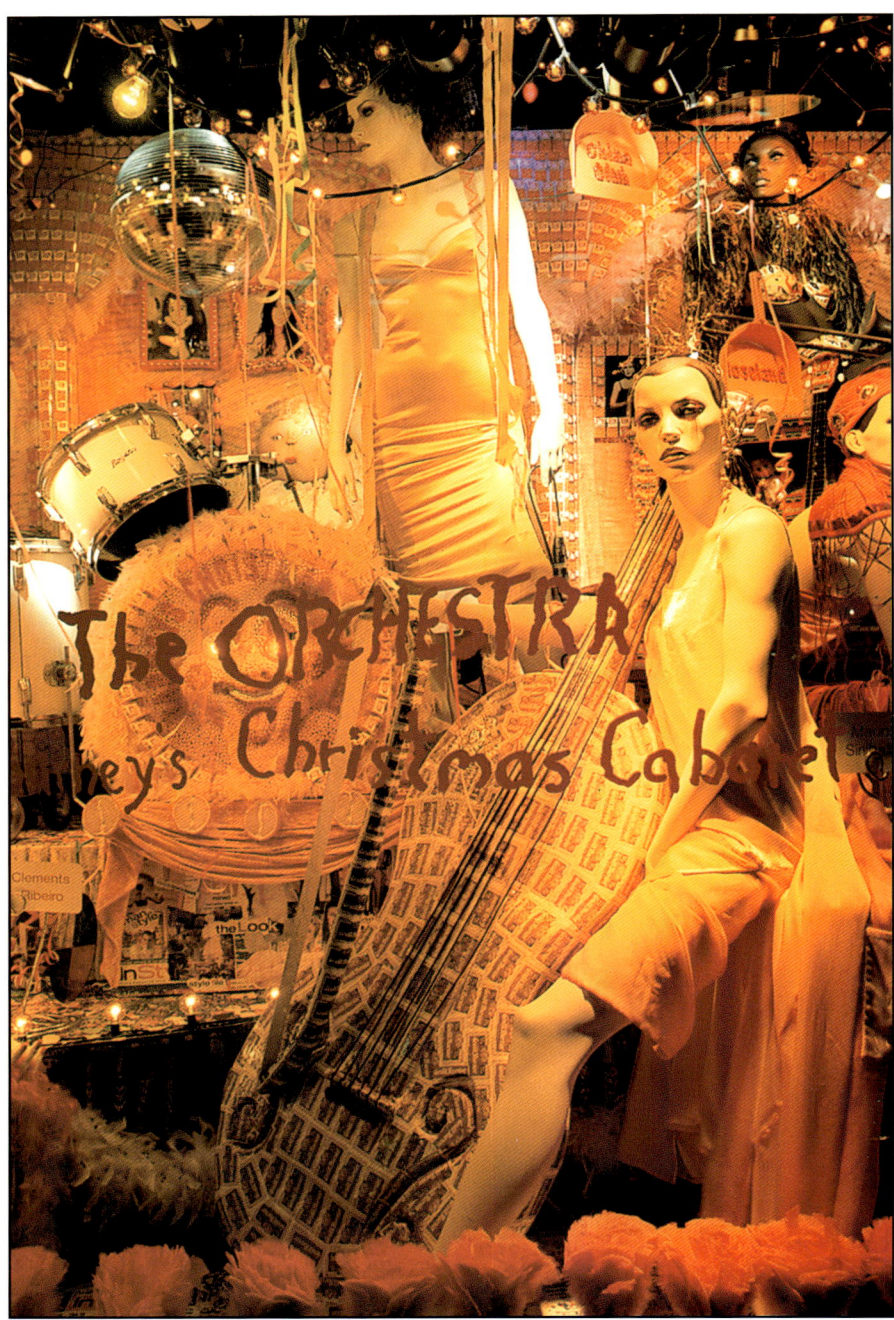

Just how far can one go before it just ain't Christmas? Barneys NY once again under the direction of Simon Doonan, pushes their viewers to the very edge with these color themed, color filled and trivia crammed holiday windows. They are a celebration of fine clothing, fantastic places, fine dining and fun! Fun! Fun! Each window features a different color and the designers have created a "proscenium" or window frame of feather dusters—of the window color—to unify the total presentation.

Crammed, jammed and squeezed into each window are designer clothes, dolls, mache figures, cafe tables and chairs, food and food wrappers, wine and liquor bottles and all sorts of everyday items that make unexpected appearances. Many are so mundane that you don't recognize them for what they are until you study each display—literally inch by inch. These are not windows to be seen in passing; they demand that you stop and study them. A real careful analysis of the displays is like taking a course in "Props 101": how to turn trite and usually discarded items into elements of wonder and amazement. All it takes is imagination, flair, a healthy dose of daring and a great big serving of humor.

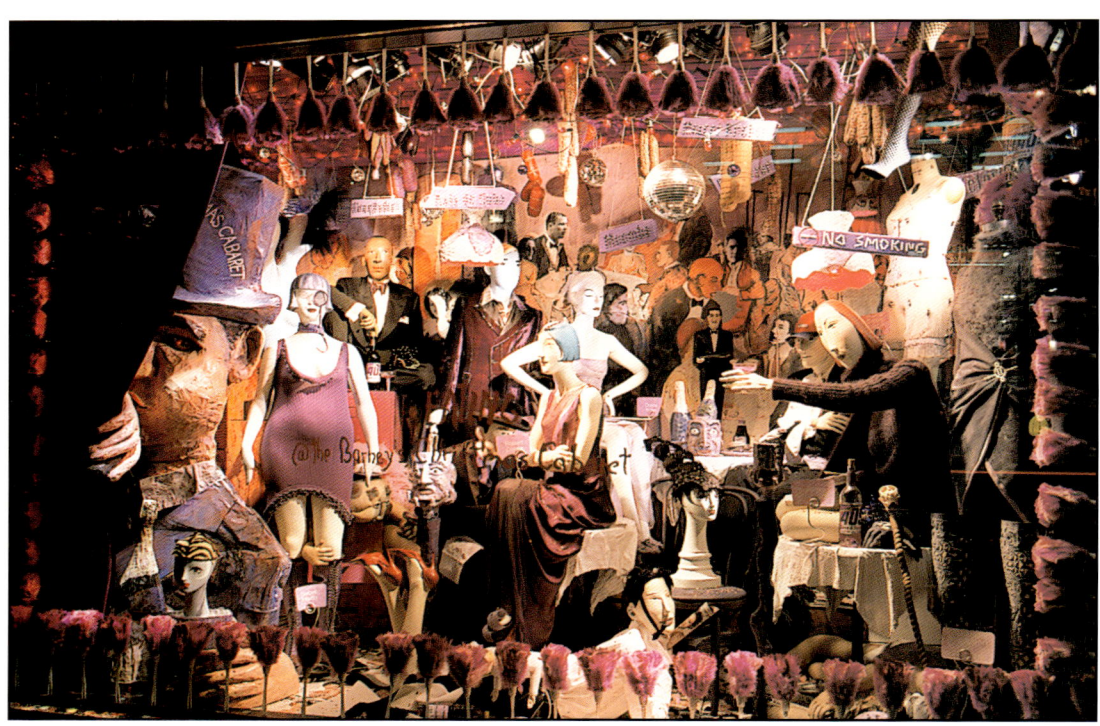

BARNEYS, (ABOVE AND LEFT)
Madison Ave., New York, NY
Creative Director: Simon Doonan
Sr. V.P. of Creative Services: David New
V.P. Creative Services: Adamo Di Gregerio

OVER THE TOP

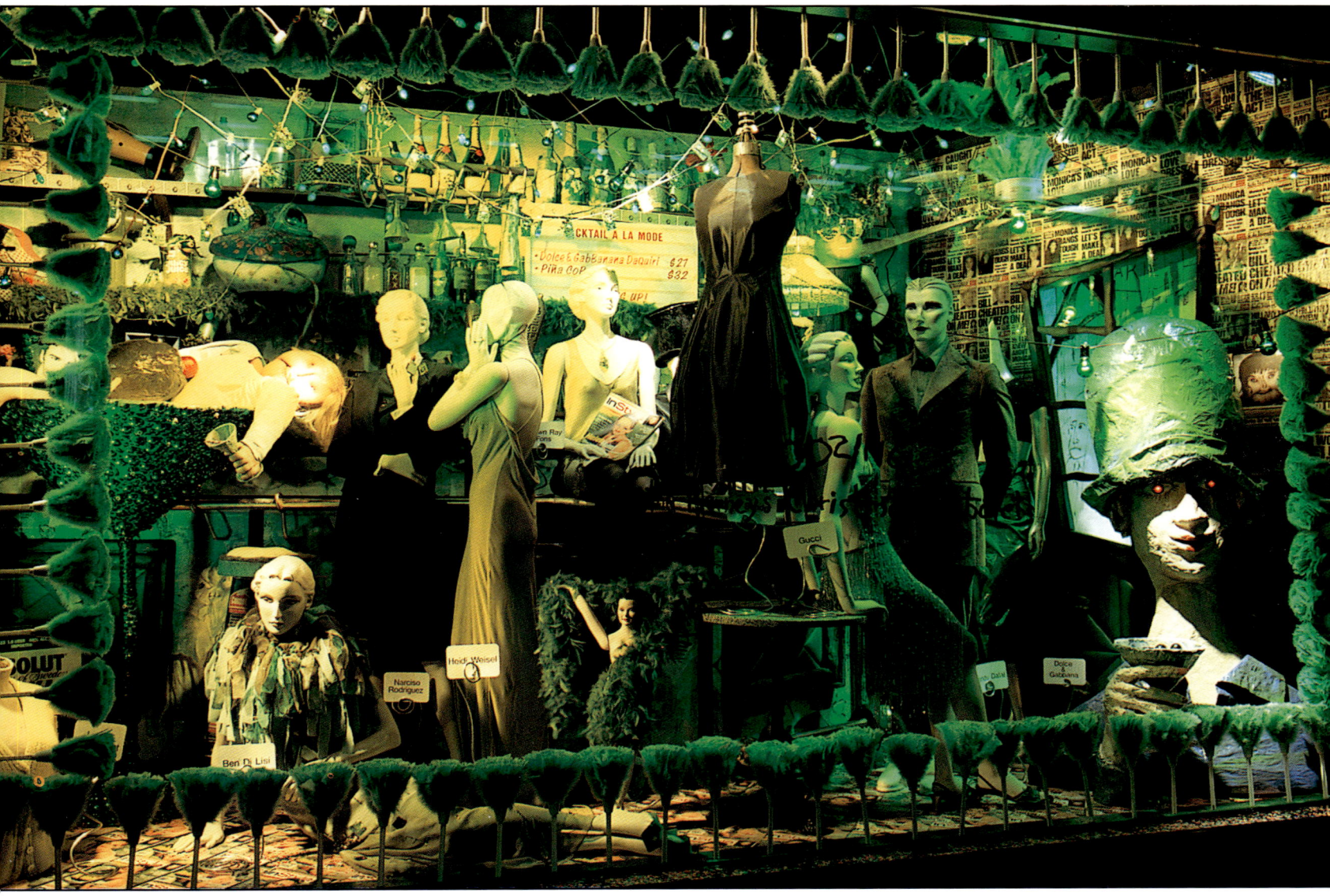

BARNEYS, Madison Ave., New York, NY
Creative Director: Simon Doonan
Sr. V.P. of Creative Services: David New
V.P. Creative Services: Adamo Di Gregerio

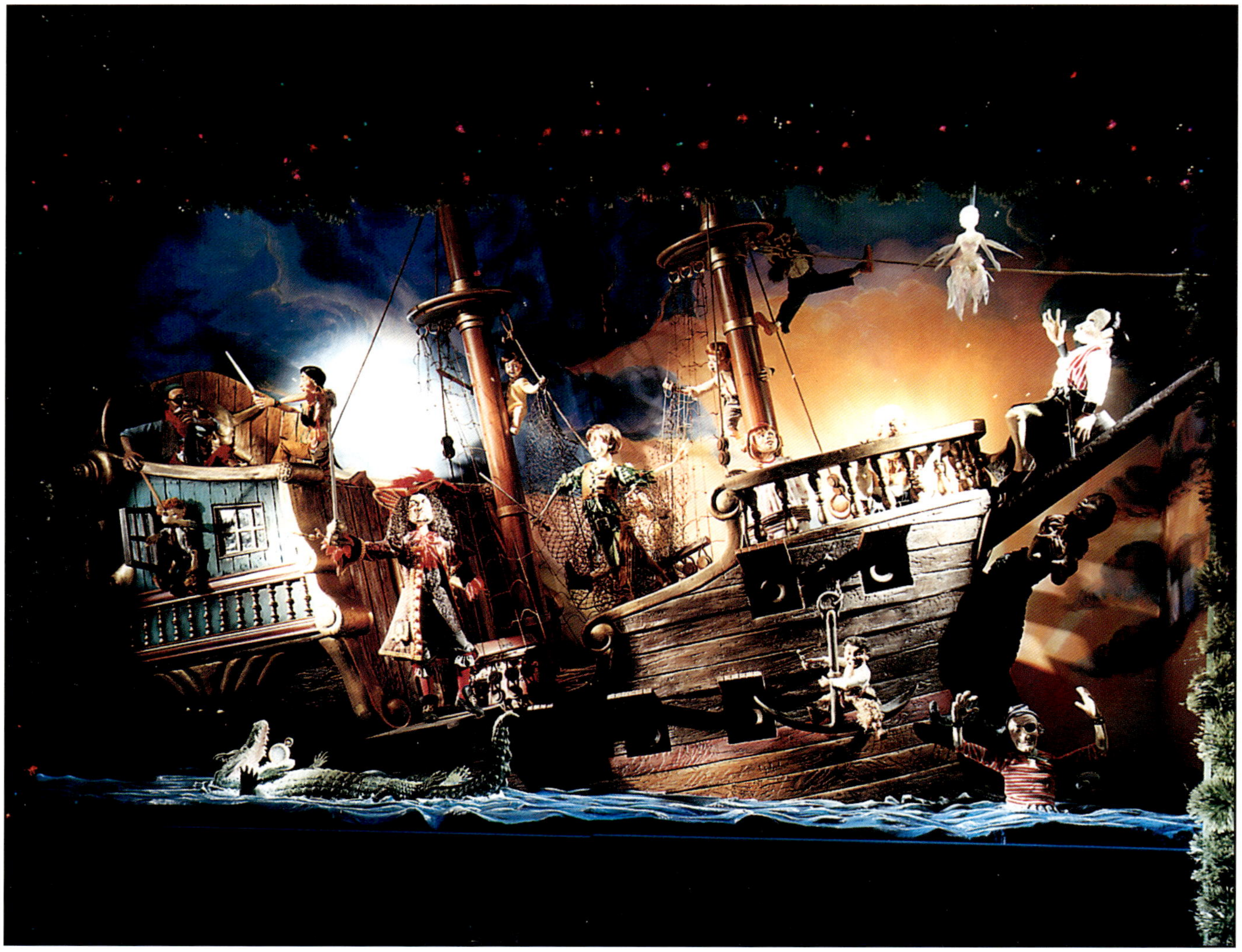

PETER PAN

Lord & Taylor's gift to New York for the holidays was a new version of the ever popular story of the boy who wouldn't grow up: Peter Pan. What added to the interest of the exciting window presentation was the tie-in with Cathy Rigby's production of the musical Peter Pan which was then being revived on Broadway.

The artists and designers of these fantasy windows recreated the essence of the story and play but did not rely on the Disney version for its imagery. Dimensional, animated figurines were dressed in velvets, brocades and fanciful costumes as well as the traditional turn of the century clothes for when the story was written. These were combined with a wealth of foliage, semi-dimensional background pieces and trompe l'oeil artwork to create the eye-popping, "story book" illustrations with depth and dimension. Music, from the play, floated out over the densely packed lines of tourists and natives who qued up for a chance to relive the fantasy of the James Barrie classic. Copy plaques, in each window, served as prompters for the parents who were explaining Peter Pan's adventures to their children.

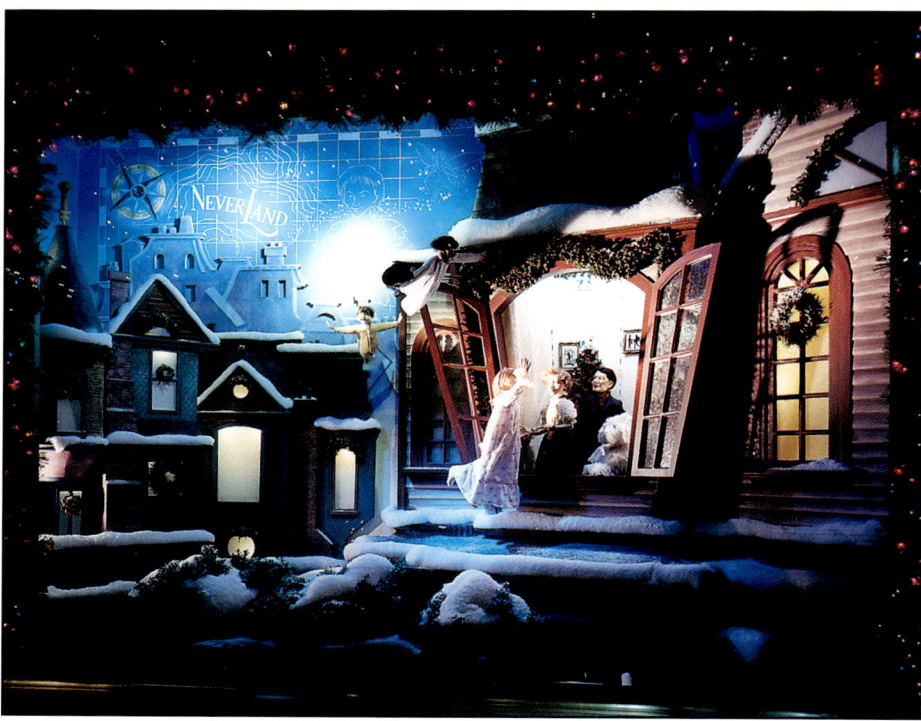

LORD & TAYLOR, (TOP AND ABOVE) **Fifth Ave., New York, NY**
V.P. of Visual Merchandising: Cal Partridge
Dir. of Windows, Fifth Ave. Store: Jan Topercer
Creative Director: Manoel Renha

PETER PAN

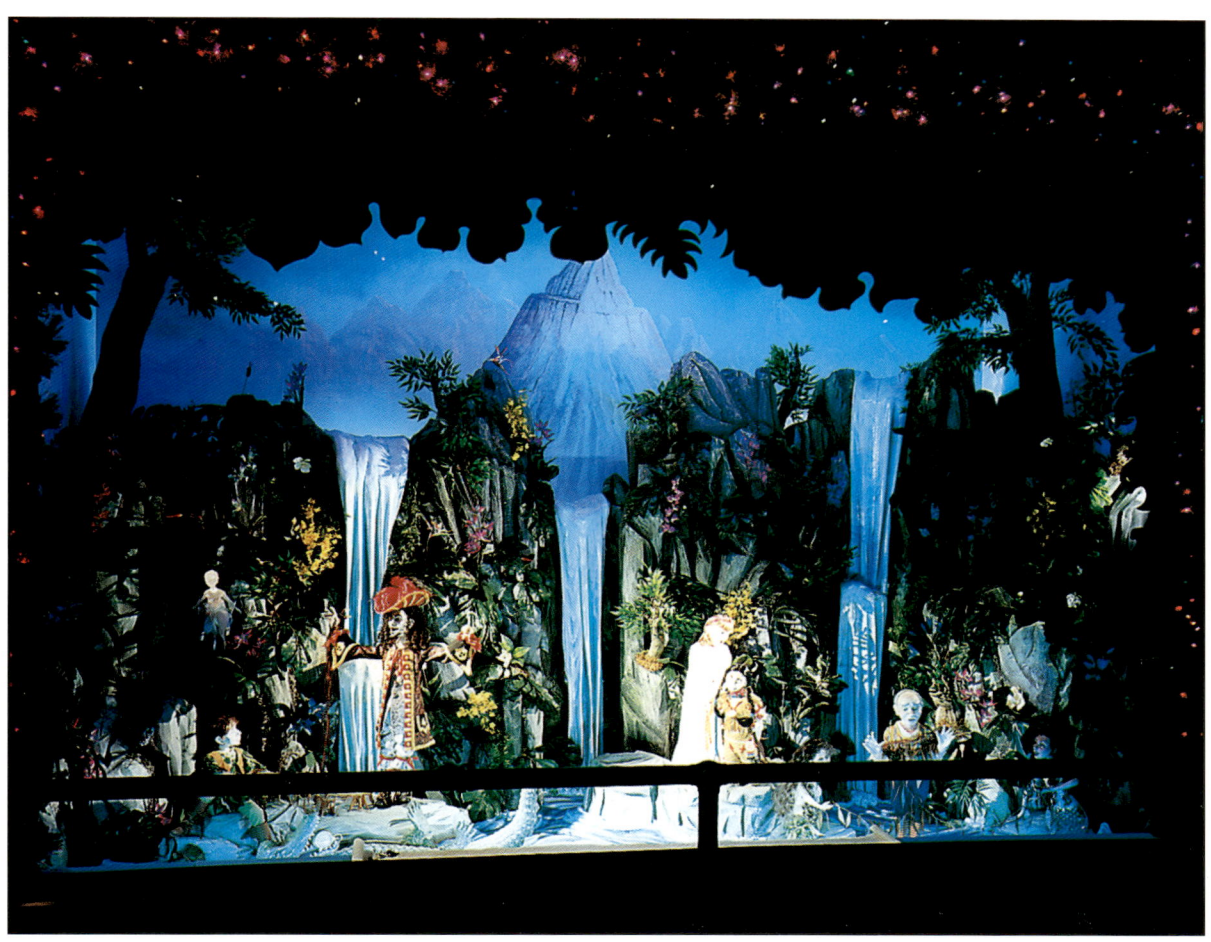

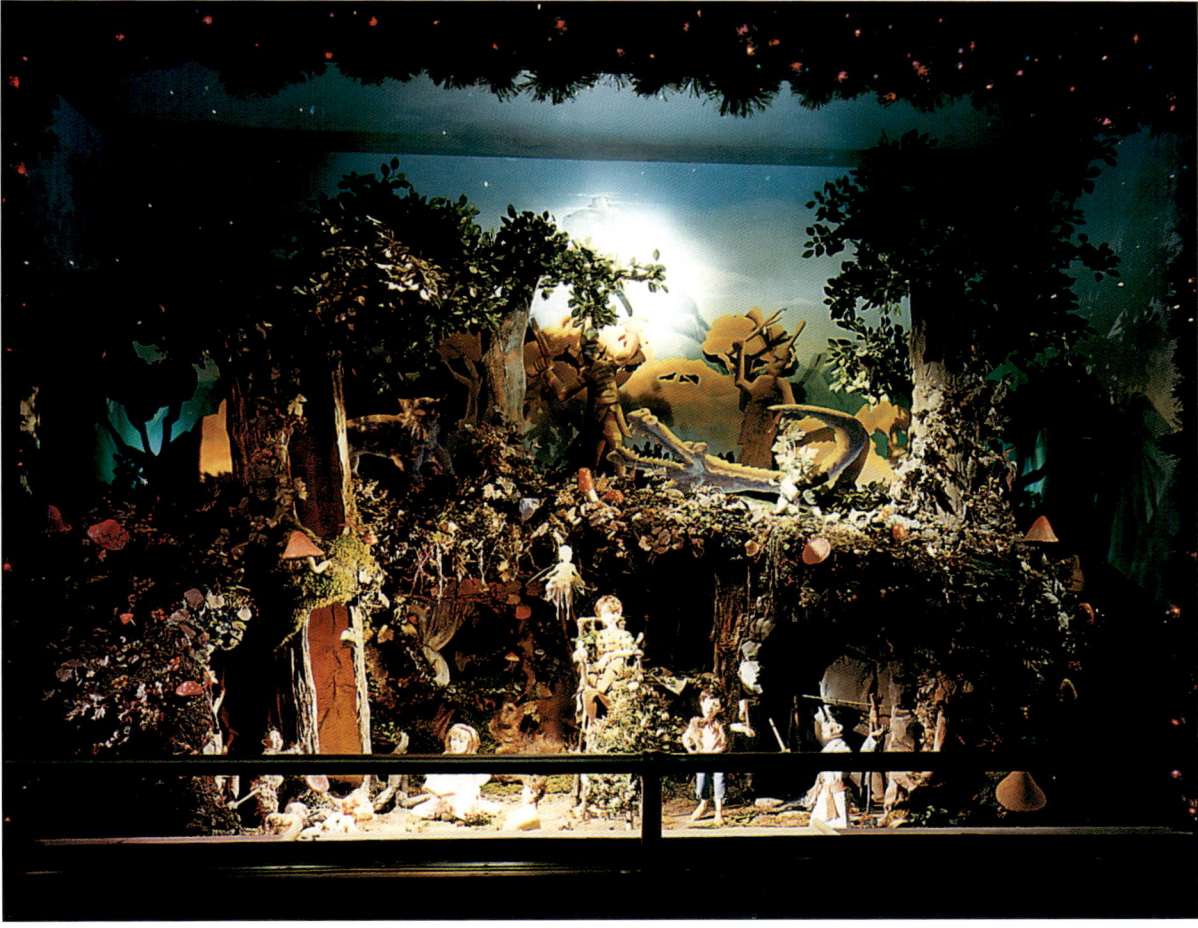

LORD & TAYLOR, (TOP AND ABOVE) Fifth Ave., New York, NY
V.P. of Visual Merchandising: Cal Partridge
Dir. of Windows, Fifth Ave. Store: Jan Topercer
Creative Director: Manoel Renha

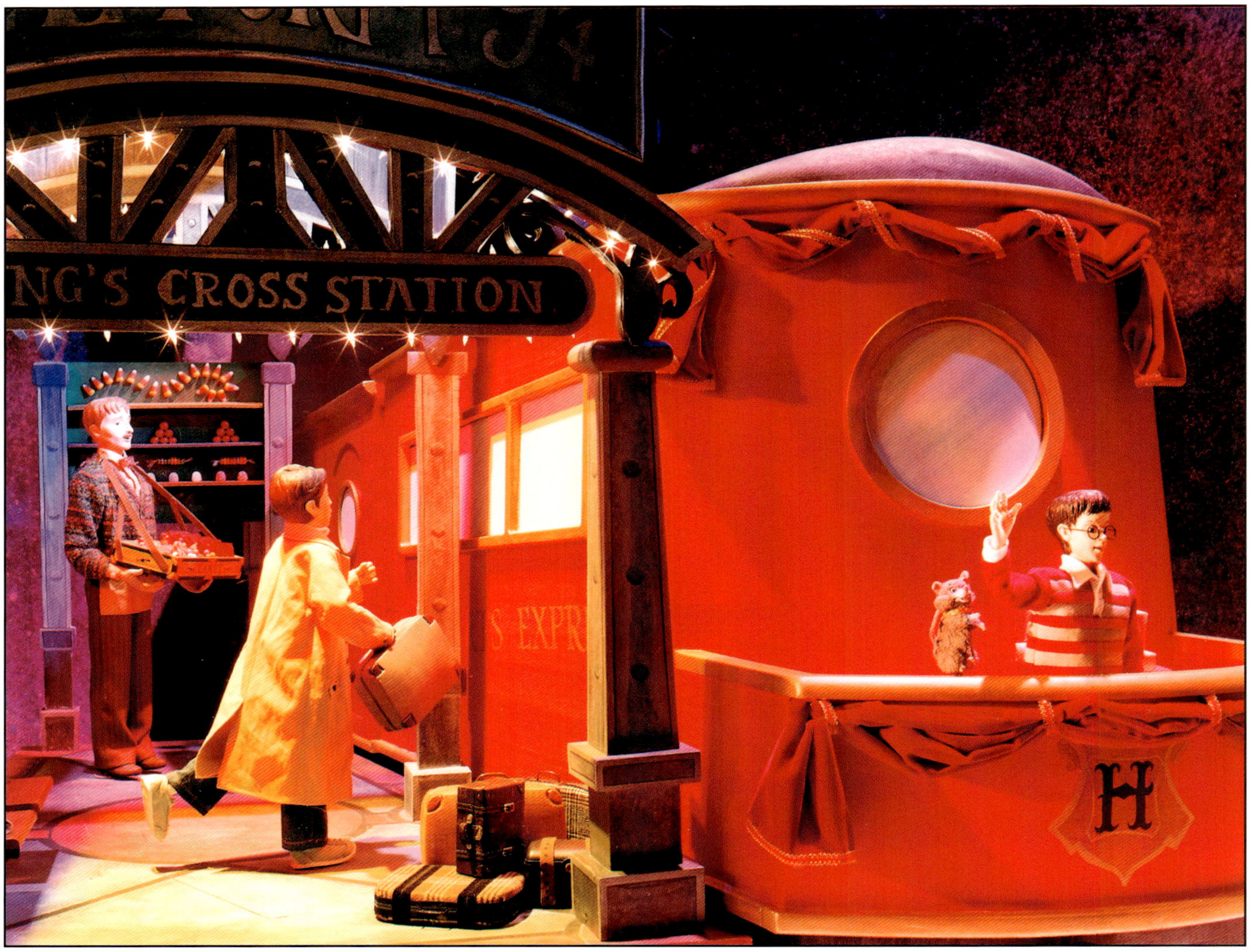

HARRY POTTER

MARSHALL FIELD & CO., (ABOVE AND RIGHT), State St., Chicago, IL
Project Design Team: Jamie Becker, Director of V.M. Marshall Field's
Amy Meadows, V.M. Manager, State St., Chicago
Donna Milano-Johnson, Corp. Specialist of Window Display, State St., Chicago
Fabricators: Spaeth Design Co., New York, NY
Props & Set Design: Kinc. Chicago IL
Photography: Susan Kezon

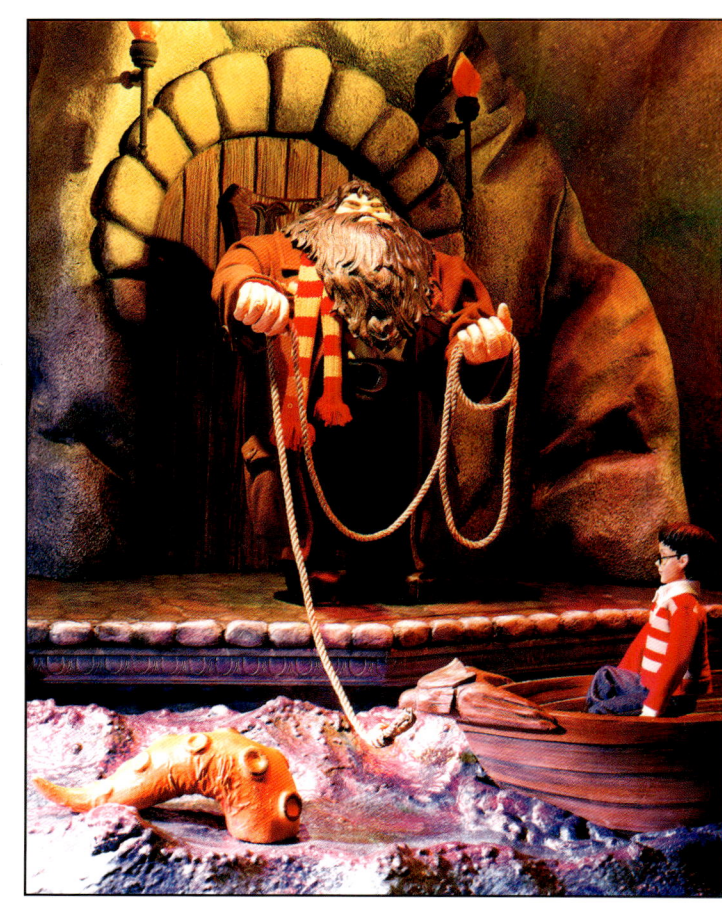

The true miracle of Christmas seems to be that people will line up in the nasty and biting cold to get a glimpse of a series of windows in which the essence of a story has been captured in four, five or six tableaux. With only the briefest of continuity provided on plaques up front (some almost impossible to read), children who may be too young to read or adults who can't see the small print without stooping way down seem to follow the story line.

In the past Marshall Field & Co. on State St. in Chicago has presented fairy tales and twice-told tales to the delight of Chicagoans who really have to brave the bitter weather to do their out-of-doors reading. This year the very popular favorite is the new sensation—Harry Potter. In a series of dimensional tableaux that combine flat artwork, dimensional props and figures, the store's design team undertook to give the public their visualization of Harry Potter and the Sorcerer's Stone. Not only do the viewers get to see Harry—based on the book's illustrations—but they can follow him through a series of adventures and meet the characters he meets as he progresses through the best selling book. Marshall Field's made a wise and popular decision in featuring Harry Potter this Christmas since the character has a tremendous following—of all ages.

HARRY POTTER

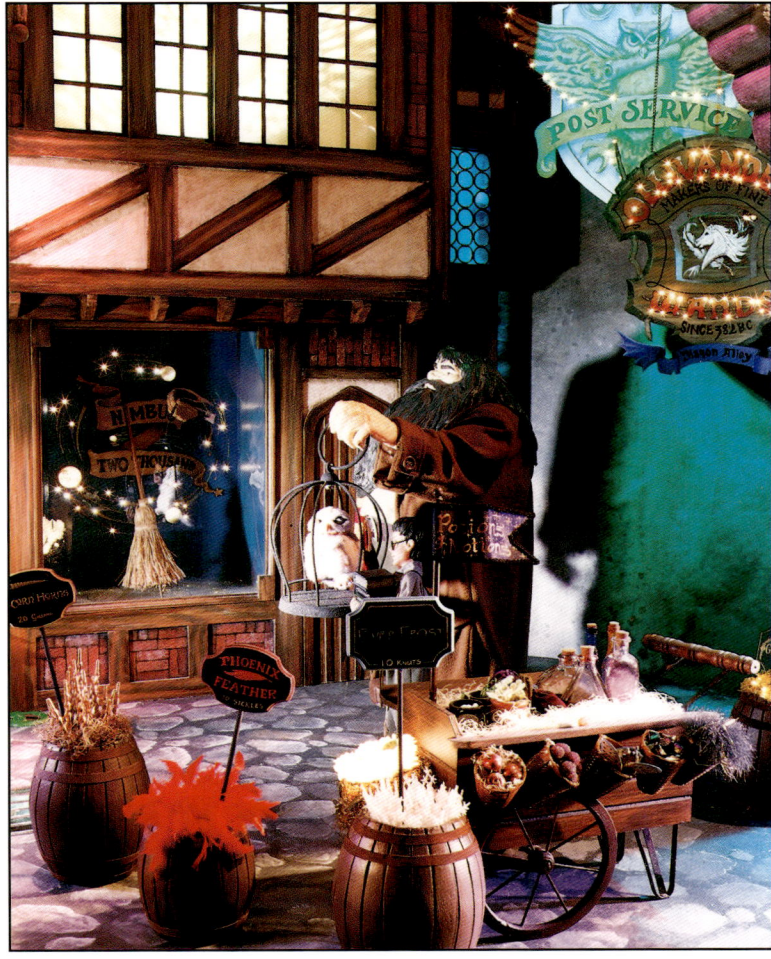

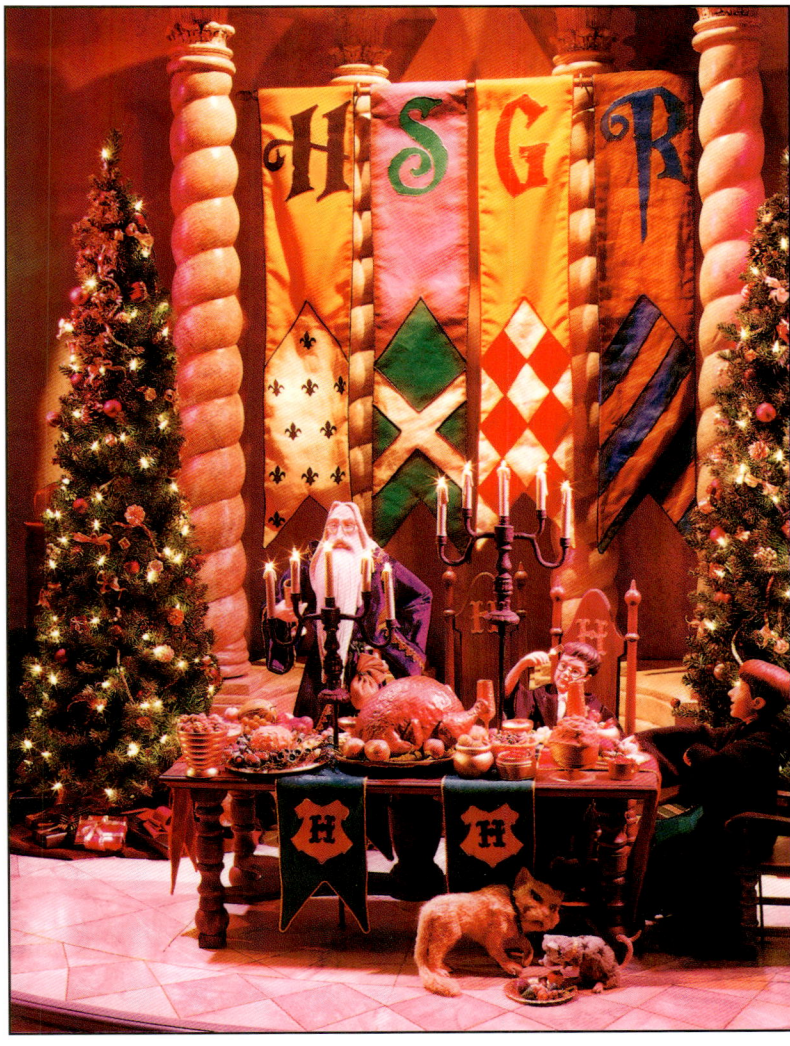

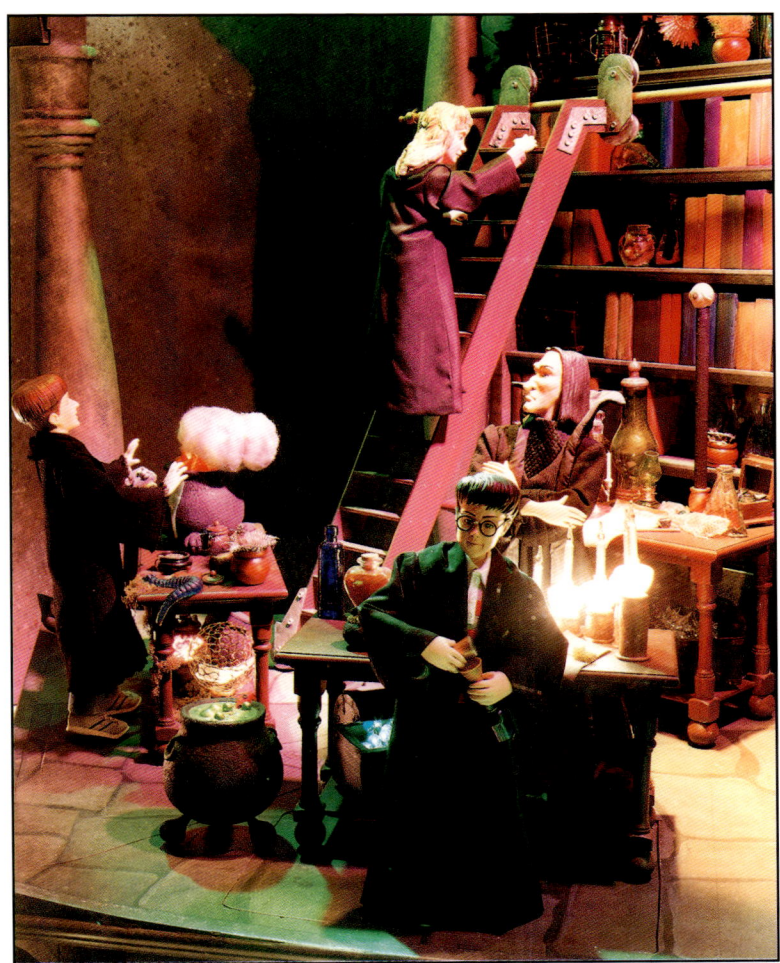

MARSHALL FIELD & CO., (ALL), State St., Chicago, IL
Project Design Team: Jamie Becker, Director of V.M. Marshall Field's
Amy Meadows, V.M. Manager, State St., Chicago
Donna Milano-Johnson, Corp. Specialist of Window Display,
State St., Chicago
Fabricators: Spaeth Design Co., New York, NY
Props & Set Design: Kinc. Chicago IL
Photography: Susan Kezon

RED

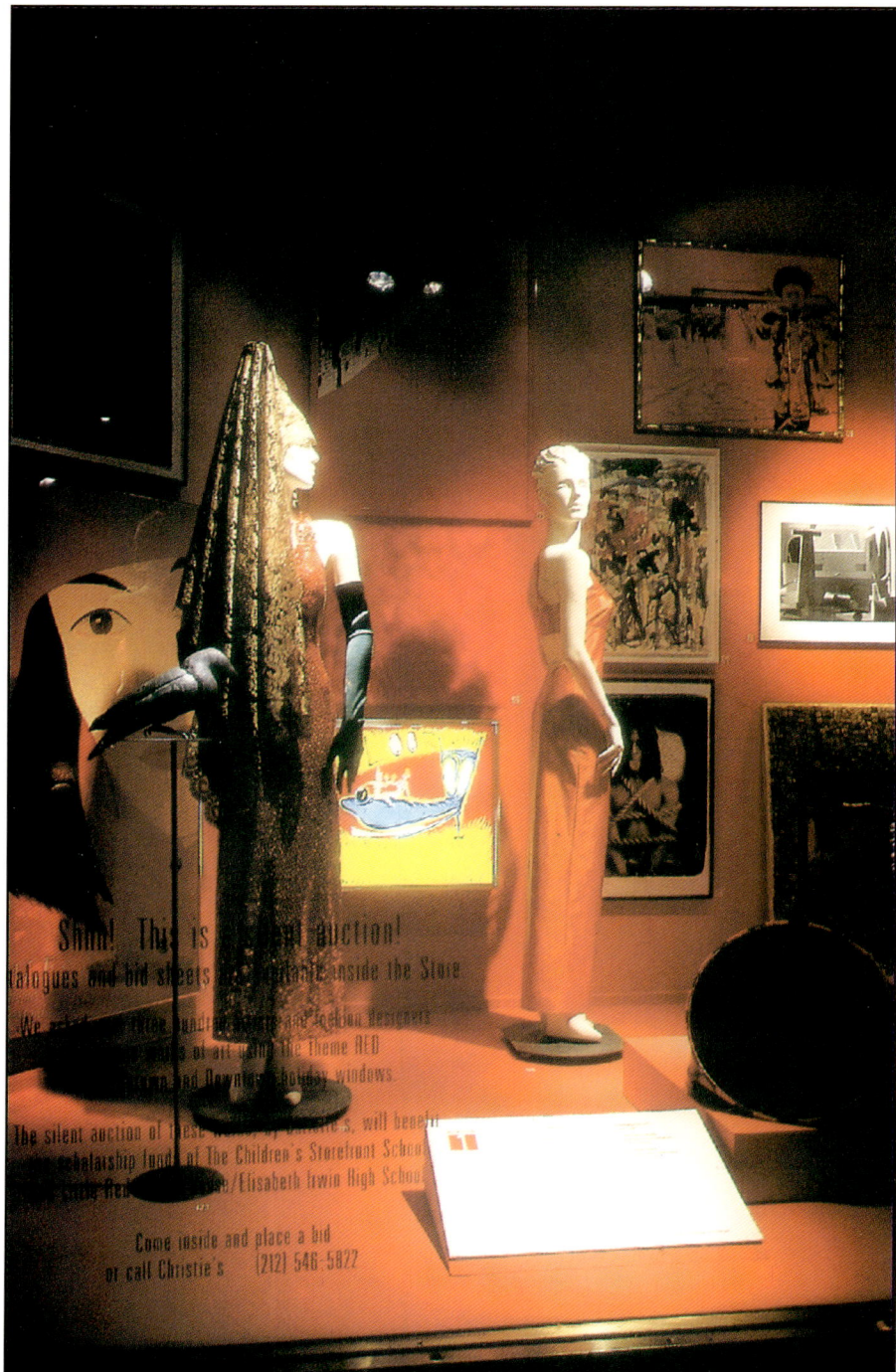

BARNEYS, Seventh Ave., New York, NY
Exec. V.P. Creative Services: Simon Doonan
V.P. Store Design/Display: David New

As part of Barneys "Red White and Blue Christmas," the red, red merchandise was tied in with an auction of artwork for charity. The vignetted settings suggested bits and pieces of "rooms" where the artwork to be bid upon was displayed on the walls, on chairs and on the floor. An assortment of redder than red gowns, worn by the stylized white mannequins, served to provide a sense of scale in the window as well as show the seasonal fashions.

At Gucci's, the headless forms literally and figuratively stepped out in red velvet tuxedos. The gold foil board dangles, against the dark walls, provide a contemporary twist to a traditional device.

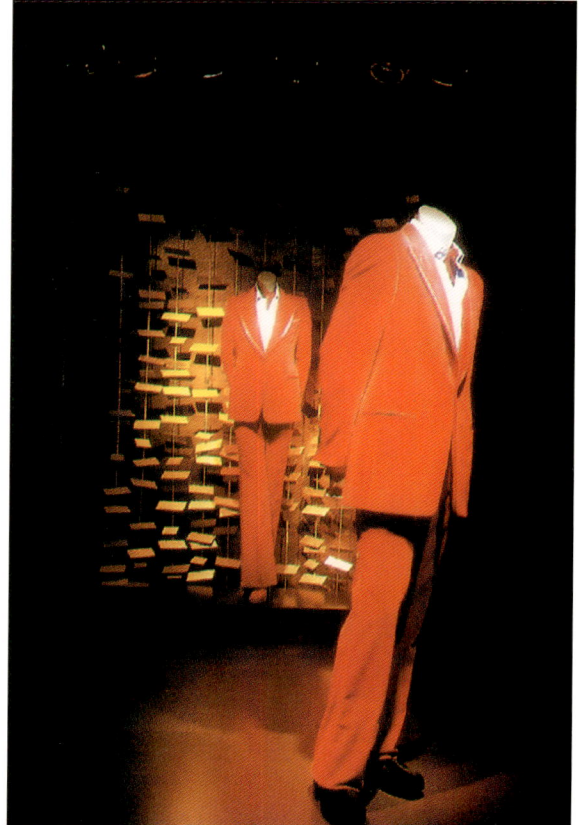

GUCCI, Fifth Ave., New York, NY
Corp. Dir. of Visual Presentation: James Knight

RED

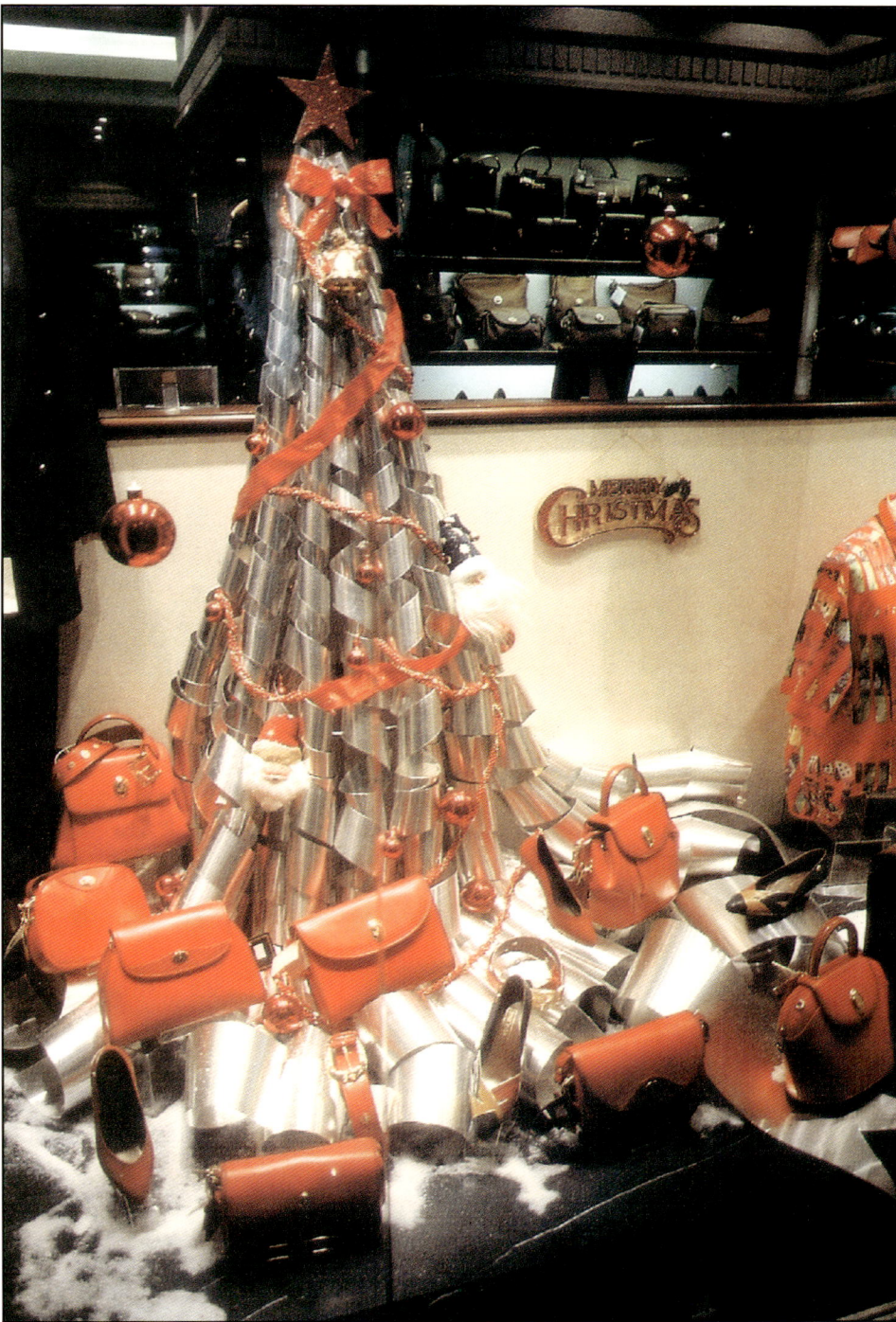

HERMES, Lot 10, Jakarta, Malaysia

Also bristling at Gucci was the red orange suit set against an ombre panel flooded with red/orange light. The headless form holds a spray of plastic, light transmitting strands with glowing red tips. The curved tube that provides the light source for the bristles also brings the viewer's eye down to the assemblage of shoes in the spotlight.

Hermes promotes the red shoes, bags, belts and other small leather accessories in their open window in Lot 10 in Jakarta. The silver foil ribbon wrapped tree serves to "hold" the overflow of merchandise together and the metallic streamers on the floor seem to unwind as they undulate in and through the assembled product display.

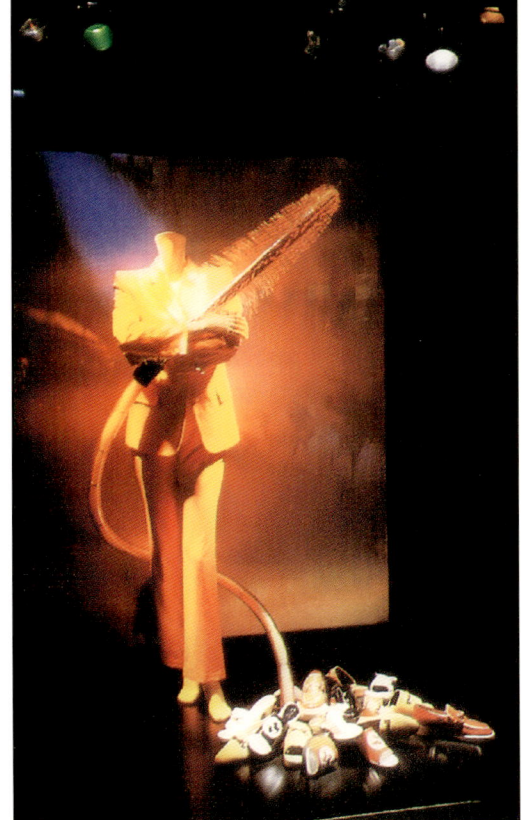

GUCCI, Fifth Ave., New York, NY
Corp. Dir. of Visual Presentation: James Knight

RED & GREEN

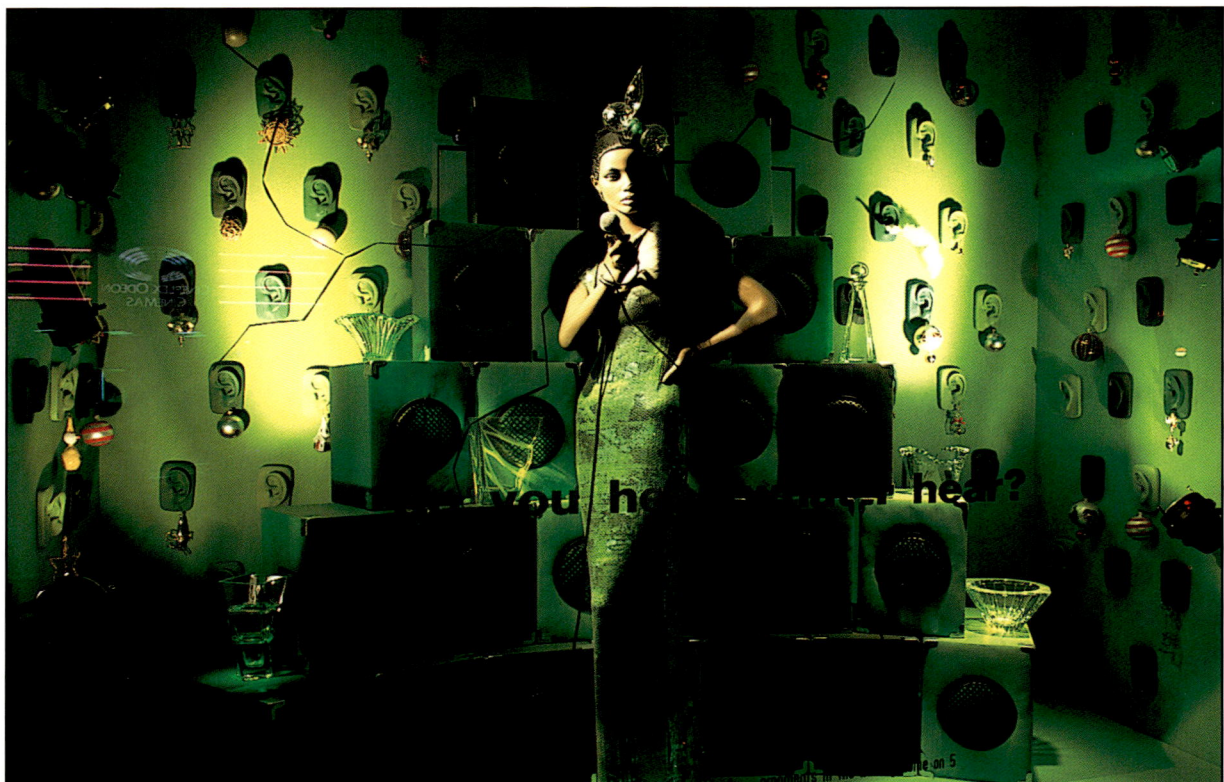

BLOOMINGDALE'S,
(LEFT AND BELOW LEFT)
Lexington Ave., New York, NY
V.P. of Visual Merchandising:
Jack Hruska
Creative Director: Mike Fisher
Window Manager: Harry Medina

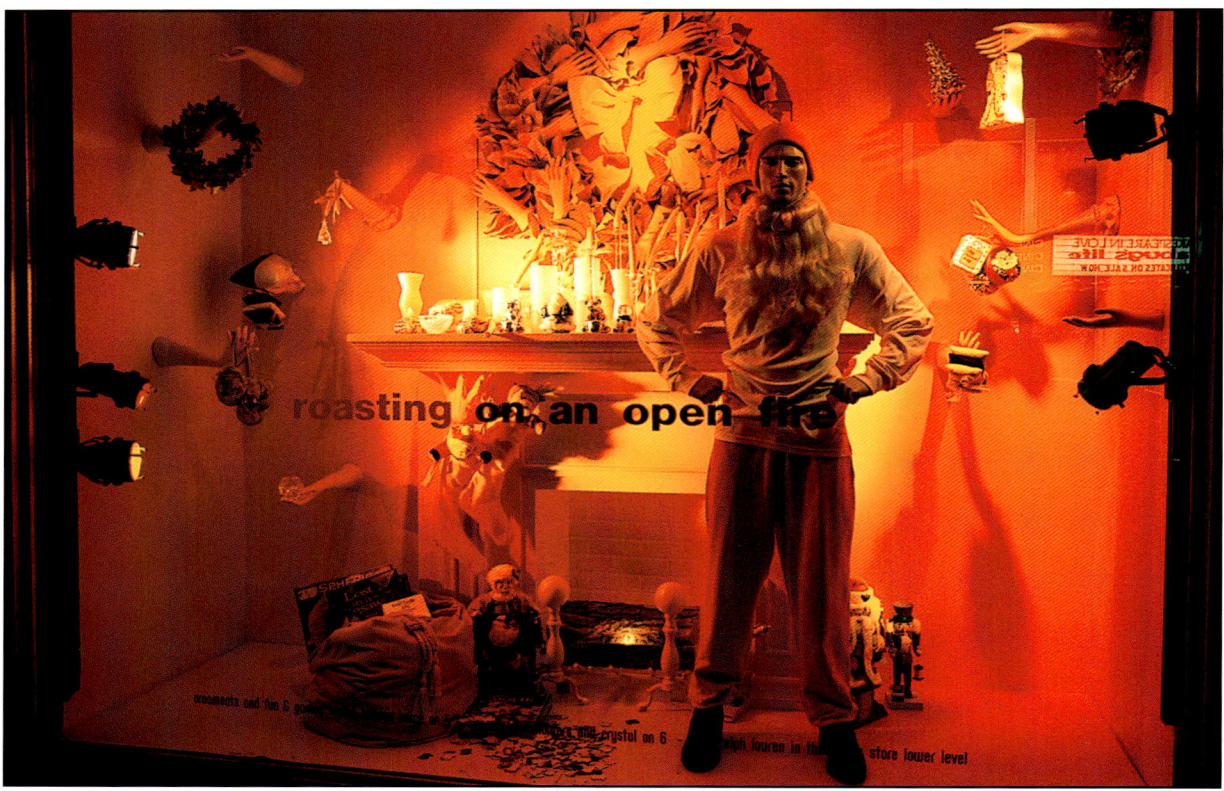

Using bright, sharp colors that varied from window to window, Bloomingdale's windows ask the questions and the proceed to provide the answers—visually. In the surreal "Do You Hear What I Hear?" the green colored walls are polka dotted with green tinted ear plaster molds and a Christmas tree of piled up green audio speakers. The mannequin in the elegant green gown is singing into a mike and her voice has "shattered" the front glass.

"Roasting on an open fire" calls for hot reds, oranges and yellows—a fireplace and hands reaching out, holding out and stretching out for gifts, gift bags, boxes and ornaments. Note the handy wreath over the mantle. It's another example of the reuse of old but still viable pieces, parts and props. The setting glows!

Taking the cue from "Lighten up—it's only the holidays," thousands of bee lights sparkle, twinkle, shimmer and shine in this tinsel backed window. The iridescent/crystal tree is resplendent in lights as is the mannequin whose gown is pinpointed with accents of light.

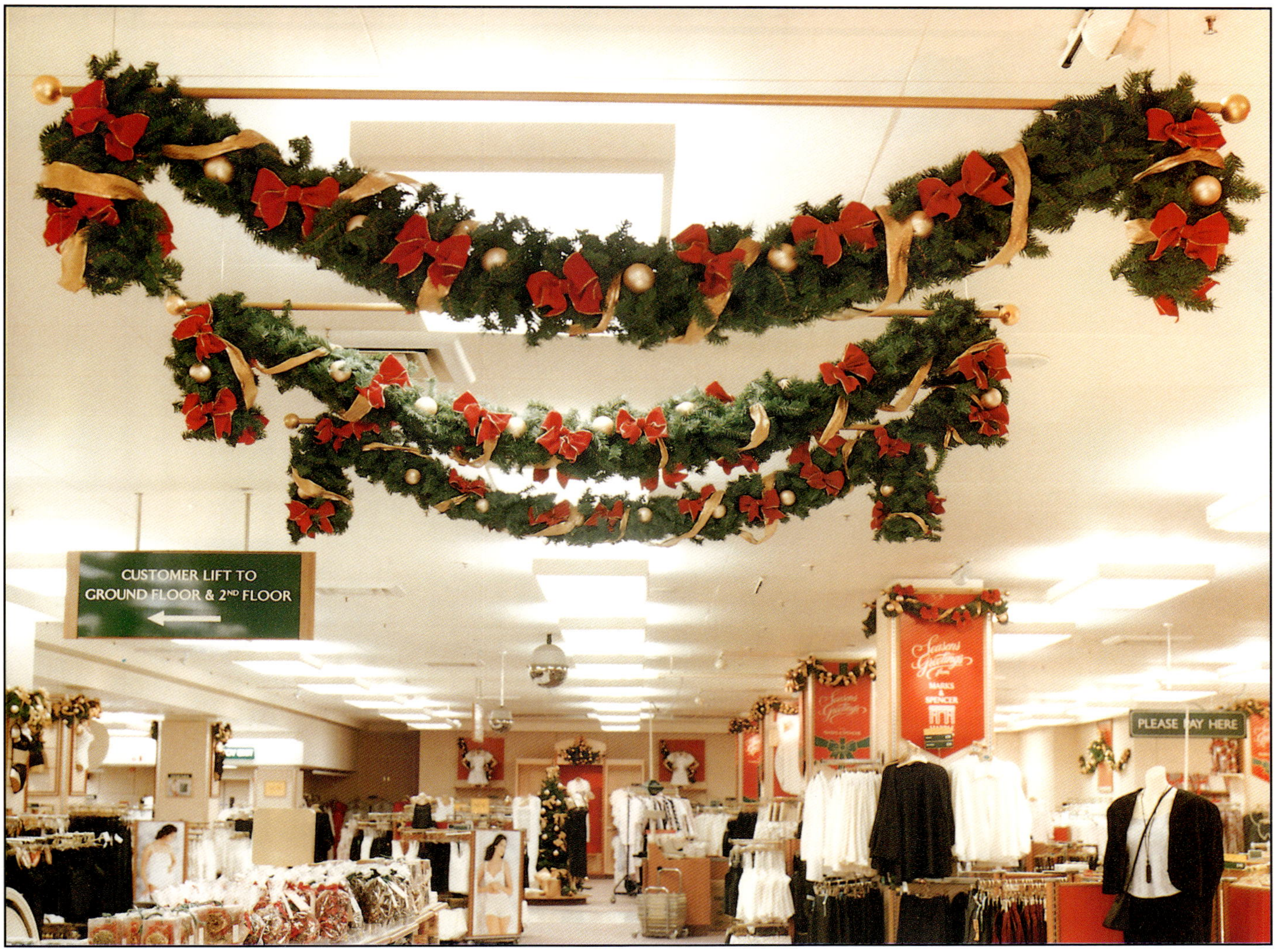

RED & GREEN

MARKS & SPENCER, Oxford St., London, UK
Designed & Executed: Barthelmess, Germany

Down to the basics: RED & GREEN!! No fuss—a little flitter—a touch of gold and a ribbon or two but when all is said and seen—it is the bright red and pine green that says Christmas. Here are two interior trims created by and executed by Barthelmess of Germany for two Oxford St. stores in London.

Marks & Spencers' trim consists of red fabric banners on the columns and green foliage swags trimmed with red bows and gold ribbons and ornaments. Green trees trimmed only with the gold ornaments and ribbons appear on the floor. Smaller variations of the aisle swags trim the columns that are covered with the banners.

For the BHS store, the green foliage swags overhead are decorated with red and green gift wrapped boxes and red and gold ornaments plus bee lights. Note how the red and green motif was continued on the walls and on the painted fixtures in the Trim-A-Tree shop. Giant gift boxes—also wrapped with ribbon—serve as counter high display tables. Matching Christmas trees—see foreground—complete the red and green look

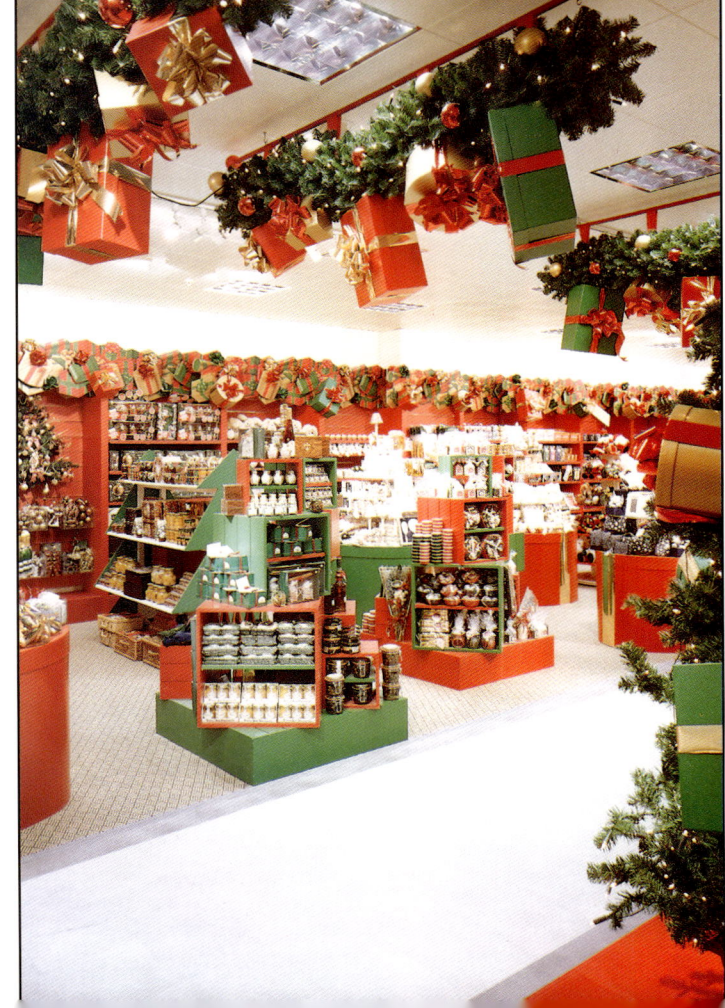

BHS, Oxford St., London, UK
Designed & Executed: Barthelmess, Germany

RICH & ROCOCO

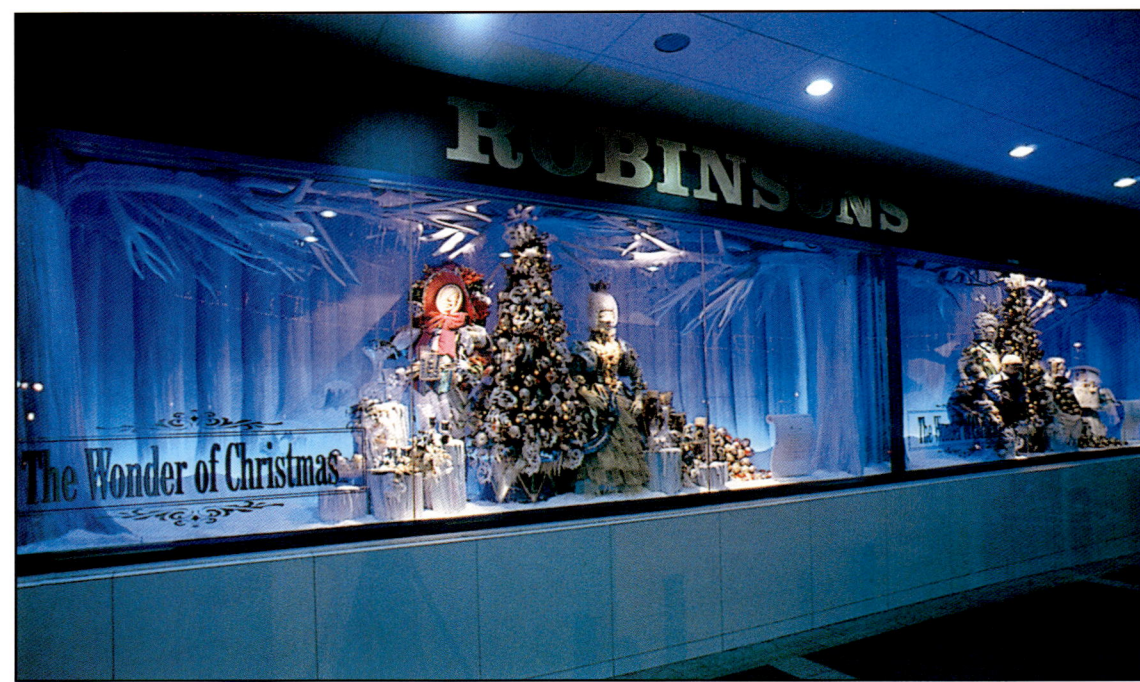

ROBINSON & CO.
(LEFT AND BELOW) **Singapore**
General Manager: Lena Phua

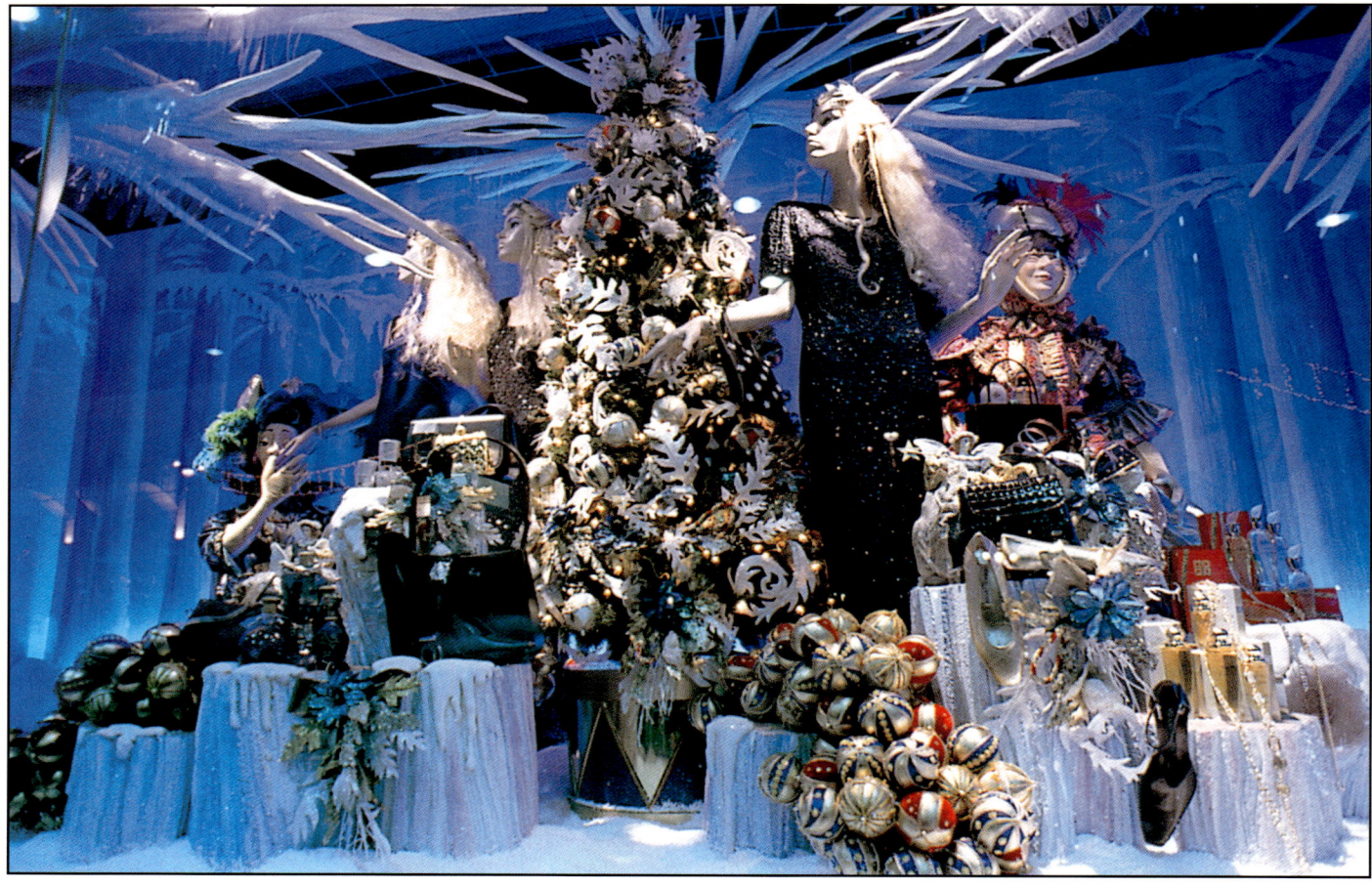

The Robinson & Co. store in Singapore greeted this holiday season with a series of lush, and romantic Rococo style mache figures that held court amid the cool, icy splendor of ornaments and foliage. They joined the store's mannequins who were dressed for the partying season. Icy spikes of snow covered bare branches criss crossed through the fabric draped and blue illuminated windows. The vertical drape folds suggested a forest of icy tree trunks in some far away and foreign place—certainly not tropic and hot Singapore. White pearlescent ornaments filled the Christmas trees as well as the swags and garlands that carried through over the fabric draped risers in the window. Scrolls, in each setting, told another part of the fairy tale and explained the characters and the happening.

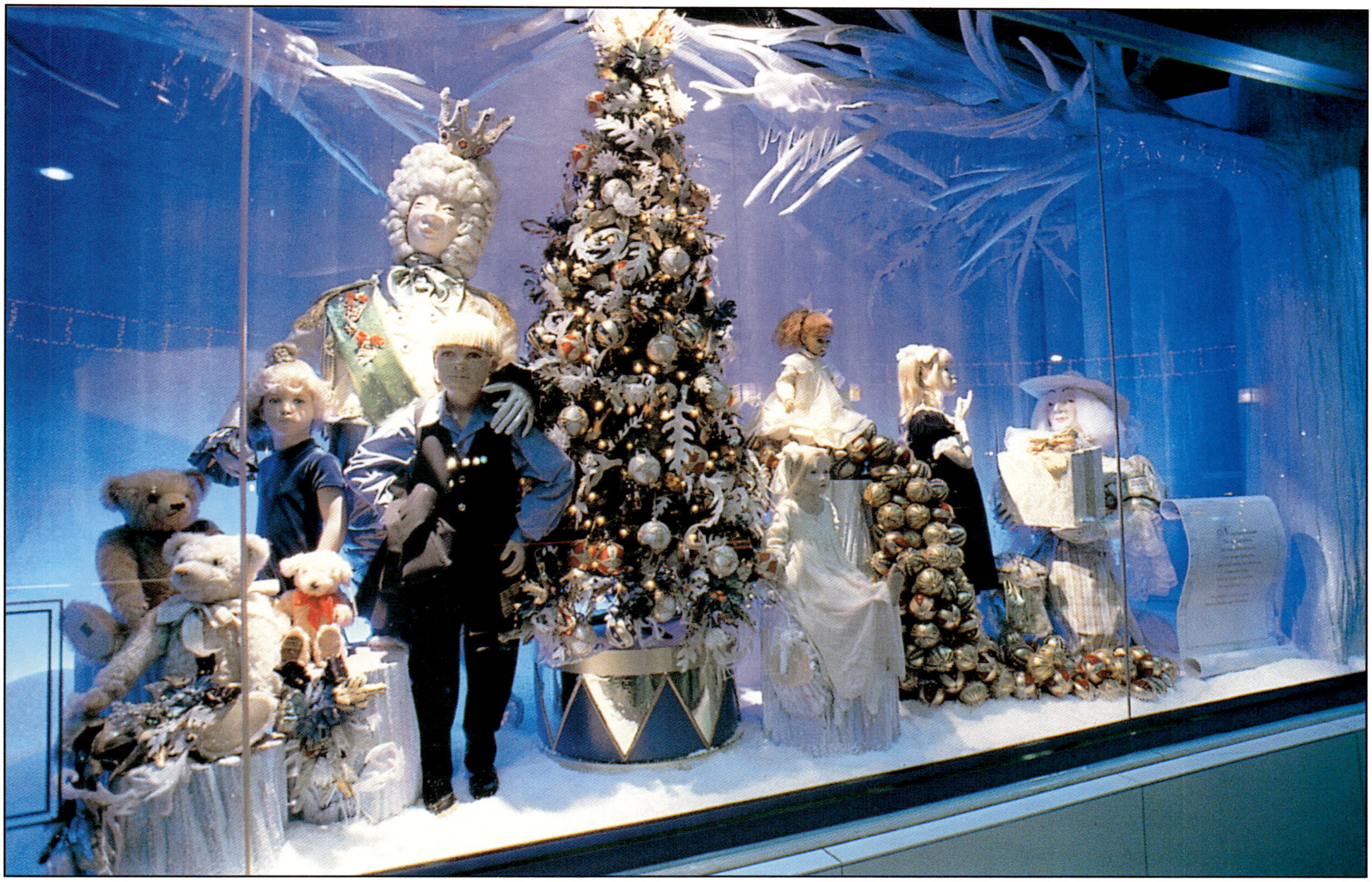

RICH & ROCOCO

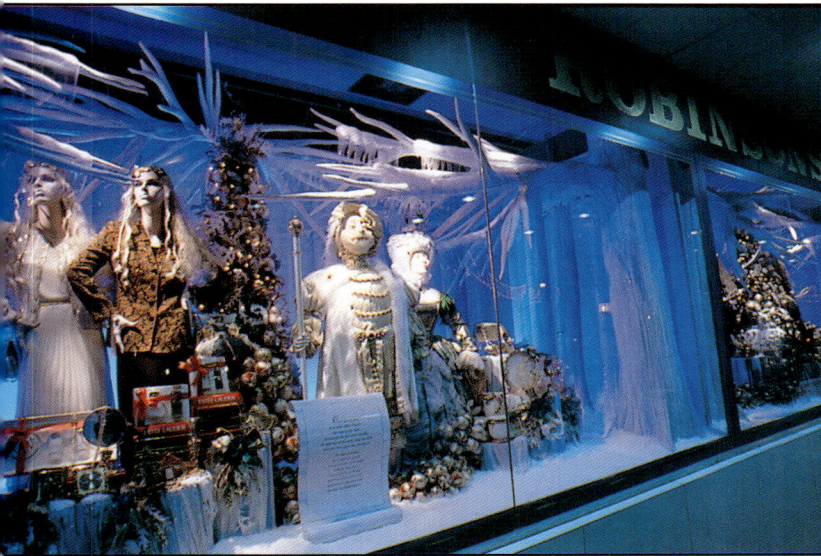
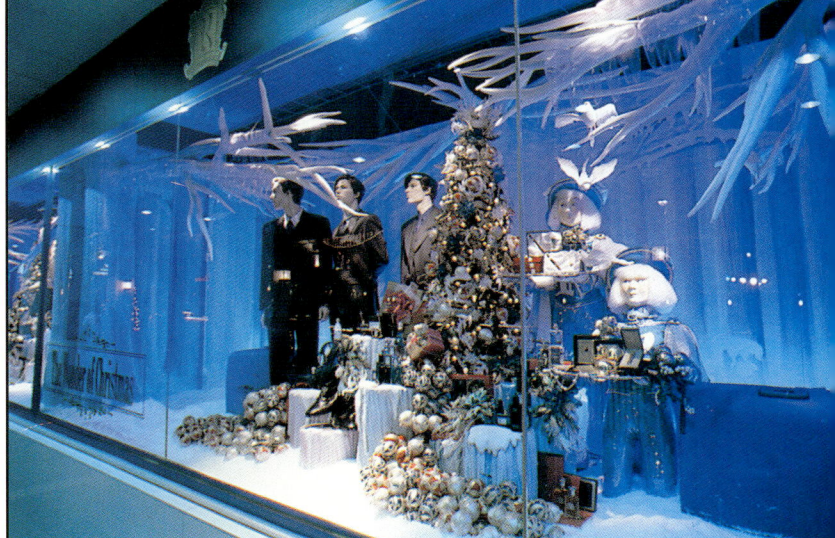

ROBINSON & CO., (ALL) Singapore
General Manager: Lena Phua

SANTA

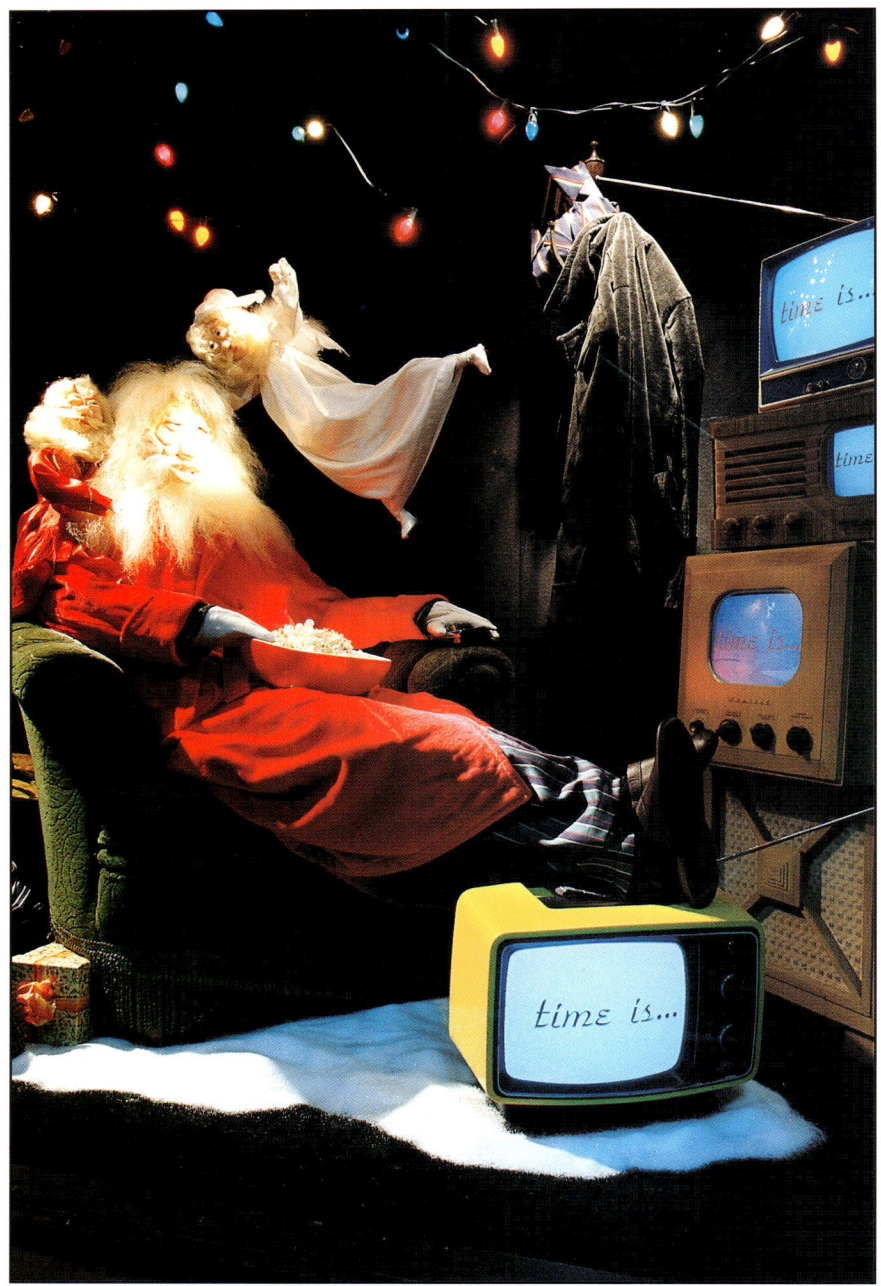

Paul Stuart's display department is composed of magicians, illusionists, and very talented artists. This past Christmas they presented us their own fashion-oriented "Christmas Carol" and Santa—not Scrooge—was invited to take a Time Trip but only into the immediate future.

The traditionally red suited Santa is awakened by the spirit of "Get With It." Santa then is shown on this voyage of self discovery in a series of black-black windows trimmed with swags of colorful strings of lights stretched across them. Santa not only gets to try on and try out some of the Paul Stuart outfits but also rummages through miles and miles of giftable items of haberdashery. Look carefully and you'll see the clock motif reappear in these windows along with some furry creatures. The propping is kept to a minimum but the merchandise is at a maximum. Santa carries a collection of fancy vests on a twig pole. He rests on a gilt throne and is inundated with ties, gift boxes, and shiny ornaments. Santa climbs a step-ladder and the rungs are immediately filled with shirts and shoes. Santa can't help but try on a new top coat and then check it out in a pier mirror. In a gender change, Mrs. Claus is seen manipulating a Santa marionette surrounded by women's fashion accessories.

As the signs say—"The Time Has Come"—and so the time comes when Santa has to get down to the serious task of gift wrapping all the wonders he beheld in his time trip through Paul Stuart's holiday windows.

PAUL STUART, (ABOVE AND RIGHT)
Madison Ave., New York, NY
Creative Director: Tom Beebe
**Co Visual Managers: Jerry Fredella &
Michael Verbert**
Team: Thomas Dang Vu

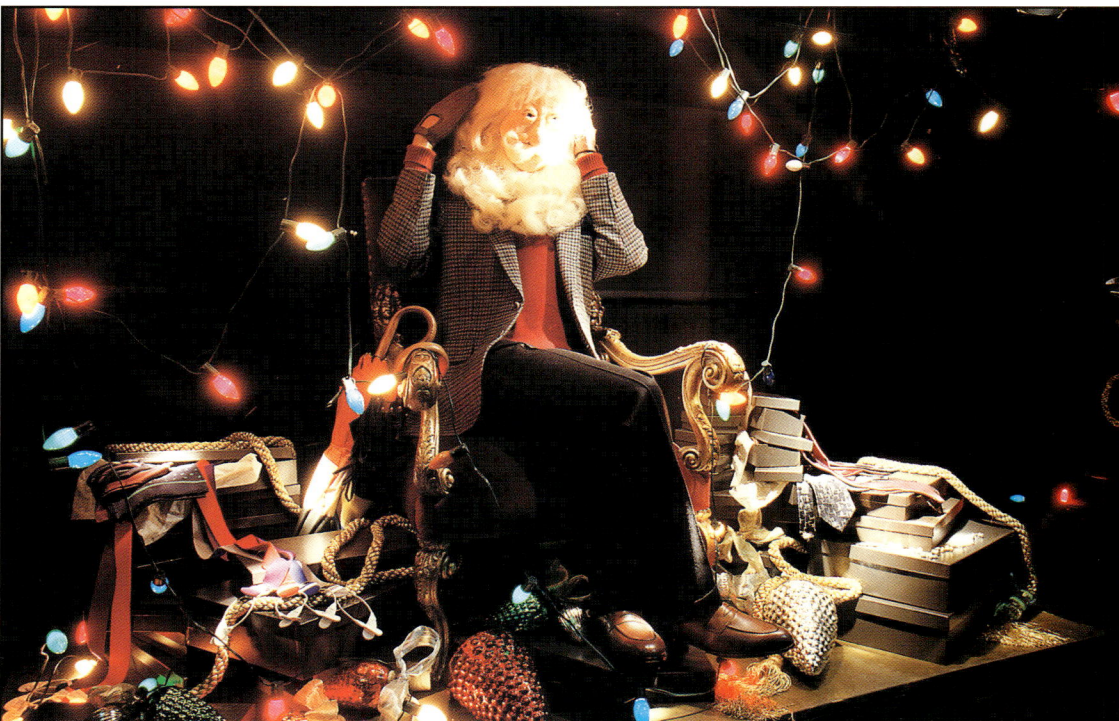

SANTA

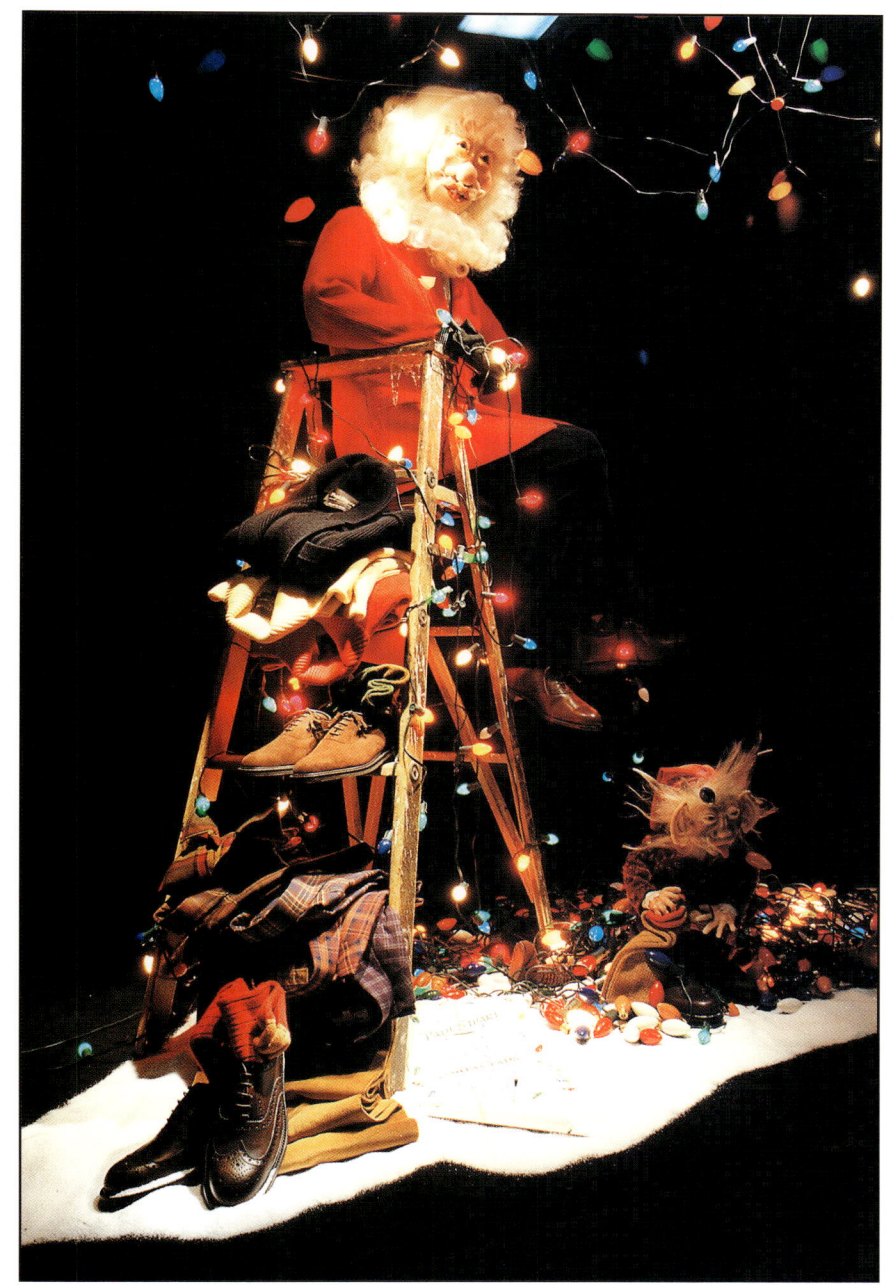

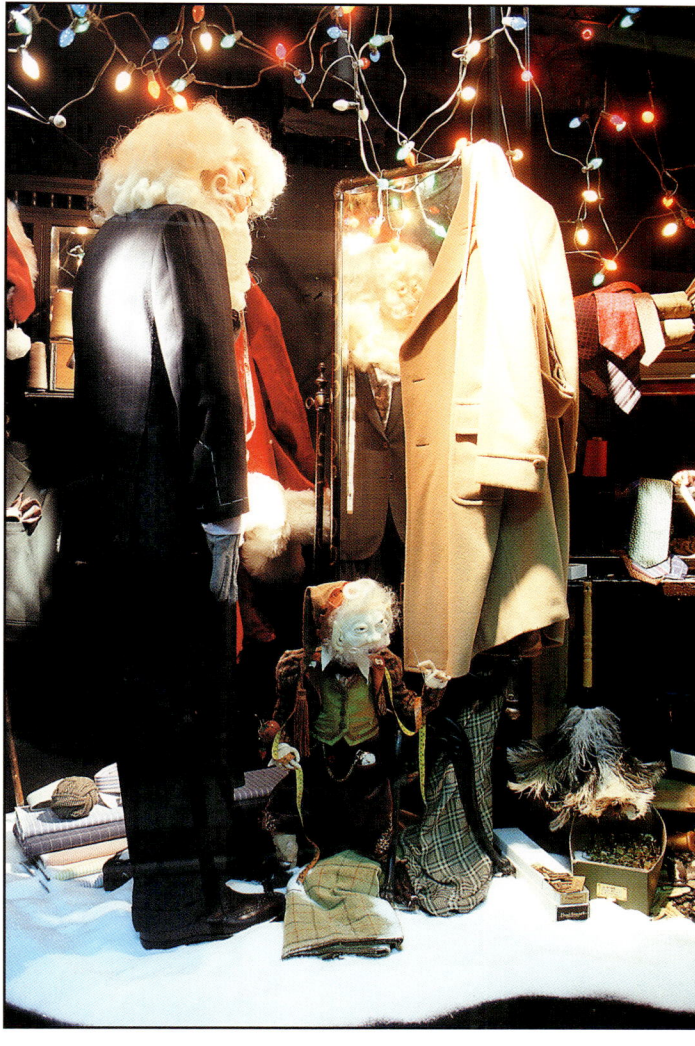

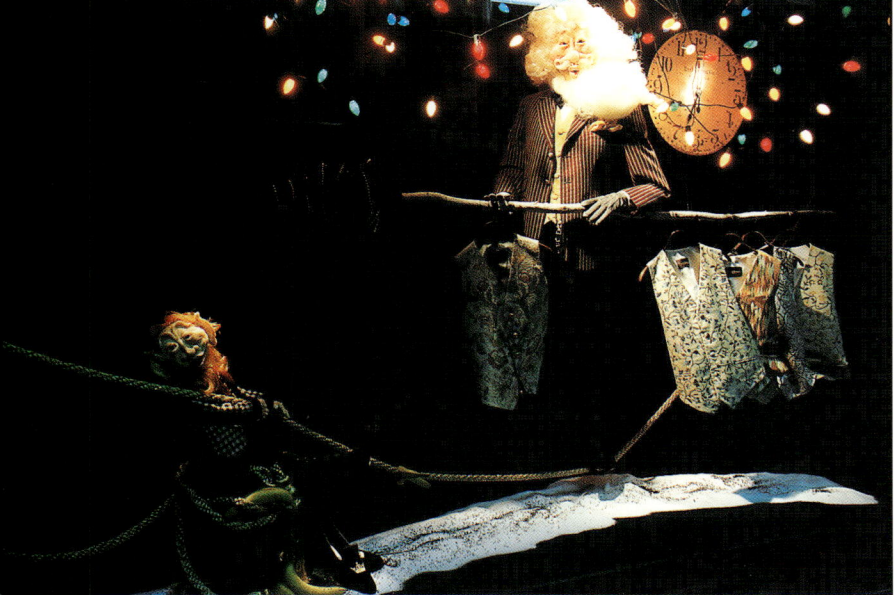

PAUL STUART, (ALL) Madison Ave., New York, NY
Creative Director: Tom Beebe
Co Visual Managers: Jerry Fredella & Michael Verbert
Team: Thomas Dang Vu

TIME TRAVEL

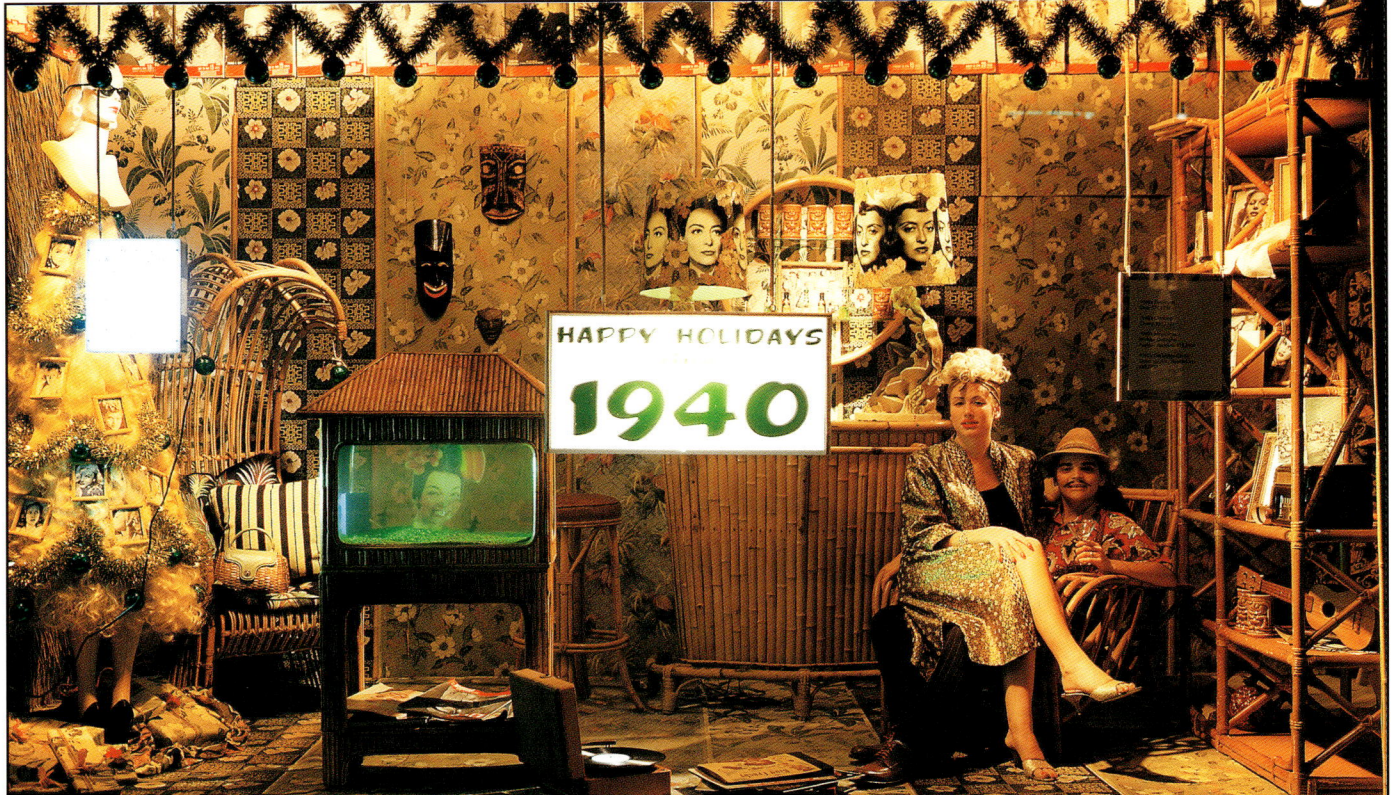

BARNEYS, (ABOVE AND RIGHT)
Madison Ave., New York, NY
Creative Director: Simon Doonan
Sr. VP Creative Services: David New
VP Creative Services: Adamo Di Gregerio

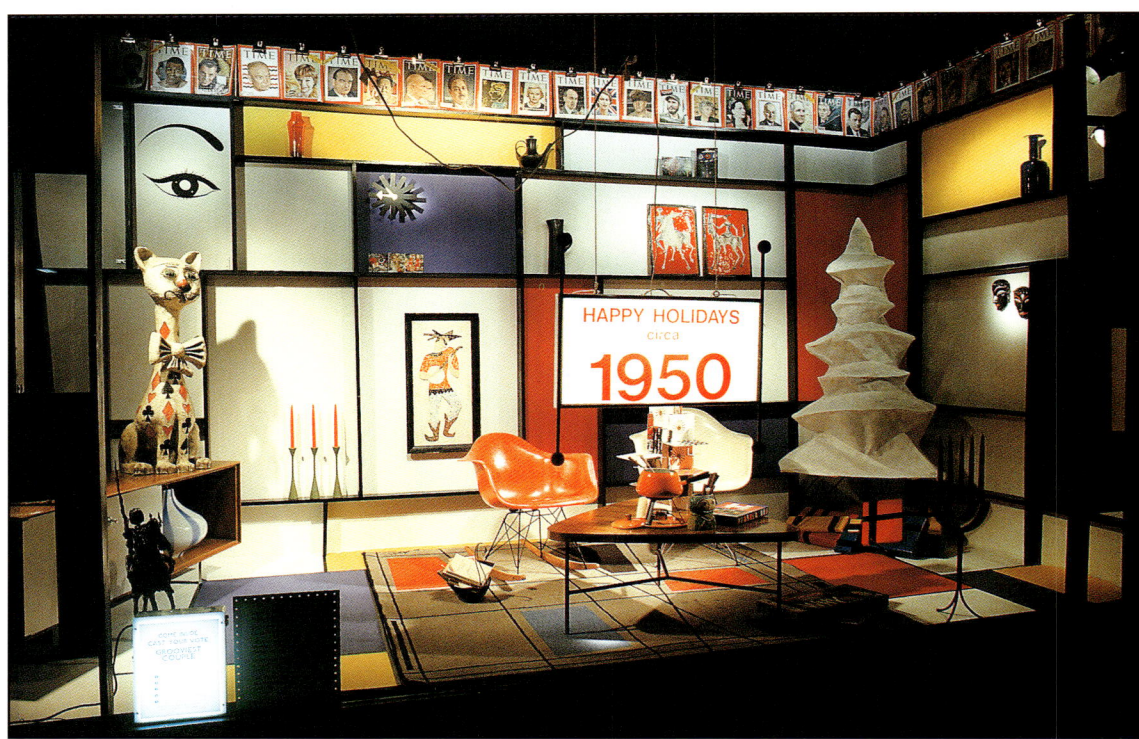

Barneys took us "Back to the Future" and really went retro in a great big way. Simon Doonan, Barneys' creative director, did it again by visiting the last decades of the previous century and doing an intense and thorough job of filling the windows with the smells, tastes, looks, dreams, fantasies and realities of those bygone but not so distant days. The windows presented the decades—from 1940 to 1980 and each window recreated the aura of that decade.

Adding a real retro touch—something that was "big" back in the 1930s when jobs were scarce and people would do anything reasonably honest to make a dollar—was the addition of real, live people—dressed in the fashions of the particular decade, to "live" in the window and do "things" such as dance, play games, interact—the way they did then. Using students from the Fashion Institute of Technology who were dressed from hair-do to toe in the look of the chosen moment, the window dwellers were in step with the time they personified and each decade's setting was right for the clothing selected.

A fun idea of going back in time and letting young people who weren't around back then step into the shoes of their parents and grandparents and recall "the good old days."

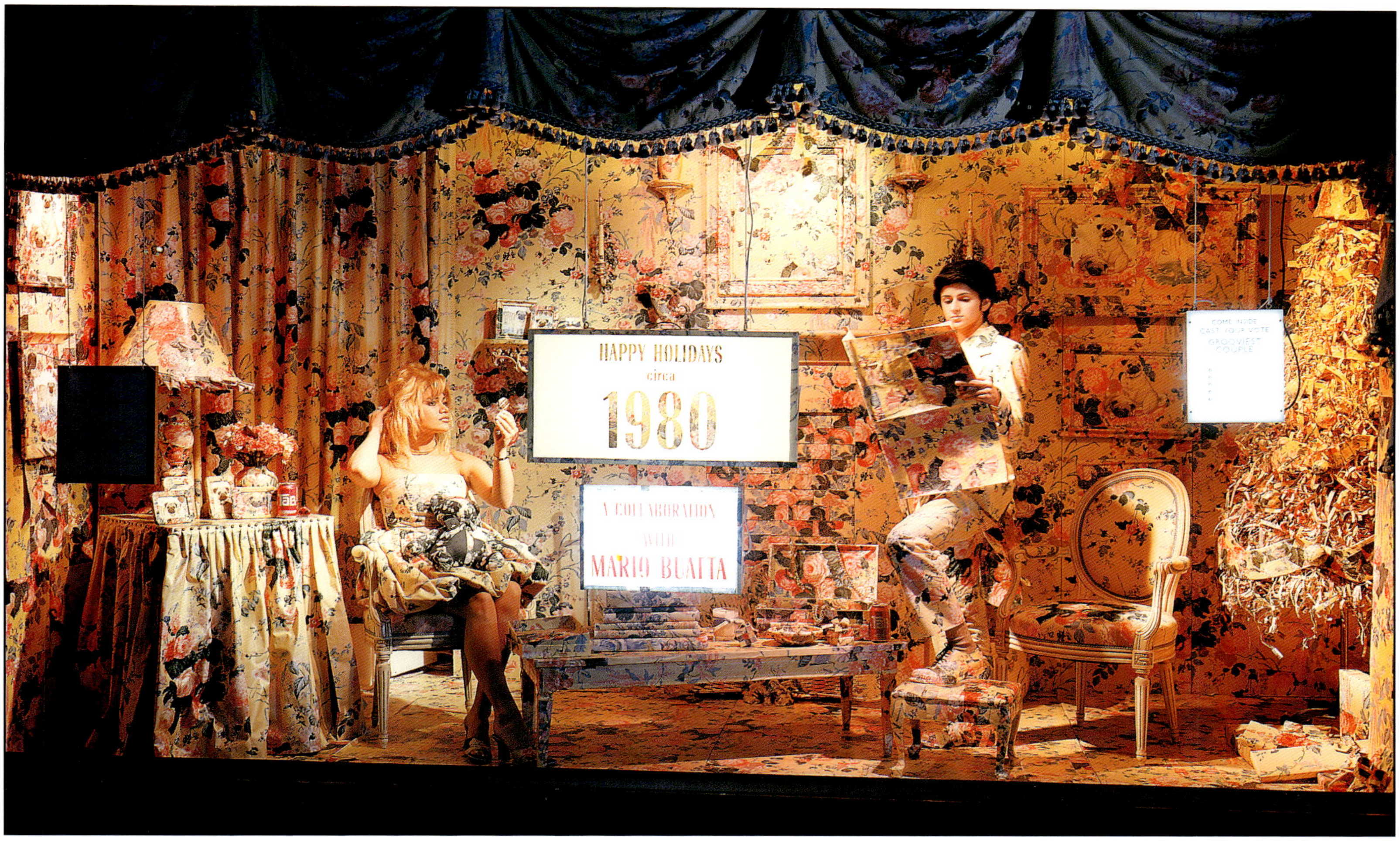

TIME TRAVEL

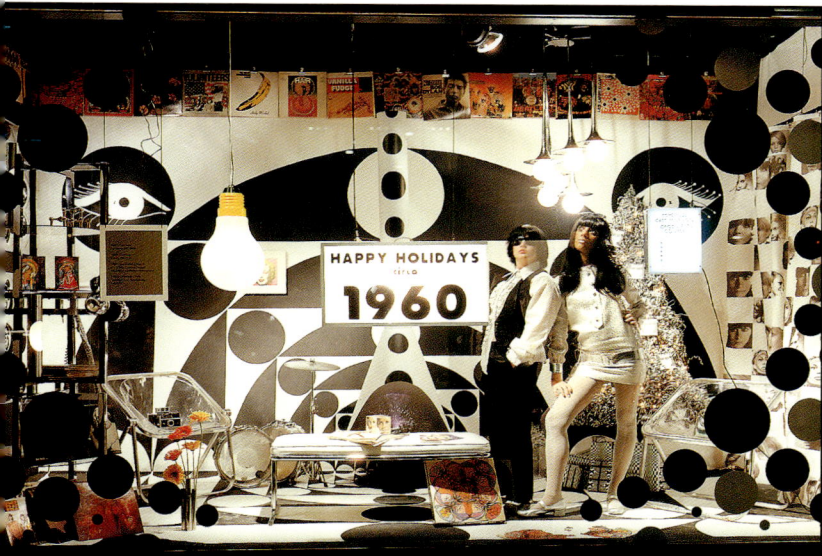
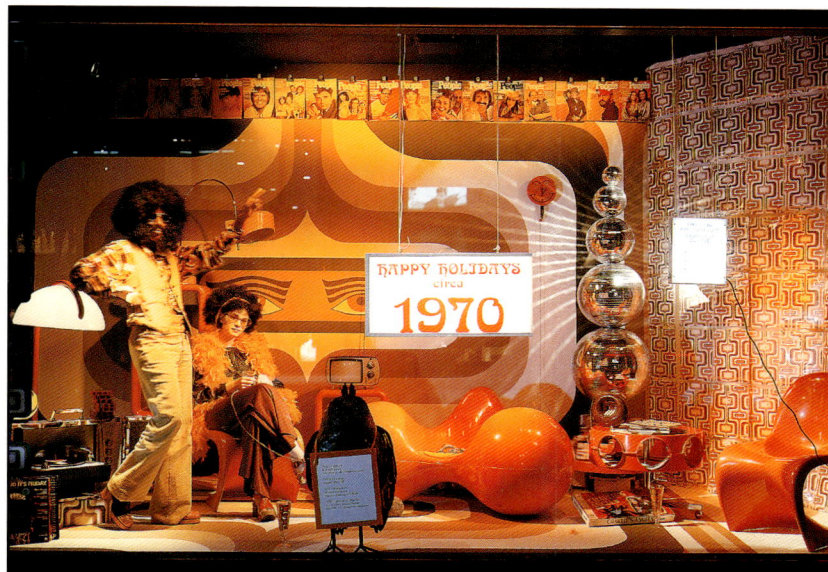

BARNEYS, (ALL) Madison Ave., New York, NY
Creative Director: Simon Doonan
Sr. VP Creative Services: David New
VP Creative Services: Adamo Di Gregerio

VIGNETTES

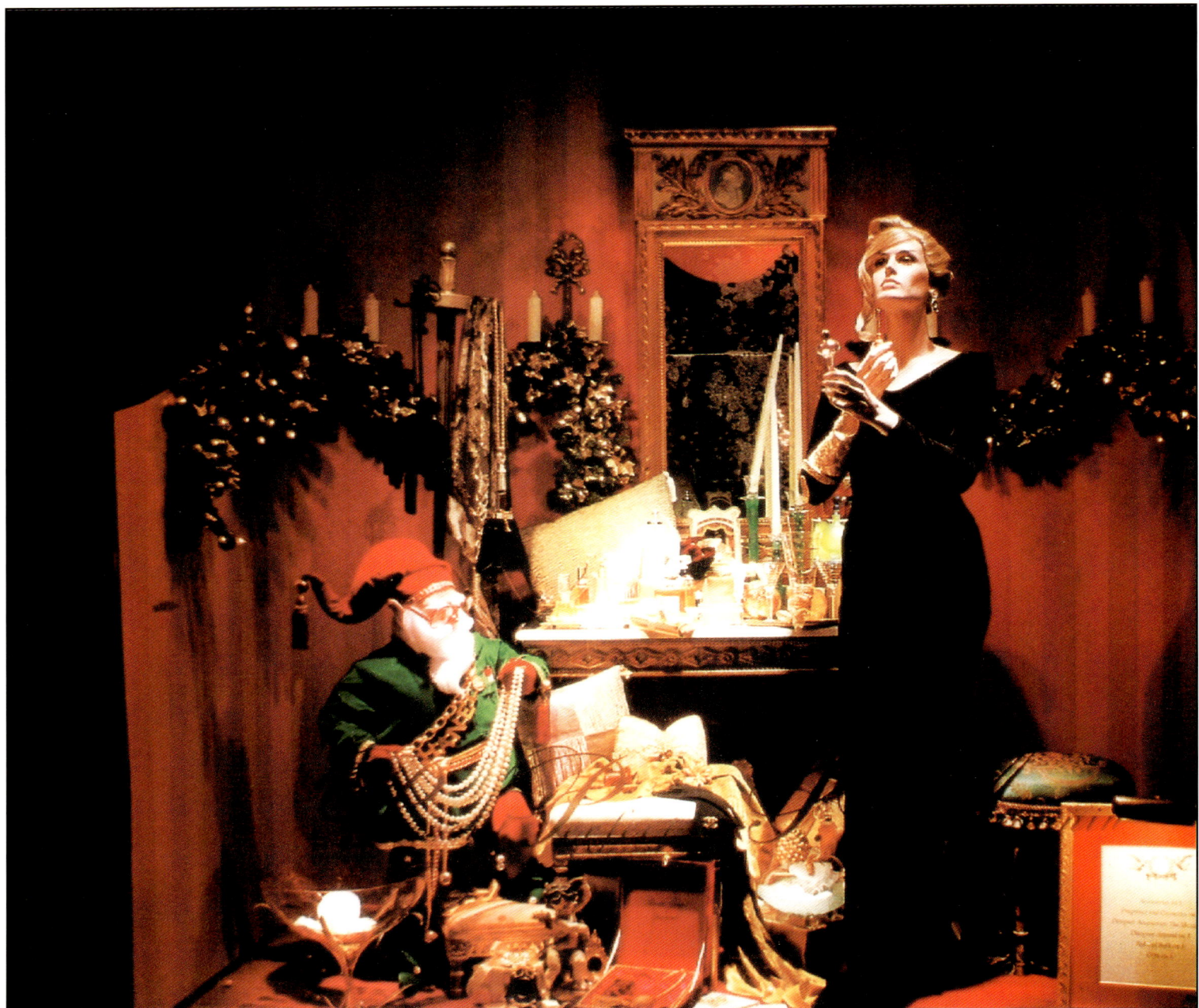

I. MAGNIN, San Francisco, CA
Visual Director: Linda Fargo

For reasons to merchandise for the holiday seasons—for giving or gifting—for presents—it makes no matter what the tense is or if the grammar is perfect, not when the concept is "Present Perfect."

I. Magnin, on Union Square in San Francisco, brought the store and its merchandise to glowing life with these brilliantly illuminated, bright red window settings filled to over-brimming with gift suggestions. Each window was targeted at another family member—another age group—lifestyle or area for gifting.

Red velvet draper, pulled back to reveal the room interiors, served as prosceniums or window frames that united the battery of windows as well as focused the shopper's eye onto the merchandise display. The red interiors varied from button-tufted, satin upholstered walls to library walls filled with predominantly red covered volumes—to heavily draped and festooned velvet walls—to red flocked striped papers or block letter decorated wall coverings. In some windows red and green velvet and satin dressed Santaish elves helped with the holiday preparations or stacked the merchandise or just pointed out some of the featured products. Gift boxes, wrapping paper, appropriate furniture and accessories all added to the festive settings.

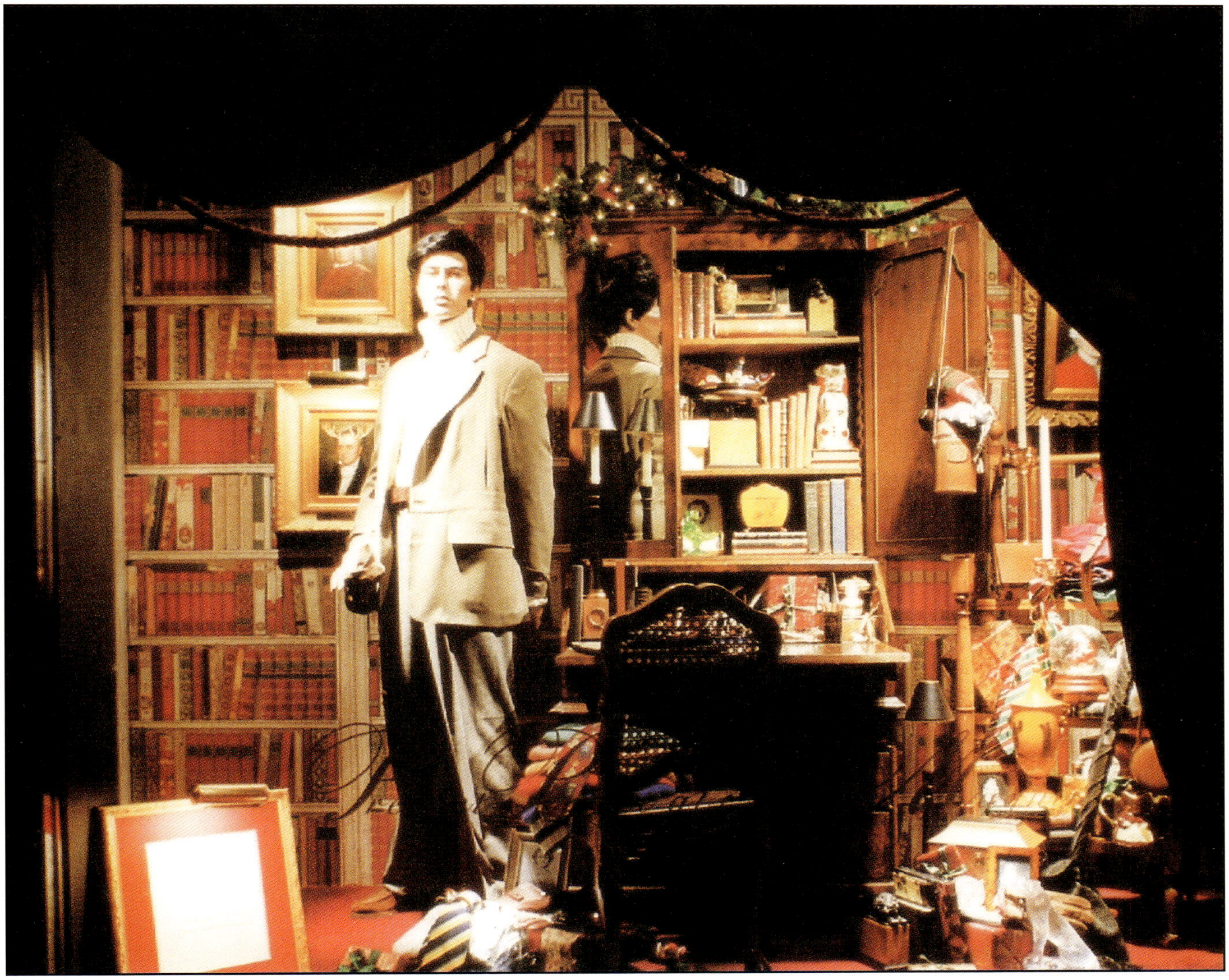

VIGNETTES

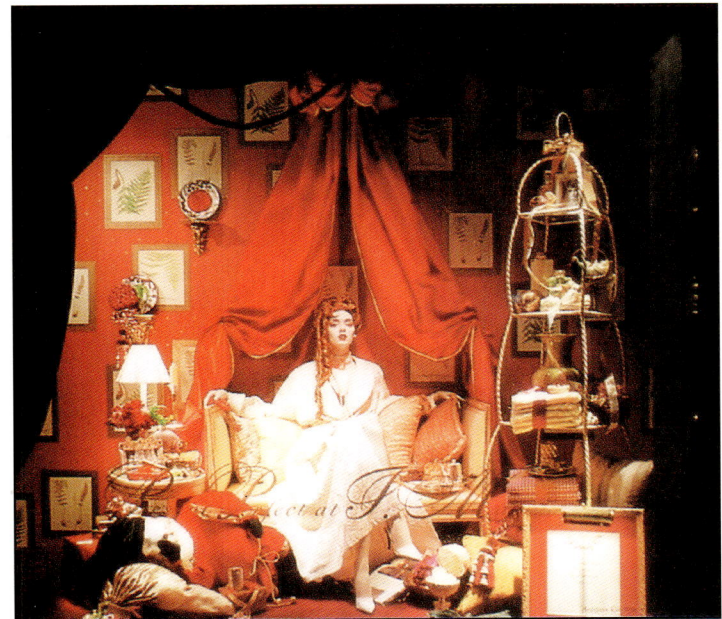
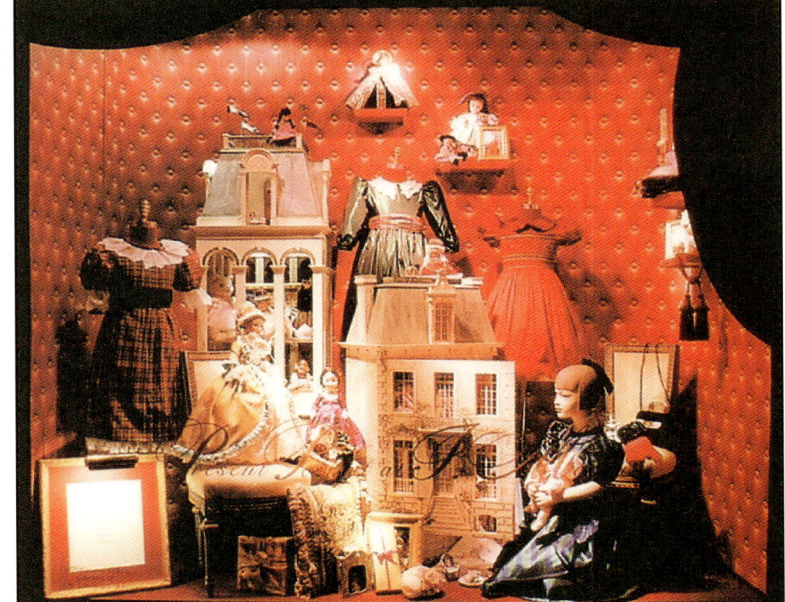

I. MAGNIN, (ALL) San Francisco, CA
Visual Director: Linda Fargo

VISIT TO SANTA

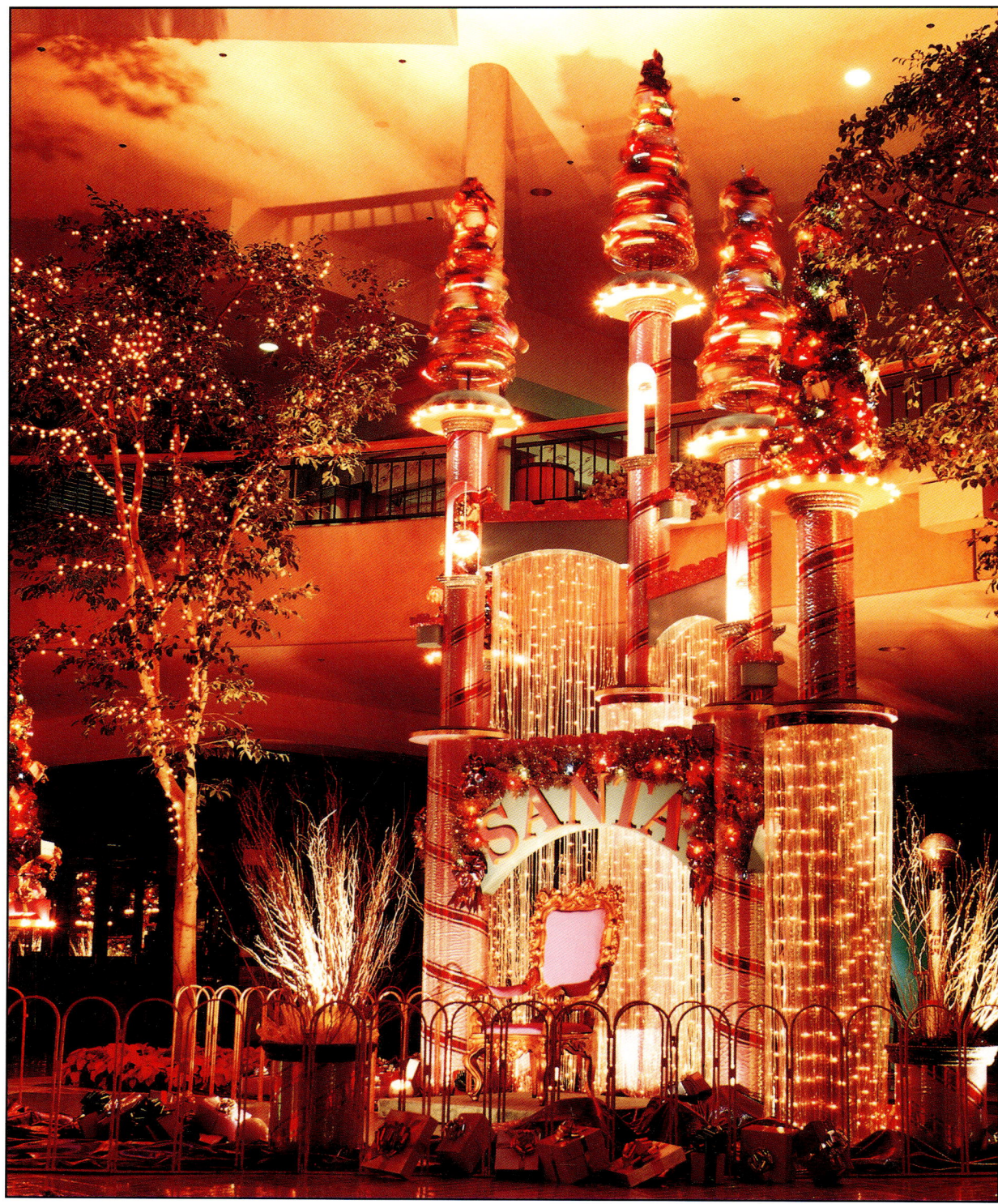

MONTEBELLO TOWN CENTER, Montebello, CA
Mall Marketing Director:
Deborah Blackford
Design & Construction:
The Design Centre, Wichita, KS
Exec. Director & Designer:
Curtis Harshfield

Nobody can ever say—"be it ever so humble"—about Santa's home. Santa is at home and receiving youngsters in his throne room in malls ands department stores all over the world. It wouldn't be Christmas without a visit to Santa's Castle all shiny and bright, full of color, animation, lights and excitement. On these pages we have selected a few of the truly outstanding settings that have delighted children across the country.

The Design Centre in Wichita, KS, created this fabulous castle that certainly outshines anything the Wizard of Oz could have hoped for. Located in the central space of the Montebello Town Center in Montebello, CA—just outside of Los Angeles—it dominates the space as it reaches up past the second level and is visible from almost anyplace in the mall. The candy cane towers are topped with candy laden trees that spin and spin while hundreds of strands of bee lights are enmeshed in clear plastic curtains to add shimmer and shine to the gold and hot pink throne which is raised up on a stage. The stage is banked with hundreds of gift wrapped boxes and the ficus trees that are part of the mall's landscaping are wreathed in more sparkling dots of light.

VISIT TO SANTA

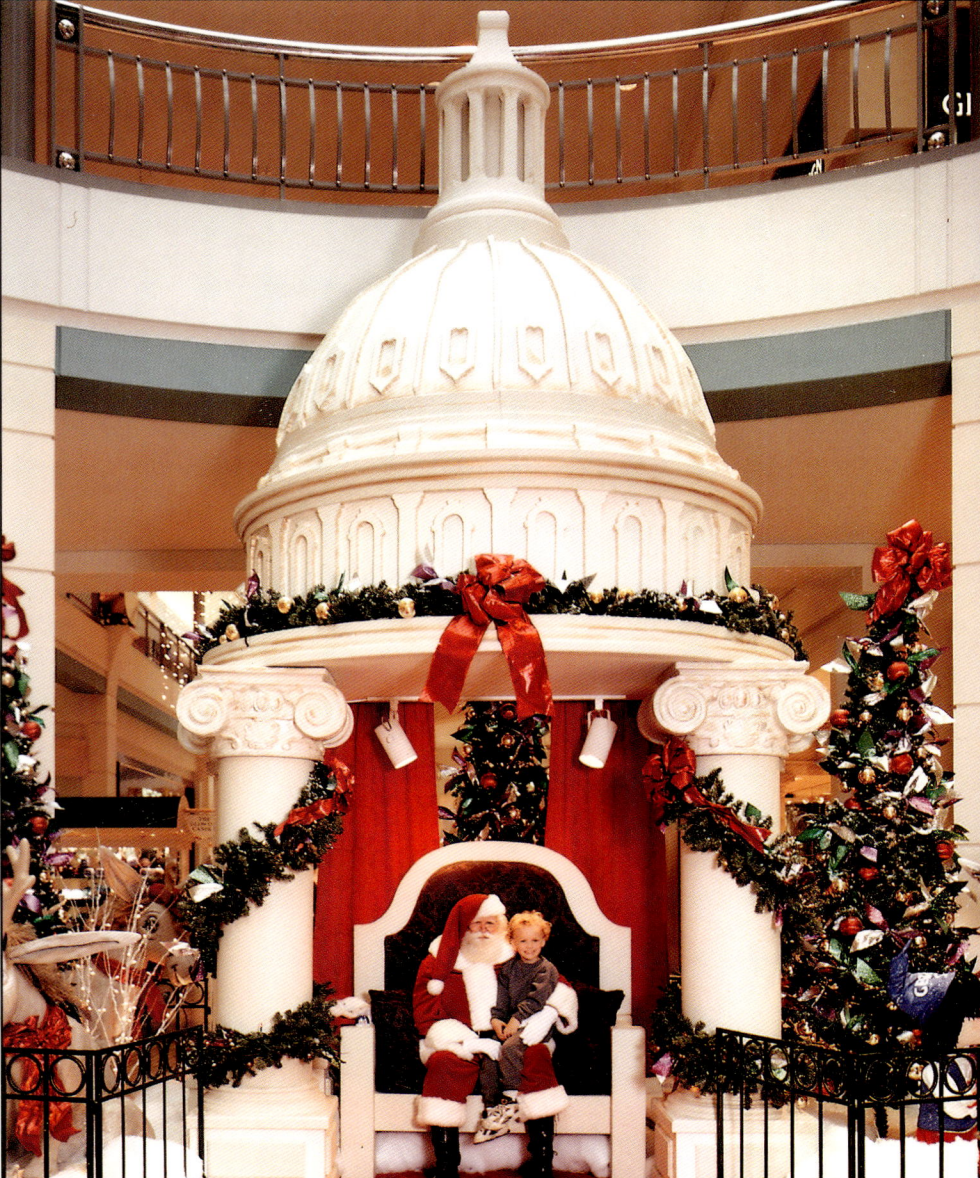

Tyson's Corner Center in McLean, VA, is just across the Potomac from Washington, DC and so it is not too surprising or shocking that Santa has moved into the Capital building for the holidays.

The all-white, easily recognized, dome topped structure is actually a half sphere resting atop four exaggerated Ionic columns. Red velvet drapery and green garlands enriched with colorful ornaments and lights are used to highlight the open structure. Santa's mammoth throne faces the traffic while on the opposite side, a giant Christmas tree is set between the drapes. A fun note in the rear view of the dome with a presidential caricature looking out from behind one of the louvered shutters. Atop his head—what else?—a red Santa hat.

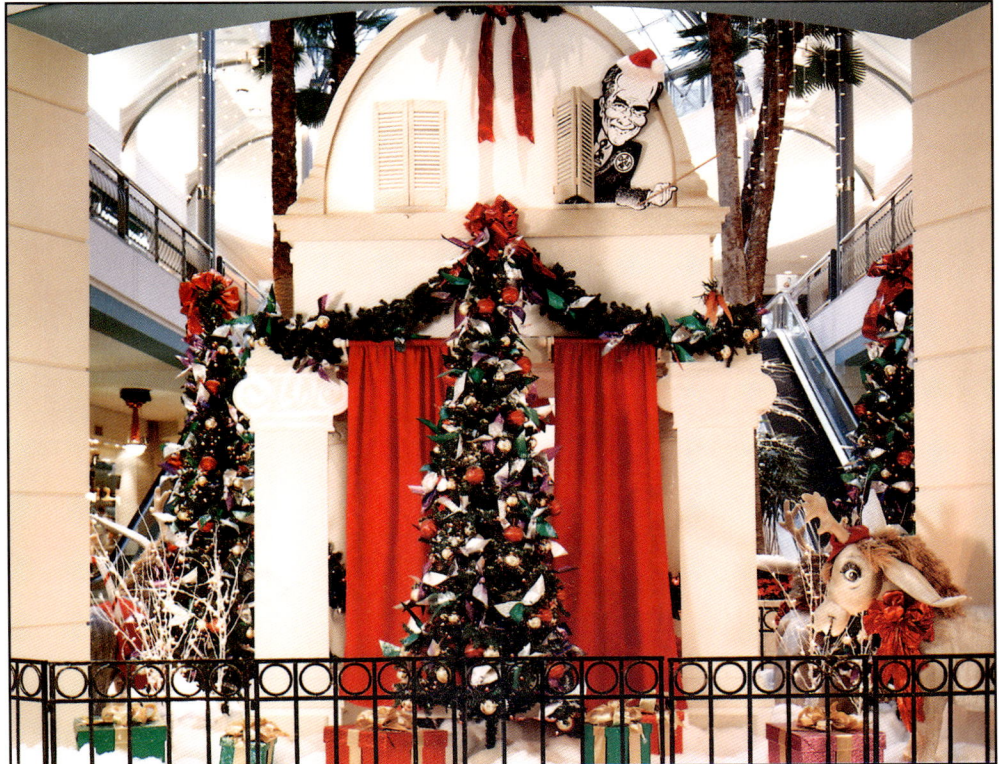

TYSON'S CORNER CENTER, (ABOVE AND LEFT)
McLean, VA
Marketing Director: Charlotte Ellis
Consultant: Robin Miller
Design & Execution: The Design Centre, Wichita, KS
Exec. Director & Designer: Curtis Harshfield

VISIT TO SANTA

A visitor to Crestwood Plaza in St. Louis is in for a candy and ice cream treat—and everything sweet and pastel to match. Giant candy canes and peppermint sticks, heroic scaled candies wrapped in pink, green, yellow, blue and red cellophane—and that is only the entrance to Santa's Ice Cream Parlor Castle. From anywhere in the mall the visitors—especially the children—can see the three scoops of ice cream tower topped with a blob of whipped cream and a luscious cherry. Colossal cones—also filled to overflowing with ice cream—stand guard against the multi-colored structure that rises up in waves of assorted pastel fresh colors. Icing the house are more giant candies, candy canes and gingerbread cookies. What kid could not want to taste this treat?

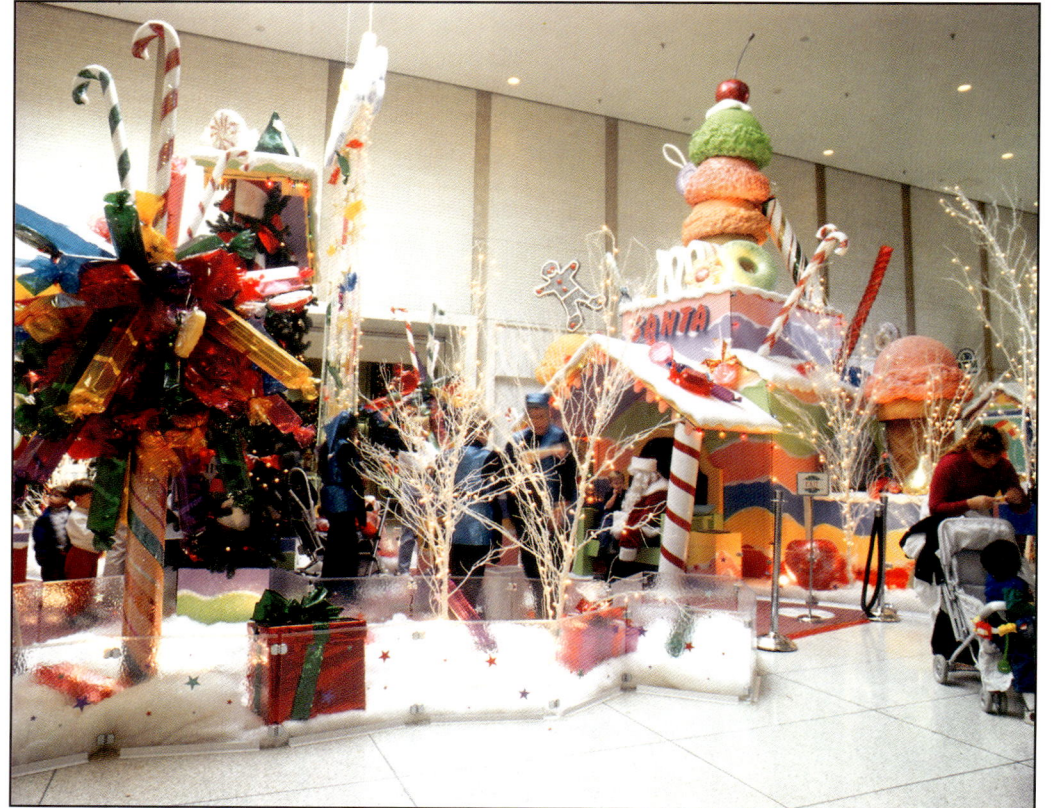

CRESTWOOD PLAZA, (ABOVE AND LEFT)
St. Louis, MO
Marketing Director: Kristin Schalk
Design & Fabrication: The Design Centre, Wichita, KS
Exec. Director & Designer: Curtis Harshfield

WHITE CHRISTMAS

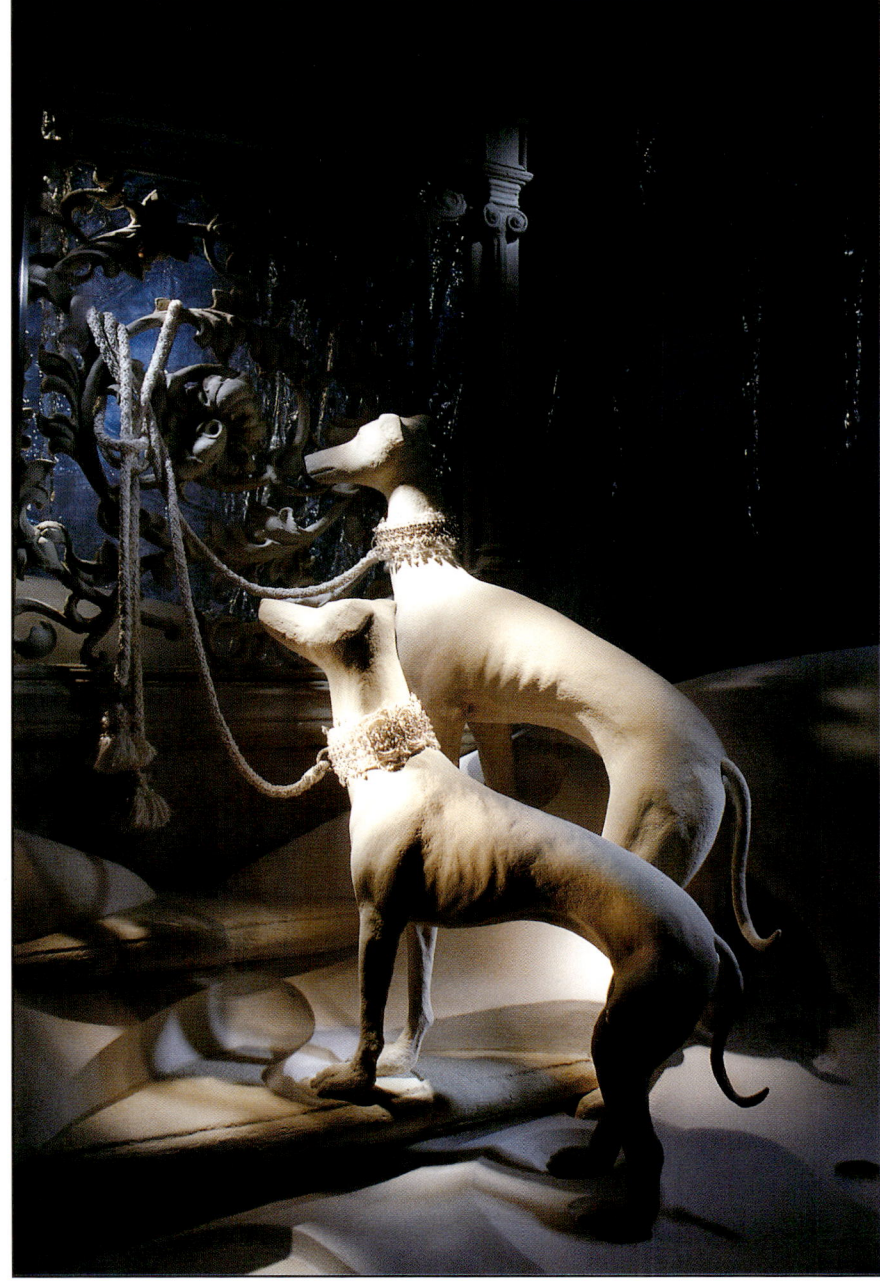

TIFFANY, Fifth Ave., New York, NY
Display Director: Robert Rufino

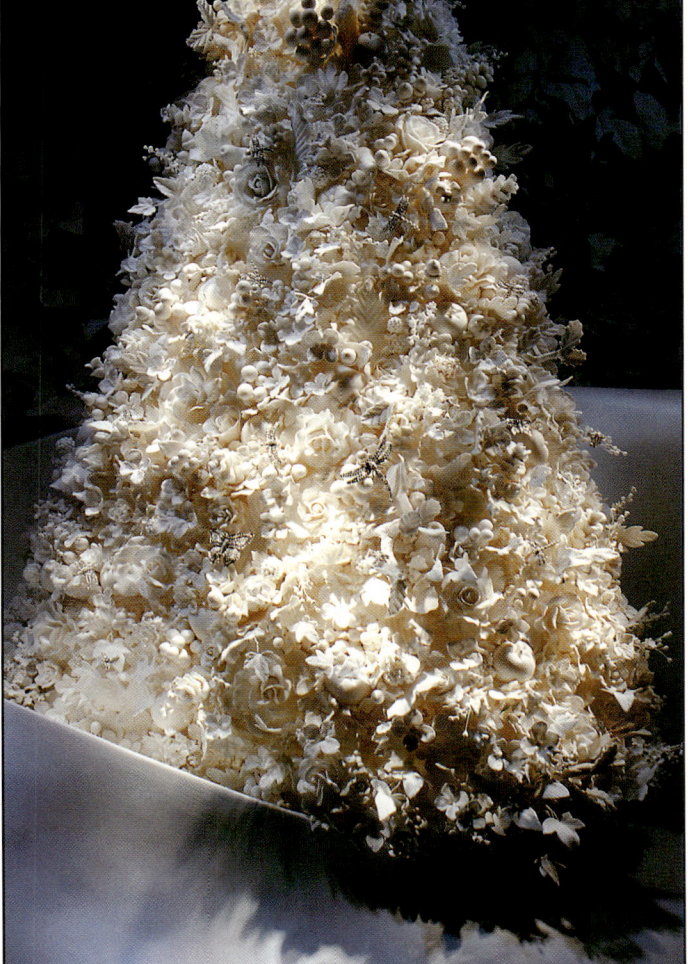

For the small precious shadow boxes that Tiffany is noted for, here are two of the small, precious displays that were on view for Christmas.

The elegant whippet dogs are tethered on to a swirling wrought iron, architectural gate. Through the openings, the cool, deep blue background can be seen. The "dog collars" are adorned with the famous Tiffany jeweled pieces.

The white tree is made up of roses, ribbons, bows, fruits and foliage—all in a matte white—and designed to attract, draw and eventually snare the jeweled insects, butterflies, wasps and such. They become the "ornaments" of this very special Christmas tree.

WHITE CHRISTMAS

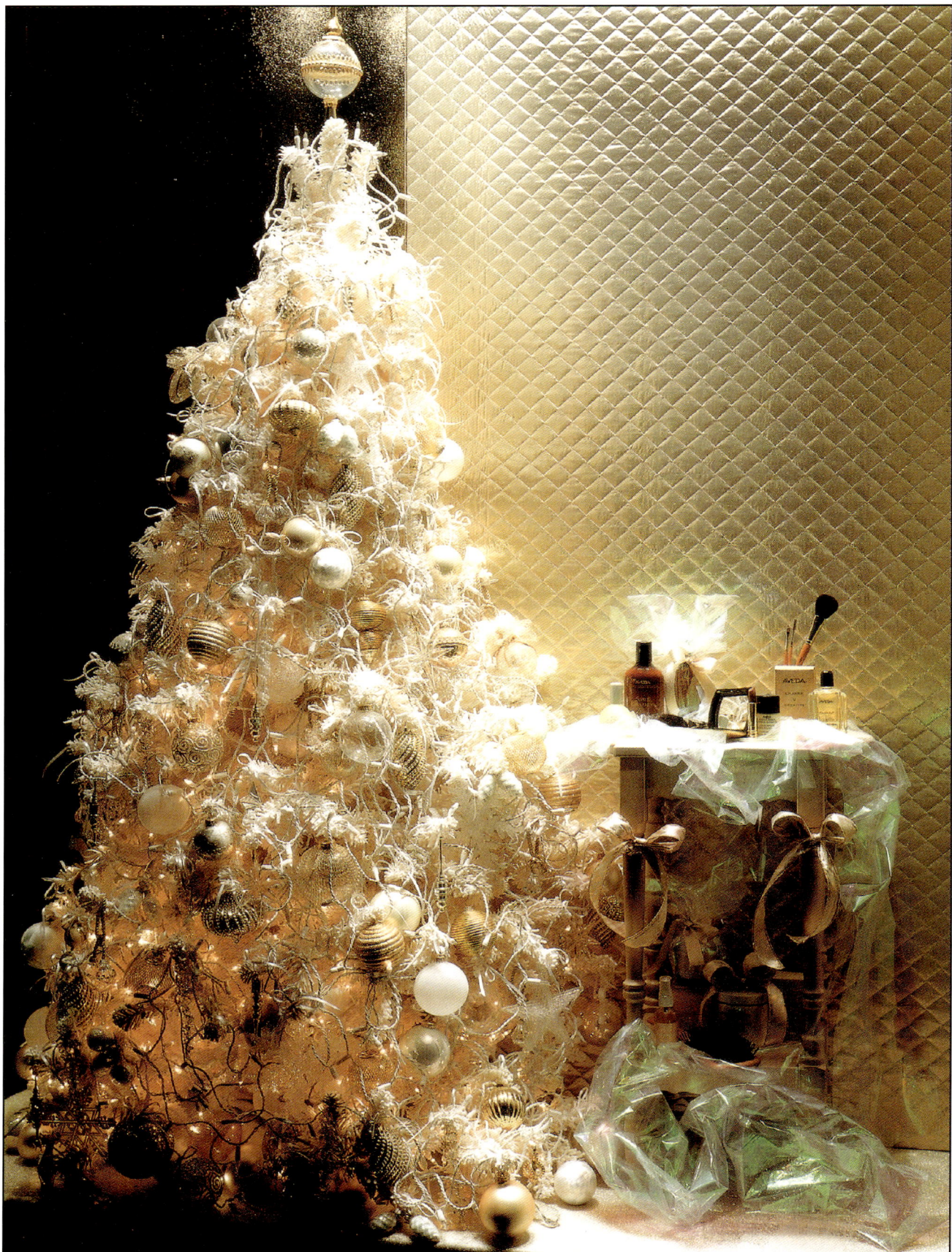

A SALON, Broadway, New York, NY

What would Christmas be without Christmas trees? Here are some display set-ups that take a stylized and decorative approach to the traditional; greenery and did the trees up in white, clear and neutral beige.

The A Salon's lush, fully trimmed tree is lavishly touched with gold and the window is backed up with a panel of quilted silver material.

Crystal clear plastic brush trees accentuate the vertical line as they complement the black gown in the small Celine window.

Bergdorf displays its myriad colored ornaments and decoratives on the white snow floor while the trees, formed of coiled natural vining, supplies a neutral accent. Natural branches frame the front glass.

WHITE CHRISTMAS

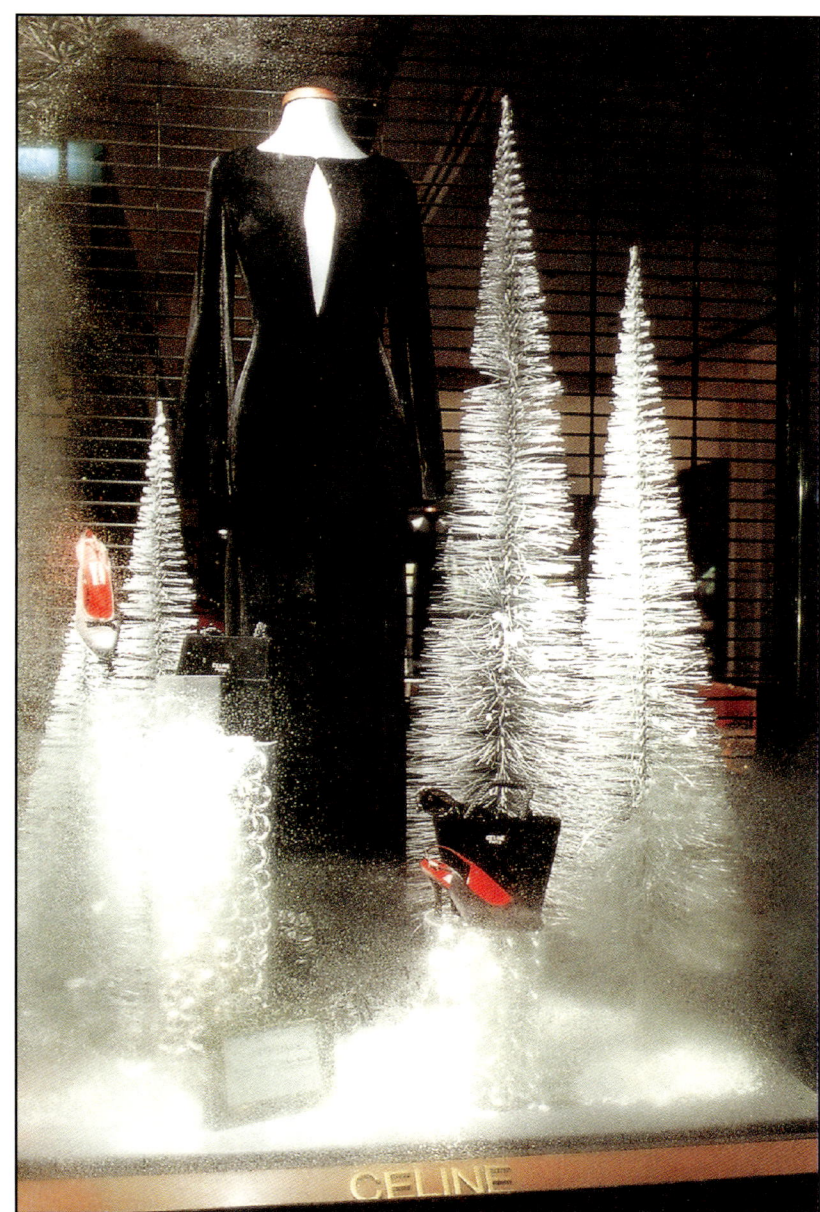

CELINE, Madison Ave., New York, NY

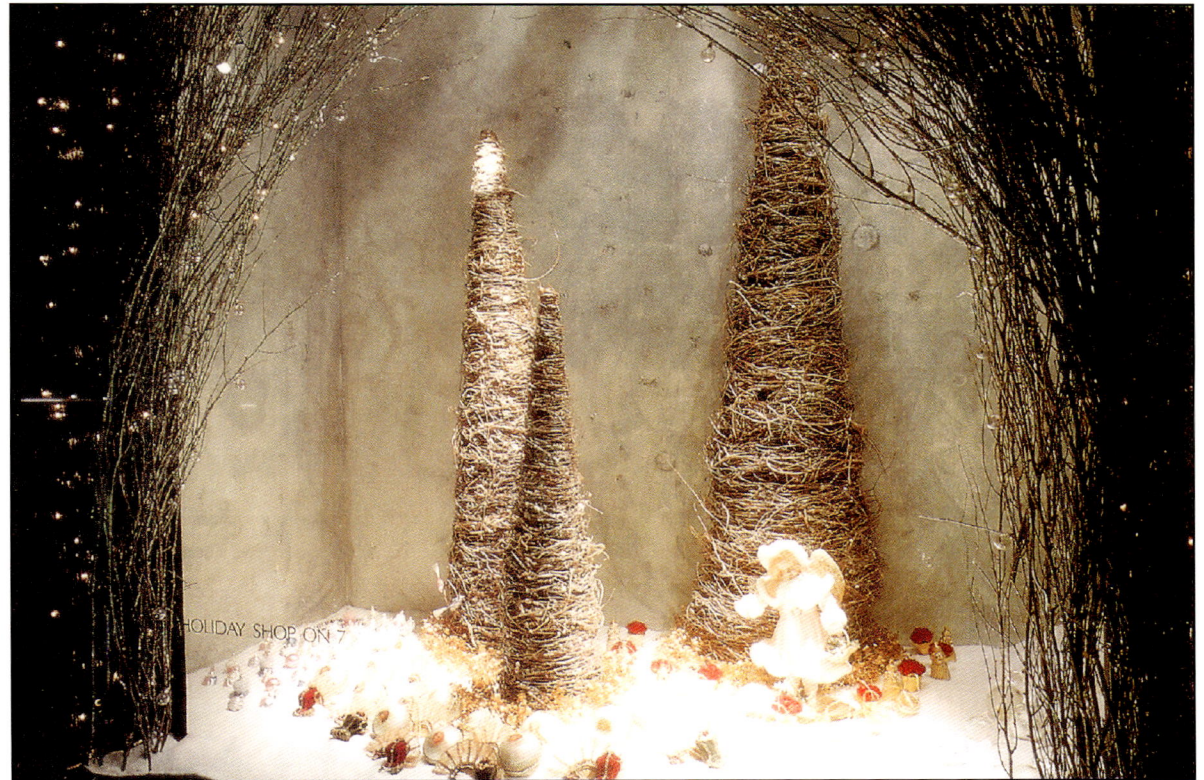

BERGDORF GOODMAN,
Fifth Ave., New York, NY
V.P. Visual Presentation:
Linda Fargo

Retailers

CHRISTMAS comes but once a year, but for anyone associated with retail, this holiday-of-holidays is experienced more as *"twas many months before Christmas and all through the store, marketing was making holiday plans galore."*

And we do mean many months before! With Christmas in July no longer a novel concept for consumers and Christmas in June, close behind, Christmas in January and February is increasingly common for those of us behind the scenes. It's not just because the selling season is longer; it's because the ideas are surfacing in new forms, such as comarketing situations that may involve one or more partners and the complexities of integrated marketing, which can necessitate even longer lead time than usual.

Add to these new marketing vehicles the variety of advertising, promotion and marketing tools that have become standards in many a retailer's Christmas effort, and you can see that in terms of potential, the possibilities—and the potential—for success are boundless.

And that is precisely the reason behind the section on retail stores that follows. We invite you to join us on a veritable shopping trip that will ultimately bring you the most effective ways to present your best gift-giving ideas to your customers. Some of you do it through your holiday catalog, others through special events, some with an all-out multimedia campaign. But whatever route you take, on the pages that follow you'll find detailed case histories complete with first-person interviews, describing how some of the most successful retailers are celebrating Christmas in their stores.

At one end of the spectrum is the big picture. Marshall Field, Daytons, Hudsons, whose elaborate multimedia, multifaceted promotion "How the Grinch Stole Christmas" illustrates the myriad selling tools possible from a single idea—community programs, in-store shops, special themed merchandise, shopping bags, advertising—even a theater production that drew more than a half-million people. Now, chances are you may not mount an event of this magnitude, but that is not the point. What is important is how a concept can be extended or adapted to specific uses—and perhaps, even more importantly, how this smorgasbord of a campaign may contain the nucleus of a single idea for an event or for an advertising direction that just happens to be right on target for your store.

You may want to try something you haven't tried before, as did The Disney Store for its "102 Dalmations" campaign. It launched its first national television advertising campaign and its first targeted newspaper effort as well, in addition to its usual sales inducements.

And yes, you can teach an old dog new tricks. Take that retail mainstay—the holiday catalog. The vehicle for a jam-packed storehouse of gift-giving ideas? Think again. American Eagle Outfitters did. You won't believe what's packed into the pages of its catalog.

On the pages that follow you'll also see examples of work that carries on the great tradition of Christmas and the great tradition of retailers such as Bergdorf's, Jacobsons, Laura Ashley and Neiman Marcus—each in a class by itself.

In addition to the in-depth retailer case histories, you'll find a variety of ideas with a specific media focus—creative photography, shopper-stopping copy, beautifully "wrapped" layouts—in short, a complete Christmas package of what you need to spark your most glittering Christmas ever. Have a merry time!

DAYTON'S   MARSHALL FIELD'S   HUDSON'S

From a Children's Classic, A Merry Celebration for All

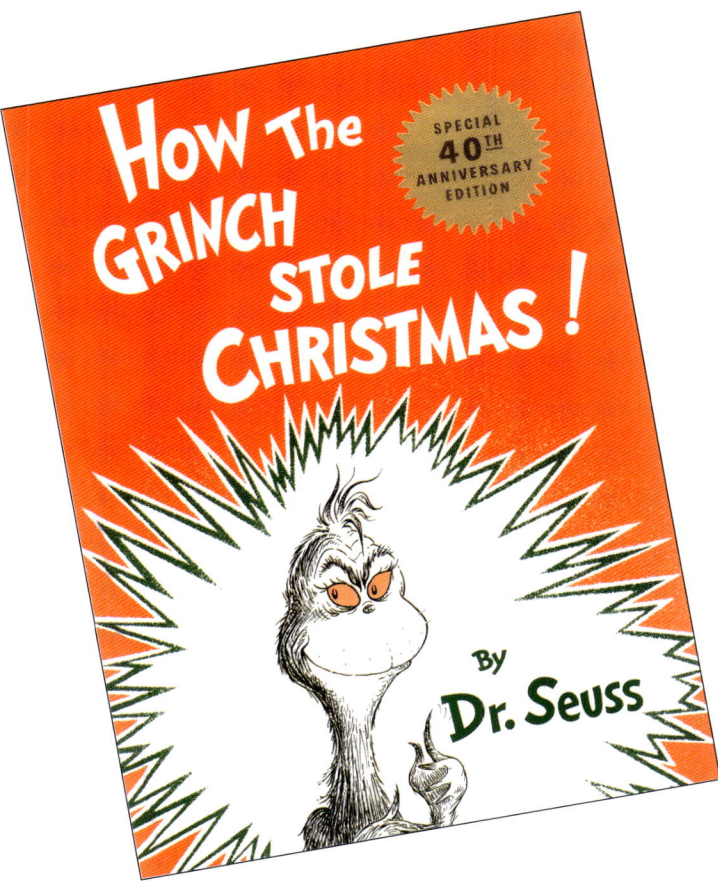

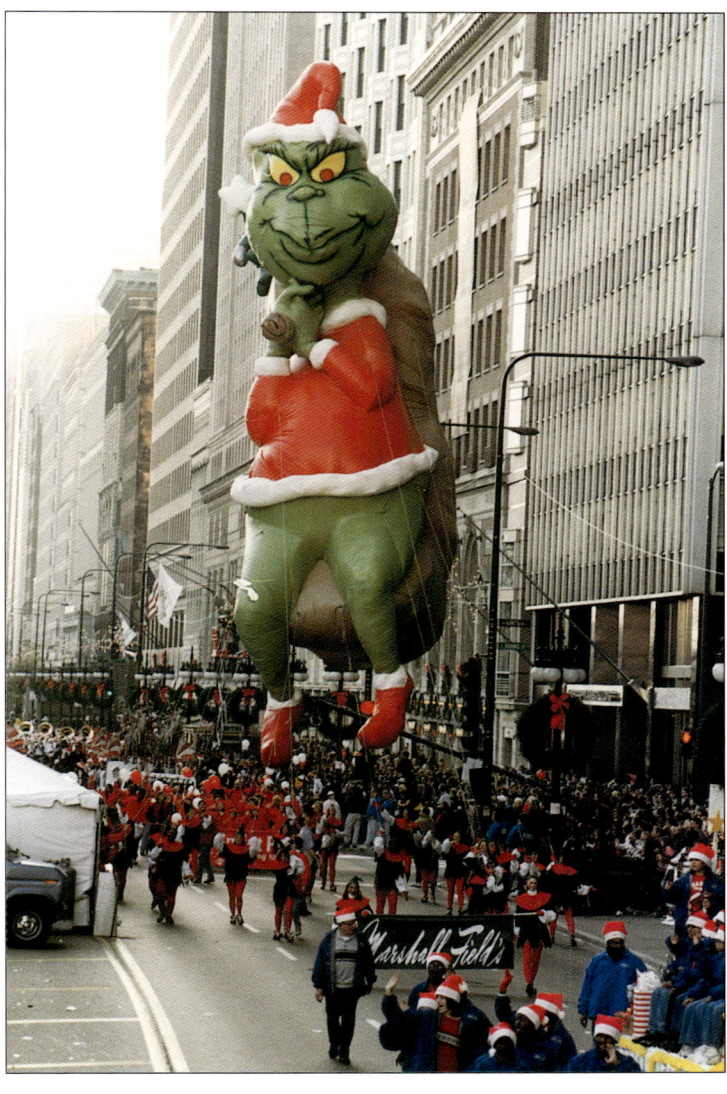

THE CLASSIC Dr. Seuss tale, *How the Grinch Stole Christmas*, emerged as a full-blown extravaganza as the 1998 holiday theme of Dayton's, Hudson's and Marshall's Field's. "We always try to start with the big picture," says Dayton's creative director, John Remington. "The most immediate was to put together a "fun box" of what we would like to do to bring Seuss into the stores." Grinch goings-on subsequently showed up in everything from shopping bags and displays to merchandise and Seuss Shops.

Layering the various elements were the department store chains' "gifts to the community." Hudson's featured the Grinch with a fabulous float in Detroit's Thanksgiving Day Parade. In Chicago, Marshall Field's carried out the Grinch theme on its towering Christmas tree in the State Street store. And Dayton's, Minneapolis, sponsored The Children's

DAYTON'S   MARSHALL FIELD'S   HUDSON'S

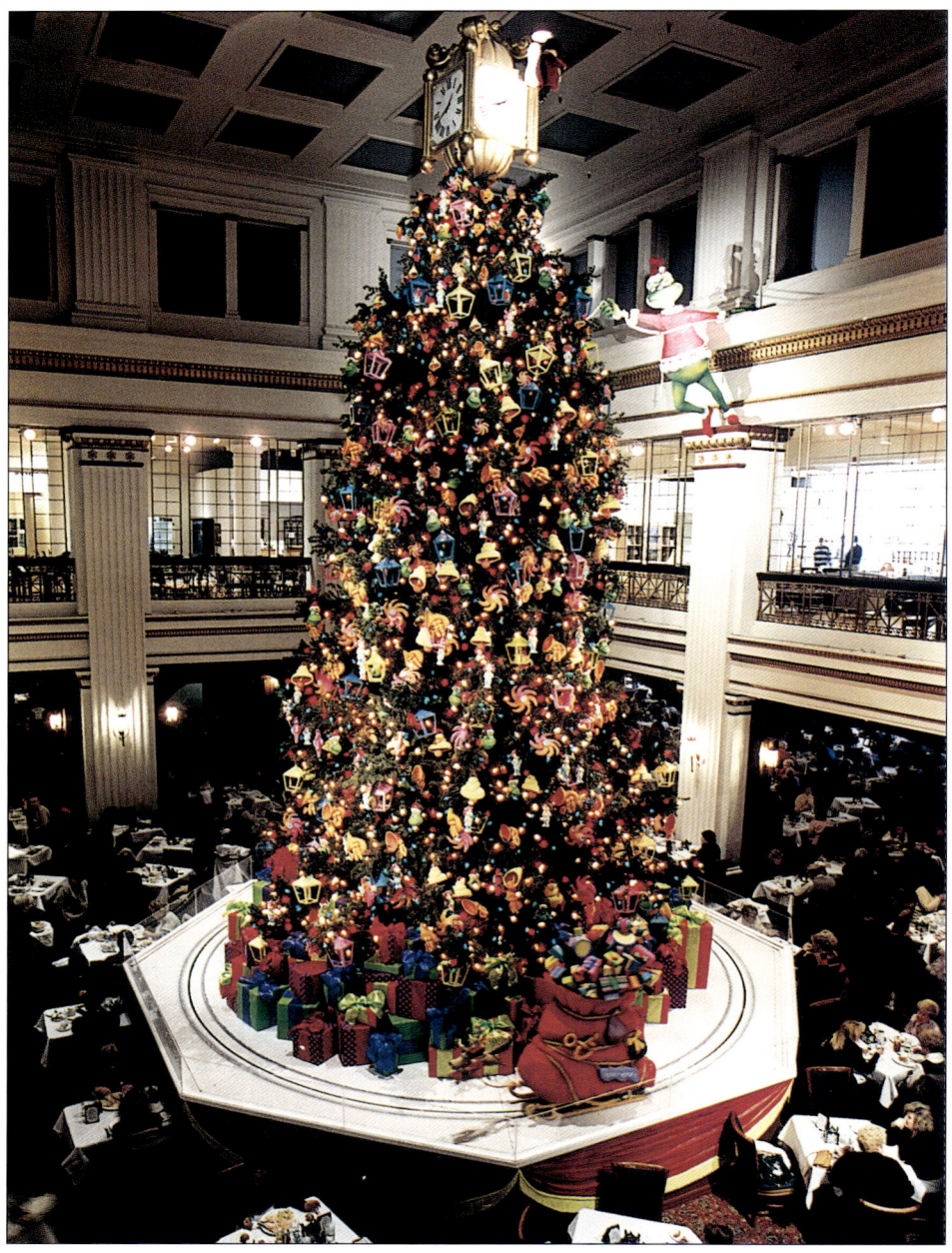

Three stories tall, Marshall Field's Great Tree was decorated with more than 1,000 Grinch-themed ornaments, including the Grinch himself. Just like in the tale, the Grinch tried to steal the Great Tree. He was suspended from the grid on the eighth floor with his rope in hand tugging on the tree.

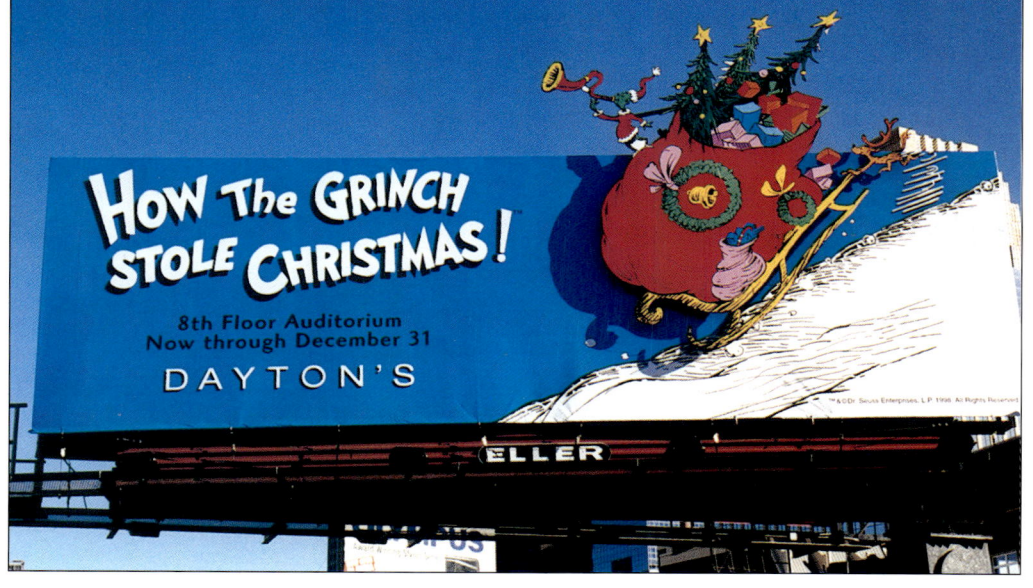

An "over-the-top" 3-D animated billboard in which the sleigh appeared to "rock" was part of the big picture in Minneapolis.

DAYTON'S MARSHALL FIELD'S HUDSON'S

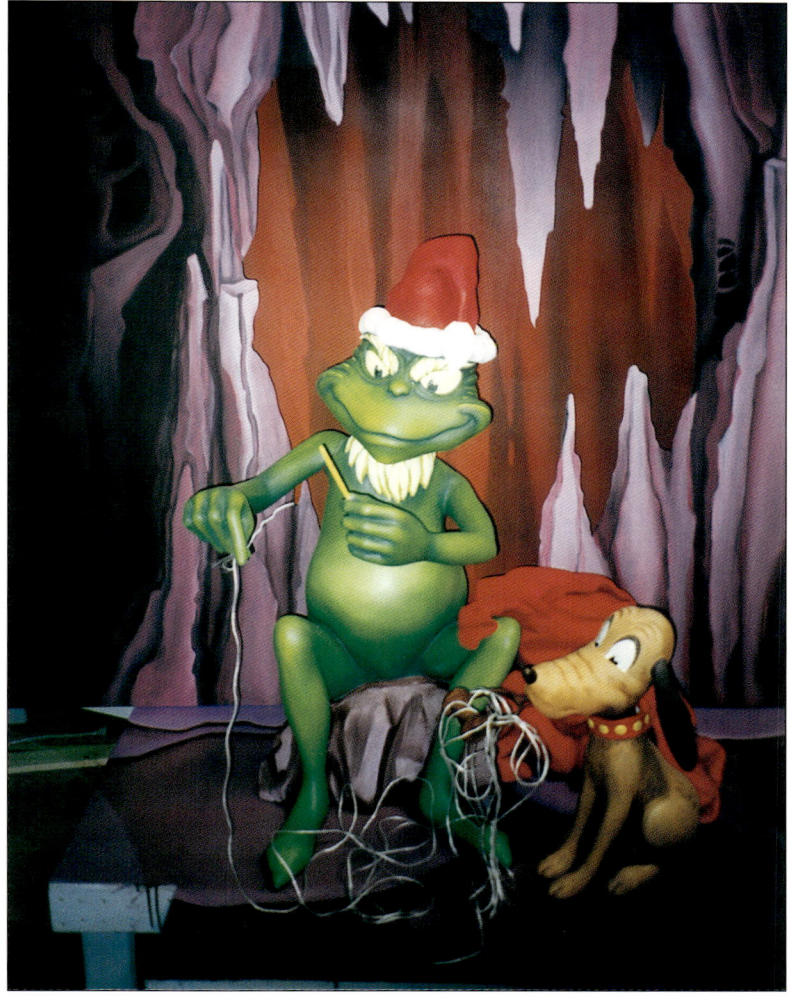

Dayton's auditorium show used 109 three-dimensional characters to trace the Grinch saga.

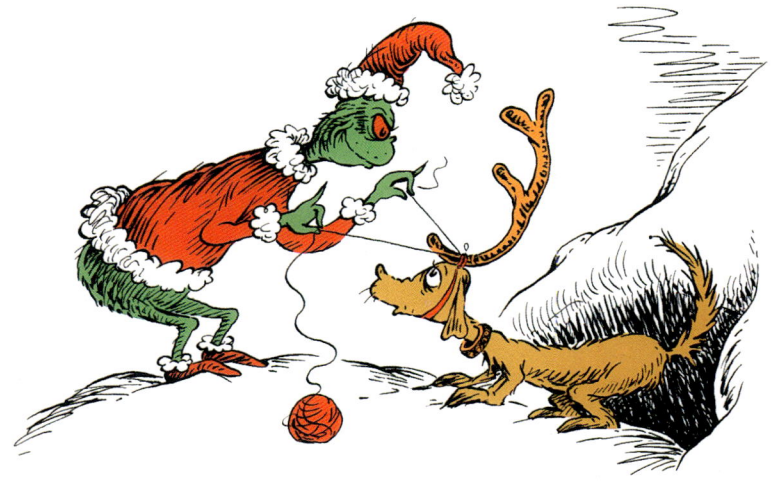

Theatre Company's production of (what else?) "How the Grinch stole Christmas." One of the last stores in the country with an auditorium, Dayton's made the most of it. For the store's 36th annual animated holiday display, the special events team brought Dr. Seuss' illustrations to life with a 23-vignette walk-through display. A mindboggling 558,000 people saw the auditorium show — the largest attendance in 32 years.

What happens to advertising based on a children's story? Says Remington, "Grinch is obviously juvenile so it wouldn't work with a Chanel gown. But the advertising had to be organic to the whole program, so we refined it. The gift strategy was to take a star that was in his illustrations and use it as an element in the gift ads with the tasty line 'Oh, the gifts you will find!' The star became an icon."

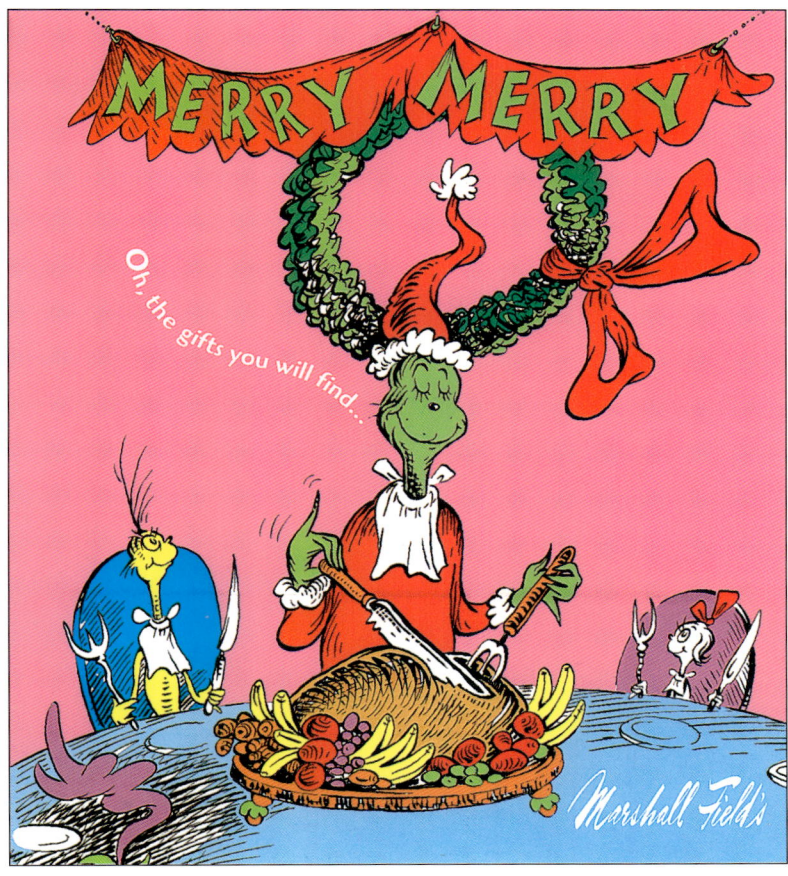

Eye-catching shopping bag.

DAYTON'S MARSHALL FIELD'S HUDSON'S

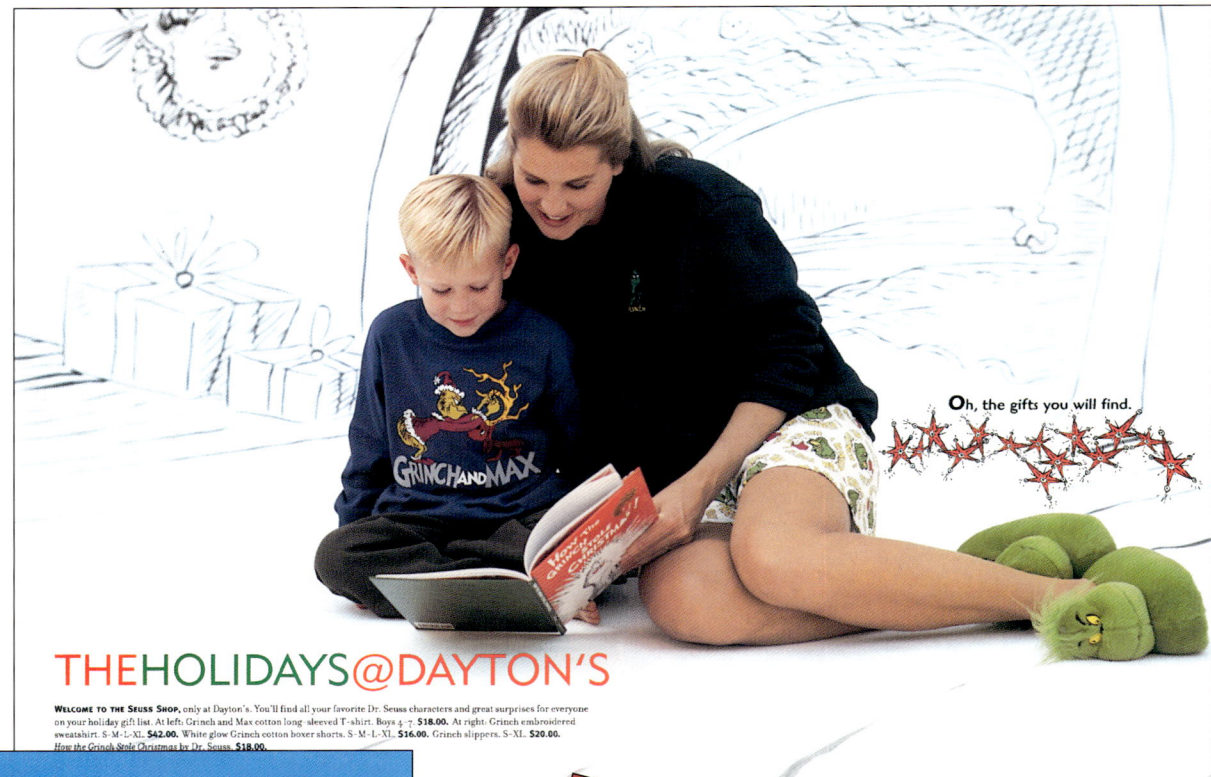

The gift ad strategy in a magazine ad with the "Seuss star" icon.

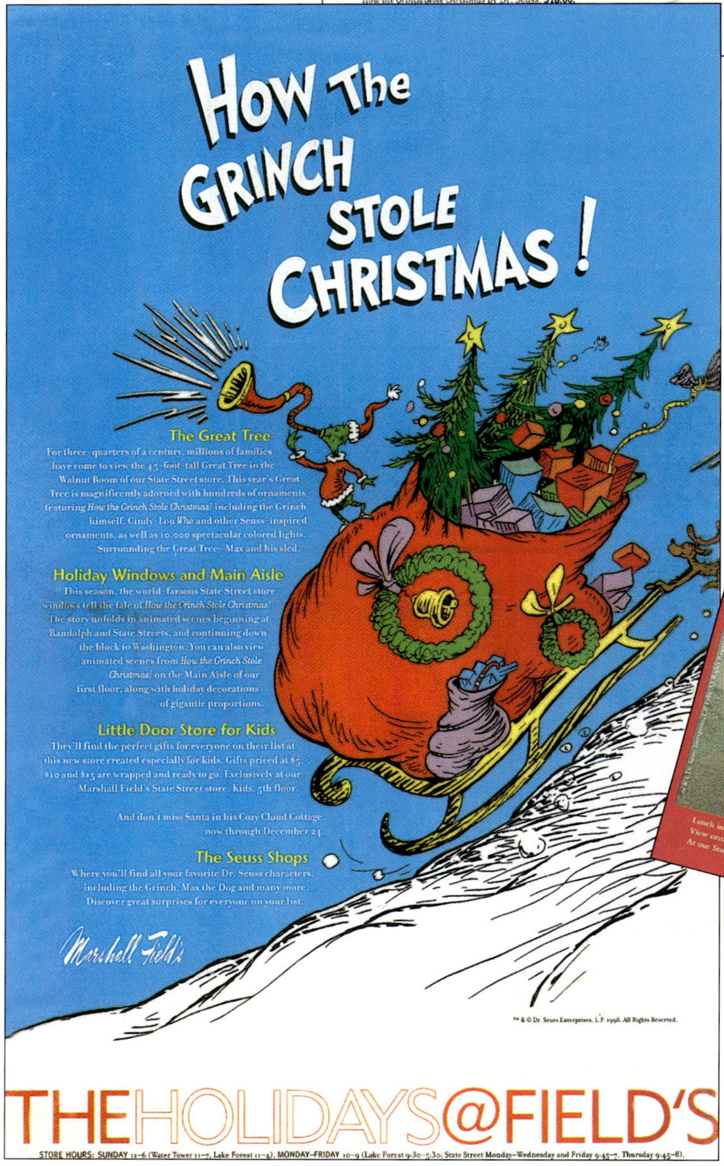

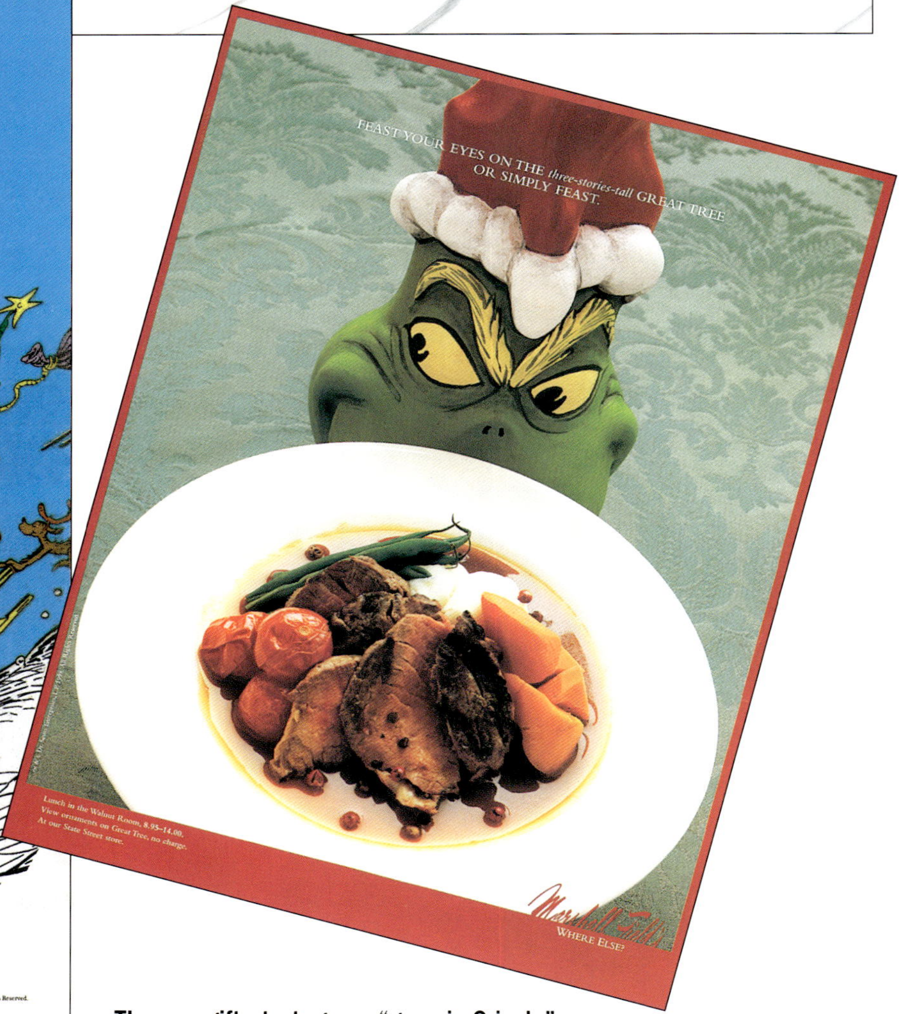

The non-gift strategy — "generic Grinch." Newspaper ad (left) and magazine (right).

DAYTON'S MARSHALL FIELD'S HUDSON'S

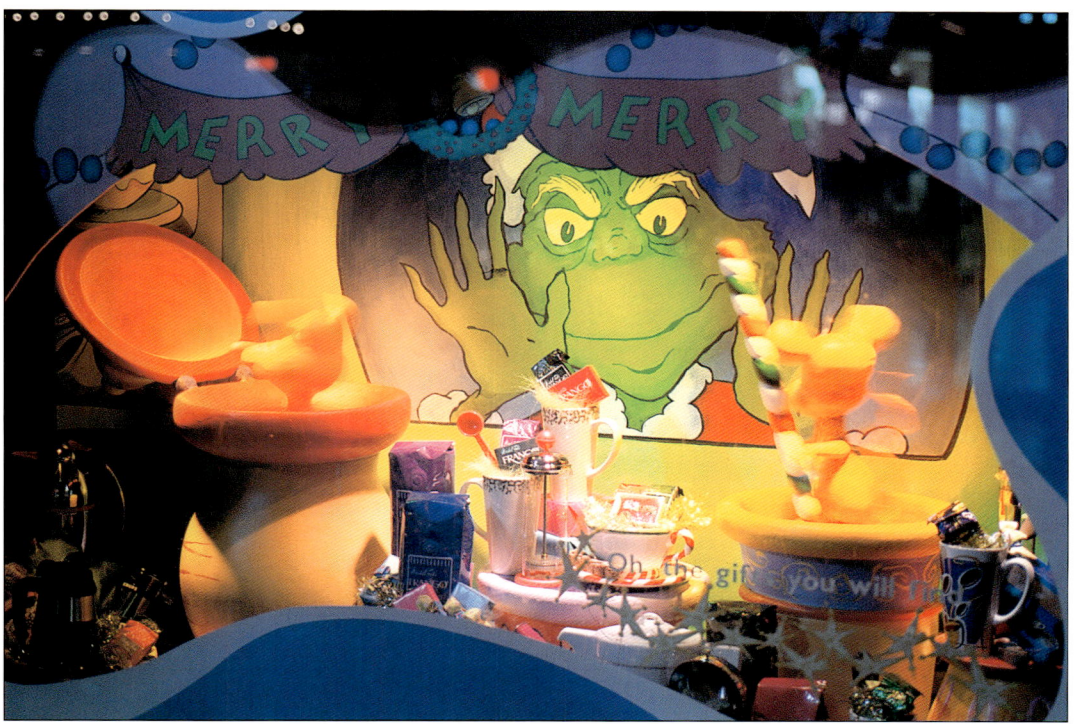

Dayton's Minneapolis store windows on Nicollet Mall

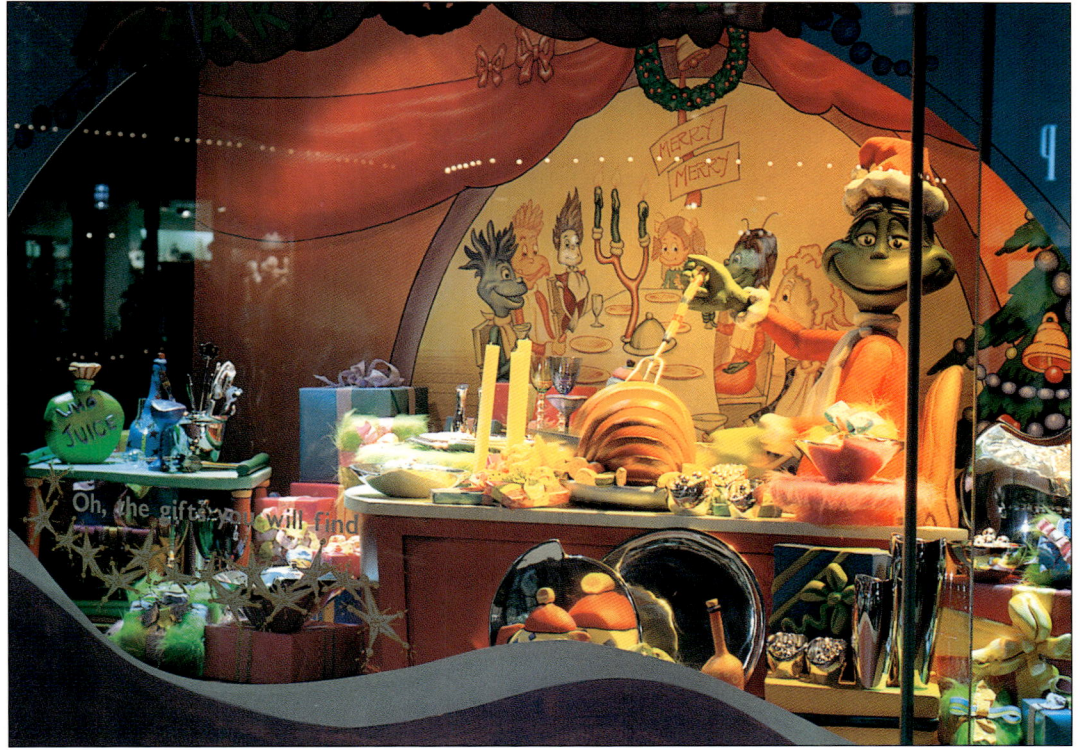

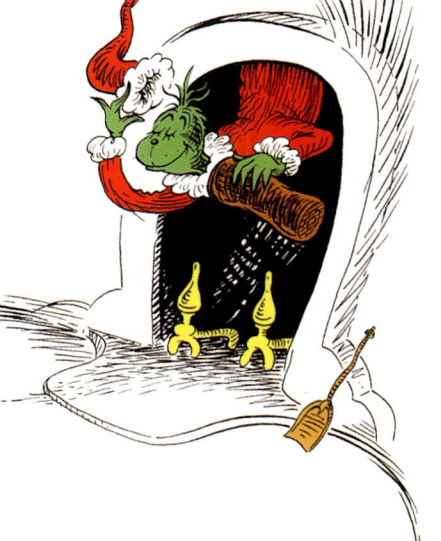

Daytons, Minneapolis, MN
MARKETING MANAGER: **Kim Brenny**
SR. CREATIVE MANAGER: **Connie Soteropulos**
CREATIVE DIRECTOR: **John Remington**
COPY CHIEF: **Vicky Iacarella**

DISNEY STORE

102 Reasons to Celebrate Christmas

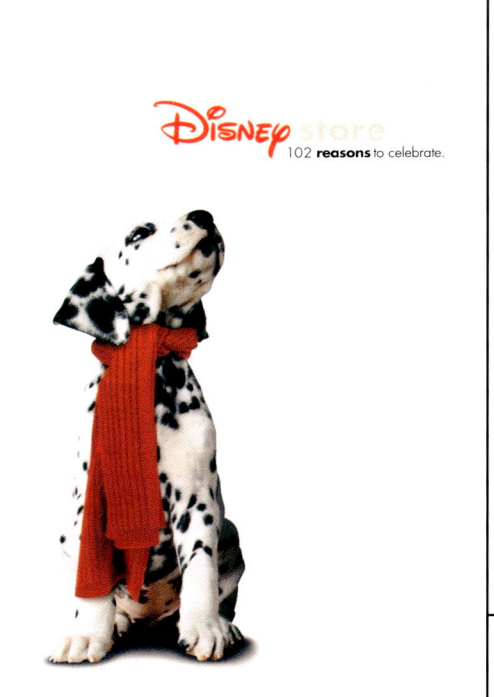

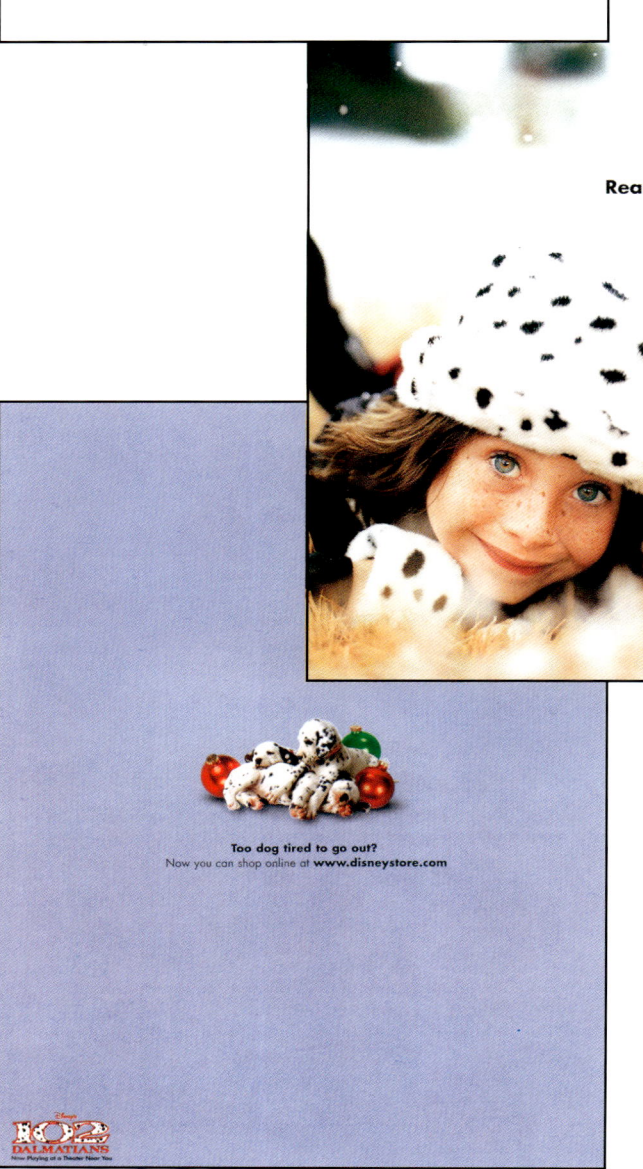

LAST CHRISTMAS people were seeing spots before their eyes. Lots of spots, as the Disney Store "went to the dogs" with Dalmatian-inspired merchandise and a multimedia campaign giving customers 102 reasons to shop for the holidays.

The campaign was timed to coincide with the Thanksgiving release of the Walt Disney Pictures movie, *102 Dalmatians*.

Christmas shoppers were first alerted to why there were "102 reasons to visit the Disney Store this holiday season" on November 16, when the chain launched its

DISNEY STORE

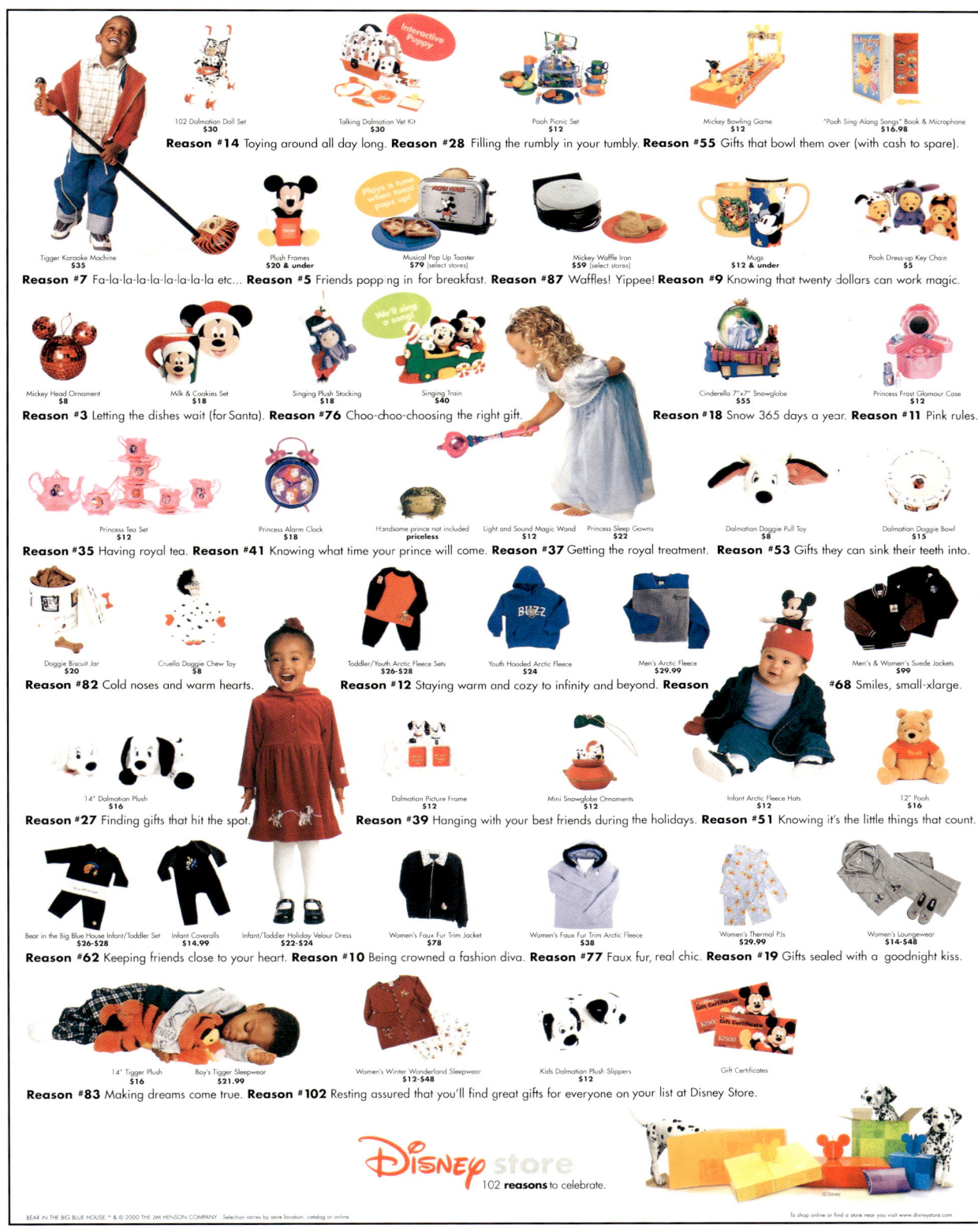

first national television advertising campaign.

The 30-second spot, ran for more than a month on national network and cable television, reaching more than 90% of the target audience of women 25 to 49 years of age. "We are making our big holiday statement with our great Dalmatian product," said Sondra Haley, vice president of marketing for the Disney Store. "These dogs are capturing the hearts of our guests and by utilizing them in our commercial, they will help keep the Disney Store top of mind holiday season."

"We have always been interested in running television advertising and found the tie-in with the *102 Dalmatians* movie made the most sense for our business, as it was mutually beneficial for the Disney Store and our stu-

DISNEY STORE

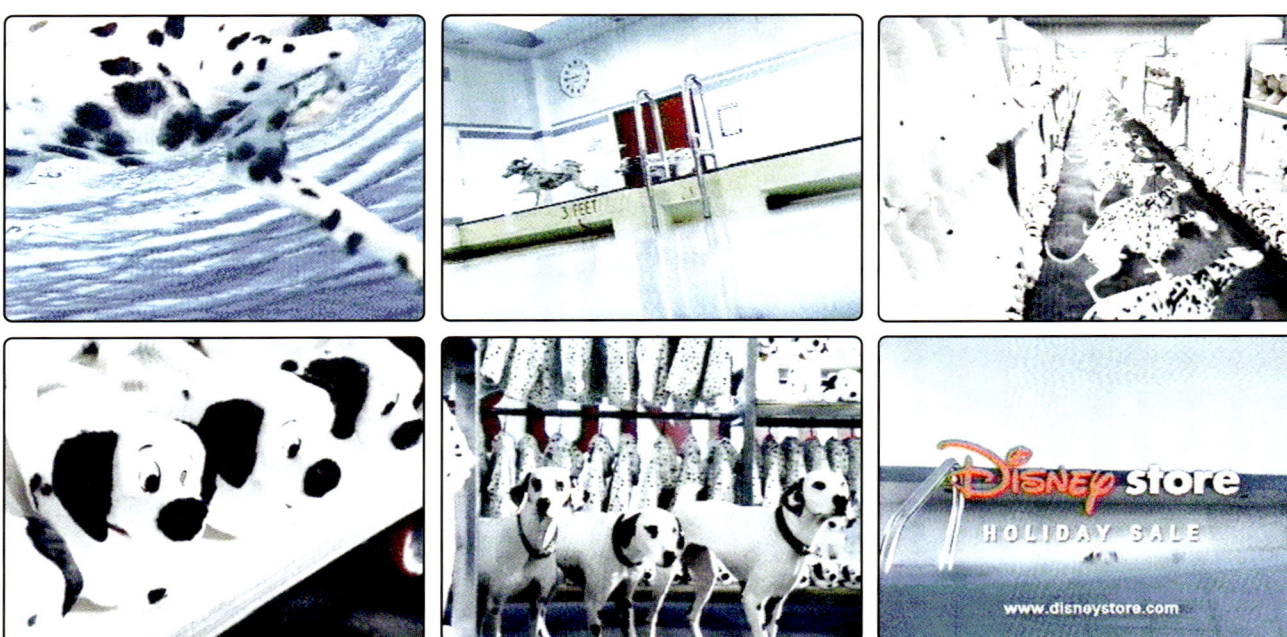

The 30-second spot featured Dalmatians taking a soothing swim in a crystal clear pool before shaking off their spots onto the Disney Store's hottest seasonal clothing, plush animals and accessories.

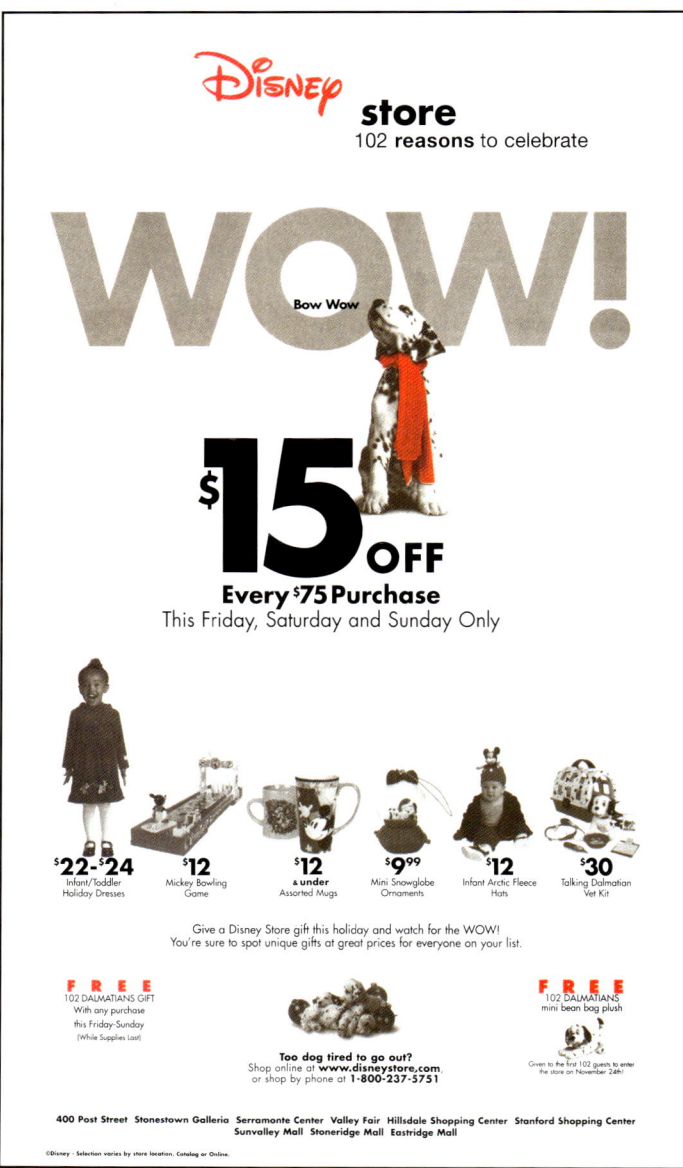

dio partner," says Jan Genovese, director, marketing. "Anticipating a competitive holiday season, we were armed with great Dalmatian merchandise and knew we needed to come to the table with an innovative and entertaining message to reach our audience."

In addition to its first national TV advertising, the holiday campaign marked another first for the Disney Store. Whereas the chain had used newspaper advertising for special store events in the past, Genovese notes, "This is the first time we have advertised Disney Store product in targeted newspapers across the country." The ad ran in 23 newspapers on November 23 and 24 in New York, Los Angeles, Chicago, Philadelphia, San Francisco, Boston, Detroit and Atlanta.

There was also plenty going on in store. Besides novel Dalmatian designs (everything from toddler dresses to mini snow-globe ornaments, doggie biscuit jars and a sensor dog that performed when applauded to a bomber jacket with spotted faux-fur collar, paw print zipper pull, and Dalmatian pup patch), there were other incentives to visit. On November 24 every Disney Store in the United States gave a mini bean-bag plush Dalmatian to the first 102 guests to enter the store. On November 25, every Disney Store in Canada and Puerto Rico got into the act as well. The mini bean-bag plush giveaway (with the traditional Dalmatian spots, black ears and a commemorative blue collar printed with 102 Dalmatians and 11/22/2000, the date of the movie release) was designed to o celebrate the beginning of the

DISNEY STORE

102 Reasons #1

MUSIC: (JINGLE-ISCIOUS)

ANNCR: One-hundred and two reasons to visit a Disney Store for the holidays"...

VARIOUS KIDS: The Disney Store has gifts that you cannot find at other places. (And) they give you great gift boxes, that have 3-D pop-up faces.

My mom says "Disney plush toys can last for many years," which is good because my brother likes to pull on Mickey's ears.

There's gifts for under 20 bucks, for every generation. The holidays are twice as fun with Disney decorations.

ANNCR: Give a Disney Store gift to someone this holiday and watch for the "WOW"! From the crankiest Scrooge, to the sweetest little princess, Disney store gifts will steal the heart of everyone on your list...and our new 3-D character gift boxes let you shop and wrap in no time at all. Plus, with any purchase this weekend, you'll get a free 102 Dalmatians collectible pin, while supplies last.

VARIOUS KIDS: There's character pajamas, and grown-up sleepwear too. It's fun to watch your parents sleep with Tigger and with Pooh.

ANNCR: Do all your holiday shopping now through Sunday and save $15 off every $75 purchase. See store for details. Find the Disney Store nearest you at disneystore dot com.

102 Reasons #2

MUSIC: (STORYTIME, CHILDLIKE)

ANNCR: One-hundred and two reasons to visit a Disney Store for the holidays"...

VARIOUS KIDS: The Disney Store has special gifts for every generation. More gifts than there are spots on all 102 Dalmatians.

There's toys for just 12 dollars, even more stuff under 20. You can give the bestest presents, without spending all your money.

My Dad says Disney clothes last long, 'cause that's the way they're made. He wants a Mickey Jacket...

(whisper)...the one that's made of suede!

ANNCR: Give a Disney Store gift to someone this holiday and watch for the "WOW"! From the crankiest Scrooge, to the sweetest little princess, Disney store gifts will steal the heart of everyone on your list...and our new 3-D character gift boxes let you shop and wrap in no time at all. Plus, with any purchase this weekend, you'll get a free 102 Dalmatians collectible pin, while supplies last.

VARIOUS KIDS: You can search the world for special gifts, on sea and air and shore. But the coolest gifts, exclusively are at the Disney Store.

ANNCR: Do all your holiday shopping now through Sunday and save $15 off every $75 purchase. See store for details. Find the Disney Store nearest you at disneystore dot com.

102 Reasons #3

MUSIC: (STORYTIME, CHILDLIKE)

ANNCR: One-hundred and two reasons to visit a Disney Store for the holidays"...

VARIOUS KIDS: There's lots of gifts and toys and stuff for under 20 bucks. For the mailman a Dalmatian, and your teacher Donald Duck.

Your best friends and your relatives deserve a Disney treasure. Like shots of you in picture frames, they'll want to keep forever.

There's classy clothes for grown-ups, thermal nightshirts, Arctic fleece. And holiday decorations full of Disney joy and peace.

ANNCR: Give a Disney Store gift to someone this holiday and watch for the "WOW"! From the crankiest Scrooge, to the sweetest little princess, Disney store gifts will steal the heart of everyone on your list...and our new 3-D character gift boxes let you shop and wrap in no time at all. Plus, with any purchase this weekend, you'll get a free 102 Dalmatians collectible pin, while supplies last.

VARIOUS KIDS: There's pretty princess gowns, made to keep your princess glowing. And pretty mini snow globes made to keep your whole year snowing.

ANNCR: Do all your holiday shopping now through Sunday and save $15 off every $75 purchase. See store for details. Find the Disney Store nearest you at disneystore dot com.

---

holiday shopping season, as well as commemorate the movie's release. The stores also offered an exclusive 102 Dalmatians pin, or a movie poster, with every purchase over Thanksgiving weekend.

The Dalmatian theme was extended to a catalog-type piece and website as well. The tagline to lure customers to the site is "Too dog tired to go out? Now you can shop online at www.disneystore.com." During Thanksgiving weekend, visitors to the website received a free 102 Dalmatian commemorative pin—$6 value—with any order. Immediately following Thanksgiving weekend, customers who purchased $75 or more received a 10% discount with their order.

The direct mail piece with "102" gift ideas arrived in homes on November 28. According to Genovese, the Disney Store's in-house database was utilized to distribute 700,000 pieces to affinity guests and collectors.

During the same time period, radio commercials ran in Top 8 markets—New York, Los Angeles, Chicago, Philadelphia, San Francisco, Boston, Detroit and Atlanta.

No wonder everyone was seeing spots before their eyes. There were even billboards on both coasts—in Los Angeles and in New York's Times Square.

See Spot run!

Disney Store, Glendale, CA
VICE PRESIDENT, MARKETING AND PUBLIC RELATIONS: **Sondra Haley**
DIRECTOR, MARKETING: **Jan Genovese**
DIRECTOR, CREATIVE MARKETING: **Steve Gross**
AGENCY: (print) **In-house**
BROADCAST: **Dexter Fedor,** The Walt Disney Company, **Jarl Olsen,** Fuel Productions
DIRECTOR: **Jarl Olsen**
PRODUCER: **Carolyn Casey**

AMERICAN EAGLE OUTFITTERS

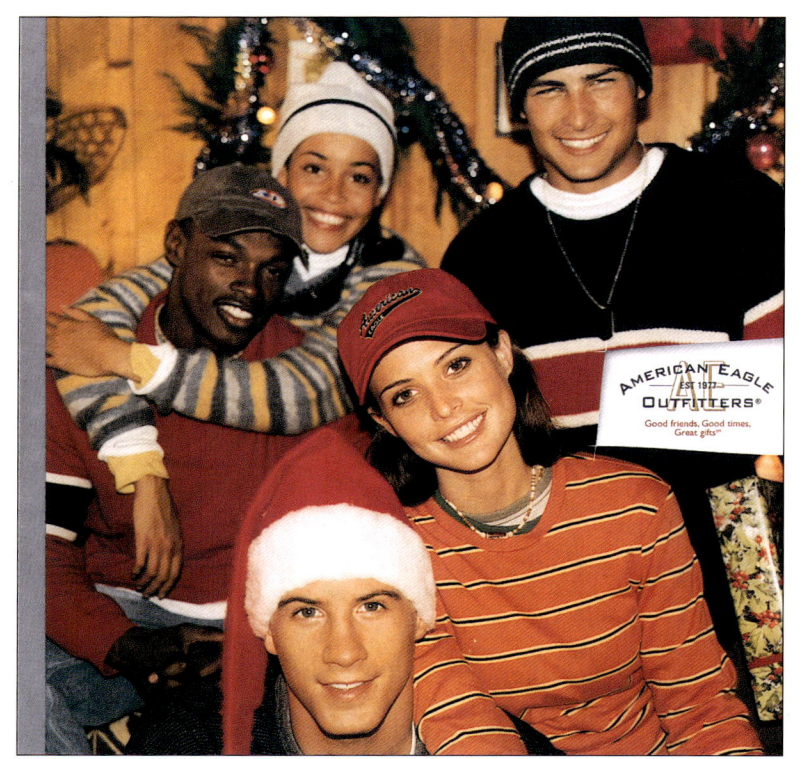

Good Friends. Good Times. Great Gifts.

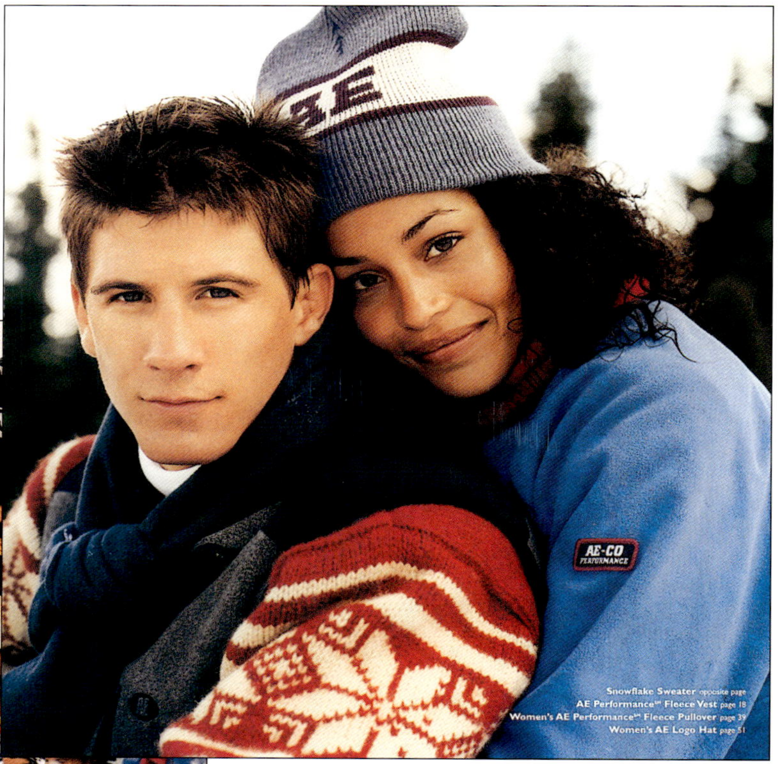

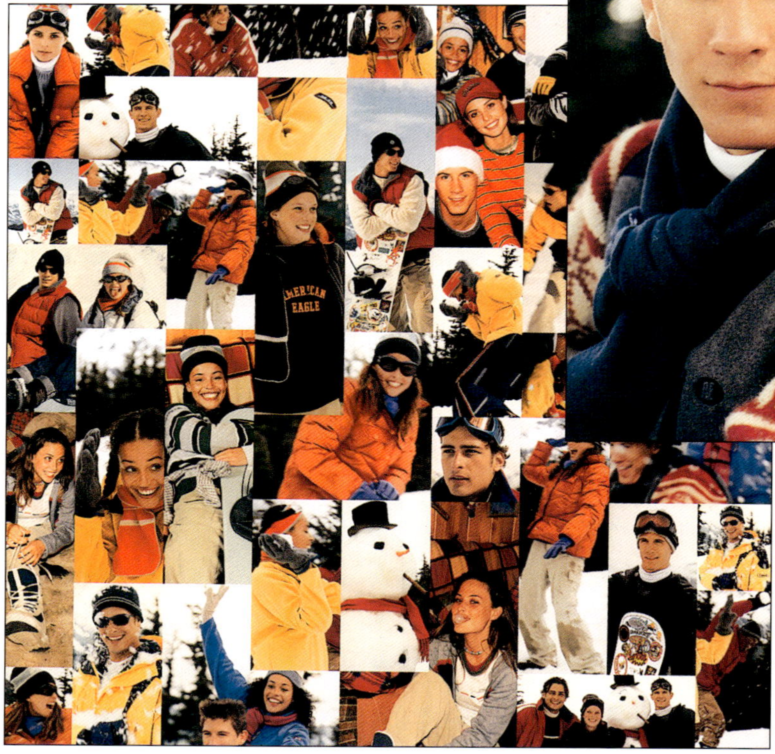

EVERYTHING ABOUT American Eagle Outfitters' 56-page holiday catalog and mailers is good fun. *And* smart marketing. Unlike Abercrombie & Fitch with which it's sometimes compared, American Eagle Outfitters seems to make a point of diversity. The catalog is packed with a wide variety of offerings.

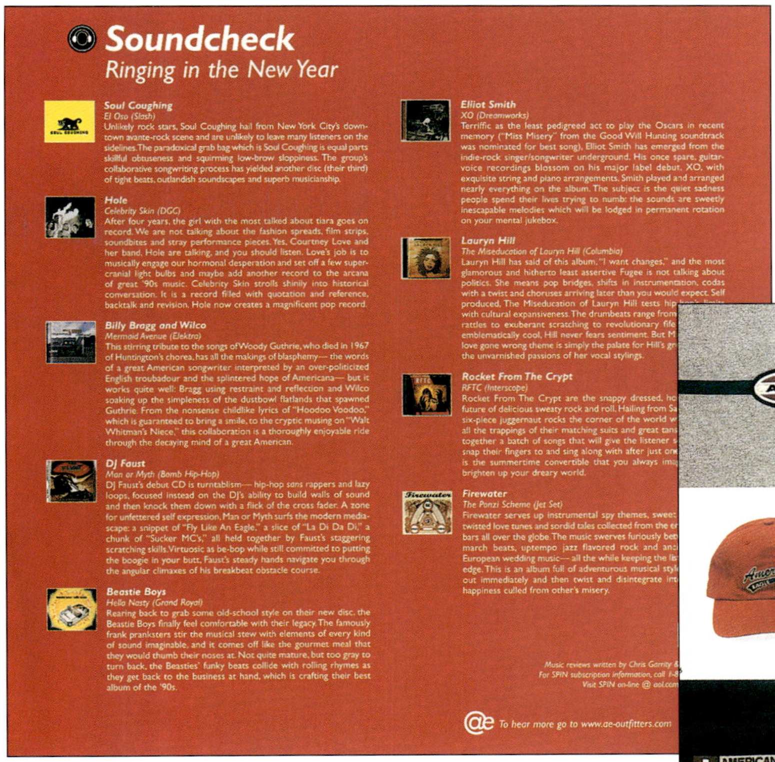

AMERICAN EAGLE OUTFITTERS

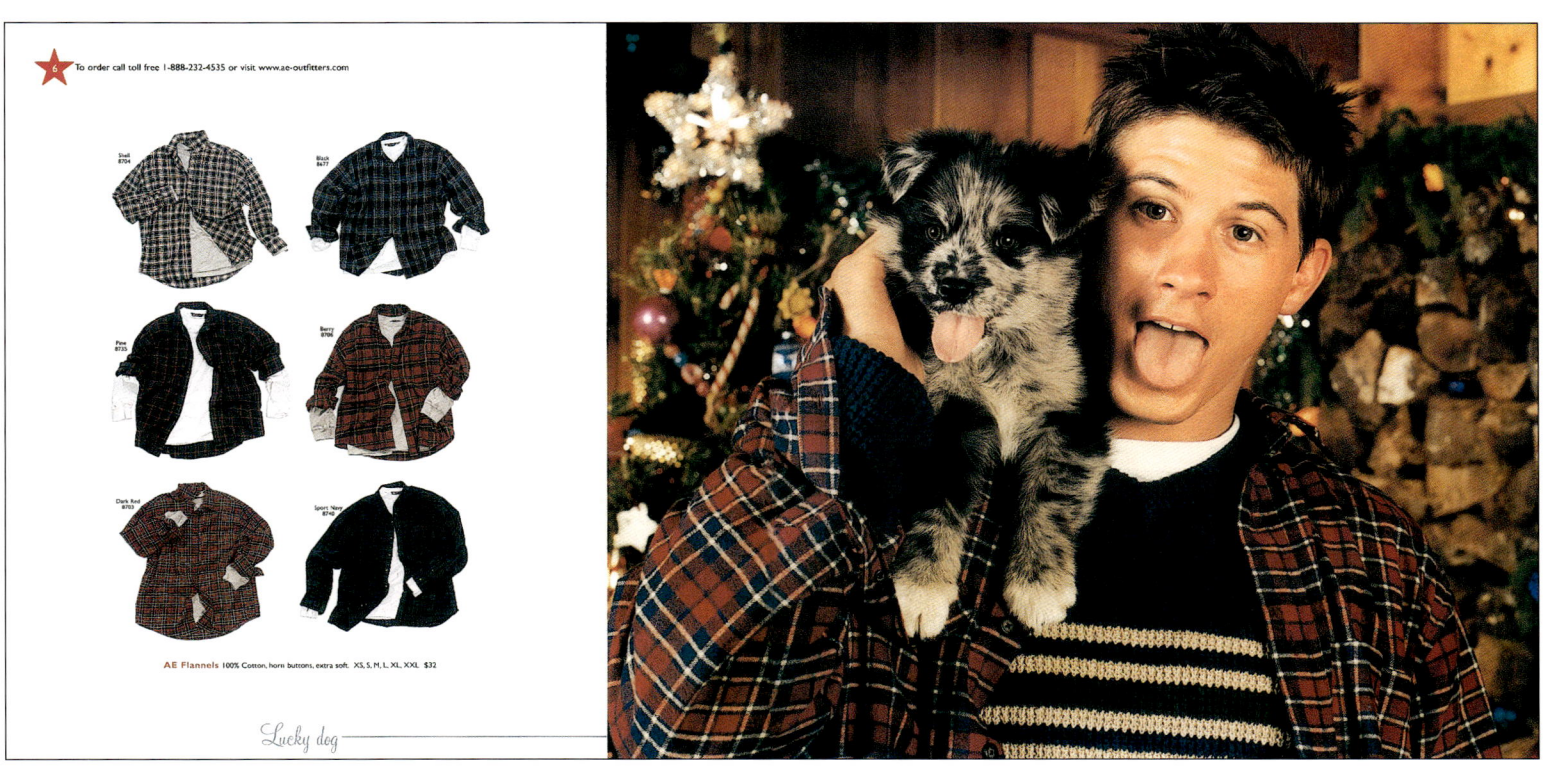

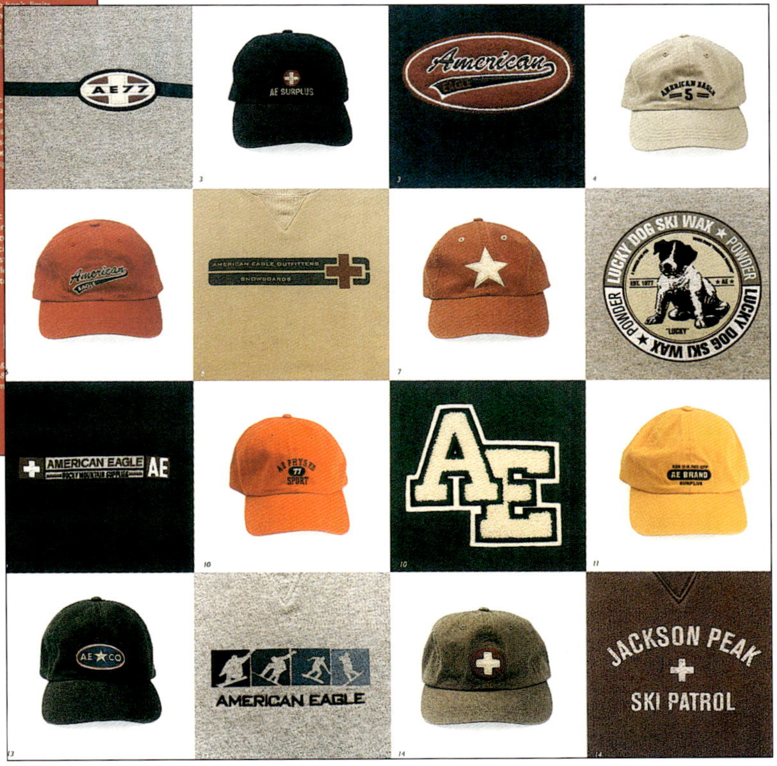

There are reviews of CDs, movies, books, an interview with a pop star, a size chart with instructions for measuring, a limited edition snowboarding poster, horoscopes, and lest we forget, lots of colorful sportswear to live it up in. The items look terrific, whether photographed on models or off-figure,

AMERICAN EAGLE OUTFITTERS

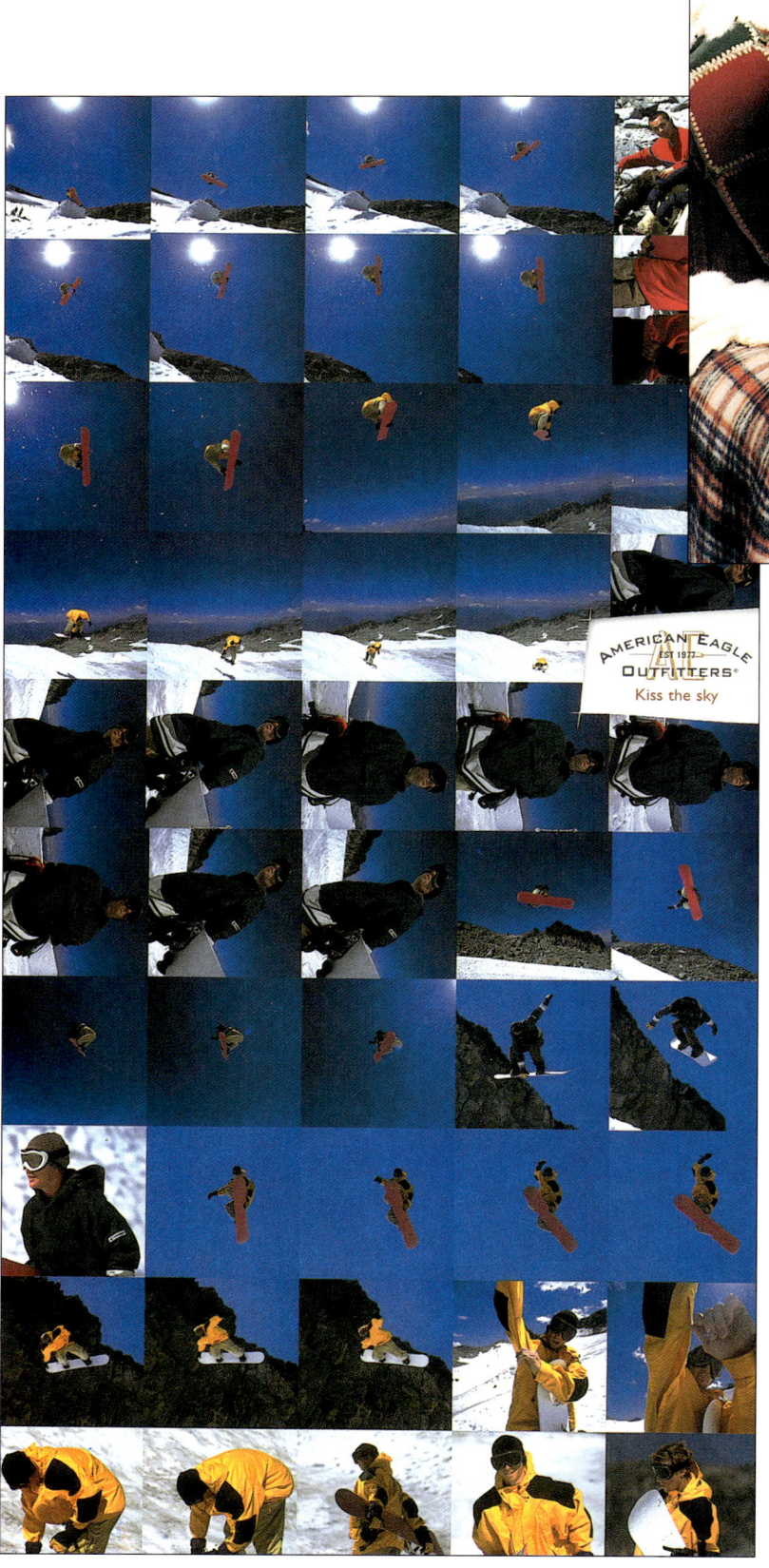

where they appear animated. In fact, the whole catalog looks like it's jumping for joy. There's even an extra holiday treat for those placing an order online — a "Shop In Your Underwear" mousepad.

Fun to look at, fun to read, right down to the final page where accompanying the usual credits are lists headed "Sounds that inspired the making of this book" and "Things consumed during the making of this book."

American Eagle Outfitters gets a lot of mileage from the catalog shoot. The photos are used in various ways in its direct mailer pieces. The mailers are unusual in that while the format is the same, the photos aren't.

AMERICAN EAGLE OUTFITTERS

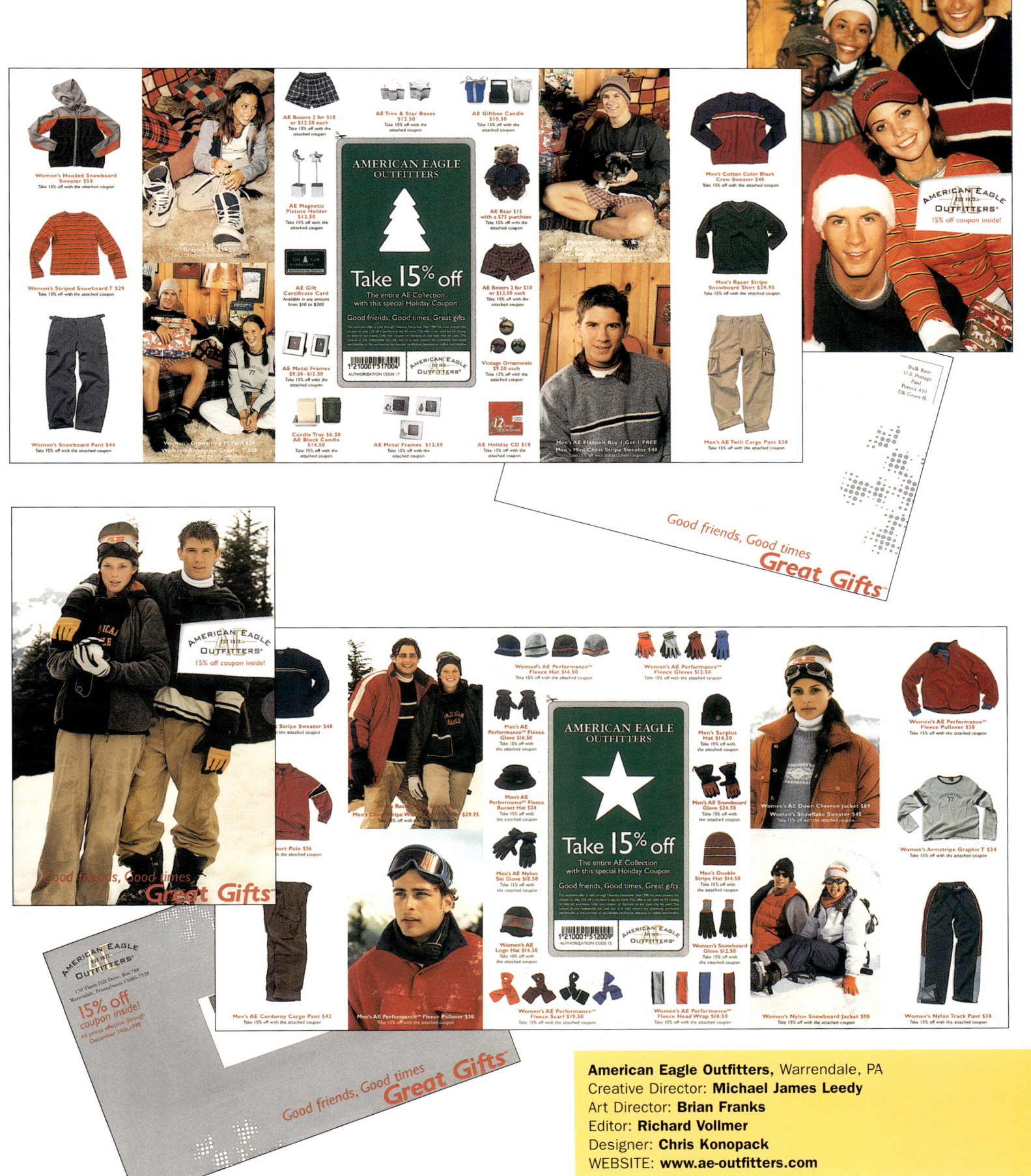

American Eagle Outfitters, Warrendale, PA
Creative Director: **Michael James Leedy**
Art Director: **Brian Franks**
Editor: **Richard Vollmer**
Designer: **Chris Konopack**
WEBSITE: www.ae-outfitters.com

BERGDORF GOODMAN

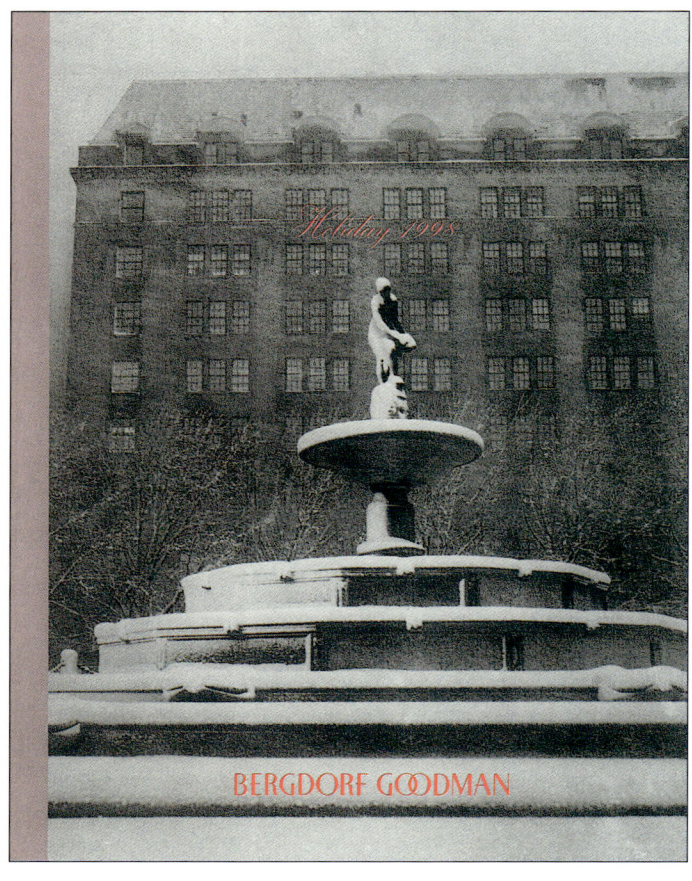

The cover was a production in itself, the result of a five-color process using b/w half-tone art, PMS colors, screens and half-tones.

THE CHRISTMAS CATALOG, without question the most important catalog of the year, is a mammoth undertaking—a complex process that by its very magnitude boggles the mind. Between meeting with management, developing the creative, working with vendors, getting the right items, coordinating the shoot, trying to "think Christmas" and stay cool when the season says something else entirely, producing a Christmas catalog is quite an accomplishment. To do it according to plan with style and panache can feel

A Christmas Spectacular

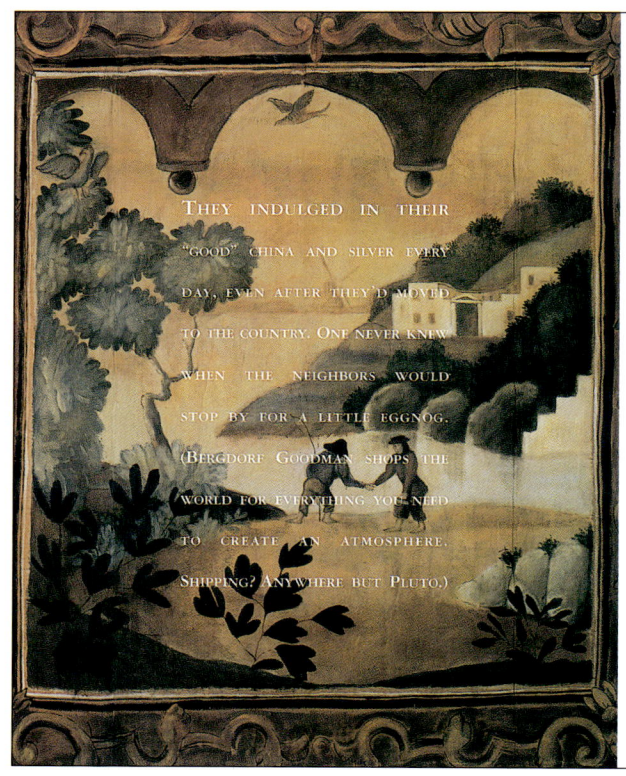

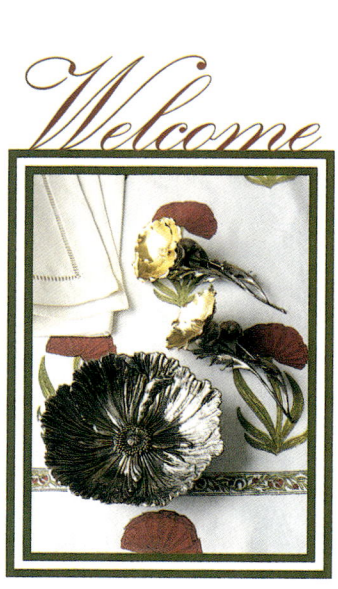

BERGDORF GOODMAN

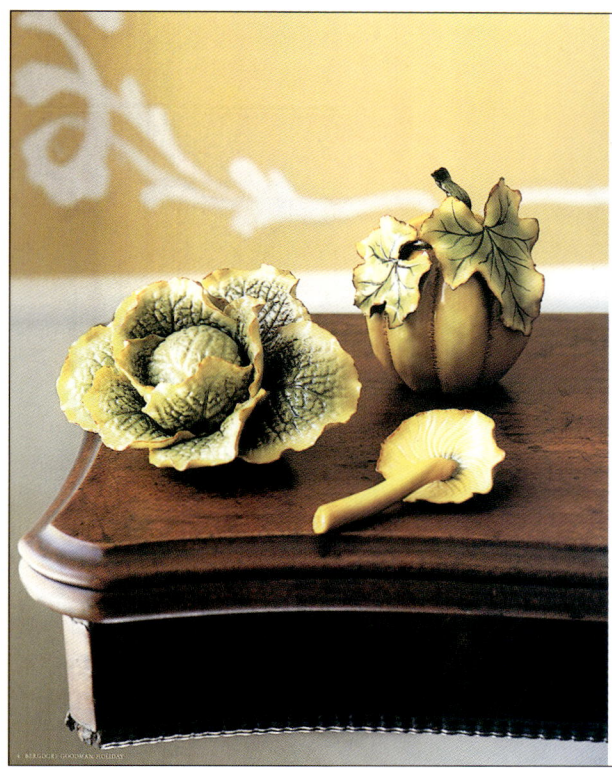
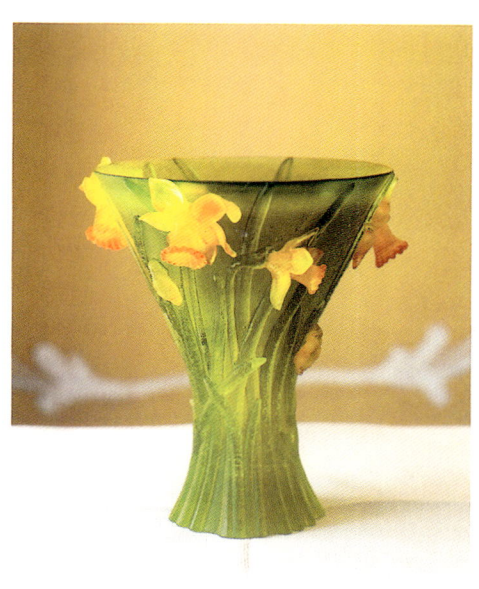

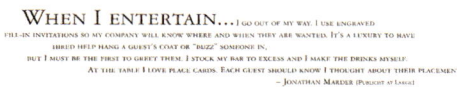

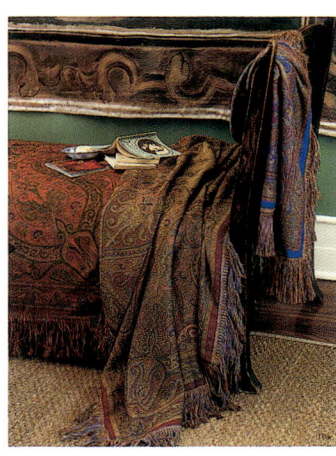
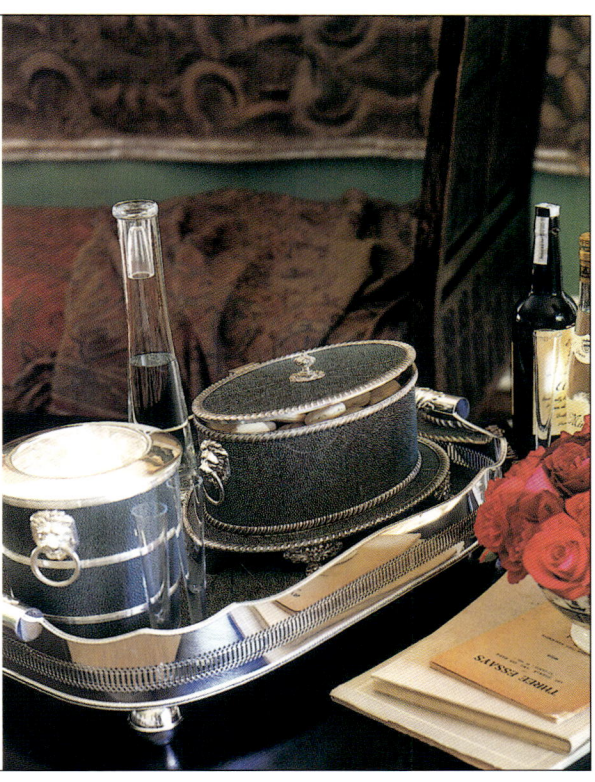

like a miracle, which is part of what Christmas is all about anyway.

Done in house, Bergdorf Goodman's Holiday 1998 catalog is both elegant and inventive. In this case, you definitely can judge a book by its cover. Shimmering in silver, the luminously romantic photograph depicts Manhattan at its most magical, heralding more treasures to come. Inside are 134 pages that while visually related… are never predictable. As Rebecca Wong Young, Bergdorf's creative director, says when enumerating the various creative talent — photographers, stylists,

BERGDORF GOODMAN

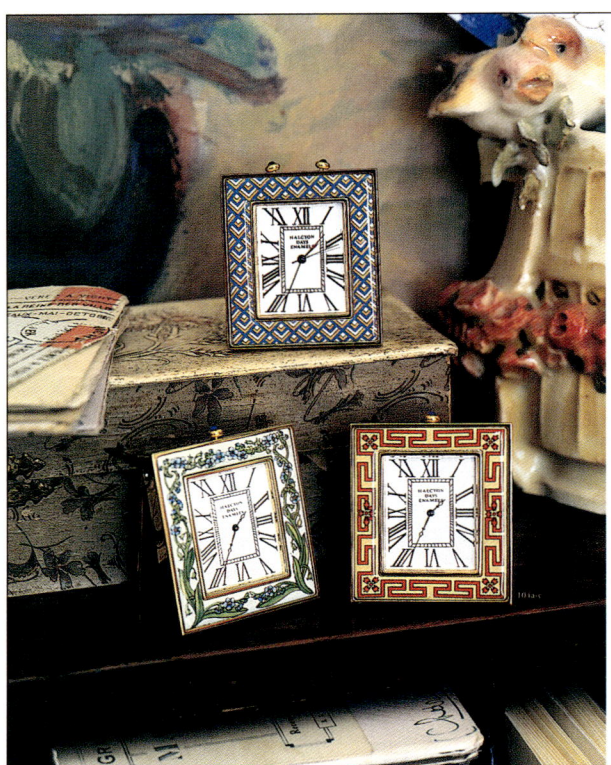

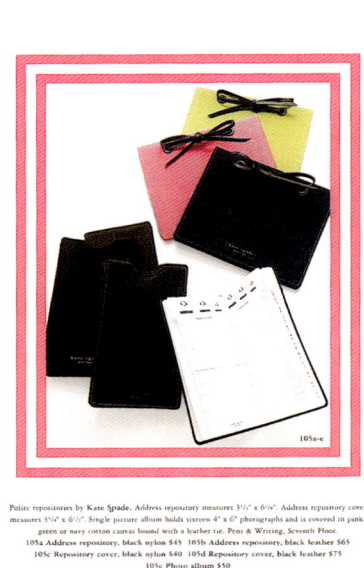

Petite repositories by Kate Spade. Address repository measures 3½" x 6⅛". Address repository cover measures 3⅝" x 6½". Single picture album holds sixteen 4" x 6" photographs and is covered in pink, green or navy cotton canvas bound with a leather tie. Pens & Writing, Seventh Floor.
105a Address repository, black nylon $45 105b Address repository, black leather $65
105c Repository cover, black nylon $40 105d Repository cover, black leather $75
105e Photo album $50

Opposite page: Petite clocks by Halcyon Days suit desktop, side table or bedside. Enameled cases with integral hinged brass stands and accurate quartz movements. 2" high x 1½" wide. Made in England. Stationery Gifts, Seventh Floor.
104a Art Deco style clock in blue/yellow $225 104b Greek key clock in red/yellow $225
104c Forget-me-not clock in green $225

While frames are a familiar graphic, in Bergdorf's artful hands, they become a fashion statement.

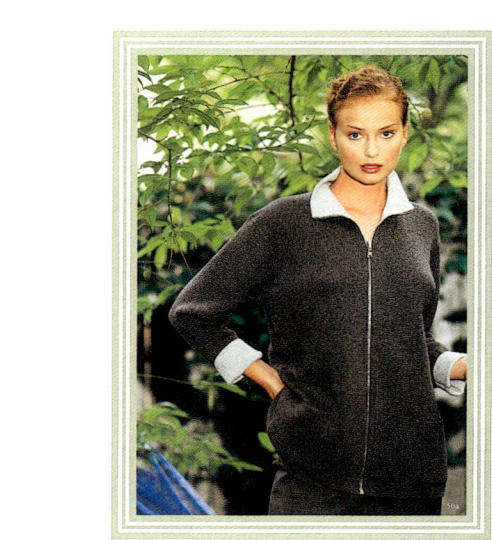

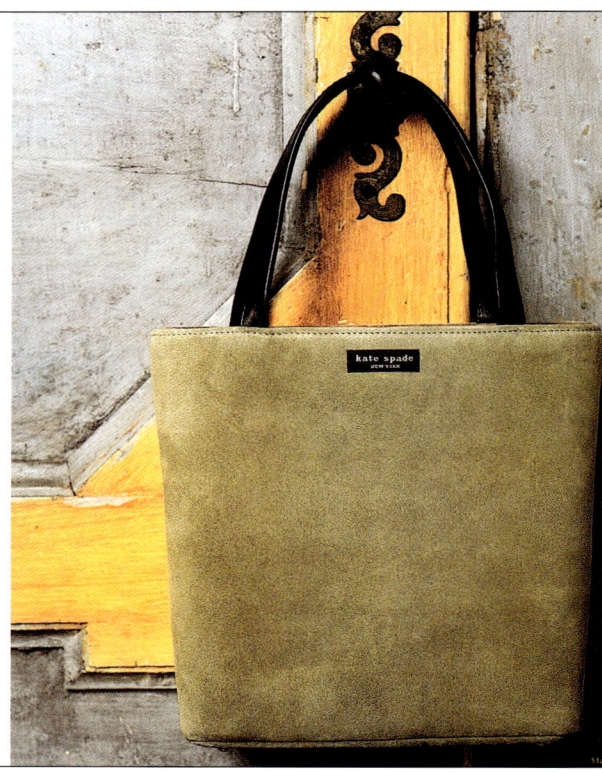

Reversible cashmere by Malo. Zip-front jacket, with just a hint of Lycra® spandex for shape, reverses from medium grey to light grey. Made in Italy for sizes S,M,L. Designer Sportswear, Third Floor.
96a Jacket $1,475

Opposite page: Fresh color from Kate Spade. Italian calf suede handbag in our exclusive shade of lime. Also available in black. 10" high x 12" wide x 3" deep. Made in the USA. Handbags, On Seve.
51a Handbag $275

illustrator, guest editors, etc.— who went into producing the catalog, "As you can imagine, the list goes on... I think it's one of the main reasons the book resulted in a rich, unformulated collection of pictures, stories, and above all, elegance that is uniquely Bergdorf Goodman."

Not surprisingly, it took many months to produce. According to Young, shooting began last May.

Holiday 1998 was mailed nationally and internationally to the Japanese market, and, yes — it was done on time.

BERGDORF GOODMAN

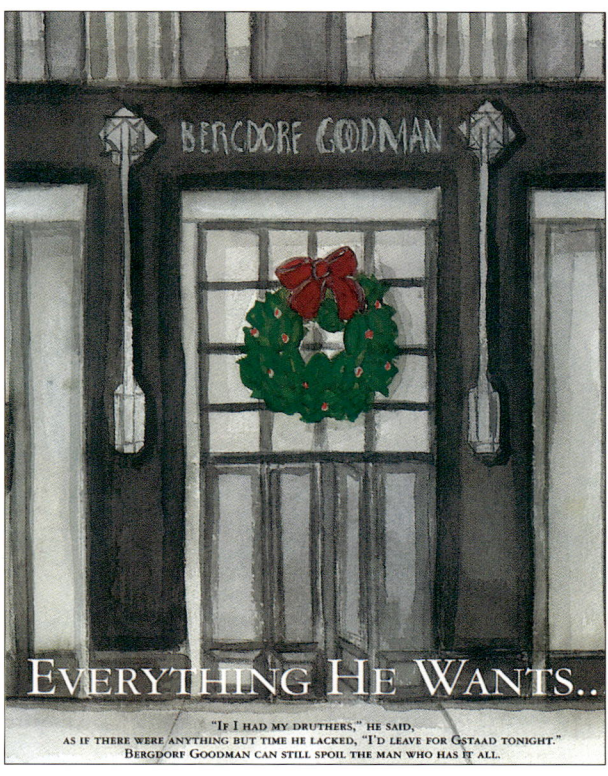

Distinctive illustrations of Bergdorf's facade were used as dividers to separate the women's and men's sections. The copy is written in the same personalized style used in Bergdorf's newspaper ads.

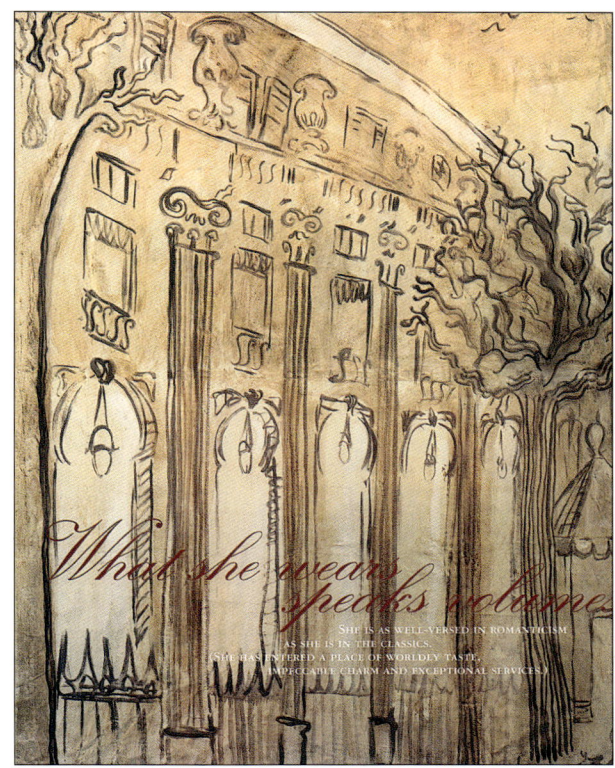

Bergdorf Goodman, New York, NY
AGENCY: **In-house**
VP, CREATIVE DIRECTOR : **Rebecca Wong Young**
ASSOCIATE CREATIVE DIRECTOR: **Laren Stover**
COPY DIRECTOR: **Laren Stover**
ART DIRECTOR: **Elizabeth Dougherty**
PRODUCER: **Jonathan Carr**

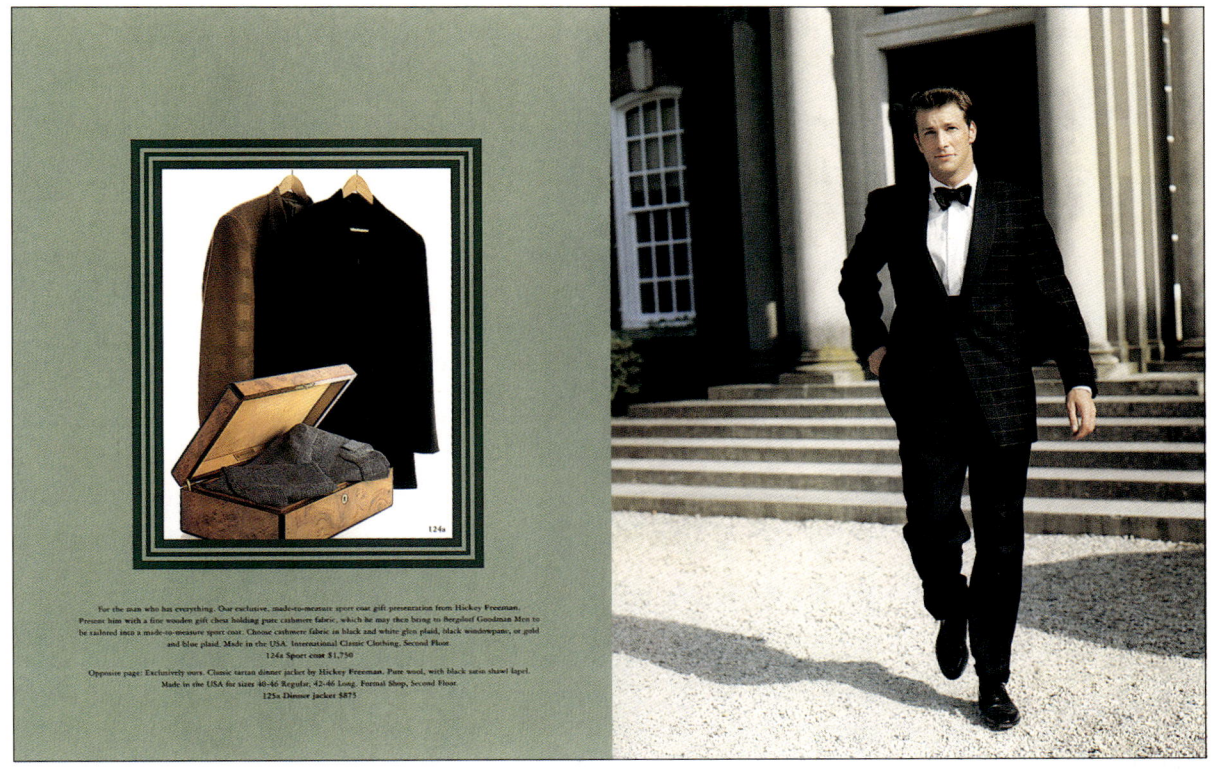

New Strategy for Holiday

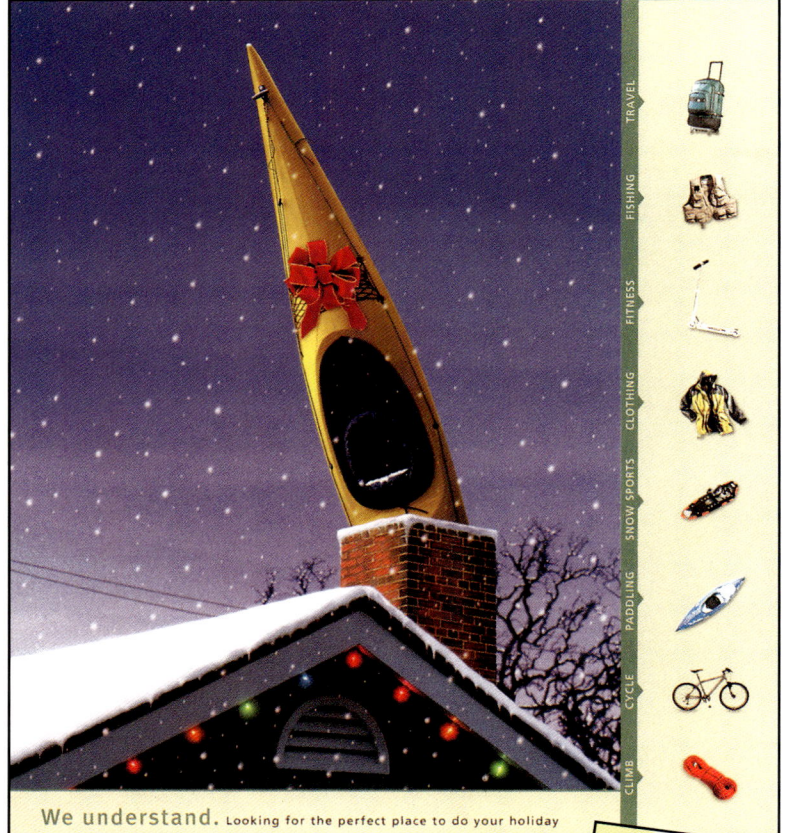

RECREATIONAL Equipment Incorporated (REI) has been around for many Christmases past. The company was founded as a cooperative in 1938 by a group of Pacific Northwest mountaineers seeking quality climbing equipment. The first 23 members each contributed one dollar to build group-buying power. At the end of the first year, 82 members received dividends.

REI is still a cooperative. In fact, it's one of "The 100 Best Companies to Work for in America" (Fortune magazine, 1998 and 1999) with a board of directors elected annually by REI members.

Anyone can shop at REI, but cooperative members—who pay a lifetime $15 fee to join—receive a portion of the cooperative's profits each year based on a percentage of their purchases.

Christmas notwithstanding, REI stores (there are some 60 of them in 24 states) are festive places to visit any season of the year. With a variety of facilities for testing equipment—including bike test trails, climbing pinnacles and camp stove demonstration tables—for visitors, being in the store is an experience in itself.

This past holiday season, REI embarked on a new adventure driven by the desire to expand the brand beyond cooperative members. Whereas the company traditionally had done most of its advertising and promotion in house, in light of the fact that competition in the outdoor equipment arena was on the rise, it turned to Copacino, the Seattle agency that had been hired to do work on its website.

"They felt that they needed to be more aggressive," says Jim Copacino, creative director. "REI

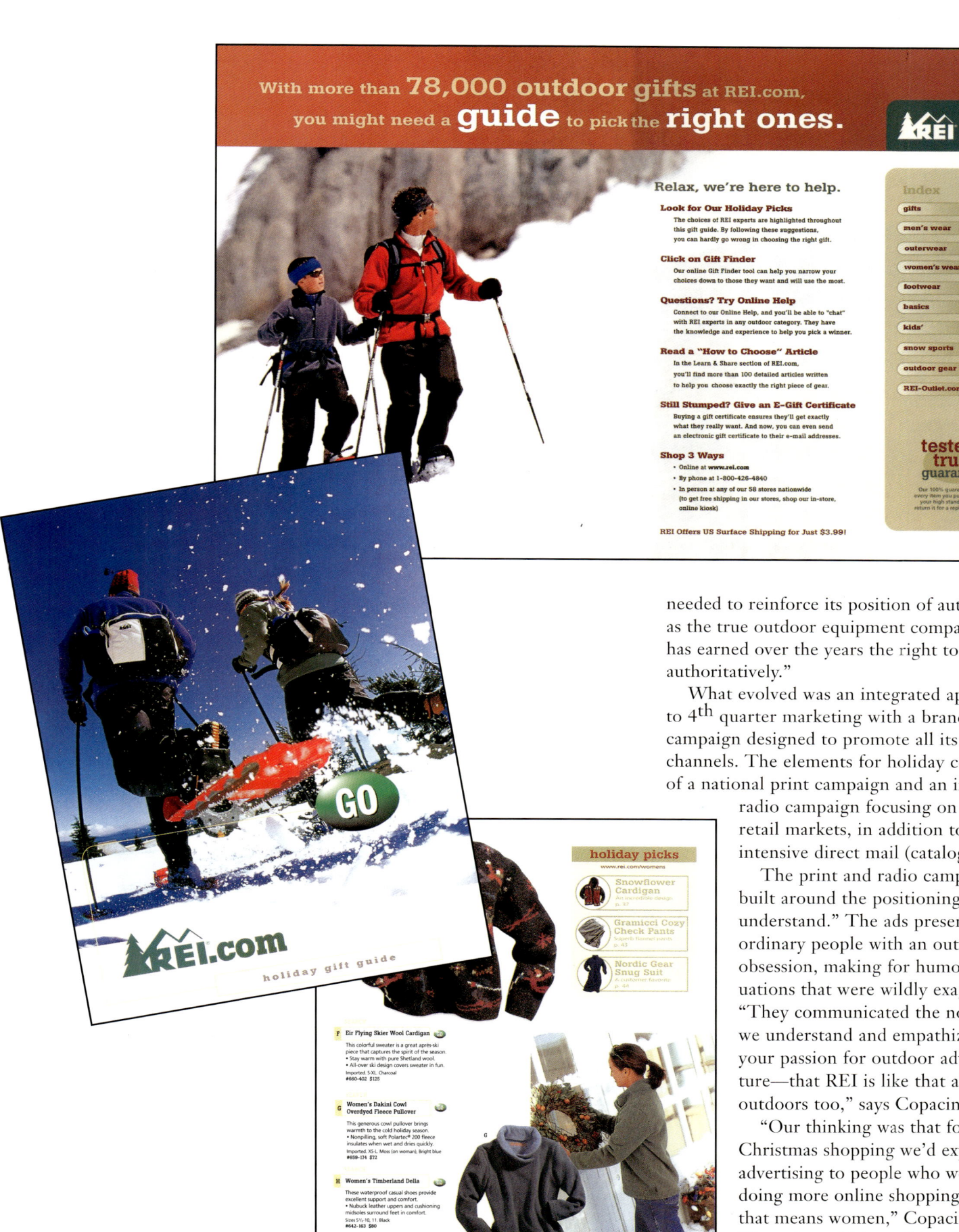

needed to reinforce its position of authenticity as the true outdoor equipment company that has earned over the years the right to speak authoritatively."

What evolved was an integrated approach to 4th quarter marketing with a branding campaign designed to promote all its sales channels. The elements for holiday consisted of a national print campaign and an integrated radio campaign focusing on key retail markets, in addition to an intensive direct mail (catalog) effort.

The print and radio campaign was built around the positioning "we understand." The ads presented ordinary people with an outdoor obsession, making for humorous situations that were wildly exaggerated. "They communicated the notion of we understand and empathize with your passion for outdoor adventure—that REI is like that about the outdoors too," says Copacino.

"Our thinking was that for Christmas shopping we'd expand our advertising to people who would be doing more online shopping, and that means women," Copacino notes. The print, which traditionally had focused on pure outdoor recreation type magazines, ran in more than a dozen national magazines such as *Rolling Stone*, *Outside*, *Men's Health*

REI

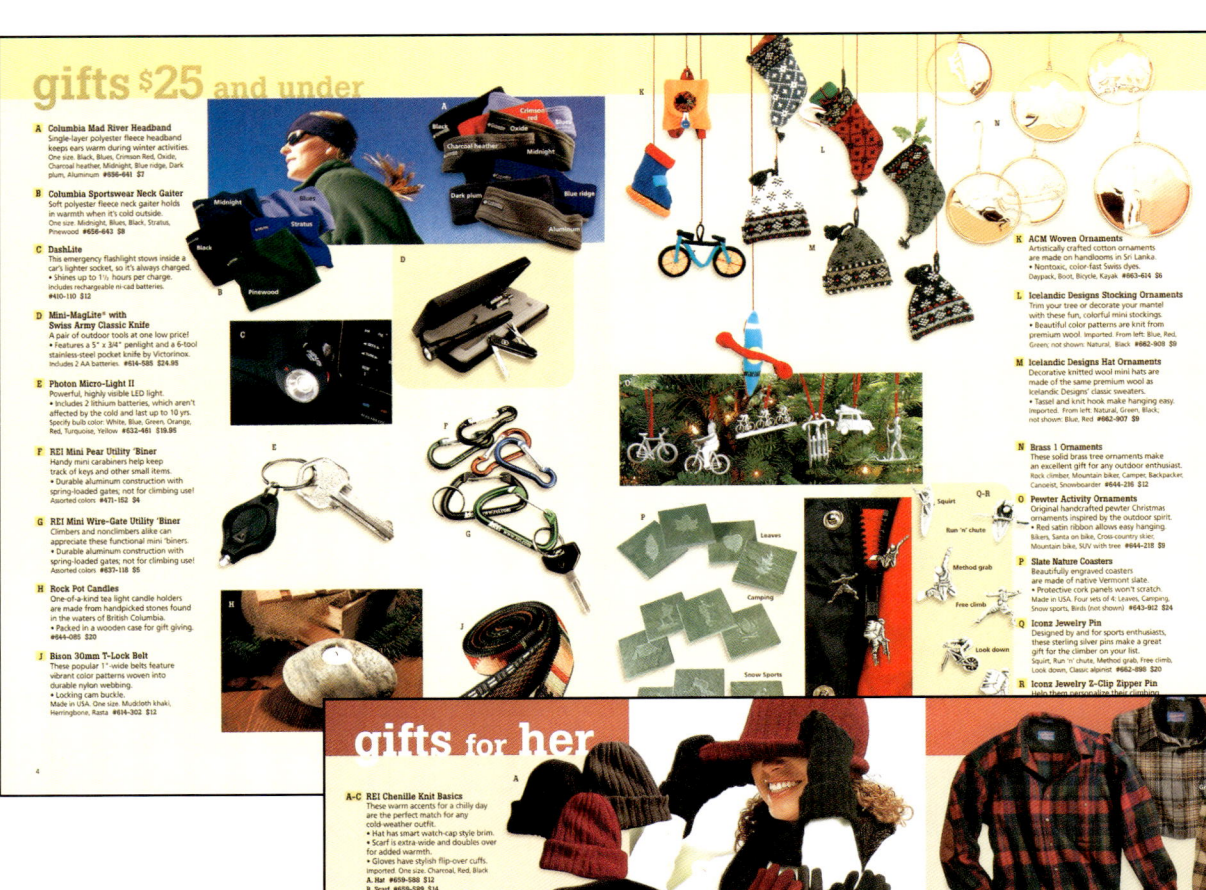

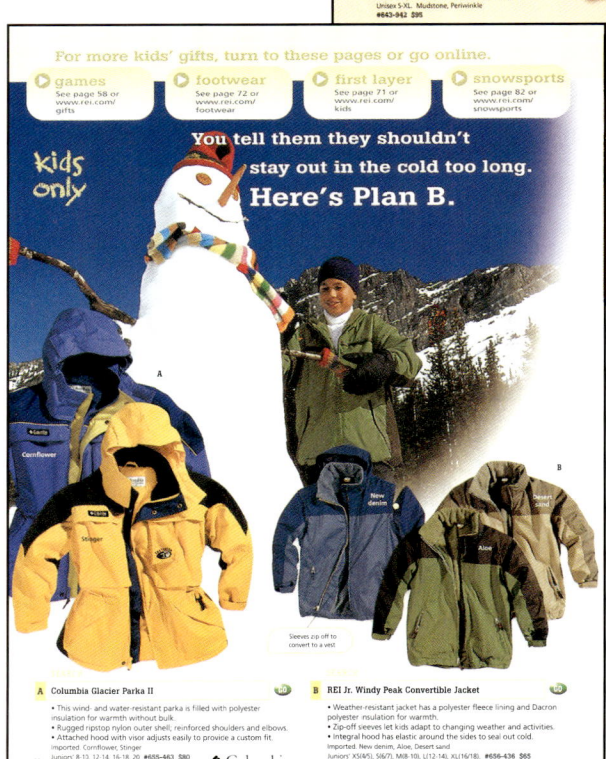

REI

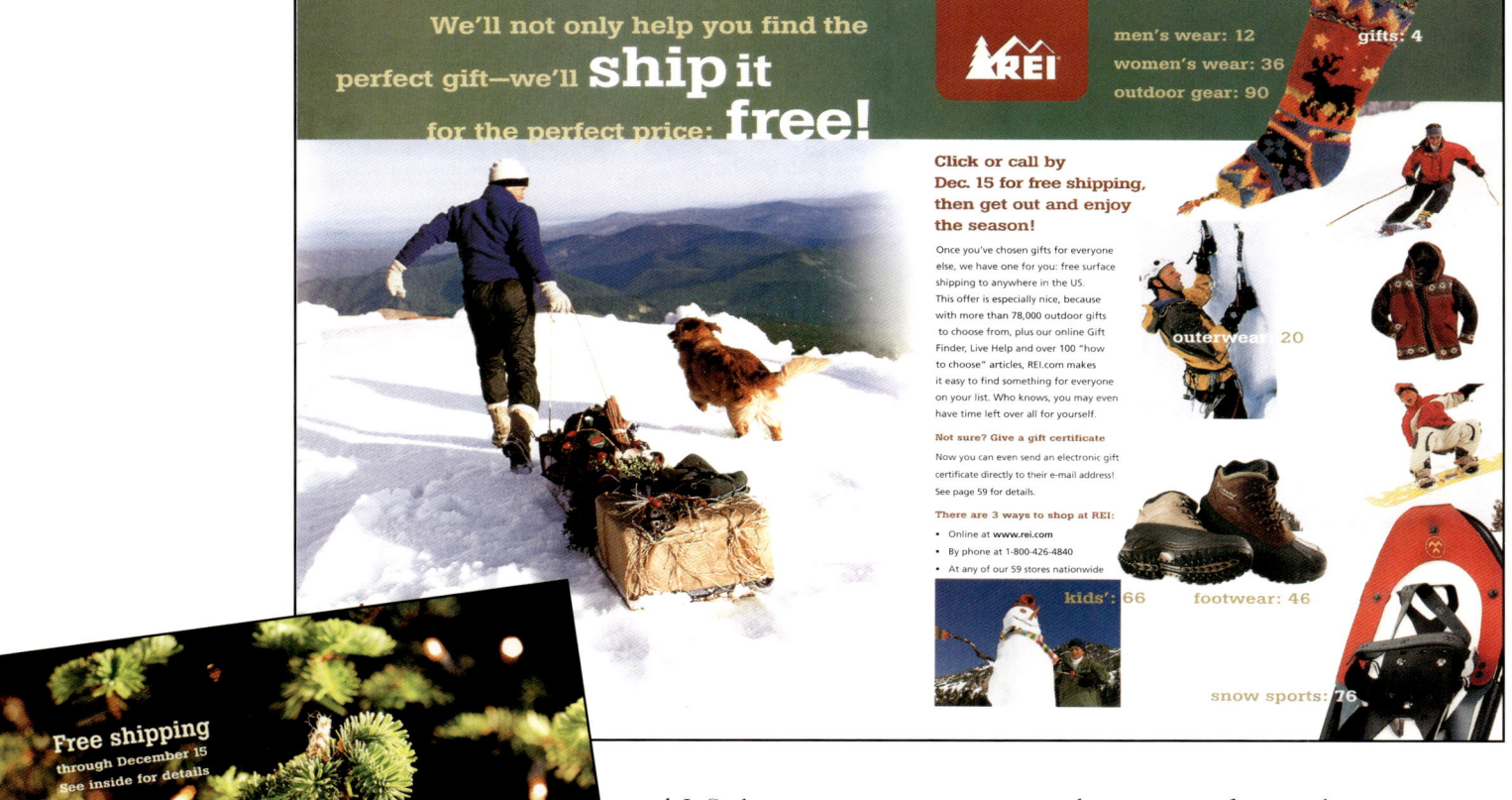

and *InStyle*.

Newspaper ads ran in December to take advantage of the holiday season and to build and retain momentum. A series of three insertions (a version of the kayak in the chimney ad) ran in daily newspapers in Denver, Seattle, Minneapolis, Portland, (OR), Phoenix, Salt Lake City, Atlanta, and San Francisco. "These are highly wired cities for Internet penetration, and usage in these markets is higher than the national norm," Copacino explains.

These efforts complemented the radio spots, which also aired in December in those markets. The overall focus was a gift-giving message.

The catalogs, which were done in-house, were filled with gift-giving suggestions, sometimes broken down into "Gifts under $25, Gifts under $50," etc. Leafing through the catalogs, one could easily find gifts for just about any-one who ever set a foot outdoors.

It's interesting to note that in terms of the portion of creative and marketing REI does internally, the company is a cooperative in more ways than one. It is so much a team effort, in fact, that no single person is credited with it.

A spokesperson for the in-house work notes that "a total of 2,321,302 catalogs were mailed largely to our online and 800-number mail-order shoppers with a small percent of those being best customers who shop our retail stores." The mailing also included some prospects from purchased lists.

There were additional efforts to promote holiday gift giving according to REI. "We offered free shipping starting the day after Thanksgiving through the 15th of December. We had signage in the stores and advertised this on the website as well as in the catalog, opt-in email and in banner advertising."

REI, Kent, WA
AGENCY (catalog): **In-house**
AGENCY (print ads/radio): **Copacino,** Seattle
CREATIVE DIRECTOR: **Jim Copacino**
BROADCAST PRODUCER: **Patti Emery**
COPYWRITER: **Ben Steele**
ART DIRECTOR: **Jerry Kopec**
MODEL MAKER: **Mike Dillon**
PHOTOGRAPHERS: **Phil Banko** (kayak), **Jane Armstrong** (wedding cake)

JACOBSON'S

Partnering for Excellence

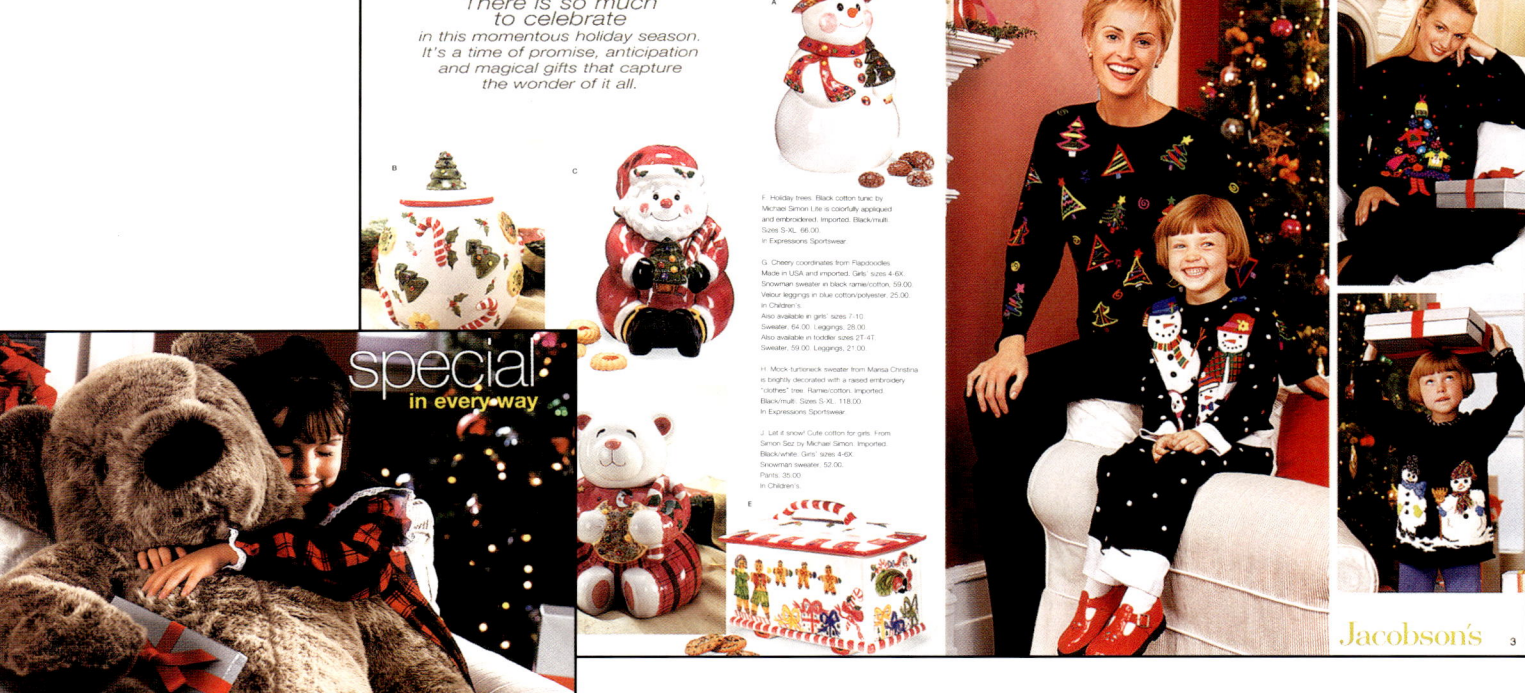

How important are covers? *Very*. This past fall/holiday will go down as having the all-time highest number of catalogs mailed. What happens when a household receives multiple catalogs in a day? The cover had better stand out! Jacobson's cover attracts attention, gives you a feeling of what the catalog is about, identifies the store and gets the reader inside. The catalog has something else vital going for it—the Jacobson's name.

AS CRITICAL as fourth-quarter sales are to a retailer is how important a holiday catalog is and how it reflects the company.

Jacobson's Holiday 1999 catalog, "Special in Every Way" (64 pages, 9" x 10¾"), goes a long way toward reinforcing the brand. This is a chain with a strong sense of who it is. "We are Family, Friendly, Fun, Fashion, Forward," says Kit Spoelstra, vice president, sales promotion director. "We offer fashion leadership and distinctive quality merchandise that gives customers the feeling our items were personally selected for them."

It's not surprising Jacobson's knows a lot about itself. Established in 1868, the six-state chain is moving on a number of fronts, not the least of which is an extensive catalog program. Jacobson's created 30 books in 1999 and anticipates approximately the same number this year.

How do they approach it? Jacobson's involves its merchants (resources) significantly in putting the catalog together. It acts as its own in-house agency, but also works with several agency partners. Spoelstra describes the process: "It starts with us 'Partnering for Excellence' by having our merchants choose the most unique, quality items for our discerning customers. We let the merchandise be our creative lead, and our layout and look is a reflection of our merchandise. With our strategy of 'Partnering for Excellence,' each book is a union of efforts representing merchants, marketing (inclusive of agency partners) and stores, with customers as our key focus."

The creative strategizing for holiday 1999 started January 1. The first order of business was meeting with the agency partners to decide who would be awarded the holiday book. New York–based Marke Communications got the nod.

"Our creative process begins with a 'turn-in' session, where our merchants present items to a review team, whose members include representatives from our partner agency, our in-house agency and Jacobson's executives," Spoelstra explains. "We then paginate the book with merchant input."

JACOBSON'S

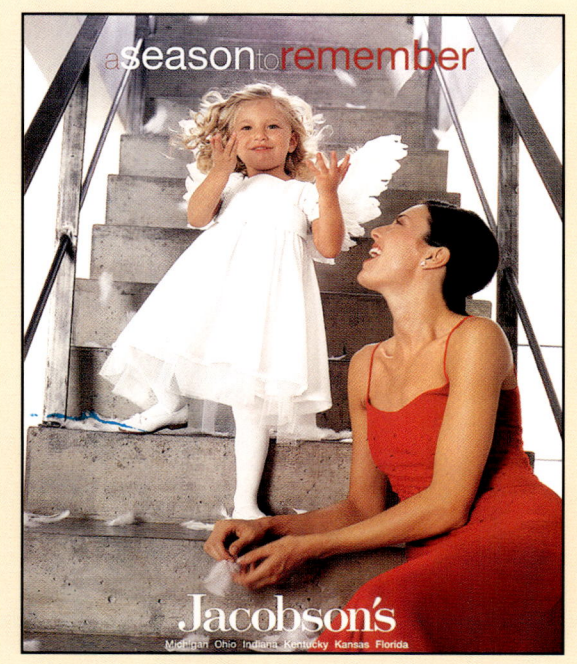
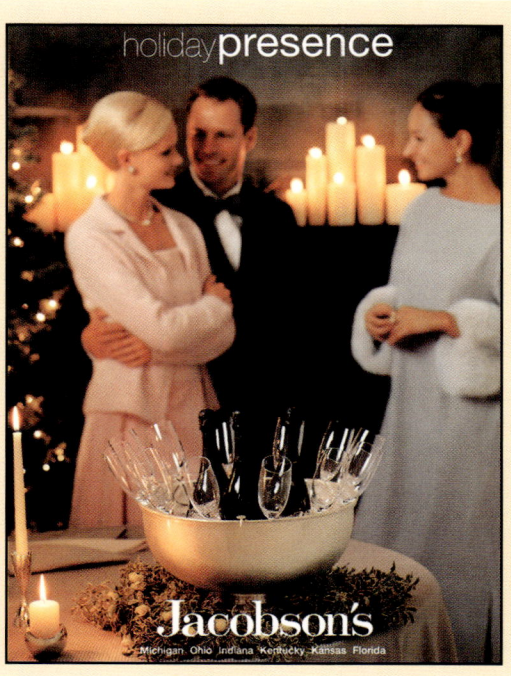

There's a carefully strategized build toward the big holiday book. A Season to Remember (left, 20 pages, 9" x 10½") was delivered at the end of September. Holiday Presence (right, 28 pages, 8⅜" x 10⅞") followed a week later.

After the turn-in and pagination, which took place for two days in mid-July, Marke Communications went to work on design, layout, photography and copy, with Jacobson's in-house agency providing creative overview and art direction throughout.

"We were especially fond of our holiday direct mail cover," says Spoelstra. "It captures the essence of what is a very special time for family and children."

Next was a meeting with the agency for film and copy review that included merchants.

Color separations were done in September and by November the holiday book was in the mail—en route to more than a half-million customers in all 24 markets, precisely as planned. Jacobson's uses its own database of existing customers and prospective customers within each market.

After that, visitors to the store would see the holiday cover poster at the entrance and around the store, along with Big Jake, the cover bear, at this home base in the children's area.

Meanwhile, Jacobson's continues to carry the holiday spirit forward and demonstrate being special in every way. When the holidays were over, there was a surplus of Big Jakes. Now the oversized teddy bear is serving as an ambassador of goodwill. Jacobson's donated more than 250 bears to charity organizations in all 24 of its markets.

The use of simple backgrounds and relaxed poses that are natural and inviting, as well as props, such as children and pets, capture the store's warmth and personality. The catalog is designed to serve primarily as a store traffic piece. There is no order form, but it does list an 800 number along with branch stores on the back cover.

Jacobson Stores Inc., Jackson, MI
EXECUTIVE VICE PRESIDENT MARKETING/STORES: **Jim Rodefeld**
VICE PRESIDENT, SALES PROMOTION DIRECTOR: **Kit Spoelstra**
AGENCY: **In-House**
AGENCY PARTNER: **Marke Communications**, New York
WEBSITE: **www.jacobsons.com**

ALLOY

All They Want for Christmas

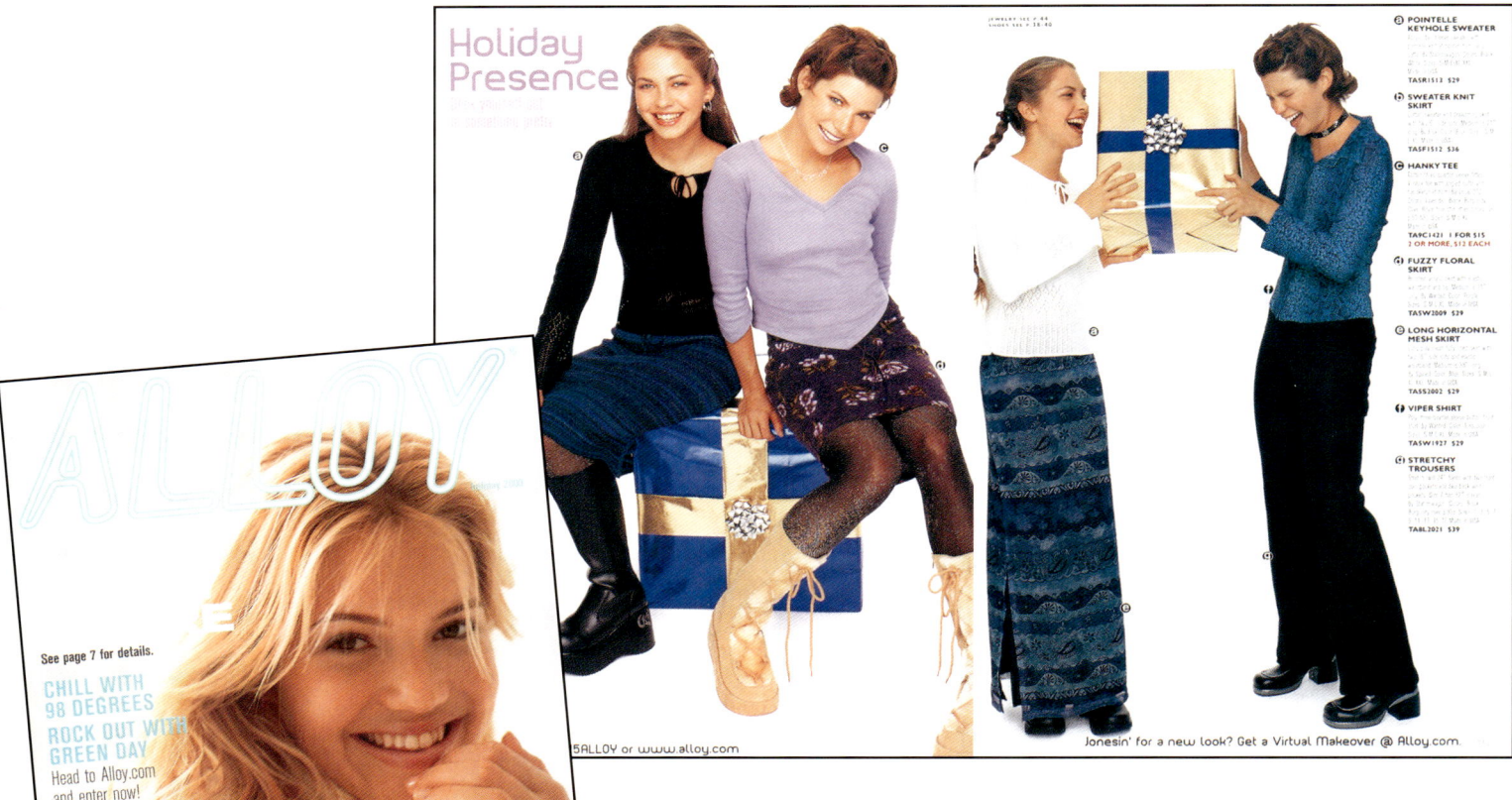

IN TODAY'S WORLD, there are few things changing faster than one, the tastes of teenagers and two, the fortunes of dot.com companies, many of whose sales performance during the holidays fell far short of expectations. Alloy is an example of a company that has managed to master both the vicissitudes of the teen market and the rose-colored-glasses aura of the Internet, becoming, in the process, one of the real dot.com success stories.

What has made Alloy succeed where so many others have failed? "We didn't get obsessed with just being online," says Matt Diamond, CEO. Instead the company designed a business model that focused on building a brand across multiple channels.

"We look at Alloy as a teen media company," says Diamond. "We're not just selling products, we also have the ability to connect with this demographic in the content area." That translates into a relationship with its young customers that is very attractive to advertisers and strategic partners.

"We have two very strong brands," says Diamond. "We have six million names in our database who either have bought from us or requested a catalog."

Becoming the convergence company it is today has been an interesting process. Alloy started as a website in 1996, but quickly decided it needed a real world presence. In 1997, the company launched a catalog. Then in 1999 another key piece of the business model was put in place when Alloy acquired CSS, a catalog company that sells apparel and sports equipment to teenage boys.

Alloy now has its own book imprint, some titles of which have been made into movies. The effort to attract more Gen Y boys to its catalog and website is working. (The split is currently 60% female, 40% male.) Moreover, the company has been receiving 4,000 to 5,000 new requests for catalogs every day.

Every month more than a million teens

The holiday catalog was used to promote features on the website.

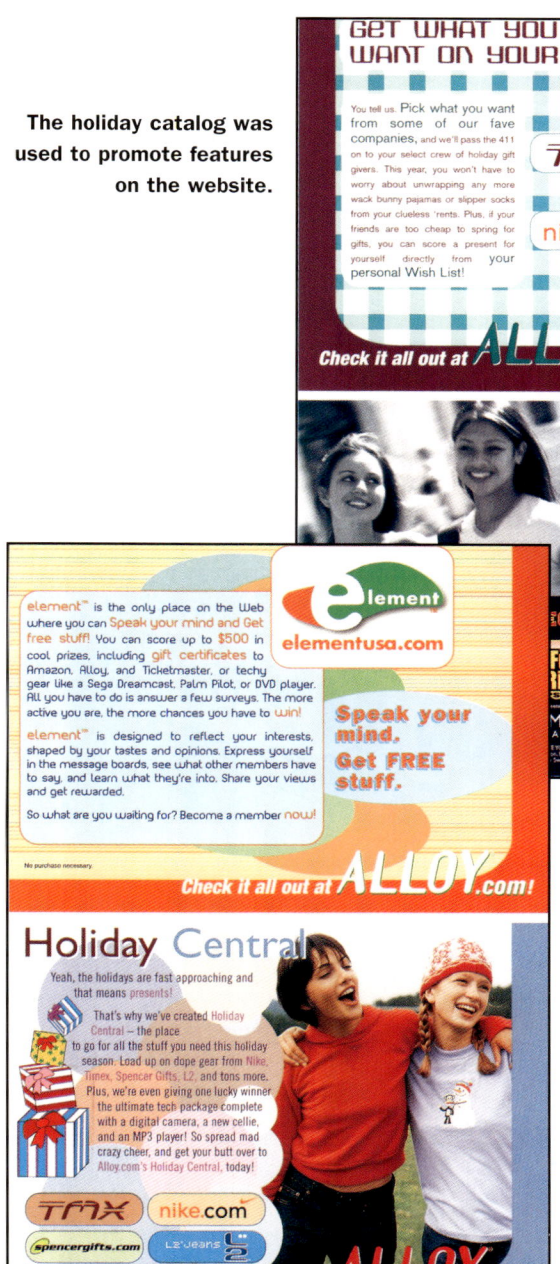

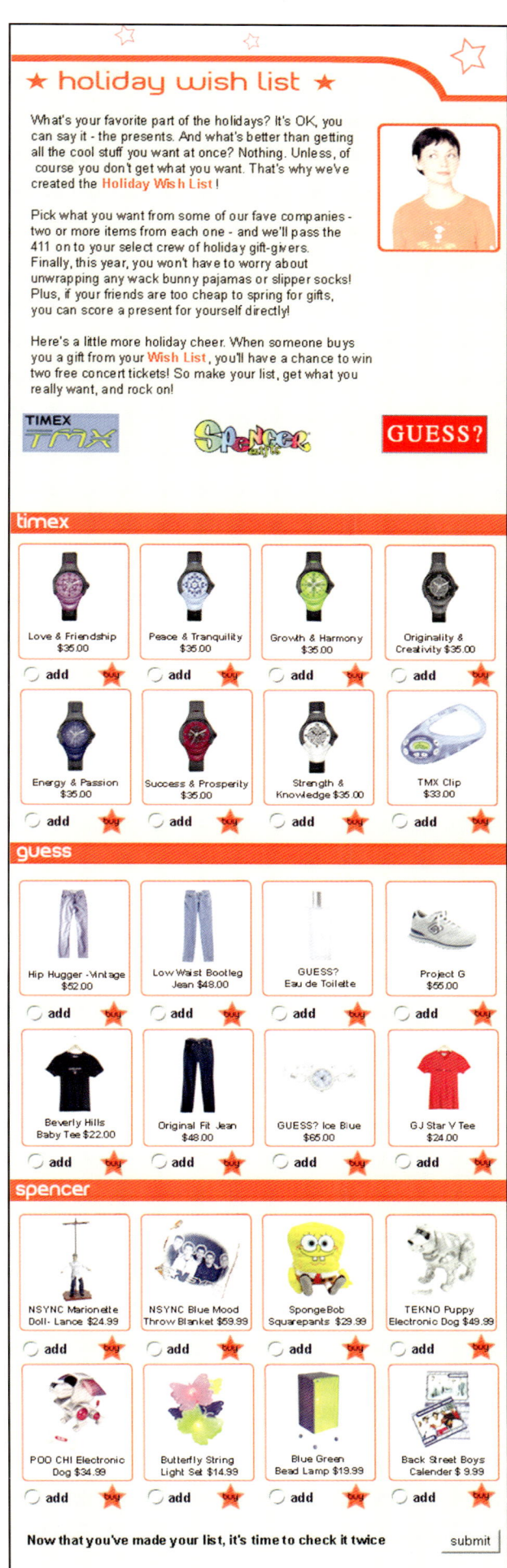

The website's holiday wish list made getting everything they wanted for Christmas easy.

log on to the Alloy website. The attractions are manifold—an identifiable community, content, commerce and entertainment—each with a dizzying array of choices. Some visitors to the website browse around. Others might take a quiz to win prizes, chat, shop, or play games. Diamond likens time spent on the website to very much what teenagers do at the mall. "They will chat with friends, check out the gossip, play a couple of games, browse around and shop."

So when the time came for these millions of Alloy-allied teenagers to do their holiday shopping, they did what they do virtually every day—checked out the catalog and browsed the website.

The Holiday catalog was mailed to five million teens. It had basically the same hip

ALLOY

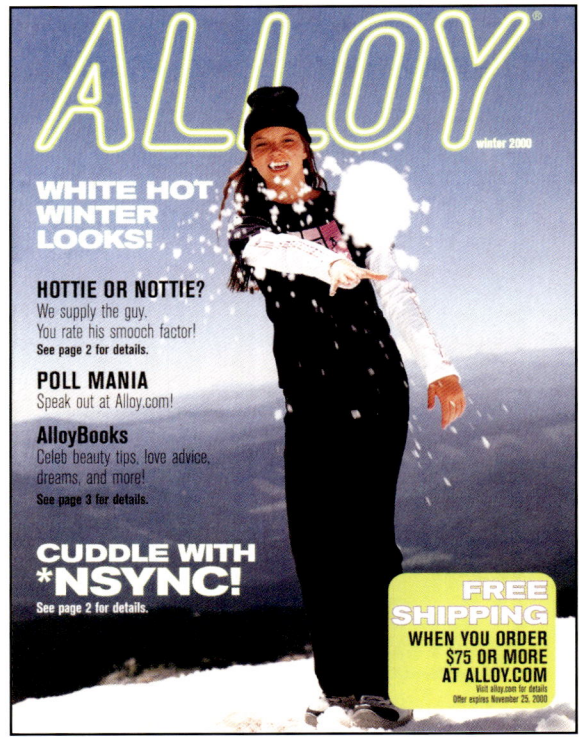
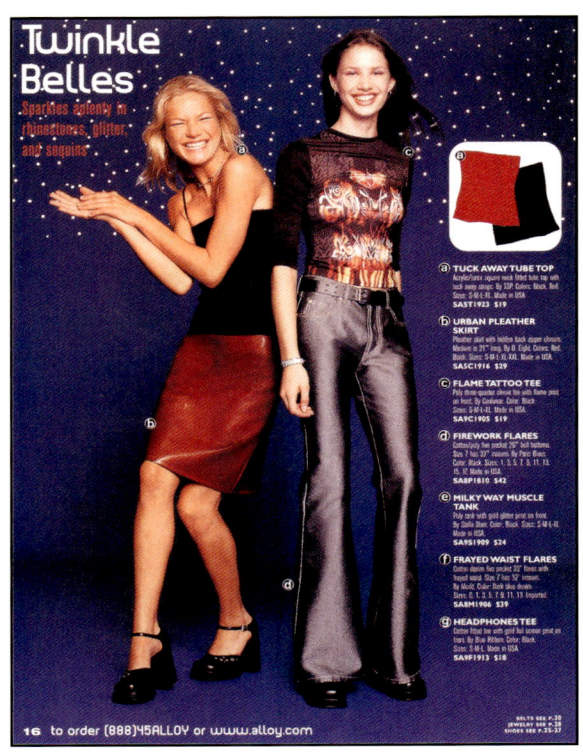

look of all Alloy catalogs with some notable additions. Besides being decked with everything a teen could want from the hottest holiday clothing and accessories to concert merchandise and bedroom furnishings, it presented the website's "Holiday Central" feature as the place to go for "all the stuff needed for the holidays." The idea was to send readers to the site for further shopping and the opportunity to win "the ultimate tech package—a digital camera, a new 'cellie' and an MP3 player."

The catalog also informed readers about the website's "Wish Lists," where teens could actually e-mail their parents and friends a list of what they wanted for the holidays. Apparently, that's just what its audience was wishing for.

According to Diamond, "The wish list was very successful. Over 100,000 e-mails were sent by teens to their parents. Thousands of orders were generated!"

Other holiday specific campaigns included opt-ins. One popular opt-in was the Wall-of-Fame program with Kodak. Users sent in holiday pictures of themselves showing them with what they were "famous for" for posting on Alloy's "Wall-of Fame."

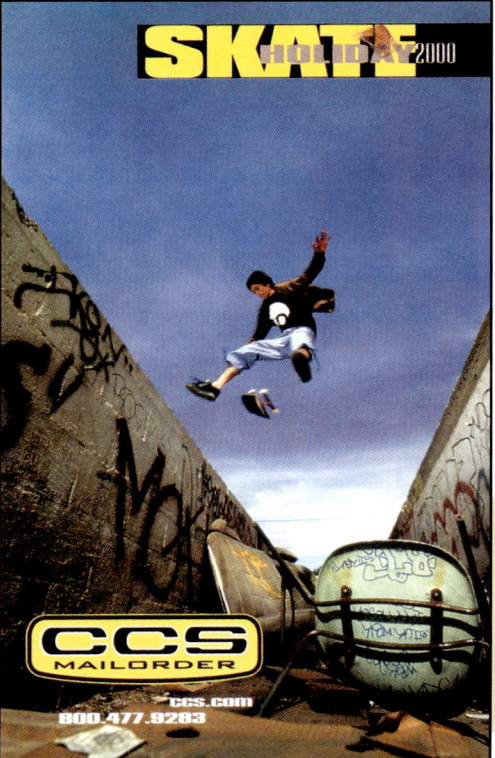
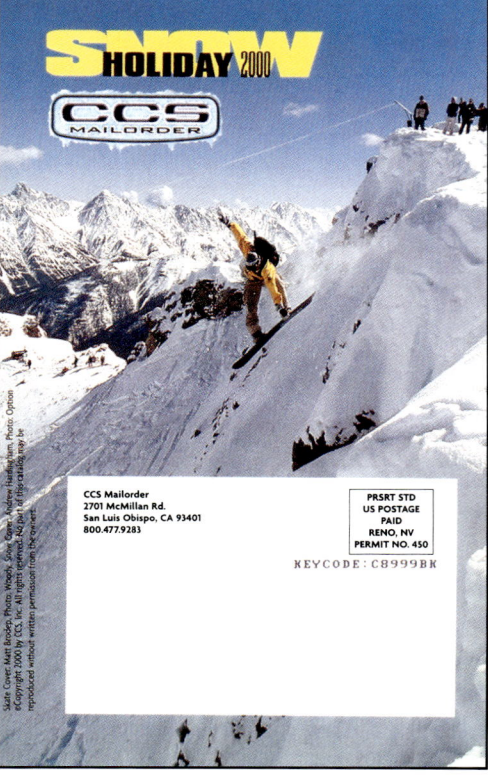

Alloy Online, New York
CEO: **Matt Diamond**
VP MARKETING AND SPONSORSHIPS:
Samantha Skey
CFO: **Sam Gradess**
COO **Jim Johnson**
AGENCY: **In-house**

TOYS "R" US

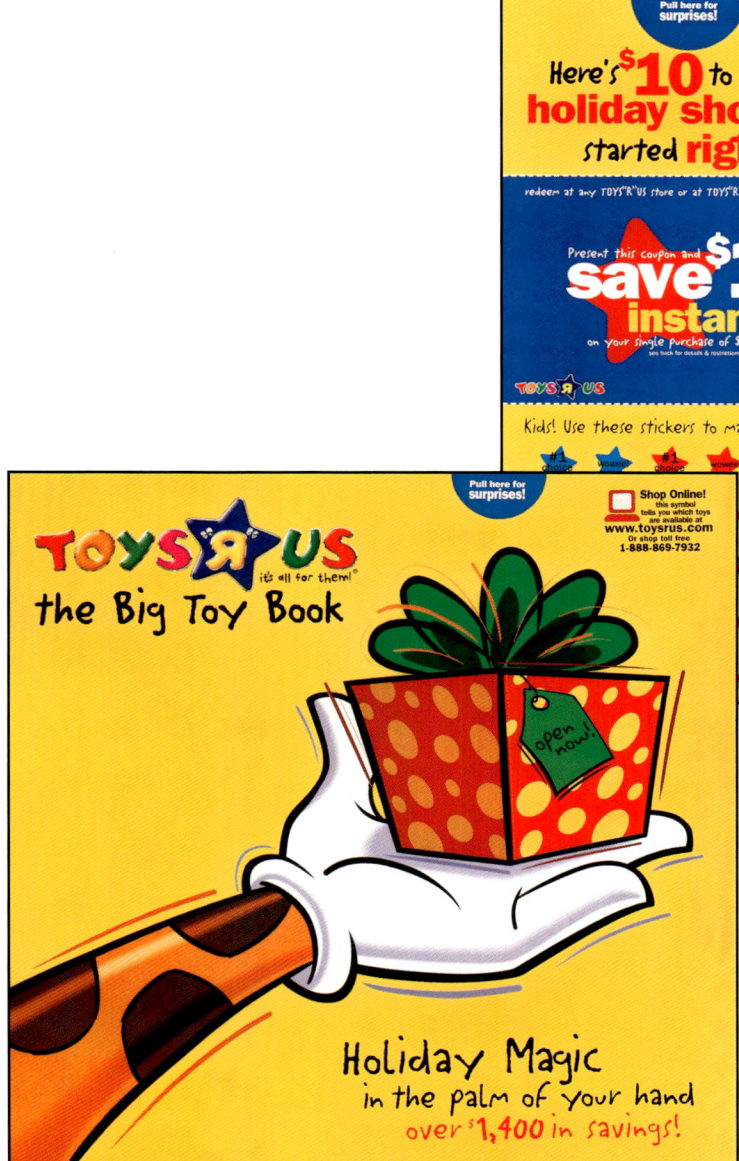

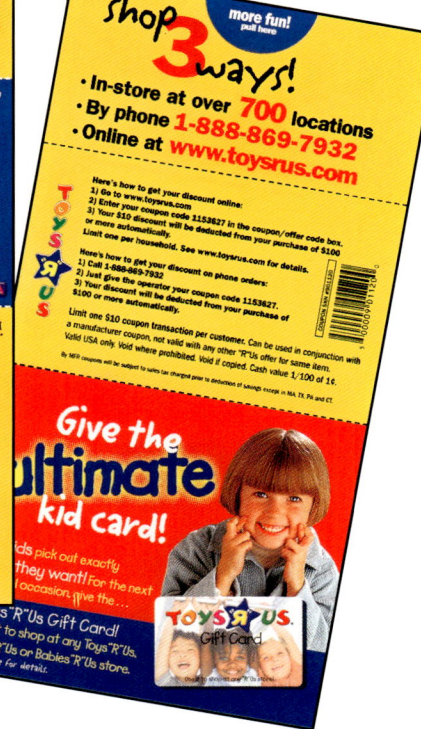

Front and back of the insert.

COMPANY: Toys "R" Us
DIMENSIONS: 9⅝" x 9⅝"
NUMBER OF PAGES: 68
WEBSITE: www.toysrus.com

"Pull here for surprises!" the blue tab instructs. Doing so reveals: a $10 off coupon, stickers for kids to mark their choices with, and information on the Toys "R" Us gift card. In addition to the hot toy of the season, the first spread (below), features a page of coupons. There are three such coupon pages in the catalog.

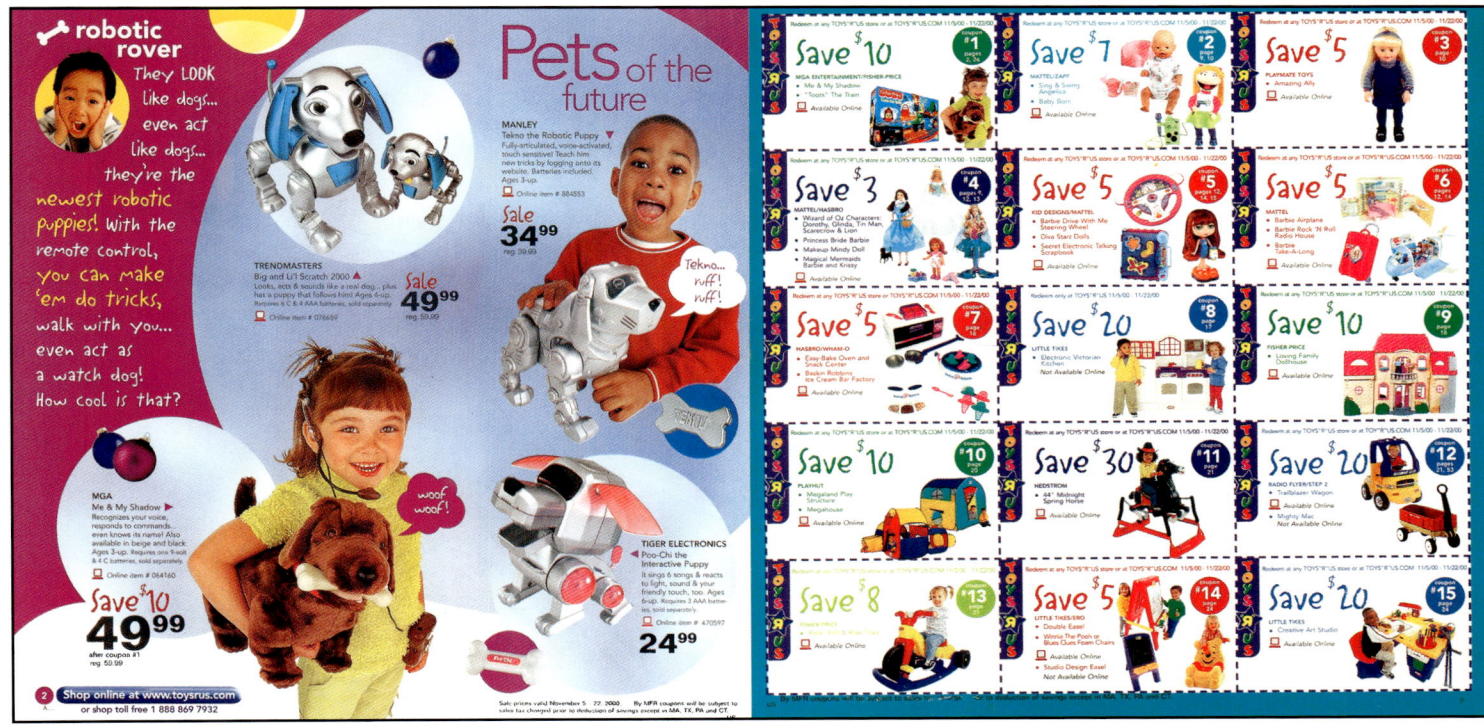

Perfection

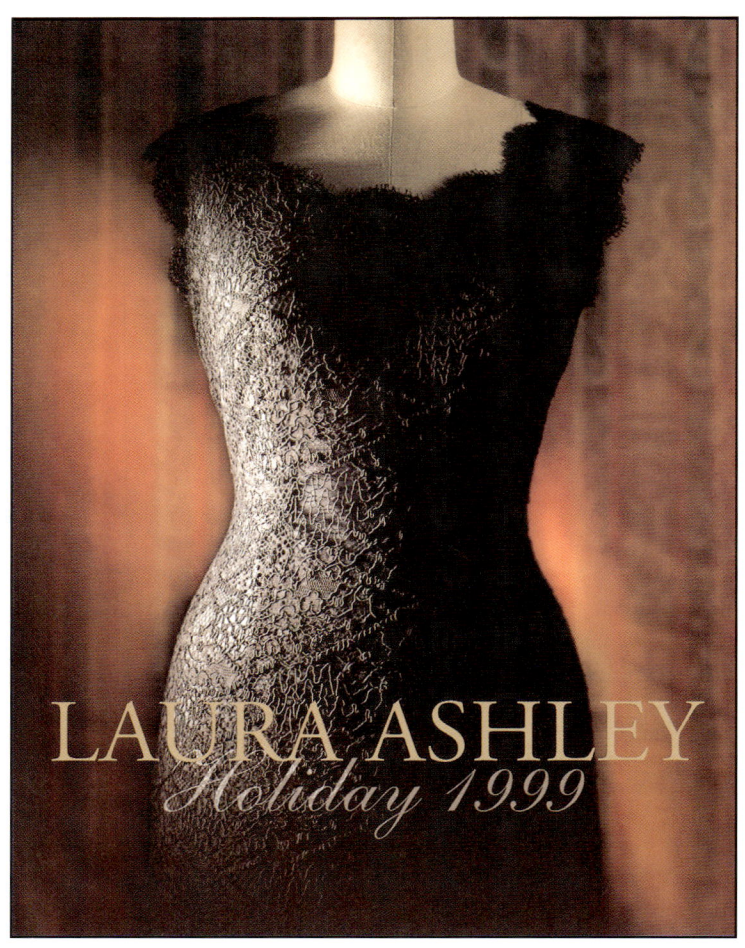

Laura Ashley

Laura Ashley has always had a proper bearing, which the holiday catalog reflects beautifully. Everything is expertly photographed; the colors are lush, the signature prints pop. Even the script typeface has just the right tone.

DIMENSIONS: 8³/₄" x 10⁷/₈"
NUMBER OF PAGES: 24

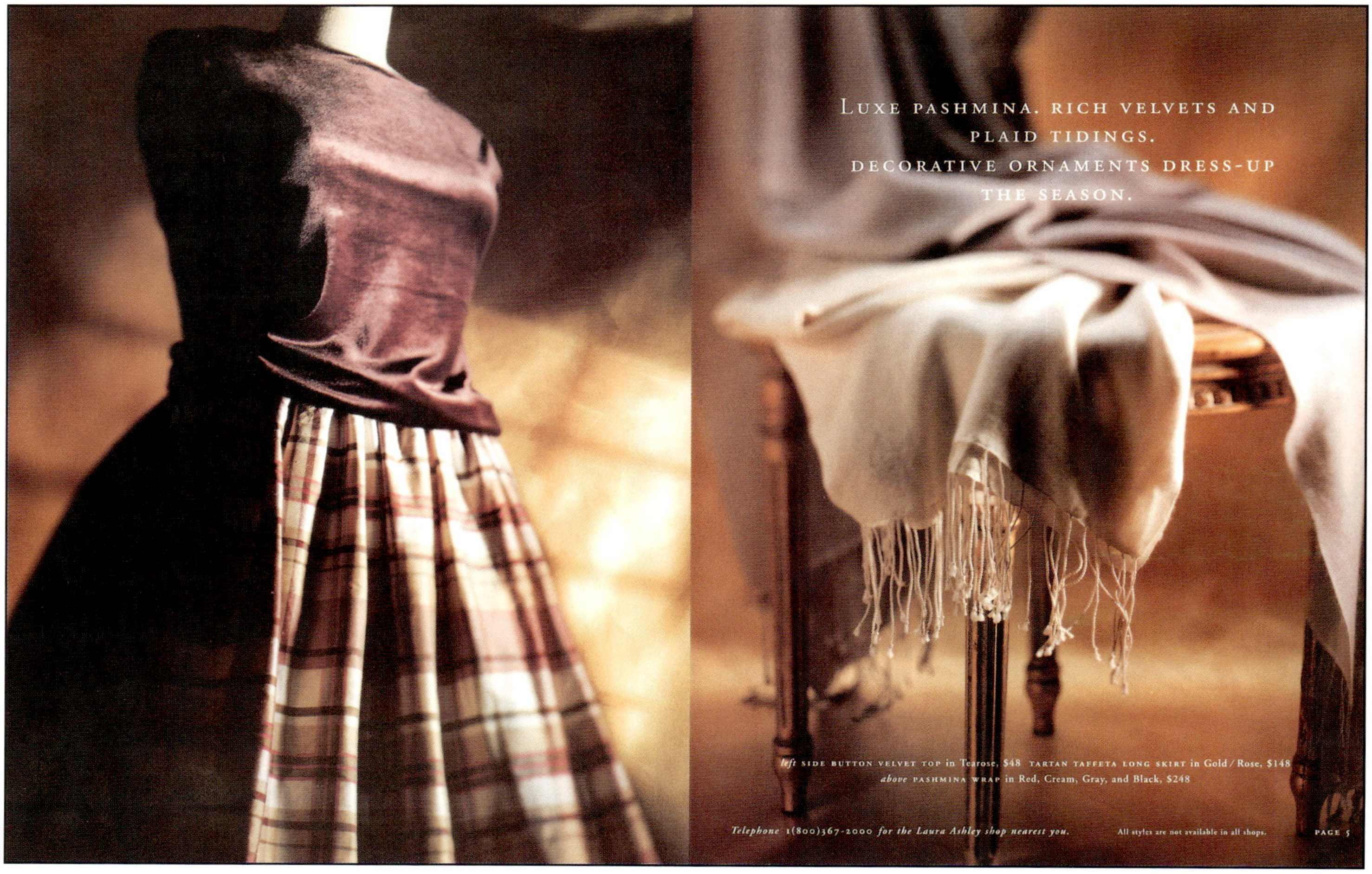

Interspersed with the merchandise pages were various opportunities for customers to support charitable organizations. Here, in conjunction with World Vision, a goat, mule, ox or cow (the real ones) can be purchased for the use of the livestock dependent peoples of Africa.

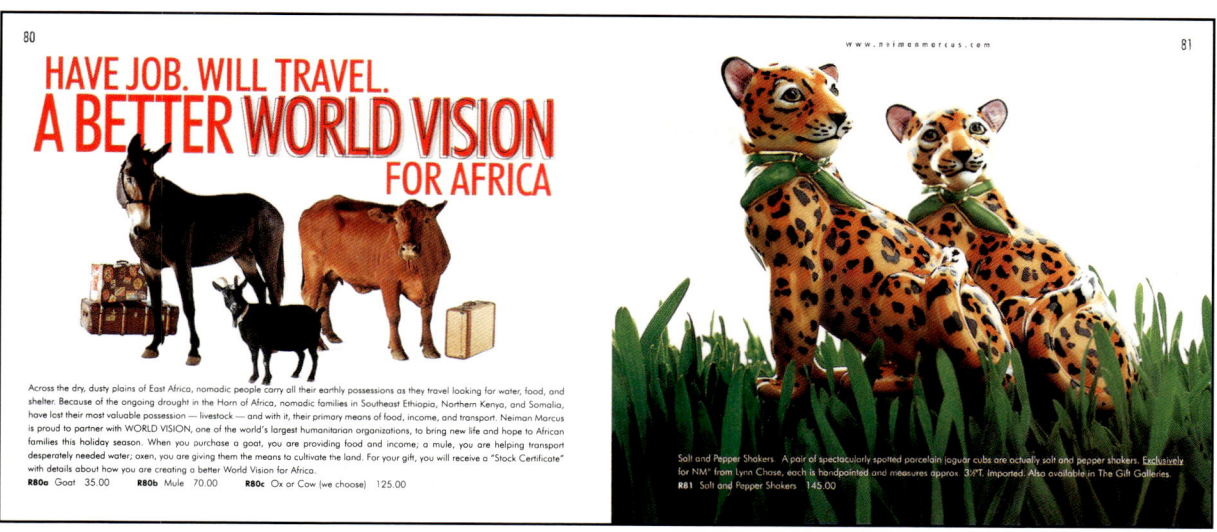
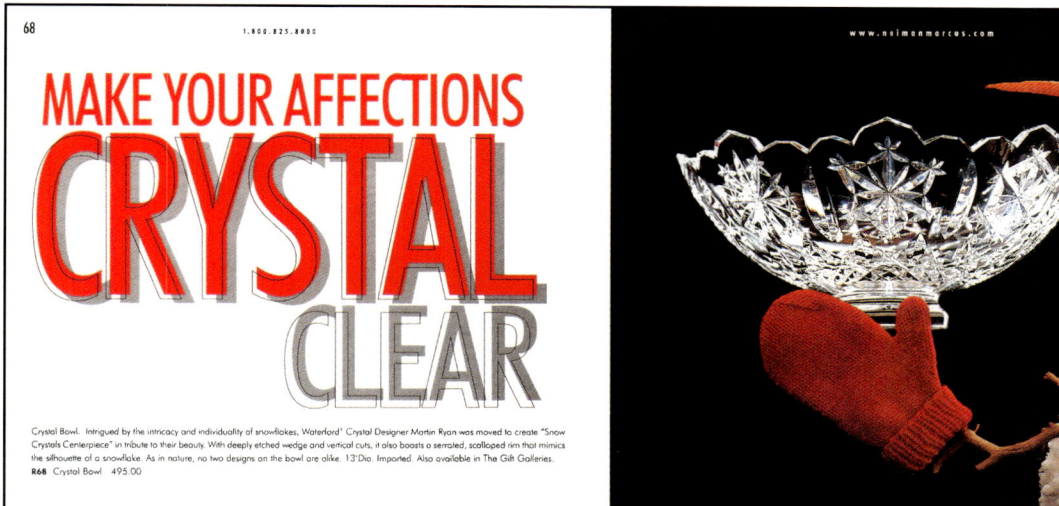
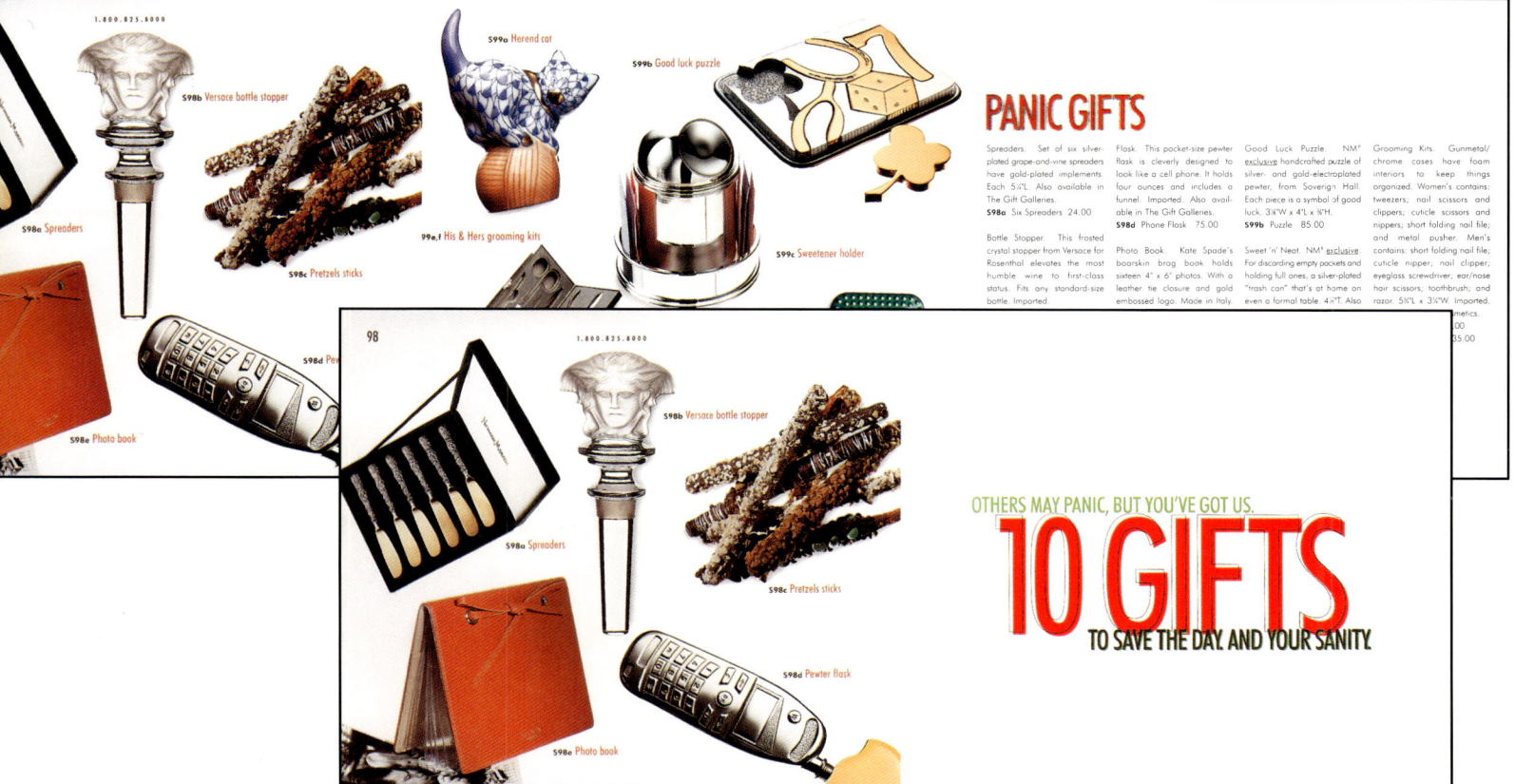

Serious Fun

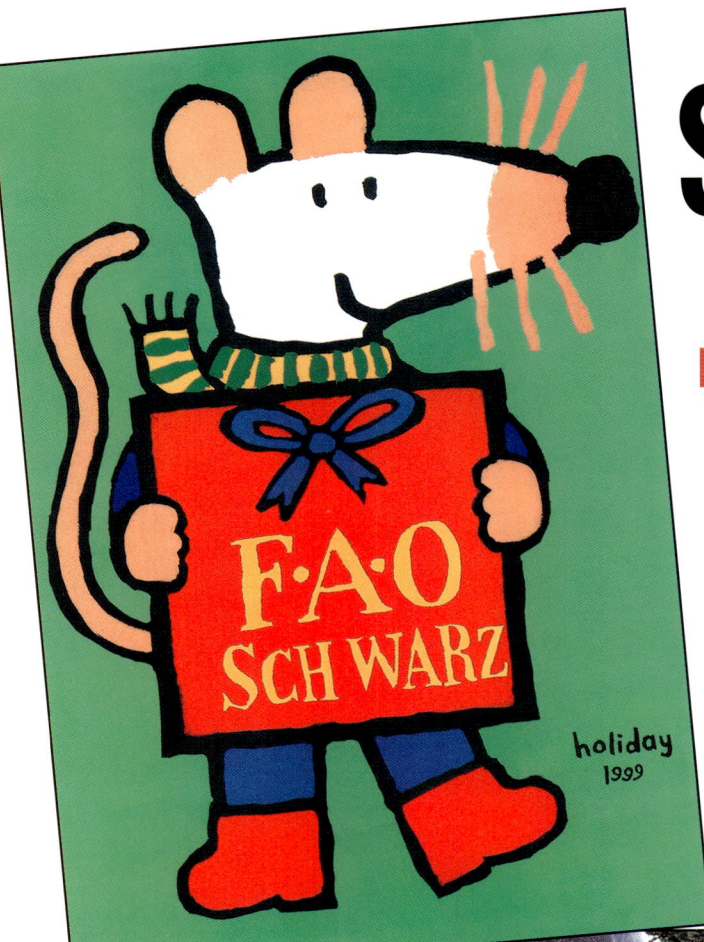

FAO Schwarz

The "package" on the front cover of the catalog opens up to reveal a toy chest of toys. That's just the beginning. The stars are out in the famous store's catalog, for a cause. Mary Tyler Moore promotes the store donating a portion of its sales to ASPCA. Whoopi is here advocating literacy, and the Duchess of York represents her cause, Chances for Children, an organization that helps children in need, to which the store donated a portion of sales of the Little Red Doll.

DIMENSIONS: 7 1/2" x 10 7/8"
NUMBER OF PAGES: 100

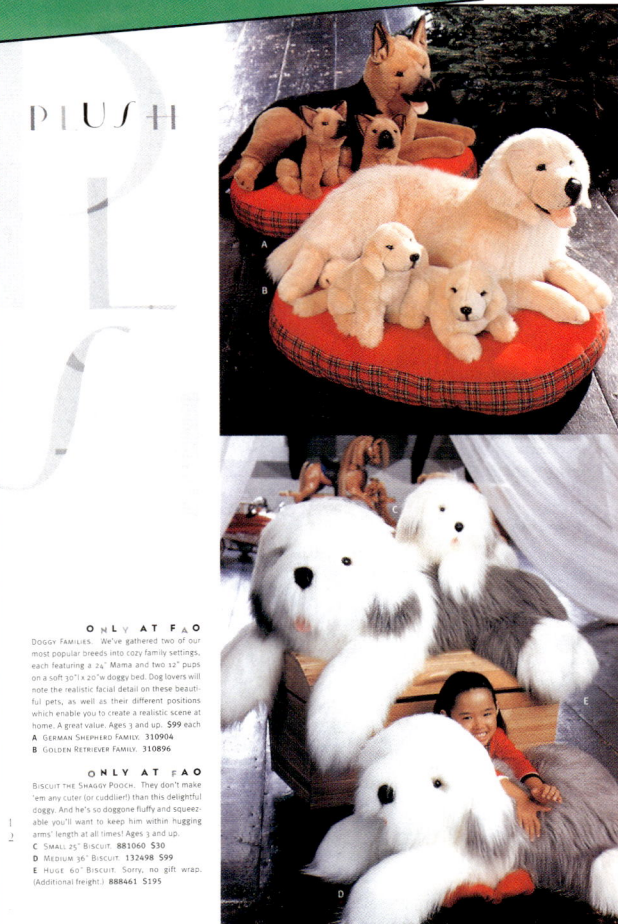
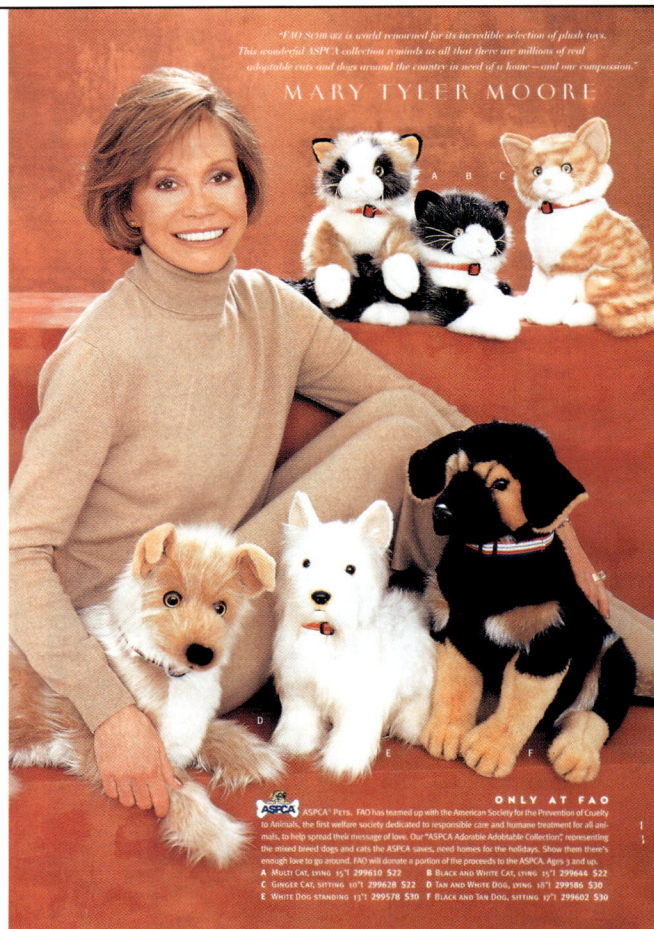

FAO SCHWARZ

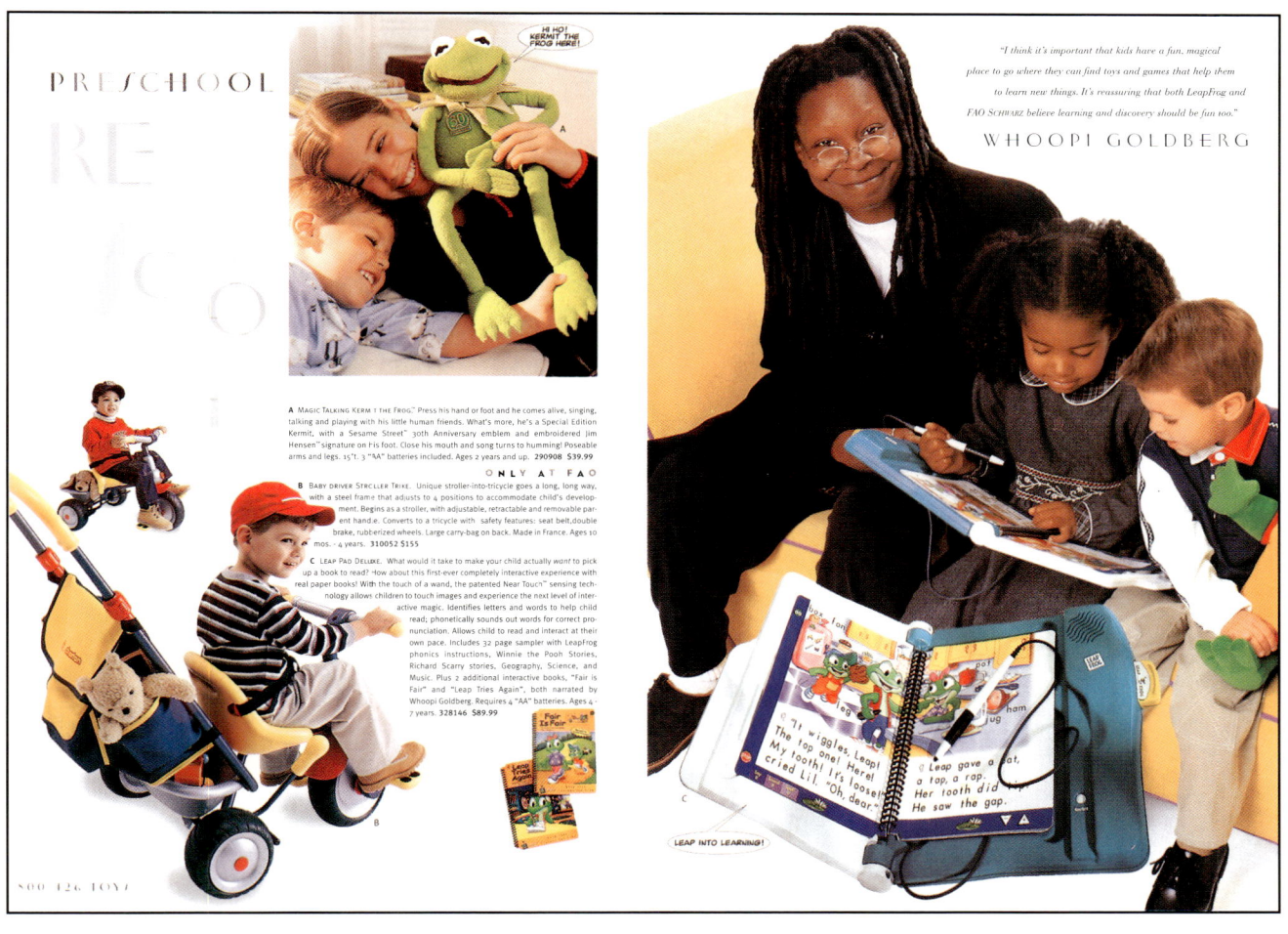

PRESCHOOL

> "I think it's important that kids have a fun, magical place to go where they can find toys and games that help them to learn new things. It's reassuring that both LeapFrog and FAO Schwarz believe learning and discovery should be fun too."
>
> WHOOPI GOLDBERG

A **MAGIC TALKING KERMIT THE FROG.** Press his hand or foot and he comes alive, singing, talking and playing with his little human friends. What's more, he's a Special Edition Kermit, with a Sesame Street 30th Anniversary emblem and embroidered Jim Hensen™ signature on his foot. Close his mouth and song turns to humming! Poseable arms and legs. 15"t. 3 "AA" batteries included. Ages 2 years and up. 290908 $39.99

ONLY AT FAO

B **BABY DRIVER STROLLER TRIKE.** Unique stroller-into-tricycle goes a long, long way, with a steel frame that adjusts to 4 positions to accommodate child's development. Begins as a stroller, with adjustable, retractable and removable parent handle. Converts to a tricycle with safety features: seat belt, double brake, rubberized wheels. Large carry-bag on back. Made in France. Ages 10 mos.- 4 years. 310052 $155

C **LEAP PAD DELUXE.** What would it take to make your child actually *want* to pick up a book to read? How about this first-ever completely interactive experience with real paper books! With the touch of a wand, the patented Near Touch™ sensing technology allows children to touch images and experience the next level of interactive magic. Identifies letters and words to help child read; phonetically sounds out words for correct pronunciation. Allows child to read and interact at their own pace. Includes 32 page sampler with LeapFrog phonics instructions, Winnie the Pooh Stories, Richard Scarry stories, Geography, Science, and Music. Plus 2 additional interactive books, "Fair is Fair" and "Leap Tries Again", both narrated by Whoopi Goldberg. Requires 4 "AA" batteries. Ages 4-7 years. 328146 $89.99

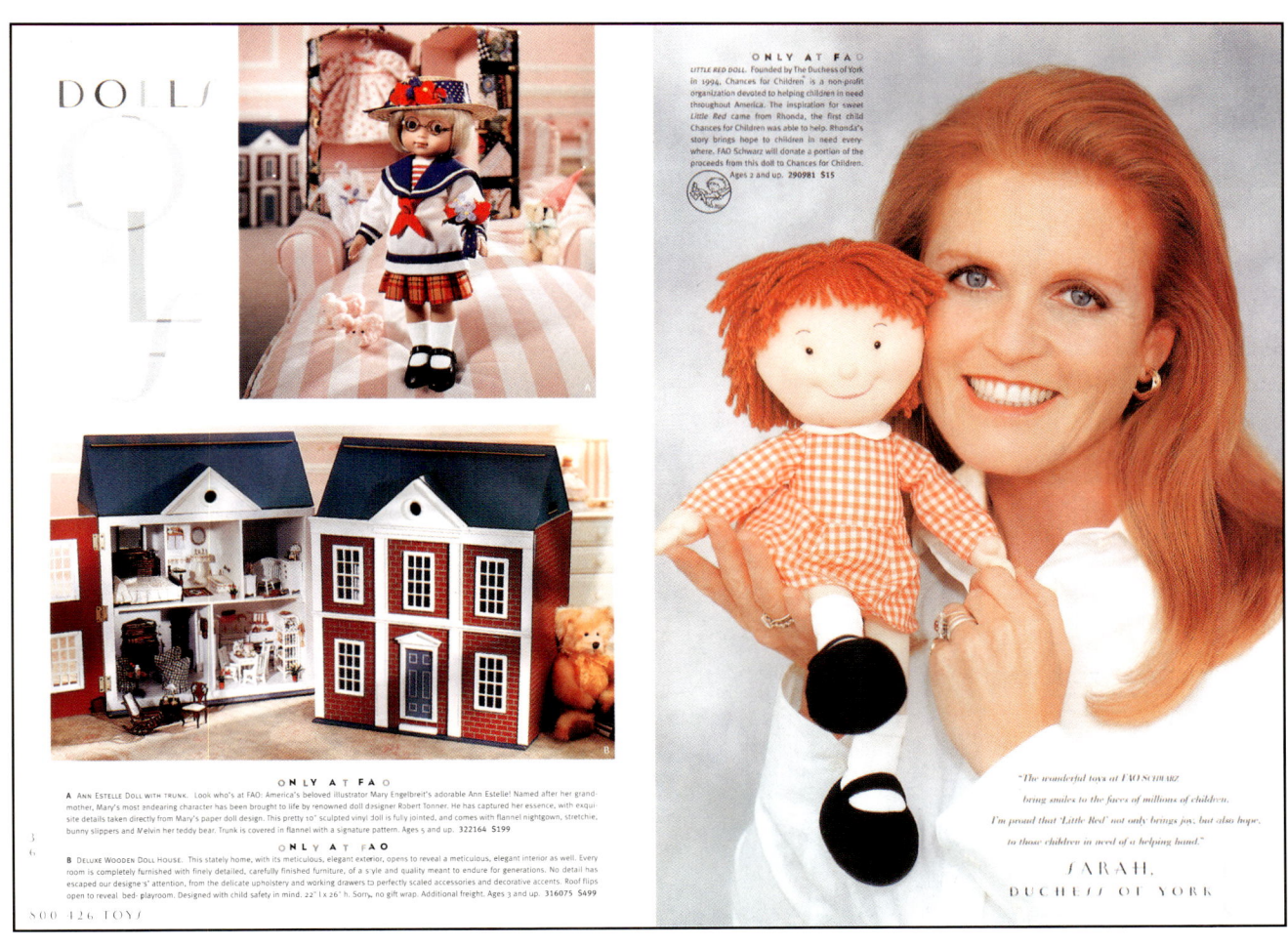

DOLLS

ONLY AT FAO

LITTLE RED DOLL. Founded by The Duchess of York in 1994, Chances for Children is a non-profit organization devoted to helping children in need throughout America. The inspiration for sweet Little Red came from Rhonda, the first child Chances for Children was able to help. Rhonda's story brings hope to children in need everywhere. FAO Schwarz will donate a portion of the proceeds from this doll to Chances for Children. Ages 2 and up. 290981 $15

ONLY AT FAO

A **ANN ESTELLE DOLL WITH TRUNK.** Look who's at FAO: America's beloved illustrator Mary Engelbreit's adorable Ann Estelle! Named after her grandmother, Mary's most endearing character has been brought to life by renowned doll designer Robert Tonner. He has captured her essence, with exquisite details taken directly from Mary's paper doll design. This pretty 10" sculpted vinyl doll is fully jointed, and comes with flannel nightgown, stretchie, bunny slippers and Melvin her teddy bear. Trunk is covered in flannel with a signature pattern. Ages 5 and up. 322164 $199

ONLY AT FAO

B **DELUXE WOODEN DOLL HOUSE.** This stately home, with its meticulous, elegant exterior, opens to reveal a meticulous, elegant interior as well. Every room is completely furnished with finely detailed, carefully finished furniture, of a style and quality meant to endure for generations. No detail has escaped our designer's attention, from the delicate upholstery and working drawers to perfectly scaled accessories and decorative accents. Roof flips open to reveal bed-/playroom. Designed with child safety in mind. 22"l x 26"h. Sorry, no gift wrap. Additional freight. Ages 3 and up. 316075 $499

> "The wonderful toys at FAO SCHWARZ bring smiles to the faces of millions of children. I'm proud that 'Little Red' not only brings joy, but also hope to those children in need of a helping hand."
>
> SARAH,
> DUCHESS OF YORK

RALPH LAUREN

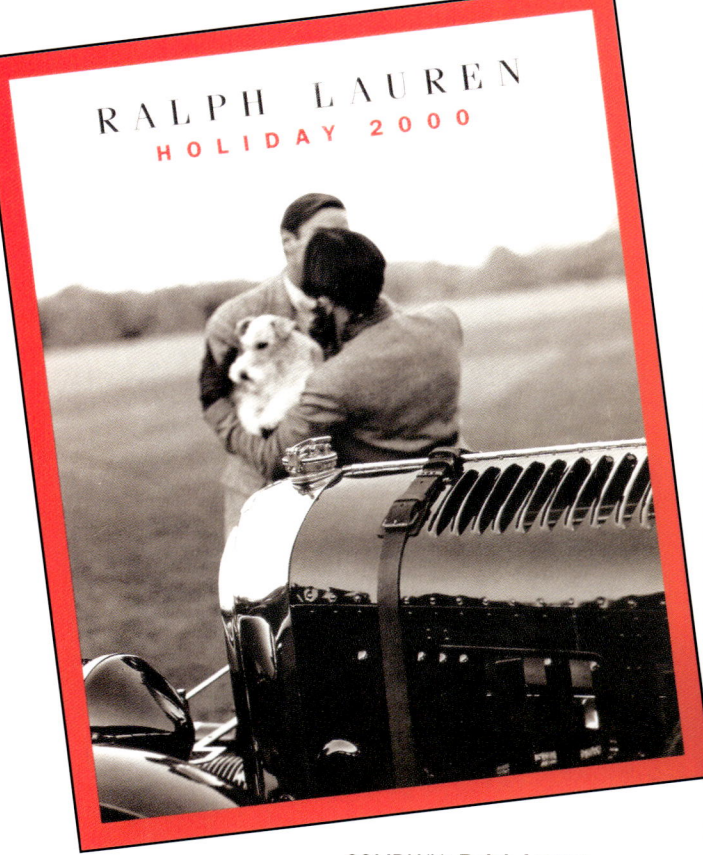

COMPANY: **Ralph Lauren**
DIMENSIONS: 8 1/2" x 11"
NUMBER OF PAGES: 20
WEBSITE: **www.polo.com**

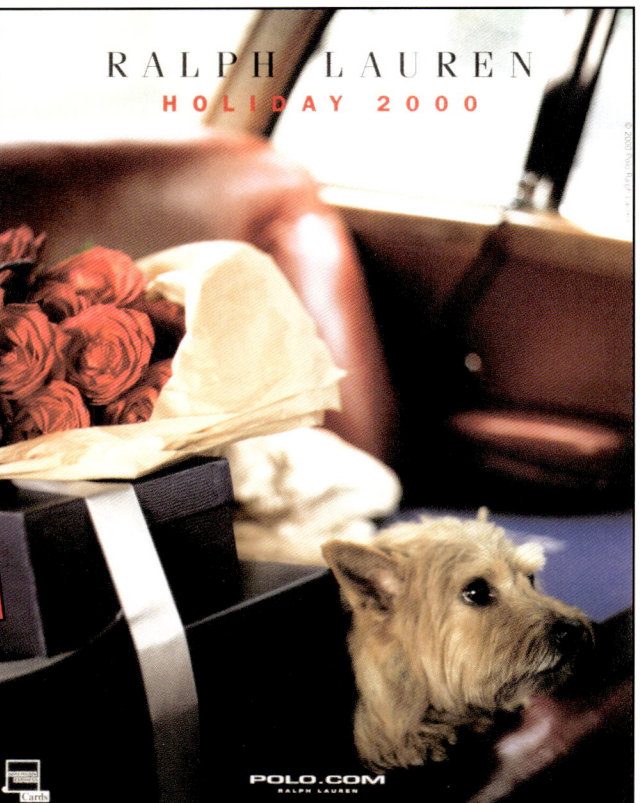

Back cover.

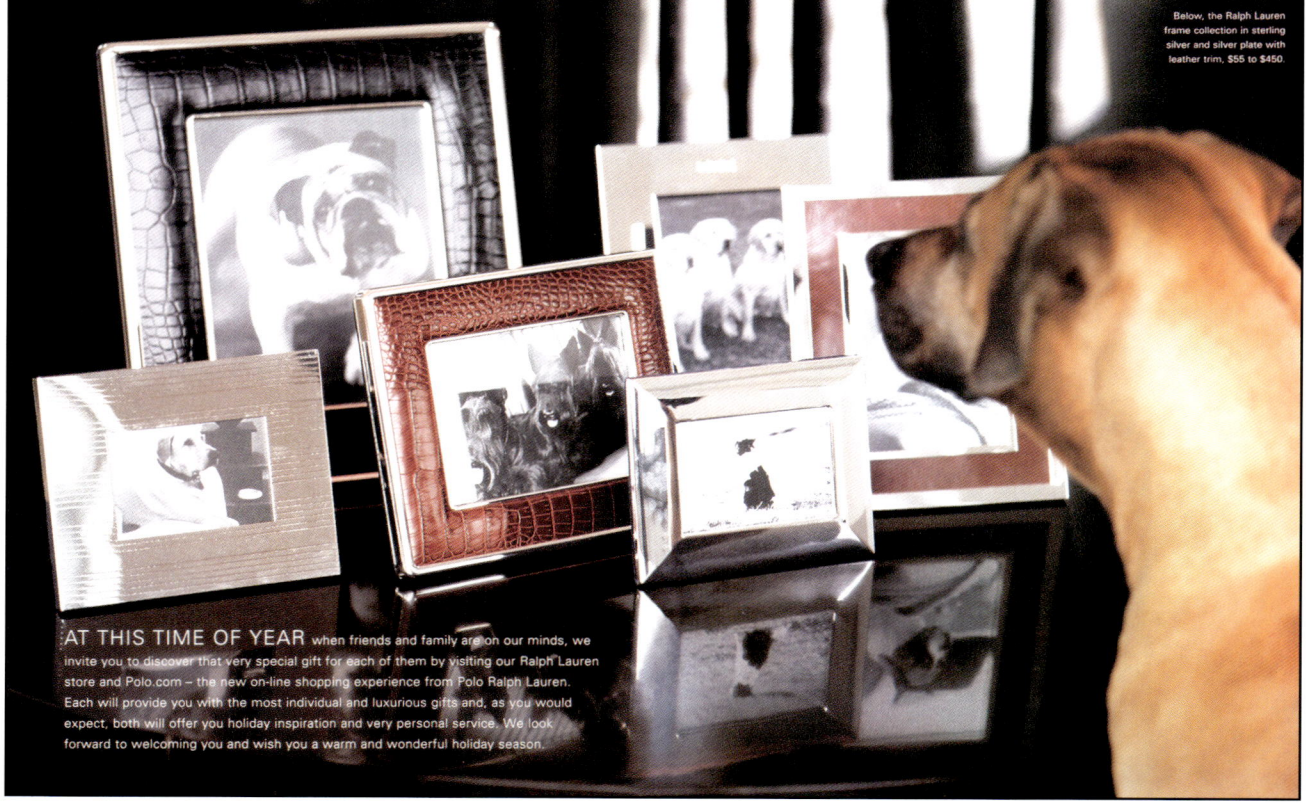

Dogs rule with Ralph Lauren—big dogs, little dogs and spotted dogs. The catalog also has an interesting mix of full-color and black-and-white photography, adding to the mood set by the vintage car used as a prop.

RALPH LAUREN

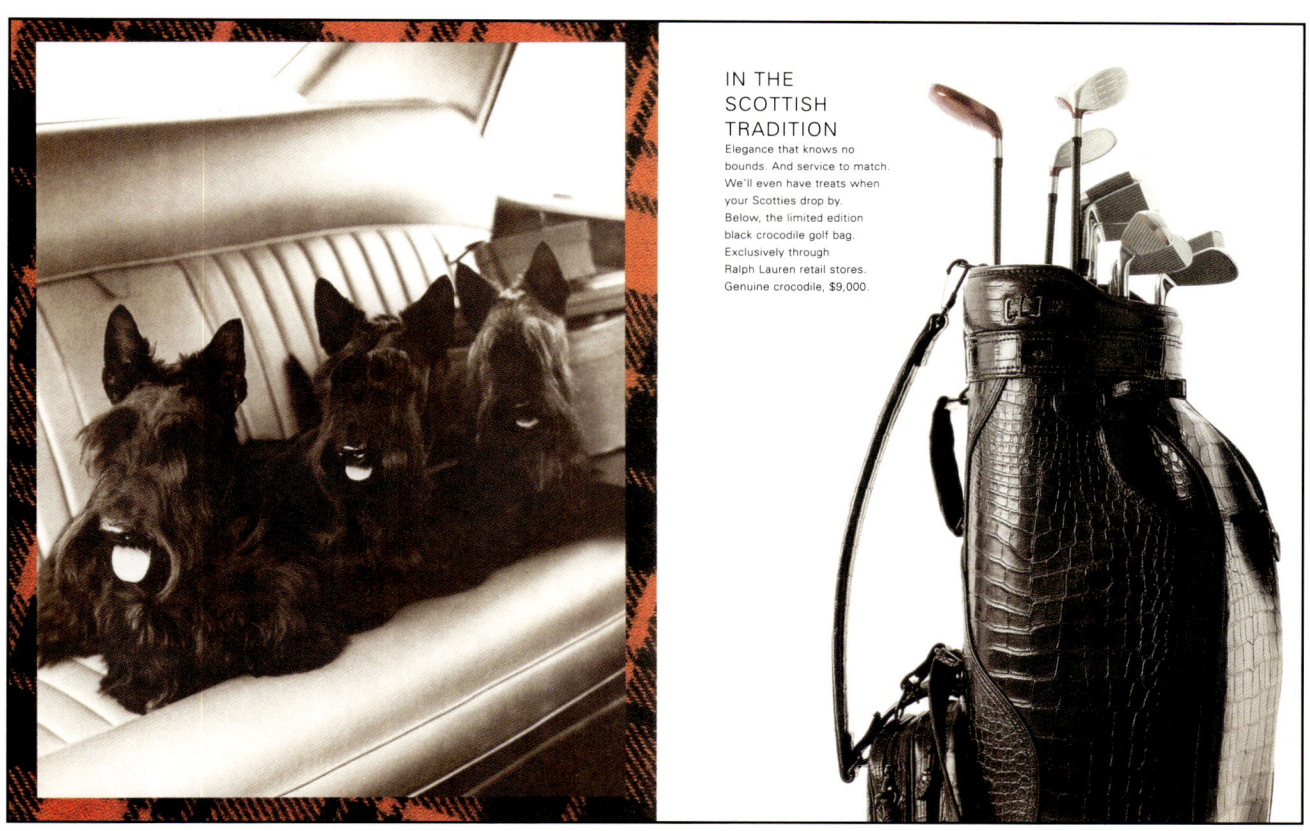

IN THE SCOTTISH TRADITION

Elegance that knows no bounds. And service to match. We'll even have treats when your Scotties drop by. Below, the limited edition black crocodile golf bag. Exclusively through Ralph Lauren retail stores. Genuine crocodile, $9,000.

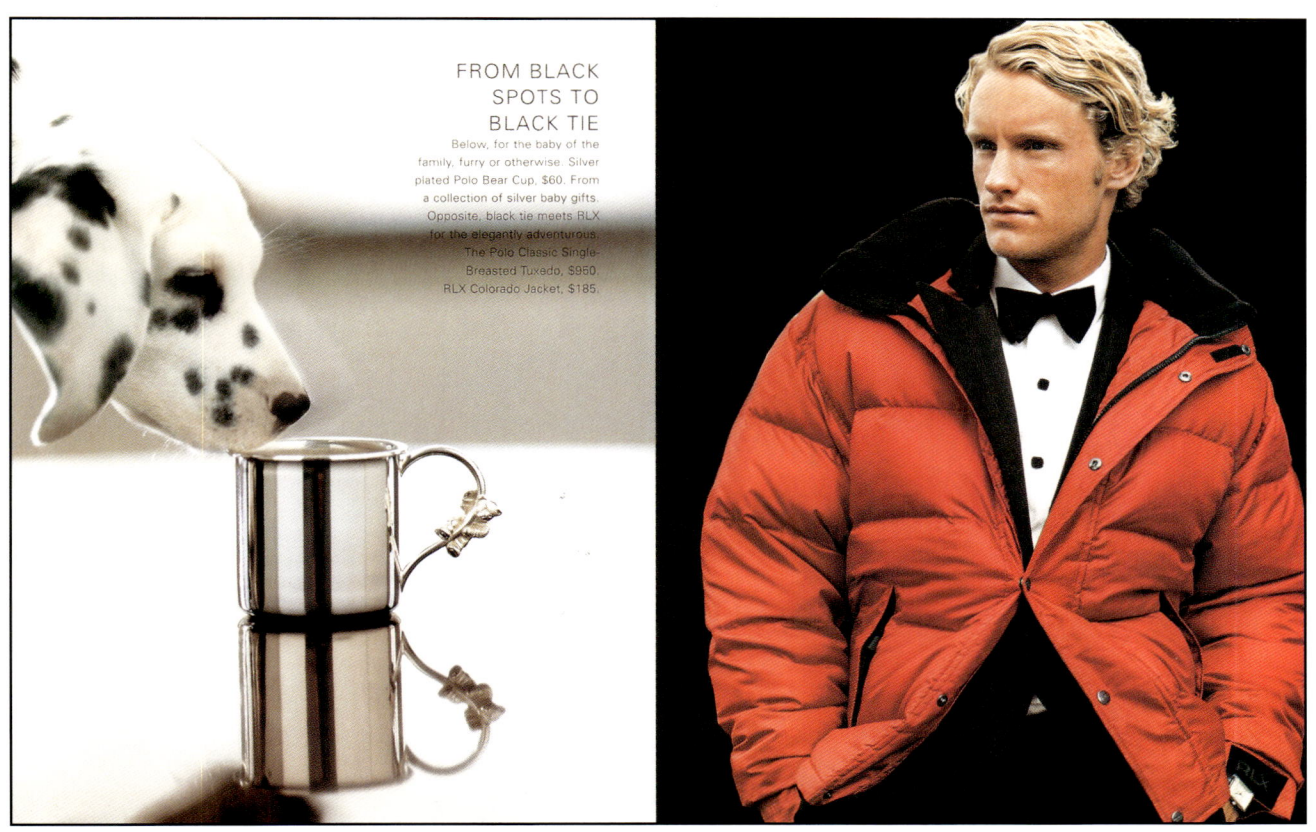

FROM BLACK SPOTS TO BLACK TIE

Below, for the baby of the family, furry or otherwise. Silver plated Polo Bear Cup, $60. From a collection of silver baby gifts. Opposite, black tie meets RLX for the elegantly adventurous. The Polo Classic Single-Breasted Tuxedo, $950. RLX Colorado Jacket, $185.

ORGANIZED LIVING

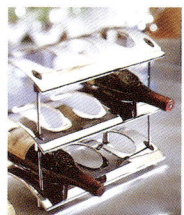 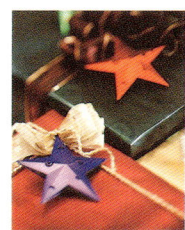 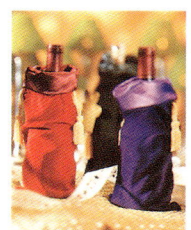

holiday 2000

Organized Living

COMPANY: **Organized Living**
DIMENSIONS: 8 3/8" x 10 7/8"
NUMBER OF PAGES: 24

There's no place like home for the holidays and there's no catalog that evokes that home for the holidays mood quite like this one, from Organized Living. From the the table scattered with wrapping paper, cheese and champagne, to the gift closet stuffed with presents, this catalog makes one yearn for that mythical home of the imagination.

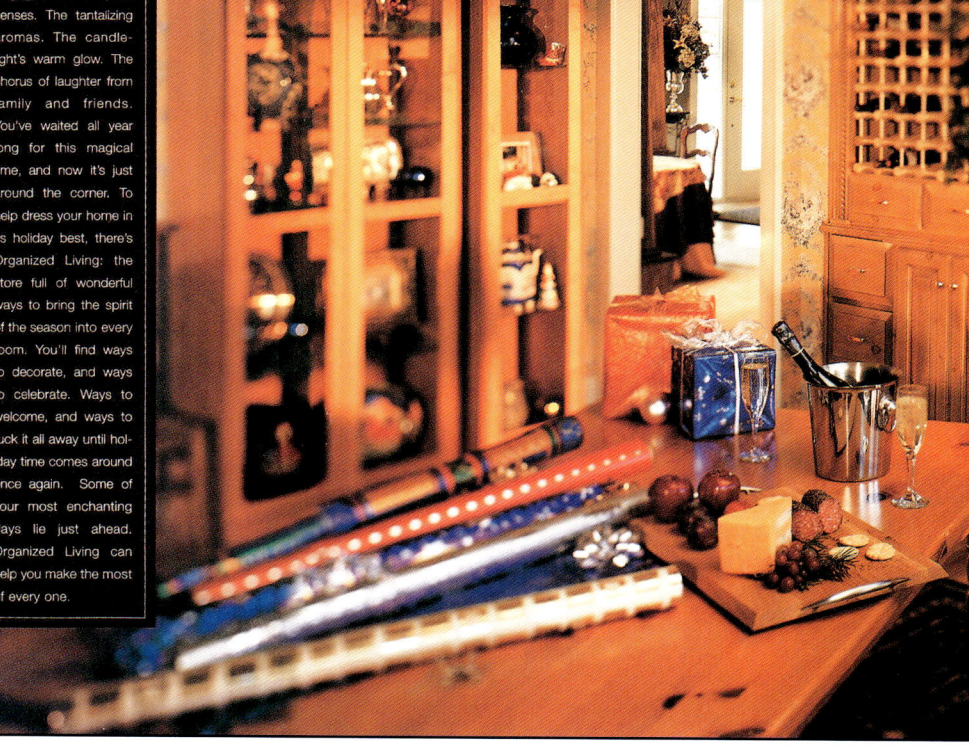

Extendible Wine Rack
You'll want to drink a toast to this elegant wine rack for many reasons. Made of New England hardwood, it creates a safe and attractive storage spot for your prized vintages. What's more, the precision-fitted racks are flexible, expandable and built to grow along with your wine collection.

13"w x 13"h x 11"d 12-Bottle Rack (150015) **$26.95**
40-Bottle Rack also available (shown at right)

Mesa Cutting Board
Slice the holiday turkey to order on this beautiful solid oak cutting board. Flanked by two graceful satin steel handles, it also doubles as a sturdy serving tray for wine and cheese. The non-skid rubber feet elevate the tray above the table or counter top to prevent scratches.

13"w x 19"h x 1 1/8"d (159921) **$89.00**

Cherry Curio Cabinet
A classic way to showcase favorite mementos from holidays past. Simple lines and clean styling allow this curio cabinet to mingle with any decor and feel at home in any room. The rest of the year, the sturdy, adjustable glass shelves hold everything from books to your pottery collection.

Two-Door Cabinet (161315) **$499**
35"w x 76 1/2"h x 17 1/4"d
Single-Door Cabinet (151323) **$349**
19 3/4"w x 76 1/2"h x 17 1/4"d

Ice Bucket /Wine Cooler
Everything gets chilled to perfection in this elegant polished aluminum piece crafted in Italy. Use it to serve ice or to bring a special bottle of bubbly to the table in high style.

(161810) **$29.95**

There's no place like home for the holidays.

It's a season that engages all of your senses. The tantalizing aromas. The candlelight's warm glow. The chorus of laughter from family and friends. You've waited all year long for this magical time, and now it's just around the corner. To help dress your home in its holiday best, there's Organized Living: the store full of wonderful ways to bring the spirit of the season into every room. You'll find ways to decorate, and ways to celebrate. Ways to welcome, and ways to tuck it all away until holiday time comes around once again. Some of your most enchanting days lie just ahead. Organized Living can help you make the most of every one.

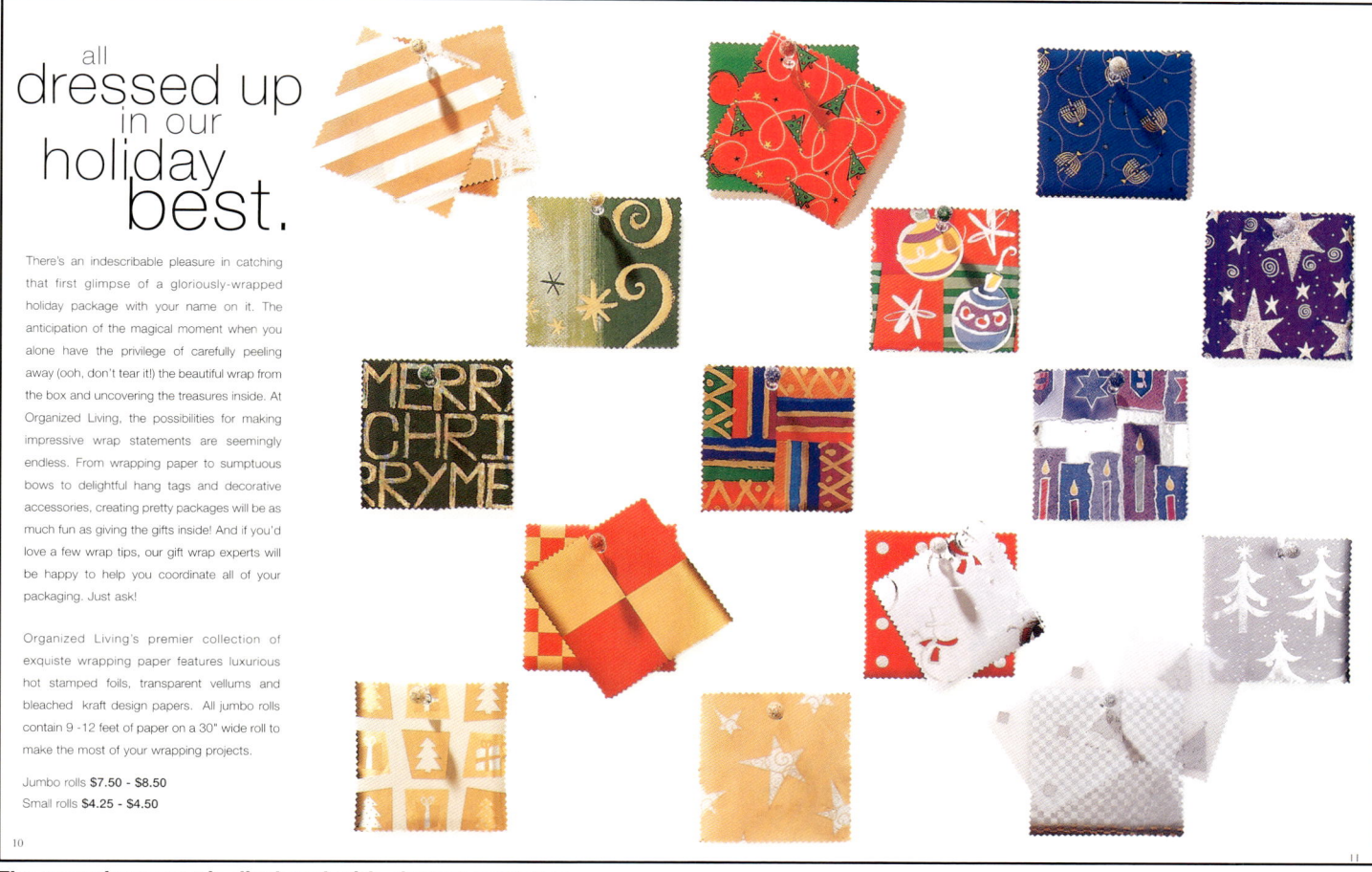

The wrapping paper is displayed with elegant swatches.

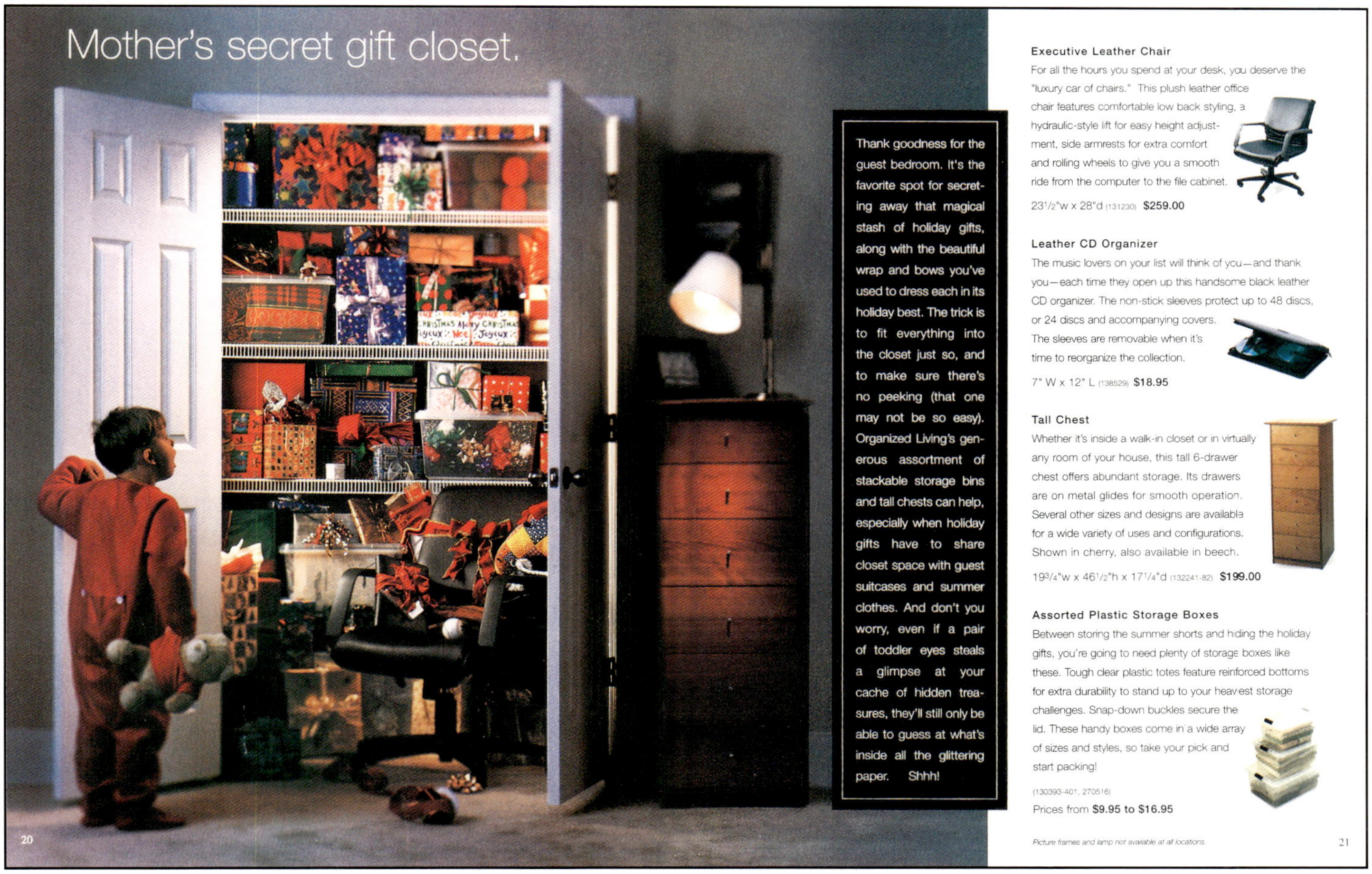

GUCCI

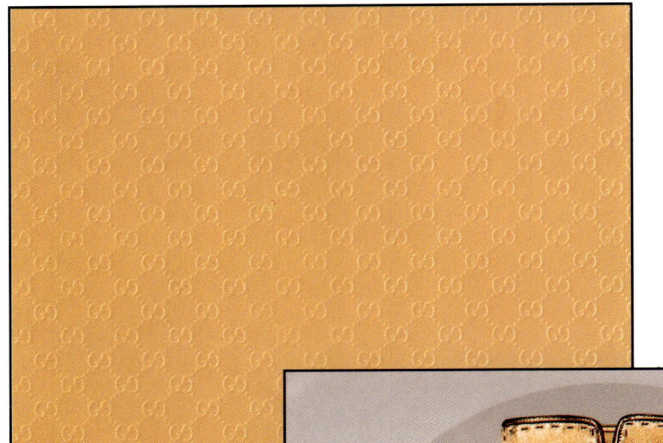

COMPANY: **Gucci**
DIMENSIONS: 8¼" x 8¼"
NUMBER OF PAGES: 56

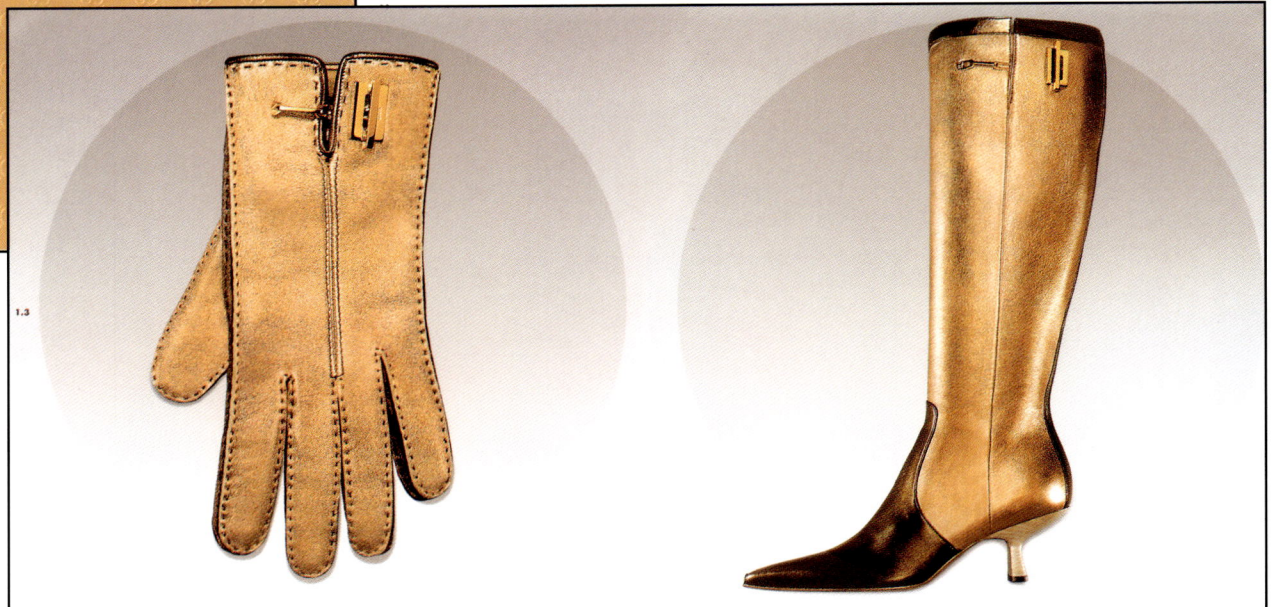

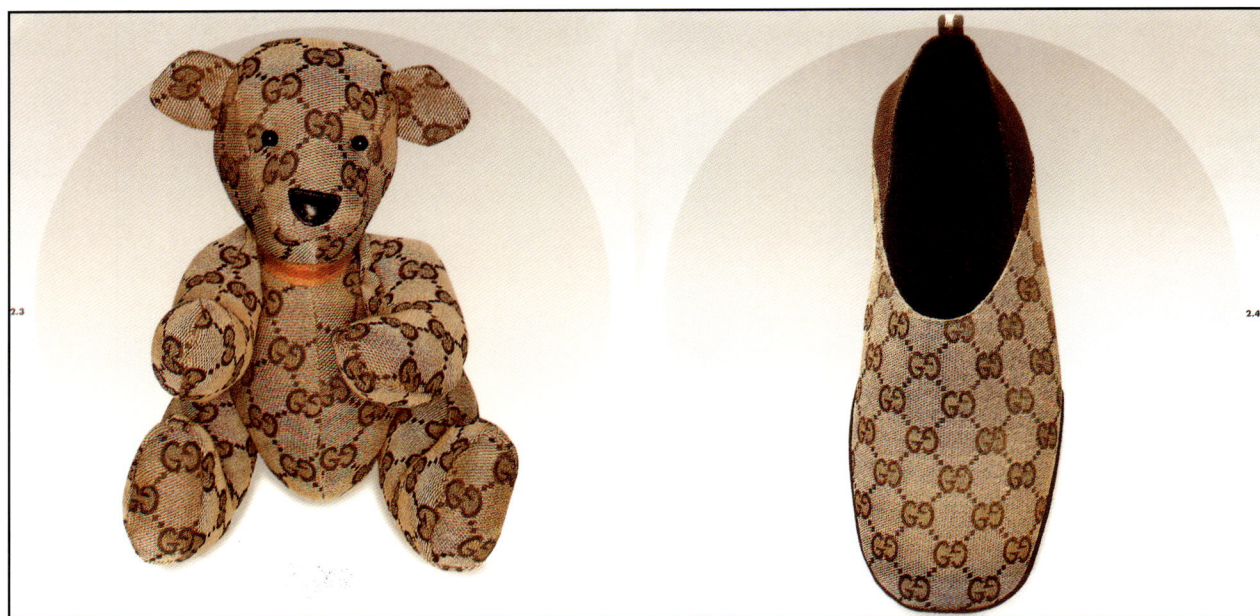

Gucci goes for the gold with its holiday catalog. Most of the merchandise shown is either gold or mostly gold and all information is relegated to pages (of gold) near the back of the catalog. The circle, and only the circle, behind each item is laminated, giving the page an added shine.

KENNETH COLE

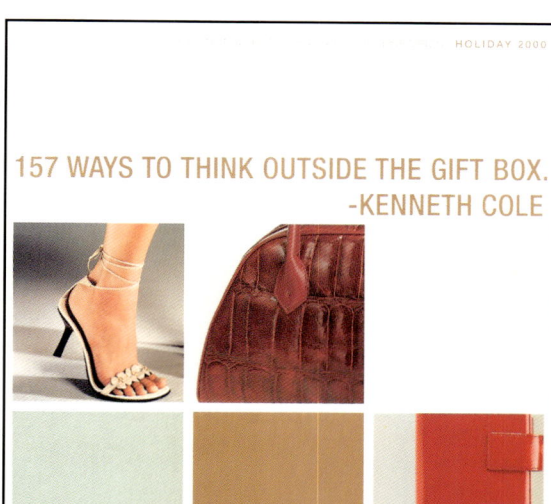

COMPANY: **Kenneth Cole**
DIMENSIONS: 7 1/2" x 10 1/2"
NUMBER OF PAGES: 36
WEBSITE: www.kennethcole.com

Here Kenneth Cole suggests "157 ways to think outside the gift box." All 157 items are consecutively numbered in the catalog, however, all items are not actually merchandise. For example numbers 4, 5 and 6 are respectively, "Stand for something," "Stand out" and "Stand under the mistletoe."

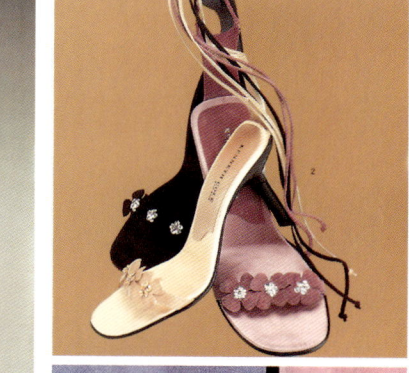

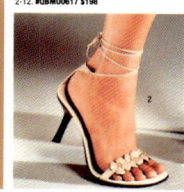

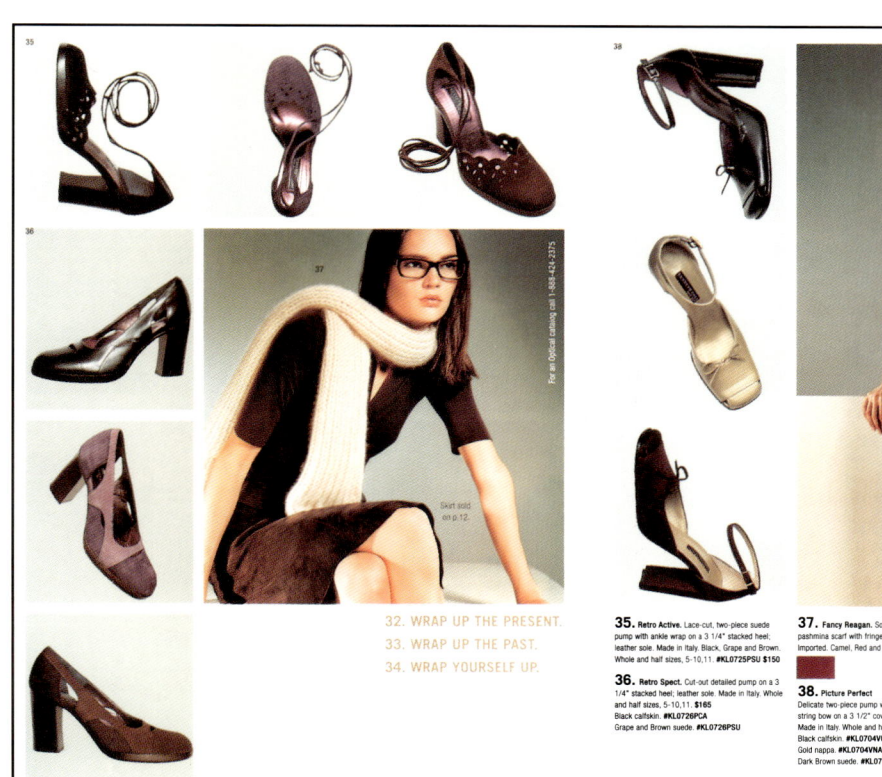

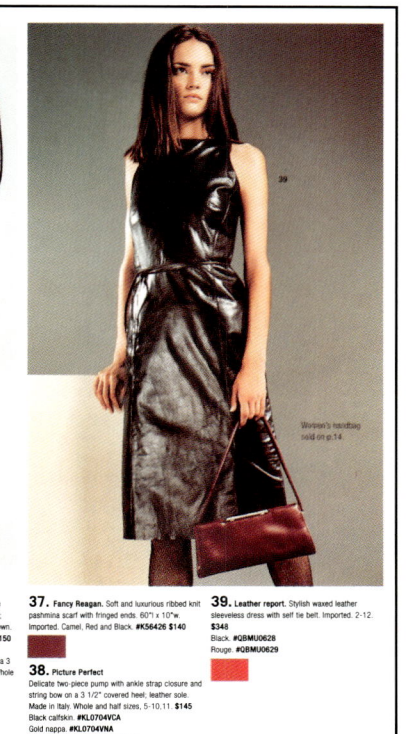

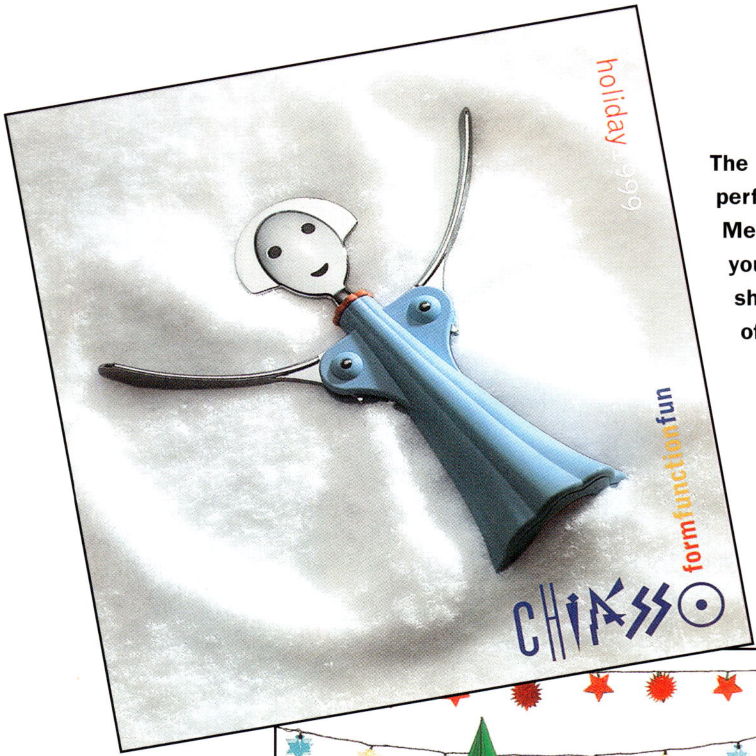

CHIASSO

The perfect snow angel; the perfect Christmas tree and/or Menorah; and the perfect gift for your perfect brother-in-law. All shown with the perfect mixture of style and whimsy.

COMPANY: **Chiasso**
DIMENSIONS: 9 1/4" x 9 1/2"
NUMBER OF PAGES: 32

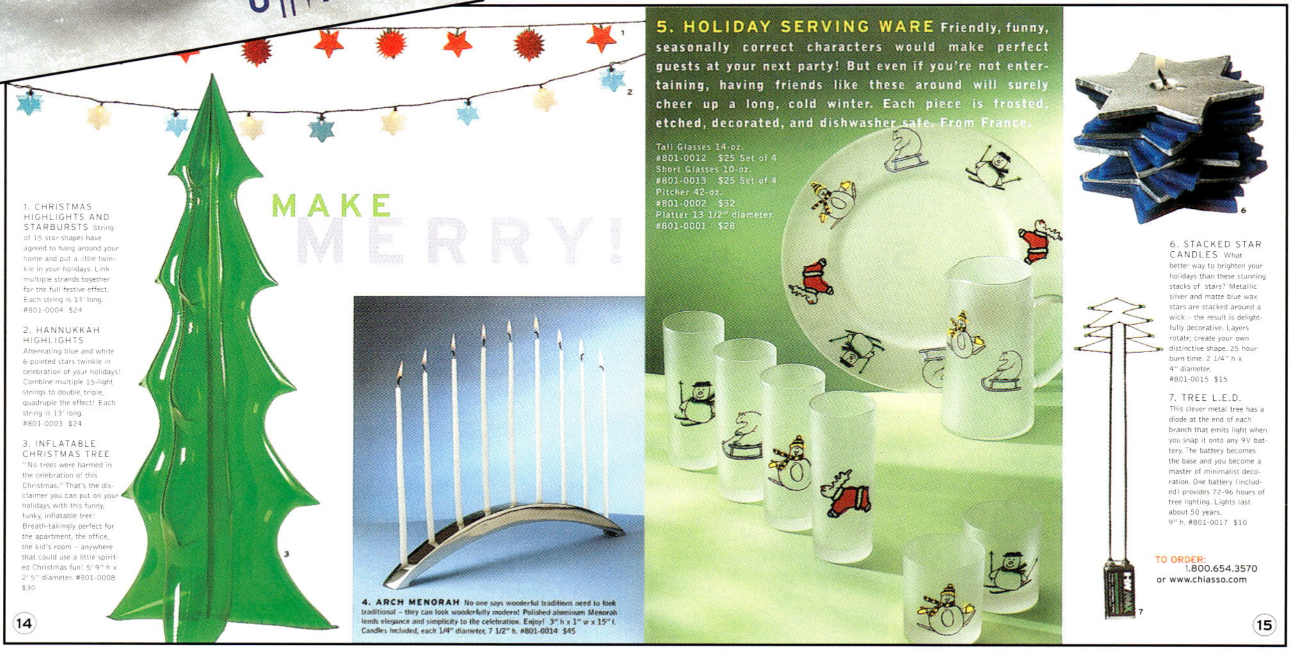

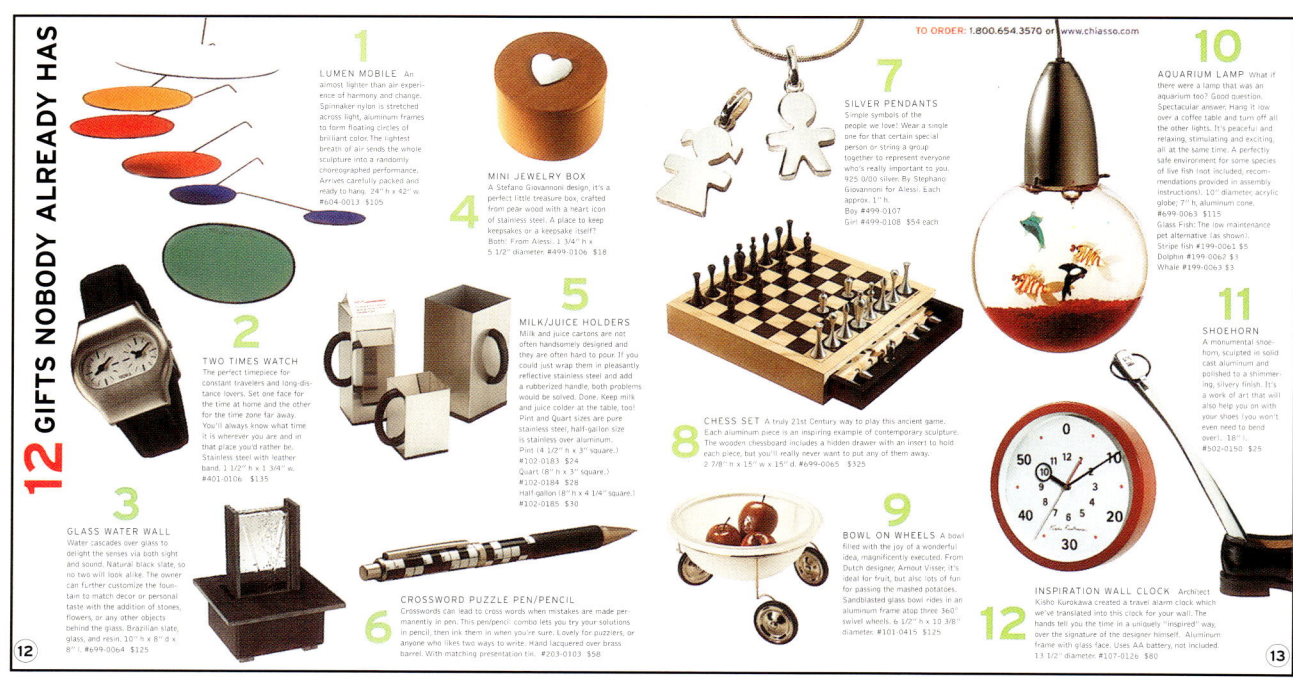

ANTHROPOLOGIE

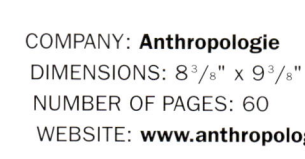

COMPANY: **Anthropologie**
DIMENSIONS: 8 3/8" x 9 3/8"
NUMBER OF PAGES: 60
WEBSITE: www.anthropologie.com

In "the gift book" from Anthropologie children play in the bedroom while their mothers share a hot drink in an unusually green garden. The "chapter titles" on the contents page are also wonderfully unusual and are explained in more detail on corresponding inside pages.

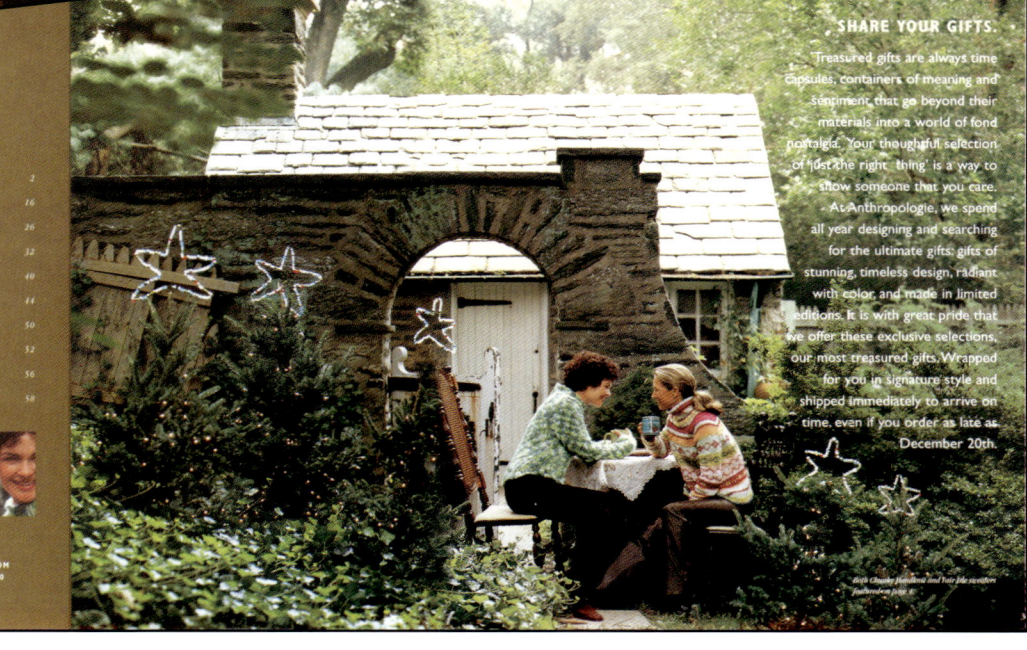

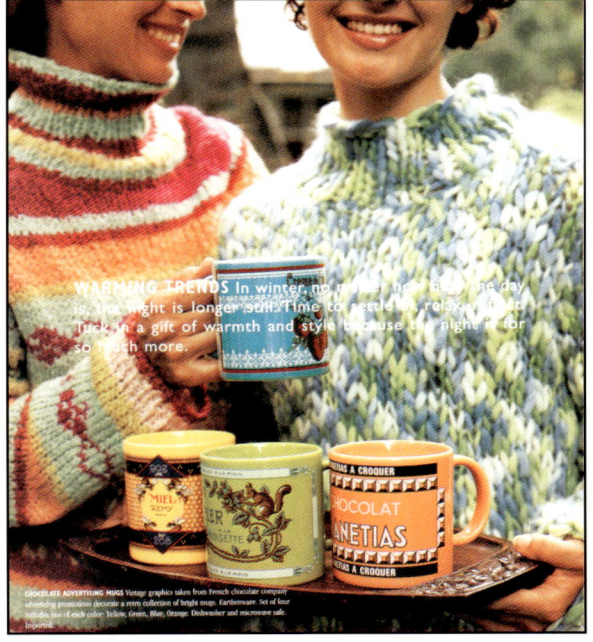

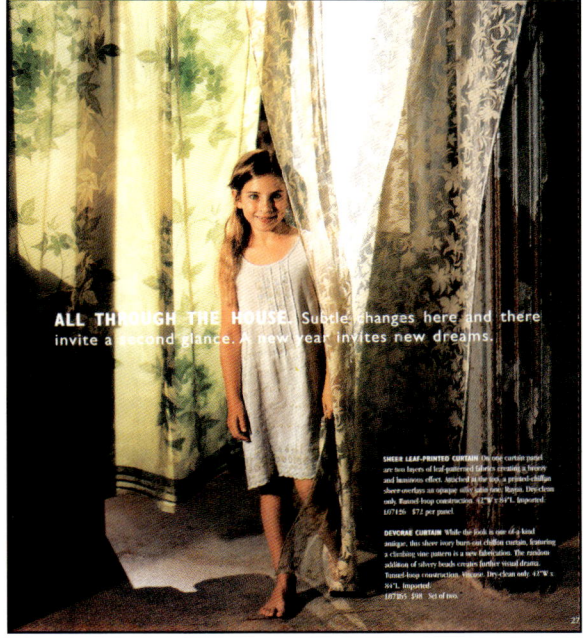

J.CREW

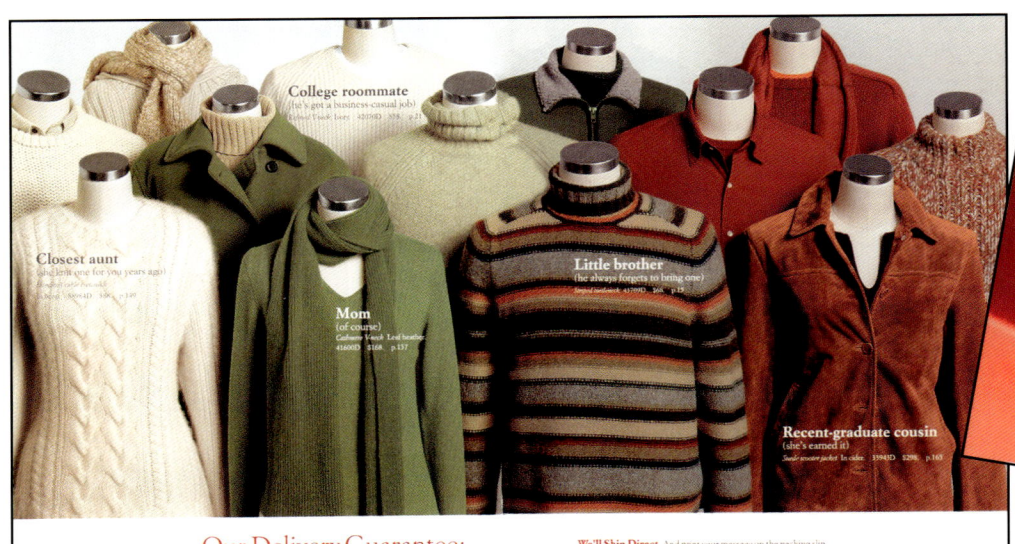

COMPANY: **J.Crew**
DIMENSIONS: 8 3/8" x 10 3/8"
NUMBER OF PAGES: 196 (red cover)
204 (white cover)
WEBSITE: **www.jcrew.com**

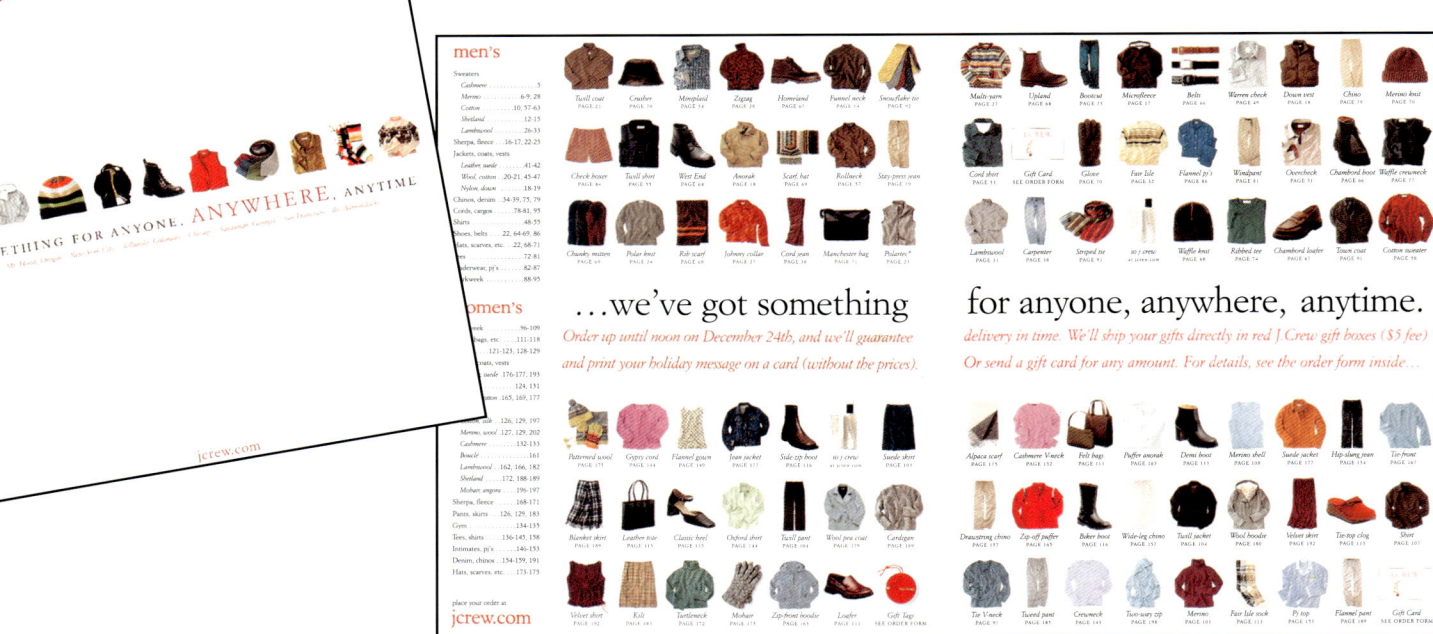

The cover of each of these catalogs from J. Crew state, "something for anyone, anywhere, anytime." However, each conveys that message differently. The catalog shown at top suggests gift ideas for various family members and friends and gives a reason why this person should receive the gift. The first spread of the other catalog (above), displays a multitude of items along with the pages on which they can be found.

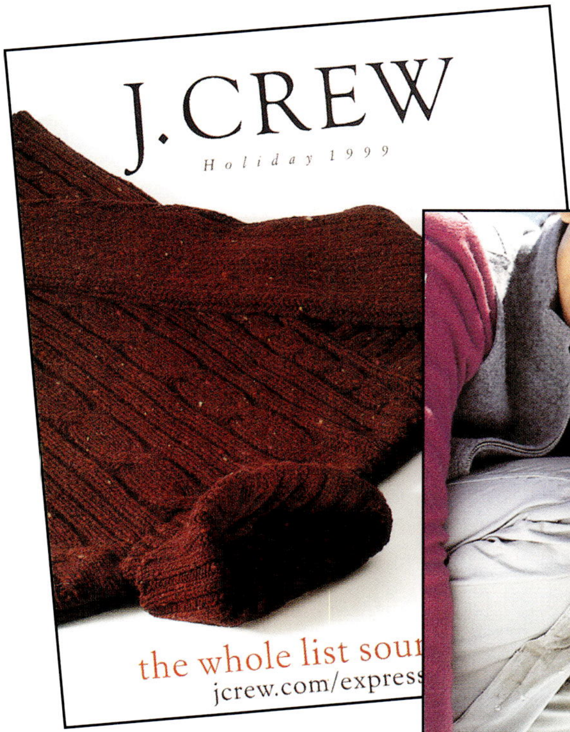

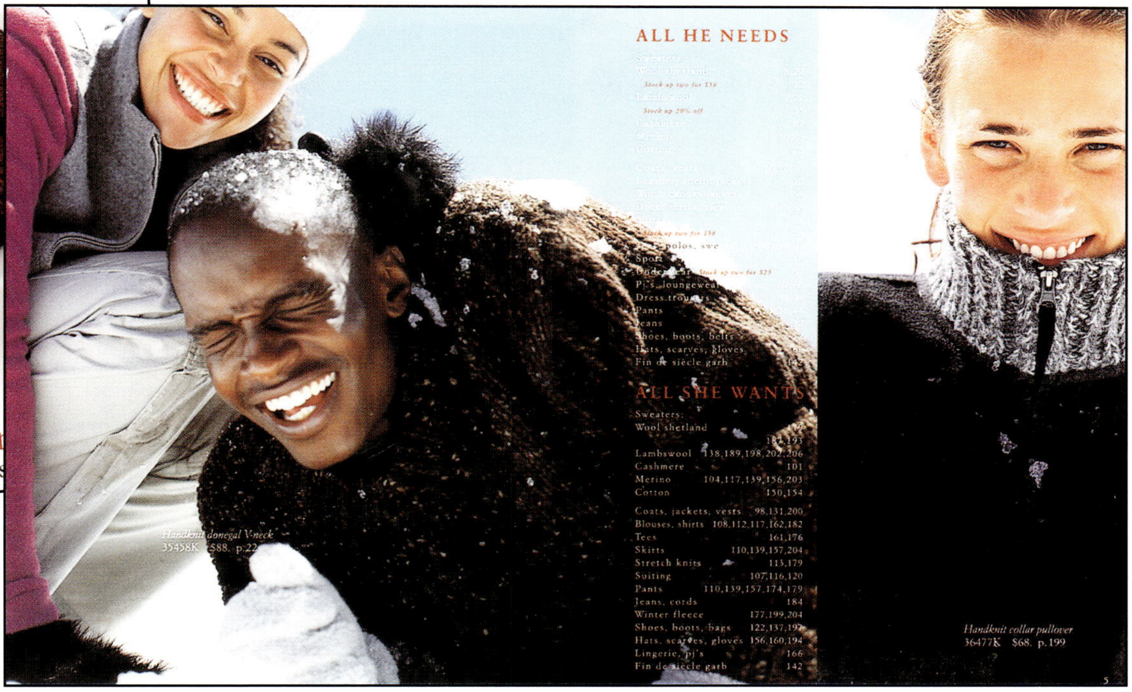

J.CREW

COMPANY: J. Crew
DIMENSIONS: 8 1/4" x 10 3/8"
NUMBER OF PAGES: 208

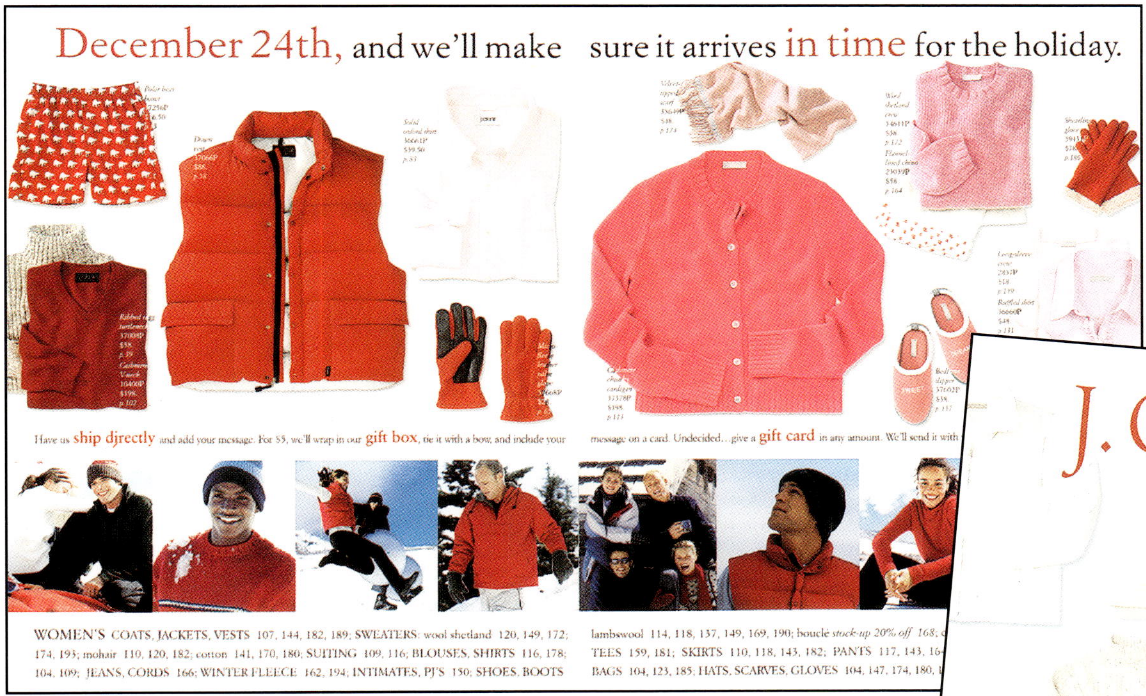

COMPANY: J. Crew
DIMENSIONS: 8 1/4" x 10 3/8"
NUMBER OF PAGES: 196

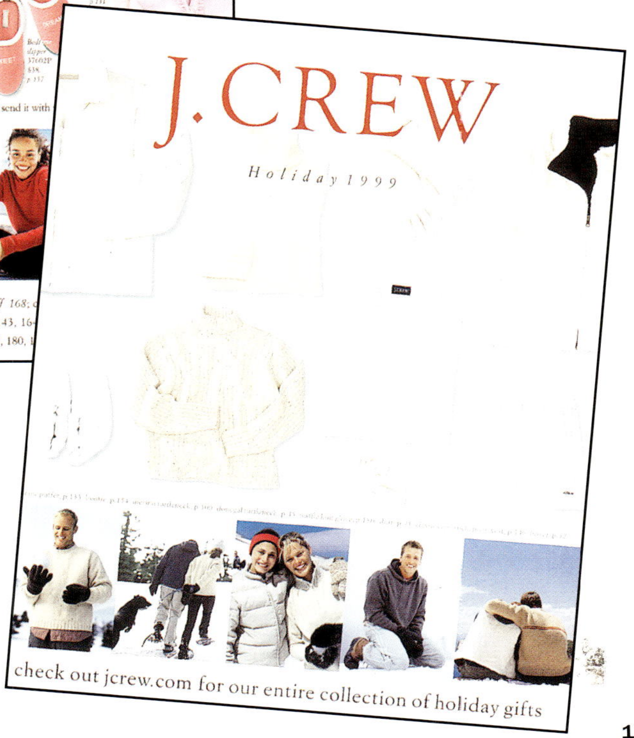

Two approaches to the contents pages from J. Crew. At top, a very straightforward listing of items and page numbers is superimposed on a photo of happy people in the snow.

Above, off-figure illustrations give specific gift suggestions while items and page numbers run along the bottom of the page. (This is the *girl's* spread, it is preceded by the *boy's* spread done in shades of, you guessed it, blue.)

POTTERY BARN

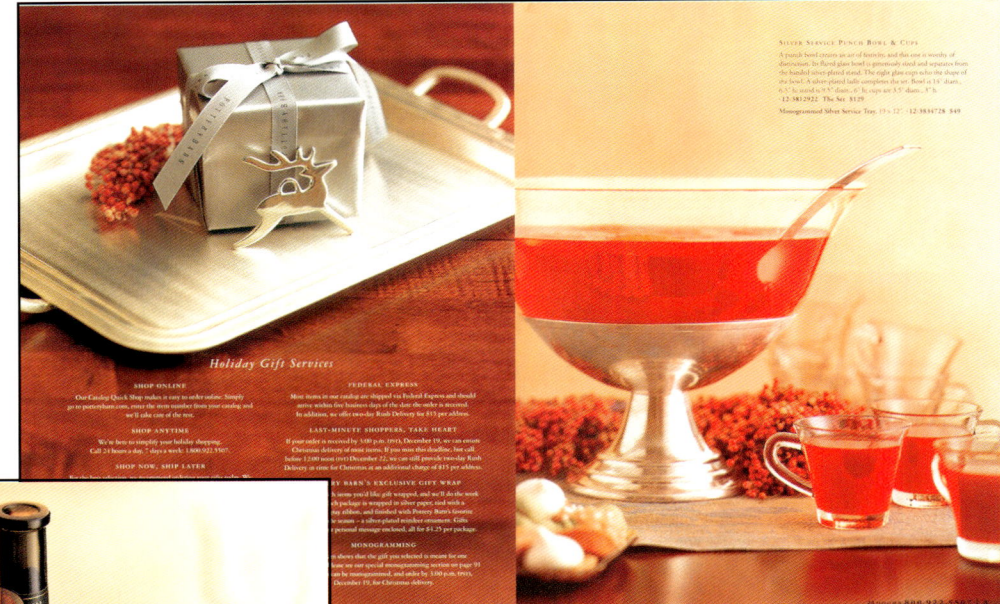

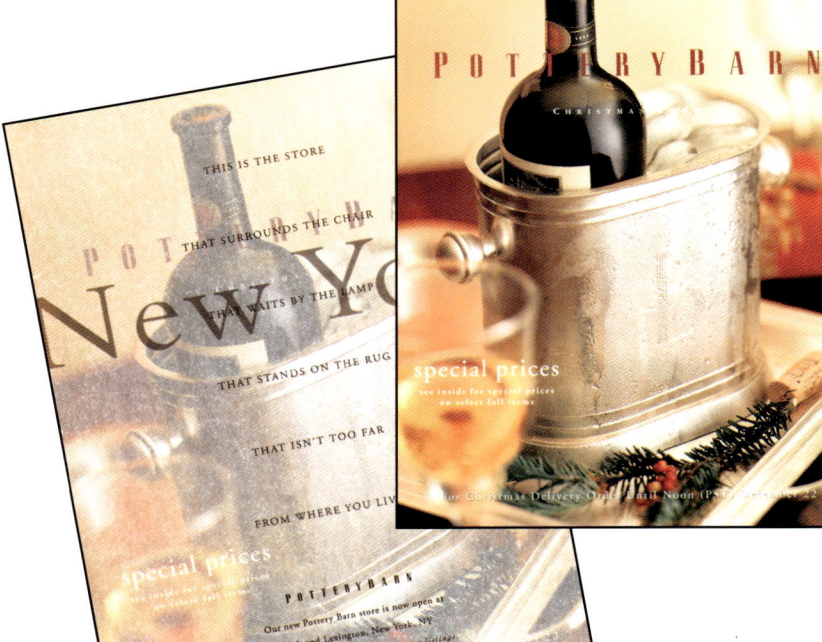

COMPANY: **Pottery Barn**
DIMENSIONS: 8 3/8" x 10 7/8" (both catalogs)
NUMBER OF PAGES: 180 (wine cooler), 184 (lamp)
WEBSITE: **www.potterybarn.com**

Stunning photography graces the covers and first spreads of these two catalogs from Pottery Barn. In the New York area both were mailed with a translucent parchment wrapped around the cover that read, "This is the store that surrounds the chair that waits by the lamp that stands on the rug that isn't too far from where you live." The parchment also announces the opening of a new Pottery Barn store in New York City.

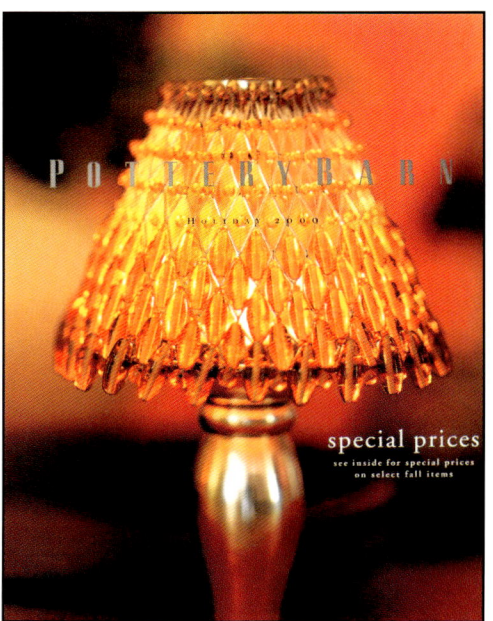

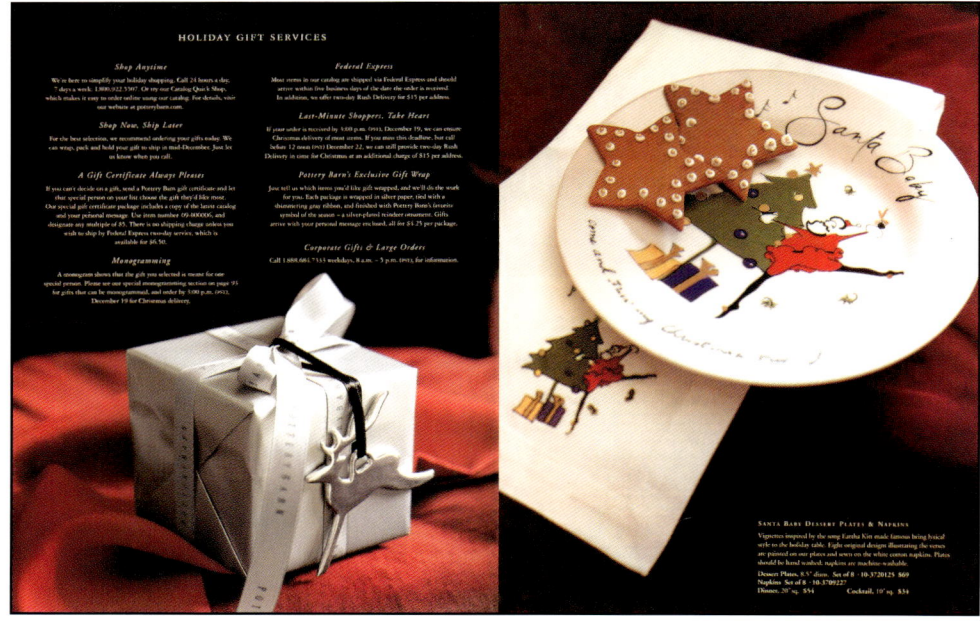

POTTERY BARN

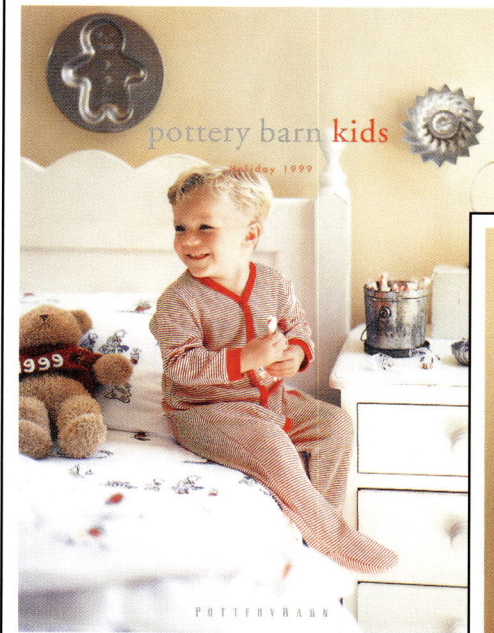

COMPANY: **Pottery Barn Kids**
DIMENSIONS: 8¼" x 10½"
NUMBER OF PAGES: 80

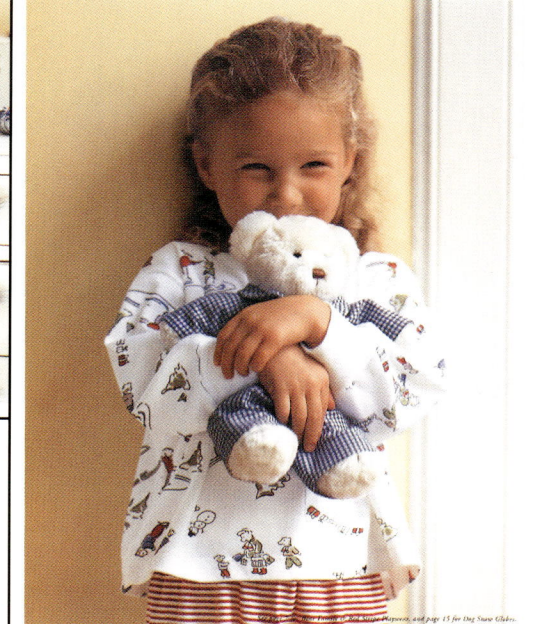 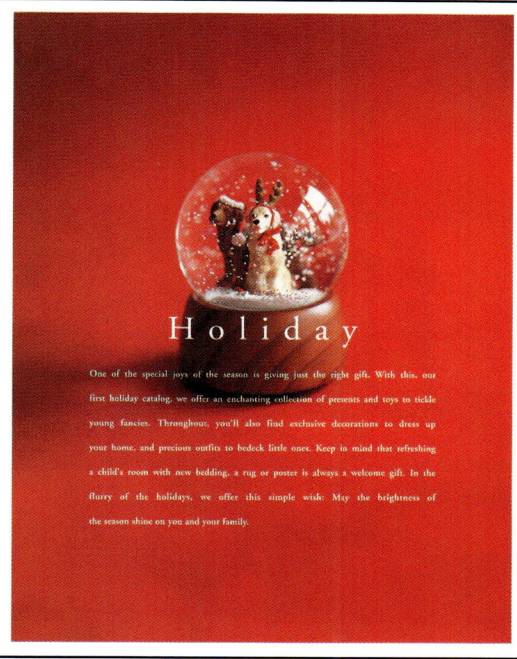

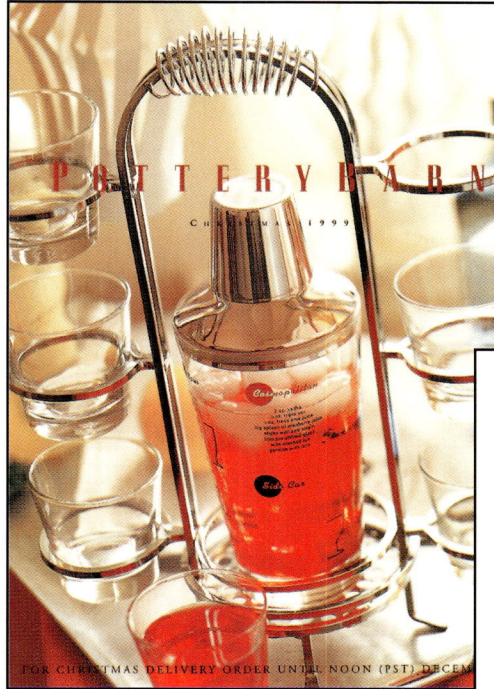

COMPANY: **Pottery Barn**
DIMENSIONS: 8³/₈" x 10⁷/₈"
NUMBER OF PAGES: 164

Pottery Barn has nudged the usual Christmas red toward the warmer side of the color wheel—giving these two catalogs a similar feel despite the very different product categories. Both introductory spreads incorporate large, eye-catching photos and elegant type into uncluttered layouts.

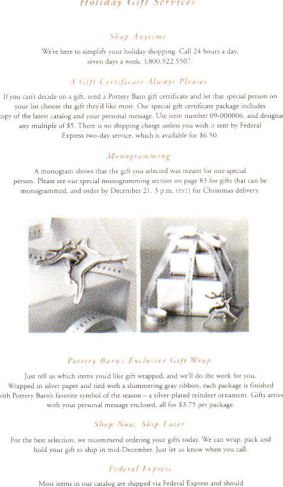 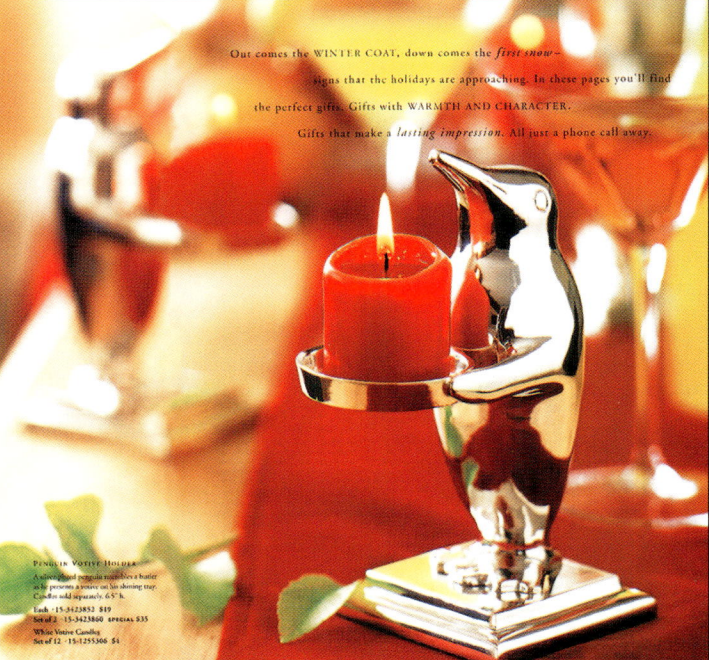

CARSON PIRIE SCOTT

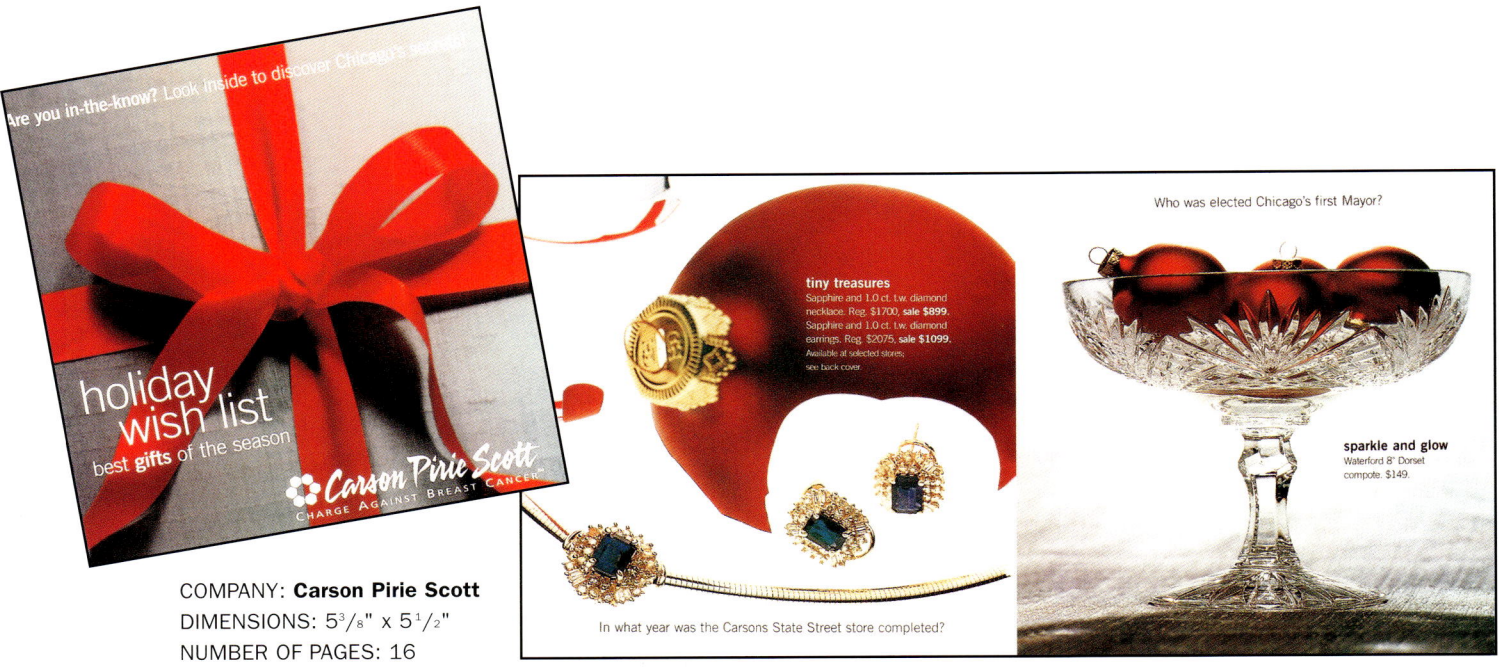

COMPANY: **Carson Pirie Scott**
DIMENSIONS: 5³/₈" x 5¹/₂"
NUMBER OF PAGES: 16

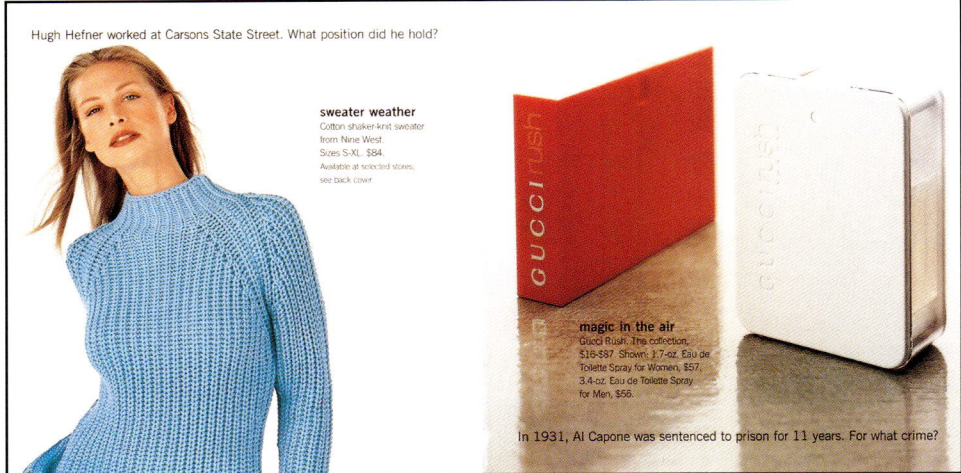

Each page of this booklet (above) includes a question about the city of Chicago. A page near the end lists the questions again with a space for each answer. Any customer who brought the completed page to a Carson Pirie Scott location during the holidays was registered to win a cruise to the Bahamas. The booklet was inserted with a magazine ad (right) that informed customers that with every charge made on a Carsons card a donation would be made to breast cancer research.

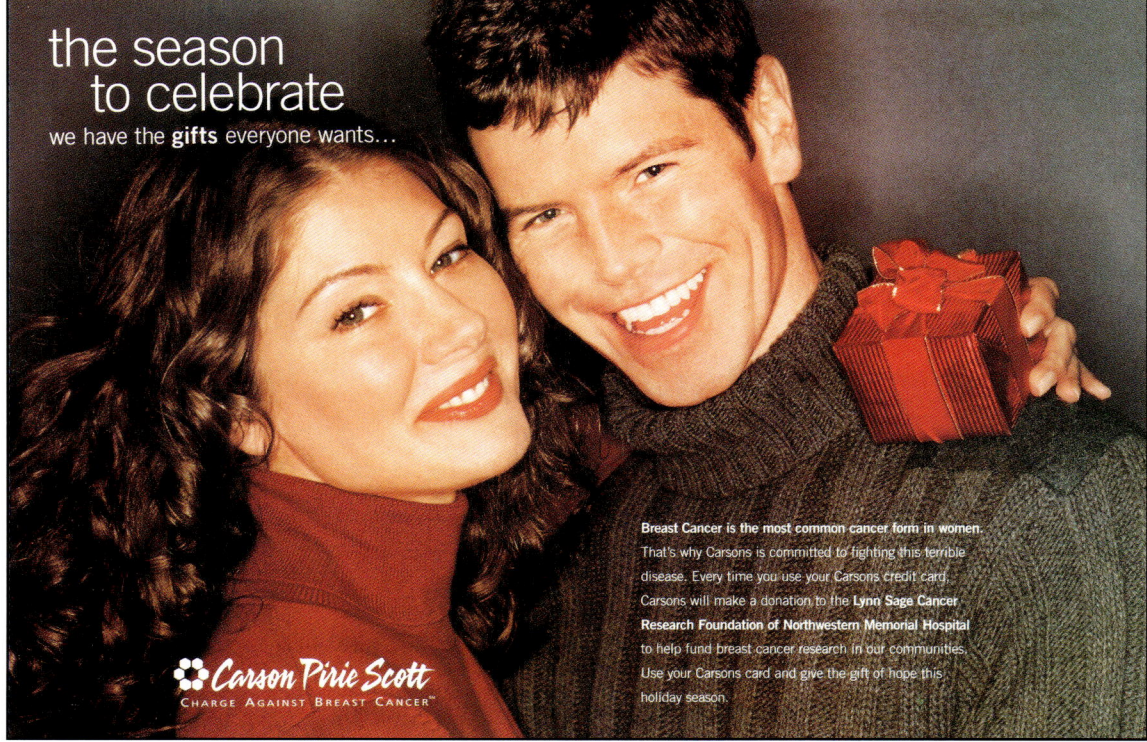

L.L. BEAN

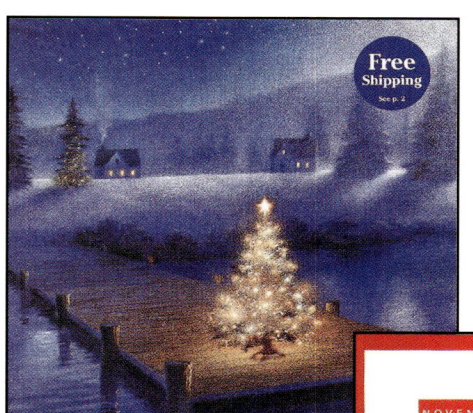

COMPANY: **L.L. Bean**
DIMENSIONS: 8" x 10 1/2"
NUMBER OF PAGES: 76

L.L. Bean provides a holiday planner with helpful reminders about when to bake the cookies and the last chance for express shipping.

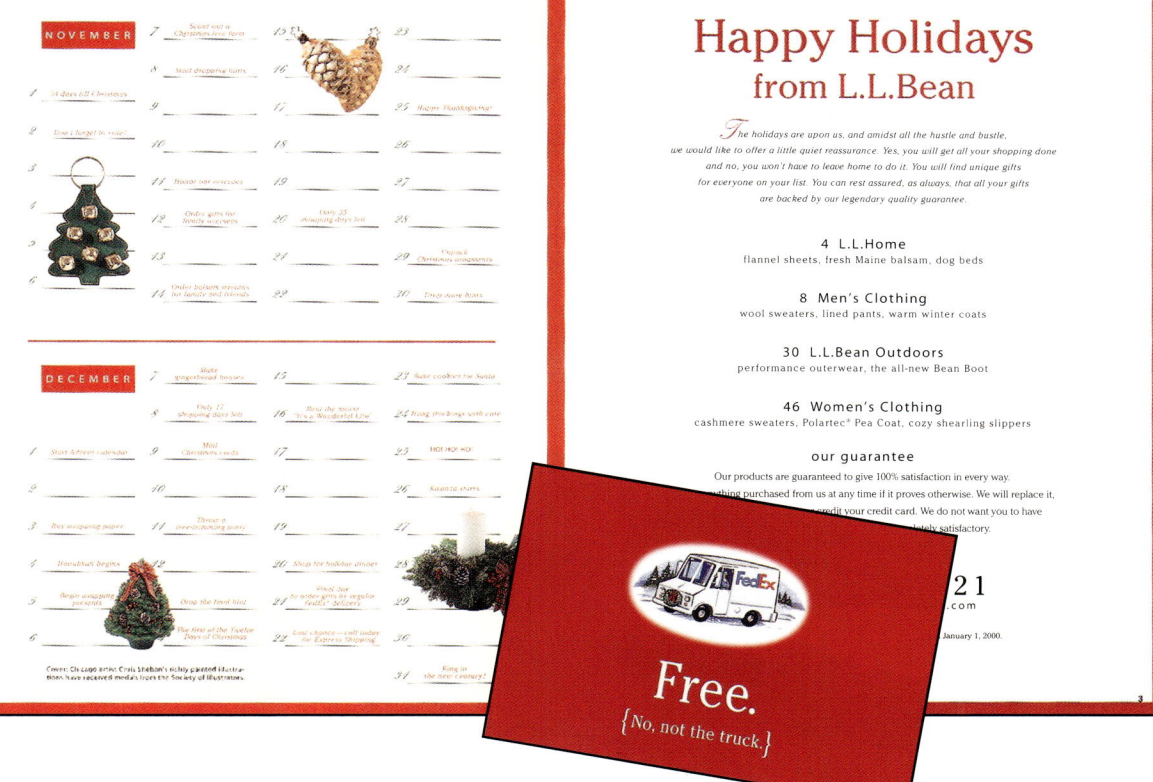

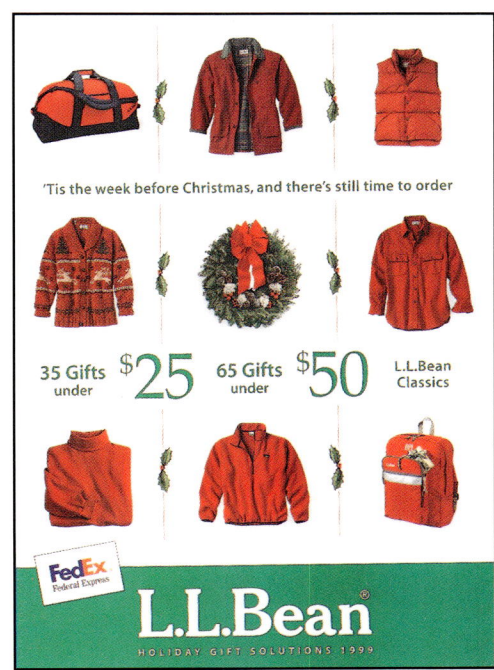

COMPANY: **L.L. Bean**
DIMENSIONS: 7 1/2" x 10 1/4"
NUMBER OF PAGES: 76

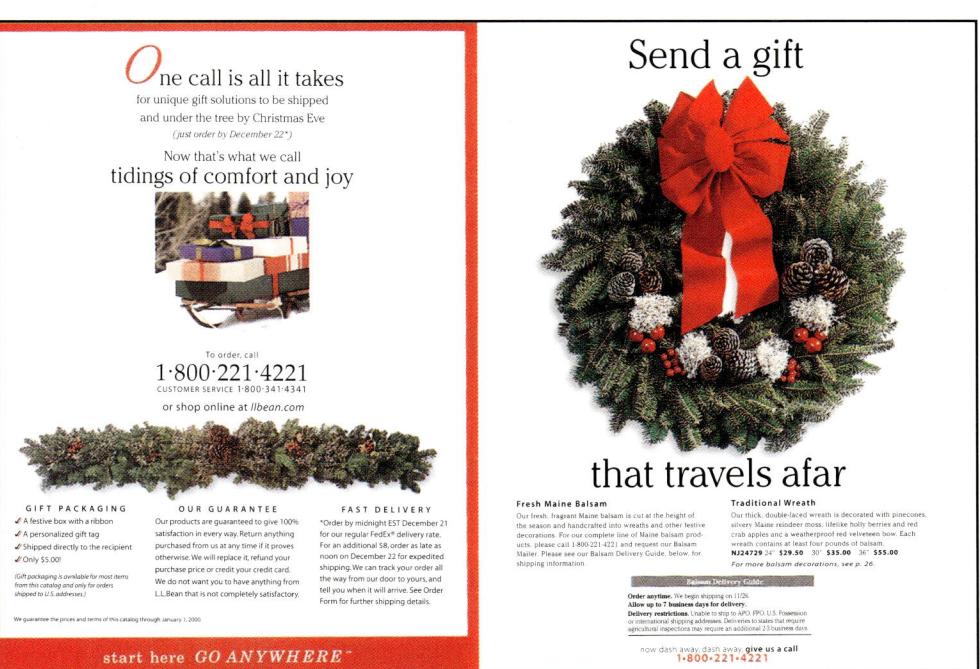

One last chance to get that gift there on time. L.L. Bean will wrap, ribbon, tag and put the gift under the tree; all the customer has to do is pick up the phone.

HENRI BENDEL

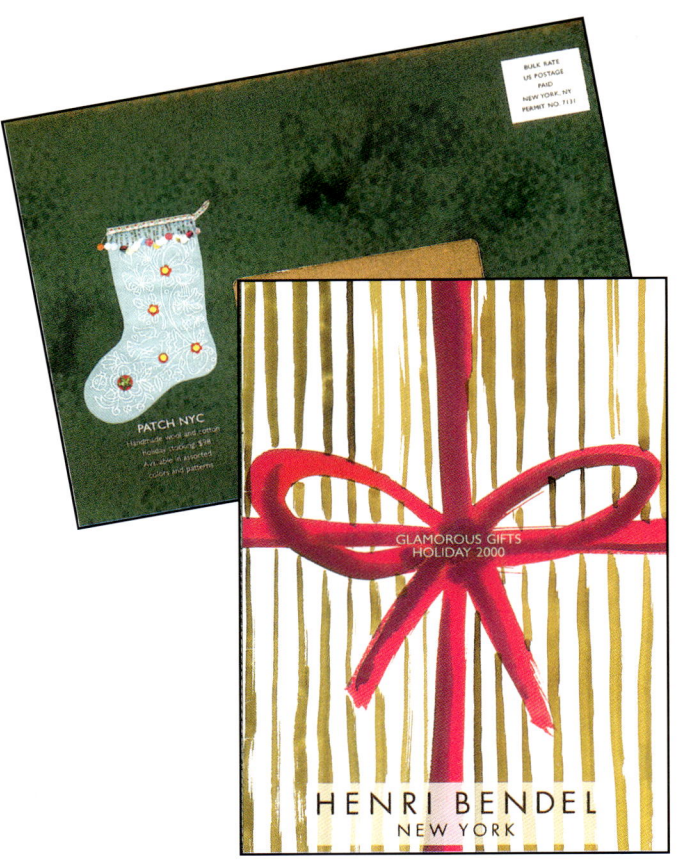

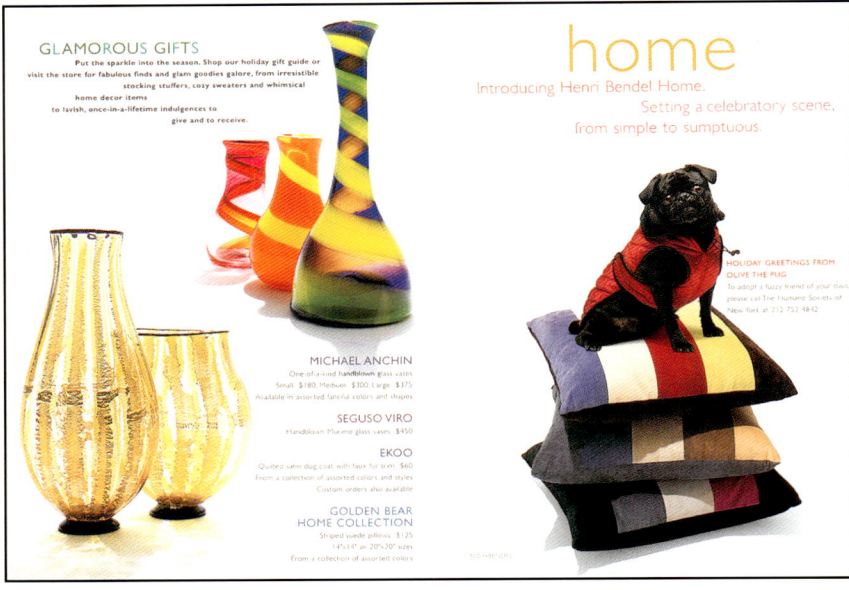

COMPANY: **Henri Bendel**
DIMENSIONS: 4½" x 6¼"
NUMBER OF PAGES: 32

The "present" on the cover of this booklet from Henri Bendel is hard to resist. Inside, festive colors help to sell the diverse gift ideas. Also included are holiday greetings from Olive the pug, and the phone number of The Humane Society of New York for those wishing to adopt their own "fuzzy friend"—perhaps the perfect gift for the home.

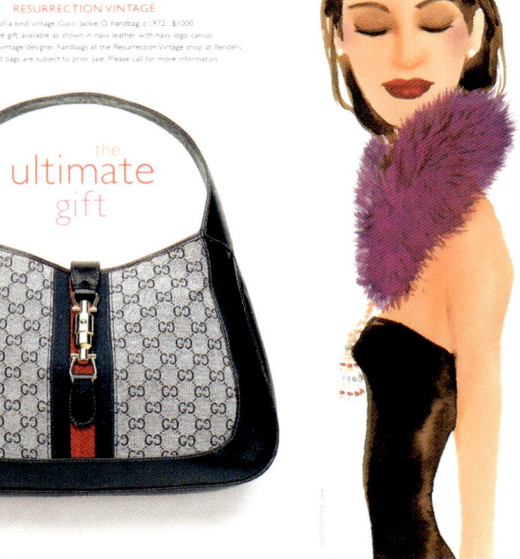

BARNEYS NEW YORK

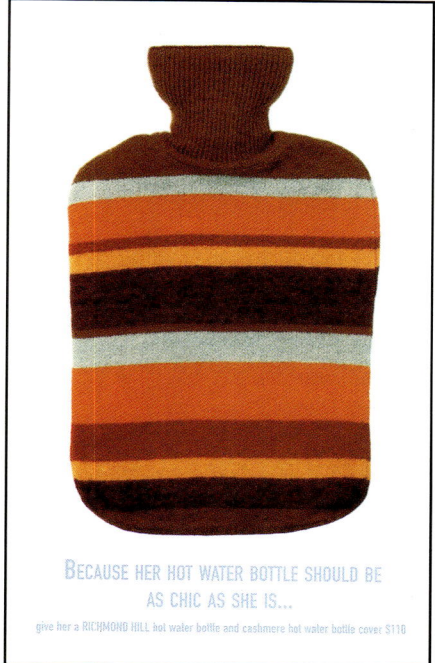
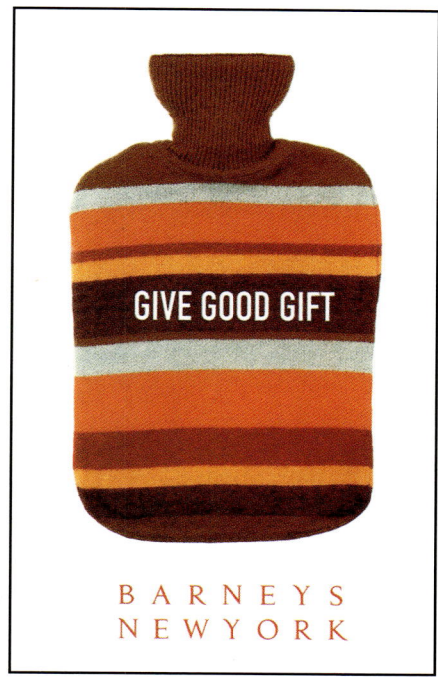

COMPANY: **Barneys New York**
DIMENSIONS: 4¾" x 7⅝" (closed)
38" x 7⅝" (fully opened)

The front and back of the piece feature the same item.

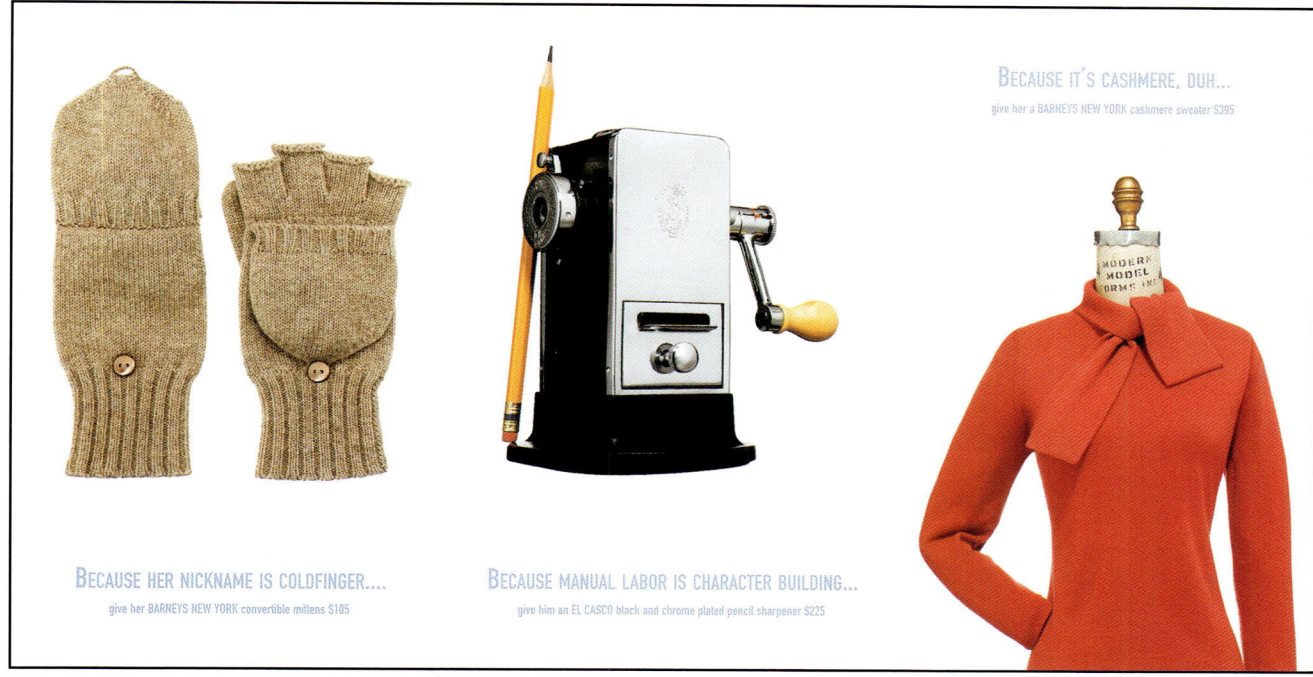

Whimsical captions accompany each gift and state a reason, if one is needed, for giving that item as a present. The gift-card panel caters to those who have given up in the attempt to decide, it reads: "Because giving gifts to discerning fashionistas and clothing connoisseurs can be a nightmare…"

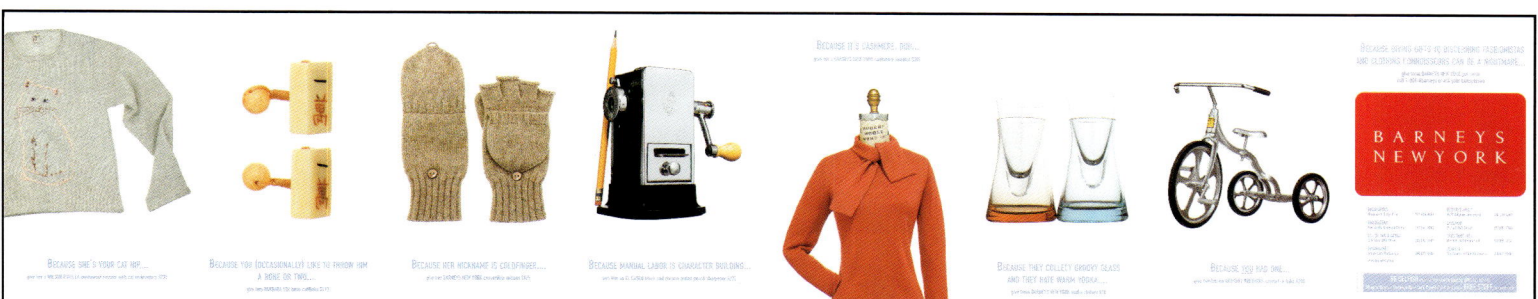

The piece fully opened.

BANANA REPUBLIC

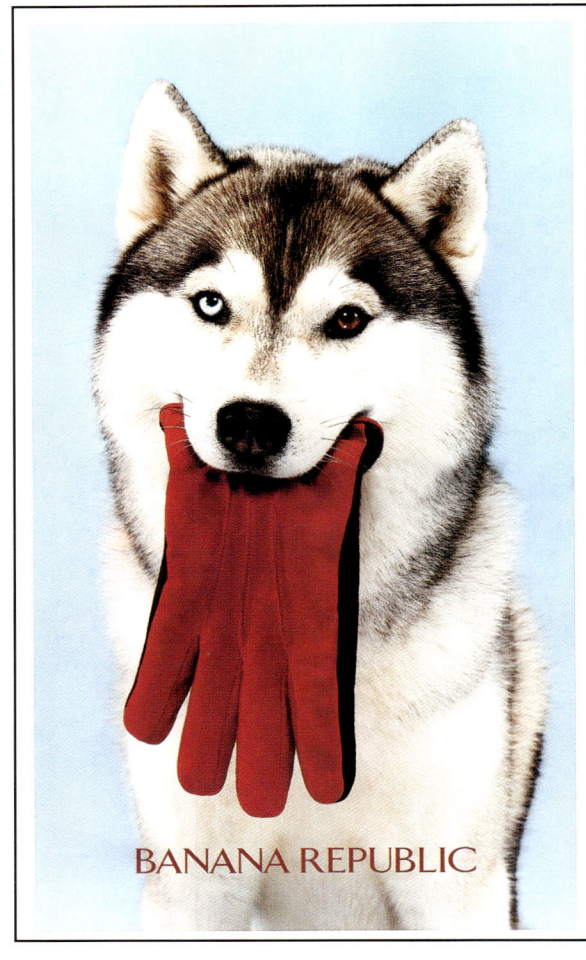

COMPANY: **Banana Republic**
DIMENSIONS: $12^{1}/_{4}"$ x $20^{5}/_{8}"$ (insert),
$8^{1}/_{2}"$ x $3^{3}/_{4}"$ (direct mail piece)
NUMBER OF PAGES: 6 (insert)
WEBSITE: **www.bananarepublic.com**

Color coordination and consistency are the key to the beauty and success of Banana Republic's holiday advertising. The color schemes of these images are closely matched whether the model is a man, woman or dog. Although a newspaper insert and a direct mail piece are shown here, the same images appeared in magazine ads, outdoor advertising and transit posters.

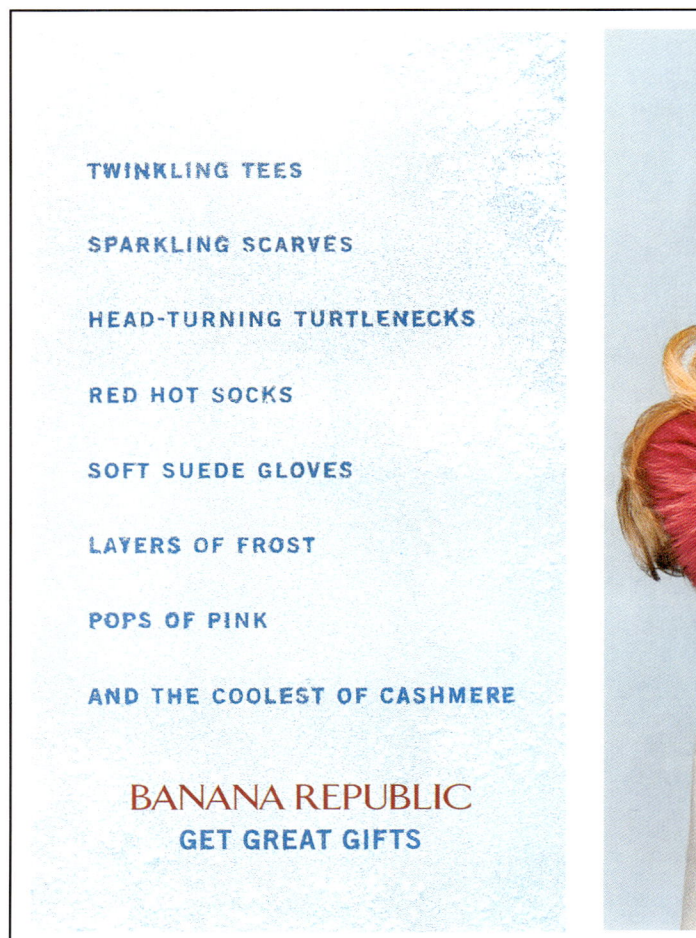
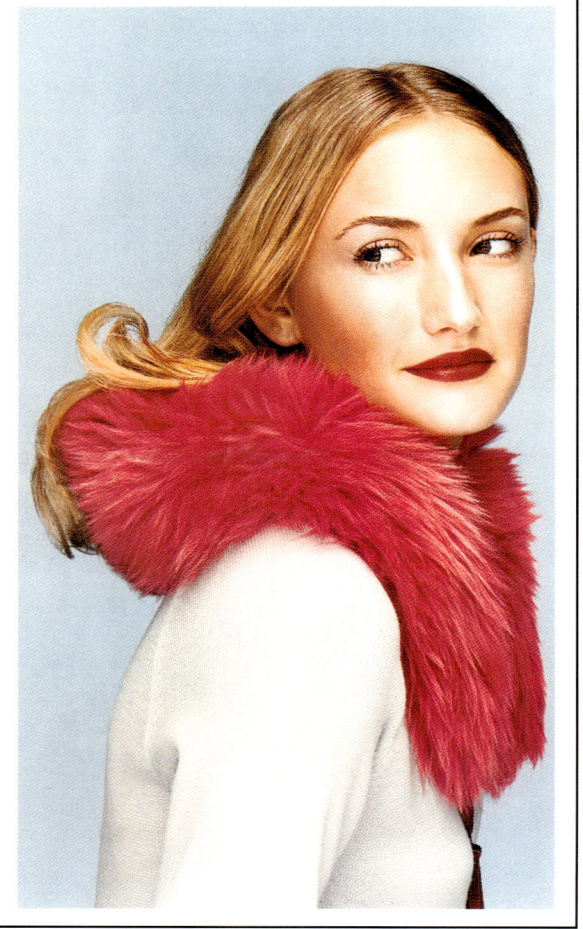

BANANA REPUBLIC

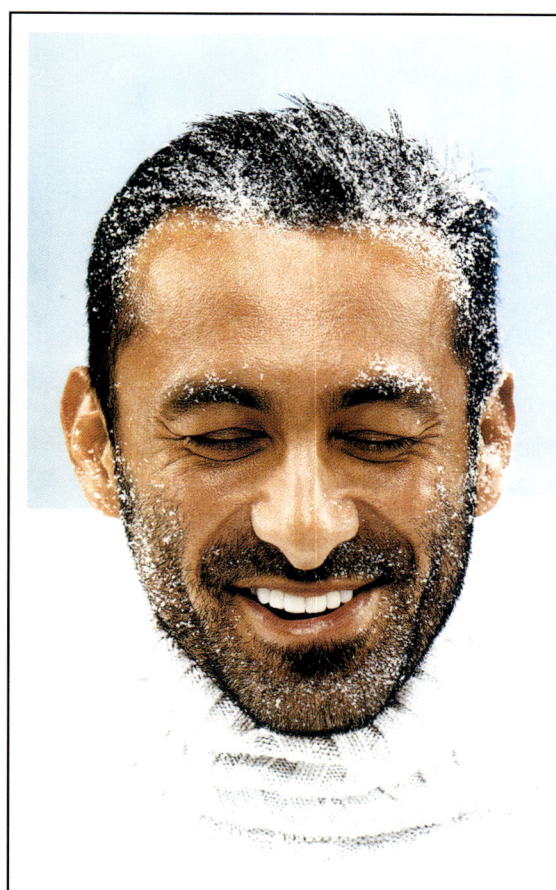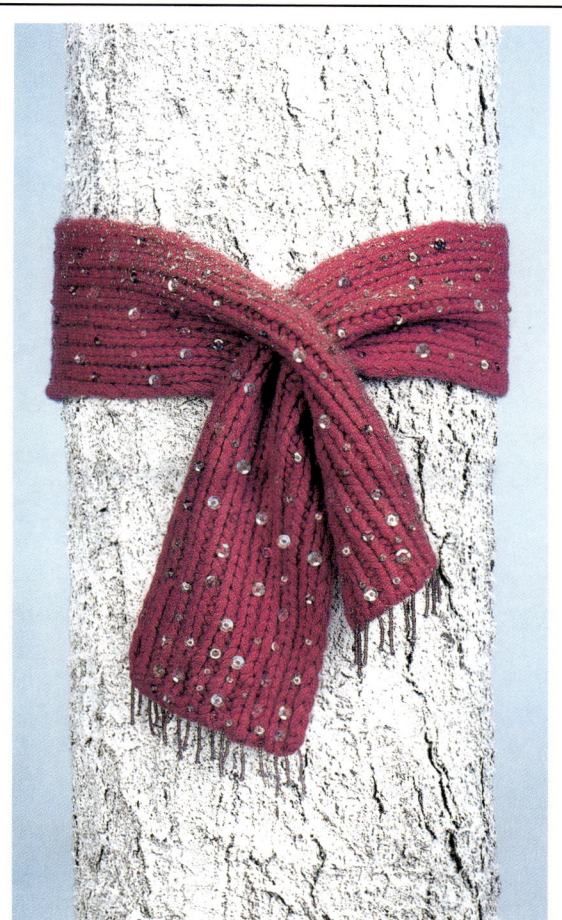

An inside spread and the back of the insert.

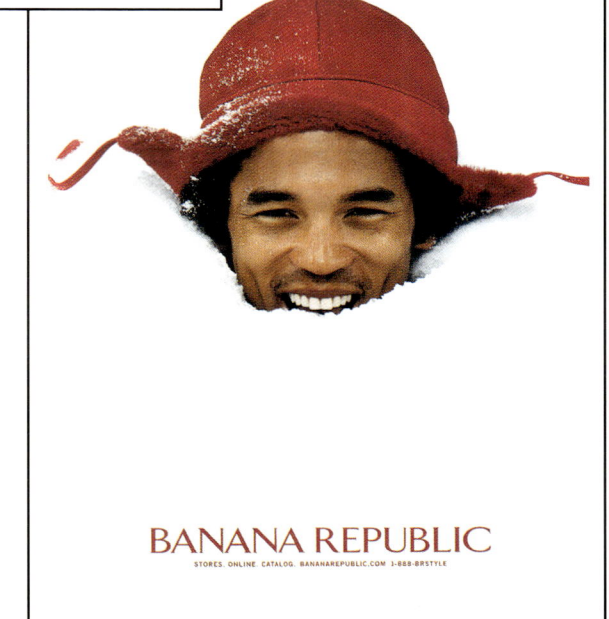

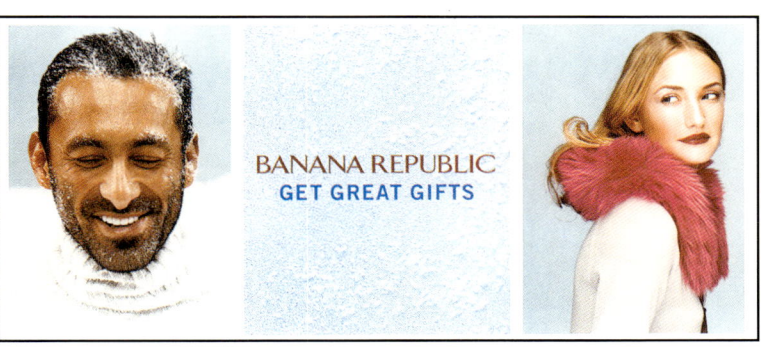

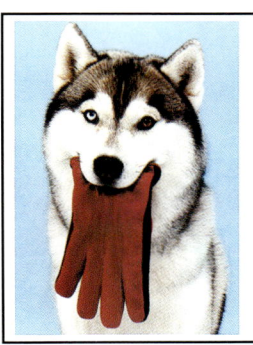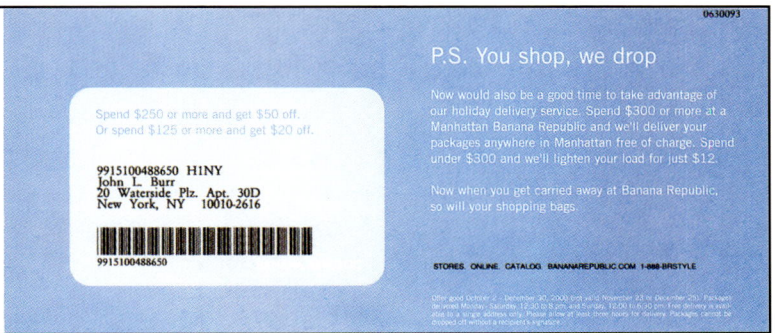

The front and inside of a direct mail piece.

Shopping Centers

DESPITE THE DIVERSITY of shopping centers, every mall, regardless of size, tenant mix, location or demographics, has one question in common—How are we going to attract customers to our center this Christmas?

The answers are as diverse. In fact, more diverse than ever, as each year we're introduced to new modes of marketing that open up exciting new ways to shine during the pivotal, make-or-break holiday selling season.

The special section that follows will take you behind the scenes of some of these sophisticated and successful marketers. These are centers that are not only venturing into new areas, but also executing the more established modes of advertising and promotion, such as catalogs and special events, with style and panache.

Our story on The Gardens at Palm Beach, for example, describes its marketing team's response to the new competition entering its primary trade area. The solution—an idea for the holidays that took innovative thinking and put it on fast forward. So forward, in fact, that The Gardens became the first shopping center in the U.S. to offer a gift of interactive family entertainment. This customized CD also involved a temporary holiday website that the mall was able to have completely underwritten by sponsors. This tool had many interesting sidelights, not the least of which was solving the problem of getting one million CDs into the hands of its customers. How did they do it? It's all right here, starting on the next page.

But what about the center that doesn't have the kind of budget a superregional like The Gardens has? This section also includes a story that takes you into the strategy behind a magazine for smaller malls to share. Three noncompeting Kravco malls in Pennsylvania have been doing it successfully for three years.

Meanwhile, the largest shopping center in the Caribbean, Plaza Las Américas in San Juan, Puerto Rico, took advantage of a special opportunity—its first Christmas after a long period of reconstruction. The center's advertising campaign used a simple icon in the center of each ad to get across the message that Plaza Las Américas is the perfect place to do holiday shopping: a quick, compelling communication.

Our neighbor to the north, Bramalea City Center in Ontario, Canada, had a brainstorm of its own—a gift registry service that was the first of its kind offered in a Canadian shopping center.

Where do people get these great ideas? From reading about what others are doing successfully. You'll see plenty of that in this section, which also includes catalogs that stand out from the crowd, such as that from The Plaza & The Court at King of Prussia—a well-orchestrated tie-in with the Philadelphia Orchestra. Then there's stunning newspaper inserts from Bellevue Square/The Plaza—to name a few.

So, read on and you can count on coming up with what we believe will be exciting ideas for your own Christmas advertising and marketing—all you could want for Christmas—and more.

THE GARDENS

High-Tech, High-Style

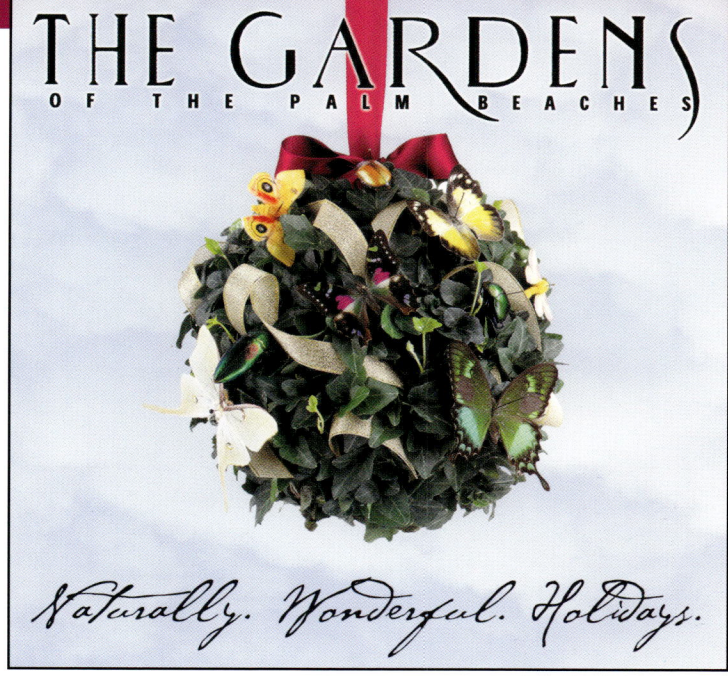

The cover for the interactive CD

THE GARDENS of the Palm Beaches, a south Florida super-regional shopping center, had new competition entering its market—a situation that motivated its marketing team to seek something for the holidays that was very forward thinking, an idea that would venture into new territory.

What The Gardens came up with made it the first shopping center in the country to introduce a new marketing concept—a gift of high-tech interactive family entertainment that enhanced the shopping experience for its customers while it marketed its retailers in a novel way.

The gift—called a "See D" by Tempo, the company that created it—was a customized compact disc that provided an interactive experience consumers could access from their personal computers. It featured jazz renditions of classic holiday music and "enhanced" entertainment highlights including holiday entertaining, fashion, travel, millennium trivia and kids' games, plus information on The Gardens' retailers and upcoming holiday events. In addition, it provided customers with a new way of exploring the thousands of options for enjoying the holidays by hotlinking customers directly to noncompeting websites that offered the products, services and information they wanted.

According to Morgan, Tempo arranged to have the CD and the cost of the temporary holiday website completely underwritten by sponsors. Sponsors included Bloomingdale's, Philips Electronics and *Travel & Leisure* magazine. In exchange for their financial investment, sponsors received a feature on the CD and a link to their website. Tempo also obtained a media sponsor for the radio and TV spots.

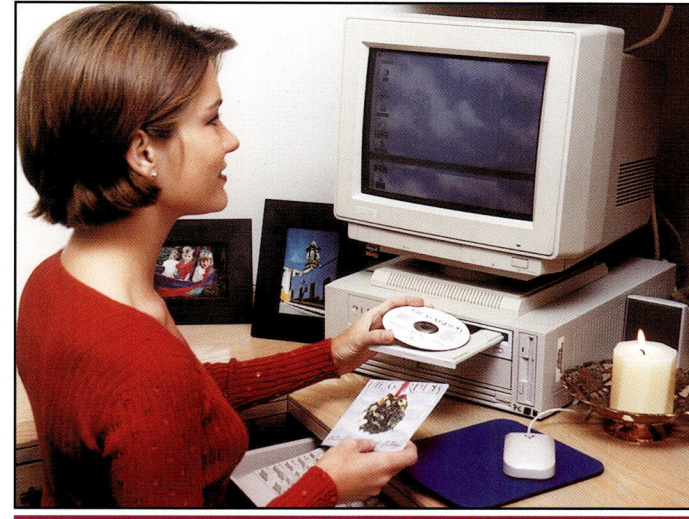

Major support went into the promoting the CD. There was a temporary holiday website, TV and radio ads and in-mall posters.

Distributing the CD presented a real challenge, however. According to Ann Morgan, marketing director, The Gardens had a total of 1 million CDs to distribute in a narrow window (Nov. 23 to Dec. 31).

How do you get 1 million CDs into the hands of your customers? One way was with local high school volunteers repre-

THE GARDENS

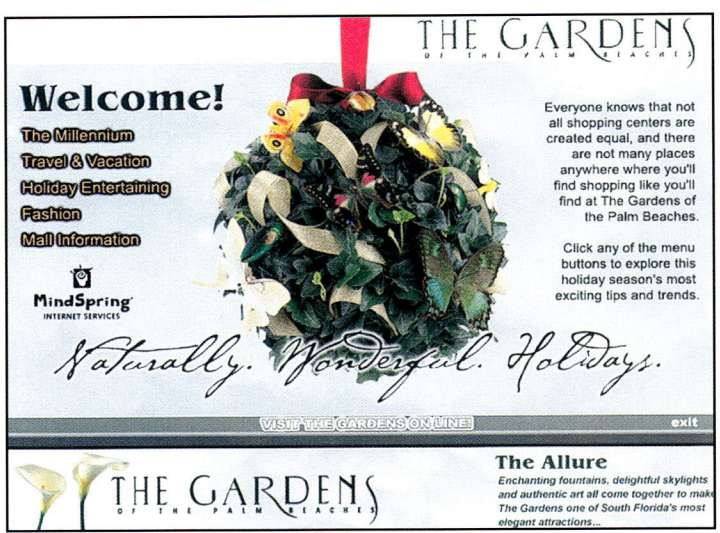
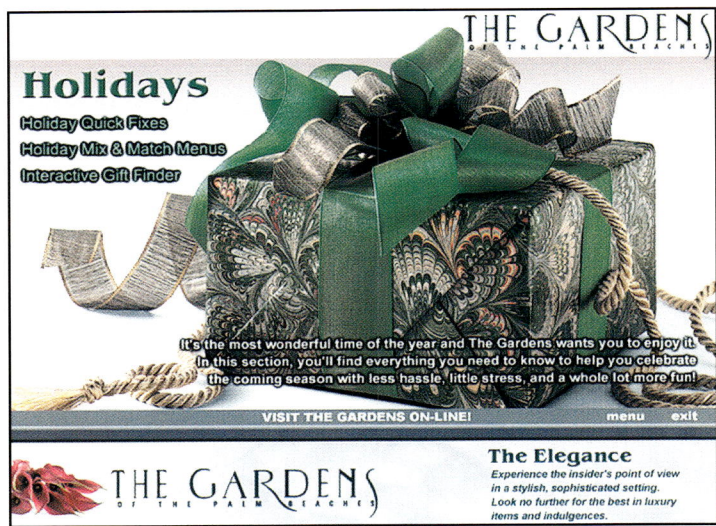
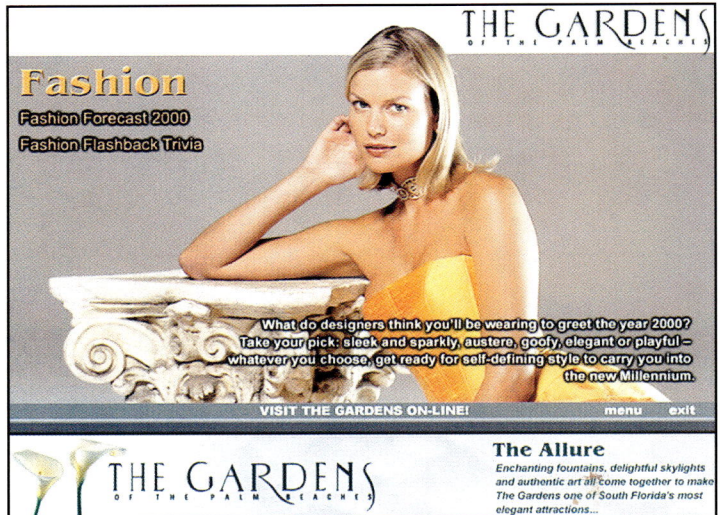
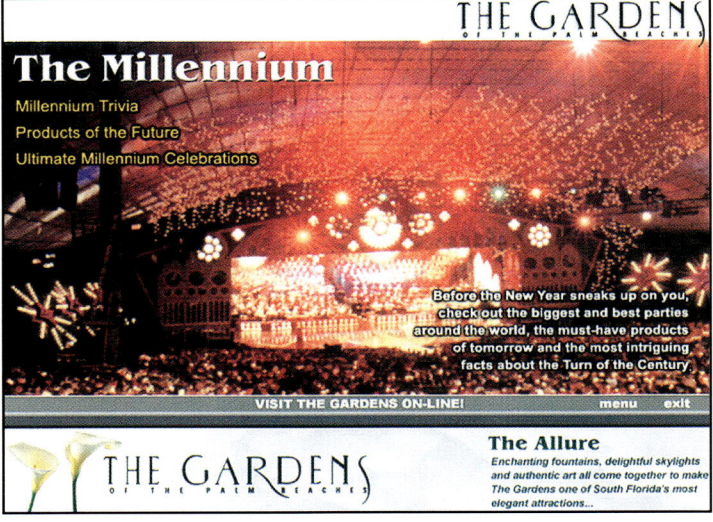

The CD offered users a wide selection.

senting various school organizations. Customers entering the mall could look for The Gardens Holiday CD Greeters—local students whose organizations received grants for their volunteering to serve as on-site distributors. Customers could also pick up the CD in stores or at the Information Desk.

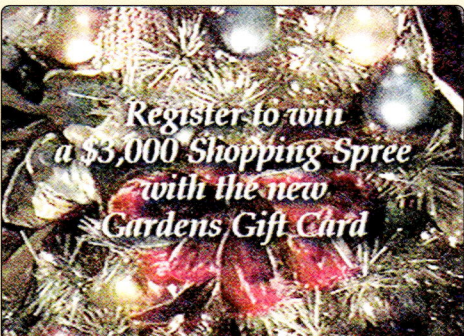

The Gardens used TV to promote the CD and the new gift card. In this spot, the package opens to reveal a CD.

But when you're talking in terms of a million, this was just the tip of the iceberg.

Getting the CDs out became a whole management team effort. "We designed a very specific distribution program and tracked it in detail," says Morgan. "We all had a hand in its coordination and the tracking was very important because of the limited time period."

The real challenge, though, was inserting hundreds of thousands of CDs into newspapers. "The newspapers we used had never inserted a CD, so it took a lot of investigation to be sure it could be done," says Morgan. "All of them were hand inserted."

Daunting as it was, it was clearly worth it. "Everybody was talking about this CD all through the holiday season," Morgan reports. "It was so new and unique that it really created a stir. I still get calls from people who are using it."

As new as the interactive CD was, The

THE GARDENS

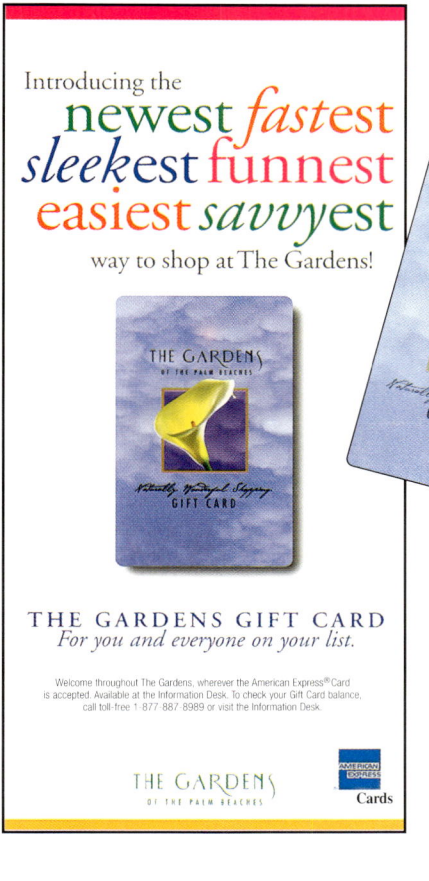

One of the first malls in the country to introduce the gift card concept, The Gardens offered a special holiday designed edition. Created in partnership with American Express, the card offered another way for consumers to give a gift.

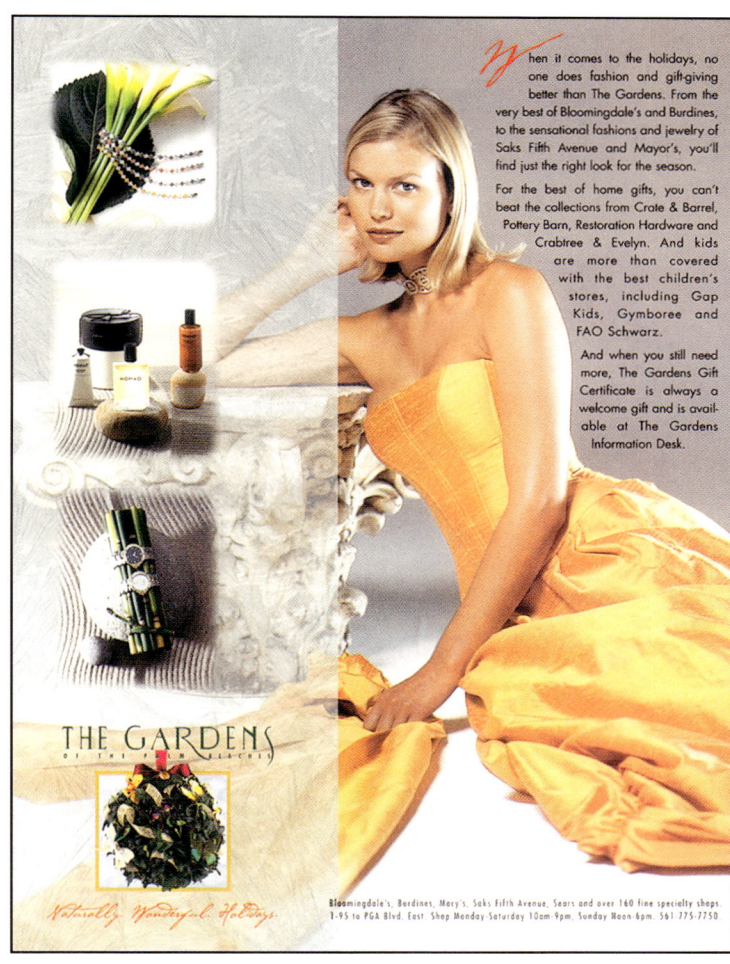

The copy in the magazine ad works in the names of the stores by relating them to merchandise. The ad ran in *Palm Beach Illustrated* magazine.

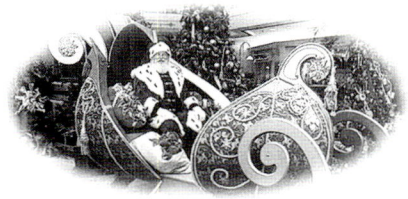

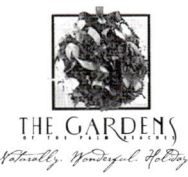

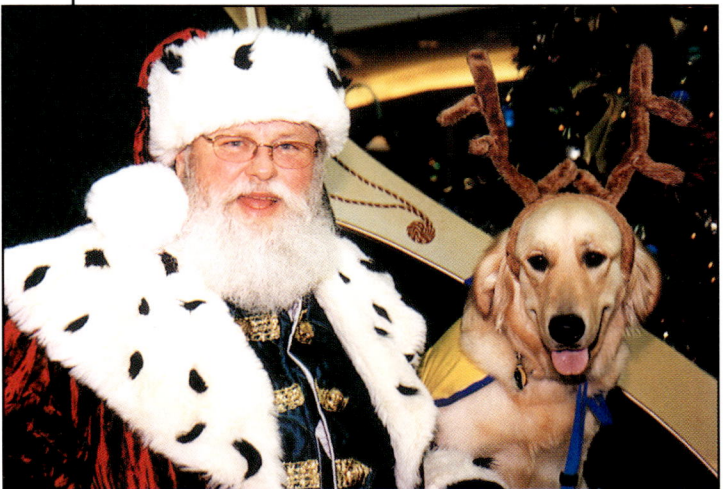

Proceeds from all portrait sales on Nov. 20 were used to benefit a national organization that trains dogs to help the disabled.

THE GARDENS

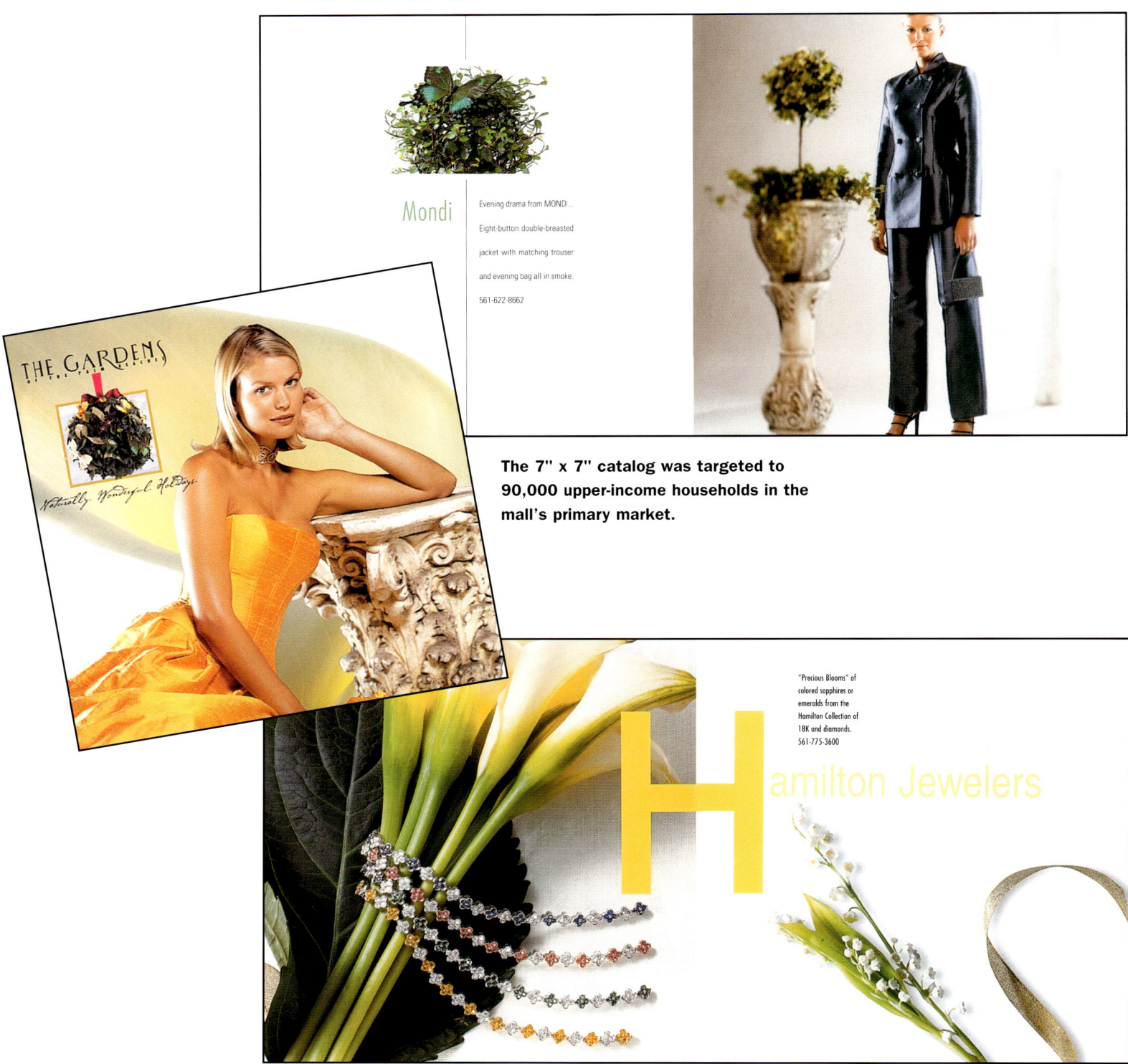

The 7" x 7" catalog was targeted to 90,000 upper-income households in the mall's primary market.

The Gardens of the Palm Beaches, Palm Beach Gardens, FL
OWNER/MANAGER: **Forbes/Cohen Properties,** Southfield, Michigan
DIRECTOR OF OPERATIONS: **David Haysmer**
MARKETING DIRECTOR: **Ann B. Morgan, SCMD**
SPECIAL EVENTS DIRECTOR: **Karen Grosser**
AGENCY (print/graphics): **2M&G Marketing Arts,** Tiberon, CA
CD PRODUCTION: **Tempo, Inc.,** Atlanta
CEO: **Bob May**
TV/RADIO PRODUCTION: **Parallax Productions,** West Palm Beach, FL

Gardens still utilized traditional marketing vehicles such as its holiday catalog. However, unlike many catalogs that pick up their participating vendors' artwork, The Gardens catalog presented each vendor photographed in the same style. With few exceptions, the vendors were presented as spreads. All the stores in the center were listed in the catalog. "We like to control the creative tone of the catalog because we feel like it gives us more a consistent image," says Morgan. "It's a good tool for us to reinforce our brand."

We were curious to know if their stores had trouble giving up creative control over their usual advertising image. Morgan conceded, "It does take some finesse, but the retailers know our work."

THE GARDENS

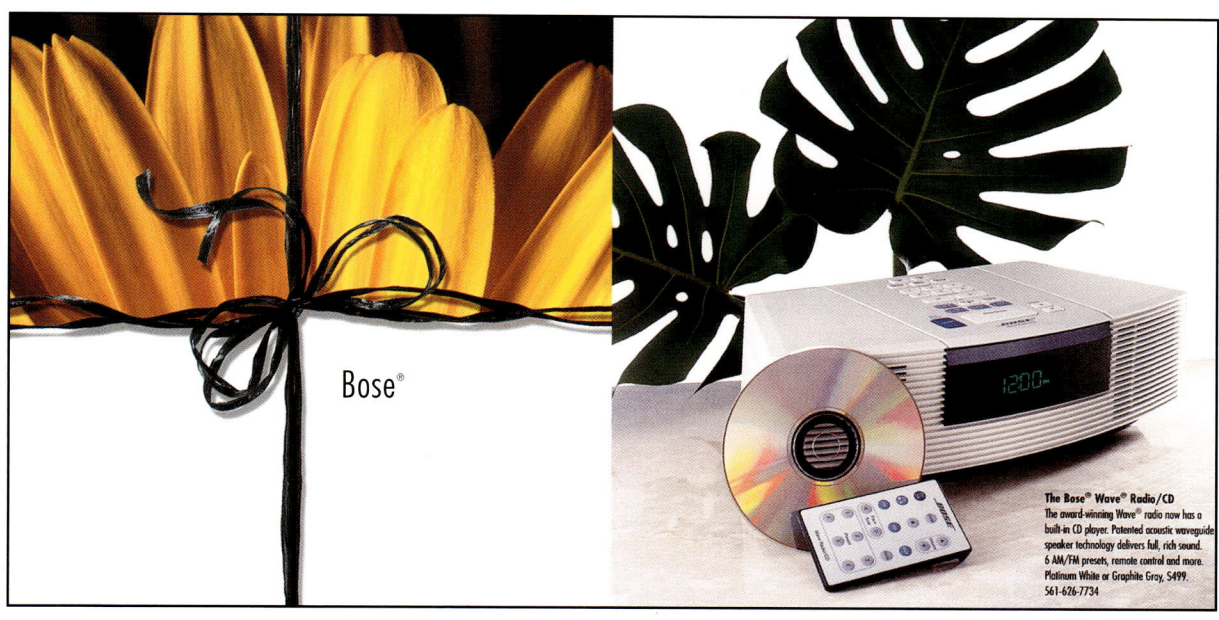

Bose®

The Bose® Wave® Radio/CD
The award-winning Wave® radio now has a built-in CD player. Patented acoustic waveguide speaker technology delivers full, rich sound. 6 AM/FM presets, remote control and more. Platinum White or Graphite Gray, $499.
561-626-7734

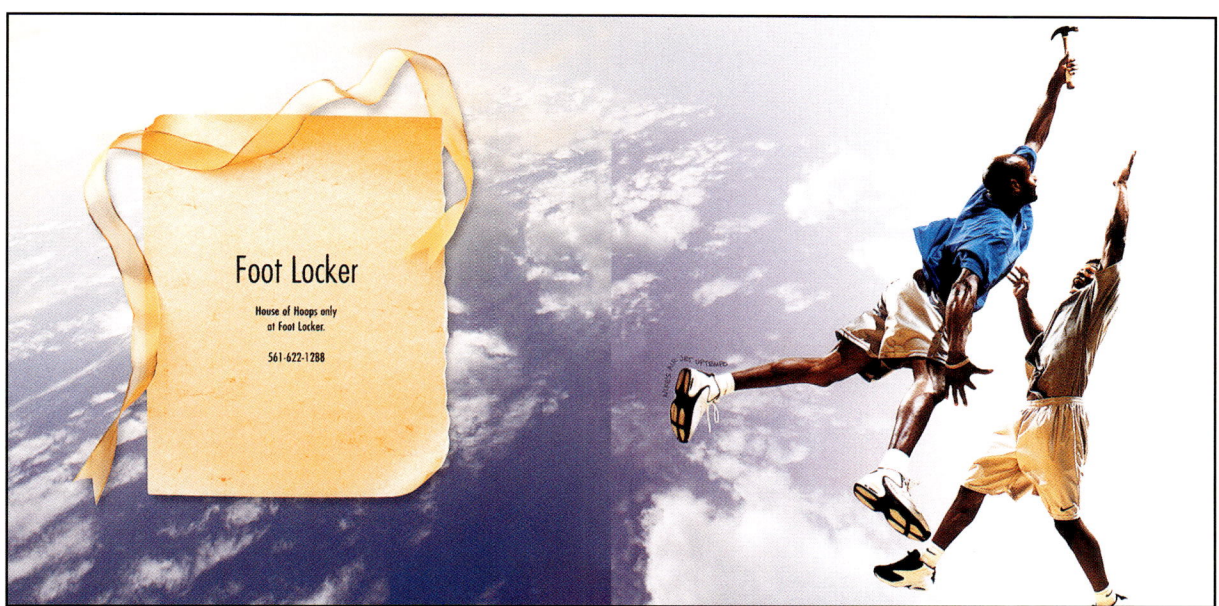

Foot Locker

House of Hoops only at Foot Locker.
561-622-1288

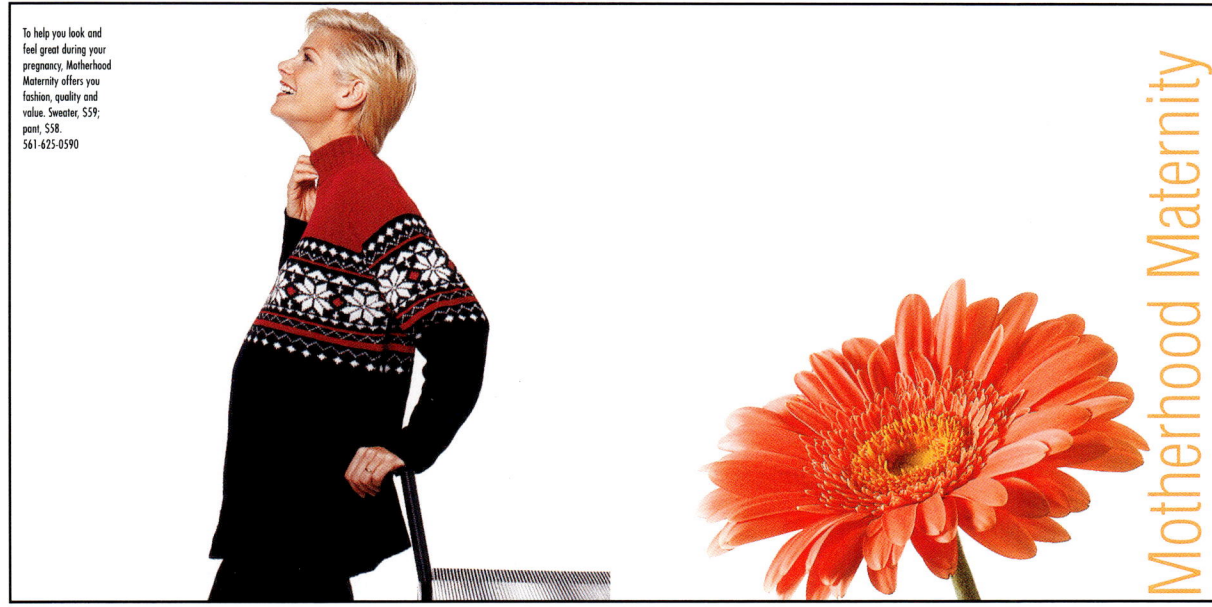

To help you look and feel great during your pregnancy, Motherhood Maternity offers you fashion, quality and value. Sweater, $59; pant, $58.
561-625-0590

Motherhood Maternity

KRAVCO COMPANY

Sharing the Holidays

Lehigh Valley Mall/Montgomery Mall/Quaker Bridge Mall

With Christmas a time for sharing—three non-competing Kravco malls in Pennsylvania did exactly that with The Mag, a syndicated catalog with specific customization. Now in its third year of publication, the new Mag reflects some notable changes at the same time it fulfills its original objectives.

"The goal was to create a magazine for smaller malls to share. These malls don't have the budget to do their own, so this is much more cost efficient for them," says Lorna Rudnick, president of Lorel Advertising. "The other goal was to create a magazine that had enough customer appeal that it wouldn't go from the mailbox to the trash!"

Whereas the original Mag had a glossy magazine feeling, chock full of merchandise and with some store ads, Holiday 2000 has a warm, user-friendly sensibility about it—the kind of magazine you'd want to keep around your home. One reason is the addition of a number of how-to features that range from making Christmas stockings to ideas for gift wrapping to baking something special for the holidays. "We wanted to personalize it," says Rudnick. "with *your* family, *your* fashion, *your* home, and basically get away from the clutter."

The publication represents a real team effort between the agency and the malls. The three-month process started in August with the agency going through the stores in each mall to find similar type stores, so they can be grouped in categories. Rudnick explains that they then sent a letter to the stores, telling them they were putting together The Mag for holiday and would like to include them, and send a stylist out to the store to pull merchandise. "As long as they're willing to let us photograph that's all they need to be in the book," she says.

Lorel's creative people comped the look and feel they wanted including the cover. Next, they brought the marketing managers of the malls in together. "We made a presentation to them of what we wanted this book to look like, which basically was about simplicity, and getting away from the clutter, and how we'd like to do it," Rudnick explains. "We went through the editorial pages to give them a general overview, and they suggested stores they'd like to see included in the book. We do it all as a team."

The mall managers were asked for their input and what else they would like to see done. "It was their idea to have the gift list," says Rudnick. "We also discussed what to give away. Everyone agreed on wrapping paper."

With the exception of black plates changes for the type (store listings, mall information, etc.) 25 of The Mag's 28 pages are identical. The exceptions are

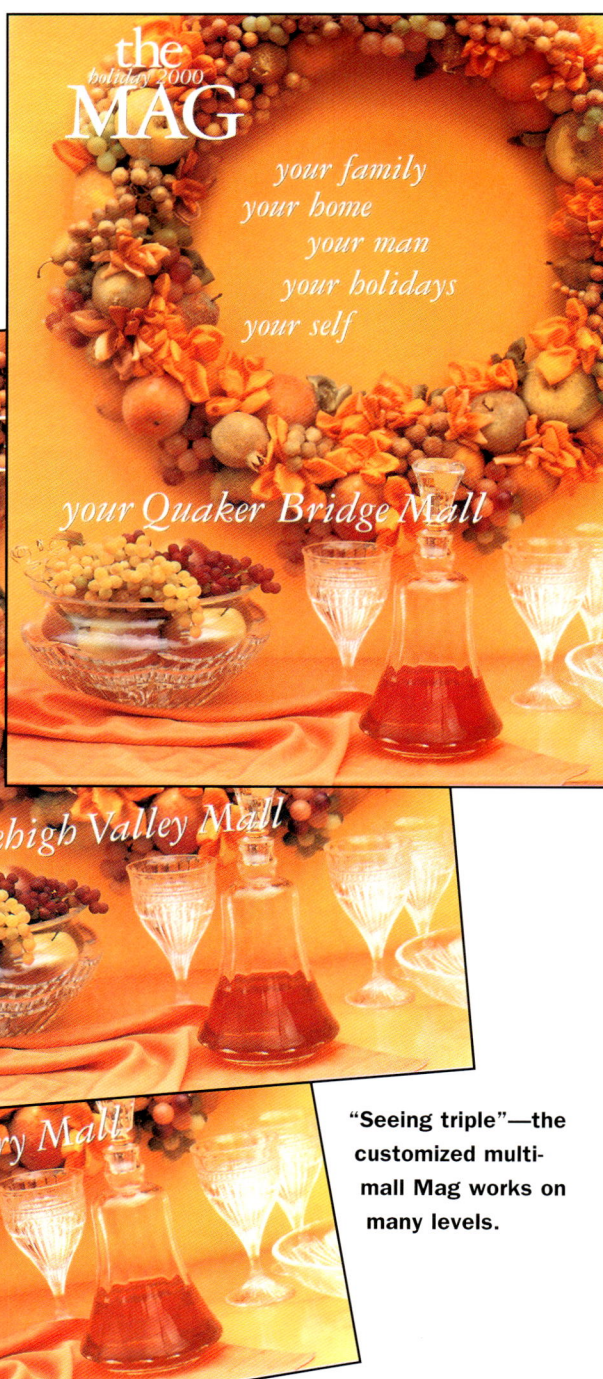

"Seeing triple"—the customized multi-mall Mag works on many levels.

page three which has a photo of the mall manger and special events and the page devoted to each mall's community cause.

The Mag arrived in 50,000 homes the first two weeks of November. The mailing list was made up of each mall's data base and lists that that met criteria for households provided by the mall marketing people. "They looked at their research and gave us the zip codes they wanted," explains Rudnick.

"There was great feedback from both customers and mall merchants who loved the way their merchandise was presented, and the magazine's connection with their community," says Rudnick. "There was a huge response to the free holiday wrap. They ran out of it in a week!"

Approximately 7,000 sweepstakes were returned for all three malls. Coupon returns for the individual stores ranged from 100 to 1000, depending on the store and the type of coupon. "The marketing people reiterated to me how excited the customers felt about The Mag," says Rudnick. "They said customers actually stopped them in the mall and said I recognize you from your photo in The Mag and I want you to know I think this is a great piece!"

Lehigh Valley Mall

MARKETING MANAGER: **Betsy Harting**
Montgomery Mall
MARKETING MANAGER: **Brooke Fellus**
Quaker Bridge Mall
MARKETING MANAGER: **Felicia Pollaro**
MANAGER/DEVELOPER: **Kravco Company**
AGENCY: **Lorel Advertising,**
King of Prussia, PA
PRESIDENT: **Lorna Rudnick**

KRAVCO COMPANY

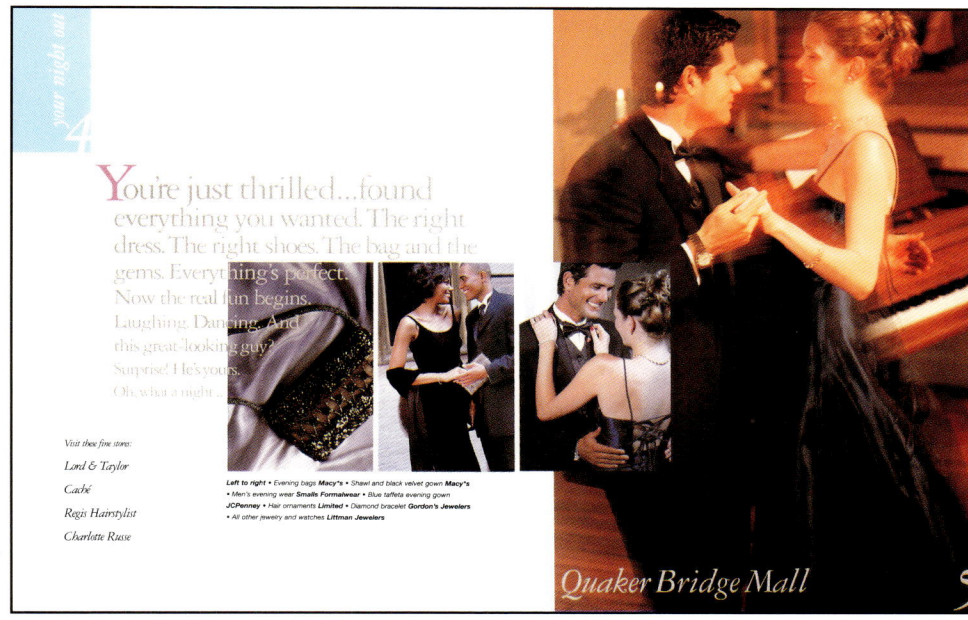

The opening spread with a welcome from the mall manager was customized for each mall.

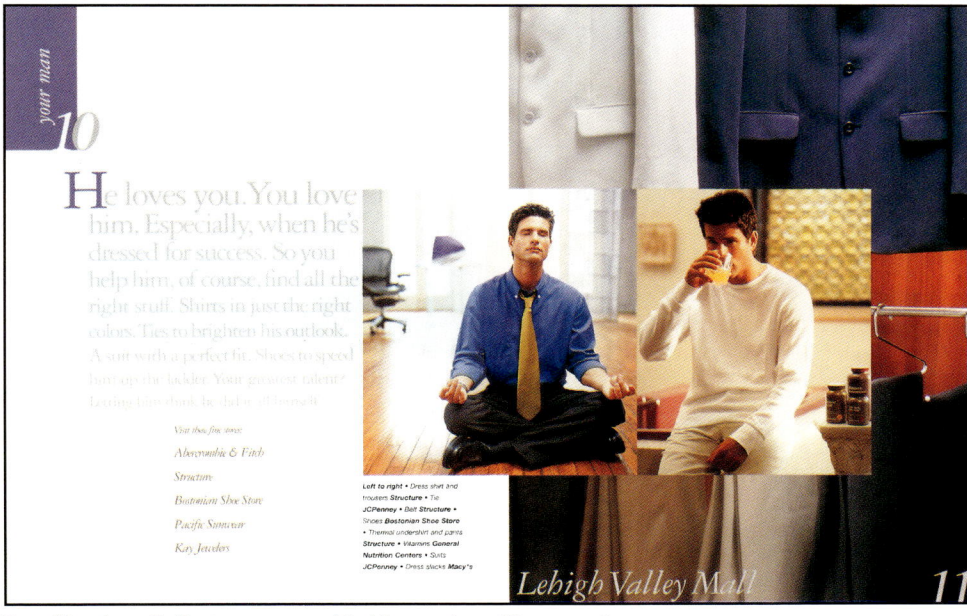

Specific store listings were provided by each mall's manager.

KRAVCO COMPANY

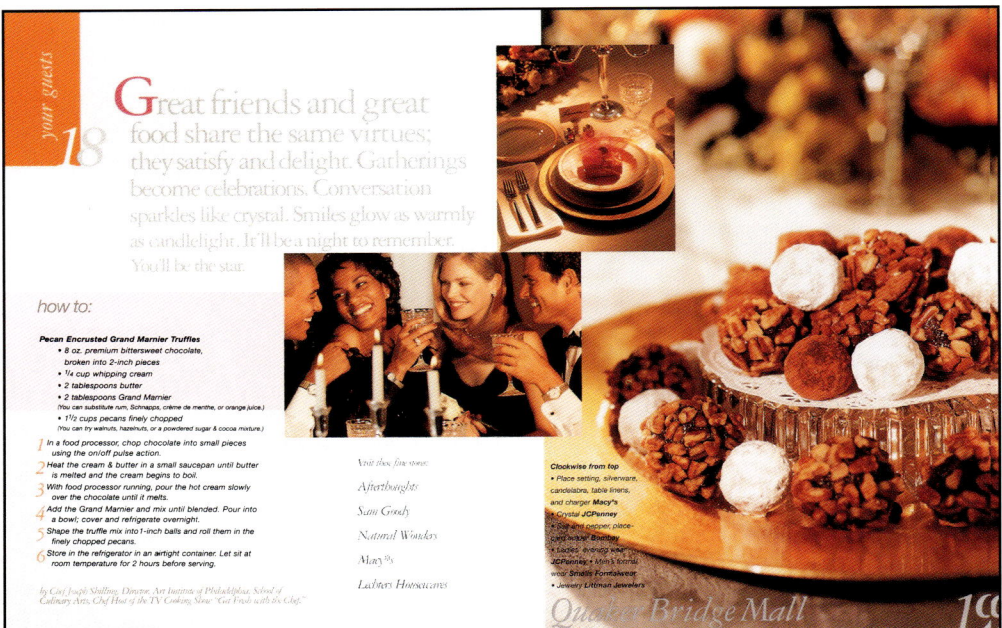

Everything about the Holiday 2000 Mag says "Keep me!" This recipe is just one of countless devices.

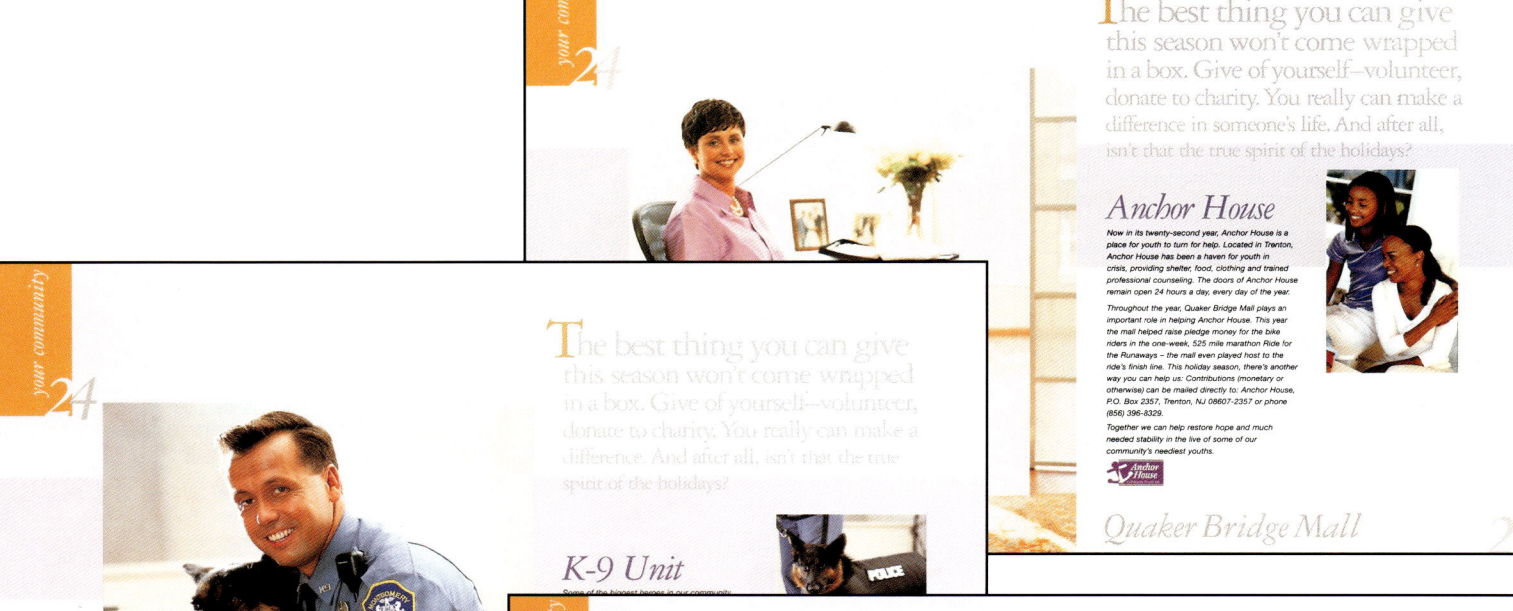

Some events and causes differed from mall to mall.

156

KRAVCO COMPANY

Special stockings anyone can make—another how-to device to make sure the Mag was "a keeper."

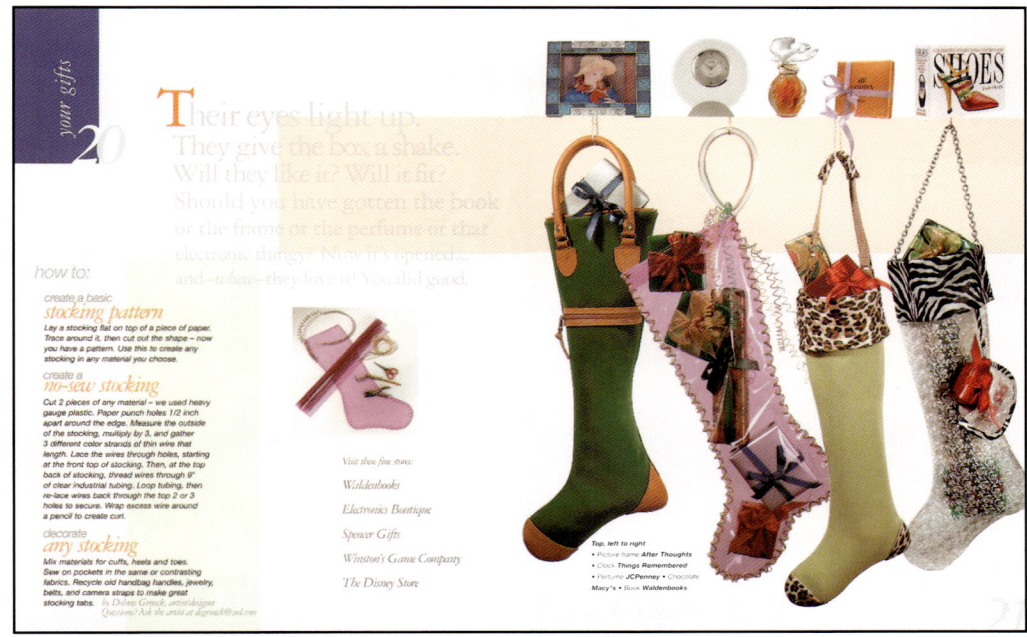

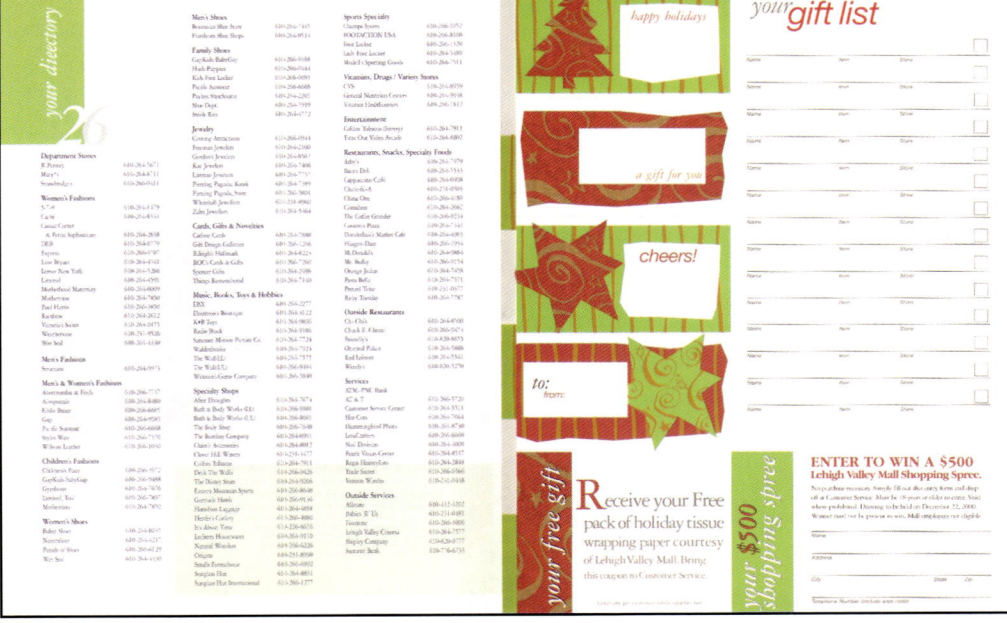

The inside back cover folded out to reveal some special touches. In addition to the gift list, there are savings coupons customized for each mall, gift tags and the sweepstakes entry form to win a $500 shopping spree.

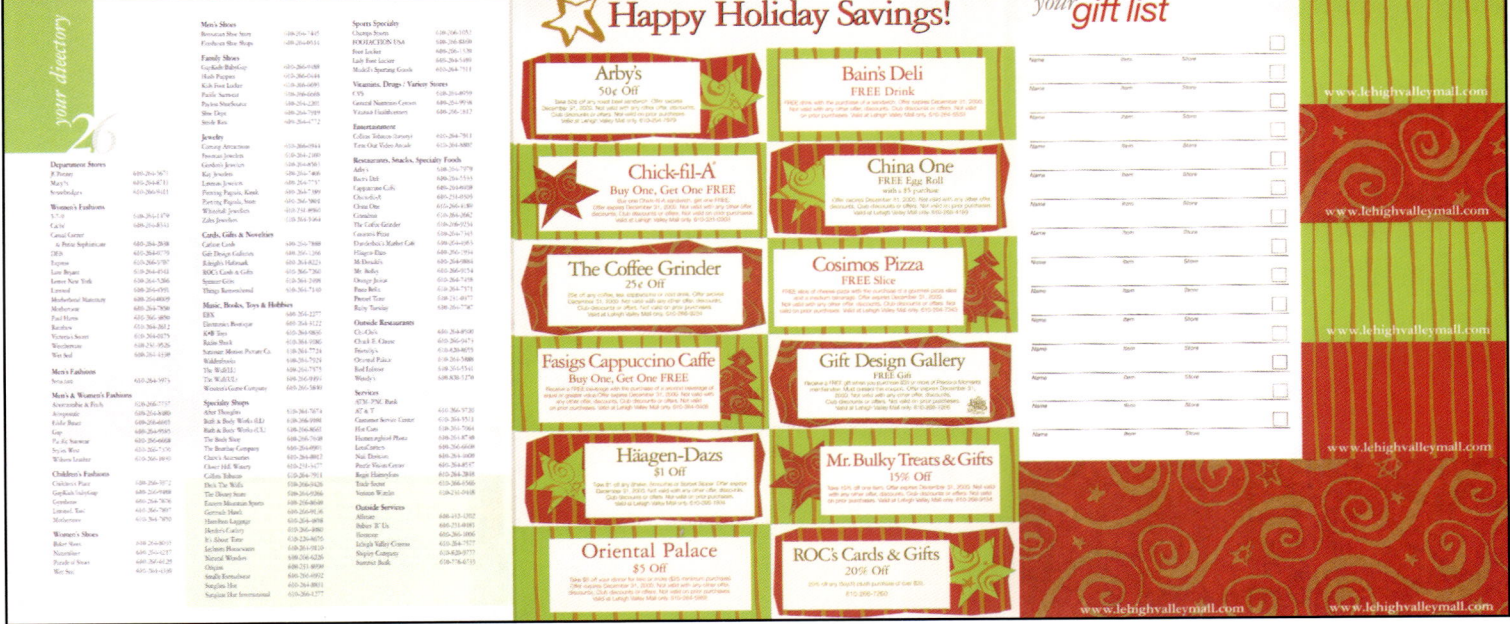

PLAZA LAS AMÉRICAS

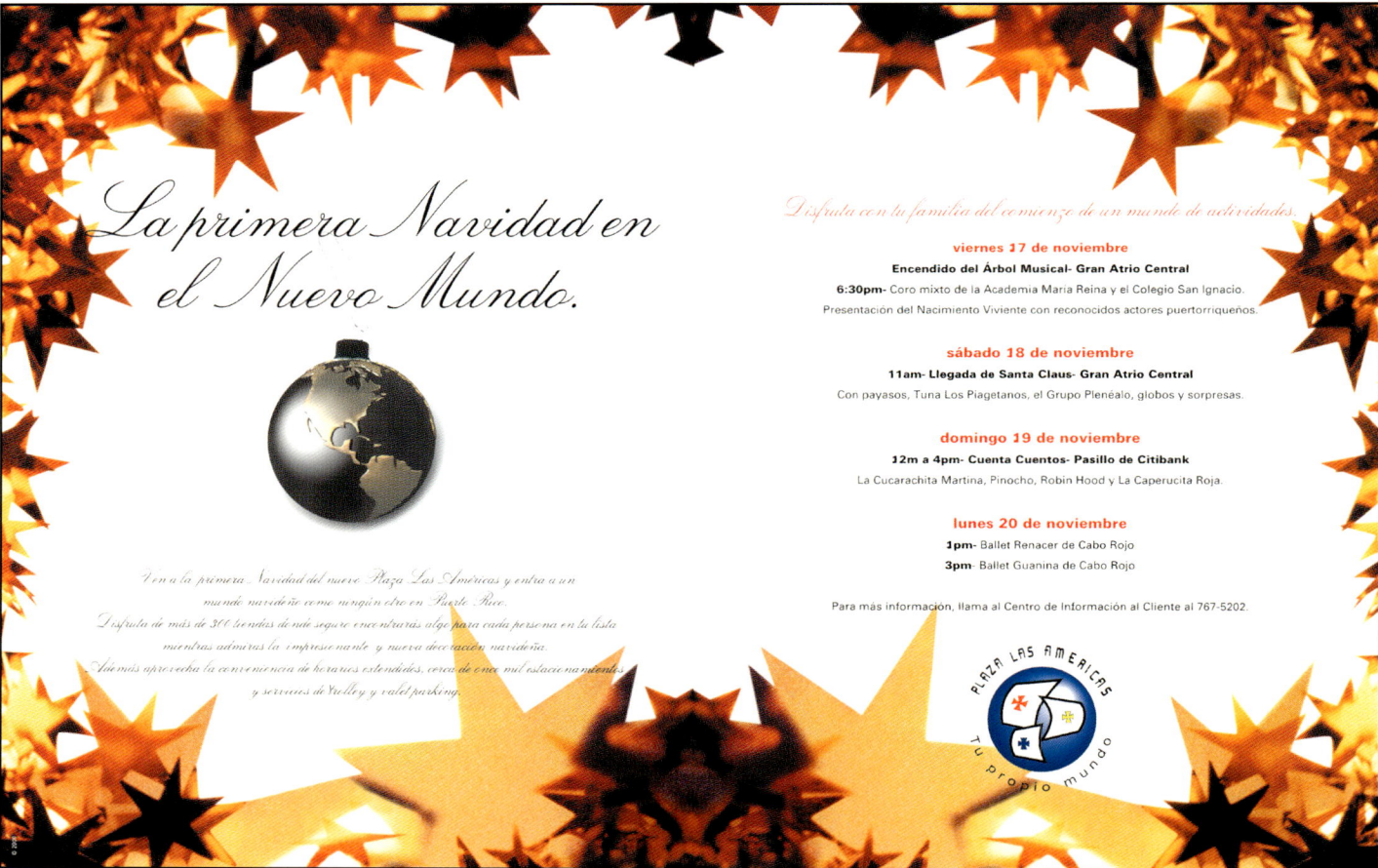

Headline Translation: The first Christmas in the New World.

Christmas in the 'New World'

THE LARGEST SHOPPING center in the Caribbean, Plaza Las Américas in San Juan, Puerto Rico, is home to more than 300 stores including the first Macy's outside the continental United States. Plaza, as it is commonly called, is so popular that more than half of the island's residents go there for major shopping trips—even though that major trip may take them 80 miles or more to reach the mall.

"Here it is part of the culture," says Vanessa Cordero, marketing director. "Plaza has been part of Puerto Rican life for 30 something years. It has always set the trend for the rest of the shopping centers."

And it is continuing to set trends with a major expansion—a project that has had considerable impact on the way the center marketed itself for the fall relaunch and the holidays. Cordero explains: "Plaza had been under construction for eight years, which was an inconvenience to customers. Although statistics don't show it, we assume a lot of people stayed away during the construction process. The center has been transformed, so it was very important for us to show this new product in a different way." Management was particularly sensitive to the effect the sheer size of the center might have. "We didn't want people to be scared. We needed to show this new world, which is beautiful. But we wanted the campaign to get more in touch with our customer, to make this new world their world."

Hence, the campaign slogan developed by Plaza's ad agency Marti, Flores, Prieto & Wachtel, was "Tu Propio Mundo" ("Your own world"). The strategy would be to convey it consistently throughout.

Advertising for the relaunch kicked off in the fall with the "New World" TV campaign. Its objectives were threefold: To reinforce an emotional attachment between consumers and the center, generate interest

PLAZA LAS AMÉRICAS

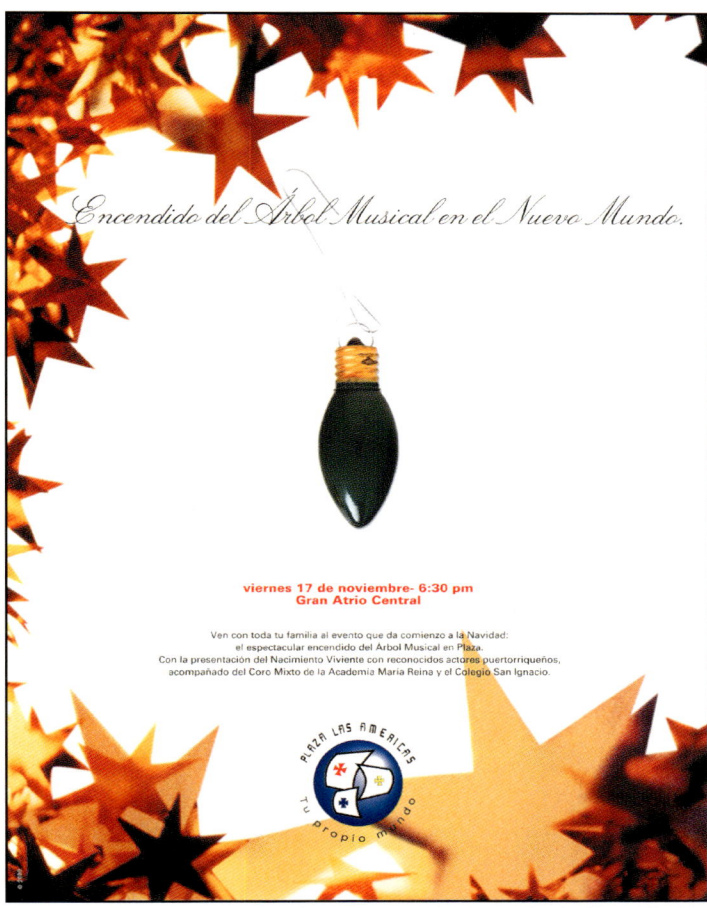
Headline Translation: The lighting of the musical tree in the New World.

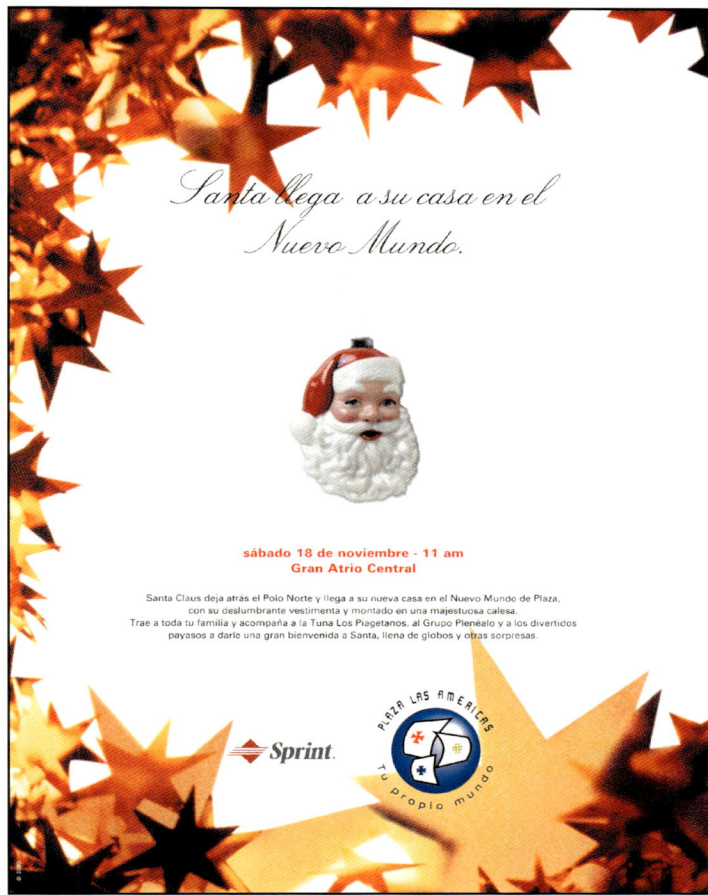
Headline Translation: Santa arrives at his home in the New World.

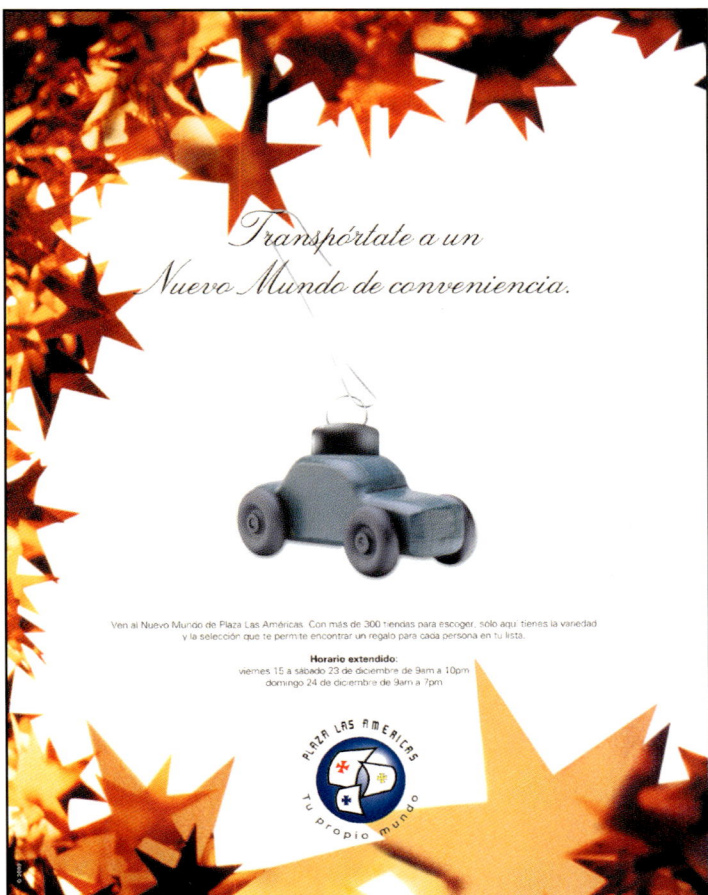
Headline Translation: Drive to a New World of convenience.

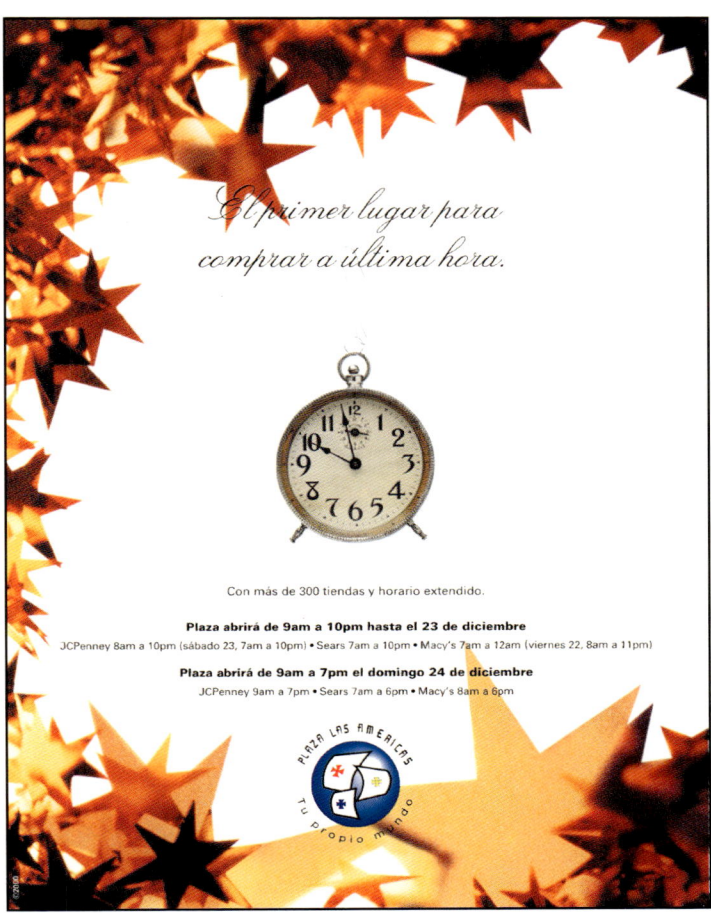
Headline Translation: The first place for last minute shopping.

PLAZA LAS AMÉRICAS

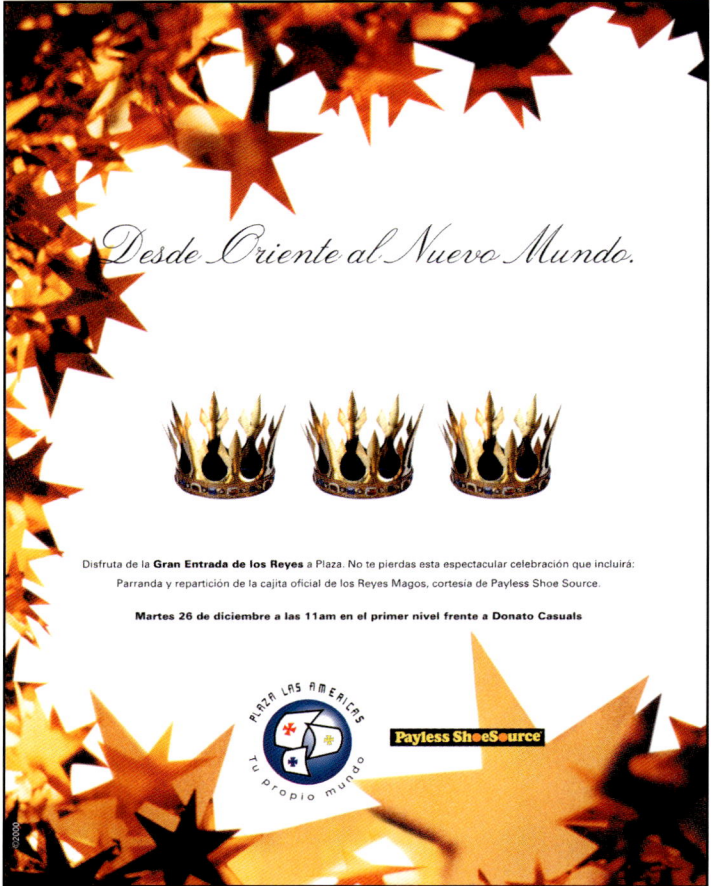

Headline Translation: From the Orient to the New World.

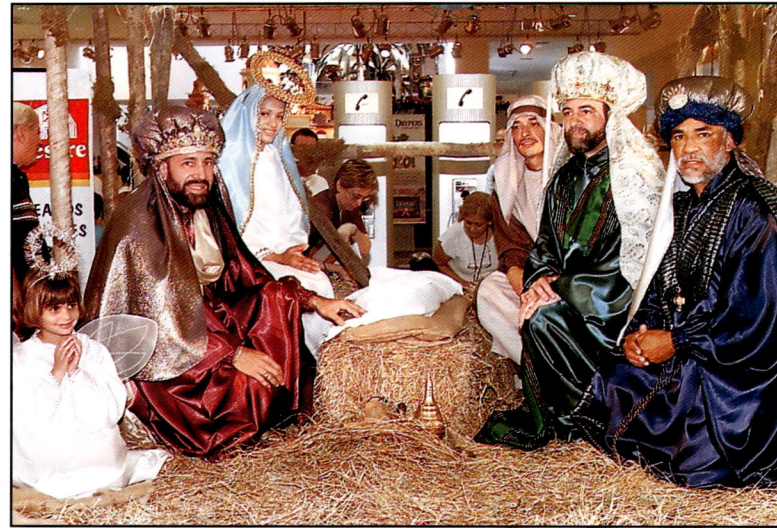

Held early in the morning on December 26, the Three Kings celebration is a Plaza tradition.

and expectation around Plaza's remodeled facilities, and inspire curiosity among consumers and invite them to "rediscover" the "New World" of Plaza.

"It was very important for us to reposition Plaza as a new institution, as a new product." says Cordero. "TV is our strongest medium because our market is the whole island. TV gives us that reach, so even though the actual relaunch was in September and October, we kept the New World TV for holiday.

For the print advertising, the center wanted to create a campaign that established Plaza Las Américas as the perfect place to do holiday shopping. Because of the center's recent reopening, the campaign sought to invite consumers to enjoy the benefit of the first Christmas at the new Plaza Las Américas.

Since the campaign had to communicate several messages (gift-with-purchase, Santa's arrival at the mall, additional parking spaces), the agency needed to create a look that would give some coherency to such diverse messages. It was decided that the best way to achieve this was to use simple icons (a small car to represent parking spaces, a cookie to represent the opening of new restaurants) and turn them into Christmas ornaments. The campaign launched close to Veterans Day in the highest circulation island-wide newspaper.

Plaza was an "event-full" place to be for the holidays too. In-mall festivals, celebrations, shows and exhibits are held often at the center, adding to the festive environment and providing an incentive for Plaza customers and visiting tourists (there are many at Christmas time!) to come and linger. (Customer time at the mall is almost two hours per customer, which is almost double the U.S. norm.) "People expect events for the holidays," says

Plaza Las Américas, San Juan, Puerto Rico
OWNER: **Empresas Fonalledas, Inc.,** San Juan
MARKETING DIRECTOR: **Vanessa Cordero**
ASSISTANT MARKETING DIRECTOR: **Mari González**
ADVERTISING AGENCY: **Marti, Flores, Prieto & Wachtel (MFP&W),** San Juan, Puerto Rico
CREATIVE DIRECTOR: **Juan José Junoy**
COPYWRITERS: (Christmas campaign) **José Mendez,** ("New World" TV) **Alice Quillinchini**
ART DIRECTORS: (Christmas campaign) **Angie Fernández,** ("New World" TV) **Agustín Fernández** SENIOR ACCOUNT EXECUTIVE: **Annette Ramírez**

PLAZA LAS AMÉRICAS

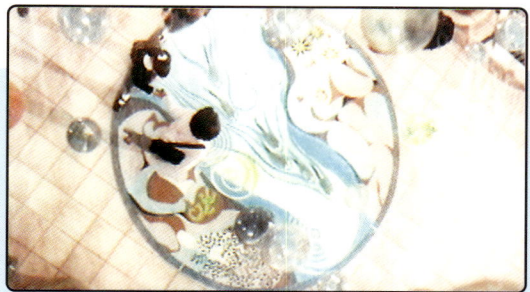

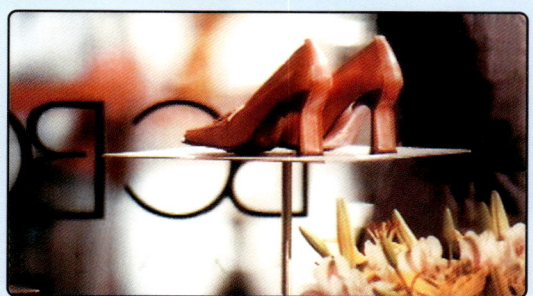

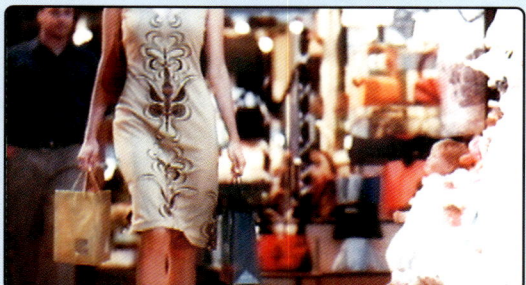

This spot is almost like a tourist ad with its emphasis on "discover the new world." The idea is that everyone has their own experience there. In the beginning, the viewer doesn't know what place is being talked about. There are impressive landscapes, and sports imagery (for ex, a surfboard in a surf shop shot close up, visuals of the center's floor medallions with people walking over. The viewer doesn't know its Plaza until the end when there's a shot of shoes in a window and a woman with shopping bag is revealed. A voiceover describes this as "a place with you in mind... discover your own world, the new world of Plaza.

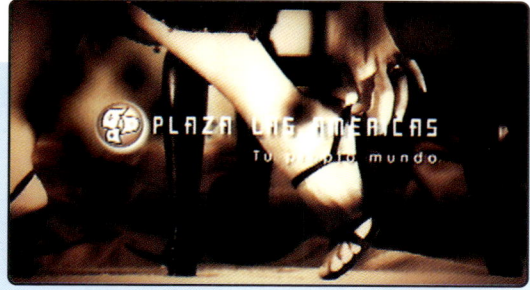

One TV spot, done in sepia, is all about pampering oneself. A woman is preparing to go out at night, putting on perfume, putting on lipstick, etc. A saxophonist plays in the background. The signature presents Plaza Las Américas as where a woman can find everything for pampering herself.

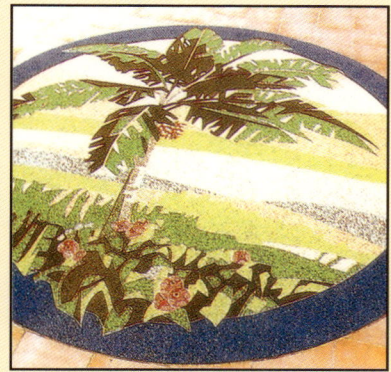
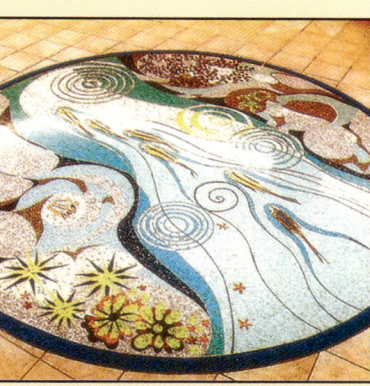

Local artists created medallion artwork as floor designs for Plaza's four atriums.

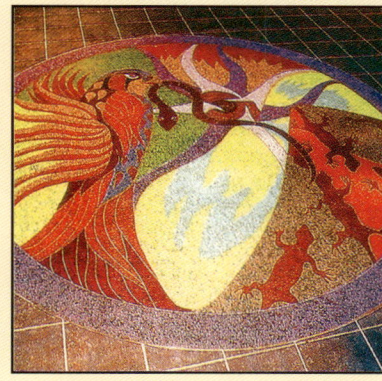
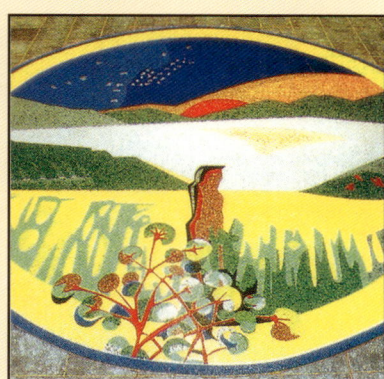

Cordero. "One unique event we do is our nativity event, a very special spiritual event prior to Santa's arrival that's usually celebrated on the Friday or Saturday night prior to Thanksgiving. On that special day, we light up the decor. No other shopping center does it."

Another event that's unique to the center is the celebration in preparation for the arrival of the Three Kings. There is a photo program in which children are given a shoe box with the tradition of the Three Kings printed on it. "It's one of the traditions we try to keep alive here," says Cordero. "It's a very children-oriented holiday in which children save a shoe box for January 5 (Jan. 6 is Three Kings Day) when they go out and fill the shoe box with grass, and put it under their bed so the camels can eat."

Response to these events and to the new Plaza Las Américas was cause for celebration in itself. "I can tell you we had a lot of visits from people we hadn't seen for a while," says Cordero. "In terms of sales we did very well. It was a very tough year. It was a lot of work. At the end of the year we looked back and we were happy!"

BRAMALEA CITY CENTRE

Very Gifted

Located in Ontario, Canada—not so far from "North Pole country"—Bramalea City Centre did some Santa-like work itself for holiday '99. The super-regional shopping center launched a program that helped consumers get the gifts they wanted using a gift registry service that's the first of its kind offered in a Canadian shopping center.

Designed to make gift-giving easier for the shopper and more enjoyable for the recipient, the gift registry worked like this:

Shoppers were encouraged to visit their favorite stores in the mall, select items they would like to receive for Christmas, complete a Gift Idea card in the store and return it to the Customer Service Centre, or the gift-wrapping kiosk. Then they spread the word that the gifts they wanted were listed at Bramalea.

Ray Casey, vice president and general manager, is the first to say that as registeries go, this was definitely a low tech version. The marketing was sophisticated but the actual gift registry was not. The lists were not computerized or part of any database. They were simply sheets of paper that had been filled out by the registrant and kept on file at the Customer Service desk. Simple!

Bramalea provided the registrants' family and friends incentives to check out what was on the list. Gifts purchased from the Gift Registry would be wrapped for free and the purchaser given a $5 Bramalea City Centre gift certificate. Presumably, a number of these potential gift givers would also participate in the Gift Registry.

"Like all good strategies we wanted to come up with a Christmas program that worked on a number of different fronts at one time," says Casey. "Initially what we wanted to do was simplify the gift-giving process for shoppers and increase sales. If you're out selecting gifts for yourself, you're likely to be a little more generous than givers would be. You tend to go one step up."

The program's objectives were to maximize sales, increase store traffic, reduce the number of gift returns, and most important—generate happy customers who got the gifts they wanted for Christmas. What Casey calls, "a guaranteed win-win scenario for shoppers, their friends and family and mall tenants."

The strategy was to expand awareness of the mall's shops and selections. "Most people have a certain pattern," says Casey. "They tend to park in the same area and tend to shop in the same area. We wanted to bring shoppers to new and different areas of the shopping center, to actually walk through stores they might not have looked at before." Not only did the new service do a job of getting people to register, but it built awareness for those people who came to purchase gifts for friends and family who were listed.

The Gift Registry program had other benefits. It served as a pro-active marketing

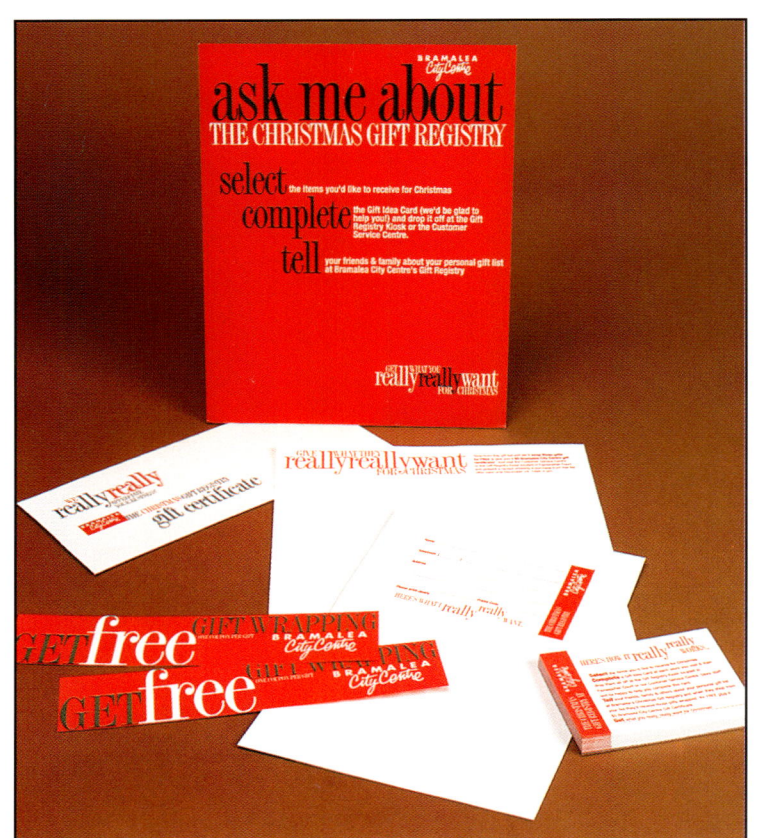

Stores displayed easels and Gift Idea Cards featuring the Gift Registry.

BRAMALEA CITY CENTRE

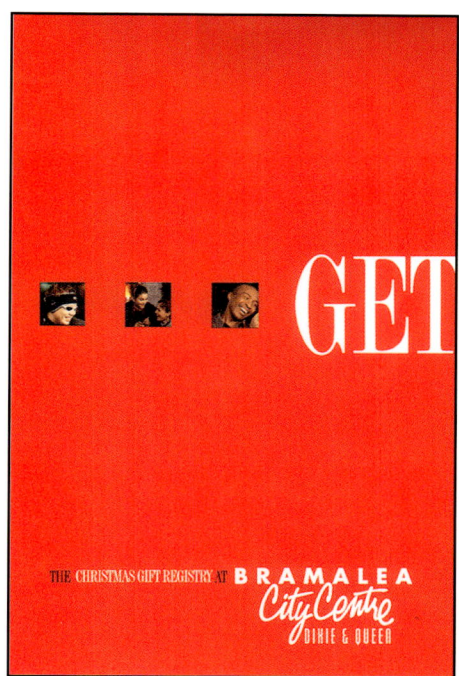
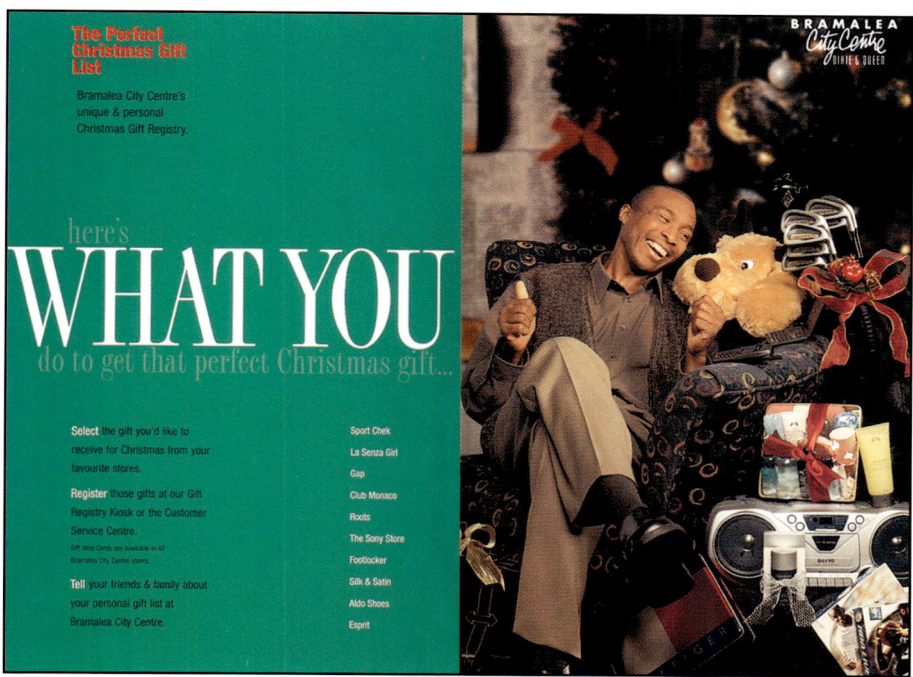
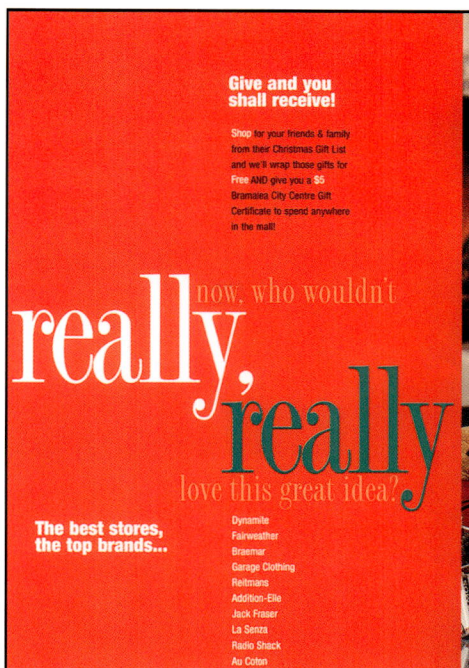

The campaign creative supported the message by featuring products and all shopper groups. The direct-mail piece was distributed to 70,000 homes in the primary market.

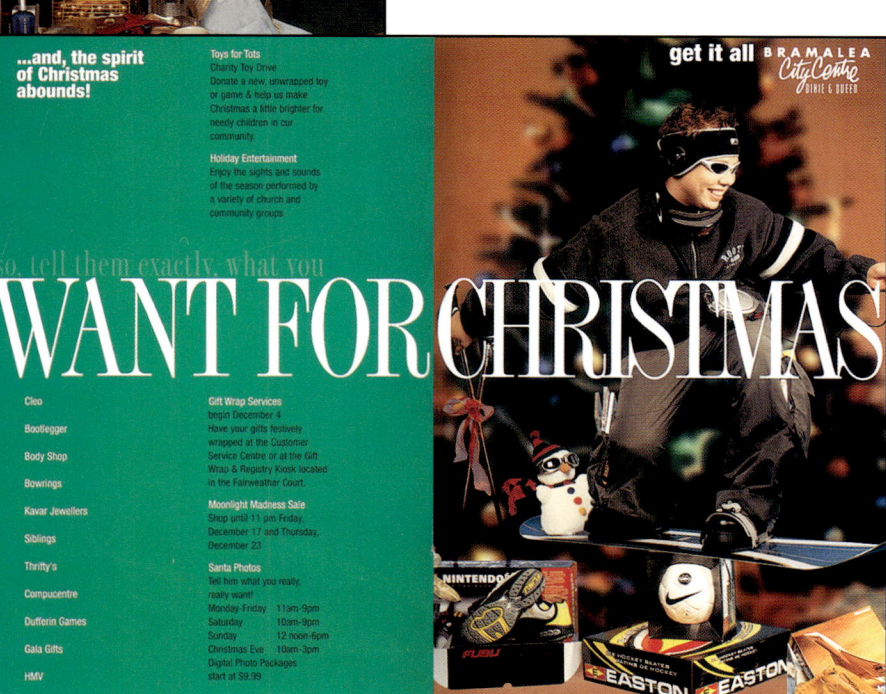

Radio Spot :30

VOICE 1: When it comes to Christmas shopping, my husband is completely lost.

VOICE 2: I know what you mean. If you ask for a nightgown, you know what you'll get...

VOICES 1 AND 2 (TOGETHER): Skimpy lingerie!

VOICE 2: This year I'm going to Bramalea City Centre and get what I really, really want for Christmas.

VOICE 1: You must mean the new Christmas Gift Registry.

VOICE 2: That's right! I just go to all my favorite stores and list the gifts I want on the Gift Idea Card. Anybody can check out my list at the Gift Registry Desk and go shopping. It's absolutely foolproof.

VOICE 1: Even for my husband?

VOICE 2: Absolutely!

VOICES 1 AND 2: This Christmas we're getting what we really, really want from Bramalea City Centre.

A three week radio flight started November 22.

Radio Spot :30

I can't believe some of the stuff I got for Christmas last year! It was either the wrong color, wrong size or just plain, well, wrong.

This year that's going to change. I'm going to Bramalea City Centre and get what I really, really want for Christmas!

They have this incredible, new program called the Christmas Gift Registry. You simply visit your favorite stores, complete the Gift Idea card, and send everyone you know to the Registry Desk for your personal Christmas list. What a system! I just know this year I'm going to get it right.

This Christmas, I'm getting what I really, really want from Bramalea City Centre.

Radio Spot :30

Don't you just hate what your parents get you for Christmas? They get the worst stuff! Socks, underwear... where do they get these ideas?

This year, I'm going to Bramalea City Centre and get what I really, really want for Christmas!

They have this radical new thing called the Christmas Gift Registry. You just go to all your favorite stores and write down what you want. Anybody can check out your list at the Gift Registry Desk and then go get it. It's amazing!

So this Christmas, make sure you get what you really, really want from Bramalea City Centre.

---

vehicle to prevent customer defection that could result from the closing of Eaton's, one of the center's three anchors, and the October opening of a new shopping center. Despite these developments, Casey reports a 4% increase in sales nonetheless. The Gift Registry program enabled Bramalea to provide a shopping benefit that other shopping options couldn't. Further, it not only helped set the center apart from the competition but increased market reach and awareness, because registrants would tell their friends and family both in and outside the market area to shop for them at Bramalea.

What make the success even more impressive is the circumstances under which it was done. "In October, we found ourselves without a marketing director," says Casey. "Responsibility for putting this program together fell to myself and Sharon Quigley" (the assistant marketing director).

In early November a general merchants meeting was held to introduce the program. "The assistant marketing director and I personally visited every store in the center (260) to make sure the retailer was thoroughly briefed on the concept," notes Casey. "If they didn't buy into the concept, we didn't want disappointment. We wanted each merchant to understand the potential for increasing sales and that it would be much easier to sell up and accessorize and add items to the list."

With its house in order, Bramalea turned to aggressively supporting the Gift Registry with a holiday ad campaign built around the line "Get what you really, really want for Christmas."

"When our ad agency presented the idea to us we jumped on it immediately," says Casey. "I have young children so it's not uncommon to hear 'what I really, really want,'" he adds. "It appeals to the child in all of us."

The highly visible advertising appeared on billboards, transit shelters and in newspapers and was also supported by a direct-mail campaign, a three-week radio program and in-store promotion.

It's remarkable what Bramalea accomplished in a short time under difficult circumstance and a budget of $200,000. The materials not only communicated the gift-registry program clearly, but by repeatedly using the same images (thereby increasing cost-effectiveness), every element continually reinforced the other. The copy was tweaked to maximize each communication opportunity. For example, each of the three

BRAMALEA CITY CENTRE

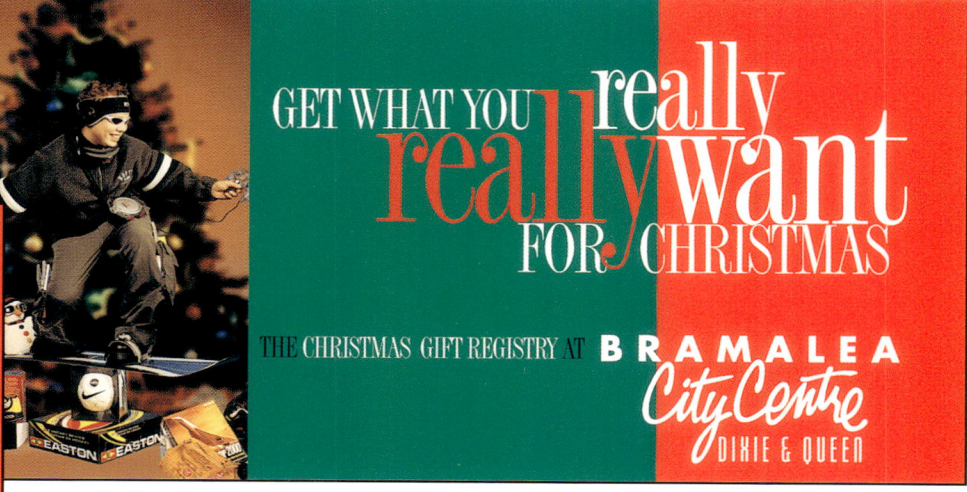

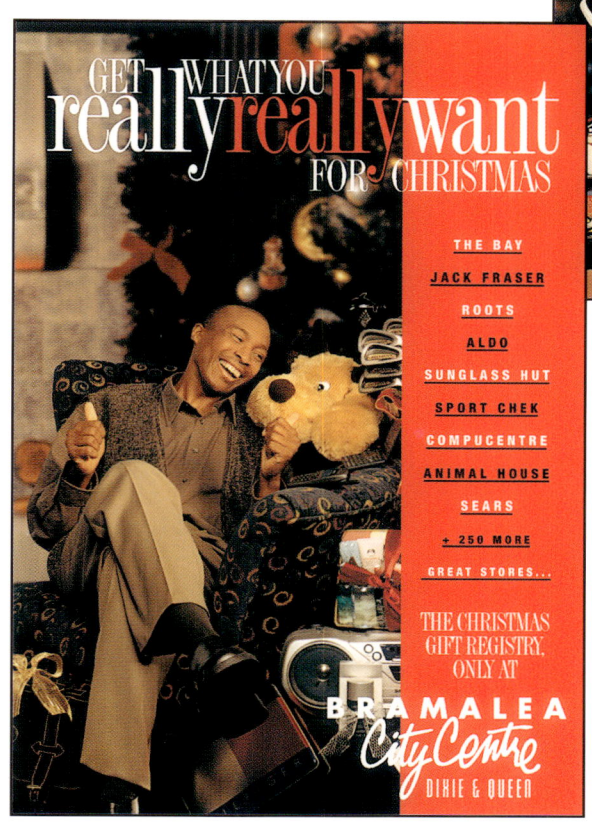

The six-week outdoor campaign features strong images and a catchy familiar message. A total of 16 billboards and 27 transit shelters got the word out. The copy on the transit shelter poster at left highlights store names, promotes shopping via the Gift Registry and communicates services and events.

The bold headline with its call to action could be adapted to a number of different messages. Even Santa is a supporter. Note the reference to Gift Wrap & Registry Kiosk. Every element works off the others.

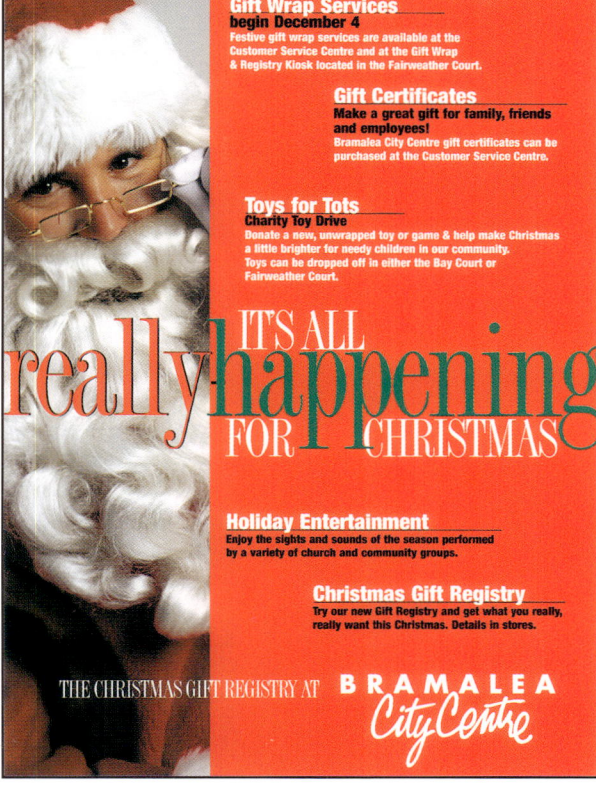

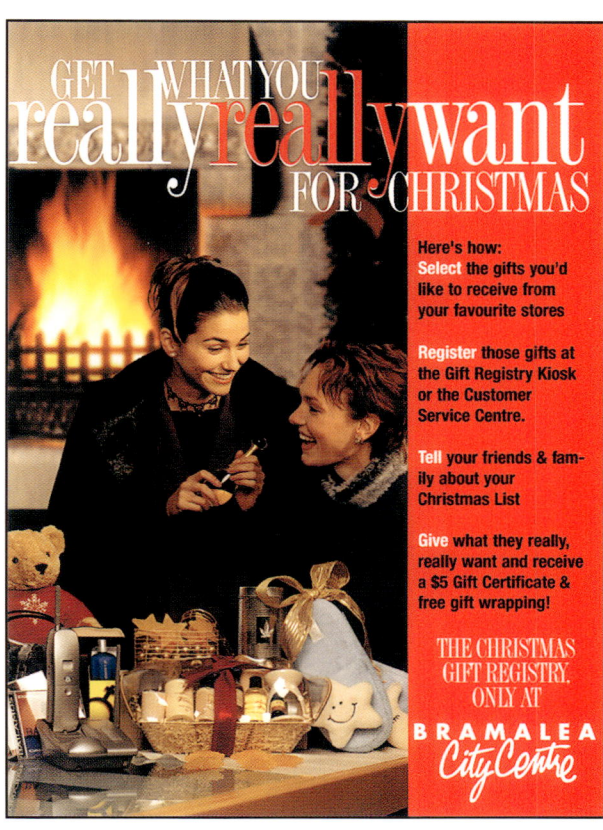

BRAMALEA CITY CENTRE

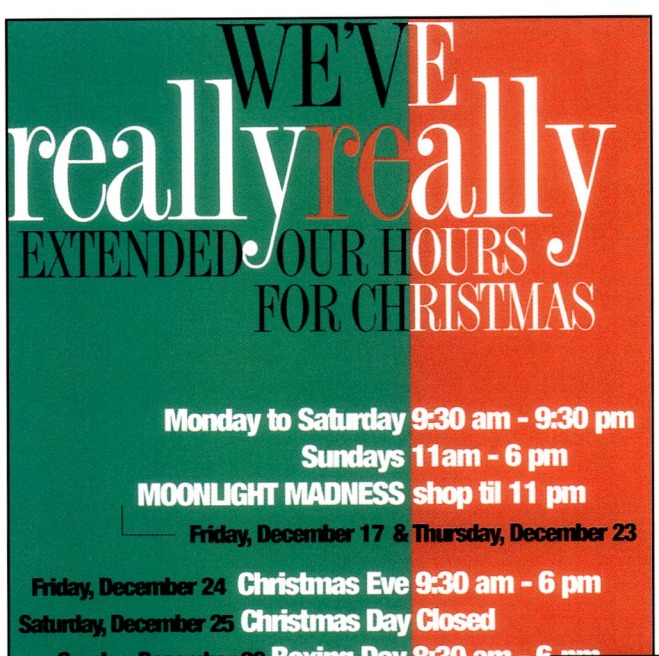

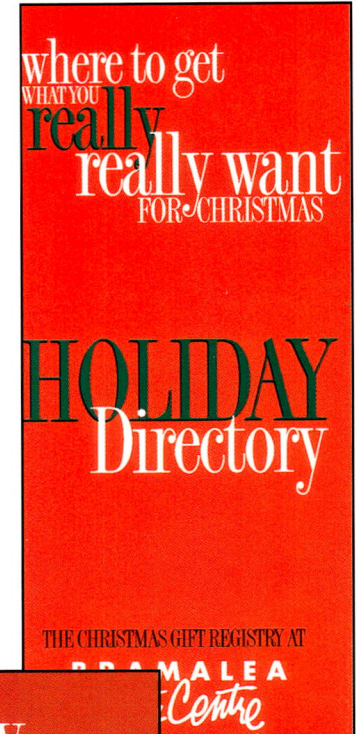

In-mall materials included decals and the store directory (right).

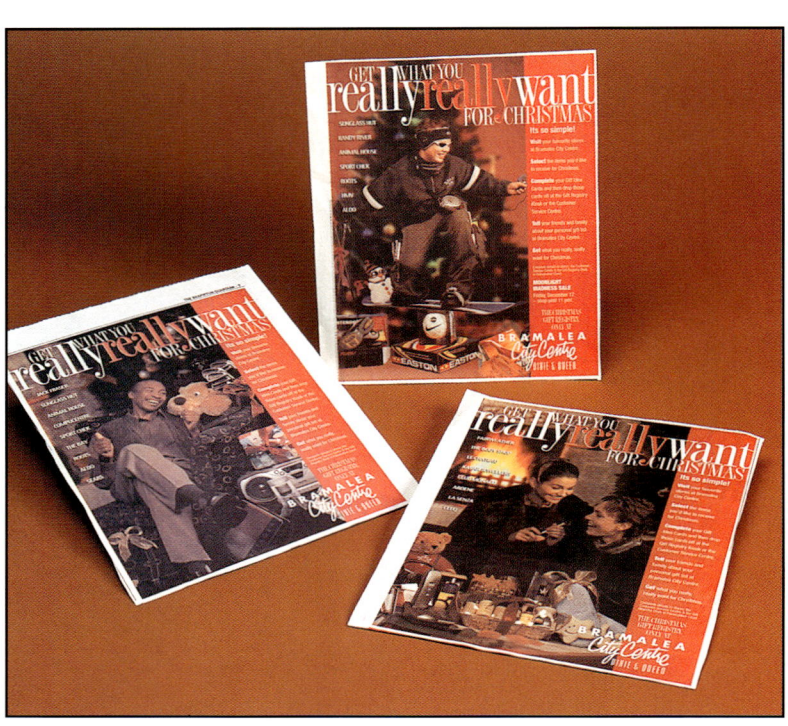

Some examples of the nine 1/4 page newspaper ads that ran in the *Brampton Guardian*.

images for transit-shelter ads lists different stores."We did that to boost awareness of what we have in the mall," says Casey. "We've renovated or added approximately 70 stores over the last 24 months and we wanted our customers to know that we have these name brand stores in the center."

It could be said that Bramalea got what it really, really wanted too. Besides the rise in sales, more than 1,200 customers submitted lists with items selected from an average of three or four different stores. In total, 135 stores were represented on the "Best Gift List."

Bramalea City Center, City of Brampton, Ontario, Canada
VICE PRESIDENT/GENERAL MANAGER: **Ray Casey, SCSM**
MARKETING DIRECTOR: **Scott Harris, CMD**
ASSISTANT MARKETING DIRECTOR: **Sharon Quigley**
AGENCY: **G/Comm Marketing Inc.,** Mississauga, Ontario
GROUP ACCOUNT DIRECTOR: **Cheryl Cardon**

SOUTH COAST PLAZA

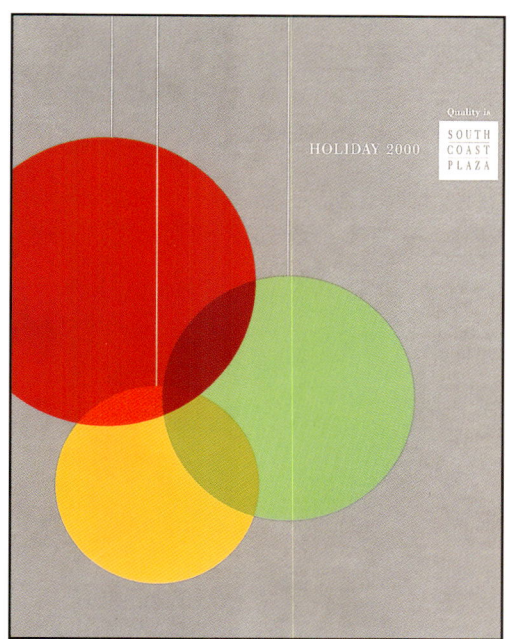

COMPANY: **South Coast Plaza**
DIMENSIONS: 7³/₄" x 10"
NUMBER OF PAGES: 122
WEBSITE: www.southcoastplaza.com

Silver adds elegance to both the cover and first spread of South Coast Plaza's holiday catalog. Inside, the catalog is divided into eight chapters—each a different gift category. The bright colors that are used to code each chapter are first introduced on the contents page. For ease of access, the colors are then carried onto the first page of each chapter and onto a bar running along the right-hand side of each spread.

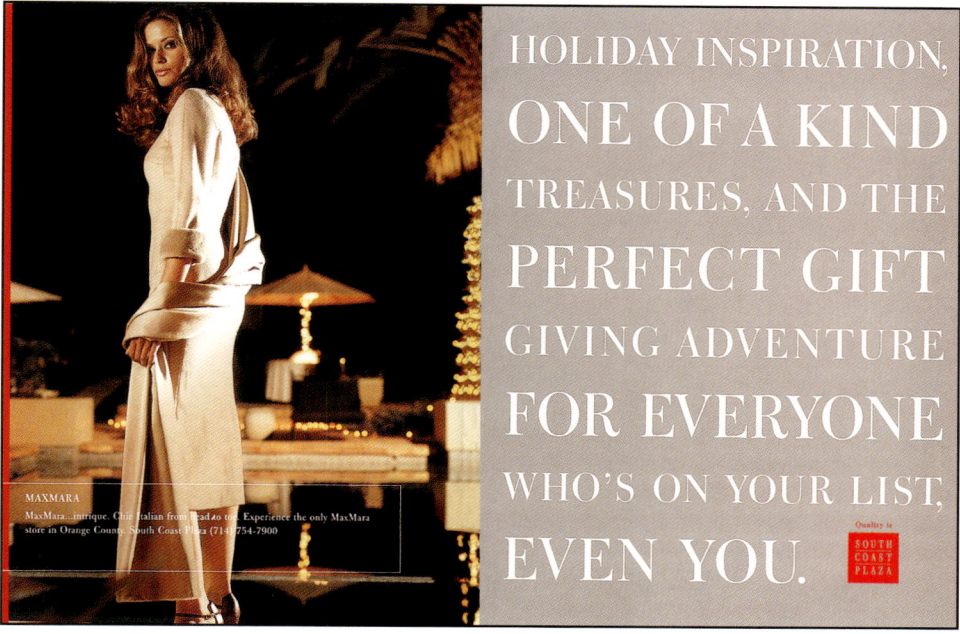

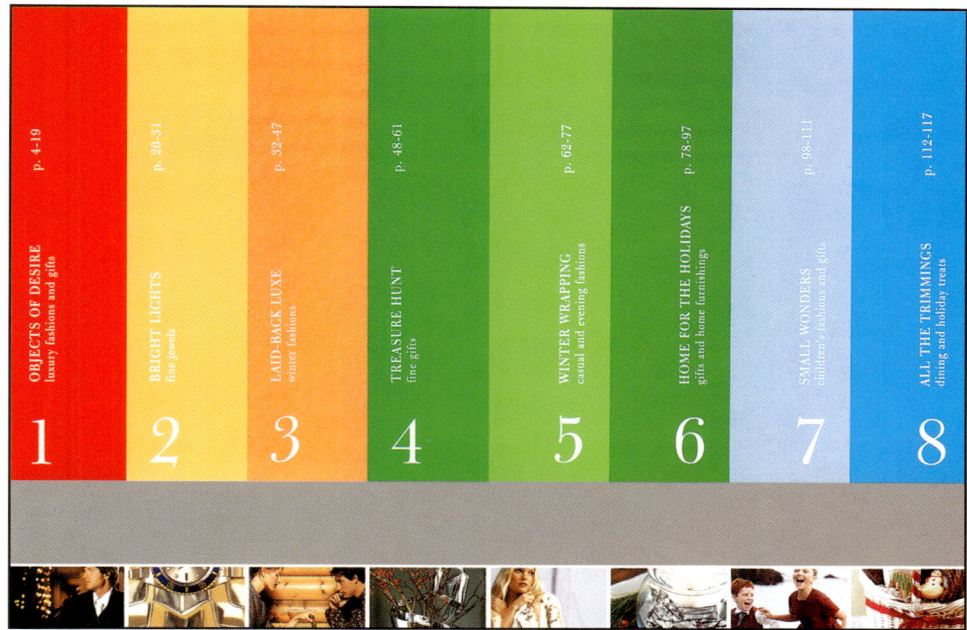

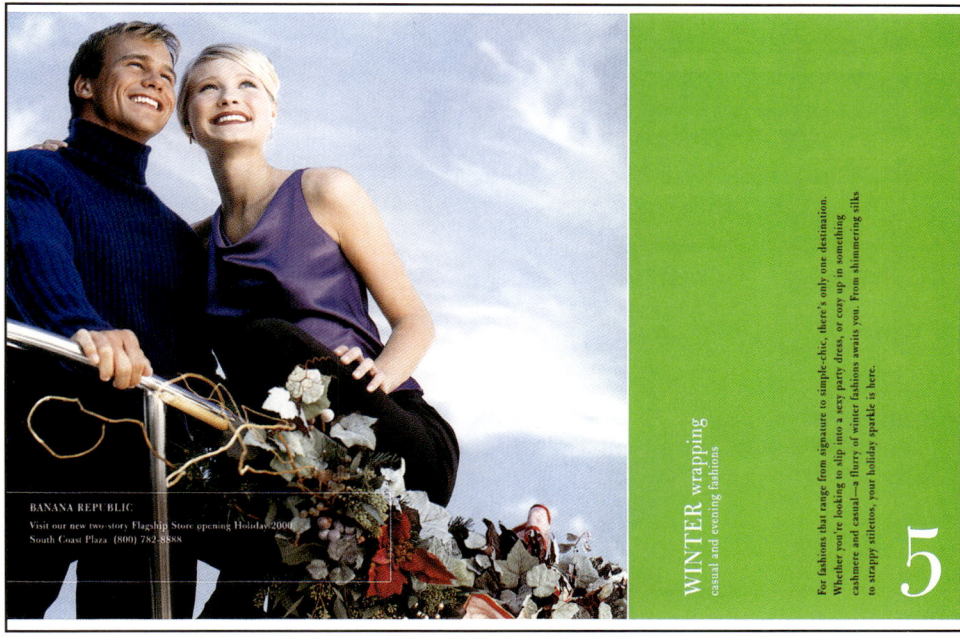

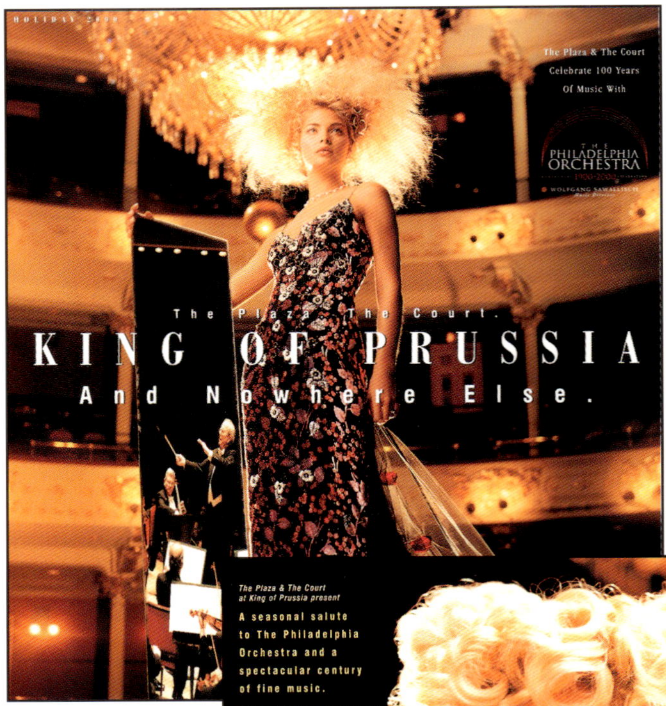

KING OF PRUSSIA

COMPANY: **The Plaza & The Court at King of Prussia**
DIMENSIONS: 10⁷/₈" x 11³/₄"
NUMBER OF PAGES: 52
WEBSITE: www.kingofprussiamall.com

King of Prussia's holiday catalog is a comprehensive tie-in with the Philadelphia Orchestra—an orchestra that has had much excitement surrounding it lately. In November of 2000 they celebrated their 100th birthday, and in December 2001 they will be moving to a new concert hall. The first spread (below), is packed with relevant information.

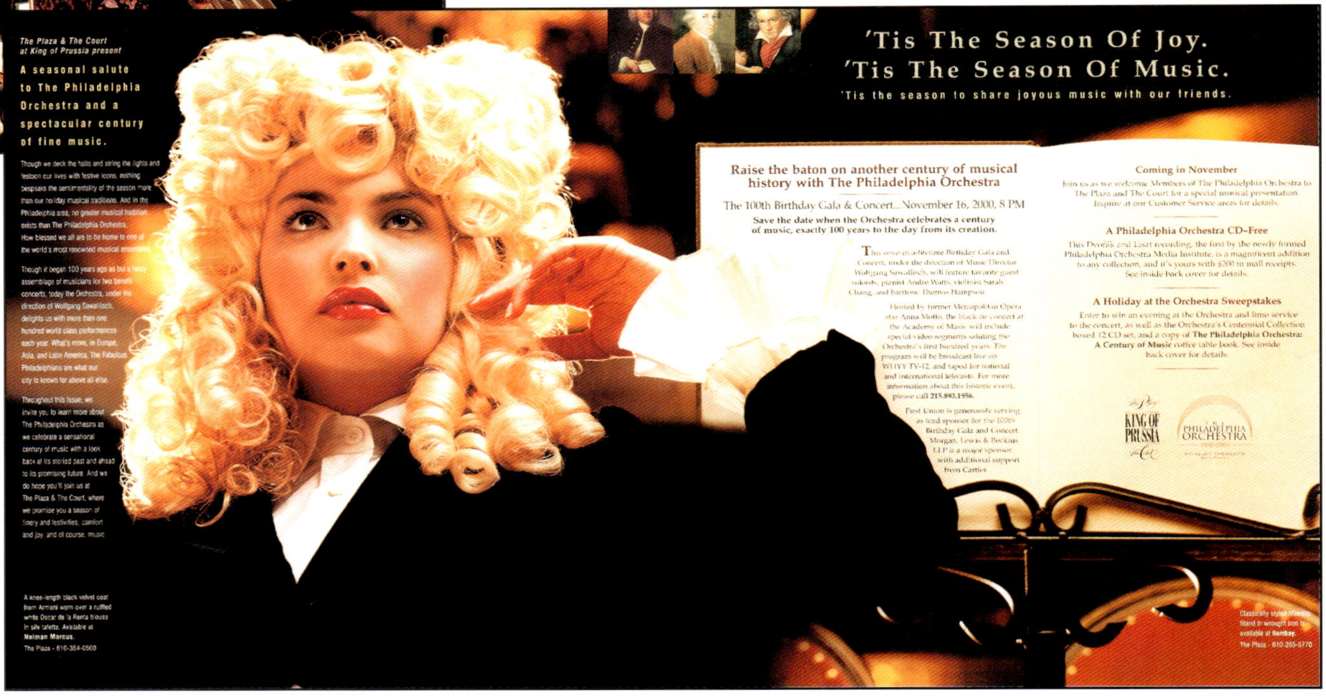

While the model on the cover (above), stands on the stage of the Academy of Music, the backdrop for several inside pages is the construction site of the new hall, The Kimmel Center for the Performing Arts. Sidebars throughout the catalog pertain to the orchestra.

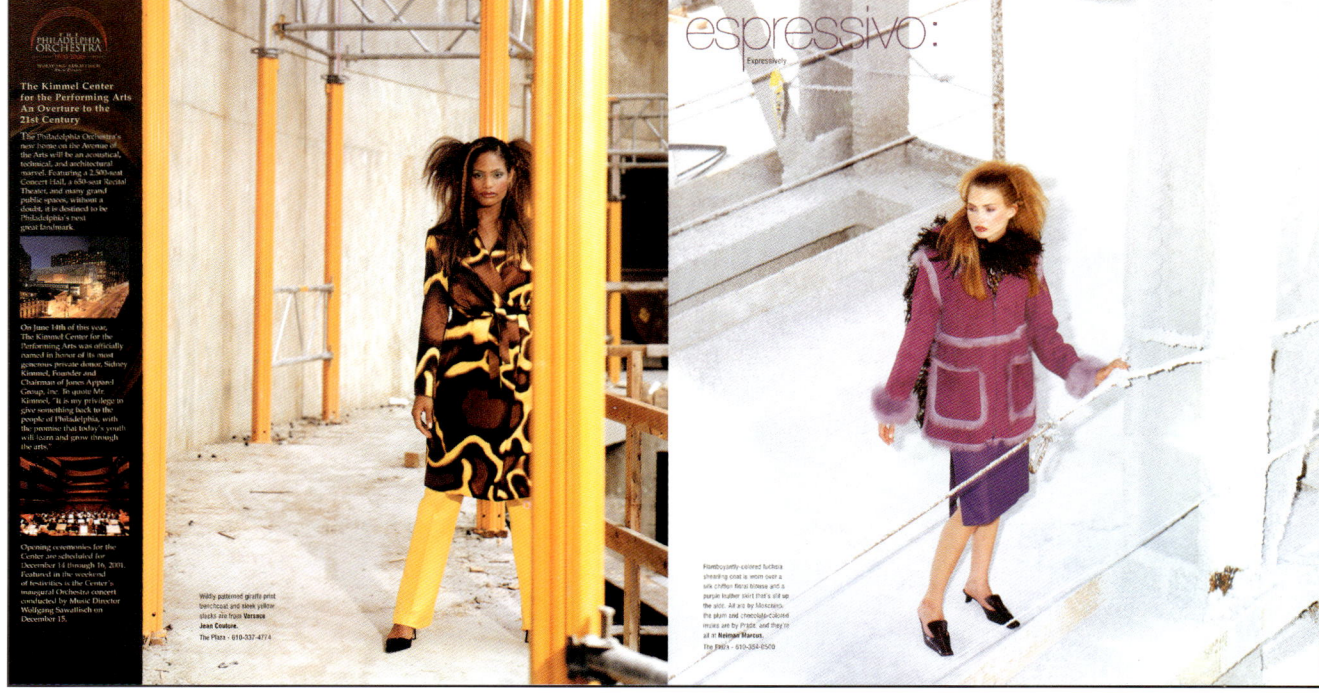

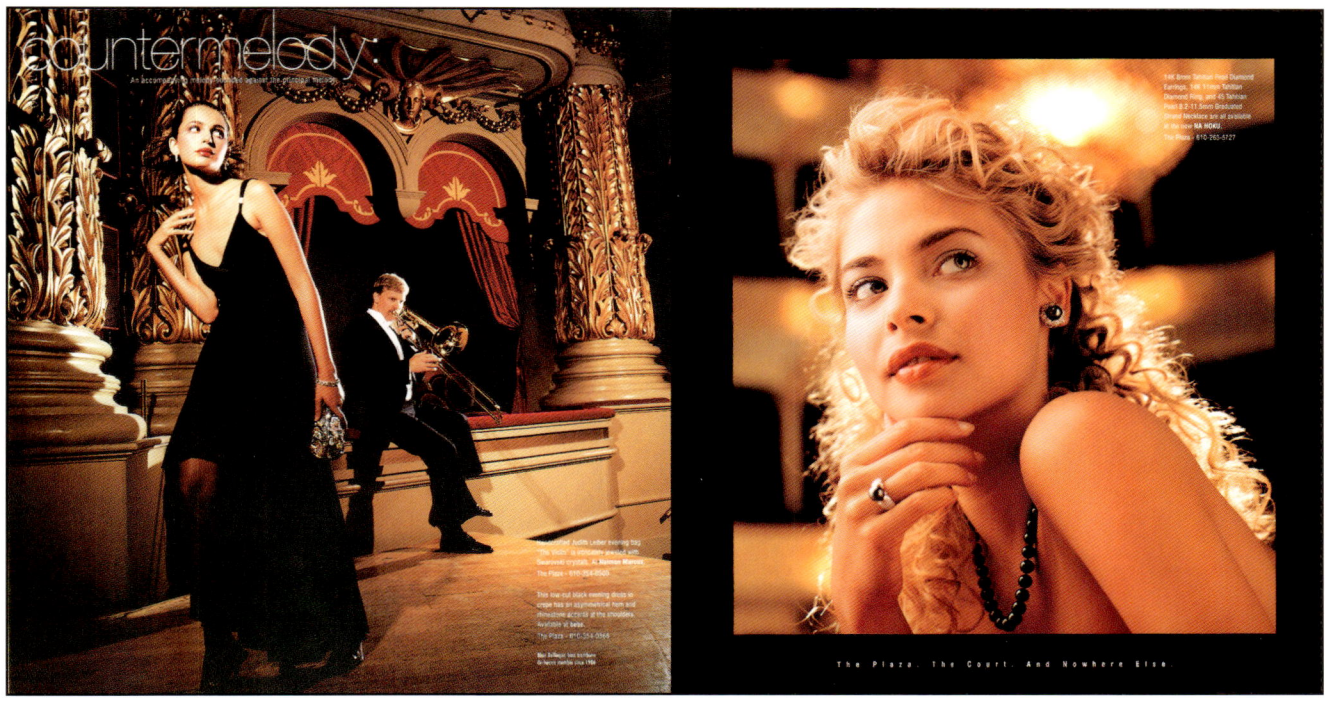

Members of the orchestra appear on several pages of the catalog. Above, in the background, is Blair Bollinger, bass trombonist, and below, three other members help children with their music lessons. Most of the pages are headed with a musical term, this one is, appropriately, "allegro," meaning fast and cheerful. The merchandise in each photo is identified with unimposing captions.

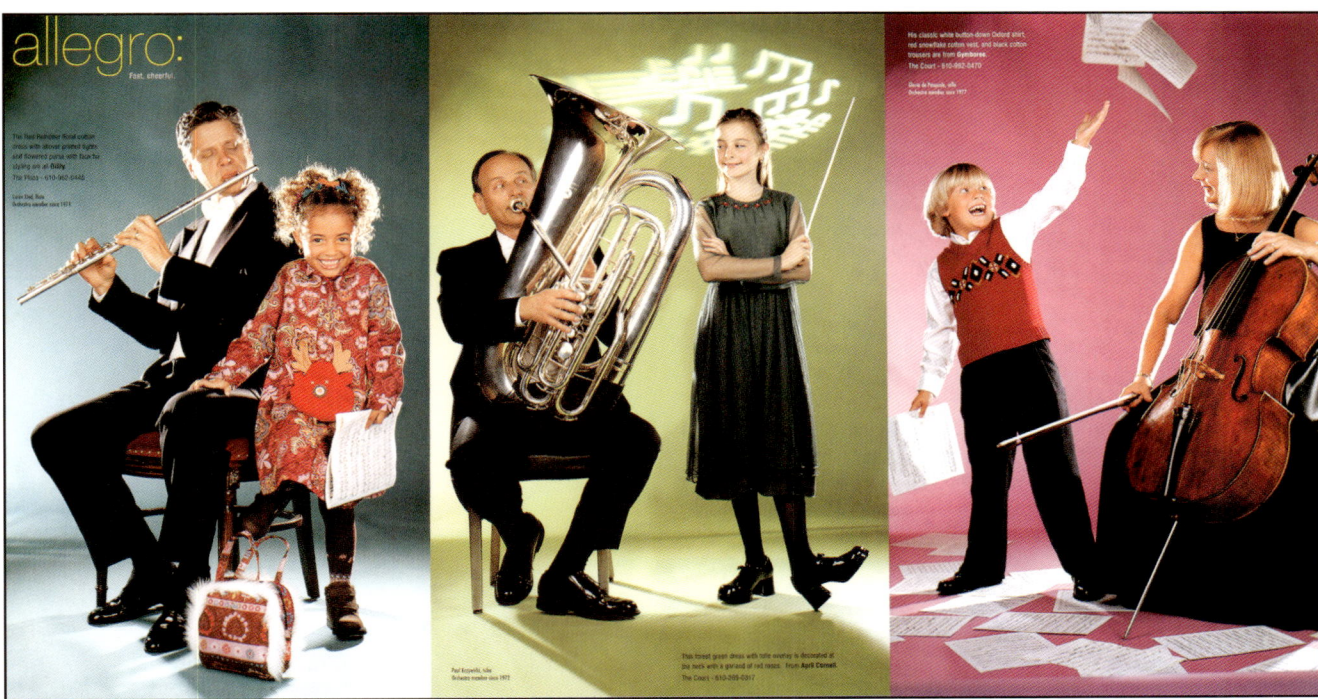

HILLSDALE

Present Perfect

Hillsdale

Another beautiful catalog from Hillsdale—and never the same thing twice. Some of the highlights of this holiday catalog are a cartoonlike graphic, beautifully designed bleed photos and a tasteful way of listing the relevant stores on each spread that gets noticed without shouting.

DIMENSIONS: 9 ¾" x 12"
NUMBER OF PAGES: 40

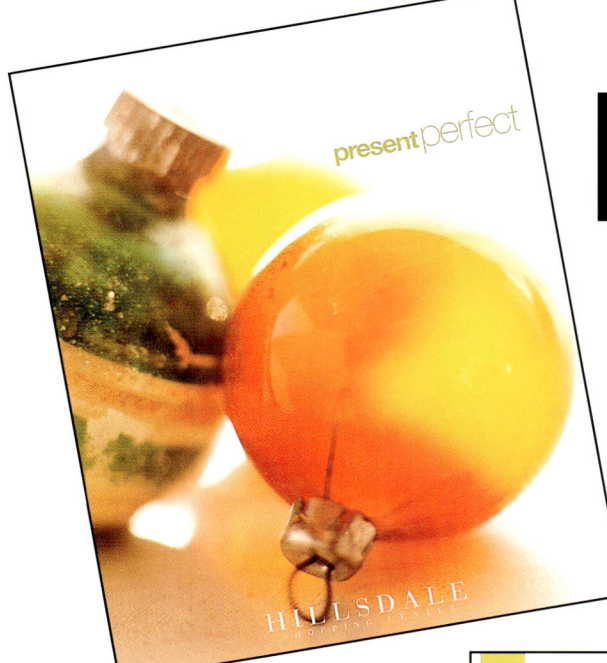

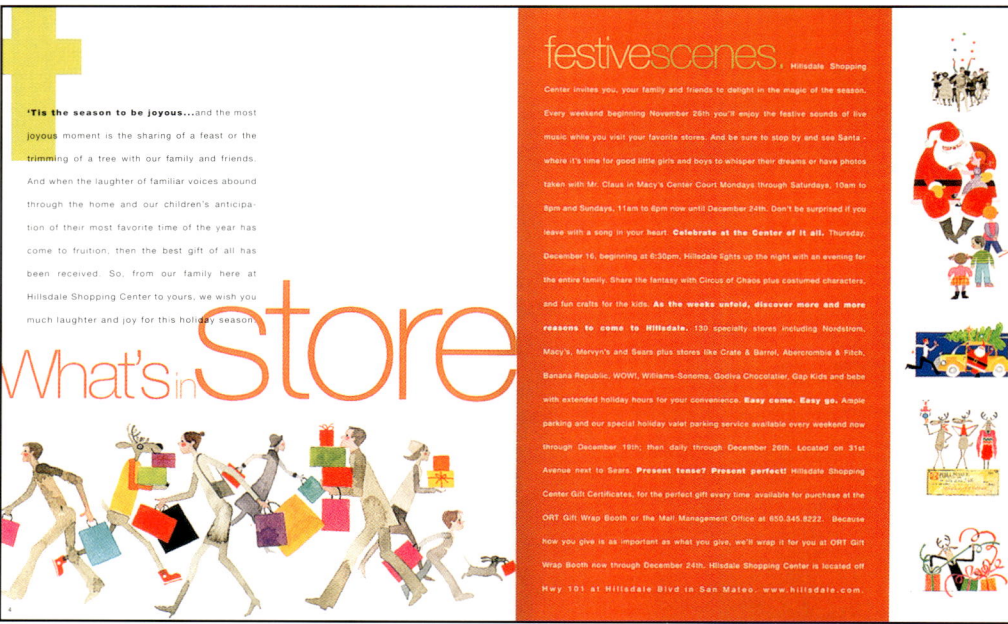

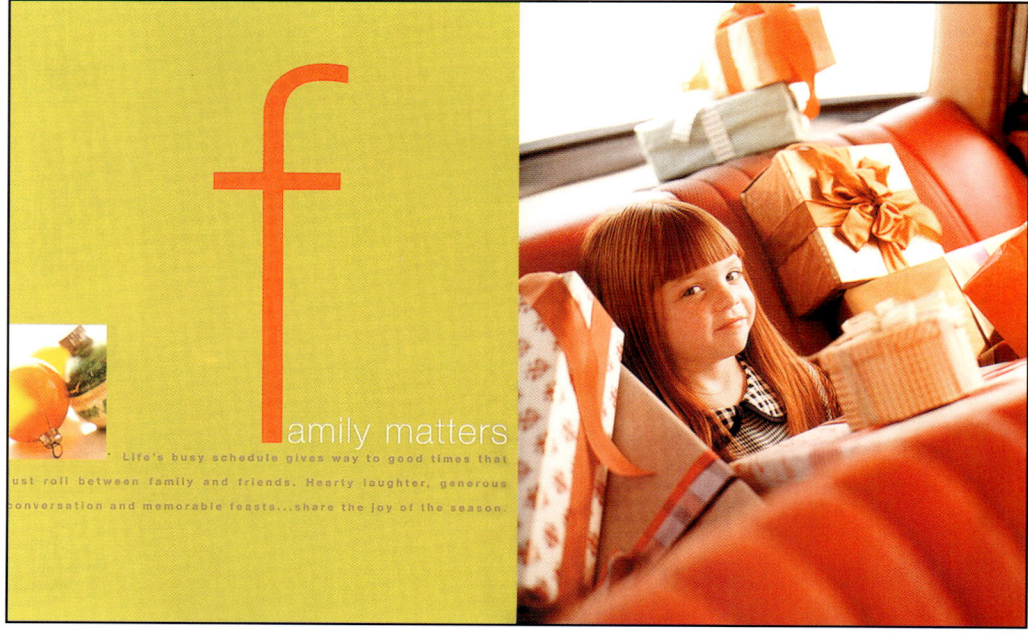

HILLSDALE

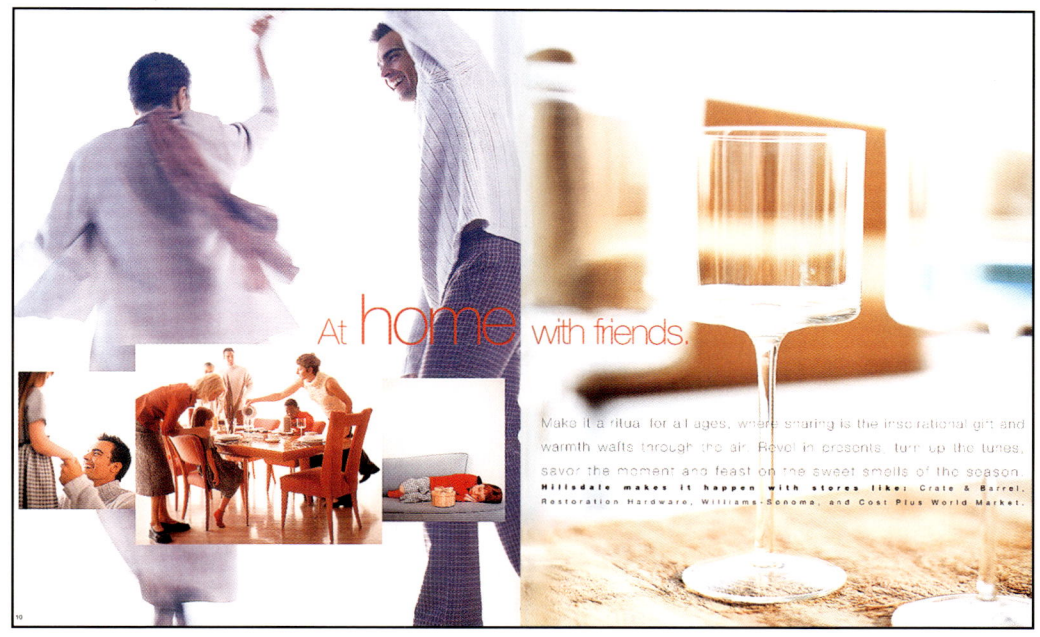

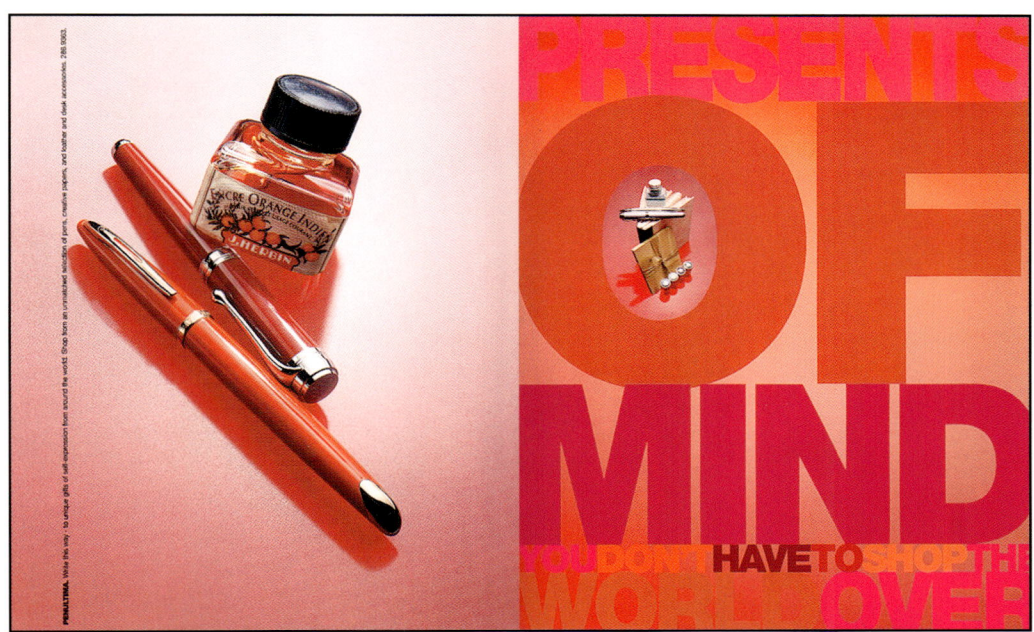

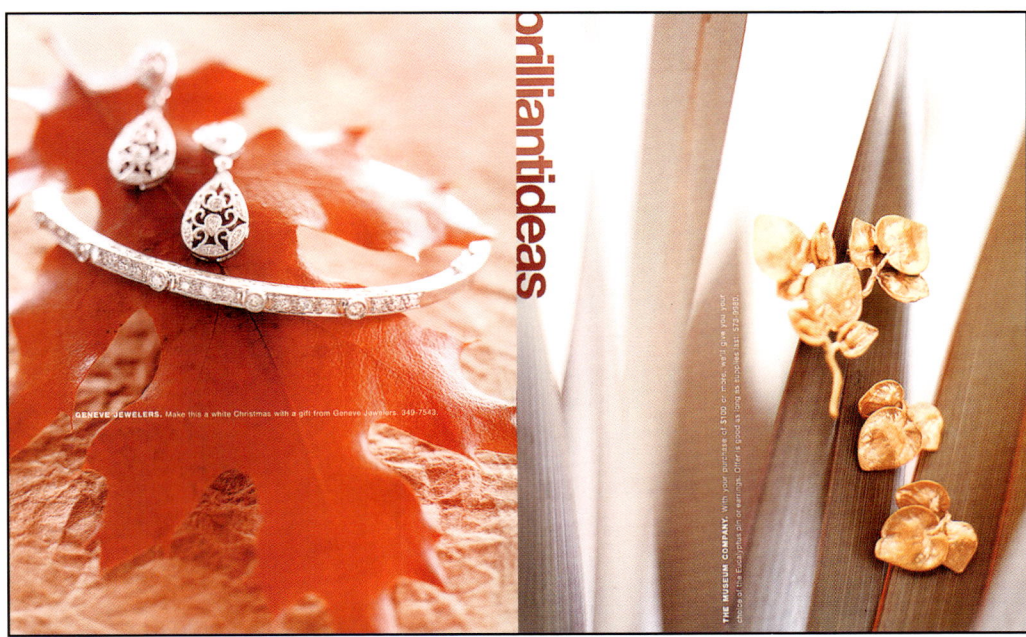

SOUTH SHORE PLAZA

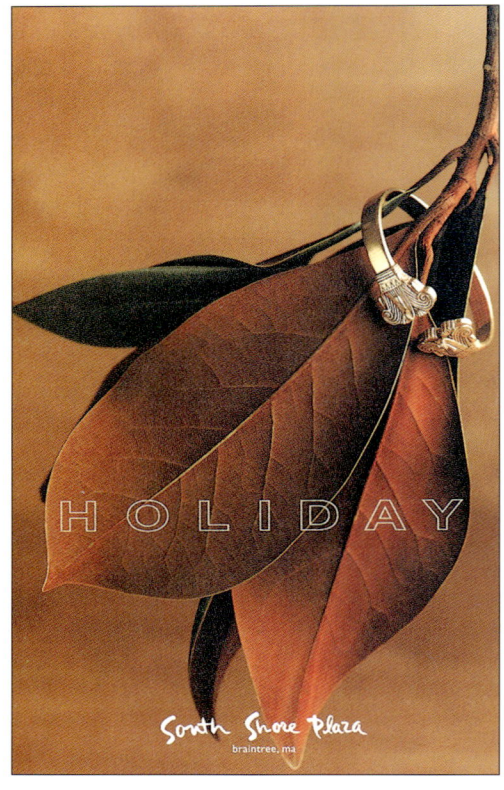
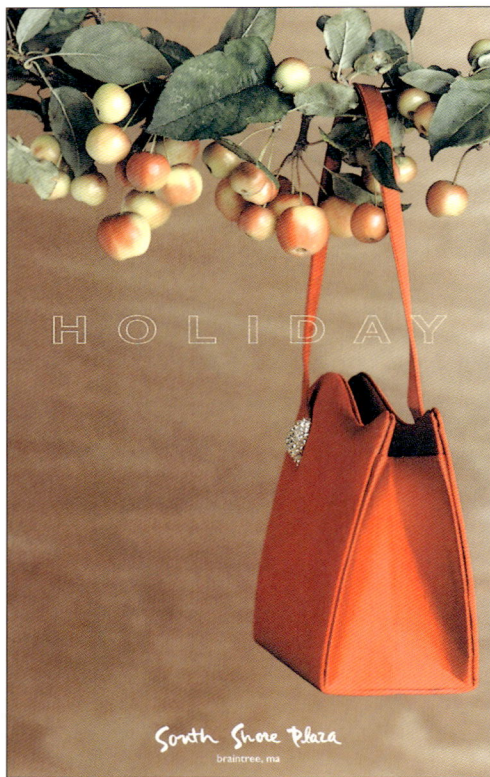
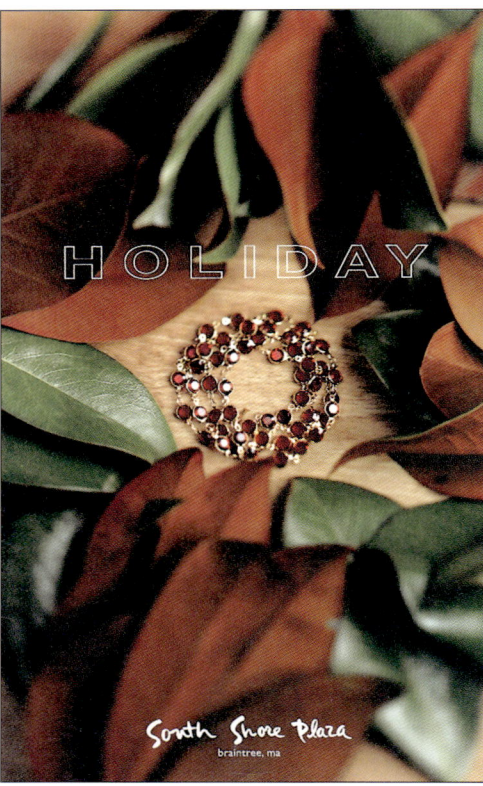
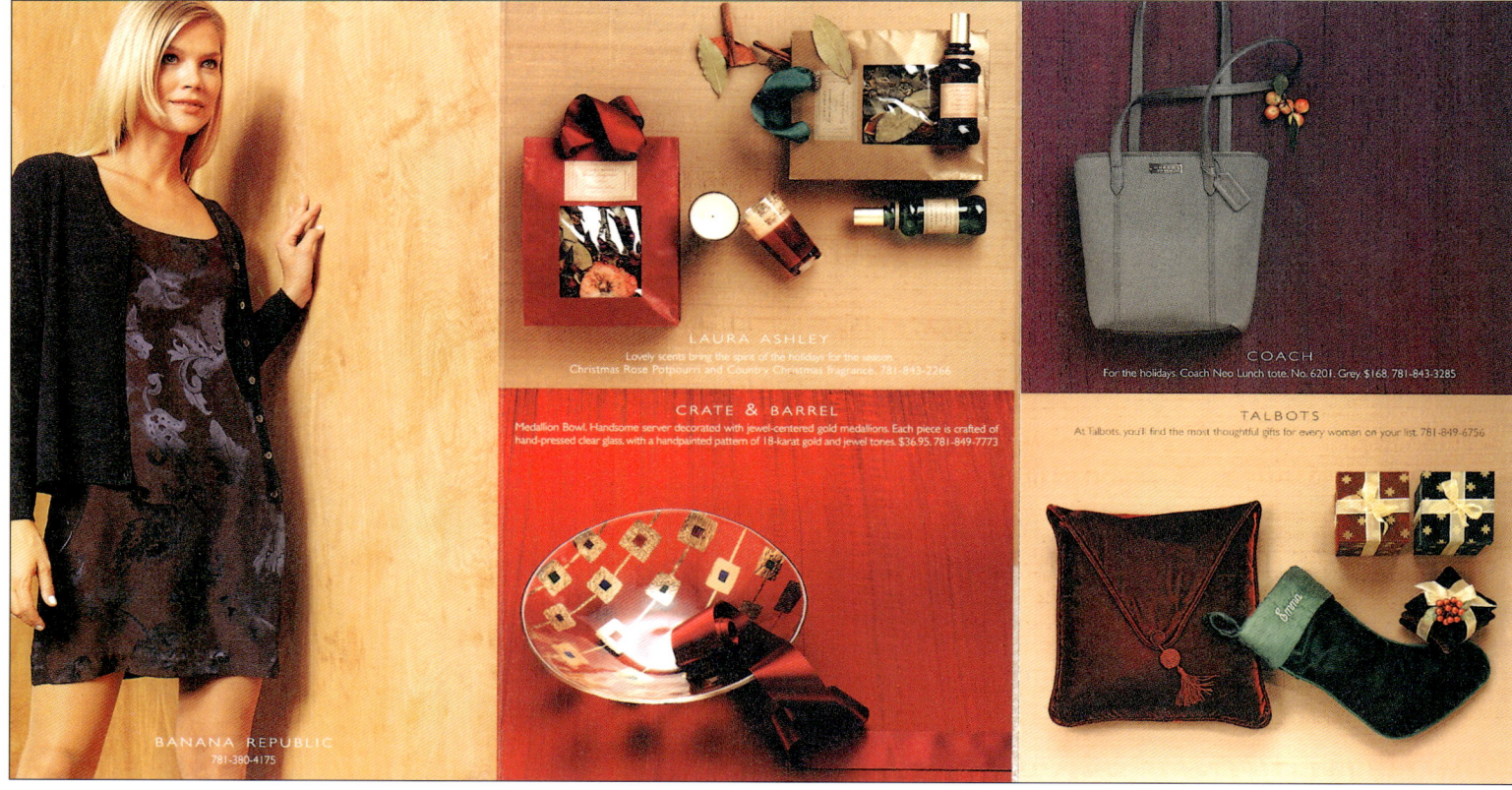

Shown at top are the covers of three direct mail pieces produced by South Shore Plaza. Also shown are select inside panels from the mailer at top left. Each piece measures 24$\frac{1}{4}$" x 8" fully opened (five panels) and folds to 5" x 8."

BELLEVUE SQUARE/THE PLAZA

Cover and inside page from 12-page newspaper insert. Cover image was also used on magazine ads.

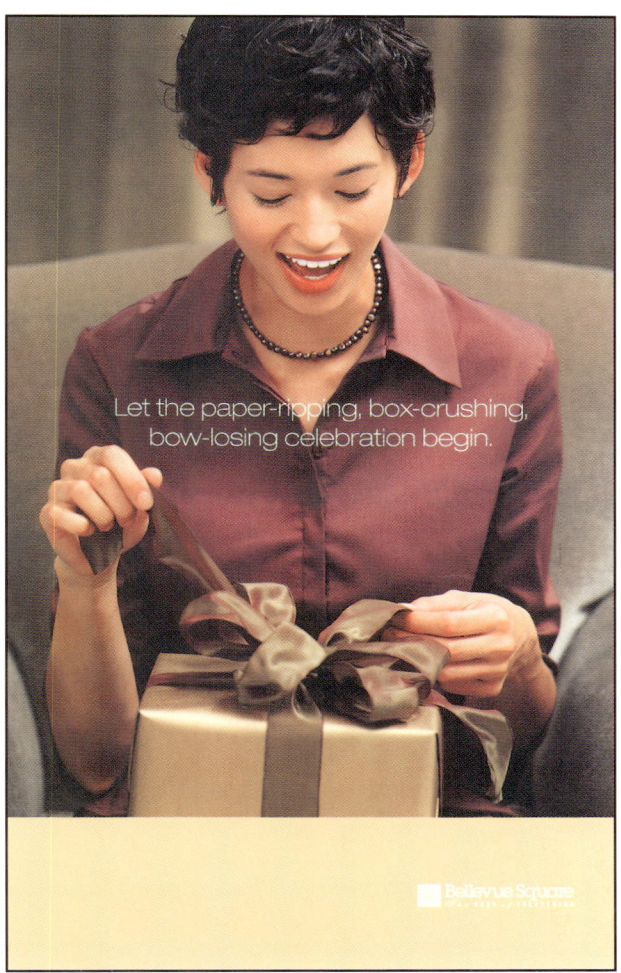
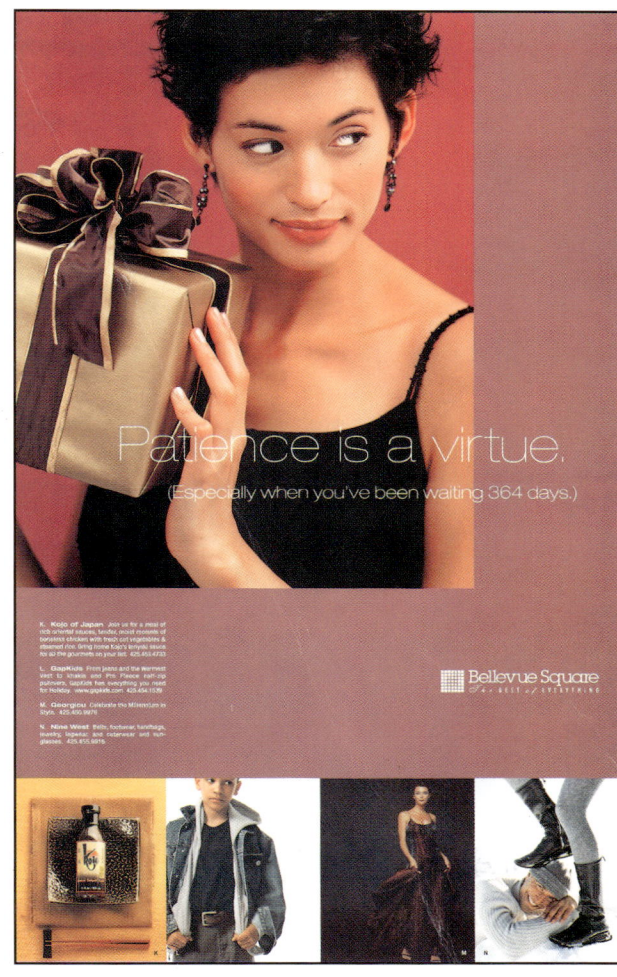

Covers from two, 10-page newspaper inserts.

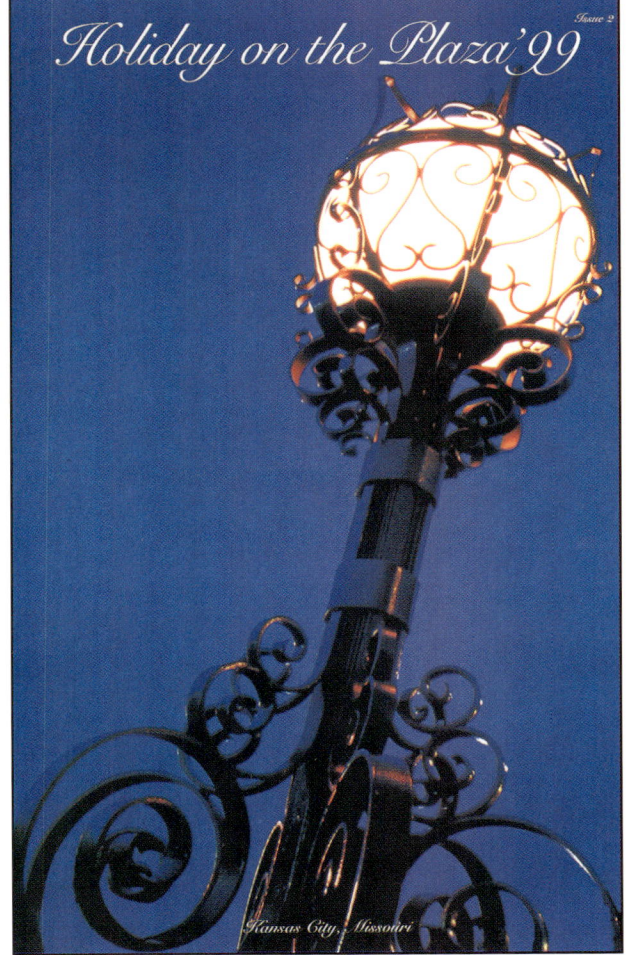
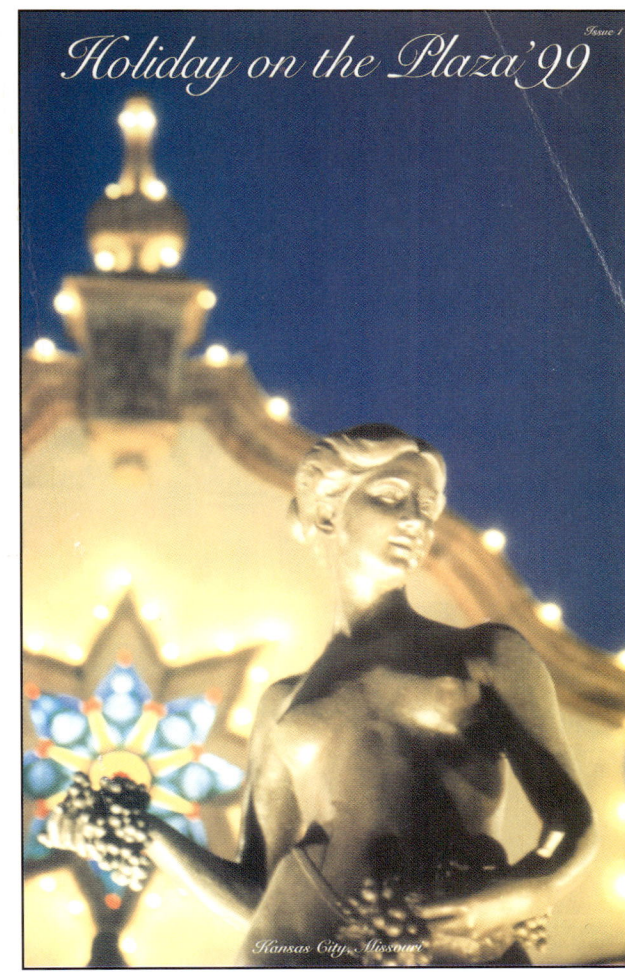

NEWSPAPER ADS

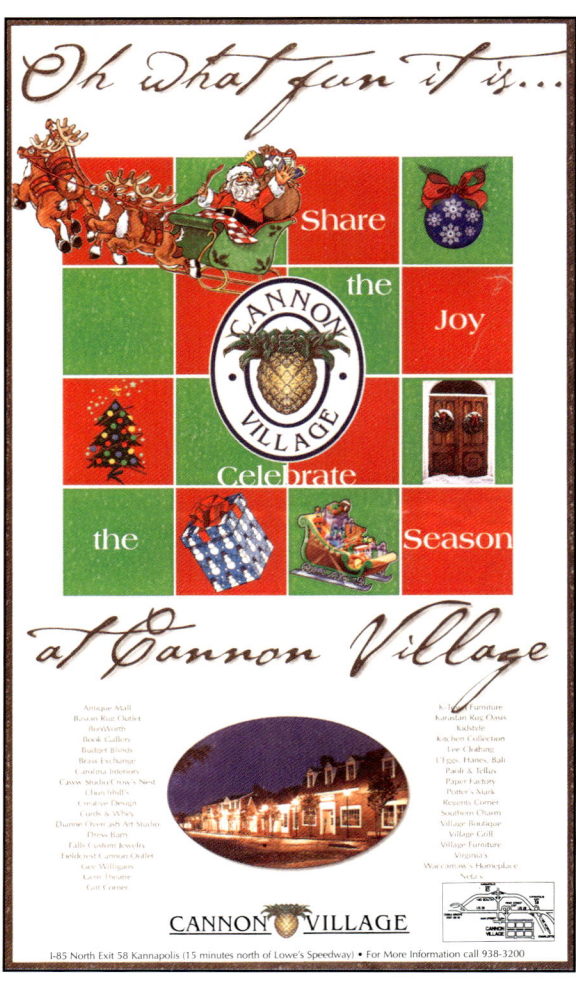
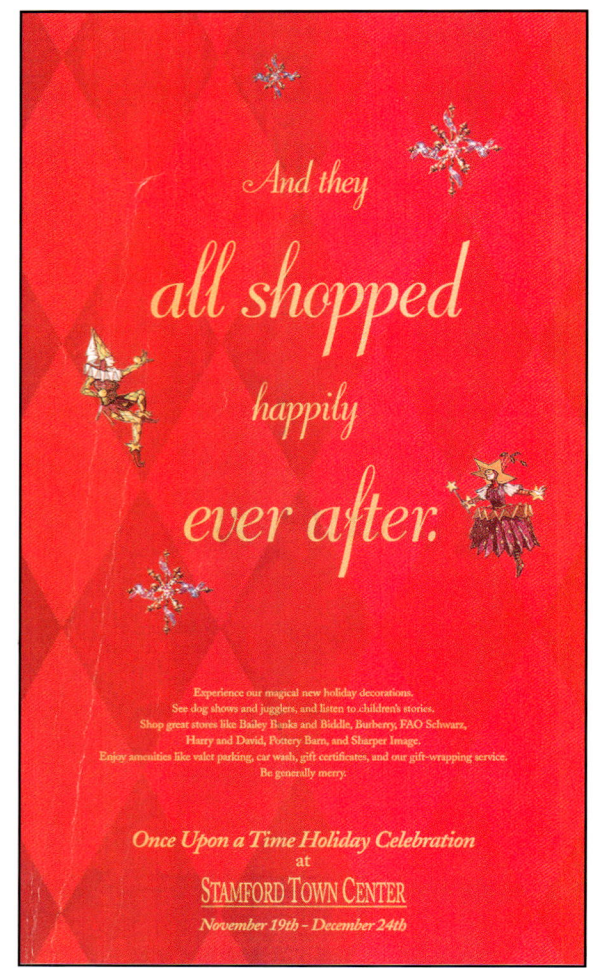
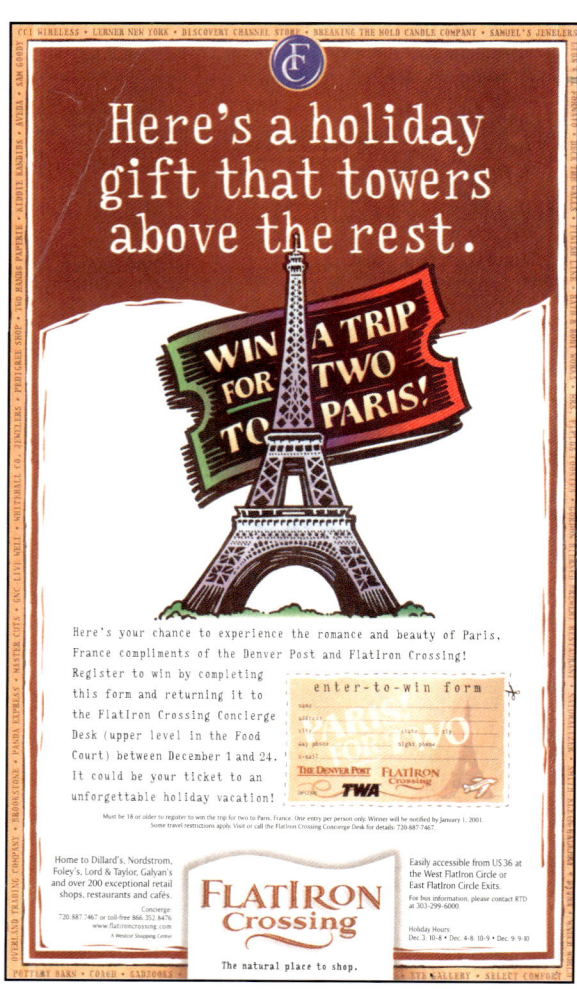
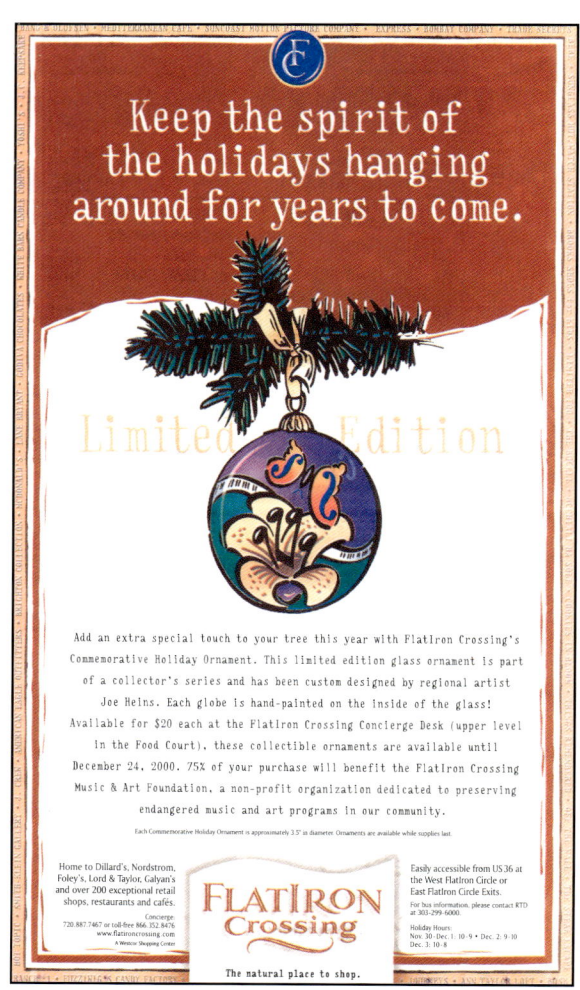

NEWSPAPER ADS

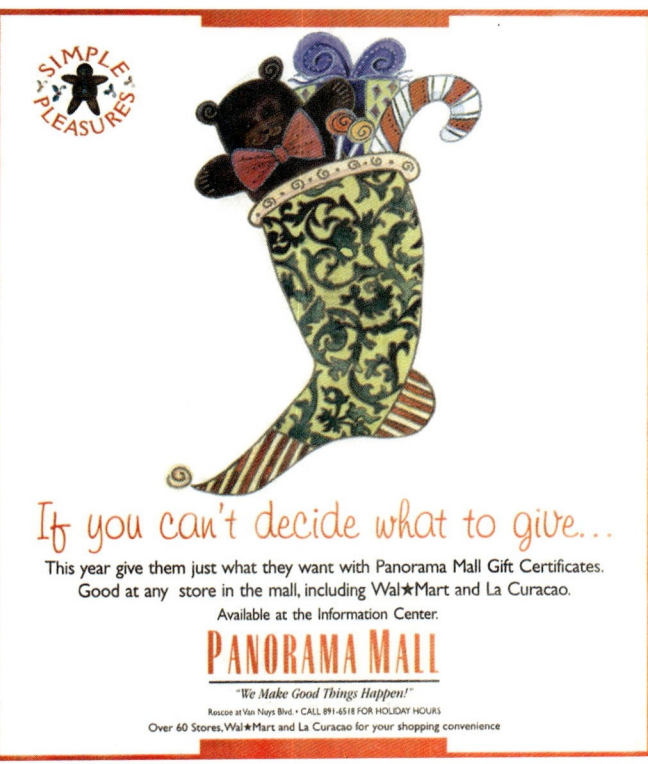

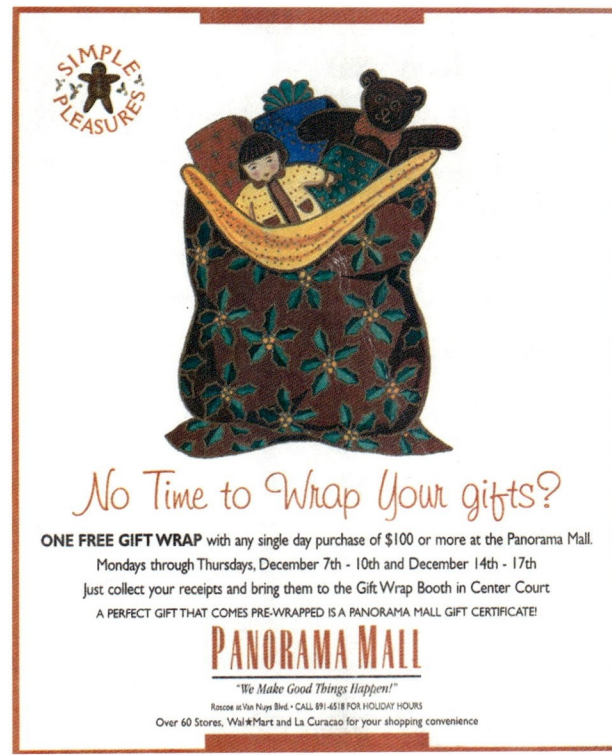

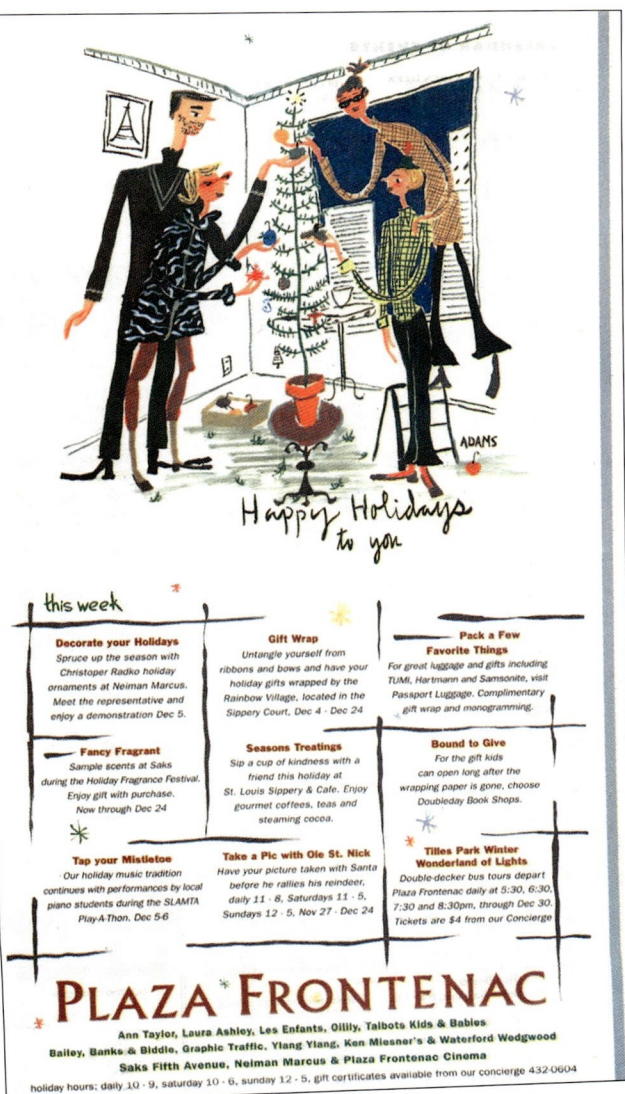

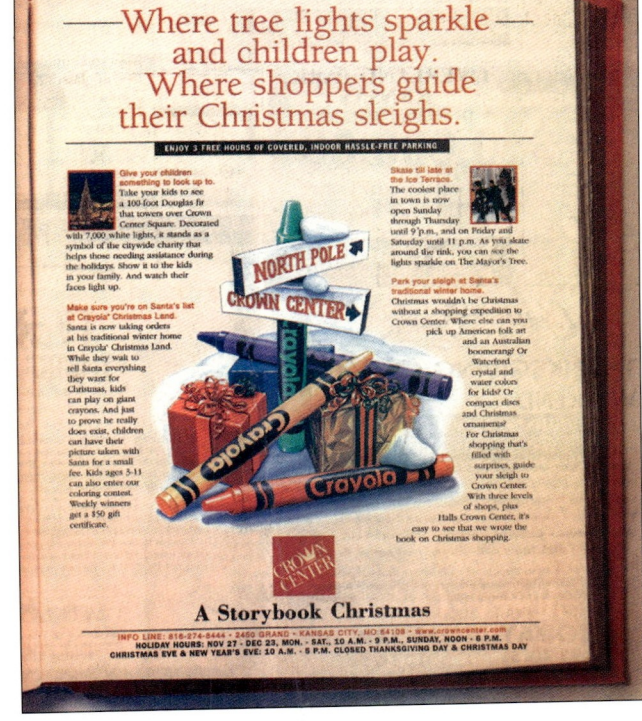

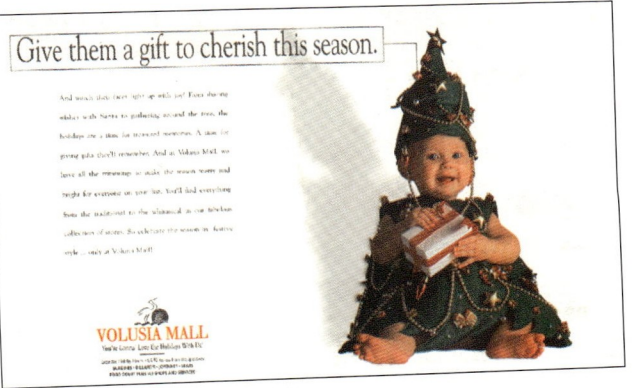

Index

A
Alloy, 120
American Eagle Outfitters, 106
Anthropologie, 137
A Salon, 94

B
Banana Republic, 146
Barneys, 72, 73, 78, 86, 87, 145
Baybrook Mall, 29
Bellevue Square/The Plaza, 173
Bergdorf Goodman, 16, 17, 35, 42, 44, 45, 56, 59, 95, 110
Berreta, 24
BHS, 81
Bloomingdale's, 38, 39, 41, 80
Bramalea City Centre, 162
Burberry, 71

C
Cannon Village, 174
Carson Pirie Scott, 52, 53, 142
Celine, 95
Chiasso, 136
Coach Store, 11
Crestwood Plaza, 92
Crown Center, 175

D
Dayton's Marshall Field's Hudson's, 97
Disney Store, 102

E
Eidhoven Mall, 29
En Toto, 42
Escada, 08, 14, 70
Euro Disney, 29

F
FAO Schwarz, 128
Flatiron Crossing, 174
Froehlich Furs, 12

G
Gucci, 11, 78, 79, 134

H
Henri Bendel, 40, 48, 49, 144
Hérmes, 79
Hillsdale, 170

I
I. Magnin, 88, 89

J
Jacobson's, 118
J. Crew, 138

K
Kenneth Cole, 135
King of Prussia Mall, 168
Kravco Company, 154

L
Laura Ashley, 124
Lisbon Mall, 28
L.L. Bean, 143
Loewe, 10
Lord & Taylor, 20, 21, 74, 75

M
Macy's, 26, 27, 60, 61
Mark Cross, 11
Marks & Spencer, 81
Marshall Field & Co., 76, 77
McRae's, 54, 55
Miss Jackson, 46
Moga, 58
Montebello Town Center, 90

N
Neiman Marcus, 126

O
Organized Living, 132

P
Palais Royal, 15
Panorama Mall, 175
Paul Stuart, 36, 37, 43, 64, 65, 84, 85
Plaza Frontenac, 175
Plaza Las Américas, 158
Pottery Barn, 140

R
Ralph Lauren, 43, 130
REI, 114
Robinson & Co., 82, 83

S
Salvatore Ferragamo, 10, 22, 23, 32, 33
Sevigne, 13
Sherle Wagner, 57
Sony, 25, 47, 59
South Coast Plaza, 167
South Shore Plaza, 172
Stamford Town Center, 174
St. John, 14, 34, 47

T
The Gardens, 149
Tiffany, 50, 51, 93
Toys "R" Us, 123
Tyson's Corner Center, 91

U
U.K. Shopping Mall, 28

V
Volusia Mall, 175

W
Wathne Ltd., 24

Z
ZCMI, 18, 19, 62, 63, 68, 69
Zegna, 25